CONSTITUTIONAL REFORM IN THE UNITED KINGDOM

CONSTITUTIONAL REFORM IN THE UNITED KINGDOM

DAWN OLIVER

OXFORD
UNIVERSITY PRESS

OXFORD

UNIVERSITY PRESS

Great Clarendon Street, Oxford OX2 6DP

Oxford University Press is a department of the University of Oxford.
It furthers the University's objective of excellence in research, scholarship,
and education by publishing worldwide in

Oxford New York

Auckland Bangkok Buenos Aires Cape Town Chennai
Dar es Salaam Delhi Hong Kong Istanbul Karachi Kolkata
Kuala Lumpur Madrid Melbourne Mexico City Mumbai Nairobi
São Paulo Shanghai Taipei Tokyo Toronto

Oxford is a registered trade mark of Oxford University Press
in the UK and in certain other countries

Published in the United States
by Oxford University Press Inc., New York

© Dawn Oliver 2003

The moral rights of the author have been asserted
Database right Oxford University Press (maker)

First published 2003

British Library of Cataloguing in Publication Data
Data available

Library of Congress Cataloging in Publication Data
Data available

ISBN 0–19–876546–0 (pbk)

3 5 7 9 10 8 6 4 2

Typeset by RefineCatch Limited, Bungay, Suffolk
Printed in Great Britain by
TJ International Ltd., Padstow, Cornwall.

Preface

The United Kingdom is going through a period of profound constitutional change. Much of this has been brought about by legislation passed since the Labour government came to power in 1997. The Human Rights Act, the Scotland Act, the Northern Ireland Act and the Government of Wales Act were all passed in 1998. 1999 saw a Local Government Act, the Greater London Authority Act, and the House of Lords Act. The Freedom of Information Act, the Political Parties, Elections and Referendums Act, and another Local Government Act followed in 2000. But a process of constitutional reform had been started well before 1997, and the previous administration had embarked on reforms to the machinery of government, to the regional dimension of government policy, and on some parliamentary reform. A number of reforms have been introduced by administrative measures not supported by legislation, notably in the field of civil service organization and the regulation of standards of conduct.

These reforms raise important issues about the nature of democracy and citizenship in the UK, and principles of good governance, and the role of the law in the UK's constitutional arrangements. These are the themes that we shall be pursuing in this book. Though these developments raise complex and important theoretical issues, I have been mainly concerned with practice and with the practical implications of constitutional reform. The references in the text should enable readers to pursue the subjects to a deeper level if they need to. I have tried to bring together some of both the legal and political science literature on these issues. This is not a textbook. I have been selective in choosing the particular aspects of the constitutional reform process that seem to me to raise major issues, and I have assumed that readers will be familiar with the basics of the United Kingdom's Constitution.

An overarching question in the book is the extent to which the UK is moving from a political Constitution (borrowing the phrase from John Griffith in his *Modern Law Review* article of that title in 1979), to a law-based constitution, and what the implications are of what I see to be a move in that direction. This raises important issues about the role of the courts, the pros and cons of judicial review, and whether we need a new Supreme Court, or reform of the system for the appointment judges.

Although I am in favour of certain further reforms, it is not the purpose of this book to press for them. Instead I have sought to look beyond the fact that some reforms that would in my view be desirable are unlikely to be implemented, and to speculate on the implications of this for the future. For instance, in my view proportional representation will not be introduced for elections to the House of Commons; the House of Commons will not be able to improve its scrutiny of legislation or its holding government to account to any great degree; the House of Lords will become less able to perform scrutiny functions when, as will probably happen, substantial numbers of its members are elected; tensions caused by the fact that devolution is asymmetrical and that England has been left out of the arrangements will increase; when different parties are in control at Westminster and Scotland or Wales relationships between these levels of government are likely to become confrontational; local authorities will not be given greater independence, or be elected by proportional representation; the judges will expand their judicial review jurisdiction into what have been considered to be 'non-justiciable' matters in response to their statutory functions under the Human Rights Act, the European Communities Act, and the devolution legislation, and thus the areas of judicial deference will shrink. It is not the case that if no further reforms are introduced the system will continue to operate as it does at present. Inaction, like action, generates responses and knock-on effects. I have considered what the implications of these possibilities are generally, and for the role of the judiciary in particular. In brief, if, as I expect, our politicians are not able to improve the political mechanisms for holding government to account and thus maintain the political Constitution, the role of the judiciary will increase, and the move to a law-based system will accelerate. I do not myself think that this is as desirable as a properly functioning political system would be, but in the absence of a properly functioning political system a judicialized system based on constitutionalism is essential, and it is already developing.

It was my original intention that this book would be a second edition of my book *Government in the United Kingdom. The Search for Accountability, Effectiveness and Citizenship* which was published in 1991. However so much has happened since then and the focus of discussion about the Constitution has changed so much that this is in effect a new book. However, I have found the framework of the earlier book useful and anyone who read it may recognize some of the points and themes.

A number of colleagues and friends have generously given me their comments on earlier drafts of various chapters, in particular Rodney Austin, Stephen Bailey, Gavin Drewry, Oonagh Gay, Brigid Hadfield, Robert Hazell, Jeffrey Jowell, Andrew Le Sueur, Ian Loveland, Ben Seyd, Sir Michael Wheeler-Booth, and Barry Winetrobe. I am most grateful to them. But responsibility for all shortcomings is mine entirely. I wish to record my thanks to Jeffrey Jowell, who as head of department granted me study leave from March to September 2002, without which I would not have been able to complete the book for a couple of years. I am grateful to colleagues who covered for me during my period of leave. The manuscript—if that is not an out-of-date word—was up to date as of September 2002, but I have added references to later material where possible.

Dawn Oliver

University College, London
January 2003

Detailed Contents

PART III INSTITUTIONAL REFORMS

Table of cases

Table of statutes

Page references in **bold** indicate that the text is reproduced in full.

PART I

THE BACKGROUND TO CONSTITUTIONAL REFORM

1

The Project: Modernizing the UK Constitution

This book is about the reform, often referred to as 'modernization', of the British constitution. The Labour Government which came to power in 1997 was committed to modernizing and reforming the UK constitution in a whole range of ways. For instance, the agreement reached with the Liberal Democrats in the run-up to the 1997 general election included a commitment to 'modernize' the House of Commons (*Report of the Joint Consultative Committee on Constitutional Reform*, 1997, paras. 64–74). The government presented its proposals for devolution to Scotland, Wales, and Northern Ireland, the moves towards a regional dimension in England, reforms to Parliament and to local government and reforms to 'how the government itself works' as 'modernizing our democratic framework' (Tony Blair in *Modernising Government*, Cm. 4310, 1999, at p. 4; see Chapters 13–15). 'The delivery of efficient, high quality, local authority services is fundamental to the Government's modernisation agenda' (*Working Together: Effective partnering between local government and business for service delivery*, Department for Transport, Local Government and the Regions, December 2001).

Our purpose in this book is to consider what 'modernization' means, and in particular, what concepts of constitutionalism, democracy, citizenship, and good governance emerge from the reforms which have been put in place since the late 1980s—the process of constitutional reform has been continuous, and major reforms were introduced well before New Labour embarked on a process of modernization in 1997. We shall also consider proposals for further reforms that are on the active political agenda in the early 2000s.

It is important to bear in mind that there has been no master plan or coherent programme for the reform of the UK constitution, either in the changes that were introduced under the Conservative administrations from 1979 to 1997, or since Labour came to power in 1997 (see Brazier, 1998). No coherent 'vision' of democracy or citizenship or good governance or constitutionalism has informed the various actors who have brought about the changes with which we shall be concerned. The reforms have often been introduced as pragmatic responses to political pressures and perceived problems, on an ad hoc, incremental basis. For instance, the Conservative government introduced public service reforms in response to its sense of frustration at its inability to implement its policies effectively, which it attributed to civil service inflexibility. John Smith committed the Labour Party to a bill of rights in response to concerns about the undermining of civil and political rights under Mrs Thatcher's government, for instance in her changes to trade union and public order law (see Ewing and Gearty, 1990). The policy of devolution to Scotland was adopted in part in response to loss of electoral support for Labour in Scotland to the Scottish National Party. Removal of most of the hereditary peers was Labour's response to the in-built Conservative majority in the House of Lords. All this is not to say that the reforms have been undemocratic or unwise, only that the reasons for implementing them have been largely political. There are many good ideas for constitutional and other kinds of reform that never get onto the political agenda. It is political pressure and sensitivity that push good ideas—and sometimes bad ideas—to the top of the agenda rather than the intrinsic merits of those ideas.

The fact that the reforms have been piecemeal and have not been part of a master plan nor conscious steps towards an ideal or model constitution means that they have been in many respects incoherent and incomplete. This has generated tensions in our governing arrangements. For instance, although most of the hereditary peers have been removed from the House of Lords, neither the government nor the opposition parties has a coherent view about what the composition of that House should be and how if at all it should be further reformed. Devolution is highly asymmetrical, with different powers being enjoyed by elected bodies in Scotland, Wales, and Northern Ireland. England, so far, has been left out of the arrangements. Both of these issues therefore remain, unresolved, on the agenda and there is as yet no constitutional 'settlement' in the UK.

In this chapter we sketch in some background issues—what do 'constitution' and 'constitutionalism' mean in the UK, and what are the characteristics of the Westminster model which have given rise to pressures for reform. Many of the debates about constitutional reform revolve around the relative importance of the political as opposed to legal regulation of politics, and to what extent political activity should be regulated—juridified—in non-legal ways. Answers to this question depend upon the cultural aspects of the system of government, notably the importance of trust and comity between state institutions.

The next two chapters will explore what concepts of democracy, citizenship, and good governance influence debates about constitutional reform in the UK. Subsequent chapters will look in some detail at many of the reforms that have been implemented and others that have been proposed, trying to extract from them evidence of how these concepts are being developed in the actual practice of government in the UK, and to understand the overall direction of modernization. In the last two chapters we shall first sum up the findings in previous chapters and, secondly, focus on the extent to which the UK is moving from a political Constitution to a law-based system or 'constitutionalism' and the implications of such a shift.

Does the UK have a Constitution? What Does it Consist of?

First we need to face up to the fact that the United Kingdom does not have a 'Constitution' in the way that almost all other countries do (see Munro, 1983). An imaginary visitor from Mars or even from the USA might ask: how can you discuss the modernization of the UK's constitution when it has no Constitution? The answer lies in the fact that the word 'constitution' has a number of meanings. For people in the USA their Constitution—and the capital C is useful—is the basic law and founding document both of the state, which was formed from a federation of previously independent sovereign states, and of their system of government. It is true that the UK has no such basic law or set of laws gathered together in one document, but it is certainly a state and it has a functioning and rather sophisticated system of government which is regulated substantially by law: in that sense it has a Constitution. Those laws are written down, not in one singe document but in a number of Acts of Parliament, conventions, decisions of the courts, and scholarly writings that have identified the most important rules, whether enforceable by the courts or not, which govern how we are governed.

But a Constitution in the American—or German or French or Canadian—sense is different from the UK arrangements in more important ways than the fact that the system is written down in a single document. In countries with written Constitutions the document is normally regarded as the source of all state power, and since it is the source of that power it also defines and limits it. Further, in most democracies there are independent institutions such as the Supreme Court of the USA or the Conseil constitutionnel and the Conseil d'etat in France, which can enforce the Constitution, even against the legislature or the executive. They can determine whether the government or the Parliament has exceeded the limits of the powers they possess under the Constitution and set aside laws or decisions that breach the Constitution. In the UK the position is different. The courts do have power to determine whether bodies created by statute have exceeded their powers, and thus for instance they may hold that the Scottish Parliament or a local authority has acted unlawfully. But the power of the Parliament of the UK is not limited by a basic law or Constitution. This is why a written Constitution is normally more than the writing down of the basic rules of the system of government, for in all other Constitutions the powers of the organs of state are substantially defined and therefore limited by the Constitution.

The legislative supremacy—sometimes called the sovereignty—of the UK Parliament is a creation of the courts. It is, as we shall see, virtually unlimited. It is unlimited in two particularly important ways. First, the UK Parliament may make almost any law (the exception is that a statute that is incompatible with European Community law will not be applied by the courts). Second, and this is where UK arrangements differ substantially from those in most other democracies, the UK Parliament can, from a legal point of view, pass any law on simple majorities in a series of readings in the two Houses of Parliament or exceptionally, in the House of Commons alone, and royal assent. By contrast, in most written Constitutions certain fundamental rules, such as those protecting the independence of the judiciary, or the powers of states in a federation, or human rights, may be amended only if there are special majorities for the changes in the Parliament, or referendums have been held indicating consent by the electorate to the changes.

Most of the powers of the government of the UK, the Crown or 'Her Majesty's Government' as it is called, are derived from Acts of Parliament. But it still derives many of its special powers from the royal prerogative, which is the residue of what used to be the absolute power of the monarch in relation to law-making, government, and adjudication. Yet further powers of the Crown derive from the fact that it is recognized at common law as a legal person with many of the legal capacities of ordinary persons, including the power to make contracts and to own and dispose of property. In these respects it differs quite radically from governments in states with Constitutions whose powers are granted, and therefore limited, by their Constitution (see Chapter 11 for further discussion of the common law powers of the Crown).

It would of course be possible to write down the most important current rules of the UK Constitution in the sense of its system of government, and to pass a Constitution Act containing them (see Brazier, 2001). There would be difficulties in doing so, as decisions would have to be made about which rules should be included in the Act and which need not be. And many rules that are unwritten at present would not be easy to express precisely in a text, so there could be disagreement about what the rules actually are. A major difference between common law systems and civil law systems is that in common law systems judicial decisions are often infused with unarticulated principles or values that are not definitively articulated or reduced to a text, and the courts may resort to those values and principles in making decisions, especially in hard cases. It is not so easy for judges operating in a codified civil law system to resort to such principles to inform decisions.

Perhaps only the rules that are currently enforceable in the courts could be written down if the UK were to adopt a written Constitution; but that would give a very peculiar picture of our system. It would be necessary to decide, for instance, whether the Constitution Act should require that all Ministers be members of one or other of the Houses of Parliament, or whether that rule—the rule which gives us a parliamentary executive, one of the most important aspects of the system—should remain, as it is now, a non-statutory constitutional convention.

If a Constitution Act were passed, the UK would then have a written constitution— but the small c is significant. Unless a Constitution were adopted as a basic law that was itself the source of state power and prescribed how it could be changed, the rules could later be changed by Acts passed by simple majority in Parliament, and the Constitution Act would rapidly become out of date and therefore rather misleading. We shall see in Chapter 5 that a concept of a 'constitutional statute' appears to be developing in UK law and if this is the case it is likely that a Constitution Act, as a constitutional statute, could only be altered by a subsequent inconsistent Act if that later Act provided that the Constitution Act was amended or part of it was repealed in express terms. This doctrine would prevent inadvertent change to the Constitution, but it would not provide very strong protection. Most people assume that a Constitution cannot be easily changed, and they are right as far as other written Constitutions are concerned. But they would be wrong about the UK constitution if the current system were simply written down and passed as a Constitution Act.

Constitution then has many meanings. In this book we are considering for the most part the actual system of government in the UK, based on a combination of conventions, traditions, Acts of Parliament and Acts of devolved bodies, regulations and decisions of the courts. It includes a number of values and principles many of which are reflected in rules but are not separately written down in legal form—a good example is the Seven

Principles of Public Life elaborated by the Committee of Standards in Public Life in 1995 (Cm. 2850. This will be referred to in later chapters).

One of the side effects of the fact that the UK does not have a Constitution and that much of governmental activity is conducted under common law rather than statutory or Constitutional powers, is that the system can be changed or reformed in many respects without the need even to secure the passage of legislation through Parliament. Of course many of the most important reforms to the system have required legislation—devolution of powers to Scotland, Wales, and Northern Ireland and the protection of civil and political rights in the Human Rights Act 1998 are the major examples. But many significant reforms have been made without recourse to legislation—reform of parliamentary procedures, reform of the civil service and of public service delivery, the formulation of codes setting down standards of conduct in public life, and establishing new public bodies, for instance. There will be examples of all of these in later chapters. Reform or modernization of the system goes far beyond the headline-grabbing statutory reforms mentioned above and into almost every corner of government.

The Westminster Model

It will be helpful at this point, for those who are unfamiliar with it, to summarize the main features of the UK's constitutional arrangements, drawing out the points at which modernization has been mooted and the changes that have been made since the mid-1980s. It was at about that time that the then Conservative government under Mrs Thatcher began to recognize that some of the problems it faced in seeking to improve the economy and the operation of government were institutional and constitutional—the problem was not simply to formulate and implement the right substantive social or economic policies. Since then there has been a wide range of reforming activity, some of it achieved under the authority of statutes, and some by internal changes and the use of codes and other non-legal measures.

Any account of a system of government is selective and represents a particular interpretation of reality. My interpretation is essentially that of a lawyer with an interest in politics. Other commentators from other disciplines or other countries might well summarize and interpret the UK's constitutional arrangements differently. Thus this account of constitutional arrangements in the United Kingdom focuses on the traditional Westminster system. It is inevitably something of a caricature. We shall note, after giving this account, that there are other current dimensions to the system, on which we shall draw in subsequent chapters.

As of the mid-1980s the main characteristics of the UK system had changed little since Dicey published his *Introduction to the Law of the Constitution* in 1885—the centenary being perhaps another reason to start at this period in our account. Since the mid-1980s few aspects of the constitution have been untouched by reform and change.

Dicey identified two 'pillars' in the British constitution, parliamentary sovereignty and the rule of law. The legislative supremacy of Parliament—Dicey's first pillar—is now recognized to be subject to the primacy of European Community law, but in other respects Parliament's sovereignty is still regarded as sacrosanct, both by the UK's courts and by the political elites. (It is discussed in Chapter 2.) There is a strong liberal tradition among the political elites in the UK, which means that although Parliament is legally sovereign, legislation that interferes with civil liberties has been something of a rarity, though by no means unknown.

Until the late 1990s the UK system of government was highly centralized and commonly regarded as 'unitary'. The Northern Ireland Assembly at Stormont established in 1922 having been dissolved in 1972, there was no elected body in the United Kingdom with primary legislative power apart from the Parliament in Westminster. Since 1998 elected bodies have been created with primary legislative power in Scotland and Northern Ireland, and there is an elected Assembly and executive in Wales. The UK, once regarded as a unitary state, is now recognized as a union state in the sense that it was created by the successive unions between England and Wales, Scotland, and Ireland, and which the Republic of Ireland left in 1922. The countries which form the United Kingdom of Great Britain and Northern Ireland are currently reasserting their own identities in various degrees and ways and the constitution is reflecting this.

In the Westminster Parliament the majoritarian first past the post electoral system operates so that the party in government will almost invariably have the support of a majority in the House of Commons and can generally be certain of getting its legislation through that chamber. The pattern has been of one-party governments for many decades, with Conservatives and Labour alternating in office. Only exceptionally has any other party been in a position even to enter into a coalition or pact with one of the two main parties. Most recently Conservative Prime Minister John Major was relying on the support of Northern Irish MPs in 1996 and 1997, and before then, from 1974 to 1976, the Labour government had a pact with the Liberals to allow it to command a majority in the House of Commons.

Until the reform of 1999 only the Conservatives could count on a majority in the second chamber, the House of Lords, which consisted of hereditary and life peers (and Church of England Bishops). Governments could rely on the Salisbury Convention (according to which a 'manifesto' bill, foreshadowed in the governing party's most recent election manifesto and passed by the House of Commons, should not be opposed by the Second Chamber on Second or Third Reading) to push through its legislation in the House of Lords and this mitigated the effect of the Conservative majority for Labour governments. In 1999 most of the hereditary peers were removed by the House of Lords Act, 1999. The position as of 2002 is that no one party has a majority in the House of Lords and government must rely on the Salisbury Convention and on winning the support of cross-benchers or members of other parties in the House—where party discipline is looser than in the Commons—or on the Parliament Acts, which enable bills to receive the royal assent without the consent of the House of Lords after thirteen months, to get its business through.

Broadly, the system enables the governing party to obtain from Parliament the legislation it needs to implement its policies, even if these do not command the support of a majority of the electorate. The implications of this for democratic theory are explored in the next chapter and Chapter 7. In practice 'effective government' has prevailed over 'representative government' where the two values conflict (see Birch, 1964). But given the two-party system, when political polarization takes place, as happened in the 1980s, successive governments can change policies radically, resulting in pendulum swing politics, which can be destabilizing for the economy. A point here is that proportional representation could change this (see Finer, 1975; Bogdanor, 1981).

Much of the British Constitution rests on conventions rather than on positive law. The parliamentary executive, which is the central characteristic of the Westminster system is based entirely on convention. Only by convention must the Prime Minister be a member of the House of Commons, and all Ministers be members of one or other House of Parliament. Only by convention is Parliament dissolved at the request of the Prime Minister. Convention regulates the Queen's appointment of a Prime Minister to form a government once an incumbent Prime Minister has resigned. Many more aspects of the UK's system of government are regulated by conventions, and this has led to the Constitution being regarded as a customary one. The system thus places much greater reliance on political and conventional rather than legal checks on the exercise of governmental or parliamentary power than most other democracies: there has until recently been no system of constitutional review. This tradition of reliance on political rather than legal checks and balances is a major theme in our discussions of the modernization of the British Constitution, to which we shall return later in this chapter and indeed throughout the book. Since the devolution of power to Scotland, Wales, and Northern Ireland in 1998, however, the courts have had the power to review the exercise of powers by the devolved bodies, in order to determine whether they have exceeded the powers granted to them by the devolution Acts. The courts also have the power to determine whether UK law and acts of the government are compatible with European Community law. Thus there is some constitutional review jurisdiction in the UK.

As far as Dicey's second pillar of the constitution, the rule of law, is concerned, a strong independent judiciary has been developing its jurisdiction in judicial review—in the UK, not American, sense: while the courts will not strike down legislation of the UK Parliament on the grounds of lack of constitutionality (save for incompatibility with European Community law), they have been expanding their jurisdiction to quash decisions made at all levels of government on grounds of illegality, irrationality, and unfairness. Under the Human Rights Act 1998 they have the power to quash decisions that are in breach of Convention rights—the civil and political rights in the European Convention of Human Rights which have been incorporated into UK law—save where the breach is expressly authorized by an Act of Parliament (see Chapters 5 and 6 below).

The political culture in the UK is strongly committed to the rule of law in the sense of the principle of legality, with internal arrangements in place to secure that government action is legally justified, and almost invariable compliance with court orders if a public body is found to have acted unlawfully (but cf. the Home Secretary's disobedience to a court order in *M. v. Home Office* [1994] 1 AC 377, discussed in Chapter 11). Recently the courts have been developing a new doctrine of fundamental constitutional rights which, while not entitling them to disapply an Act of Parliament, imposes a burden on Parliament to use express and clear words if it wishes to authorize interferences with these rights. This doctrine is discussed further towards the end of this chapter and in Chapter 5.

The UK joined the European Community on 1 January 1973. As a result of membership, considerable legislative and policy-making power has been passed to European Community institutions that are not themselves democratic in the sense of being directly elected; nor are they strongly accountable to directly elected European Community bodies. The legal obligation of British courts to give effect to the decisions of these bodies raises issues about alternative justifications for political authority, apart from election. Broadly these justifications are contractarian or functional: part of the deal the UK has done with the European Community and the other member states is that Community law should be given effect, whether or not it has popular consent as is the case in relation to the legislation passed by the institutions of the member states. The UK is in a contractual relationship with its European partners and, so the argument goes, it has accepted that the benefits of membership justify the UK contracting to give effect to the laws of the Community. An additional justification is functional—the Community could not function without the doctrine of primacy of European Community law, and this has been recognized by member states when agreeing to the terms of membership. These issues will be considered further in Chapter 4.

A liberal interpretation of the Westminster model

The UK's constitutional arrangements may be interpreted in various ways. On one view it implies a theory of democracy that is majoritarian, representative, and liberal. It is *majoritarian* in that—subject to European Community law—it permits the passing of any legislation on the strength of simple majorities in Parliament. And it implies that the wishes of a majority of the electorate may be given effect in legislation and that this will be democratic even if, for instance, the legislation interferes with the rights and freedoms of individuals, or discriminates against certain sections of the population or certain areas of the country or undermines important principles that are generally regarded as 'constitutional' in a normative sense, such as the independence of the judiciary. The system is also *representative* in that it channels public participation in government through Parliament and other elected bodies, and thus through elections and the political parties. It does not make explicit provision for other more direct forms of public participation in government, although a number of statutes do afford participatory opportunities, as we shall see in later chapters. The assumption of the system is that the central forum for public participation in UK politics is the party-dominated House of Commons.

The system is also *liberal*, in that the legal system permits individuals freedom of activity unless some positive law, normally a statutory provision, authorizes interference with the liberty. The term 'liberalism' is sometimes used to imply a preference for a market economy, but the UK system is not necessarily liberal in that sense. It is perfectly possible within the law for a socialist or social-democratic system to be put in place in the UK.

The strong liberal tradition affords considerable freedom of activity to individuals. Importantly it permits extensive freedom of speech and association so that individuals are free to form not only new political parties but also other associations of civil society which can discuss and engage in deliberation about public affairs. But the system implies or assumes that ministerial responsibility to Parliament provides an adequate check against abuse of political power; it also seems to assume that all governmental power is exercised by democratically accountable bodies—Ministers, elected bodies in Scotland, Wales, and Northern Ireland, and local authorities in particular. As we shall see this is not the case and much power is exercised by quangos (see Chapter 17) and via networks and partnerships involving private not-for-profit bodies, non-governmental organizations, and commercial companies.

Before devolution, the attachment to the unitary nature of the system seemed to imply that government, through the parliamentary system, could properly promote the aggregated public interests of the whole of the United Kingdom, rather than supposing that different regions, nations, or areas might have different public interests or public interests that could be differently aggregated, or that bodies directly accountable to the people in the nations and regions might be better placed to decide on the balancing and aggregation of public interests and private interests in those areas than the government and Parliament in London.

It is not the case that this model of representative liberal majoritarianism was, or is, the only model or theory of governance operating in the British system. There are parallel, residual elements of the pre-democratic, authoritarian era still in place, as in the surviving powers under the royal prerogative, exercisable by ministers without the prior consent of Parliament, in relation to foreign affairs, defence, some aspects of home affairs, and the like. There are also extensive areas of public activity in which political and democratic checks do not operate, or not strongly, as in the activities of quangos (see Chapter 17). In these areas there are not strong legal or administrative law checks either, a point to which we return in later chapters. There are also parallel emerging strands of a republican and extra-parliamentary theory of democracy, involving direct public participation in policy-making, and public deliberation as a prelude to decision-making—a model that will be considered in some of the chapters that follow.

Alternative narratives about the operation of the system: networks and governance

This Westminster majoritarian representative liberal model is not the only possible account that could be given of the reality of the UK constitution. Other accounts have been given by political scientists since the Second World War as, within the formal Westminster system, practice and power relationships change and parallel systems develop. In the 1960s and 1970s some commentators focused on the growth of corporatism, arrangements whereby government negotiated policy with the two sides of industry on matters such as investment, wage restraint, job security, and the like (Middlemas, 1979). These arrangements bypassed Parliament. Ministers were not in any real sense accountable either to Parliament or the courts for their policies under these negotiated arrangements. A literature developed in America which considered that these arrangements and the participation of pressure groups in politics and policy might be positively democratic, and in the United Kingdom commentators began to write of a post-parliamentary democracy (Richardson and Jordan, 1979). But there were concerns that the habit of consultation and bargaining with labour and capital resulted in the capture of government by sectional interests and the subjection of the public interest to vested interests. This led in turn to a paralysis of public choice (Beer, 1982). The Thatcher government elected in 1979 dismantled the apparatus of this corporatist system, putting an end to negotiations with the trade unions and employer or capitalist interests, reasserting, formally at least, the primacy of the parliamentary system.

From the early 1990s the Conservative government started to alter the role of the state, moving away from the provision of public services towards a role in facilitating the availability of those services—'steering, not rowing' in the words of Osborne and Gaebler (1992). In the 1990s commentators (Marsh and Rhodes, 1992; Rhodes, 1997) began to note the operation of networks between bodies of various kinds, including governmental bodies such as government departments and local authorities, but also special-purpose bodies—quangos—and private or voluntary bodies contracted to provide services to the public. The policy of the Labour government since 1997 has been to encourage the use of networks to achieve policies. We shall come across them in later chapters, notably chapters on Ministers, the Civil Service, Quangos, Local Government, and Devolution, and a few words of explanation may be helpful here. Taken with the privatization of many functions formerly performed by government and the abandonment of some of the responsibilities undertaken by the state—the funding of students in university education, payment of unconditional benefits to young unemployed, for instance—they contribute to a what has been called a process of 'hollowing out' of the state (Rhodes, 1994).

Networks may be formal or informal, public or private. In reality networks are likely to exist in any political organization: the old school tie 'network' in England was notorious, as was the Oxbridge network. There are many more such unofficial and opaque networks. Webs of connection and influence grow up between donors to parties and sponsors of political projects, even between parties and their MPs and councillors. Such networks may manifest themselves in 'cronyism' as personal friends or acquaintances are appointed to public bodies or as members of the second chamber, or in attempts to mandate elected representatives. As we shall see, this kind of opaque network has been increasingly discouraged in the UK through codes of conduct and other normative devices over the last two decades or so.

Other networks are more open and formal and can be harnessed in support of government policy. There is a pervasive and complex set of organization-based networks, many of which operate *within* state bodies. The internal arrangements between departments and their executive agencies, or between the Treasury and other government departments are examples of these internal networks (see Daintith and Page, 1999).

Policy is often formulated and public services are commonly delivered through intergovernmental agreements, funding arrangements, or formal or informal contracts between governmental bodies, departments, teams within departments, executive agencies, local authorities, and a wide range of non-governmental bodies such as charities, not-for-profit organizations, and companies. The mechanisms used are commonly contractual or quasi-contractual—arrangements such as public service agreements, public private partnerships, private finance initiative arrangements. These will be considered further in later chapters. In fact the use of contract and pseudo-contract as an instrument of government goes back to the days of corporatism (Harden, 1992).

Networks may be classified in various ways. A policy network is the dependent relationships that develop between organizations and individuals that are in frequent contact in particular policy areas. An issue network is a 'communications network of those knowledgeable about policy in some area, including government authorities, legislators, business people, lobbyists and even academicians and journalists' (McFarland, 1992, 70). Jackson (2001) sees networks as being about government 'brokering' the provision of public services. He suggests that the old dichotomy between bureaucracy/control/ hierarchy and competition/contract was simplistic and what is required is network relationships based upon cooperation and participation rather than competition and control.

The Westminster model or theory of democracy, with its assumption that government makes policy and delivers services and is accountable to Parliament for doing so, and the hierarchical organization of the civil service, does not take sufficient account of this sphere of network activity. It is a sphere of political and governmental activity that operates outside, often in parallel with and sometimes in tension with, representative democratic processes. It is not as yet well theorized and the issues of accountability, effectiveness, and balancing of conflicts between public and private interests that it raises have not yet been fully explored and resolved (Morison, 1998).

This use of networks to deliver public policy has effected a shift away from government to governance. Rydin (1999) suggests that:

Whereas government implies hierarchical relationships between tiers of the state, a strong element of top-down control and a firm boundary between the state and outside organisations, 'governance' points to the proliferation of quasi-governmental agencies and the growing formal role of organizations outside the state within the policy process.

He is making an institutional distinction here between the formal state and other bodies which are involved in governing or delivering policy or public services.

Governance then is about relationships between government, market operators and civil society (see generally Lewis, 2001; Newman, 2001). A strong trend in the last twenty years has been for government to seek to cooperate with the voluntary sector and commercial enterprises in order to implement their policies. Examples of working through commercial arrangements include: the contracting out of local authority refuse collection; the private finance initiative, involving private capital in building and managing aspects of hospitals and other institutions; public private partnerships for the improvement of London Underground, for instance. There are also many areas in which cooperation with the charitable or voluntary sector is built into policy on the delivery of services—service level agreements involving voluntary and non-governmental organizations in the provision of residential care home services and others. This is particularly prevalent and encouraged in local government (see Chapter 16).

In fact there is now in the UK a pervasive network of autopoietic—self-regulating and autonomous—systems, a series of complex public private relationships that developed as a consequence of marketization (Morison, 1998, 524). As Kickert (rather heavily) puts it, 'top-down government steering is increasingly being replaced by self-responsibility and autonomy of social institutions, and theories of central governance from super-ordinated positions are being replaced by theories of inter-organizational networks and non-compulsive co-operation' (Kickert, 1993, 262). This needs to be taken into account in identifying and then seeking solutions to constitutional and governance problems. To the extent that they fall outside the checks and balances of the representative system, the provisions for openness, accountability, and promoting trust and trustworthy conduct are either absent, or extra-parliamentary. The liberal reform agenda with its focus on reinforcing representative democracy does not engage with these issues.

Pressure for Reform of the Westminster Model

From the mid-1960s, and particularly from the mid-1980s, there had been a growing sense that the system of government needed reform in various ways, and this has been reflected in a literature from lawyers, political scientists, and practising politicians. Most of these commentators have been concerned to reinvigorate the liberal Westminster model, but some (see Morison, 1998) have urged the need to build a more participatory, deliberative and communitarian—republican—system (see further discussion in the next chapter).

A summary of the perceived problems in the operation of the Westminster model will serve to put the reforms that have been made into perspective. It is a bit of a caricature, but it brings out the main issues. Starting with the United Kingdom Parliament, there is concern that it is unable or unwilling to scrutinize government policy and legislation adequately. This means that much legislation is passed that has not been properly scrutinized by Parliament, so that it is not well drafted, nor well thought out. This is put down to the operation of the party and electoral systems. Party discipline is strong and the first past the post system normally guarantees one party a majority in the House of Commons. Backbenchers of the governing party are generally unwilling to oppose their party (but cf. Norton, 1980), and the opposition parties appear to oppose on principle, which can stimulate intransigence on the part of government in the legislative process. The operation of the convention that Ministers are responsible to Parliament is seen to be undermined by the party system and by the facts that the government has first claim on Parliament's time, and Ministers themselves determine what information should be given to Parliament, and whether and how to answer questions.

There have also been concerns about the style and working practices of the House of Commons. Procedures are complex and hard for outsiders to understand. Some of them have been plainly ridiculous, like the use of the opera hat to raise point of order on a division. But the working hours of the Commons, most of whose work was done until recently in the afternoons and late into the evenings, were not social or family-friendly. This may have contributed to another concern about the Commons, the very few women members. Here the practices of the parties in selecting candidates made it difficult for female candidates to be put up in winnable seats and exacerbated the under-representation of women.

These pressures have resulted in some reforms to parliamentary procedure, though there remains a full agenda of possible further reforms, both to parliamentary procedure and to the electoral and party-funding systems. The scrutiny of legislation is, of course, solely the responsibility of Parliament and there is no equivalent body to the Conseil constitutionnel or the Conseil d'etat in France with power to scrutinize legislation before it is passed for its drafting and workability, or its compatibility with constitutional norms or international human rights or other obligations or European Community law. The merits of such bodies will be considered—briefly—in Chapter 18. The House of Commons has sought to modernize its working hours and practices to make it more family-friendly. And legislation has been passed to make it easier for a female candidate to be selected and remove the earlier rule which held that all-women short lists of candidates, for example, were regarded as illegally discriminatory.

There is also concern about the impact of European Community or European Union policy on the UK and at the fact that Ministers are subject to few controls on the commitments they enter into on behalf of the UK at European Council meetings, a matter that will be explored further in Chapter 4. This concern has even been reflected in some support for the adoption of a written Constitution for the UK that could introduce additional protections for our constitutional arrangements against European Community encroachment, of the kind that the constitution of, for instance, Germany provides. Such a move to a written constitution would represent a radical departure from the Westminster system if it were to subject Parliament's legislative competence to particular procedural or substantive limitations before legislation of a 'constitutional' kind could be passed.

By the mid-1980s there had been a succession of decisions against the UK Government in the European Court and Commission of Human Rights at Strasbourg, which fuelled concern that our domestic law protection of human rights was inadequate, and that this country was exposed to international criticism when its law and practice were found not to come up to these standards. This exposure has been a factor in the passage of the Human Rights Act 1998, which gives the UK courts the power to protect civil and political rights and to determine whether our law is compatible with the European Convention on Human Rights (see Chapter 6).

Further, it was increasingly felt that the degree of centralization of government in the UK was too great. Pressure was coming from Scotland and Wales for devolution—pressure which had originated in the late 1960s and had resulted in abortive attempts to legislate for devolution in 1976 and 1978. These pressures resurfaced in the 1990s and led to the devolution legislation of 1998, which established elected bodies in Scotland, Wales, and Northern Ireland (see Chapters 13–15). It is worth noting here that these arrangements are not fully consistent with the traditions of the Westminster system. They are not solely about revitalizing that system, as many of the reforms have been, but also about moving towards a less confrontational, more deliberative, and communitarian system in those countries. But the arrangements all maintain the legislative supremacy of the Westminster Parliament, and in that respect they do represent adherence to the Westminster model.

In the mid-1990s, standards of conduct in public life became an issue for the press and the public, with scandals about Members of Parliament accepting payment for asking parliamentary questions, and concern about the exercise of unregulated ministerial and Prime Ministerial patronage in the making of public appointments. This has resulted in increased regulation of ministers and Members of Parliament, though through 'soft law'—codes of various kinds—rather than by statute. The reforms in Parliament have been made by the introduction of a Code of Conduct for MPs and a stricter requirement to register their interests, and the appointment of a Parliamentary Commissioner for Standards to monitor compliance with the rules on behalf of the House of Commons. These arrangements seek to uphold the aspect of the traditional Westminster representative model which requires Members of Parliament and others in public positions to exercise their powers for the general public good and not for their own or other private interests. But the introduction of even this degree of formalized self-regulation represents a departure from the liberal tradition of reliance on political mechanisms based on trust to regulate political behaviour, a point which we shall return to later in this chapter.

The Juridification of Politics

The pressure for reform of the Westminster model has raised issues to do with the regulation—juridification—of government activity. Politics—in the sense of what elected politicians do—is regulated in a range of ways in the UK. Much political activity is governed by statutes, which commonly grant powers to ministers whose decisions can, if necessary, be enforced through the courts; the exercise of such powers is commonly made subject to appeal to the courts or judicial review, procedures through which the courts may prevent ministers—and others exercising public functions—from exceeding or abusing their powers. It has been memorably said that the law acts as both a green—empowering—light and a red—controlling—light for government (Harlow and Rawlings, 1997). But as has already been noted, much activity, especially in central government and Parliament, is neither regulated by Acts of Parliament nor subject to judicial review. Instead it is regulated by 'soft law' or 'quasi-legislation' (see Megarry, 1944; Ganz, 1987), such as codes of conduct and, central to the UK's Constitution, constitutional conventions which are non-legal rules of political morality and have often been textless, in the sense that they are not authoritatively written down.

Until about the 1980s many of the rules and principles governing political activity were unclear, or not written down or if written down they were not published. Some of these rules are summarized in Erskine May (1997), the 'bible' of parliamentary practice, and unpublished documents such as what is now known as the *Ministerial Code*, which was—and still is—no more than guidance drawn from lessons of previous governments about Cabinet government and ministerial pitfalls, and had no legally binding effect. But many of the principles and values by which politicians were supposed to be guided were unwritten. Despite this they were generally understood and observed. However, for reasons which will be noted in the chapters that follow, since the 1980s very many new and old soft law rules have been devised, written down and published in the form of codes, concordats, and so on. There has in effect been a process of juridification of politics, and this will be one of the focuses of discussion in this book.

Examples from each of the areas with which we are concerned will serve to illustrate the different forms that juridification can take.

- The House of Commons has imposed by *resolution* a requirement on ministers that they should not, other than in exceptional circumstances, enter into any new commitments in the Council of Ministers of the European Community until the Commons scrutiny process has been completed (this is known as the *scrutiny reserve*). A similar resolution applies to the House of Lords' scrutiny process (see Chapter 10).

- The government issued a *Code of Practice on Access to Government Information* (2nd edn, July 1997) which, in the absence of a Freedom of Information Act (until 2005) sets out the rules for giving or refusing access to information (see Chapter 8).

- In 1996 the House of Commons adopted by resolution a *Code of Conduct* incorporating the Seven Principles of Public Life drafted by the Committee on Standards in Public Life, with *Guidance* attached (see Chapter 9).

- By House of Commons *resolution* 'Short money' is paid to the opposition parties, which may be spent only on parliamentary activity. 'Cranbourne money' has been paid for similar purposes to the opposition parties in the House of Lords since its *resolution* of 1996 (see Chapter 7).

- The two Houses of Parliament passed *resolutions* on ministerial responsibility shortly before the dissolution of Parliament for the general election in 1997 (see Chapter 9). The House of Commons resolution was then incorporated into the *Ministerial Code*, which regulates the conduct of members of the government (see Chapter 11).

- The *Civil Servant Management Code* is promulgated under the Civil Service Order in Council. It contains the *Civil Service Code* setting out the rules of conduct of civil servants. These form part of the terms and conditions of employment of civil servants (see Chapter 12).

- The UK government and the devolved executives in Scotland, Wales, and Northern Ireland agreed on a series of *Memorandums of Understanding* and a number of *Supplementary Agreements* (Concordats) setting out how relations between the different levels would be conducted. These agreements seek to avoid potential conflicts between institutions (see Chapter 13).

- Local authorities are required by the Local Government Act 2000 to *adopt their own codes of conduct* containing *General Principles of Conduct* which have been approved by the Secretary of State and endorsed by Parliament (see Chapter 16).

- The Commissioner for Public Appointments issues a *Code of Practice for Public Appointment Procedures* which includes seven principles for public appointments including ministerial responsibility for appointments (see Chapter 17).

- The Lord Chancellor voluntarily issues a document *Judicial Appointments* setting out his own criteria and procedures for making these appointments (see Chapter 18).

It will be seen then that these codes (and there are many, many more) are used across a wide spectrum of government, they may or may not be drawn up with statutory authority, and they may or may not be subject to parliamentary or ministerial approval. They are in fact generally obeyed, although they are not enforceable in the courts. But their use, as we shall see, can undermine trust, they can have unintended consequences and they may impose disproportionate burdens on those regulated by them.

Judicializing politics

There has also been a considerable shift since the early 1990s in the direction of subjecting political processes and decisions to formal 'hard law' regulation that is enforceable by the courts—judicialization. This is a particular form of juridification.

Judicialization has come about largely as a result of Acts passed by the UK Parliament, notably the devolution legislation and the Human Rights Act. These Acts specifically give jurisdiction to the courts to enforce the provisions in statutes, many of which regulate political activity and decision-making. In addition the courts themselves have developed their jurisdiction in judicial review, so that many political decisions are reviewable by them at common law, even in the absence of specific statutory authority for judicial review (see Chapter 5). The most obvious and strongest example of the courts judicially reviewing political decisions is the position in European Community law, where British courts exercise a power to disapply legislation of the Westminster Parliament that is incompatible with European Community law (*see R. v. Secretary of State for Transport, ex parte Factortame (No. 2)* [1991] 1 AC 603; *(No. 5)* [2000] 1 AC 524; see Chapter 4). We have already noted that the justifications for this power are contractarian or functional. Whatever the justifications, the fact that political power—the power to legislate either through Parliament or in the form of secondary legislation (statutory instruments) or Orders in Council—is now subject to control by the courts where European Community law issues arise is a major departure from the earlier position that the courts could not disapply an Act of Parliament.

Devolution too has resulted in judicialization of politics. The devolved bodies in Scotland, Northern Ireland, and Wales are subject to statutory limitations on their powers: their competence is limited so that they may not act or legislate contrary to European Community law or the European Convention on Human Rights, nor in areas of competence reserved to the UK Parliament. The devolution legislation also includes some measures subjecting the formation of the executive and committee arrangements in elected bodies to legal regulation in a way that does not apply to the UK Parliament or government. These bodies then are liable to have their acts, decisions, or laws disapplied by the courts. In other words the political activity of these bodies is subject to court-enforced legal regulation. They have their own written constitutions. Again, as with the European Community, the justifications put forward for the limits on the powers of these bodies are partly contractarian and functional rather than democratic. A deal has been done between these countries and the United Kingdom, including England, that certain powers are transferred to bodies elected in Scotland, Wales, and Northern Ireland. The UK itself could not function effectively unless there was judicial review of possible excesses of power by the devolved bodies, as the UK government needs to be protected from liability to the EU for breach of European Community law by the devolved bodies and from accountability to the European Court of Human Rights for breach of the European Convention on Human Rights by the devolved bodies, and from being found to be in breach of its other international obligations. Further, certain aspects of the law of the UK would become unworkable if different laws were in force in different parts of the UK.

Comity, trust, and juridification

The effective working of the Westminster system has traditionally relied heavily on comity between institutions, especially between the courts on the one hand and government and Parliament on the other hand. Quite apart from the courts' own doctrine of parliamentary sovereignty, through which they defer to Parliament, the courts recognize that the two Houses of Parliament have exclusive cognizance of their own proceedings, which means that the courts will not interfere in those matters (see generally Erskine May 1997, ch. 11; Bradley and Ewing, 2002, ch. 11). Thus, the courts will not entertain a claim that an Act of Parliament was not duly passed (*Edinburgh and Dalkeith Railway v. Wauchope* (1842) 8 Cl and F 710; *Pickin v. British Railways Board* [1974] AC 765). Both Parliament and the courts would regard it as a breach of parliamentary privilege if the courts were to do so. This position was reached after a series of conflicts between the courts and the House of Commons in the nineteenth century (see *Stockdale v. Hansard* (1839) 9 Ad and E 1; *Sheriff of Middlesex* case (1840) 11 A and E 273; *Bradlaugh v. Gossett* (1884) 12 QBD 271, Erskine May, 1997, ch. 11). By way of resolution of the conflict, a stand-off was reached between the courts and Parliament. The courts assert a jurisdiction to determine whether a privilege claimed by Parliament exists, but if it exists they will not interfere in its exercise. (The devolution legislation protects Acts of the devolved legislatures from judicial review on the ground that due procedures were not followed in the course of the legislative process, thus extending similar protections to those enjoyed by the Westminster Parliament to these bodies.)

Thus because of the courts' and Parliament's position, internal parliamentary political activity is entirely self-regulating, though as we shall see the system has come under criticism for the way it has dealt with instances of untrustworthy behaviour (Chapter 9). The courts have also traditionally been reluctant to undermine comity between themselves and Parliament or government by intervening in substantive policy-laden political decisions—in the sense of controversial and value-laden decisions requiring political expertise that they lack—for instance in the field of national security and defence (see for instance the *Council of Civil Service Unions v. Minister for the Civil Service* [1985] AC 374, discussed in Chapter 5; and *R. v. Ministry of Defence, ex parte Smith* [1996] QB 517) unless, of course, their intervention is clearly required by legislation. (Under the Human Rights Act the courts are required to adjudicate on such issues if they involve interferences by ministerial decisions with Convention rights, such as the right to respect for private and family life and non-discrimination: see Chapter 6. This duty may well undermine the comity between the courts and the government.)

The concern to preserve comity between Parliament and the courts is voluntary. This is borne out by Lord Woolf's reference in *R v. Parliamentary Commissioner for Standards, ex parte Al Fayed* ([1998] 1 WLR 669, at 670G) to the court's 'self-denying ordinance in relation to interfering with the proceedings in Parliament'. He refused an application for judicial review of the Parliamentary Commissioner for Standard's findings in a complaint of breach of the standards of conduct expected of MPs (see Chapter 9).

Comity works both ways, and government and Parliament observe a number of conventions designed to preserve good relations with the courts, including the *sub judice* rule (see Chapter 18). Comity is a delicate relationship. If it breaks down—if self-denial and self-restraint are abandoned—relations between institutions may not only become acrimonious, but they may become judicialized. For instance, until the decision in *M v. Home Office* ([1994] AC 377) the government had always complied with court orders, though their view was that they did so as a matter of grace—comity—rather than legal obligation. In that case, discussed in Chapter 9, the government had disobeyed an order of the court that the deportation of an immigrant should be delayed pending the decision in his court case, and deported him. When the Home Secretary was called to the court to answer for his disobedience to the court order, he claimed that he had not been obliged as a matter of law to comply with it. The House of Lords, after reconsidering earlier rulings to the effect that ministers could not be found guilty of contempt of court, ruled that though the Crown was immune, Ministers were not. (For discussion of the concept of 'the Crown' see Chapter 11). The change of approach by the court was facilitated by the way in which the jurisdiction of the courts over ministerial decisions had developed in the *Factortame* case (*supra*), where issues of European Community law were at stake (see Chapter 4), but one of the lessons we can draw from *M. v. Home Office* is that if a party acts in an untrustworthy way and in breach of comity—as here by disregarding a court order—it is possible that the basis of the relationship with the courts will move from trust and comity to judicialization.

There was also for many years a strong tradition of comity between central and local government (see Chapter 16). This broke down from the late 1970s. That period marked the end of the post-war settlement and consensus between the parties on matters of policy and the welfare state, and it led to sharp political divisions and partisanship, notably as between central and local government. Local authorities controlled by Labour opposed many of the Conservative government's policies, leading to concerns about the politicization of their administration and in due course to increases in the level of juridification—and judicialization—of local government.

Regard for comity in the system is essentially a cultural phenomenon, explicable by the fact that there is a high level of trust generally in British society (see O'Neill, 2002). Trust has been identified as a major factor in economic development and lack of trust as a major hindrance to development (see Fukuyama, 1995). Trust is one of the principles of good governance (see Chapter 3). A low level of trust has serious implications not only for constitutional arrangements but also for an economy. Trust is valuable 'social capital' which is hard earned and easily dissipated (O'Neill, 2002, ch. 1). So is its cousin comity.

British politicians have commonly if not always acted, or been believed to act, in a trustworthy way, and this has contributed to the culture of reliance on trust and comity, and the fact that intense juridification of politics has been avoided in the UK—until recently. The increase in juridification, including judicialization, in the period with which we are concerned is largely due to public or governmental perceptions of an increase in untrustworthy behaviour among politicians. As O'Neill (2002, ch. 1) observes, we cannot be objectively sure that there has been an increase in untrustworthiness, but there appears to be that perception.

Opinion polls suggest that the public *say* that they trust Members of Parliament and other politicians less than they used to. But, O'Neill suggests, in practice they are still trusted. What is commonly called a crisis of trust is in fact a culture of suspicion, not only suspicion of government on the part of the people, but between state institutions. The culture of suspicion has given rise to 'an unending stream of new legislation and regulation, memoranda and instructions, guidance and advice, which floods into public sector institutions' (O'Neill, 2002, ch. 3). Thus juridification has been treated as the solution to what is perceived to be a problem of untrustworthiness. But some kinds of juridification run risks of undermining the level of trust in society by encouraging a culture of suspicion, and even increasing untrustworthy behaviour. O'Neill suggests that other mechanisms need to be devised that will foster trust and trustworthy behaviour, matters that will be considered in the discussion of good governance in Chapter 3.

In the chapters that follow particular examples of the increase in juridification and judicialization over the last twenty years or so will be noted. They will show that there has been an erosion of a culture of trust and comity as underpinning constitutional arrangements in the UK, and their replacement by suspicion, inter-institutional, and intra-institutional conflict, and central control which undermine pluralism and responsibility.

The Politico-Legal Debate

The trends towards juridification and in particular judicialization of politics have given rise to a debate about the relationship and proper balance between politics or politicians and law or the courts in our constitutional arrangements, a politico-legal debate. On one side of the debate the preference is for political rather than judicially enforced legal checks on government; on the other side political checks are regarded as inadequate and needing to be supplemented by legal checks in the form of judicial review—judicialization. Ultimately the debate is about the nature of the constitution. Does it have, or should it have, normative content? To what extent should political activity—the activity of elected representatives—be subject to legal controls enforced by the courts? It may be useful to introduce the arguments briefly here.

Many of the writers who favour political over legal checks are distrustful of judges, whom they regard as hostile to socialist values and often inclined to favour the powerful against the poor and the state against the workers (see Griffith, 1979, 1993, 2000, 2001; Ewing and Gearty, 1990; Ewing, 2001*a*; Tomkins, 2002). They exhibit a greater degree of trust in politicians than do those in favour of increased judicial supervision of government. The latter claim that the development of legal checks is 'constitutional' in a normative sense, while the former tend to regard the Constitution as lacking normative content, being no more that the outcome of past conflicts between differing groups and interests in society.

A good place to start in the case for political controls over political activity and against recourse to law and the courts, at least for those of us who are lawyers, is Griffith's seminal lecture in 1979 entitled 'The Political Constitution'. In 1979 Griffith was concerned particularly with the campaign that was then being waged in favour of the enactment of a Bill of Rights for the UK and possible further constitutional reforms such as devolution (Scarman, 1974; Hailsham, 1976, 1978). Griffith criticized Lord Hailsham, the then shadow Lord Chancellor, for wanting to 'institutionalize the theory of limited government' (Hailsham, 1978, 226) because such a development would produce conflicts between the government and Parliament on the one hand and the courts on the other. This aversion to conflict between the courts and the other branches of government has been noted in the discussion of comity in the previous section of this chapter. Griffith argued—and still does so—that conflicts about rights, for instance, are essentially political conflicts (Griffith, 1979, 14), that law is politics by other means (Griffith, 2001, 59), and furthermore that judges are not suited to resolve such conflicts, even with the aid of a Bill of Rights (see also Griffith, 1991). This is partly because he sees in past decisions of the courts evidence of illiberal instincts, which run counter to the spirit of Bills of Rights. He purports not to be opposed to civil and political rights, only to giving the judges the right to decide whether an interference with those rights on public interest grounds is justified. He regards these as essentially political decisions, and states: 'I believe firmly that political decisions should be taken by politicians' (see also Ewing, 1999a). It is not clear, however, to what extent Griffith would accept that politicians be constrained in their decision-making by rules that are not enforceable by the judges.

In his later writings (Griffith, 2000) Griffith has identified the lack of resources and advice available to judges as equipping them less well than politicians to make decisions about the public interest and the balancing of rights against public interests. Politicians have more experience than judges of public opinion, and judges are ill-equipped to deal with the increasingly political arguments that are put before them in cases where an individual is challenging governmental decisions, and to come to informed judgments. Griffith here suggests that it is not a question of whether it is constitutional or unconstitutional for judges to make political decisions, but rather a question of lack of qualification to do so. He also suggests that judges have their own interests in taking on additional powers in relation to government, influenced by their self-aggrandizing belief in 'the values of the common law under the benign influence of Her Majesty's judges' (Griffith, 2001, 42).

Griffith's objections to Bills of Rights and generally to transferring to the judges decisions that are made by politicians are not only political and pragmatic. They are also philosophical. In his view rights are no more than political claims, and the law is not and cannot be a substitute for politics (Griffith, 1979, 16). His response to those who argue for the constitutional protection of rights is to challenge the concept that anything is 'constitutional' in a normative sense. For him 'The constitution is no more and no less than what happens' (p. 19). He rejects the idea that there is a democratic deficit and that this justifies an increase in judicial power. He considers that it is the responsibility of political institutions to determine the shape of the Constitution and the part to be played in it by the judiciary. 'In a democracy to believe otherwise is a dangerous error' (Griffith, 2001,

66–7). He thus has more trust in the will and ability of political institutions to discharge their responsibilities than commentators on the other side of the argument.

Griffith's approach is similar to that of many other commentators, from the worlds of the law, politics, and philosophy. Waldron (1999) too argues that democracy requires that political decisions be taken by politically accountable persons rather than by the courts. This is particularly the case in relation to qualifications to individual rights. Waldron's position is that in a country with a culture of liberty we should be hesitant about the enactment of any canonical list of rights, particularly if the aim is to put that canon beyond the scope of ordinary political debate and revision (p. 212). He rejects the general idea of a Bill of Rights—even, by implication, the New Zealand technique of an ordinary Act of Parliament which can be impliedly or expressly repealed by later legislation—and he rejects even more strongly the idea of an entrenched Bill of Rights. (Here it is worth noting, in anticipation of our discussion in Chapter 6, that the UK Human Rights Act 1998 is not entrenched.) However, later in his book Waldron seems to concede that some procedural protection for rights and other legislation might be justified—such as delay or 'slowing down' for a period before a recently enacted principle can be reversed, as long as it does not privilege certain rights (e.g. civil and political rather than social and economic rights) or undermine majoritarianism (pp. 301, 305–6).

Waldron's approach is heavily based on an assumption of a liberal culture and he does not suggest that in a country without such a culture the entrenched protection of rights would be wrong. But his assumption also seems to be that suitably liberal cultures do exist in Western democracies such as the United States or the United Kingdom—an assumption that I myself am not too confident about. At the time of writing suspected terrorists have been held on the authority of the President of the USA by the American army in Guantanamo Bay, outside the USA, without trial for many months (see *R. (Abbasi) v. Secretary of State for Foreign and Commonwealth Affairs and Secretary of State for the Home Department*, [2002] EWCA Civ. 6 November 2002; Chapter 5); and the UK Anti-terrorism, Crime, and Security Act 2001 authorizes the indefinite detention without trial of foreign suspected terrorists who cannot be deported (see further Bellamy, 1999, 2001; Pettit, 1999; Crick, 2000).

Griffith's views are in many ways preferences for the least worst way of making decisions in society. He is sceptical about politicians and politics and about judges and the law, but he prefers politics because the electorate can pass judgement on it. Another more positive way of looking at politics is as the best protection against tyranny and oligarchy, both of which preclude politics. Crick argues that politics is 'essential to genuine freedom' (Crick, 2000, 18). Tomkins (2002) urges that 'Politics is something which should be celebrated, not castigated. For politics is what makes us free'. The freedom he has in mind is freedom from domination, whereas the freedom that commentators and judges often have in mind when restricting the powers of politicians is the freedom to be left alone by the state.

Clearly if there were no politicians, no politics, and no elections, the courts and law could not counter tyranny or oligarchy. Indeed the tyrant would seek to use the courts and laws to suppress politics and the rights or freedoms of individuals. Equally though, if there were only politicians and no courts or no judicial review there would be a risk of politicians oppressing their opponents or minorities. A balance has to be achieved as to the extent to which political activity is regulated by law and the courts. Both politicians and the courts have a role in seeking and adjusting this balance. And the importance attached to the UK tradition of preserving and enhancing trust and comity will be influential in setting and resetting the balance.

Much of the debate about the balance between political and legal checks has been generated by the prospect and, since 2000, the reality of a Human Rights Act (see Chapter 6). The Human Rights Act 1998 (which came into force on 2 October 2000) enables the courts to quash decisions by Ministers and other public authorities or private bodies exercising public functions, if they interfere with the civil and political rights that are set out in the articles of the European Convention on Human Rights that have been incorporated into UK law (see Appendix). But the Act does not enable decisions that are authorized by statute to be set aside if that would involve disapplying the statute. Thus the Act protects political decisions embodied in statute, but not political decisions taken by Ministers and other public bodies where they have a choice about whether to act in breach of Convention rights. This is a halfway house between the Griffith view that judges should not adjudicate on any political decisions and the more commonly found approach in democracies with written Constitutions and entrenched bills of rights, where there is often provision for breaches of rights to be remedied by an independent referee, whether the courts or a council of state or constitutional council.

While the UK legal establishment has generally been in favour of the Human Rights Act, there is an impressive body of sceptical opinion about it. Ewing (2001a), for instance, argues that the Act raises liberty to a higher legal status than equality, thus reinforcing judicial preferences for the former and hostility to social and economic rights which can promote equality. He is particularly scathing about the judges who 'wax lyrical about individual rather than popular sovereignty and who are now empowered to reassert those claims against the other branches of government' (p. 116).

Those in favour of judicial rather than political resolution of where the balance between individual civil and political rights and public interests should lie generally have different concepts of democracy and the constitution from those on the political side of the politico-legal debate. We consider these concepts of democracy in the next chapter, but here it suffices to note that broadly the divisions of opinion are between majoritarian-ism on the one hand, and a view that democracy necessarily involves the idea that individuals and especially minorities should be protected from the majority acting through politicians on the other hand; between a view that a Constitution, being only 'what happens', does not have normative content; and a view that a constitution does contain rules and principles that are there because they are thought to be right and better than other rules; and between a view that the balance between individual rights and the public interest is best weighed up by politicians, subject only to being held to account in Parliament, and a view that this is better done objectively in a court. There is greater scepticism among those on the legal side of the debate about the willingness of Parlia-ment to hold Ministers to account on these matters than is the case on the politics side, and greater faith in judges' competence to weigh up the balance, on the basis of adver-sarial procedures and evidence, coupled with deference to politicians on highly sensitive matters, which stems partly from the tradition of comity, discussed above.

It is perhaps worth noting here that the culture of reliance in the UK on political decision-making, and the relative non-judicialization of politics is unusual in the Western democracies. Almost all of them have written Constitutions which give either the ordinary courts or a Supreme Court (as in the USA) or a Constitutional Court (as in Germany) or a Constitutional Council and a Council of State (as in France) the power to determine whether an act or proposed act is compatible with the Constitution, including any bill of rights. In most of these countries this is a matter of pride. In some, notably the Scandinavian, countries the courts' power to set aside statutes is seldom exercised. The arguments in favour of such arrangements are, in broad terms, that democracy is not simple majoritarianism but requires the legal protection of rights and of constitutionality, that politicians can be expected to want to interfere with individual rights for reasons of self-interest or self-preservation rather than in the public interest, and they should be hindered from doing so; that neither Ministers nor Parliament can be trusted themselves to uphold the Constitution and rights, as it may seem to them to be better to subordinate them to other interests; that periodic elections are not sufficient to provide guarantees against abuse of power; and that judges or members of constitutional councils are well qualified to do so. There are in effect different cultures and different understandings of the culture, different levels of trust, and different weights given to comity in these countries, from the understanding of the culture and level of trust and the importance attached to comity of those in favour of the political Constitution in the UK.

Towards Constitutionalism?

In the last five years or so courts in the UK and some legal commentators (Jowell, 1999, 2000; Steyn, 1999; Elliott, 2002) have been interpreting the ways in which the system is developing as a move, which they generally welcome, in the direction of a theory of limited government which they refer to as 'constitutionalism' (see Chapter 5). By limited government is meant either that Parliament is limited in its legislative capacity by procedural or substantive restrictions (which is not the case in the UK save in relation to European Community law), or that government is so limited, or both. The limitations cover interferences with what the courts regard as 'fundamental rights' and other principles of a constitutional kind such as are found in Magna Carta, the Bill of Rights, 1689, the Act of Settlement, 1700, and other important Acts of Parliament.

It is often said that a Parliament needs to have unlimited powers as only so can popular sovereignty find expression. For some popular sovereignty in this sense is the essence of democracy (see discussion in Chapter 2), and constitutionalism in the sense of limited legislative capacity is anti-democratic. But constitutionalism in the sense of a Parliament constrained in its freedom to legislate—for instance to legislate in breach of human rights—is also said to be essential in a democracy. The point is that different concepts of democracy are being relied on by those on each side of this argument. (The operation of concepts of democracy in the UK will be explored in Chapter 2 and subsequent chapters.)

The particular form of constitutionalism to which the courts have been referring in recent cases is liberal, and the point needs to be made at the outset that the term 'constitutionalism' could be applied to other kinds of arrangement. A system which put substantive equality before liberty, for instance, might be termed 'social democratic constitutionalism'. The uses of the term 'constitutionalism' by those in favour of limited government as being linked to liberalism has attracted considerable hostility. Tomkins, for instance, in his review of Barendt's *Introduction to Constitutional Law* (1998) objects to the assumption that the general principles of the British constitution are principles of *liberal* constitutionalism and that this is the only form that constitutionalism can take (Tomkins, 1999, 529, 534). It is indeed true that other, often parallel, current concepts of constitutionalism find expression in our system—republicanism or participative constitutionalism, or communitarianism for example (see Chapter 2).

Although constitutionalism seems to be discussed currently among lawyers more than politicans, it is fundamentally a political theory. Lord Steyn (1997) has suggested that:

[T]he principle of constitutionalism . . . is neither a rule nor a principle of law. It is a political theory as to the type of institutional arrangements that are necessary in order to support the democratic ideal. It holds that the exercise of government power must be controlled in order that it should not be destructive of the very values which it was intended to promote (at p. 87).

It is worth noting here that the emphasis is on controlling the exercise of government power, not of legislative power. Although Steyn maintains that the theory is a political one, it entails that some controls over government power will be exercised by the courts. Constitutionalism affords to the courts a greater role than Griffith and others who support the political Constitution would probably accept.

One of the many implications of this concept of constitutionalism is that pressure for a constitutional court, democratically acceptable methods of appointment of judges and clarification of the roles of the Lord Chancellor become of importance, matters which will be considered in Chapter 18.

The interest among the UK legal establishment in constitutionalism reflects a trend in a number of other countries, especially countries like New Zealand and Israel which, like the UK, have customary Constitutions, and other countries whose legal system is based on the common law. The position and attitude of UK courts on the question of legal control of the executive, even of American-style judicial review of legislation (which permits the Supreme Court to strike down unconstitutional legislation), may move in favour of judicial control as contacts between courts in different jurisdictions increase. Steyn (2002) in the 2001 Holdsworth lecture noted that there has been a renaissance of constitutionalism in Australia, Canada, India, New Zealand, and South Africa. A dialogue is taking place through their judgments between Supreme Courts of constitutional democracies, notably in respect of human rights issues, in which the Appellate Committee of the House of Lords participates. In their capacity as members of the Judicial Committee of the Privy Council the Law Lords hear appeals from Commonwealth countries including countries in the Caribbean and New Zealand. Judges of the Court of Appeal and the High Court, and of inferior courts and tribunals, regularly visit courts in other jurisdictions and receive visiting judges from other jurisdictions. Among the Law Lords currently are a retired President of the Court of Appeal of New Zealand and several South African born members who have practised in South Africa. No doubt as a result of their knowledge of and contact with other systems, judges find themselves indulging in the irresistible exercise of comparative law. Judges in the UK cannot fail to be influenced by the experiences of judges in countries with written Constitutions and a more legalistic approach, where less trust is placed in comity and politics than in the UK.

An interest in constitutionalism in other countries is also surfacing in academic journals, and legal commentators and courts in the UK may well be borrowing from overseas experience in reinterpreting the UK's arrangements (see for instance Joseph, 1998, 2000; Barak, 1999; Weinrib, 1999). In Chapter 5 we shall explore constitutionalism further, and in Chapter 20 we shall draw together the points about constitutionalism and the political Constitution that emerge from discussion in the chapters that follow and try to reach some conclusions about the nature and implications of this trend.

That completes our survey of the background to the period of constitutional reform in which the UK finds itself and some of the debates that it has generated. We turn in the next two chapters to three themes that have run through much of those debates, changing concepts of democracy, citizenship, and good governance. Part II will consider citizen-centred reforms to the relationship between the individual and governmental bodies, notably the Human Rights Act, the introduction of new forms of election, the use of referendums, and the regulation of parties and party funding, and a Freedom of Information Act, coming into effect fully in 2005. In Part III we consider reforms affecting particular institutions, including Parliament, government, the devolved bodies, local authorities, quangos, and the judiciary. And in the last two chapters we draw together threads from previous chapters to try to reach conclusions about what modernization has meant, how democracy, citizenship, and good governance are evolving, and to what extent the political constitution is becoming a law-based system imbued with a theory of constitutionalism.

2

Themes: Democracy and Citizenship

Three themes recur in debates about the reform of the UK constitution: how the concepts of democracy, citizenship, and good governance are developing and how they should be reflected in our constitutional arrangements. Given the importance of these themes, it will be helpful to consider the issues they raise before proceeding in the next two sections of this book to discuss particular aspects of the working of the system and its reform. There is no very clear or single meaning to each of the three concepts. In practice ideas from former periods still influence our understanding of them. An obvious example is the way in which the concept of the 'subject', dating from feudal times, is still used when a more current term would be 'citizen' or—depending on the context—'national'. Also, these three concepts overlap to a considerable degree, and they are interrelated. They should be mutually supportive—democracy should support good governance, citizenship should support democracy, and so on.

In this chapter we consider the related theories of democracy and citizenship as they are developing in the UK. Our discussion of democracy concentrates on institutional and procedural issues to do with representative and participatory democracy. Citizenship is the relationship between individuals and the state and civil society, especially the rights and duties of individuals and the ways in which they can participate in political processes. There is thus substantial overlap between the two concepts. In discussion of participatory democracy the emphasis will be on how state bodies can or should promote participatory processes, while the discussion of citizenship will focus on the legal rights and responsibilities of individuals and provisions that promote social cohesion and civil society. The next chapter discusses the third concept, good governance.

Democracy

Many items on the constitutional reform agenda have been concerned with democratizing the system of government. We focus here on the concepts of democracy and democratization that are reflected in British constitutional arrangements and the debates about reform in the UK, rather than on broader issues of democratic theory (on which see for instance Craig, 1990; Loughlin, 1992). In practice debates about the reform of the British system of government have focused on a number of interrelated issues. We shall discuss them and the concepts of democracy that they imply in turn.

Representative democracy and parliamentary sovereignty

The United Kingdom is a representative democracy, in that the House of Commons, the dominant chamber of Parliament, is elected, and government Ministers are required to be Members of one or other House of Parliament. This is not the only form that representative democracy can take. Presidential systems, in which the head of government is separately elected and is disqualified from membership of the legislature, as in the United States, are also representative democracies. Each country's arrangements evolve in response to its history and culture, and the UK's arrangements reflect this strongly. However, a common requirement in all representative democracies is that there should be universal adult suffrage—though the age at which the right to vote is acquired may vary, and some exceptions are normally made, for instance for the insane or prisoners. All votes should be of equal value in a representative democracy—political equality is another essential. (In Chapter 7 we consider the operation of electoral systems in Britain, in which there is an issue as to the equality of votes for minority parties under the first past the post system that is used for the House of Commons elections.)

The UK Parliament is legally sovereign (save in relation to European Community law—see Chapter 4) and we shall consider shortly what model of democracy this characteristic implies. The legislative supremacy of Parliament is in practice a fundamental legal and cultural aspect of British parliamentary democracy. The courts, government, and Parliament and the general public recognize and accept the doctrine (see generally Goldsworthy, 1999; MacCormick, 1999; cf. Allan, 1993; Elliott, 2002). However, the Parliament of Scotland before the Treaty of Union of 1707 did not claim absolute sovereignty and there is some discontent in Scotland with the assumption that the Westminster Parliament inherited the English character of sovereignty rather than the Scottish concept of limited power.

For lawyers, parliamentary sovereignty means, in brief, that the legislature may pass legislation on any subject matter, and the courts will give effect to that legislation (see *Cheney v. Conn* [1968] 1 All ER 779). Generally if two measures conflict, the most recently passed one impliedly repeals the earlier one, so it is open to the present Parliament to alter laws passed by its predecessors simply by passing another Act (*Ellen Street Estates v. Minister of Health* [1934] KB 590). Generally if it wishes to change a previous Act Parliament must do so by Act of Parliament. However, the courts require the use of very clear words in an Act which interferes with fundamental or constitutional rights or the Convention rights that are protected by the Human Rights Act 1998 (see discussion of constitutionalism in Chapter 5) and recently it has been suggested that only words expressly repealing earlier provisions can be effective to do so in respect of 'constitutional statutes' (see Laws LJ in *Thoburn v. Sunderland City Council* [2002] 3 WLR 247, and discussion in Chapter 5). Laws LJ suggested in the case of *International Transport GmbH Roth v. Secretary of State for the Home Department* ([2002] EWCA 158, [2002] 3 WLR 344) that the British system was 'at an intermediate stage between parliamentary sovereignty and constitutional supremacy' (at para. 71), but it would be a revolutionary step for the courts to go so far as to hold that an Act that expressly repealed a previous 'constitutional' provision should not be given effect and it seems most unlikely that they would do so.

There is debate about whether the doctrine of sovereignty is judge-made, a creation of the common law, or whether it stems from judicial recognition of a custom of acceptance of parliamentary primacy, recognition that is shared by others in power (see Goldsworthy, 1999, ch. 11 for a summary of the debate). In my view it is a matter of recognition, based in custom and culture.

Five main justifications may be put forward for parliamentary sovereignty. They are not all based on theories of representative democracy and they do not all require UK style sovereignty, in the sense of the power to make any law in proceedings requiring only simple majorities in the two Houses of Parliament.

First, the need for a centre of authority in a state. An implication of a doctrine of sovereignty in a constitution is that it is necessary for the citizens to be clear about who is the ultimate authority and whose orders should take priority over others where there is a clash. Unless it is clear who the sovereign is, and unless the sovereign is generally obeyed, a state of lawlessness and disorder is likely to prevail. There needs to be a *grundnorm* or ultimate rule of recognition in a legal system, and in the UK the *grundnorm* is parliamentary sovereignty (Kelsen, 1949; Hart, 1994). We are not concerned here to argue out whether a single authority is necessary or not, although we shall see in later chapters that theories of shared or divided sovereignty are surfacing in relation to the European Community, and in the development by the UK courts of their jurisdiction in judicial review. The point is that this justification is not necessarily a *democratic* justification for sovereignty. It has its origins in pre-democratic Hobbesian concerns about what we would now call good governance.

Secondly, sovereignty may be justified on the ground that Parliament is the institution through which the popular will finds expression, and the 'sovereignty of the people' is given effect. This is in effect a democratic and republican justification. Many written Constitutions expressly recite in their preambles that the people are sovereign. But many of them do not subscribe to a doctrine of parliamentary sovereignty on British lines. Most written Constitutions provide either that certain of their provisions cannot be changed at all, or that they can only be changed if there is a special majority for change in the Parliament, or if a majority of voters in a referendum were in favour of change. Constitutional provisions protecting civil and political rights, the independence of the judiciary, and the autonomy of states in a federation are commonly protected in these ways. There is no such special protection in the UK constitutional arrangements.

Neither popular sovereignty nor the popular will are *in practice* treated as the justification for parliamentary sovereignty in the British system. Griffith put it pithily:

In this country we have stayed clear of one bit of nonsense which is commonly advanced in countries as diverse in their political structures as the Chinese People's Republic, the Soviet Union and the United States of America. I mean the view that sovereignty resides in the people who delegate it to their politicians who hold it in trust for them. (Griffith, 1979, 3)

A claim by a British government that its policies were in accordance with the general or popular will and *therefore* it was democratic for Parliament to put its policies into effect by legislation would be particularly unconvincing where, as has been the case invariably for at least a century, no party has won a majority of seats in the House of Commons on a majority of the votes cast in the most recent election. But even if a government were to win a majority of seats in Parliament on a majority of the votes cast in an election, that fact alone would not mean that what the government proposed to do was generally accepted to be substantively democratic. If it did, then opposition would be anti-democratic, and that is not how opposition is in practice regarded in the UK. Democracy in the UK, in other words, is not simply a matter of procedure—the election of the legislature by universal suffrage and its right to pass any law on simple majorities—but is commonly regarded as also having substantive content.

Does the fact that the parties publish election manifestos affect the credibility of the popular sovereignty argument in favour of the UK's concept of the legal sovereignty of Parliament? After general elections the winning party claims a mandate for its policies, and the Salisbury convention requires the House of Lords not to oppose manifesto bills at second or third reading (see Chapter 10). The basis of a government's claim to be entitled to implement manifesto commitments is that the manifesto contained summaries of what the party proposed to do, and the electors have approved those proposals. But it is of course accepted that members of opposition parties are entitled to oppose the government's proposals, even if they were in the manifesto. In practice the fact that a policy was included in a manifesto does not add up to a claim to be entitled to give effect to the popular will, only to a claim that this is what the government considers to be the right thing to do, and that it is legitimate for it to seek to do so because it won the election, the voters knowing full well what the party would do. Opposition parties are not considered to be guilty of seeking to frustrate the popular will when opposing government. They are doing their constitutional job in requiring a government to justify and defend its policies, and their MPs are exercising a right to give or refuse consent to legislation, exercising their own judgement on behalf of their constituents. In practice, then, popular sovereignty is not treated as a *democratic* justification for parliamentary sovereignty in the UK.

Third, parliamentary sovereignty may be regarded as desirable and consistent with democratic principles because it imposes constraints on the powers and freedom of action of the *executive* by making it accountable to Parliament. Parliamentary sovereignty amounts to a veto power that may be used against the government. It is part of a system of checks and balances, and it protects individuals against domination by the executive. This is one of the rationales advanced for sovereignty that does appear to prevail in the UK. When legal sovereignty passed from the King to the King-and-Queen (William and Mary)-in-Parliament with the Glorious Revolution and the Bill of Rights 1689, there was no implication of popular sovereignty, only of control of the executive. The House of Lords was not, of course, elected, and it was certainly not 'popular'. The Commons were also not elected in a way that would then have been considered 'democratic'. Indeed, democracy was regarded as a dangerous concept until well into the nineteenth century. The Glorious Revolution of 1689 was about subjecting executive power—the King—to a range of limitations that secured that certain laws could not be changed, and things could not be done without the consent of the Commons and Lords in Parliament assembled. Thus the provisions of a statute cannot normally be changed by a simple majority vote in one or even both Houses of Parliament (see *Bowles v. Bank of England* [1913] 1 Ch 57) and one of the most significant points about the transfer of sovereignty from the monarch to Parliament in the seventeenth century was the fact that Parliament imposes fairly elaborate procedural requirements on its legislation, whereas the monarch had powers to alter the law summarily by proclamation (but cf. the *Case of Proclamations* (1611) 12 Co. Rep. 74, noted in Chapter 5). Bills have to be read three times in each House, there is a committee stage for detailed line by line scrutiny, scrutiny by the Joint Committee on Human Rights of the two Houses for compatibility of a bill with the European Convention on Human Rights, scrutiny by the committees on delegated legislation and scrutiny by the Constitution Committee of the House of Lords for its constitutional implications. (However, there is increasing use of 'Henry VIII clauses' in Acts, which enable Ministers to amend Acts of Parliament by orders that are laid before Parliament but do not need to go through the usual legislative process for statutes: see for instance the discussion of remedial orders in Chapters 6 and 19.)

The justification for parliamentary sovereignty in the late seventeenth century was not, then, a desire to give effect to the popular will, but rather to secure that government was conducted through and in accordance with law, that laws were made in a procedurally appropriate way, and to secure government by consent—the consents being those of the Commons and the Lords. The Commons were supposed to decide in accordance with their own judgements of what was in the public interest and not to be mandated by their constituents or patrons (Burke, 1776). They were not regarded as mouthpieces for the expression of the popular will.

In the nineteenth and twentieth centuries, as the franchise became universal, the concept of representative democracy developed. Ministerial responsibility was an important element of the theory, securing that government was accountable to Parliament (see discussions in Chapters 9, 10, and 11). Representative democracy was given effect through the conventions that all ministers should be members of one or other House of Parliament, that the Commons should have control of supply, and that Ministers owe it to Parliament to account for and explain the actions and decisions of their departments. The government as a whole is expected to stand by its policies, and if a government is defeated in the Commons on a vote of no confidence it should resign. The underlying tenets of representative democracy in the UK are, then, that the Queen's government has to be carried on but that the executive should be accountable to Parliament, rather than that government is to be conducted in line with the 'general will' as was—and remained until after the Second World War—the theory in many Western European democracies. But the effectiveness of the checks and balances to which the executive is subject has become weaker as the party system and the electoral system ensure that the government can almost always get its way in Parliament.

The constitutions of the member states of the European Community, all of which are accepted to be democratic—that is a condition of membership—reflect a range of concepts of democracy that differ from one another and in particular from the British position, in a number of ways. In Germany, notions of popular and parliamentary sovereignty were rejected in the aftermath of Nazism, and under the post-war Constitution the powers of the Parliament are limited and in some respects subordinated to the powers of the Länder—the states that form the federation. The German Parliament's laws are subject to constitutional review by the constitutional court, the Bundesverfassungsgericht. France and Italy are unitary states and their Parliaments' legislation, too, is subject to constitutional review. The French Conseil constitutionnel can scrutinize a bill that has been passed by the Parliament (a *loi*) for its compatibility with the Constitution, and if it finds the *loi* to be incompatible it may not be promulgated by the President. Once promulgated a *loi* cannot be challenged in the ordinary courts (Bell, 1992, 29–56; see Chapter 5). In sum, many other Western democracies, notably Germany, Italy, France, Spain, abandoned Constitutions based on the general will and parliamentary sovereignty in the aftermath of fascist regimes after the Second World War, and they have introduced systems of constitutional review of legislation. To them this is a strong positive feature of their democracies. Parliamentary sovereignty UK style is not essential in a system that may be regarded as democratic in the world order. It is peculiarly British, reflecting a particular history and culture.

The democratic theory that developed in the late nineteenth and twentieth centuries in the United Kingdom was, then, that government ought in a democracy to be accountable to—and dismissible by—the elected representatives of the people. As we shall see a number of issues on the current constitutional reform agenda are responses to concern that this theory is no longer reflective of the reality. In practice Parliament does not control the executive. The executive governs through Parliament. Pressures to reform the electoral system and the operation of ministerial responsibility through reforms of the select committees of the House of Commons are concerned to make the theory of democratic accountability to a representative elected body real. Devolution seeks to move accountability closer to the electorate—to introduce a degree of subsidiarity (see discussion in Chapters 4 and 13)—modifying the theory of ministerial responsibility to take account of the special needs and interests of Scotland, Wales, and Northern Ireland. The devolution arrangements preserve the formal legal sovereignty of the UK Parliament and thus the power of the British government, but informal understandings in practice constrain the exercise of this sovereignty. The Human Rights Act represents something of a move away from the primacy of ministerial responsibility to Parliament, by seeking to give additional, judicial protection to individuals against the actions of the executive, though that Act too preserves the formal legal sovereignty of the UK Parliament.

A fourth justification for parliamentary sovereignty in the sense that the courts will give effect to any Act of Parliament (unless it is incompatible with European Community law) is that it preserves comity between the legislature and the courts, and thus it promotes trust between those in power and, in turn, it promotes good governance. This rationale finds expression in legal doctrines that have been developed by the courts. For instance, respect for parliamentary privilege and deference to Parliament and the executive where cases raise issues that are not justiciable because they are highly politically sensitive or the courts lack the expertise to deal with them, or where issues of proportionality arise under the Human Rights Act (see Chapters 5 and 6). Where courts are empowered to strike down legislation passed by a Parliament, the relations between Parliament and the courts, and indeed between government and the courts, are likely to be strained. This can reduce trust and undermine Parliament's and government's—and public—respect for the rule of law.

A fifth justification that may be advanced in favour of parliamentary sovereignty is that in the eyes of the electorate legislation passed or approved by Parliament is legitimate because the House of Commons is elected. Thus they are likely to be disposed to obey it. It would not be regarded as legitimate for judges to have the power to strike down or disapply Acts of Parliament and ultimately court orders purporting to do so may become practically unenforceable against individuals or the state. Ultimately the government might refuse to obey orders disapplying Acts made by the ordinary courts. This would be the position in France, where public law decisions may generally not be reviewed by the courts but are reviewed instead by administrative tribunals or the Conseil d'Etat. The latter has a higher status than the courts in France and its members have special expertise in these matters. It is unlikely that the French government would be willing to obey orders from the ordinary courts quashing its decisions.

Good governance requires that the law should be voluntarily obeyed in practice, for else there will be a need for excessive coercion, or there will be disorder and alienation resulting from unequal subjection to the law. This too would undermine the rule of law. We have already noted that there are many democracies in the world in which the courts do have the power to strike down legislation that is incompatible with the Constitution— the USA, Canada, Australia, and Germany are examples. It is not regarded as illegitimate for the courts to do so in those countries. It is a feature peculiar to the British constitutional and political tradition that it would be regarded as illegitimate for our courts to strike down Acts of Parliament. But cultural norms can change, external conditions may force change—for instance, membership of the European Community—and this particular norm is not immutable (Bradley, 2000).

To summarize, the need to give effect to the popular will does not form part of the theory of democracy that is current in the United Kingdom. Nor is parliamentary sovereignty in the sense that the UK Parliament is entitled to pass legislation by simple majority on any subject matter, justified as an essential element of a functioning democracy. The United Kingdom's concept of parliamentary sovereignty is unusual in this respect among Western democracies. Democracy, even in the UK, is not an absolute. Adherence to the doctrine of sovereignty or legislative supremacy of the UK Parliament is essentially a cultural phenomenon. The nub of the theory of democracy at the level of the UK is that the government should be accountable to Parliament, especially to the House of Commons, the elected chamber, and that a web of accountability measures should be in place to secure that government is carried on broadly in the public interest, shows respect for human rights, and is in accordance with principles of good governance, discussed in the next chapter.

Participatory and deliberative democracy

The point was made in Chapter 1 that many of the recent reforms to the British Constitution have been designed to reinvigorate the Westminster system of representative democracy by reforming the framework within which it operates. This model assumes that the electorate participates in government primarily through voting and holding ministers to account via MPs in Parliament. In this aspect of the Constitution the political parties are dominant. This form of participation could be made more effective with a more proportionately representative electoral system, such as has been introduced in the devolved bodies (these will be discussed in Chapters 7 and 13–15) and by improved public rights of access to information (see Chapter 8), so that better-informed electoral choices may be made. The protections of free speech and freedom of association that had been developed at common law and under the Human Rights Act also facilitate effective participation in the representative system by keeping the political process open (see Hart Ely, 1981).

There is however another model of constitutionalism and democracy which suggests that the system should facilitate a *process* of democracy rather than just establishing a *framework* for democracy (Morison, 1998). Democratic process involves citizen participation in government and deliberation about policy that is not entirely channelled through party-dominated elected institutions. Participation in government can take many forms and result in greater or lesser influence on the final decision. For instance:

- opportunities to put forward one's views for consideration by officials;
- rights to be consulted and have one's representations responded to, which would entail rights of access to information;
- rights to vote on decisions.

These rights may be exercisable either by individuals or by membership groups and organizations in civil society, such as trade unions, environmental groups, and the like.

The advantages of processes of this kind include the fact that participation, in the sense of consultation and being listened to on the part of those affected by possible policy changes, may result in better-prepared and thought-out proposals being implemented. This approach accepts that the government or other public body—for instance the local authority—has the primary responsibility for policy, but seeks to improve its quality and accountability by facilitating participation. Voting on questions in referendums, for instance, on the other hand should result in decisions that have the support of those affected, but it does not follow from the fact of popular support that the decisions will be wise or successful.

Deliberative democracy is a variant of participatory democracy. It envisages that citizens will actively discuss together and with officials the solutions to problems. The purpose, again, is to improve the quality of decisions, but also to enable a learning process to take place in the citizenry that will improve understanding of the complexities of the decisions that government has to take which will help to legitimate decisions. Agreement on important values can also emerge from the process of deliberation. Thus deliberation—like other forms of participation—is developmental.

We shall see in some of the chapters that follow that a number of devices are being developed to increase public participation in and influence over decision-making outside the representative democracy system. Quangos are being pressed to have representative boards and to consult their users. Arrangements in Northern Ireland seek to involve citizens outside the normal political parties in debates and discussions of policy, through the civic forum, for instance. Citizens' juries, internet referendums, and other direct democracy techniques based on computer-based communication are used from time to time (see Sixth Report of the Select Committee on Public Administration, *Innovations in Citizen Participation in Government*, HC 373, 2000–1; Morison, 1998).

Recently the use of 'deliberative participation' or deliberative polling has spread. This differs from normal consultation or participation because the emphasis is not on providing a 'snapshot' set of views or answers but rather on getting groups of citizens to think about their experiences and priorities, to look at the problems of providing public services, and to frame their own suggestions and recommendations for policy makers to consider. As the Public Administration Committee (PASC) put it: 'In short, people are asked to deliberate, listen to evidence and get involved'. Experience shows that this kind of participation can help public bodies to make more effective allocations of resources (see HC 373, 2000–1, *supra*, para. 50).

The PASC also looked at 'e-governance', which enables individuals to communicate with government and obtain information through the Web, and 'e-democracy' which could be used for deliberative consultation, with members of the public contributing as and when they felt they had something useful to say. Overall, in its consideration of new technologies the PASC concluded that, carefully used, they were tools which offer the possibility of greatly improving the accessibility and use made by citizens of public participation opportunities—though care should be taken to secure that individuals without their own access to the internet could have access in other ways (para. 67; see also Walker and Akdeniz, 1998; Hansard Society, *Technology: Enhancing Representative Democracy?*, 2002. Hansard Society Commission, *The Challenge to Parliament*, 2001).

The PASC's conclusion in the light of the evidence it received about new forms of participation was that the period since the mid-1990s had seen an explosion of interest in involving the public more frequently, more extensively, and in much more diverse ways in the conduct of decision-making within the public services. They welcomed the commitment of many public servants to overcome problems and make new advances in participation (*Report* at para. 75).

In its response (see HC 334, 2001–2) the government accepted many of the committee's proposals, acknowledging the importance of public participation. It asserted that a number of its policies were designed to increase participation, including its code of practice on written consultation for central government, and its attempts to promote interest in politics in civil society, for instance through citizenship education in schools. The PASC felt however that the government had not taken sufficient notice of the low turnout in the 2001 election that had intervened between the publication of their *Participation* report and their response, and suggested that a Democracy Commission should be established to consider how the crisis in public participation could be resolved. (This proposal has not been accepted by government.)

Participatory arrangements may be regarded as threatening, and therefore they may be opposed, by existing representative institutions. An example is the hostility to the proposals by the Royal Commission on Reform of the House of Lords that unelected party-aligned members of the reformed House should be appointed by an independent

Appointments Commission. This was seen as threatening by the parties who insisted that they should themselves have the exclusive right to appoint people of their choosing who might support them in the House (see further on this the discussion in Chapter 10). Another interpretation of the proposal for independent appointment would be that it should enhance the participatory aspect of democracy by securing that voices which do not make themselves heard through the political parties—the voices of women and members of ethnic minorities, of the politically uncommitted expert, of industries and sectors of the economy, culture and society that parties do not select for election—would have voices in the second chamber and, most importantly, voices to which government would have to respond in that chamber. But the parties were unable to appreciate and understand this argument for appointment.

Participatory democracy may be facilitated by information and communication, a subject considered in Chapter 8. This is recognized in the discussion of the need for 'e-democracy' and establishing websites, for instance for quangos, European Community institutions, and other public bodies. As the *European Governance* White Paper (COM (2001) 428, Brussels, 25.7.2001) put it 'Providing more information and more effective communication are a pre-condition for generating a sense of belonging to Europe', and 'The aim should be to create a transnational "space" where citizens from different countries can discuss what they perceive as being the important challenges for the Union' (p. 11; see Chapter 4).

Many visions of a deliberative and participatory democracy do not explicitly envisage formal legal provisions for participation. Within a system in which the law guarantees freedom of association and expression the image is often of individuals and institutions of civil society—the professions, pressure groups, trade unions, the voluntary sector, and so on—spontaneously engaging in discussion and consultation with a receptive government about policy and administration. In fact the law has an important role in promoting participatory democracy. The preferences of politicians for political decision-making outside legal controls will have to give way to legal, often judicialized mechanisms if participatory democracy is to develop effectively. Consultation and discussion are pointless if the officials who have the power to make decisions are not obliged to take account of advice and information that emerge from consultation and respond to it. Loose political conventions are not a sufficient guarantee that due account is taken of these processes.

There are numerous statutory and common law requirements for consultation and other procedures which encourage participation and deliberation. To take some simple examples, individuals who will be affected adversely by administrative decisions—for instance to deprive them of a licence or a public office—have legally enforceable rights to be informed in advance of the decision of any concerns about them, to be given an opportunity to put their own side of the case, and often to be given reasons for the decision (see further discussion of judicial review in Chapter 5). In the law of planning and compulsory purchase interested organizations and members of the public frequently have the legal right to take part in statutory public inquiries, to see the reasoned report of the inquiry inspector, and to appeal against, or apply for judicial review of, the eventual decision if there was a legal error. There are many statutory provisions for local authorities, regulators, and government departments to consult widely, often specifically with consumer groups, about policy. As we shall see in the chapters on devolution, civic forums on which representatives of civil society who are not party aligned have voices form part of the statutory devolution arrangements. The regional chambers in England include in their membership people drawn from various interests in the region, as do Regional Development Agencies. The networks through which much policy is delivered include partnerships with private and voluntary sector organizations.

For some proponents of deliberative and participatory democracy, the age of the 'parliamentary state' is over. Peter Mandelson MP observed in a lecture in 1998 that: 'it may be that the era of pure representative democracy is coming slowly to an end' (*Times*, 20 March 1998, quoted in Morison, 1998, 514). On this view, a move to a participatory system is essential if power is to be controlled and exercised in the public interest. It is already clear that the Westminster Parliament does not and cannot control large parts of the state, for a range of reasons. The executive controls Parliament rather than vice versa. Parliamentarians lack the time and resources to exercise effective scrutiny of the activities of government and of the many other public bodies which exercise public power. The reality is that much power is exercised by private or quasi-state bodies, which Parliament and other elected bodies cannot control. The traditional focus in representative democracy theory on Parliament and government serves to distract attention from these other sources of power.

The role of elected bodies would be relatively diminished, in formal terms at least, under a more participatory constitutional arrangement, though if one were to accept the view that Parliament and government have already become of lesser importance than they were, say, fifty years ago, the real reduction in their role would be not so great. But the role of the law and the courts could well be enhanced under participatory arrangements, both to protect and define rights of participation, and to clarify what the effect of decisions reached through deliberation and other forms of participation might be. It may prove difficult to increase the legal, statutory provisions for the facilitation and regulation of participatory and deliberative processes if politicians who are responsible for legislating for more participation see it as threatening to their own positions and the representative system. A balance between the two systems will have to be found, especially since responsibility and effectiveness can be undermined by participation, a matter considered in the discussion of good governance in the next chapter.

Lewis (1999) suggests that 'individual branches of the law need to be re-examined to see how far they can be redesigned to give force to the rights of citizens to a greater degree of participation in all forms of social organisation' (p. 29; and see generally Campbell and Lewis, 1999). But it is clear that legal provisions on their own cannot bring about a more participatory system. A culture of participation—a citizenship culture—is needed, and this depends upon levels of trust in society and upon sensitivity on the part of government and institutions of civil society to the cultural conditions in which different kinds of participation flourish or fail to thrive (Perri 6, 1999). Though law has an important role in promoting participatory democracy, it is a largely cultural matter. This point will be followed up in the section of this chapter on citizenship.

Criteria for evaluating democracy: can it be audited?

There is then no single or simple notion of democracy in the United Kingdom. There are many strands of theory running alongside one another, and the system is in a state of flux between a predominantly representative model and a developing participatory system. There are tensions between the two. The project known as the Democratic Audit of the United Kingdom has sought to formulate objective criteria for auditing democracy and political freedom. They identified two overriding criteria, political equality and popular control, supported by participation, accountability, representation, and responsiveness; and they developed a series of criteria for testing systems for the degree of democracy. Using these criteria the Audit has carried out exercises in auditing the UK system for its protection of human rights, and the extent to which political power is subject to democratic control. In *Three Pillars of Liberty* (1996) Klug, Starmer, and Weir used a *Human Rights Index* of evolving international human rights standards as benchmarks against which to audit the UK position. While concluding that 'British citizens live in a democracy' the audit found that the system was subject to a pattern of systemic weaknesses (p. 304). As we shall see in Chapter 5, and at other points in this book, the UK courts too have been drawing on international instruments, notably the European Convention on Human Rights, in developing the law relating to human rights. In securing the passage of the Human Rights Act 1998 the government was consciously incorporating internationally accepted principles into domestic law.

In the second Democratic Audit volume, *Political Power and Democratic Control* (1999, ch. 1; see also Beetham, 1994) Weir and Beetham identified four components as being crucial for any functioning democracy: free and fair elections; open, accountable, and responsive government; civil and political rights and liberties; and a democratic society. The chapters that follow will be considering these components. The last component, the democratic society, is about the socio-cultural and politico-cultural realities in a community. It is premised on the assumption that the quality and vitality of a country's democracy will be revealed in the character of its civil society as well as its political institutions, a point to which we return in our discussion of citizenship. A 'democratic society' includes the idea that there should be some minimum agreement on the political nation, tolerance of difference, an emphasis on a flourishing associational life whose activities are also democratically accountable, social and economic inclusion, and confidence of citizens in their own capacity to influence the collective decisions that matter for their lives (Weir and Beetham, 1999, 14).

Weir and Beetham then break these components down into a set of thirty Democratic Audit Criteria (DAC) or questions. There is not the space here to set them all out, but a picture may be obtained from the Democratic Audit's own summary of what they are about. The first five DAC examine the inclusiveness and independence of elections, how equal citizens are in elections, and turnout in elections. They ask, for instance 'To what extent do the votes of all electors carry equal weight, and how closely does the composition of Parliament and the programme of the government reflect the choices actually made by the electorate?' (DAC4; see further the discussion in Chapter 7). The openness and accountability criteria include the questions 'How far is the executive subject to the rule of law and transparent rules governing the use of its powers?' (part of DAC11; see Chapter 8). On rights and liberties the Audit asks 'How clearly does the law define the civil and political rights and liberties of the citizen, and how effectively are they safe-guarded?' (DAC19; see Chapter 6). And the questions about a democratic society include 'How far are all citizens able to participate in economic, social and cultural, as well as political, life?'(DAC29).

The Audit concluded that the system was 'good in parts'. It does not reach a satisfactory standard against all of their democratic criteria by any means. But they admit that democracy is not an absolute, democracy and governmental effectiveness sometimes have to be weighed against one another, and no system has ever been or ever will be perfectly democratic. We shall refer to this exercise in auditing democracy at other points in our exploration of the modernization of the UK constitution (for instance, the Democratic Audit criteria have been used by the select committee on public administration in relation to quangos—see Chapter 17).

Citizenship

The second theme in our consideration of constitutional reform is the developing concept of citizenship. The term has many meanings. In ordinary parlance it is commonly used to refer to the status of being a legally recognized national of a state or a commonwealth (see the *New Oxford Dictionary of English*). There are thus three important variables in discussions of citizenship; (i) which individuals are to be regarded as citizens, (ii) what entities are they to be regarded as citizens of, and (iii) what rights and responsibilities flow from the status of citizen. Not every person in a state will be regarded as a citizen of that state, and some people may be regarded as citizens of entities other than states—members of a federation, for instance, or the European Union, neither of which is a sovereign state in the normal sense in international law. Those who are citizens of states may, however, have few *special* rights and responsibilities as a result of that status, and others residing in their states may have many of the same rights and responsibilities. These are all matters regulated by law. Another sense in which citizenship is used refers to participation in civil society—'active citizenship', for instance.

There is no explicit legal status of citizenship in the United Kingdom in the sense in which we are considering it here. In English legal usage citizenship is connected with immigration law (see Dummett and Nicol, 1990). The various grades of British citizenship are concerned with the right to enter and remain in the United Kingdom. These rights do not of themselves give even the full British citizen any rights other than the right to come and go from the United Kingdom and, in certain circumstances, to vote. The right to vote, however, is shared with many who are not British citizens. The legal status known as 'citizenship' then is negative rather than positive, and Gardner has gone so far as to suggest that 'immunity from the various disabilities which attach to alien status provides a "definition" of the content of British citizenship' (Gardner 1990, at 65). Citizenship may be acquired at birth, or through naturalization under the British Nationality Act 1981 and other statutory provisions.

Individuals benefit from many rights regardless of whether they are legally British citizens. The rules are complex, but in principle all—including illegal immigrants—who are in the country are subject to the law and entitled to the equal protection of the law, including the Human Rights Act. Many non-British citizens living lawfully in the United Kingdom (EU nationals and others) are entitled to receive public services such as school education, health services, and housing on the same terms as British citizens. Citizens of the Republic of Ireland have had the right to vote in British parliamentary elections since the formation of the Republic. Commonwealth citizens living in the UK have the same right to vote in UK elections as British citizens. Since 1999 European Union citizens resident in the UK have been entitled to vote in European Parliament and other elections in the UK. Rights to participate in the political process do not depend then to any great extent on being a British citizen. In this respect 'the United Kingdom has moved away from the nationality citizenship model' (Gardner, 1990, 68).

But the term 'citizen' may also refer to a national of a commonwealth, in the sense of an aggregate or grouping of states or other bodies. It is in this sense that the term 'citizen of the European Union' is used, for instance (see Chapter 4). This novel kind of citizenship—quasi-citizenship would be a better term—gives the individual rights against or in relation to institutions other than and outside his or her own state, such as rights to vote for members of the European Parliament, to petition the Parliament, to apply to the European ombudsman, to have access to the European Court of Justice where Community law is at stake (a right not exclusive to citizens of the Union), and rights to diplomatic protection from other member states of the European Union.

Citizenship and rights

Despite the absence of an explicit statutory status of citizenship outside the ambit of immigration and nationality law, citizenship in a social and political sense does have considerable legal content in the UK. In identifying that content it is convenient to go back to what is still the seminal work on the subject, the set of lectures delivered in 1950 by T. H. Marshall, Professor of Social Institutions in the University of London, entitled *Citizenship and Social Class* (Marshall, 1950). Marshall divided citizenship into three parts, political, civil, and social. By the political element of citizenship he meant the right to participate in the exercise of political power as a voter, or as an elected Member of Parliament or a local authority. By civil citizenship he referred to the rights necessary for individual freedom—liberty of the person, freedom of speech, thought and faith, the right to own property, and the right to justice or access to the courts. Civil and political rights are part of an essentially liberal or liberal democratic concept of citizenship.

Marshall's third aspect of citizenship was the social element 'by which I mean the whole range from the right to a modicum of economic welfare and security to the right to share to the full in the social heritage and to live the life of a civilised being according to the standards prevailing in society' (Marshall, 1950, 11)—a citizenship of inclusion. Marshall saw the welfare state as the guarantor of this social element. It was legally enforceable social rights which gave practical content to the legal and political rights of the citizen, by making it possible for civil and political rights to be exercised and for the citizen to participate in society. This was a social democratic concept of citizenship. Although social and economic rights are provided for by law to an extent in the UK, unlike many civil and political rights since the HRA came into force they do not have special legally protected or constitutional status (save to an extent in European Community law: see Chapter 4). In Chapter 6 we shall consider the extent to which social and economic rights could have such protection and the implications that would have for citizenship theory. Dahrendorf considered that rights forming the citizenship of entitlement that Marshall elaborated must be unconditional. Citizenship was 'above all a set of entitlements, rights. Rights lose their quality if they become conditional . . . citizenship rights . . . stipulate unconditional entitlements, and . . . any condition detracts from their quality' (Dahrendorf, 1988, 117–18).

Proponents of the constitutional protection of civil and political rights may envisage a high degree of economic freedom for individuals, stressing the importance of enterprise to the economy and the ability of individuals to fulfil their potential (see Hayek, 1960; Nozick, 1984). For this school of thought democracy is a means to the end of protecting individuals against interference by the state and securing that it provides only the minimum range of services, those that can only be performed by the state—defence, foreign policy, and the maintenance of law and order, which includes the protection of individuals' civil and political rights. For them, an essential, if not *the* essential, feature of a democracy is that individuals are protected from state interference by certain fundamental and legally enforceable civil and political liberties.

But the special legal protection of individual civil and political rights may also be justified in liberal terms on other grounds. For our purposes an important rationale is that rights such as freedom of expression and association secure that government can be criticized, that support of government and opposition to it can be effectively organized, its actions made open, and that it can thus be held to account for its actions. (See also Hart Ely, 1981 for a similar rationale for rights in the USA.) Civil and political rights form part of the web of accountability in the British version of democracy (see below).

Since Marshall wrote, ideas about the extent of citizenship rights have developed to include environmental rights (for instance, to an unpolluted environment), and cultural rights (access to the arts, freedom to maintain particular cultural traditions). The European Charter of Fundamental Rights, discussed in Chapter 4, also shows how the concept of rights deserving special legal protection is expanding to include broadly social, economic, and environmental rights. As we shall note in Chapter 6, in the UK these rights have tended to be regarded as less justiciable than civil or political rights, in that the judges may lack competence to make decisions about the allocation of state resources. These rights can be highly politically contentious, raising major issues about public expenditure and taxation, which again is taken by advocates of the political constitution to be a reason why they should be left to the politicians (see Chapters 1, 20).

At the time that Marshall was writing the civil, political, social and economic elements of citizenship were well protected in law and respected in practice: the post-war consensus extended to social, and economic policy, and the liberal-democratic tradition treats the civil and political freedoms of citizens as central to the system. However, in the 1980s and 1990s the consensus broke down, and some of the elements of the citizenship of entitlement as conceived by Marshall were eroded. The weaknesses of the legal and political foundations of this conception of citizenship were exposed. Concern about this process contributed to the enactment of the Human Rights Act 1998, which gives additional protection to civil and political—but not social or economic—rights. A point to which we shall return is that political polarization tends to lead to juridification and judicialization of matters that would be left to politicians in a consensual political atmosphere.

The social and economic elements of citizenship were reduced or made conditional in various ways in the 1980s and 1990s, as governments sought to reduce public expenditure and discourage a dependency culture by reducing the availability of some cash benefits (unemployment benefit and others), removing others from certain classes of claimant (unemployed young people, for example), and imposing conditions on eligibility for others. This reflected not only a desire to limit public expenditure and keep taxation low, but also changing notions of citizenship, which involved increasing the responsibilities of individuals to work and provide for themselves and their families where possible. A side effect of this removal of entitlements has been the creation of an underclass of very poor, often unemployed and unskilled people. The policy has implications for social cohesion in that it denies some people the opportunity to participate in the political process and the life of the community, especially if those policies also result in the alienation of sections of the population. Concern about this was behind the new Labour government's adoption of a policy on social inclusion in the late 1990s.

The citizen as consumer?

In 1991 Prime Minister John Major launched the *Citizen's Charter* (Cm. 1599; see Deakin, 1994; Bynoe, 1996; Oliver and Drewry, 1996; Drewry, 2002; see further Chapter 12) which committed the government and its departments, and agencies and other public bodies, to prioritize the needs and interests of individuals as consumers of public services. The Charter was mostly concerned with procedural matters rather than with the substantive quality of public services, though it did include rights to compensation for passengers from train operators whose services were late. Individuals were entitled to be informed, in sectoral charters produced by each public service, what their rights were (for instance, the time within which medical appointments should be offered), and how to complain if these requirements were not met. They were entitled to know the names of the officials they were dealing with. The sectoral charters also emphasized the obligations of individuals, for instance to pay their taxes promptly, to keep medical appointments, and so on. An objective of the initiative was to emphasize the interests of 'consumers' of public services over those of employees in these services, and to make it possible for consumers to bring pressure to bear on services about which they had complaints. Overall the intention was that services should improve in these matters without additional funding being made available to them, on the assumption that they were being run inefficiently and for the convenience of those working in them—a public-choice theory assumption.

The initiative thus introduced a new consumer dimension to citizenship, which was criticized as a perversion of the very concept of citizenship as an essentially political status (see Barron and Scott, 1992). More recently the focus has shifted to 'Best Value' and '*Service First*' in the provision of public services (see Chapters 12, 16) with less emphasis on reducing costs, and more on the quality of these services.

Citizenship and responsibilities

Citizenship is not generally understood to be simply a matter of rights and entitlements. It is reciprocal, and involves individuals owing duties to the community, having responsibilities (see Selbourne, 1994). These duties may be either legally imposed, or voluntarily undertaken as a result of a sense of solidarity with and commitment to others. The principal, and well-recognized, direct legal duties of the citizen include the payment of taxes, jury service, and service in the armed forces if required. These duties are, ultimately, legally enforceable.

But in the changed political climate of the 1990s additional legally backed up obligations of citizenship began to be mooted—duties to work for example (Mead, 1986, Mead and Field, 1997), to bring up one's children in acceptable ways (Oldfield, 1990, 181) and to send them to school. The provision that parents could be made liable for their children's offences contained in the Criminal Justice Act 1990 reflected this view. These duties might not all be directly legally enforceable through sanctions imposed by the courts, but they could be just as effectively made compulsory through techniques such as the legally authorized withholding of benefits by the state from those who do not perform their duties to its satisfaction.

This trend continued after the election of the Labour government in 1997. Policy moved in favour of encouraging individuals to take more responsibility for their own lives and for their communities. The originator of this approach was Professor Tony Giddens, who elaborated his concept of citizenship in his book, *The Third Way* (1998). According to this set of ideas, the individualism that had developed in recent years was associated with the retreat of tradition and custom from our lives, a process which has liberated individuals from some of the fixities of the past. In the new situation old-style social solidarity had been weakened and in its place it was necessary for individuals to accept responsibility for their own lifestyles. Giddens argued that individualism needed to be balanced by duties of individual responsibility and mutual obligation. What were previously regarded as unconditional entitlements to benefits for those in need could create perverse incentives to dependency. They should be replaced with the idea that it is the role of the state to enable people to be self-sufficient and to provide ways out of dependency. These ideas have been reflected in a number of reforms since 1997, including changing to the systems of unemployment and disability benefits so as to build in conditions and incentives to encourage claimants to find work and escape from dependency. The paradigm citizen is, amongst other things, self-supporting.

Civil society and citizenship

A modern concept of citizenship has to include a sense of belonging to the national, local, and functional communities in the country—social cohesion or 'civil citizenship' in other words. Social cohesion means that individuals are likely to accept that they have obligations—whether legal or purely social and moral—of respect and consideration towards one another, including members of their families, employers or employees, and members of the social organizations to which they belong, for instance. It also generates trust. Citizenship is not solely a matter or legal rights and responsibilities. It is also social and cultural. It will be remembered that the Democratic Audit identified a 'democratic society' as an important element in a democracy, and this included 'civil society'. Social cohesion and a strong civil society are linked to 'active citizenship'. As Heater has put it: 'He who has no sense of a civic bond with his fellows or of some responsibility for civic welfare is not a true citizen whatever his legal status' (Heater, 1990: 182). We can see the implications of a lack of this sense in the troubles in Northern Ireland, and in the alienation of some members of the ethnic minorities from the mainstream of national life. Giddens (1998) too was concerned that civil society should be cherished; equality should be promoted in order to foster senses of social cohesion; and the vulnerable need to be protected.

Citizenship is also related to Foucault's concept of 'governmentality' (1979). This concept shifts the focus implied by the word 'government' away from political institutions, their law-making power and the individual as being subject to law—a top-down concept—towards the freedom of individuals and their consensual relationships, not only with the state but also with other organizations of civil society. On this view citizenship is a cooperative and ethical concept. As Foucault puts it:

[I]f you try to analyse power not on the basis of freedom, strategies, and governmentality, but on the basis of the political institution, you can only conceive of the subject as a subject of law. One then has a subject who has or does not have rights, who has had those rights either granted or removed by the institution of political society, and all this brings us back to a legal concept of the subject. On the other hand, I believe that the concept of governmentality makes it possible to bring out the freedom of the subject and its relationship to others—which constitute the very stuff of ethics. (Foucault, 2000, 300)

This concept of governmentality fits neatly with governance, the reliance by government on networks and civil society to formulate policy and secure the delivery of services (see further Morison, 2001, especially in relation to Northern Ireland). It also draws together concepts of democracy and citizenship, illustrating how our three themes are interconnected.

Institutionally local authorities could have a role in promoting social cohesion and good relations between communities in their areas if they were allowed the resources and freedom of action to do so. This is a role—promotion of community well-being—given to them under the Local Government Act 2000 (see Chapter 16). The evolving system of decentralization to national and regional assemblies (Chapters 13–15) may promote the sense of identity with the communities in those areas.

Citizenship in the social sense involves a sense of identity, and increasingly individuals experience multiple identities which give them a sense of being citizens, even if not of the state of which they are nationals. Heater (1990) emphasized the existence and importance of multiple citizenship: a person may feel him or herself to be a citizen of Scotland, the United Kingdom, and Europe, for instance, and may derive legal rights and responsibilities from each of those citizenships. But their sense of multiple citizenship will not only be about legal rights and responsibilities, but also about being involved in social or economic networks, sharing aspects of a culture and commitment to each layer of citizenship.

The importance of social solidarity in civil society has been central to Labour policy. One of its 'joined-up government' initiatives (*Modernizing Government*, Cm. 4310, 1999) was the establishment of a Social Exclusion Unit. But the fact that solidarity formerly based on long established working-class neighbourhoods with people sharing the experience of working in mass production industry has been undermined was recognized. Civil society is less based on neighbourhood and locality than it used to be, and its organizations are more likely to be functional or based on common interests. The inability of the state—both financially and practically—to provide for all needs and to protect people and communities against crime and dilapidation was also recognized. Giddens placed emphasis on Labour pursuing a policy of 'fostering an active civil society' (Giddens, 1998, 78) arguing that 'it is just as wrong to reduce civic decline to economics, as the old left often did, as to deny the influence of poverty and underprivilege' (p. 79). State and civil society should act in partnership, mobilizing communities to practical tasks such as the refurbishment of neighbourhoods. He commended the development of the voluntary or third sector but hoped that people from poorer backgrounds could be mobilized to engage in community efforts to improve their neighbourhoods and repair the social fabric (Giddens, ch. 3).

Summary

Democracy and citizenship are closely intertwined and they are also linked to our third theme, good governance. Much emphasis has been placed in recent years on participatory rather than representative democracy, perhaps in recognition of the limits of representative democracy, especially where turnout in elections is low and the parties dominate the process, alienating those who do not feel that their views or interests can be given voice through the parties. In relationship to citizenship, the emphasis has been not only on civil and political rights but also on rethinking the terms of eligibility for social and economic provision, on encouraging independence, and on developing social cohesion and a democratic society. These points will be taken up in the chapters in the following parts this book.

3

Themes: Good Governance

The third theme that has run through much of the discussion about reform of the UK Constitution is the need to promote good governance, a term used as shorthand for a number of principles. As we shall see good governance overlaps with democracy and citizenship. It needs to be distinguished from 'governance', which is often used to refer to the use of networks for the delivery of policy (see Chapter 1). As well as being used in relation to governmental arrangements in the UK, compliance with good governance principles is generally imposed as a condition of international aid for developing countries (see for instance IMF, 1997 (*Good Governance. The IMF's Role*); Camdessus, 1998; UNESCAP, no date; see also on good governance principles Leftwich, 1993; Chartered Institute of Public Finance and Accountancy, 1994; European White Paper, *Good Governance*, COM (2001), 428).

Broadly good governance requires that government observes the following principles:

- openness and transparency;
- there should be appropriate mechanisms of accountability, whether political, legal, public, or auditing;
- there should be in place appropriate provisions to maximize the effectiveness of government; and
- public participation is to be encouraged.

Further, constitutional arrangements should promote:

- legitimacy;
- trustworthiness, which implies encouraging trust and cooperation between state institutions;
- reliability;
- an absence of corruption; and
- respect for human rights.

Many of these principles are also elements of democracy as commonly defined (for instance, public participation) and citizenship (respect for human rights). A range of techniques is employed in the UK to give effect to good governance principles, some legal and some political or administrative. Some of these are considered in detail in other chapters. Our focus here is on accountability, and on maintaining an uncorrupt system.

Accountability

Accountability has been said to entail being liable to be required to give an account or explanation of actions and, where appropriate, to suffer the consequences, take the blame or undertake to put matters right if it should appear that errors have been made (see generally Marshall, 1989; Oliver and Drewry, 1996; Woodhouse, 1997a). Accountability mechanisms are the Constitution's solution to the problem of fallibility around which the liberal-democratic tradition has been built up. Nobody and no party is infallible and no particular substantive policy can be assumed to be right. It is essential that the Constitution and the processes—the rules of the game—that it entails, recognize these factors and provide safeguards against bad government and bad governance. Decision-makers must be obliged to justify their acts and not be allowed to rely on claims that their rightness is to be assumed. It must be permissible to advance alternative policies. There must be provision for matters to be put right when things have gone wrong. The procedures and mechanisms for making processes of accountability effective are therefore central concerns of a liberal-democratic Constitution. Accountability furthers important objectives. It is supposed to promote openness, effectiveness, and public participation, and it is part of the system for safeguarding an uncorrupt system from corruption.

Responsibility and leadership are crucial elements in an accountable system. It is essential that some identifiable body takes decisions as part of his or her job and is blameworthy or praiseworthy for the results. Acceptance of the importance of accountability and participatory democracy should not undermine the equal, even greater, importance of responsibility in the system. The present arrangement in central government, in the devolved bodies, and in local government, is that certain decisions and acts are the responsibility of defined bodies—a Minister or secretary of state, a Minister or the executive in devolved bodies, the council in local government. It is their job to make decisions, to be accountable for them, and to take the credit or blame if they turn out to have been wrong. A danger in some forms of participatory democracy, or in collective decision-making in local authorities, for instance, is that if things go wrong it may not be clear whose fault, if anyone's, the mistake was. In such a system, where there has been wide consultation and participation in decision-making and the decision is exposed to serious criticism, it will be open to the committee or other decision-maker to say: 'Don't blame us. We consulted and this is what the public wanted us to do.' The fact that the public or a public wants a policy or a decision does not mean that it will turn out to be a wise or lawful or successful policy or decision. The UK tradition places a high priority on prudent, responsible decision-making (Birch, 1964).

Ultimately in the British liberal-democratic tradition it is for their stewardship of the public interest that state institutions are in practice most commonly accountable, and by this criterion that they are judged. So in considering questions such as: 'to whom is a Minister to be accountable?', 'by what criteria is an official to be held accountable?', and 'by what mechanism is accountability to be imposed?', it is important not to lose sight of the fact that the public interest is the ultimate legitimating justification for government, and accountability should promote this. As we shall see later in this chapter the divisions of responsibility between elected politicians and officials are ambiguous and this makes the imposition of accountability problematic.

It is helpful in analysing accountability to distinguish four classes of body to whom accountability is owed—accountees; these are politicians, the public, the courts, and a range of 'auditors'—the term has a special meaning in this context. We shall consider them in turn.

Political accountability

First, accountability to elected politicians. Ministers are accountable to Parliament, the Prime Minister, and the Cabinet; civil servants to Ministers; local authorities to government and Parliament. The point about this form of accountability is that it exposes the bodies to politically motivated control, to public censure through elected institutions—the House of Commons or local authorities—and in some cases to electoral risk. The criteria by which a body is judged in political accountability tend to be more fluid than the criteria imposed by, for instance, legal accountability (judicialization) or audit: in political accountability a minister or other official will be judged according to whether, for instance, their actions have met with public approval or criticism, whether they have succeeded in meeting objectives, which is often difficult to assess, such as increasing prosperity or improving public health. The procedures for political accountability are also normally less formal than those for legal accountability (in litigation strict rules of procedure have to be followed) or in audit (the ombudsmen, the National Audit Office, and the Audit Commission carry out their investigations with some formality—see below). In the case of Ministers, they are themselves members of the body to which they are accountable—Parliament—and their supporters are in the majority in the House of Commons, which weakens accountability. We should also note that the sanctions where the machinery of political accountability imposes a duty to make amends are not generally legally coercive but political: a minister's duty to undertake to put things right or to resign is a matter of convention rather than law.

Accountability to Ministers (of civil servants, for example) is open to be used, or abused, by Ministers for partisan purposes, e.g. to protect their own position or that of the government, unless there are effective mechanisms in place to prevent such abuses. There has been a trend over the last fifteen years or so to spell out and publish the limits within which Ministers must act in relations with their officials, for instance in the *Ministerial Code* (July 2001), and the *Civil Service Code* (see Chapters 11 and 12).

Other bodies that are politically accountable—to Parliament—include those in receipt of public funds, who are accountable to the House of Commons' Public Accounts Committee. This aspect of political accountability is directed to promoting the general public interest in the proper use of public money and is not normally influenced by party political considerations.

Political accountability is not always as effective as it should be. It is too easy for public bodies to avoid giving an account of their actions or making amends if found to be at fault. The 'Arms to Iraq' affair, discussed in Chapter 11, provides an example. Many of the reforms discussed in later chapters have been designed to improve political accountability: clarification of the requirements of ministerial responsibility, electoral reform, access to official information, decentralization, and other measures should all have this effect.

Political accountability, as it operates in the United Kingdom, is not always the most suitable form of accountability. This point is well illustrated by the case of the judiciary and by quangos. The judges are constitutionally insulated from political accountability for the way in which particular cases are decided. But it does not follow from this that no accountability should be imposed on judges, or on those responsible for the system of justice. In practice judges are accountable in various ways, but rightly not to politicians, especially in respect of their decisions in particular cases. Quangos too have been estab-lished in recognition of the fact that certain activities should not be directly subject to political accountability. There are, as we shall see, a range of forms of accountability and within each form a variety of particular mechanisms; an important aspect of the Consti-tution is securing that the most appropriate forms or combination of forms, of account-ability are applied to public bodies.

Public accountability

The second form of accountability which we shall consider is to the general public or to interested sections of the public. Ministers, Members of Parliament, councilors, and other public officials are in practice under obligations to explain and justify their actions to the public, and they may find themselves obliged through pressures of criticism and embar-rassment to make amends where errors have been made. Elected bodies are publicly accountable through the ballot box.

But 'the public' is not monolithic. There are different publics with different needs and wishes in the nations and regions of the United Kingdom; and yet, with the exception of a weak tier of local government, until the devolution arrangements took effect in 1999 there were no institutions to respond to these different publics. The public is also divisible in other ways, for instance in relation to different categories of consumer of public services—acutely and chronically ill patients, sufferers from different ailments, for instance—or different interest groups, and these interests may not always have effective 'voices' through which their interests may be made known and responded to.

'Consumer' accountability is a relatively new form of public accountability that developed from the 1980s. Both Conservative and Labour governments in this period have taken steps to increase the influence of consumers of public services over their quality and method of delivery, for example by introducing choice, providing infor-mation, and giving consumer representatives (parents of school children) rights to par-ticipate in decisions (on school governing bodies for instance). The desirability of strengthening the position of consumers of public services is now recognized across the political spectrum (Deakin and Wright, 1989; *Modernizing Government,* Cm. 4310, 1999), though the concept of citizenship that it implies, the citizen as a market operator rather than a political actor with civil responsibilities, has proved controversial (see for instance Barron and Scott, 1992; see Chapter 2).

The effectiveness of accountability to the public or publics depends on the availability of information—openness. An ill-informed public cannot hold government to account for its care of the public interest. Hence the freedom of the media to report on matters of public interest, and public rights of access to official information and freedom of speech are crucial to the effectiveness of this form of accountability (Chapters 6 and 8).

The sanctions available to the public through which they can give 'teeth' to mechanisms of public accountability range from transfer of 'custom' elsewhere by exercising choice ('exit'), through the pursuit of complaints and grievance procedures, for instance via the various ombudsmen in the system, to the withholding of electoral support, which can effectively deprive parties in government or local authorities of a majority; and the withdrawal of cooperation resulting in loss of legitimacy without which it is in practice impossible for government to operate effectively without itself resorting to coercive measures.

As with political accountability, public accountability is not always appropriate. Some matters must be kept confidential and therefore immune from public scrutiny (certain matters to do with national security, the detection and prevention of crime, sensitive foreign relations). Consumer accountability can undermine the ability of government to provide services efficiently and effectively if it subordinates the general public interest to the interests of consumers. Nor is it necessarily in the public interest that a government should owe particular duties of accountability to sectional interests within the public— local authorities to ratepayers, for instance (see *Bromley London Borough Council v. GLC* [1983] 1 AC 768 for instance, and Chapter 16). So the design of constitutional mechanisms should be such as to secure that public accountability does not undermine effectiveness, and that it does not promote sectional interests at the expense of the general public interest.

Legal accountability/Judicialization

Thirdly, legal accountability, normally accountability to the courts. The legal accountability of public bodies is an important aspect of the rule of law. The duty to obey the law, enforceable by action in the courts at the instigation of those affected by the actions of public bodies, imposes an obligation on a public body to explain and justify its actions in legal terms if sued in the courts or subjected to judicial review, and to make amends if found to have transgressed.

The legal accountability of public bodies needs to be put in perspective in this discussion. In important respects it differs from that of the private sector. Public bodies, or more precisely bodies exercising public functions, have many special legal powers—to grant and refuse licences, to levy taxation, to acquire property compulsorily, and so on. But they are also subject to special legal duties to secure that their actions are lawful in a narrow, technical sense, that they do not interfere with human rights without legal justification and that their discretionary powers are exercised fairly and rationally (see Lord Diplock in *Council of Civil Service Unions v. Minister for the Civil Service* [1985] AC 374; see Chapter 5).

An important respect in which legal accountability differs from other forms is that the remedies and sanctions are coercive: generally public bodies can be compelled by the courts to perform their legal duties and to refrain from unlawful acts.

As with political and public accountability, accountability to the courts is not always the appropriate form. Pursuing actions in the courts is expensive and time-consuming and often alternative methods of resolving disputes will be more appropriate, for instance, via an ombudsman. There are problems over whether judges are competent to decide on the legality of government action and whether political or administrative accountability would therefore be more appropriate. The political Constitution ends where judicial review is exercised. The judges themselves are conscious of this, and they regard certain matters as not 'justiciable' (*Council of Civil Service Unions v. Minister for the Civil Service* [1985] AC 374), for example disputes about national security, diplomatic matters, and foreign affairs, and they are usually willing to defer to politicians and give them a margin of discretion when making politically charged decisions (see Chapter 5).

Audit, inspection, and administrative accountability

Fourthly, there is audit and, linked with it, inspection and administrative accountability in the sense of accountability within and between governmental agencies. (We have already noted the use of the technique of audit by the Democratic Audit.) Until recently audit has been connected with the function of professional examination of financial accounts, and auditors have been non-political experts in accounting. The National Audit Office, which is responsible for the audit of most government expenditure, reports to the Public Accounts Committee of the House of Commons, so that political accountability and audit come together in this field. The government accepts that: 'An effective system of accountability of the Executive to Parliament, backed up by rigorous processes of audit, reporting and scrutiny, is fundamental to the proper operation of a Parliamentary democracy' (Cm. 5456, 2002; see also *Holding to Account* (the Sharman Report), 2001).

The term audit and the techniques associated with it have come to be used in relation to non-financial matters. Environmental audits involve assessing the impact of development on the environment; teaching quality audits involve examining the procedures for assessing the quality of teaching; and there are value for money audits, intellectual property audits, stress audits, and so on. There has in effect been an audit explosion (Power, 1994, 1999). Audit and inspection rely heavily on the formulation of relatively concrete criteria against which performance can be measured. These criteria may be set out in statute, as is the case with audit under the National Audit Act 1983, or, more commonly, in 'soft law' form, such as performance indicators or PSAs.

In the context of this discussion of the kind of body to whom a person is accountable, 'auditor' and 'inspector' are useful terms to denote a range of non-political, expert public bodies, not limited in their operations to financial auditing and accounting. Bodies such as the Parliamentary Commissioner for Administration, the Commissioners for Local Administration (the local government 'Ombudsmen'), the National Audit

Office, the Audit Commission, the Treasury, and various other bodies are concerned for the most part with non-political—i.e. non-party and non-partisan—matters such as maladministration leading to injustice, efficiency, effectiveness, value for money, and meeting Public Service Agreement (PSA) targets (see below and Chapters 11 and 12).

It is only in the last twenty years or so that attention has focused on these mechanisms of accountability, many of which operate within government, or between government agencies as well as between government and independent agencies. This form of audit has been quite developed in Sweden, for instance, for many years—and it is in some respects a substitute for political accountability (McDonald, 1992a,b; Richardson, 1982). This kind of operation may be conceptualized nowadays as 'regulation inside government', to borrow the title of one of the leading monographs on the subject (see Hood et al., 1999; see also Daintith and Page, 1999). The accountees operating these mechanisms are for the most part non-political and professionally qualified, and they are concerned with particular and closely defined aspects of government. As Hood et al. put it, they are 'waste-watchers, quality police, and sleaze-busters'.

It is helpful to distinguish here between internal and external audit and inspection mechanisms. The internal mechanisms—for instance the Treasury's imposition of accountability on other Whitehall departments—may be viewed as forms of self-regulation. (These have been mapped and analysed by Daintith and Page, 1999.) The Select Committee on the Treasury in its Third Report of the session 2000–1 (HC 7303) *HM Treasury* found that the Treasury had become over-powerful in its influence over the strategic direction of government, and by the use of PSAs. (A brief explanation of PSAs may be helpful here. They form the conditions on which departments and other bodies receive extra funds from the Treasury. The policy is that extra investment from the Treasury is conditional on clear objectives, higher standards, improved productivity, and the reforms needed to delivery of the modern and efficient services the public needs (Cm. 4181, 1998, Foreword).) The first PSAs were issued in 1998 (see *Public Service Agreements 1999–2002. Public Services for the Future: Modernization, Reform, Accountability,* Cm. 4181, December 1998). They were updated in July 2002 (see further Chapter 11).

The Treasury Committee report found that the Treasury had increased its influence over the affairs of spending departments to an unacceptable extent. Witnesses suggested that the interventionism of the Treasury in other departments was undermining both the Treasury's own effectiveness in its core work, and the effectiveness of departments. The Committee recommended, *inter alia*, that the Treasury's own targets, which it used to hold spending departments to account, should be externally validated (para. 34), that the Treasury's influence in government should be decreased by altering the balance of membership of the Public Services and Public Expenditure Cabinet Committee (para. 38), and that the Treasury itself should be accountable to the departmental select committees (para. 50).

The *external* auditing relationships between public bodies involve auditing by bodies independent of the body giving the account: the Comptroller and Auditor-General, the National Audit Office, the Parliamentary Commissioner for Administration, the Audit Commission are examples. Since 2002 the government has adopted a policy of requiring independent inspection of public service providers to determine whether they have met their PSA targets. Many of these procedures are linked in with political accountability: the Comptroller and Auditor General is an officer of Parliament and works with the Public Accounts Committee; and the Parliamentary Commissioner for Administration, also an officer of Parliament, works with the Select Committee on Public Administration.

These external auditors have statutory coercive powers enabling them to gain access to documents and information about the matters under investigation. But the sanctions in this form of accountability are not generally legally coercive: the recommendations of the Parliamentary Commissioner for Administration and the Commissioner for Local Administration (the Ombudsmen) are advisory only. The Comptroller and Auditor-General and the National Audit Office, in their reports on value for money, cannot impose legal sanctions. But they are taken very seriously by government departments. The principal weapons of these agencies are publicity and embarrassment, so there are links here with public and political accountability. These are often backed up by political pressures. The Select Committee for Public Administration can apply pressure on ministers to comply with the Commissioner's recommendations, and in practice this is usually effective. The Public Accounts Committee also has strong influence in securing that notice is taken of the reports of the National Audit Office.

Audit and inspection have, then, become fashionable forms of accountability, but they have a number of disadvantages.

- Imposing an audit or inspection regime on activity implies a lack of trust in the organization or its members: lack of trust can generate untrustworthiness or loss of commitment to the activity (see Power, 1999, ch. 6; O'Neill, 2002).

- Audit or inspection can be inflexible as compared with negotiation between organizations in a network, which they have come to replace in many areas, such as local government (Loughlin, 2000).

- Audit can best measure quantity, not quality (Oliver and Drewry, 1996).

- Audit imposes considerable costs on those being audited.

- The criteria by which audit takes place can be difficult to define.

- Audit and inspection can have unintended adverse consequences.

- The auditors and inspectors themselves and their processes need to be open to audit and inspection.

What we can draw from this is not that audit or inspection are bad things, but that, as with other forms of accountability, proportionality in the sense of avoiding unnecessarily burdensome requirements is an important consideration (Power, 1999).

Webs of accountability

Often accountability is imposed in more than one form and is directed to several bodies: for example, local authorities are publicly accountable to their electors and consumers of their services; they are politically accountable to central government (which provides the bulk of their funds), and to the parties to which members belong; they are audited and inspected by the District Auditor and the Commissioner for Local Administration; and they are legally accountable to the courts. Each form of accountability involves measuring actions or decisions against different criteria, thus creating a complex web in which the varying tensions ought to promote, overall, good governance.

But '[T]oo much accountability can be as problematic as too little. Certain organizations operate in a dense web of accountability demands which undermine its capacity to fulfil primary objectives' (Flinders, Richards, and Smith evidence to the House of Commons Select Committee on Public Administration, quoted in Sixth Report of the Select Committee on Public Administration, HC 209, 1998–9, *Quangos*, at para. 102). To take an example close to the author's experience, the upward accountability of universities to the Higher Education Funding Councils is imposed through the quinquennial research assessment exercises, the periodic teaching quality assessments, and auditing of internal procedures. The processes involve peer review which should protect universities from political interference. But the processes are bureaucratic, and they impose substantial costs in terms of staff time and resources on the universities which might be better spent on teaching and research.

Accountability mechanisms also have to be balanced so as to promote the overall objectives of the enterprise. Accountability processes can have unintended consequences, particularly where different objectives contradict one another or where the targets or criteria for accountability have been ill-thought-out and contain perverse incentives. A crude example is provided by the bus driver whose performance was assessed according to the punctuality of his arrival at the terminus at the end of the route. Asked why he had driven past a queue of passengers at a bus stop, his reply was that he would have arrived late at the terminus if he had stopped to pick them up. To return to the universities, the research and teaching quality assessment exercises introduce incentives in the system in favour of universities concentrating resources on research, which is rewarded by the HEFCE, and diverting energies away from teaching, where there are no special rewards for high quality (see also Committee for Public Accounts 46th Report *Inappropriate Adjustments to NHS Waiting Lists*, HC 517, 2001–2, and discussion in Chapter 12).

In search of intelligent accountability

It was noted in Chapter 1 that accountability can undermine the level of trust and even increase untrustworthy behaviour in society. O'Neill (2002, ch. 3) suggests that there seems to be no evidence that public trust is reviving as a result of the increase in regulation and accountability in the system, and she asks whether continuing expressions of mistrust suggest that we are imposing the wrong sort of accountability. She points out that some accountability mechanisms conflict with others and are incoherent and that this invites compromises and evasions and undermines both professional judgement and institutional autonomy. The pursuit of ever more perfect accountability provides citizens and consumers, patients and parents with more information, more comparisons, more complaints systems, but it also builds a culture of suspicion and low morale, and may ultimately lead to professional cynicism—and then we would have grounds for public mistrust. She suggests that what is needed is 'intelligent accountability', with more attention paid to good governance as a whole rather than over-concentration on accountability. Institutions need to be allowed some margin for self-governance within a framework of financial and other *reporting*. 'Serious and effective accountability . . . needs to concentrate on good governance, on obligations to tell the truth and needs to seek intelligent accountability. If we want a culture of public service, professionals and public servants must in the end be free to serve the public rather than their paymasters.' An emphasis on reporting rather than auditing (except for financial propriety) could indeed counteract the distorting effects of targets, performance indicators, and the like.

Accountability then is about constructing a framework within which public bodies are forced to seek to promote the public interest and are compelled to justify their actions in those terms or in other constitutionally acceptable terms (justice, humanity, equity); to modify policies if they should turn out not to have been well conceived; and to make amends if mistakes and errors of judgement have been made. The question, 'to whom is accountability owed?', is often crucial to the good working of the Constitution, as are the criteria against which a person's conduct is measured, and whether those criteria have been reduced to writing in legislation or a code, and the design of the mechanisms of accountability. Choices have to be made about the balance between the different forms of accountability—whether legal accountability is to be preferred to political accountability, or whether a number of forms of accountability can operate in parallel. But there are many ways in which accountability can go wrong, and finding the right mechanisms of accountability and the right balance between overlapping mechanisms and 'webs' for each particular body giving the account and function is a subtle and complex business. In the chapters that follow we shall note how accountability works in practice and what some of the major pitfalls are.

Maintaining an Uncorrupt System

Trustworthiness and an absence of corruption are essential components in a good governance system. In the UK the commitment to an incorrupt and honest administration finds expression in the public service ethos, which has become deeply embedded since the nineteenth-century Northcote Trevelyan reforms of the civil service. It has recently been elaborated as Seven Principles of Public Life, which have been adopted in a number of codes of conduct. Those principles are selflessness, integrity, objectivity, accountability, openness, honesty, and leadership (see First Report of Committee on Standards in Public Life, Cm. 2850, 1995). The ethos applies to public employees, elected members of Parliament, the devolved bodies, and local authorities, and possibly even to those in the private sector performing public functions or delivering public services (see PASC report, *The Public Service Ethos*, HC 263, 2001–2).

There is no firm definition of corruption in public life (Heywood, 1997, 5–10). Broadly in the general understanding in the UK political corruption consists of interference with the proper exercise of judgement and discretion by holders of public office. It can include the misspending of public money, but it also includes such matters as the giving or taking of bribes in exchange for favourable treatment, or giving in to pressure or threats from sectional interests in the exercise of public functions, or the making of appointments not on merit but on grounds of personal favouritism. It covers activity of varying degrees of seriousness, from 'ethical lassitude' (Mancuso, 1993, 180) via 'slackness' (Committee on Standards in Public Life, first report, 1996) and sleaze, the most serious forms being the taking of bribes, to fraud. Not all of such acts are unlawful, though they are widely perceived as corrupt or improper, and even in the absence of legal controls there are commonly soft law or cultural (public opinion and peer group pressure for instance) controls of inappropriate conduct.

Philp (1997) comments that any definition of political corruption presupposes a notion of *uncorrupt* politics, which might differ from country to country, depending on the culture. He cites the scandal in the Legislative Assembly in New South Wales in 1988 as illustrating how conduct that may be regarded as improper by some commentators would be regarded as part of the nature of politics itself by others. The new premier of New South Wales, Greiner, having created an Independent Commission against Corruption (ICAC) that was designed to prevent a range of corrupt practices including the exercise of illicit political patronage, reached an agreement with an independent MP, Metherall, who was opposing the government at a time when it had no majority in the hung parliament. The agreement was that Metherall would resign his seat and be immediately appointed to a well-paid position in the NSW public service. Greiner was the subject of a censure motion in the legislative assembly for this deal, but his response was that if what he had done was contrary to the law, then 'that is, for practical purposes, the death of politics in this State . . . I am not sure . . . that those standards are going to produce a workable system of democracy' (quoted in Philp, 1997, 21). The ICAC found that the arrangement was the partial exercise of official functions and constituted a breach of trust, contrary to the anti-corruption legislation. (Eventually the NSW Court of Appeal found that the ICAC report was in excess of jurisdiction and a nullity and that the conduct did not constitute reasonable grounds for dismissal under the Act.)

In the UK there is a fairly widely agreed notion of uncorrupt politics, expressed in some of the Seven Principles of Public Life noted above, against which allegedly corrupt conduct can be measured. This conforms to what Philp classifies as the liberal model of politics, which focuses on ways of ordering the structures of rule so that those entrusted with political power will act in the interests of those whom the state was founded to protect, and will not usurp that power for their own ends. This model sees corruption as the weakening of ethical constraints on individual conduct in public office and consequent abuse of political power for individual gain.

On the question of public appointments—the issue in the New South Wales case—the liberal model of an uncorrupt system will normally require that they be made on merit, but less rigorous criteria may be tolerated on the grounds that effective government relies on a degree of cooperation which can only be brought about by allowing some partisan interest within political institutions. This is an interesting perspective on appointments of special advisers, discussed in Chapter 12, or to the House of Lords, discussed in Chapter 10, neither of which are made on impartial assessment of merit, and both of which attract considerable public criticism.

There is no evidence of *endemic* serious corruption in the sense of the bribery or blackmail of public decision-makers in the United Kingdom. However, there has for long been a degree of corruption in local government, particularly in relation to the taking of bribes for grants of planning permission and in the police, and this has surfaced from time to time in prosecutions. There have been scandals over fraud and corruption in quangos. And, as we shall see (Chapter 9), there was consistent concern about sleaze in the House of Commons and other public bodies in the early 1990s. The Transparency International *Corrupt Perceptions Index 2002* placed the UK tenth in the world out of 102 countries.

In some European countries, notably Italy, in countries in Africa including Kenya and Nigeria, in the Indian subcontinent, and in South America, to name but a few places, there is a serious problem of endemic corruption (see Transparency International, *Corrupt Perceptions Index*, 2002). It is beyond the scope of this chapter to seek to identify the reasons why some countries suffer from corruption and others do not do so, but the point for our purposes is that it would be foolish to assume that the United Kingdom is immune from such problems and it is important that appropriate mechanisms are in place to prevent corruption from taking root (see Heywood, 1997).

There are a range of legal provisions dealing with political corruption in the UK. The giving or taking of bribes (except to or by Members of Parliament) is a criminal offence under the Prevention of Corruption Acts. Judicial review of decisions made corruptly or in breach of proper standards of conduct would be a remedy for those adversely affected by an improper decision. Misfeasance in a public office, which would include corruption and other abuses of power, is a tort (see *Three Rivers DC v. Governor and Company of the Bank of England* [2000] 2 WLR 1220, HL). Misbehaviour in a public office is a crime at common law (*R. v. Bowden* [1995] 4 All ER 505). In practice however there have been very few prosecutions or civil actions for corruption of these various kinds. It is of course impossible to say whether or not there is much undetected corruption, but it is probably the case that there is little of it.

An absence of corruption, or to put it more positively, an uncorrupt political system, is largely a cultural phenomenon. The press has an important role in investigatory reporting of corrupt or improper practices which serves both to uphold the public service ethos and as a deterrent. But press activity has also spawned a culture of suspicion which could undermine trust and trustworthiness (O'Neill, 2002; see Chapter 1). Concern about 'sleaze' and this developing culture of suspicion lay behind the decision to appoint the Committee on Standards in Public Life in 1995.

The Committee on Standards in Public Life

In the mid-1990s concerns started to be expressed about standards of conduct in many areas of public life. The particular problem which precipitated the taking of steps to promote proper standards was the 'cash for questions' affair in the House of Commons (see Chapter 9) but there were a number of other areas of concern. The government finally responded to such concerns, and this triggered action on a number of fronts to define and improve the upholding of appropriate standards of conduct in public life. Pressure from the press and public opinion for sleaze to be dealt with led to the appointment of the Committee on Standards in Public Life, chaired by Lord Nolan, a Law Lord:

To examine current concerns about standards of conduct of all holders of public office, ... and make recommendations as to any changes in present arrangements which might be required to ensure the highest standards of propriety in public life (HC Deb., 25 October 1994, col. 758).

In its first report in (Cm. 2850, 1995) the Committee found that:

We cannot say conclusively that standards of behaviour in public life have declined. We can say that conduct in public life is more rigorously scrutinized than it was in the past, that the standards which the public demands remain high, and that the great majority of people in public life meet those high standards (Summary, para. 2).

But the Committee concluded that:

[T]here are weaknesses in the procedures for maintaining and enforcing . . . standards. As a result people in public life are not always as clear as they should be about where the boundaries of acceptable conduct lie. This we regard as the principal reason for public disquiet. It calls for urgent remedial action (Cm. 2850, 1995, Summary, para. 2).

Public disquiet—suspicion was the term used by O'Neill in the 2002 Reith Lectures on *A Question of Trust* (2002)—was to be dispelled through juridification of various kinds. This first report included a statement of the Seven Principles of Public Life, which have since served to inform the drafting of codes of conduct in a wide range of areas.

The House of Commons and the government responded fairly promptly to the findings of the Nolan Committee in its first and subsequent reports, and since 1995 a number of measures have been introduced across many aspects of public life (Parliament, Ministers, civil servants, the NHS, local authorities, non-departmental bodies, for instance) by way of remedial action. The main technique has been the adoption of codes of conduct. These are for the most part 'soft law' in the sense that their breach does not lead to prosecution or directly legally enforceable sanctions. The Committee also recommended the appointment of independent officials to secure the observance of codes of conduct and this led to the appointment of the Parliamentary Commissioner for Standards, the Commissioner for Public Appointments, responsible for monitoring appointments, and other bodies responsible for standards in local government.

Formalizing the public service ethos?

The Public Administration Select Committee of the House of Commons (PASC) has also been concerned about upholding standards of conduct. In *The Public Service Ethos* (HC 263, 2001–2) it recommended a public service code that would govern all those providing public services. Significantly the PASC based its proposals on acknowledgement that public services may be provided both by public bodies, such as government and its executive agencies, quangos, devolved bodies and local authorities, and by private sector bodies, often acting in partnership with government or local authorities. Good governance should therefore include provisions for securing high standards of conduct by all those involved in the networks through which public services are delivered. The PASC recommended that all those providing public services should be bound by the public service ethos, which should be expressed in a code which had parliamentary backing. The code should include a statement of the Seven Principles of Public Life. In addition it should lay down the following requirements of those providing public services:

- They should observe at all times the ethical standards expected of public servants and public service bodies.
- They should make themselves accountable through elected representatives and other means for their policies and performance with the highest standards of openness and transparency.
- They should aim to deliver public services that match in quality the best private equivalents, including standards of customer care. Where there is no private sector equivalent, best practice in the public sector should be matched.
- They should treat public service workers and users fairly and equitably, and involve them as much as possible in service issues.
- They should respect at all times the right of the citizen to good administration as set out in the Charter of Fundamental Rights of the European Union, and his or her right to safe, reliable public services (see Chapter 4).
- Proper redress should be made where maladministration has taken place.
- They should remember at all times that public service means serving the public, not serving the interests of those who provide the service, and work collaboratively with others to that end.

However, the PASC was concerned that the externally imposed measurement culture—the culture of audit and accountability—might damage the public service ethos. 'There is a danger that such a culture can erode trust and damage the values of professionalism' (para. 44). This chimes with the concerns expressed by O'Neill (2002) about devising appropriate mechanisms to promote trust and trustworthy behaviour, countering the culture of suspicion that has developed. A code of this kind would amount to a relatively mild form of juridification which, coupled with reporting duties, could underpin the public service ethos without undermining it in the way that detailed targets, performance indicators, and other measures can do. On the other hand it could spawn further codes elaborating on the principles and add to the burden of regulation that O'Neill suggests can actually encourage rather than dispel suspicion.

The government rejected the proposal for a new Public Service Code on the grounds that, though the public service ethos was key to delivery of services, such a code might be inflexible and inappropriate for certain services, and codes tend to codify existing stand-ards rather than be aspirational. The government's preference was to staff working in public services to formulate their own codes, and to rely on a range of arrangements, including frameworks for accountability, devolution, and delegation of responsibility, flexibility, and customer choice (Public Administration Select Committee First Special

Report, *The Public Service Ethos: Government's Response to the Committee's Seventh Report of Session 2001–2*, HC 61, 2002–3).

Overall finding the right balance between accountability on one hand and trust on the other is difficult and it is hard to know whether the right balance has been achieved. Power suggests that audit has become 'a leading bearer of legitimacy and this must be so because other sources of legitimacy, such as community and state, are declining in influence' (1999, 147). But society, he says, needs to be capable of knowing when to trust, when to trust trust, and when to demand an audited account (1999, 146; see also O'Neill, 2002).

Summary

Good governance issues will arise in most of the chapters that follow and we shall see that accountability and trust are recurring concerns. In the next chapter we shall find that good governance is also an issue in the European Community. Apart from accountability and trust, other ingredients of a good governance system, openness, and respect for human rights are considered in separate chapters. Concern for effectiveness runs through many of the other chapters.

4

The United Kingdom in the European Union

The reform of the British Constitution cannot be treated without regard to the fact that the United Kingdom has since 1 January 1973 been a member of the European Community (EC) and, since the Maastricht Treaty of 1992 (2001 Cm. 5090) of the European Union (EU). (The EC and the EU have shared institutional frameworks although they are formally distinct organizations.) In this chapter we shall be mainly concerned with the implications of Britain's membership of the EC and the EU for our themes of democracy, citizenship, and good governance in the UK, and for the process of judicialization of the Constitution. In order to do so we shall have to consider briefly the working of the EC and EU institutions and the 'democratic deficit' in the EC in relation to the UK's own constitutional arrangements (see generally Hartley, 1998; Birkinshaw, 2001*b*; Barnett, 2002, chs. 8, 9; Craig and de Burca, 2002; Douglas-Scott, 2002). The House of Commons European Scrutiny Committee published a report on *Democracy and Accountability in the EU and the Role of National Parliaments* (HC 152, 2001–2) in June 2002 and reference will be made to their recommendations to highlight some of the issues. In the space available we shall not be able to go into these in any detail.

Background—the European Community and the European Union

First, a brief explanation of what the European Union and Community are and how the United Kingdom became a member. The European Union consists of three 'pillars', i.e. there are three separate fields of governmental activity, each of which uses a different process. The EC is the first pillar, governed by the amended EEC treaty, now renamed the EC Treaty. Common foreign and security policy make up the second pillar. Police and judicial cooperation make up the third pillar. In relation to the second and third pillars decisions are reached by intergovernmental negotiation between member states, whereas in relation to the EC decision making is by the Community institutions—the European Commission, the Council, the Parliament, and the European Court of Justice.

The European Union is both an international organization and a supranational body. The original European Economic Community was formed by the Treaty of Rome 1957— and so it is an international organization. Since its inception a number of further treaties have added to the competences of the institutions, created new institutions, and enabled new members to join. There are two principal treaties. The 'Treaty Establishing the European Community' (sometimes colloquially known as the 'Treaty of Rome', or 'EC Treaty' for short) and the Treaty *on* European Union made at Maastricht in 1992. Both these principal treaties have been amended, most recently by the Treaty of Amsterdam, 1997 and the Treaty of Nice, 2001 (which, though signed, is not yet ratified at the time of writing). The numbers of articles of the Treaties have changed as a result of successive amendments, and the article numbers given below are those of the version of the Amsterdam Treaty, known as the Treaty on European Union, 1997 (the TEU).

Primacy and direct effect or European Community law

Unlike other treaty organizations such as the United Nations, the terms of the European treaties as interpreted by the European Court of Justice require members to subordinate their sovereignty and that of their Parliaments to the Community institutions, and to give direct effect and primacy to European law. It is in this respect that it is a supranational organization. The giving up of part of their sovereignty—i.e. the power of their Parliaments to legislate contrary to the Terms of the EC Treaty—by member states was a necessary ingredient of the deal between the member states to set up what was initially known as the Common Market, and later evolved into the European Community.

It is the position of the European Court of Justice (ECJ) that European law should be enforceable in the courts of the member states and that it prevails over the laws, including the constitutional laws, of members states, including of course those of the UK. The ECJ's position was stated in the seminal case of *Van Gend en Loos v. Nederlandse Tarief Commissie* ([1963] CMLR105, 129), as follows:

The Community constitutes a new legal order of international law, for the benefit of which the states have limited their sovereign rights, albeit within limited fields, and the subjects of which comprise not only Member States but also their nationals.

In the *Simmenthal* case ([1978] ECR 6290)—decided after the UK had joined the Community—the ECJ maintained that every national court must apply Community law in its entirety and protect rights which the latter confers on individuals, and must accordingly set aside any provision of national law which may conflict with it, whether prior or subsequent to the Community rule. (See also *Costa v. ENEL* [(1964] ECR 585.) Those whose Community law rights have been infringed are entitled to seek remedies in the courts, and this right has been instrumental in the development of the rule of law in the EC. Thus European law has direct effect in member states, and primacy over the domestic law of member states.

European institutions: Who and what do they represent? Are they democratic?

A question about European institutions is who they represent, whose interests they promote, and in what sense, if any, they are democratic. The principal institutions and their functions are as follows.

First, the European Parliament. The members of the European Parliament (MEPs) are directly elected by list-based systems of proportional representation (see Chapter 7) to represent 'the people of Europe'. They sit in party, not national, groups. A problem is that the people living in Europe are not themselves a single 'demos' or 'ethnos' in the sense of a nation, race, or nationality. It is self-evident that there are many peoples in Europe, and there will be divergences of interest and identity between different peoples of Europe on different matters, and indeed between different sections of the people of Europe. The European Parliament therefore has to seek to aggregate a wide number of conflicting interests. (So of course do all elected legislatures.) But the overall objective of its activities, to promote the interests of the people of Europe, not of the people or peoples or nations of the United Kingdom and other member states is hard to achieve when people have such diverse interests.

Originally the European Parliament's role in the European Community's legislative process was very restricted; for instance, it had rights to be consulted by the European Commission on many proposed measures, and a right of veto in relation to some. However, its powers have been successively increased by the Maastricht Treaty and the Amsterdam Treaty so that it now has extensive legislative powers. Its participation in legislation is commonly by way of 'co-decision', when it operates as an equal partner with the Council (see below) and passes the majority of European laws. The legislative processes are complex, and include consultation of and cooperation with the Parliament by the Commission (see below). The Parliament does not, however, have any right of legislative initiative. The European Scrutiny Committee of the House of Commons in its report of June 2002 (HC 152, 2001–2) found that these aspects of the arrangements were inappropriate and proposed that co-decision should not be extended until a more effective and transparent set of procedures had been devised. Among other things, the Parliament may adopt the Commission's proposed budget, or reject it by a majority of its members and two-thirds of the votes cast if there are important reasons to do so—Article 272 TEU.

Second, the Council, formerly known as the Council of Ministers. European laws are in fact made by the Council (Articles 202, 203, TEU)—in collaboration with the Parliament. Each member state is equally represented on the Council. The relevant minister of the government of each member state attends their meetings. The Presidency of the Council rotates among member states in six-month terms. This then is the forum in which the interests of member states are represented. Decisions on proposals for legislation—directives, regulations, or decisions—are put to the Council by the Commission, having passed through the cooperation or co-decision procedures involving the Parliament and having been considered by the Council's expert working groups, and by the Committee of Permanent Representatives (COREPER). The Council usually meets in private and it is often not therefore known on what terms decisions are reached and what bargains are struck between the members. The Council may decide many issues by qualified majority, and the availability of qualified majority voting will be extended under the Treaty of Nice from 2005. Member states do not generally have vetos in the Council, and the interests of individual states may therefore be overridden. In practice voting is not often required as consensus will have been achieved in preparatory negotiations.

The House of Commons European Scrutiny Committee urged in its report on

Democracy and Accountability in the EU and the Role of National Parliaments (HC 152, 2001–2) that the presidency should no longer rotate in six-month periods but that the President should be elected for a two-year term, and the Council's legislative meetings should be held in public. They proposed that the President should be subject to parliamentary accountability through joint meetings of national parliamentarians and MEPs.

Third, the European Commission. The Commission is the nearest European equivalent to the government of Europe. There are twenty commissioners appointed for renewable periods of five years. Each member state has one commissioner and no state may have more than two. The Commissioners and the Commission are required to act in the general interest of the Community as a whole and should be independent in doing so. They must neither take nor seek instructions from any government or other body (Article 213(1) TEU). The main functions of the Commission are to initiate proposals for legislation to be considered by the Parliament and Council as sketched in above. The Commission also has responsibility for ensuring that the laws of the Community are implemented and enforced, and it may take enforcement proceedings in the European Court of Justice (Article 211, TEU).

The Commission is accountable in various ways to the European Parliament and the Council, but this does not add up to democratic accountability in any way comparable to the accountability of executive bodies in the UK and other member states. The nominations of Commissioners are made by their member states. The Council, with the nominee for President, adopts the list of persons, and this is submitted to the Parliament for approval or disapproval, which takes place after committee hearings and questioning. But the Parliament has no role in the allocation of portfolios to individual Commissioners—this is a matter for the President of the Commission. In early 1999, the European Commission was forced by political pressures to resign en bloc after an independent report found extensive fraud and corruption in the Community and accused the Commission of failing to control it.

The House of Commons European Scrutiny Committee proposed that the powers of the Commission should be strictly defined by the Council and the EP and its political and legislative powers should be confined to those for which there was clear justification. Given the tendency for the Commission to expand its powers a subsidiarity watchdog should be established to deal with concerns that the Commission was exceeding its competence. In effect there is here support for a Constitution for Europe designed to keep its institutions within bounds (see below).

Fourth, the European Court of Justice and the Court of First Instance. These are the courts of the Communities. The ECJ has both jurisdiction over references from the courts of member states and original jurisdiction. It is in effect the top court on European law matters for the UK and other member states. The Court has been highly influential in developing the legal system of the Community, elaborating the principles of the primacy of European law over the law of member states, including their Constitutions, noted above, identifying common principles and values in European law, holding that unimplemented directives have direct effect against state bodies, and developing a right to damages against a member state for breach of community rights. It has in other words developed the rule of law as a fundamental principle in Europe.

Fifth and lastly, the European Council consists of the heads of government of the member states, who meet together as a 'summit' about four times a year to provide the necessary impetus for the development of the Union and define its general political guidelines (Article 4, TEU).

The European Community's institutional arrangements acknowledge the existence of the different interests of the people and peoples of Europe, of the member states, and of the Community as a whole. The Community is developing procedures and mechanisms to balance the conflicts between these interests. It operates alongside the internal arrangements of member states. While it is widely acknowledged that there are serious democratic deficits in the Community, there is no consensus about how they may be remedied. The House of Commons European Scrutiny Committee proposed that the deficit should be remedied by increasing the openness of EU institutions in their operations and reconnecting the EU with citizens via national Parliaments. These should, for instance, have increased opportunities to scrutinize proposed European legislation and hold their own governments to account for their decisions at Council meetings. There should be joint meetings of national parliamentarians and MEPs to scrutinize the Commission's annual policy strategy and work programme and question the Commission on it. They also proposed re-examination of the method of election to the Parliament, expressing a preference for first past the post (see Chapter 7) as it would re-establish relationships between citizens and their MEPs. And they were in favour of clearer statements of principles setting out what the EU is for and how it can add value.

It may be that there is no way in which an organization such as the EU can be effective and at the same time more than minimally democratic. Increasing the influences of the Parliaments of the member states could serve to protect the interests of the states but paralyse the Community. Increasing the powers of the European Parliament could undermine the position of the national Parliaments and governments and would be resisted for that reason.

This raises the issue to what extent good governance arrangements can be a substitute for democracy, or compensate for a democratic deficit? One problem is that without democratic accountability it is hard to stop a good governance system from being undermined and corrupted. But it is conceivable that a suitably enforced set of anti-corruption laws, and provisions for wide consultation of affected interests before decisions are made, coupled with the rather tenuous democratic safeguards in the European institutions, especially an incorrupt, expert, and independent court, could achieve many of the ends which representative democracy is supposed to secure in nation states. The Laeken European Convention on the future of Europe is concerned to propose a new framework and structures for the EU which are geared to the citizens of Europe and the future development of the European Union—and to changes in the world situation—and one of its tasks will be to meet concerns about democracy in the EU (see further below, in discussion of a possible Constitution for the EU).

Law and law-making in the EU

European laws that are to be given effect in the domestic courts of the member states are to be found in the Treaties, directives, regulations, and decisions of the Commission and the case law of the European Court of Justice and the Court of First Instance. Treaty provisions have effect and give rise to rights and obligations that are enforceable by individuals who complain that their rights have been breached in British courts and the courts of the other member states to the extent that they are clear, unconditional, and not conditional on a national implementing measure (*Van Gend en Loos v. Neder-landse Administratie der Belastingen* [1963] ECR 1, and *Reyners v. Belgium* [1974] ECR 631). Directives are made by the Council and are binding on the member states as to their results (Article 249, TEU) but they are not normally enforceable in domestic courts until they have been transposed into the law of the member state. In the UK this is usually done by secondary legislation—Orders in Council. However, directives which have not been transposed, i.e. which have not been implemented or have not been effectively implemented, by a member state, may have some effect in the domestic law of the state: if the time for their taking effect has passed and the rights they create are sufficiently clear, precise, and unconditional to be capable of being applied directly by a national court (*Van Duyn v. Home Office* ([1974] ECR 1337), then they will have 'direct vertical effect'. This means that a person whose rights under the directive have been breached will have a right to a remedy from a domestic court against a state body which has breached them, for instance against the government which has failed to implement the directive. But such a directive cannot have 'horizontal effect', i.e. it cannot impose duties and liabilities upon another private body such as a private employer.

European regulations and decisions may be made by the Commission or the Council or the Parliament acting jointly with the Council. They are immediately enforceable, i.e. directly applicable, in the member states if they are sufficiently unconditional, clear, and precise, and they override or impliedly repeal inconsistent laws of the member state, including laws made by its Parliament.

When the treaties are to be amended or new treaties negotiated, an Intergovernmental Conference is held at which unanimity among member states is required for the amendments or the new treaty. Thereafter each member state takes the steps required by its Constitution before ratifying the treaty, to secure that the measures take effect in domestic law. In the United Kingdom this requires an Act of Parliament. In other states it may require a referendum (as in Ireland and Denmark) followed by legislation, or formal amendments to the country's Constitution. Thus the UK's interests and those of the other member states are protected, and only if their domestic procedures are followed can these major amendments be made. But it remains to be seen whether this process will continue to operate once the Community is enlarged to over twenty states in the next few years. It will become increasingly difficult to amend the Treaties and thus to modernize the Community when so many Members' domestic constitutional requirements are involved in implementing changes. This has given rise to discussion of whether a European Constitution is required that would both protect member states against reforms to which they do not agree and enable the Community to reform itself where needed (see further below).

We note below and in Chapters 9 and 10 the role of the UK Parliament in the scrutiny of European legislation. Other member states have their own parliamentary and other scrutiny procedures. Overall, despite improvements in the scrutiny of European legislation by the UK Parliament in recent years, the provisions for scrutiny in the member states do not impose strong accountability on this legislative activity.

Democracy in the EU?

In its White Paper on *European Governance* the Commission commented that 'the Union has moved from a diplomatic to a democratic process' (p. 29). In fact the Union is a highly bureaucratic organization (see for instance, Siedentop, 2000). How far then can this claim to democracy be justified?

First, the European Parliament has, as we have seen, become closer to a democratic legislature since 1992, consenting to many European laws on behalf of the people of Europe. There are elements of an embryonic participatory democracy developing in the EU, alongside the legislative provisions noted above. For instance, the Aarhus Convention on environmental protection, which entered into force on 30 October 2001, is concerned with environmental information and decision-making designed to secure rights to live in an environment adequate to human health and well-being. Article 1 provides that each party to the Convention (i.e. the member states and the Community) 'shall guarantee the rights of access to information, public participation in decision-making and access to justice in environmental matters' in accordance with the provisions of the Convention. In particular, an environmental impact assessment must be made of the effects of certain projects on the environment, and directives requiring this have been implemented by regulations in the UK. In *Berkeley v. Secretary of State* ([2001] 2 AC 602) it was held that the need for an EIA was enforceable, and interested parties, including charities and voluntary sector organizations, had a right to be heard and have a fully informed decision taken. For our purposes this is significant both in illustrating the development of participatory democratic procedures and in pointing up the fact that these require legislation and legal enforcement if they are to be effective, and that mere political commitments would not secure effective participatory opportunities. Participation in this kind of case also makes it harder for politicians to make policy decisions based on ideology, gut feelings, or personal preferences without justifying them concretely.

A more controversial example of participatory processes is found in the Social Chapter to the Maastricht Treaty (which the UK opted out of initially but signed up to in 1997). It envisages a role for the social partners (i.e. management and labour) in being consulted on proposals that affect them. It also entitles certain 'cross-sectoral social partners' (i.e. Union-wide union and employers' federations) to negotiate 'framework agreements' which would be given binding effect by the Council in the form, for instance, of directives, without any role for the European Parliament. The Parental Leave Directive 96/34/EC was the first to be adopted through this procedure. The Court of First Instance in the

UEAPME v. Council case, T-135/96 ([1998] IRLR 602) stated that where there is no official involvement of the European Parliament 'the principle of democracy on which the Union is founded requires ... that the participation of the people be otherwise ensured, in this instance through the parties representative of management and labour who concluded the agreement which is endowed by the Council ... with a legislative foundation at Community level.' In that case the CFI found that the bodies consulted had been representative, although UEAPME had wished to be consulted and did not accept that those consulted were representative. This procedure may well raise issues of legitimacy, therefore, and the fact that the governments of the member states in the Council have input into the decision to issue these directives—by qualified majority voting—will not necessarily legitimate these measures. Thus although there are elements of representative and participatory democracy in the EU, there are many unresolved issues as to the extent to which it is or should become more democratic, and how democracy at EU level should operate alongside democratic arrangements within member states. The development of democracy is affected by an emergent concept of European citizenship, considered below.

Subsidiarity

We have noted that the United Kingdom's membership of the European Community has transferred some of what were the powers of the British government and Parliament 'upwards' to the Community. This raises questions about a principle that is influential in the Constitutions of some member states and in the thinking of the Community, 'subsidiarity' (Wilke and Wallace 1990; House of Lords Select Committee on the European Communities Twenty-Seventh Report 1989–90, paras. 23, 24, 165; Emiliou, 1992; Douglas-Scott, 2002). This has been essentially a socio-political term rather than a legal or constitutional principle (Wilke and Wallace 1990, para. 13) but the Treaty of Amsterdam 1997 introduced a protocol on subsidiarity, thus giving the concept a legal and justiciable status (see de Burca, 1998). Increasingly then membership of the Union is judicializing our constitutional arrangements, as the UK courts and the European institutions work out their respective areas of competence (Nicol, 2001). This has reduced the relative importance of the political and customary nature of the British system when European issues are involved.

The subsidiarity principle is based on the assumption that government can be both more effective and more accountable to those affected by its actions if its functions are discharged at the lowest possible level. It may be further justified on the basis that democracy and political and public accountability are stronger within member states than at European level. It is easier to state the principle of subsidiarity than to apply it, and opinions will differ between member states and European institutions as to whether the criteria justifying European as opposed to member state action are met. Its effectiveness will depend substantially on the attitudes of member states and public opinion.

Although there are a range of ways of expressing the subsidiarity principle, it is sufficient for our purposes to adopt the *Oxford English Dictionary* definition which was adopted by the House of Lords Select Committee on the European Communities: 'a central authority should have a subsidiary function, performing only those tasks which cannot be performed effectively at a more immediate or local level.' Although this cannot yet be said to be a strong and observed principle of Community law, it is recognized in a number of provisions of the Treaties. By Article 6(3) of the TEU the Union is to 'respect the identity of its Member States'; and Article 3b EC provides that except in matters where the EC possesses exclusive competence, it is to act 'within the limits of its powers' and 'in accordance with the principle of subsidiarity'. It should take action only if and in so far as 'the objectives of the proposed action cannot be sufficiently achieved by the Member States and can therefore . . . be better achieved by the Community.' Community action 'shall not go beyond what is necessary to achieve the objectives of the Treaty.'

As the concept of subsidiarity develops in the EU, attention focuses not on the *separation* of those functions that are exercised at EU level from those that are exercised by the member states, but rather on the way in which elements in particular functions are *shared* between European institutions and member states. Thus the *Protocol on the application of principles of subsidiarity and proportionality* that was annexed to the Treaty of Amsterdam 1997 treats the principle of subsidiarity as a guide as to how shared powers are to be exercised at Community level (Hartley, 1998, 111–13). The burden lies on the Community institution proposing legislation to show why the objective cannot be met by member states and why it can be better met by European level action. The proportionality principle affects the content of legislation conferring powers on European institutions. By Article 3b TEU, where Community action is taken it 'shall not go beyond what is necessary to achieve the objectives of this Treaty'. The Amsterdam Protocol elaborates this by providing that action taken at Community level should respect national legal arrangements and traditions, and it should provide maximum scope for action to be taken by member states. The ECJ may declare a measure invalid for infringement of the principle of subsidiarity.

Thus a concept of duality of sovereignty seems to be emerging in the EU, with the member states and EU institutions interacting. This would involve a move away from the hierarchy of norms that is usually found in nation state legal systems, towards a network of norms (Schwarze, 2001*a*, 100, 300, 364–8, 372–4; Bell, 2002, 192). MacCormick (1999) suggests that the trend in Europe is towards a confederal commonwealth rather than a federal union enjoying sovereignty as a comprehensive entity.

Good governance in Europe

Good governance is an issue in the European Community as well in the UK (see Chapter 3). The Commission produced its white paper *European Governance* (COM (2001) 428; see Cygan, 2002) in response to growing concern that many Europeans felt alienated from the Union's work –the decreasing turnout in European Parliament elections and the first Irish 'No' vote on the Treaty of Nice in 2001 were given as examples of the widening gulf between the Union and the people it is supposed to serve. (The ratification of the Treaty was held up as a result of the 'No' vote in the referendum in Ireland on the ratification of the Treaty, a referendum being required by the Irish Constitution. On a second referendum in 2002 the Irish vote was in favour of enlargement and of the Treaty.) The definition of governance adopted in that document was 'rules, processes and behaviour that affect the way in which powers are exercised at European level, particularly as regards openness, participation, accountability, effectiveness and coherence' (*European Govern-ance*, 2002, n. 1, p. 8). These same five principles have also featured prominently in the British debates about good governance. The proposals in that White Paper were addressed to European Institutions, member states, regional and local authorities, and civil society (p. 9).

It will be useful to flag up some of the ways in which these principles are regarded as particularly significant and in need of implementation in the EU and how they relate to similar concerns in the UK (*European Governance*, 2001, 10). Openness is taken to include a requirement that European institutions should work in a more open manner in order to improve public confidence in complex institutions. There must be wide partici-pation throughout the policy chain, and this again is likely to create more confidence in the end result and in the institutions. Accountability involves institutions explaining and taking responsibility for their activities and greater clarity and responsibility on the part of member states and all those involved in developing EU policy at whatever level. Effectiveness involves clear objectives, an evaluation of future impact and of past experi-ence, and also depends on implementing EU policies in a proportionate manner and deciding at the most appropriate level. And finally coherence includes ensuring that policies are easily understood. Many policies cross the boundaries of sectoral policies—translated into English terminology, joined-up government is needed—and coherence requires political leadership and strong responsibility. The White Paper states that appli-cation of these principles reinforces those of proportionality and subsidiarity—though subsidiarity seems to mean taking action at the most appropriate level, which is not presumed in the White Paper to be the 'lowest' level. It may be that proportionality is replacing subsidiarity as a guiding principle in the EU.

It is significant that the proposals in the White Paper are largely about fostering confidence, recognizing that the legitimacy of the Commission and of European institu-tions generally depends on involvement and participation and means that the linear model of dispensing policies from above must be replaced by a virtuous circle, based on feedback, networks, and involvement from policy creation to implementation at all levels (p. 11). Thus in Europe as in the UK networks are recognized as being important, and some are supported by Community funding. They can link businesses, communities, research centres, and regional and local authorities. An example given in the *European Governance* White Paper (COM (2001) 428, Brussels, 25.7.2001) is the annual 'Car Free Day' in September which mobilizes around 800 cities in twenty-five countries. The White Paper resolved that the Commission would develop by the end of 2002 a more systematic and pro-active approach to working with key networks to enable them to contribute to decisions-shaping and policy execution.

The European Commission also considered the governance issues raised by centralization/subsidiarity issues in *European Governance*. It moved the concepts on by noting that the Union was based on multi-level governance in which each actor contrib-utes in line with his or her capabilities or knowledge to the success of the overall exercise (p. 35). In a multi-level system the real challenge is establishing clear rules for how competence is shared—not separated.

The White Paper stressed the important role of civil society—it mentioned for instance churches and religions communities—in giving voice to the concerns of citizens and delivering services that meet people's needs. Civil society includes trade unions and employers' organizations, which are referred to as social partners, and professional associations, charities, and grass-roots organizations (see also the Opinion of the Economic and Social Committee, *The Role and Contribution of Civil Society Organisations in the Building of Europe*, OJ C329, 17.11.99, 30).

The White Paper is however weak on implementation of its five principles. The emphasis is on the duty of member states to promote the European Community rather than on its own institutions' duties to improve their observation of the principles set out. There is no suggestion of formal ways of institutionalizing subsidiarity, for instance through a Constitution for the Community setting out the powers and competences of each level (see below). An intergovernmental conference is to take place in 2004 in which such issues will undoubtedly arise.

There are a number of applicant countries seeking to join the EC and EU. By 2001 negotiations had started with twelve countries. As and when they join membership will rise to twenty-seven states, and this will require major amendments to the EU institutions and procedures. Present arrangements, devised for a much smaller membership, would not be workable: they would not meet a number of good governance criteria, including effectiveness and accountability.

The Treaty of Nice 2001, as and when it is ratified and member states have passed the necessary legislation to fulfil their obligations under it, will introduce the changes required to deal with enlargement. The Treaty sets out the principles and methods for changing the distribution of seats in the European Parliament, for the appointment and composition of the Commission, the powers of the President of the Commission, and for a new definition of qualified majority voting in the Council. Under this new definition, a decision will have to receive at least a specified number of votes, known as the qualified majority threshold (the number of votes of each member state depends in part upon population) and it must be approved by a majority of member states. Qualified majority voting will be extended to far more areas than hitherto, and thus the veto powers of member states will be reduced.

A 'Europe of the regions'?

There has been a strong trend towards regional or subnational government in a number of the member states of the European Economic Community as minorities in Belgium, the Basque country, and other areas have asserted their rights to self-determination, and as regional populations, notably in France and Spain, have demanded a greater degree of control over their own affairs. The process of decentralization in the United Kingdom (see Chapters 13–15) has parallels in other European countries. The Committee of the Regions paper, *New forms of governance: Europe, a framework for citizens' initiatives* (CdR 186/2000) sought stronger involvement of regional and local authorities in the EU's policies, reflecting their growing responsibilities in some member states and a stronger engagement of people and grass-roots organizations in local democracy. But the *European Governance* White Paper view was that the principal responsibility for involving the regional and local level should remain with the member states (at p. 12).

EU regional policy therefore has clear implications for the UK and its devolution arrangements.

The Welsh executive joined with nine other regional governments in promoting a Declaration in response to the *European Governance* White Paper calling for greater involvement of regions in European policy formation, and urging the European Commission to consult directly with regional governments rather than through member state governments. The British government's position on devolution has been mixed. Subsidiarity is seen primarily as a principle governing relations between Europe and member states and not between member states and their own regions or nations. The asymmetrical provisions for devolution in the UK have been pragmatic responses to pressure and have not been driven by a principled commitment to subsidiarity within the UK.

European Citizenship and Fundamental Rights

Article 17 TEU confers 'citizenship of the European Union' on nationals of member states within the Union. This status complements and does not replace citizenship of the member states. The status is not very explicitly developed, although there is a growing academic literature on the potential for development of the concept and the implications of using the term 'European citizenship' when there is neither a European state nor a European 'demos' (Weiler, 1995; Douglas-Scott, 2002). If a relationship with a state is a prerequisite of citizenship, the status of 'citizen of the Union' cannot be true citizenship. At best it is quasi-citizenship of the Union, although it also represents extended citizenship rights for member state nationals within their own and other member states.

Many of the rights that go with this status are enforceable against member states rather than Community institutions: for instance the right to vote in elections to the European Parliament would be enforceable through the courts or other institutions of member states if eligible voters were denied the right to vote. Thus an important aspect of citizenship of the Union is its implications for the status of citizenship of member states. For instance, citizens of one member state lawfully residing in another must not be discriminated against in the conditions for receipt of welfare benefits—economic rights associated with Marshall's concept of citizenship (see Chapter 2) provided by the state of their residence (see *Maria Martinez Sala v. Freistaat Bayern* Case C-85, 1998). As we noted in Chapter 2, UK citizenship in the sense of nationality is primarily about the right to come and go from the UK; the other rights and responsibilities normally associated with citizenship, such as the right to vote in domestic elections and civil and political, social and economic rights, do not depend and have not depended for many years, well before the UK joined the EC, on a person having British nationality, though they may depend on other matters such as Commonwealth or Irish citizenship, residence, and so on. One aspect of citizenship of the Union, then, is that it enlarges some UK citizenship-type rights, extending them to non-nationals.

As far as the political elements of citizenship of the Union in relation to European institutions are concerned, all citizens of member states are entitled to vote where they reside in elections to the European Parliament, even if they are living in a country other than that of their nationality. Citizens of the Union have access to the European ombudsman and the right to petition the European Parliament. Community institutions and member states exercising Community competences are committed to the European Convention on Human Rights. The proclamation in 2000 of the European Charter of Fundamental Rights (on which see more below) underpins the civil, political, social, and economic rights of citizens of the Union in their relations with Community institutions or with the member states when exercising Community competences. Other citizenship-related rights include access to Council, Parliament, and Commission documents under the TEU, which the European Court of Justice may enforce (see *Interporc Import und Export GmbH v. Commission* [1998] ECH II-231), and rights of participation in EU processes, noted in our earlier discussion of democracy in the EU.

Substantive European Community law also includes many rights which are enforceable in the domestic courts of member states by individuals and companies in the EC. For instance the 'four freedoms', of movement of workers, goods, services, and capital, under the Treaty of Rome give rise to rights and causes of action that are justiciable in the member state where a right is infringed. But the priority given to these essentially economic rights is not something we would expect to find in the Constitution or citizenship laws of the member states, and its presence in the original Treaty, juxtaposed with the recent adoption of the European Charter, shows how the Community itself has developed beyond an organization committed to promoting purely economic activity to a political union based on liberal democratic ideals (see Mowbray, 1999). The Community has also, increasingly, made commitments to social rights. Some of these find expression in the European Union Charter of Fundamental Rights, to which we turn shortly, but the Community has also committed itself and its member states to the promotion of social rights, especially in relation to employment and non-discrimination. This is reflected in the decisions of the European Court of Justice in a number of cases. For instance, in *Defrenne v. SABENA II* ([1976] 2 CMLR 98) the Court stated that the equal pay provision of Article 119 of the Treaty of Rome 'forms part of the social objectives of the Community, which is not merely an economic union, but is at the same time intended, by common action to ensure social progress and seek the constant improvement of living and working conditions of their peoples. . . . This double aim, which is at once economic and social, shows that the principle of equal pay forms part of the foundations of the Community.' Thus the rights in European law of citizens of the Union extend the member states' own liberal concepts of citizenship towards a social-democratic model.

Human rights and the European Union Charter of Fundamental Rights

A major component of citizenship in relation to states is the protection of civil and political rights. The Treaty of Amsterdam of 1997 confirms the Union's 'attachment to the principles of liberty, democracy and respect for human rights and fundamental freedoms and of the rule of law, principles which are common to the Member States' (Article 6 TEU). The Treaty of Nice, when in force, will enable the Council, acting by a four-fifths majority of its members and with the assent of the European Parliament, to declare that a clear danger exists of a member state committing a serious breach of fundamental rights, and address appropriate recommendations to that member state—a process to be known as a 'preventive instrument'.

An important citizenship-related development was the proclamation by the Union of its Charter of Fundamental Rights in December 2000. This adds a social-democratic dimension to the liberal-democratic ethos of the EU. Although the Charter is declaratory only, it has important implications for the law applied in the United Kingdom. It will be remembered that British courts are also European courts when they are applying European law. Although the Charter *itself* is not binding, only declaratory, it will have some effect in UK courts.

The background to the Charter is that at the Cologne European Council of June 1999 it was resolved that 'the fundamental rights applicable at EU level should be consolidated in a Charter and thereby made more evident.' In December 2000 the European Charter of Fundamental Rights was 'proclaimed' at the Nice European Council (see Cm. 5090, 2001). It includes the classic civil and political rights, closely modelled on the ECHR, as well as social and economic rights. It was the product of a compromise between opposing views about the appropriateness and legal status of such a charter.

The arguments in favour of such a charter were broadly as follows (see Alston (ed), 1999; Fredman, McCrudden, and Freedland, 2000). The Union was moving towards being a 'people's Europe' and this should be reflected in explicit provision for it to recognize and give effect to the rights of its citizens. The status of Citizenship of the Union was recognized in the Maastricht Treaty in Article 8(1). Article 6 TEU states that 'the Union is founded on the principles of liberty, democracy, respect for human rights and fundamental freedoms' but it does not state what those principles, rights, and freedoms are. Article 6 (2) TEU commits the Union to respect fundamental rights as guaranteed by the ECHR and the constitutional traditions common to members states. The TEU now contains a new section entitled 'The Union and the Citizen' which includes chapters on employment and social policy. It was timely therefore for those principles to be stated explicitly rather than be referred to obliquely. But other developments in, for instance, cooperation in the investigation and policing of cross-border crime, were creating new vulnerabilities to human rights breaches, which a charter could avoid. Concerns about the increasing powers of both the European Court of Justice and the other European institutions could be allayed if those institutions were constrained by an explicit charter of rights. It was anomalous that the Union was laying down requirements of new members that they should have adequate protections for the rights of their citizens if the Union itself had no such protections. The EU's new responsibilities for common foreign and security policy have generated demands for third countries to respect human rights, and the absence of a charter of EU rights for its own institutions appeared illogical. As far as social and economic rights were concerned, the Social Chapter gives clear legislative competence to Union institutions in respect of certain aspects of social rights. Equality is by Article 13 EC a stated aim of the Union so that discrimination on a wide range of grounds including race, religion, age, disability, and sexual orientation, may be legislated against. It was thus consistent with accepted policy that certain social and economic rights should find expression in a charter.

These arguments in favour of the Charter have clear implications for concepts of citizenship. Although there is no European 'demos' the fact is that all the citizens of the member states of Europe, together with many third-party nationals (though their position is not equal to that of member state nationals), enjoy rights and are subject to duties and responsibilities under European law, which it is the job of the courts in each member state to apply. So the Charter will be relevant—its legal status will be discussed below—in litigation in the UK and other member states.

There were however strongly pressed arguments against the adoption of a European Charter of Rights, particularly in the UK. It was argued that civil and political rights were well protected by the European Convention on Human Rights, so that a separate charter was unnecessary. There would be difficulties if a separate charter were adopted with resultant two mechanisms, two sets of courts and other institutions responsible for the protection of the same or similar rights. There would also be opposition to the extension of the powers of the European Court of Justice as against the elected legislatures and executives of the member states. (Similar difficulties are reflected at UK level in the debates about whether judges should be responsible for protecting civil and political rights in UK law, discussed in Chapters 1 and 6.) This particular consideration raises issues as to the meaning of democracy and in particular opposing views of the merits of majoritarianism as against protection of fundamental rights (see Chapter 6).

The opposing views about the merits of an EU Charter of Rights were neatly reconciled to a degree in the proclamation of the European Charter of Fundamental Rights at the Nice European Council in December 2000. The Charter is expressed to have only declaratory effect—it is concerned to 'strengthen the protection of fundamental rights . . . by making those rights more visible in a charter' (Preamble). The Charter 'recognizes the rights, freedoms and principles' set out in the text (Preamble).

The Charter rights

The Charter is divided into seven chapters, on dignity, freedoms, equality, solidarity, citizens' rights, justice, and general provisions.

The first three chapters broadly cover the civil and political rights in the ECHR, with the addition of rights to the protection of personal data (Article 8), freedom of the arts and sciences (academic freedom shall be respected—Article 13), a right to education (Article 14), a right to choose an occupation and to engage in work (Article 15), and to conduct a business (Article 16), the right to property (Article 17), to asylum (Article 18), and freedom from collective expulsions (Article 19). Chapter III provides for equality, including broad freedom from discrimination (Article 21), a right to respect for cultural, religious, and linguistic diversity (Article 22), a right to equality between men and women (Article 23), provision for the rights of the child (Article 24), the rights of the elderly (Article 25), and the rights of persons with disabilities (Article 26).

Chapter IV is concerned with 'solidarity' or social cohesion, and provides for the rights of workers to information and consultation, to collective bargaining and actions, access to free 'placement services', protection from unjustified dismissal, a right to fair and just working conditions, and a prohibition on child labour. Article 33 protects family and professional life (maternity leave and parental leave), social security and social assistance, health care, access to 'services of general economic interest' (broadly, utilities), 'a high level of environmental protection and improvement of the quality of the environment', and a high level of consumer protection.

Chapter V makes provision for 'citizens' rights'. These include the right to vote and stand for election to the European Parliament, and at municipal elections in the country of residence. Particularly significantly for our purposes, Article 41 provides a right to good administration by the institutions and bodies of the Union. The right includes a right to be heard before an adverse decision is taken, a right of access to personal files, a right to reasons for a decision, and a right to compensation for damage caused by community institutions in the performance of their duties. Administration is thus conceived of as primarily procedural and process-oriented in this document.

Certain articles reiterate TEU provisions. Any citizen of the Union has a right of access to official documents, a right of access to the Union ombudsman, and a right to petition the European Parliament, freedom of movement and of residence, and rights to diplomatic and consular protection. Chapter VI (Justice) provides for a right to an effective remedy and a fair trial, presumption of innocence, and so on on similar lines to the ECHR (see Chapter 6).

Chapter VII contains general provisions, and these make clear that 'The provisions of this Charter are addressed to the institutions and bodies of the Union' and so it does not apply to member states unless they are implementing Union law (Article 51). It also makes clear that the Charter does not establish any new power or task for the Community or the Union. Article 52 states that the meaning and scope of rights guaranteed by the ECHR are the same as those laid down by that Convention.

The European Union Committee of the House of Lords considered that a better route would have been for the EU to be a party to the European Convention (8th Report of the Select Committee on the European Union, *EU Charter of Fundamental Rights*, HL 67, 1999–2000). Accession to the ECHR by the EU would have required treaty changes to EU competence and to the Convention itself and there was not the political will in the Community to make such changes. There will be problems however over the fact that the ECHR and the EUCFR will both be applicable in many areas of activity and there are two separate court systems—the ECJ and CFI, and the European Court of Human Rights—operating in the same subject areas.

The legal status of the Charter

We have already noted that the charter is technically declaratory, but it applies to the EU institutions and institutions of member states when implementing European law. The theory is that it does no more than set out the existing legal position. It is regarded by the UK and many (but not all) member states as essentially political and non-binding in a legal sense. Indeed, it could not possibly be binding in some of its provisions, which have no relevance to European Community law—for instance, Article 2 prohibits the death penalty. The Charter lacks the precision that is normally necessary for an instrument to have legal force. This would seem to bear out the view that it is a purely political, non-legal, document, as it was expressed to be at the Nice summit.

However, experience in common law jurisdictions and increasingly in Europe is that courts and other institutions will draw on sources, including international instruments which do not have full domestic effect, for values to support their decisions and influence the development of the law. British courts may choose to draw on the Charter to inform their decisions and develop the law of the UK in conformity with the principles and values that are made explicit, where previously they were not, in the Charter. Initially the Charter provisions may be mere make-weights which are called in aid of a decision that the judge wishes to reach in any event. But it is entirely possible that the courts will draw on the EUCFR to support the proactive development of the common law. The natural instinct of judges operating in many different legal traditions is to look for sources from which values can be drawn to assist in decision-making, even if those sources are not, in a positivist's sense, sources of law. An example is the way in which the French Conseil d'Etat has drawn on the Declaration of the Rights of Man to develop French administrative law (see Brown and Bell, 1998, 216–27). The UK courts drew on the ECHR before the Human Rights Act came into effect to develop English law compatibly with the Convention. The concept developed by the ECJ of general principles of law and grounds for review drawn from the legal traditions of member states provide good examples of this happening in European law (Hartley, 1998, ch. 5, 15). The ECJ and the CFI may choose to refer to the Charter in support of their decisions, just as they already take account of the ECHR. It will be at the least a useful guiding resource.

Comments on the Charter

The Charter has implications not only for citizenship and governance in the Union as far as the Union's own institutions are concerned—matters outside the scope of this book—but also for the United Kingdom—and other member states. The 'rights' set out in the Charter are important not only in following the civil and political rights in the ECHR, but in extending the concept of citizenship, in the Union at least, to embrace social and economic rights. They may be drawn upon by institutions in the UK, including our courts, as resources for values and principles that might guide them in making decisions in cases where no European point arises. Just as it is regarded as legitimate for our courts to draw on the jurisprudence in other common law countries such as the United States and Commonwealth countries to inform the resolution of hard cases, so the Charter may be drawn upon also. The Preamble recites that the Union contributes to the preservation and development of common values which include human dignity, freedom, equality, and solidarity, and of principles of democracy and the rule of law. The fact that the British government is a party to the charter serves to make explicit these values and principles and make them more available to our courts, even though the Charter itself is not justiciable in UK courts—unless European law is at issue. This may contribute in due course to the development of the concept of UK citizenship as well, of course, as of European citizenship. It is notable that the Public Administration Select Committee's report on *The Public Service Ethos* (HC 263, 2001–2) recommends that public services should respect the right to good administration as set out in the Charter, in non-European as well as European activity, an example of the way in which ideas of good governance can be borrowed and transplanted into new environments.

When implementing European law the UK government will be obliged to give effect to the principles declared in the Charter and this is likely to have a knock-on effect on English and Welsh, Scottish, and Northern Irish law. While on the face of it the Charter only declares and proclaims rights that already exist in the member states, many of them do not do so very explicitly. For instance, the non-discrimination provision in Article 21 goes beyond what is expressly recognized in English law, covering discrimination 'on any ground' including 'genetic features, language, . . . property, . . . age or sexual orientation.' Just as European law on remedies and direct effect influenced the development of the English law of remedies in the *Factortame* litigation (see below), leading to the acceptance by the courts of jurisdiction to award injunctions against Ministers of the Crown in *M. v. Home Office* ([1994] 1 AC 377) where no such jurisdiction had existed before (see Chapter 11), so the Charter and its effect in European law may influence the development of English and Welsh—and Scottish and Northern Ireland—law, especially the common law or areas where no statutory provisions dictate the outcome of a case. The courts may well look to the Charter for guiding principles to enable them to develop the law compatibly with these widely accepted values which have been endorsed by member states at the Nice European Council.

Towards a Constitution for the EU?

In many respects the EU already has a Constitution in the sense of a system of government. We have noted that its laws constitute 'a new legal order'. Its institutions have broad legislative competence, and many of its laws—notably some provisions of the Treaties and regulations and decisions—take effect without the need for transposition in the law of the member states. It has a directly elected Parliament with significant powers in relation to legislation, the budget, and the Commission. Its Courts have developed the rule of law for Europe, including principles of a constitutional kind, including the doctrines of primacy and direct effect of Community law. The substantive law of the Community promotes some rights which the ECJ has held are enforceable by individuals. And a concept of citizenship is evolving.

On the other hand the EU does not yet have a Constitution (note the capital C) and it cannot yet be said to be a federal state in the way that states such as the USA or Australia are federal, it does not itself possess sovereignty, nor is it a state in the normal sense in international law. To the extent that it has one, its Constitution is one of a kind—*sui generis*—as is its status as both a supra-national and international organization.

Since 2001 work has started on formulating a Constitutional Treaty which would pull together the constitutional elements of EC law and further define the relations between individuals and the EU and between member states and European institutions. The Laeken European Council held in December 2001 adopted a declaration enabling a Convention on the future of Europe to be established. The Convention is to consider, among other things, the demarcation of responsibilities between the Union and the member states, the status of the Charter of Fundamental Rights of the European Union, simplification of the treaties, and the role of national parliaments in the institutional architecture of the EU. A possible outcome of this project would be a proposal for a Constitution for the EU. The member states and the candidate countries are taking part in this project, the first meeting of which was held in July 2002, convened by Giscard d'Estaing. The timetable for the project set by the Laeken Council was that the Convention should produce a final document by March 2003, which will provide the basis for discussion at the Intergovernmental Conference to be convened in 2004. In October 2002 the British government put forward for consideration by the Convention a 'Draft Constitution for the EU' which had been produced for them by Professor Alan Dashwood of the University of Cambridge and others. A few weeks later Giscard d'Estaing published a 'preliminary draft Constitutional Treaty' containing his proposals for discussion. At the time of writing the Convention has not produced its own substantive recommendations.

Some would like to think that the EUCFR is an embryo Constitution for the EU (see generally Schwarze, 2001a). While the Charter is not binding, it does put human rights at the heart of Europe. This raises issues about the meaning of 'Constitution' and the scope of Constitutions. The Charter is primarily about the relationship between individuals and EU institutions or their own states when implementing Union law (Article 51). Constitutions need also to make provision for the establishment of state—or in this case 'superstate'—institutions, their powers and the relations between them, matters which are dealt with in the treaties. A European Constitution would also have to set out the relations between the member states and European institutions, as federal Constitutions define the relationships between the states and the federal level. A Constitution could not consist only of a Charter of Rights.

A Constitution for Europe that included institutional arrangements could help to overcome the complexity and opacity of the existing Treaties, and introduce some of the structural components that are missing, such as precise and transparent rules on the relations between organs of the EU, the Member States, and the citizens of the Union. In August 2002 the Foreign Secretary of the UK, Jack Straw, made a speech advocating a Constitution for the European Union that would set out a simple set of principles, what the EU is for and how it can 'add value', and reassure the public that national governments would remain the primary source of political legitimacy (*Times*, 27 August 2002). Schwarze suggests that there needs to be a written catalogue of human rights—which the EUCFHR goes some way to provide—and a clear statement of the distribution of the competences of the Community and member states. A more transparent and efficient organization and decision-making structures are needed, and better democratic legitimation (Schwarze, 2001a, 194–204; Schwarze, 2001b, 554).

However, there are strongly pressed counter-arguments against a Constitution for Europe, partly based on the notion that a Constitution in the sense either of an authoritative single written document or of a system of legal rules is not possible for a body that is not a nation state. This argument has been rejected in the German Constitutional Court which regards the EEC Treaty as to some extent the Constitution of the Community (BVerfGE 22, p. 296). But attempts to reduce the basic governance-related aspects of European law to one single document or source could make the arrangements unduly inflexible while also giving greater legitimacy to the Community and its institutions than some member states would accept—particularly if it undermined their own sovereignty. Even if the case for a European Constitution were presented as a means to keep the Community within bounds in order to protect the rights of the member states, as Constitutions in federal states such as the USA seek to do, it will in my view probably prove impossible for the member states to reach agreement on the terms of a *comprehensive* European Constitution, since their agendas are mixed and conflicting, ranging from pressure for further political integration to a much stronger sense of subsidiarity and the need to protect the rights of member states against encroachment by the Community (see generally Schwarze, 2001*a*).

One way of viewing European Community law is that it constitutionalizes the substantive law and policy of member states, for instance on discrimination, social policy, employment, and so on, by making it legally impossible for the Parliaments or governments of member states to alter these laws. This represents a departure from the liberal democratic tradition in the UK and many other countries, which treats Constitutions as neutral between political parties and does not dictate substantive policies. This tradition has been eroded in a number of respects in many modern democracies, including South Africa and India, which include principles of state policy or directive principles in their Constitutions, and there are pressures within the UK to give legal status to social and economic rights that is comparable to the status of civil and political rights (see Chapter 6). There is in other words a trend towards constitutionalizing substantive policies in many parts of the world.

It has also been suggested that the ways in which European law has borrowed principles from the legal systems of member states (notably principles of legality, legitimate expectations, proportionality, and legal certainty—see Chapters 5 and 6) and the ways in which the legal systems of the member states have had to adapt to membership of the Community, taken together, mean that beyond a 'new legal order', a European Constitutional Order is being born (Schwarze, 2001*a*).

The United Kingdom's Membership of the Community

Having looked generally at the EU and the demands it makes on its member states, we turn to some particular issues for the UK and the effect of membership on its domestic constitutional arrangements. The United Kingdom negotiated its entry into the Community by the Treaty of Brussels 1972. The United Kingdom's is a dualist legal system, which means that though the British government is legally free to enter into international agreements, such treaties cannot, without incorporation by statute, give rise to rights or obligations that are enforceable in our courts. An Act of Parliament was therefore required to give effect to British membership, including giving primacy to European law in our domestic courts, as required by the jurisprudence of the European Court of Justice. This international obligation was fulfilled by the passage of the European Communities Act 1972, which came into force on 1 January 1973. There was no referendum to authorize British entry into Europe, but a referendum was held in 1975 on whether the United Kingdom should remain a member and the result was a Yes. Since then further Acts have been passed by the Westminster Parliament to give domestic effect to European law as the treaties are reformed and amended.

The United Kingdom has been a fairly sceptical member of the Community from the outset, and has been chary of permitting the Community institutions to extend their powers or permitting the British government to agree to certain extensions of power without parliamentary consent. Thus the European Assembly Elections Act 1978, s. 6 provided that any increase in the powers of the European Parliament must be subject to approval by Parliament and could not be given effect by mere government ratification of a new treaty obligation.

Although under the royal prerogative the government may ratify treaties without statutory confirmation (see *R. v. Secretary of State for Foreign and Commonwealth Affairs, ex parte Rees-Mogg* [1994] 2 WLR 115), in practice the government submits new European treaty obligations to be approved by Parliament. So, for instance, the European Communities (Amendment) Act 1986, which incorporated a treaty amending the EC Treaty, known as 'the Single European Act', into UK law, authorized the increase of the powers of the European Parliament (as was required by the 1978 Act, s. 6) and also increased the scope for decision by qualified majority voting in the Council, and added new competences to Community institutions. The Treaty on European Union 1992—the Maastricht Treaty (which establishes the Union and the three pillars, provides for economic and monetary union, and also increases the power of the European Parliament)— was given effect by the European Communities (Amendment) Act 1993 and resolutions of the Houses of Parliament. Further amendments to the EC Treaty and TEU made by the Treaty of Amsterdam were incorporated in domestic law under the European Communities (Amendment) Act 1998. In November 2002 the European Parliament (Representation) Bill was introduced into the Westminster Parliament as a first step towards the implementation of the Nice Treaty. It provided for the reduction of the number of Members of the European Parliament (MEPs) representing the UK after enlargement.

Were the implications for its sovereignty (see below) appreciated when the UK joined the EU? Nicol (2001) suggests that the government, or at least the British Parliament, did not do so. Although by the time of British entry the European Court of Justice had already elaborated its doctrine of the primacy of European law, this was not fully appreciated by many MPs. Nicol attributes this to the traditional emphasis in the UK on the political rather than legal nature of the Constitution (see Chapter 1), which means that British politicians do not understand well the legal implications of what they do— including joining the EC. Nicol compares this approach with the position in Ireland, where the implications of EC membership were better understood at the time of joining, because Ireland's written Constitution required there to be constitutional debate about membership and a formal constitutional amendment. In the UK it has until recently been unusual for our politicians—or our courts—to conceptualize questions as constitutional rather than as pragmatic decisions taken by government and ratified by Parliament for reasons of national economic or other advantage. Nicol's important point is that the 'political Constitution' tradition in the UK meant, in relation to membership of Europe, that our politicians simply did not appreciate the importance of the legal aspects of membership of the EU. He compares this with the passing of the Human Rights Act 1998 (see Chapter 6) in which Parliament and the government were far better informed about the legal implications of what they were doing, although they did not take on board the links between European Community Law and the ECHR (Nicol, ch. 8).

Sovereignty and the primacy and direct effect of European law in the United Kingdom

British courts are under an obligation under the European Communities Act 1972—as in European law—to apply European law in the United Kingdom and to disapply British legislation and rules of the common law to the extent that they are incompatible with European law. Section 2(1) of the European Communities Act 1972 provides 'All . . . rights, powers, liabilities obligations and restrictions from time to time created or arising by or under the Treaties, . . . as in accordance with the treaties are without further enactment to be given legal effect or used in the United Kingdom shall be recognized and available in law, and be enforced, allowed and followed accordingly.' Section 2 (4) provides, *inter alia*: 'any enactment passed or to be passed [by the Westminster Parliament], other than one contained in this part of the Act, shall be construed and have effect subject to the foregoing provisions of this section.' Thus membership of the European Community undermines what Dicey regarded as a 'cornerstone' of the British Constitution, the legislative supremacy of the United Kingdom Parliament.

Although it was realized from the first in some political and legal circles (though not, as we have seen, generally in Parliament) that the implication of British membership of the Community was that the UK Parliament would be limited in the Acts that it could pass and expect to be applied by our courts, it was not until the landmark decisions in the *Factortame* litigation that it became clear to all concerned that this was the case: in that case the European Court of Justice found that the British Merchant Shipping Act 1988, which sought to prevent Spanish-owned fishing vessels from fishing against the United Kingdom's quotas under the Community's common fisheries policy, was contrary to Community law. As a result the Appellate Committee of the House of Lords eventually disapplied the Act, and the claims of the Spanish owners of vessels to compensation for having been denied the right to fish under the Act were upheld (see Craig, 1991). Lord Bridge, in the course of his judgment in the 1991 *Factortame* decision (*R. v. Secretary of State for Transport, ex parte Factortame (No. 2)* ([1991] 1 AC 603), commented that:

If the supremacy . . . of Community law over the national law of member states was not always inherent in the EEC Treaty it was certainly well established in the jurisprudence of the Court of Justice long before the United Kingdom joined the Community. Thus, whatever limitation of its sovereignty Parliament accepted when it enacted the European Communities Act was entirely voluntary . . . [T]here is nothing in any way novel in according supremacy to rules of Community law in those areas to which they apply and to insist that, in the protection of rights under Community law, national courts must not be inhibited by rules of national law from granting interim relief in appropriate cases is no more than a logical recognition of that supremacy. (p. 643)

In other words, the court relied on a contractarian justification for giving primacy to European law over an Act of Parliament. However, Nicol (2001) has shown that in fact parliamentarians were for the most part not aware of the implications of membership of the EU and Lord Bridge's justification was based on a wrong assumption of fact. No parliamentary consensus on the sovereignty issue existed. (It is worth noting that the British government's case in *Factortame* was that UK law was compatible with European law. They were not maintaining that the UK Parliament had, as it was entitled to do, legislated contrary to European law.)

Nicol suggests that if a contractarian justification for the decision is not persuasive, the real reason for the House of Lords' decision in this case (and in *R. v. Secretary of State for Employment, ex parte Equal Opportunities Commission,* [1995] AC 1), in which the House of Lords declared a UK statute to be contrary to European law without first referring the matter to the ECJ, is that the courts were keeping constitutional law up to date with actual constitutional practice (Nicol, 2001, 263).

Membership of the European Community, with its doctrines of primacy and direct effect, has then undermined the doctrine of the legislative sovereignty of Parliament. In particular it has displaced the doctrine of implied repeal, according to which in the event of a conflict between two Acts of Parliament the later one prevailed and impliedly repealed the inconsistent provisions of the earlier Act (*Ellen Street Estates v. Minister of Health* [1934] 1 KB 590). In the case of *Thoburn v. Sunderland City Council* ([2002] 2 WLR 247) Laws LJ made a point of stating that the European Communities Act 1972 was, by force of common law, a 'constitutional statute' which could not be impliedly repealed by a subsequent inconsistent statutory provision. The court would only treat such a 'constitutional statute' as having been amended or repealed by Act of Parliament if it was shown that Parliament actually intended to amend or repeal it.

There remain some legal arguments about whether or in what sense the Westminster Parliament retains its legislative sovereignty since the United Kingdom joined the European Community (MacCormick, 1999; Bradley, 2000; Craig, 2000; Nicol, 2001). For instance, it is assumed that the United Kingdom could lawfully (as far as the UK courts are concerned) leave the European Community and that if it did so the power of the UK Parliament to legislate on any subject matter would revive. On this approach parliamentary supremacy has not been surrendered with membership of the EU and is only in abeyance. Some lawyers consider that if the UK Parliament were to legislate incompatibly with European law and if the Act in question expressly stated that its provision should override European law, then British courts would uphold the UK statute. We shall not know what British courts would do in such a situation until this assertion is put to the test—which is most unlikely to occur, as the British government would be in breach of its treaty obligations and in serious breach of European law if this were to occur. But the practical reality is that it is not legally, politically, or economically possible for the United Kingdom to behave as an entirely independent sovereign state or for its Parliament to exercise full legislative powers for as long as the UK remains in the EU.

The UK Parliament's role in relation to the EU matters

We have already noted that there is parliamentary scrutiny of new treaty obligations through the requirements that increases in the powers of the European Parliament must be approved by Parliament and the need for new treaty provisions to be incorporated into domestic law via Acts of Parliament. However, most European law takes the form of directives, regulations, and decisions, where Acts of Parliament may not be required to give them effect. Regulations and decisions take effect without the need for further transposition, but directives normally require legislation in the member state to give them effect. In the United Kingdom this is generally done by Order in Council rather than by Act of Parliament.

There is inevitably considerable negotiation and horsetrading between member states' representatives before a measure—a directive, regulation, or decision—reaches the Council for decision. Decisions are increasingly taken by qualified majority voting, and thus representatives of member states cannot veto many provisions. British Ministers have the authority, under the royal prerogative, to bind the UK by their decisions in the Council without the need for formal endorsement from the UK Parliament—subject to the scrutiny reserve (see below). So how, if at all, are ministers in the British government accountable to the UK Parliament for the legislation emanating from the Council of the Community? What role does the British Parliament have in relation to European legislation?

The TEU of 1992 committed the governments of member states to ensure that 'national parliaments receive Commission proposals for legislation in good time for information or possible examination.' The Treaty of Amsterdam of 1997 tightened up the position by including a Protocol on the role of national Parliaments in the EU, which laid down that all Commission consultation documents and proposals for legislation should be made available to national parliaments in good time and that a six-week period should elapse between a proposal being made and its appearance on the agenda of the Council. However, in practice these documents are often not made available in good time and national Parliaments are denied the opportunity to scrutinize them properly.

The two Houses of the UK Parliament have complementary arrangements for the scrutiny of documents and proposals for EU legislation. The House of Commons has imposed a requirement on Ministers that they should not, other than in exceptional circumstances, enter into any new commitments in the Council until the Commons scrutiny process has been completed (this is the scrutiny reserve). A similar resolution applies to the House of Lords' scrutiny process. But these resolutions do not purport to prevent Ministers, once the scrutiny process is complete, from consenting to new com- mitments even in the face of reservations expressed by the committees of either House to proposed directives, regulations, or decisions. There is however considerable political pressure on Ministers to have due regard to the reports of these committees and they will be required to answer in Parliament for their decisions.

In each House reports are produced on selected issues, and government Ministers may be called on to respond to their findings and account for their conduct of negotiations in the Council and the directives that result. In the House of Commons three committees are responsible for this. The Select Committee on European Scrutiny examines European documents such as draft proposals for legislation, and reports to the House on the legal and political importance of each document. Any document which this committee recommends for further scrutiny is referred to one of two standing committees. These committees are hampered by the fact that the time available for their consideration of documents is often short as they receive them not long before the Council is due to make a decision on them. Also the task requires considerable expertise and dedication of time and it is not always possible to find backbenchers willing to make the commitment to the work of the committee. Many backbenchers are more interested in their constituency social work function and nursing their majorities than in holding the government to account for, in this context, its representation of British interests in the Council.

The House of Lords' activity in relation to European draft legislation complements that of the Commons. It is in fact more effective than the Commons' work and is highly regarded in the other member states (HC 152, 2001–2) and in the Community institutions themselves. The House of Lords' Select Committee on the European Communities, chaired by a salaried officer and member of the House, considers any Community proposal which it believes should be drawn to the attention of the House. The Committee has six subject-based committees, on Agriculture, Fisheries and Food; Economic and Financial Affairs, Trade and External Relations; Social Affairs, Education and Home Affairs; Energy, Industry and Transport; Environment, Public Health and Consumer Protection; and Law and Institutions. These subcommittees and the committee produce their own valuable in-depth, detailed reports on particular issues: see for instance the report on *EU Charter of Fundamental Rights*, 2000, a highly regarded report on the draft charter (see discussion of the House of Lords in Chapter 10).

At present the Parliaments of the member states of the EU do not have a direct institutionalized relationship with European institutions. Proposals for reform of the EU have tended to focus on strengthening the direct relationship between voters and the European Parliament and through the Parliament, enhancing the accountability of the Council and the Commission. Another approach has been to argue for an increase in the influence of the Parliaments of member states directly in relations with European institutions. In June 2002 the House of Commons European Scrutiny Committee made a number of radical recommendations for improving the accountability and transparency of the Council's decision-making, increasing the connectedness between voters and the European Parliament, and increasing the influence of the Westminster Parliament and the Parliaments of other member states. The committee criticized the 'slapdash' way in which the Council made decisions and called on them to meet in public. They argued for MEPs to be elected by first past the post rather than proportional representation to reconnect them with their electors. And they urged that the commitment to 'ever closer union' should be removed from the Maastricht Treaty so as to reduce the perception that the EU was engaged in a one-way process towards greater centralization, regardless of what citizens wanted. National Parliaments should have an enhanced role in holding the Commission and other institutions to account, thus playing a crucial role in bridging the increasingly obvious and damaging gap between citizens and EU institutions (HC 152, 2001–2). Though these proposals are unlikely to be accepted either by European institutions or the British government, both of whom would feel threatened by them, they raise important issues about the nature of citizenship in the Union, the relationship between citizenship of member states and union citizenship, and concepts of good governance that will no doubt continue to be debated.

The Convention on the future of Europe has been noted above. In response to this project the House of Commons appointed a novel Standing Committee on the Convention on the future of Europe in June 2002. Among its members were the two MPs appointed as Representatives to the Convention. Although this is not a joint committee of the two Houses, two House of Lords Alternates to those Representatives have been appointed, and other members of the House of Lords are permitted to participate in the Committee's work, though not as full members. They will monitor and report back to Parliament on the work of the Convention.

Devolution and Europe

The United Kingdom government is responsible to the European institutions for securing compliance with European law by all state bodies in the country. Thus any delegation or devolution of power to devolved bodies such as the Scottish Parliament and Executive, the Welsh Assembly and Executive, and the Northern Ireland Assembly and Executive and, potentially, regional executives in England, has to be subject to the overriding power of the United Kingdom government to compel compliance with EU law. The European Court of Justice also has jurisdiction to determine issues of compatibility of laws and executive action by any state body or 'emanation of the state' in the United Kingdom with European law. Hence there are considerable limitations as a consequence of EU membership on the powers both of devolved bodies and the UK Parliament and government, and the devolution legislation does not permit these bodies to act incompatibly with European law (see Chapter 13).

The Scottish executive, the Welsh Assembly, and the Northern Ireland executive recognize that the institutions of the European Community are where much of the real power that affects their interests lies, rather than Westminster or Whitehall. In particular, regional aid may be made available to regions via the governments of member states from the European Commission in Brussels. So these bodies have opened up regional offices there, as have the regional assemblies/chambers in England. The staffing however is minimal, and to date there is little evidence that this has benefited them.

One way in which devolved bodies in the United Kingdom have hoped to increase their influence in Europe is by being involved in negotiations and discussions within the UK government in reaching a position before negotiations with European institutions take place. There is substantial overlap of powers between the UK government and the devolved executives, and consultation is in any event essential if conflict between these bodies is to be avoided. The *Concordat on Co-ordination of EU Policy Issues* reached between the British government and the devolved bodies seeks to ensure that the latter are properly consulted on all devolved matters and can have an input into the agreed UK negotiating line (*Memorandum of Understanding*, Cm. 5240, December 2001).

Another way in which devolved bodies hope to have their voices heard and their interests considered in Europe is by participating in UK delegations to Europe. There is provision for their members to represent the United Kingdom in such negotiations, but if they were to do so it would be required that they put forward the agreed UK position and not their own preferred options if they were to differ (see Hazell, 2000b). The *Concordat* states that the UK government will only allow their input so long as they respect confidentiality and support the UK line.

The fact of United Kingdom membership of the EU has encouraged nationalists in Scotland and Wales to consider independence for their countries, in the hope that this would give them additional control over their own affairs and enable them to tap into resources in the EU directly and in their own right rather than via the United Kingdom government (MacCormick, 1999).

Summary and Conclusions

Membership of the European Union has profound implications for UK concepts of democracy and citizenship. It forces us to focus on how the Community itself can be made acceptably democratic while not undermining the system of democracy and citizenship in place in the UK. It reinforces the trend that goes back nearly a century towards a concept of citizenship that is not nationality based. It also reinforces a trend towards a rights-based citizenship, extending rights beyond the civil and political to social and economic rights.

The workings of the Community institutions and of member states when implementing Community law are in many respects far more juridified than political activity within the UK usually is. Examples include the elaborate regulation of the legislative process, with requirements for cooperation and co-decision involving the Council and the Parliament when directives are being promulgated, provisions for qualified majority voting in the European Council, the many articles in the European Charter that extend to rights that would not normally be found in constitutions in the member states, and the very extensive jurisprudence of the European Court of Justice about the implementation of European law uniformly throughout the Community. This parallel legal system is having an influence on our own political decision-making and legislative processes and has parallels in the devolution arrangements. It is also affecting the attitudes of British courts to politics, in turn increasing the juridification, including judicialization, of the UK constitution.

The possibility of the sharing of sovereignty rather than the separation of powers between Europe and its member states has parallels in the devolution arrangements in the UK. And theories of good governance in Europe mirror the debates in the UK. A multi-layered system is developing, with a complex network rather than a hierarchy of norms.

5

The Constitutional Role of the Courts

One of the questions we are asking in this book is whether or to what extent the UK is moving from a political to a law-based Constitution. In a law-based Constitution the role of the courts, or of a Constitutional or Supreme Court, is greater than in a Constitution based on politics. In this chapter we outline the current role of the courts in the UK, focusing especially on their judicial review jurisdiction and a particular aspect of that jurisdiction, the development of principles of constitutionalism. We shall focus first on judicial review generally and then on constitutionalism. Questions to do with the institutional arrangements within which the courts operate are considered in Chapter 18, including whether the UK should have a new Supreme Court.

Judicial Review

As indicated in Chapter 3, legal accountability is one of a number of mechanisms that form part of the complex system of constitutional checks and balances in the UK Constitution. Legal accountability is imposed largely via judicial review and this is the focus of discussion in this chapter. But public bodies are also subject to the law of tort and may be liable in damages if, for instance, they are found to have owed duties of care to individuals who have suffered loss as a result of negligence by the public body or if they have acted in breach of the rights of individuals or companies in European Community law (see Chapter 4). We shall draw out some of the implications of judicial review for theories of democracy, citizenship, and good governance in the UK.

The judicial review jurisdiction is 'supervisory', meaning that the court considers whether or not a public decision-maker or a body exercising a public function has acted lawfully. If it is satisfied that a decision-maker has acted unlawfully, the court cannot substitute its own view of what the decision-maker should have decided, as this would be to usurp the decision-maker's function; but the court may, in effect, require the decision-maker to re-decide, applying the law correctly, by quashing the decision, requiring the decision-maker to perform a public duty, making an order prohibiting the decision-maker from doing an unlawful act, or making a declaration as to what the law is. This judicial review jurisdiction is largely the courts' own creation, through the development of the common law. It has grown up rapidly since the 1960s as the courts have developed the principles of judicial review and expanded the classes of decisions that must be taken in accordance with these principles and the kinds of bodies that are subject to judicial review.

Judicial review is an extremely complex subject and no attempt will be made to consider it in any detail here: the issues can only be sketched in. (For full discussion of judicial review see De Smith, Woolf, and Jowell, 1995; Craig, 1999b; Jowell and Le Sueur, 1999; Wade and Forsyth, 2002). During the twentieth century the range of areas over which the government exercised control under statutory powers expanded greatly, particularly after the Second World War, and it was therefore to be expected that in time the range of subject matter over which the government might be challenged in the courts would increase. The fact that the courts were willing to develop and expand the grounds on which they would review and quash governmental decisions may have reflected a loss of confidence in the capacity of Parliament to obtain redress of individuals' grievances from government. The courts' justification for their judicial review jurisdiction was, generally, that in reviewing the decisions of government, they were giving effect to the presumed intention of Parliament that the powers it granted to government should be exercised legally, fairly, and reasonably. If an official did not observe these requirements he or she was considered to be acting beyond the powers granted by Parliament—*ultra vires*—with the results that decisions were invalid. This was essentially a democratic justification—the courts were giving effect to Parliament's will. As we shall see, however, in the last twenty years or so the courts have extended their jurisdiction to the many areas of governmental activity that are not authorized by Act of Parliament and this has raised questions about the democratic justification for judicial review.

The grounds for judicial review

The grounds for judicial review are, broadly, illegality, procedural impropriety, and irrationality, principles which were expounded by Lord Diplock in *Council of Civil Service Unions v. Minister for the Civil Service* ([1985] AC 374), known as the *CCSU* case. In addition unjustified interference with a Convention right is a ground for review—and other possible remedies—under the Human Rights Act 1998 (see Chapter 6).

It may help to give brief examples of what these three principles mean. Some cases of illegality are fairly straightforward—if a statute gives a local authority the power to purchase land other than park land, then the purchase of park land would be unlawful (*White and Collins v. Minister of Health* [1939] 2 KB 838). Other forms of illegality are more subtle. For instance, decisions should not be made for inappropriate reasons. Thus, a Minister who has a discretionary power to refer a complaint to a committee is not entitled to refuse to make a reference to a committee for political reasons, such as to avoid political embarrassment (*Padfield v. Minister of Agriculture, Fisheries and Food* [1968] AC 997). His refusal to refer the complaint would be quashed, and he would have to consider the request to refer the complaint again and re-decide, this time not being influenced by improper considerations. This would be a breach of the good governance principles of legitimacy, reliability, and trustworthiness.

Procedural impropriety involves the decision-maker not following the procedures that are laid down by statute or imposed by the courts, in order to secure fairness to those who might be adversely affected by a decision. Thus before a chief constable is dismissed he is entitled to know what is alleged against him and to have an opportunity to put his side of the case, because the decision will deprive him of his livelihood and of his reputation (*Ridge v. Baldwin* [1964] AC 40). A decision-maker should give indications of concerns about an individual's case before making a decision adverse to him, so that he may respond before the decision is made, or should give reasons for decisions if, for instance, the decision implies a slur on the character of the individual affected, or if the decision would be aberrant, so that the individual may know if he has grounds to challenge it (*R. v. Gaming Board for Great Britain, ex parte Benaim and Khaida* [1970] 2 Q.B. 417, CA; *R. v. Secretary of State for the Home Department, ex parte Al Fayed* [1998] 1 WLR 763, CA; *R. v. Civil Service Appeal Board, ex parte Cunningham* [1991] 4 All ER 310, CA). Thus judicial review requires the provision of opportunities for participation in decision-making by those affected and imposes accountability on the decision-maker to the person affected and the courts—good governance principles.

Irrationality is the most problematic and controversial of the grounds for judicial review. The test the courts apply is whether a decision was so unreasonable that no reasonable Minister could have so decided (*Associated Provincial Picture Houses v. Wednesbury Corporation* [1948] 1 KB 223, Lord Greene MR). It includes malice and bad faith. This ground differs from the procedural impropriety ground, which is concerned with decision-making procedures, and from illegality, which is a more technical ground and leaves less room than irrationality for the courts to appear to substitute their own views of the merits for those of the primary decision-maker. The irrationality ground can come close to permitting the court to reach an independent view about the merits or wisdom of a Minister's decision, and thus to usurp the role of the decision-maker. The courts seek to avoid this by deferring to the decision-maker save in extreme cases of perverse decision-making. But, especially where a decision was made by a Minister, a finding that it was, in effect, perverse, is provocative and indeed offensive to the decision-maker—more so than a finding that a decision-maker failed to take account of a relevant consideration (which would count as illegality), for instance.

The foundation of this ground for review, as it has developed since the *Wednesbury* case, is that the rule of law requires lack of arbitrariness, consistency, and respect for fundamental rights in decision-making (see Jowell and Lester, 1987) and thus the ground involves finding a balance between judicial deference to political or democratic decision-makers and the rule of law.

In the *CCSU* case Lord Diplock added a further possible ground for judicial review, disproportionality (see Jowell and Lester, 1988). A decision will be disproportionate if, for instance, interference with the rights or interests of an individual could have been reduced by the adoption of a less restrictive alternative, or if a decision imposes excessive burdens on an individual or a company. It resembles, and may in fact be but an aspect of, irrationality. Disproportionality is a ground for review in European Community law and in the law of many member states of the European Community which follow the civil law tradition, and under the Human Rights Act (see Chapter 6). English courts have until recently been reluctant to regard proportionality as a ground for review apart from rationality (save where expressly required to do so, as where some of the Convention rights under the Human Rights Act are at issue. In effect under the Human Rights Act a new ground for judicial review—unjustified or disproportionate interference with a Convention right—has been added). Their concern has been that reviewing the proportionality of government decisions might lead them to adjudicate on the merits of decisions, which they do not consider to be their function. However, with the coming into effect of the Human Rights Act the courts have become readier to use the principle of proportionality in deciding cases—even where human rights issues do not arise.

The elaboration of grounds for review by Lord Diplock in the *CCSU* case in 1985 has been overtaken by developments, not only in relation to proportionality and human rights generally, but also in the direction of principles of legal certainty, notably legitimate expectations, which have drawn heavily on principles of European Community law (see Jowell and Lester, 1988; Craig and de Burca, 2002; Hartley, 1998; Wong, 2000; Clayton, 2001; Douglas-Scott, 2001). Thus it has been held, for instance, that a health authority which promised a small number of residents in a care home for the severely disabled that it would be their home for life was not entitled to frustrate the legitimate expectation they had generated by closing the home, as this would be an abuse of power (*R. v. North and East Devon Health Authority, ex parte Coughlan* [2000] 2 WLR 622, CA). The abuse was the unreliability of the Authority in making and then breaking a promise, and the breach of the trust reposed in them (both breaches of good governance principles).

The grounds for judicial review, then, are a highly complex and developing subject. Overall they promote respect for the law, respect for the interests of individuals, consultative processes in decision-making that will affect individuals, and rationality. Judicial review protects the status and security of individuals by restraining arbitrary interference by public decision-makers, and it thus promotes both a liberal and a social-democratic concept of citizenship (Oliver, 1999). It promotes reliability, trustworthiness, accountability. These are all elements of democracy, citizenship, and good governance.

The scope of judicial review

Although much of government activity rests on statutory powers, many broadly governmental decisions are not specifically authorized by statute. As we shall see in Chapter 11, powers in relation to defence and foreign affairs and many other matters are based in the royal prerogative, a residue of powers which formally belong to the monarch but which are now exercised in her name by Ministers. Many of these powers are highly sensitive politically (diplomatic relations, treaty-making, and defence, for instance) and the courts generally regard them as being non-justiciable and will not judicially review their exercise (see discussion of justiciability in Chapter 11). However, the passage of the Human Rights Act has meant that judges may feel justified in judicially reviewing decisions taken in these sensitive areas if they interfere with Convention rights, since the Act raises the status and legal relevance of human rights and may tip the balance in favour of judicial review.

Some prerogative powers, such as management of the civil service (the *CCSU* case, *supra*) and the issue of passports (*R. v. Foreign Secretary, ex parte Everett* ([1989] QB 811) have been held to be reviewable. The mere fact that a power derives from the royal prerogative does not make it unreviewable. The test for reviewability, then, is the nature rather than the source of the power, and only if a power is on balance—and the balance has been altered by the HRA—'non-justiciable' will the courts consider it to be unreviewable (*CCSU* case, *supra*).

Many non-statutory powers of governmental bodies rest on the fact that they have control over property and assets of various kinds—sums of money that could be expended on building hospitals, roads, and the like, or overseas aid, or compensating victims of crime (as under the Criminal Injuries Compensation Scheme: see *R. v. Criminal Injuries Compensation Board, ex parte Lain*, [1967] 2 QB 864, DC; *R. v. Secretary of State for the Home Department, ex parte Fire Brigades Union* [1995] 2 WLR 1), or control of property that could be sold or let. Daintith has called the power that derives from ownership of resources *dominium* and he contrasts this with coercive power, *imperium* (Daintith, 1979). Statutes too grant both *dominium* and *imperium*. Daintith highlights how *dominium* has acquired increasing importance over the years and how its exercise can bypass parliamentary scrutiny, so that judicial review may be the only means by which it is controlled (see also Galbraith, 1983). This *dominium* power, exercised without statutory authority, stems from the fact that government has legal personality—the Crown is a corporation in law—and it therefore enjoys the same legal capacities as natural persons, e.g. to deal with property (see Chapter 11). (The case of *Malone v. Metropolitan Police Commissioner* [1979] Ch 344, discussed in Chapter 6, provides another example of a non-statutory public body having the same freedom of action as individuals.) These powers are very considerable, and they enable government to impose conditions and require certain actions from those dependent on it in ways that could be oppressive. They are particularly important where governmental bodies enter into network or partnership arrangements such as public-private partnerships, private finance initiatives, public service agreements, and so on, contractual arrangements which give government considerable discretionary power which could be misused.

The courts impose similar principles on the exercise of statutory and non-statutory powers, *dominium* and *imperium*. For instance, they have held that refusal to purchase newspapers of which a local authority disapproved for a public library was unlawful because it was influenced by an irrelevant consideration (*R. v. Ealing London Borough Council, ex parte Times Newspapers Ltd.* (1986) 85 LGR 316, DC). The boycotting of a company's products by a local authority for political reasons has been held to be unlawful (*R. v. London Borough of Lewisham, ex parte Shell UK Ltd.* [1988] 1 All ER 938).

The use of networks and partnerships with private bodies to deliver public policy dates back to at least the 1970s (see Chapter 2) and some of these private bodies may also be subject to judicial review. To this extent the courts are taking into account current developments in governance. In a celebrated case, *R. v. Panel on Take-overs and Mergers, ex parte Datafin* ([1987] QB 815) the court decided that where a private body is exercising public functions (here regulation of take-overs) it is bound by the same principles of judicial review as are public bodies. (But where a network or partnership arrangement involves a private body in providing services under contract with a public body, it may not be regarded as performing a public function and will not then be subject to judicial review: decision *R. v. Leonard Cheshire Foundation, ex parte Heather* [2002] EWCA, Civ. 366 (21 March). Thus judicial review can extend to non-governmental bodies.

In cases where private bodies are exercising public functions, and where public bodies exercise non-statutory powers, the justification, if any, for imposing duties of legality, fairness and rationality in judicial review cannot be that Parliament is taken to have intended this, since Parliament will not have been involved. The traditional justification for judicial review—that the courts are giving effect to Parliament's will—does not apply. Hence the question arises, what democratic justification is there for judicial review in such cases?

Is there a democratic justification for judicial review?

In a common law system the judges have a far greater power to develop the law than do judges in civil law systems, where there are comprehensive statutory codes and there is no doctrine of precedent, so that each judgment decides only the particular case and does not lay down principles for future cases. Ewing (2000) has argued that it is undemocratic for judges to have the common law power to develop and change the law and that the common law should be replaced by a codified system such as civil law jurisdictions have. This however is not on the active political agenda in the UK—and it is worth noting that in fact the European Court of Justice and the European Court of Human Rights are increasingly adopting the methodology of the common law to develop general legal principles, in effect exercising legislative power (see Chapters 4, 6). Even judges brought up in the civil law system are adept at using common law techniques.

There are differences of view as to the basis of the jurisdiction in judicial review in our common law system (the extensive literature includes Craig, 1990, 1998, 1999a; Loughlin, 1992, 2000a; Forsyth, 1996; 2000; Jowell, 1999, 2000; Allan, 2001; Elliott, 2001). We have already noted that the orthodox view was that the jurisdiction was justified in democratic terms in that it enabled the courts to give effect to the express or implied intentions of Parliament, but that the jurisdiction is also exercisable, on the same broad grounds of legality, procedural propriety, and rationality, where the body under challenge is exercising powers that do not derive from an Act of Parliament (The *CCSU* and *Datafin* cases, *supra*). In such cases the *ultra vires*, legislative intent approach is not appropriate. If the judges in judicial review cases were not giving effect to parliamentary intent, but instead imposing their own principles on the exercise of governmental power and their own concepts of democracy, how did the jurisdiction fit in with principles of representative democracy? Might the courts one day presume a power to disapply a statute if they felt it was inconsistent with their notions of democracy, thus taking it upon themselves to override the doctrine of parliamentary sovereignty?

These concerns were fuelled by two public lectures in the mid-1990s delivered by eminent judges, Lord Woolf (1995) and Sir John Laws (1995). They suggested that it would be legitimate for the courts to refuse to give effect to a very undemocratic Act. This position was refuted in a public lecture by the Lord Chancellor in waiting, Lord Irvine (1996).

The debate about the rationale or justification for judicial review, among academics at least, became highly charged. Forsyth (1996, 2000) suggested that the old *ultra vires* justification should be maintained, though he admits that it is in fact a 'fig leaf'. At least in the eyes of the public it looks democratic. Elliott (1999, 2000, 2001) also argues that, at least where statutory provisions are in issue, the legislative intent rationale applies. Craig, on the other hand (1998, 1999*a*, 2000) argues for the 'common law' basis for the jurisdiction, based in principles of justice and the control of public power coupled with acceptance of parliamentary sovereignty. In its origins this jurisdiction had nothing to do with parliamentary intent or the *ultra vires* rules (Craig, 1998). Jowell (2000) suggests a middle or third way, arguing that the judges are the ultimate arbiters of the way power should be exercised in a democracy, basing their decisions on constitutional principles which take account of the fact that judges are well suited to adjudicate on procedural matters but are not constitutionally qualified to make broad decisions on social and economic policy. The courts do not and should not unilaterally and arbitrarily impose substantive constraints on administrative action.

Given that the *ultra vires*, legislative intent theory cannot explain the courts' jurisdiction in judicial review where non-statutory powers are in issue, the most convincing explanation of and justification for the jurisdiction in judicial review, in my view, are that the courts are rediscovering and developing a common law power going back to the seventeenth century (see, for instance, *Bagg's case* (1615) 11 Co Rep 93b), and based in what they have considered since then to be their constitutional duty to do justice and remedy wrongs by imposing duties—for instance, duties of legality, fairness, rationality, perhaps proportionality on decision-makers. These substantive principles are not inconsistent with, indeed they promote, democratic values, citizenship, and good governance. The problem is, however, that judges are not accountable in any strong sense for their concepts of what justice requires, what are wrongs, and how they should be remedied. Judges may be wrong (though who is to decide they are wrong is not obvious unless Parliament legislates to override a court decision) or they may be unwise, ignorant, or under misapprehensions in reaching their decisions on these matters.

However, the judges' power is not entirely unfettered. As we have seen, it is limited by their own acceptance of the sovereignty of Parliament. Despite the observations in their lectures by Lord Woolf (1995) and Sir John Laws (1995), the position of the courts is that (save in relation to European Community law) they would not be justified in setting aside an express and clear provision in an Act of Parliament, even if it was incompatible with constitutional principles or with the principles of legality, procedural propriety, or rationality. If Parliament wishes to override these principles, it must say so (see discussion of constitutionalism, below).

However, judicial review can undermine comity between the courts, the legislature, and the executive, which I have suggested is one of the values underlying not only the doctrine of parliamentary sovereignty, but other aspects of the UK's constitutional arrangements too (see Chapter 2). In a number of high-profile cases the courts have exercised the jurisdiction in judicial review to quash decisions taken by Ministers who can claim to have a democratic mandate to exercise their own powers and judgements as they think fit, and to be properly accountable to Parliament rather than the courts in doing so.

For instance, in *R. v. Secretary of State for the Home Department, ex parte Venables* ([1998] AC 409, HL) the Appellate Committee of the House of Lords decided that the Home Secretary had adopted an unlawful policy in fixing a tariff period of detention for young offenders sentenced to be detained at Her Majesty's pleasure which would in no circumstances be varied by reason of matters occurring during the tariff period. This, the Appellate Committee held, should have been a matter for the courts rather than the Home Secretary. The case concerned the two young men who had been convicted of the murder of little Jamie Bulger. The court's decision raised something of a furore since the Home Secretary's decision had been popular and the court's decision was not (see Le Sueur, 1996, and discussion below). However, it was substantively consistent with the requirements of the ECHR, a point which brings out the possible conflict between majoritarianism and limited government models of democracy in the UK Constitution.

Towards Constitutionalism?

We noted in Chapter 1 that in recent years the courts have been developing explicit common law principles of constitutionalism and fundamental rights that they apply in judicial review, and potentially in other, cases. Before considering these developments it is worth reminding ourselves that many of the fundamental constitutional principles which are taken for granted by lawyers and politicians have been elaborated by the courts of common law and equity since at least the early seventeenth century. For instance, the principle that a person is free to do anything that is not prohibited by an Act of Parliament—or under the common law—was enunciated in the *Case of Proclamations* ((1611) 12 Co. Rep. 74): Sir Edward Coke CJ decided that the executive—the King— could not alter the law unilaterally by proclamation and without the consent of Parliament so as to interfere with the liberties of subjects, and that a royal proclamation that purported to criminalize activity—the manufacture of wheat starch in London—was legally ineffective. And in *Entick v. Carrington* ((1765) 19 St Tr 1029) it was held that a mere claim by government that interference with the liberty of a subject was necessary in the public interest could not justify it and such interference was only lawful if permitted by some positive law. The separation of the judicial from the executive function and of the judiciary from the executive owes much to the speech of Sir Edward Coke CJ in the *Prohibitions del Roy* ((1607) 12 Co Rep 63) in which the judges decided that cases raising issues of law should be decided by judges, who are experts in the law, and not by the King—in modern terms, the executive—who is not learned in the law.

But by no means all of the decisions of the courts on constitutional matters over the years have been durable, and many have been displaced by legislation. For instance, the decision in *Darnel's case* ((1627) 3 St Tr 1) upheld the power of the King to enforce the payment of taxation levied without the consent of Parliament by preventive arrest: this was overridden by the Bill of Rights 1689, Article 4, which provided that there shall be no taxation without the consent of Parliament.

Some of the constitutional principles in the old cases have been relied on from time to time by the courts in support of their decisions, even before the current fashion for constitutionalism. Just to take a simple example, in *Congreve v. Home Office* ([1976] QB 629) it was held that a statutory provision that a TV licence 'may be revoked' by the Home Secretary could not authorize the Home Secretary to revoke a TV licence and demand payment for a new licence because the owner had renewed his licence early in order to avoid paying an increased licence fee. The court decided that the Home Secretary had acted unlawfully in purporting to revoke the licence, because the owner had done nothing unlawful when he renewed his licence early; the revocation by the Home Secretary was an interference with the right of the owner to use his TV freely, and with his privacy in his home, it criminalized prima facie innocent conduct (using a TV without a licence is a crime), and it was in fact an unlawful demand for the payment of tax (the payment for a TV licence) which was not expressly authorized by Parliament, as it should have been under Article 4 of the Bill of Rights 1689 (per Lord Denning. The other judges delivered concurring judgments). The court drew upon a number of fundamental constitutional principles in this case, only one of them—Article 4 of the Bill of Rights—being statutory, in deciding that a discretionary statutory power had been exercised unlawfully.

By way of further example of the fact that many constitutional principles have been elaborated by the courts over the years, though the Prevention of Corruption Acts cover some possible abuses of public office, the principles that public offices are to be used in the general public interest and not in the interests of the office holder, and that office holders are to exercise their own independent judgements—the public service ethos—are based in the common law rather than in statute (see for instance *Porter v. Magill* [2001] UKHL 67, [2002] 2 WLR 37; *Bromley LBC v. GLC* [1983] 1 AC 768—see Chapter 16).

My point is that it is not new to the British Constitution for the courts to expound constitutional principles and to apply them in their decisions, though some judges—Lord Denning was one—have been more explicit than others about the constitutional dimensions to their decisions. This does not of course mean that judges are right to take on this role, only that some of the controversy surrounding the current process of exposition by the courts of constitutional and fundamental rights and principles is surprising, given the history of the matter. We return to the justifications for this activity below.

Human rights, fundamental rights, and constitutional rights

A number of decisions and comments from the judges in the last fifteen years or so illustrate the way in which doctrines of constitutionalism have been evolving in that period. They are particularly striking for the explicitness of the judgments. First, from the late 1980s the courts developed a principle that the threshold for a finding of *Wednesbury* unreasonableness (see above) was lower when human rights were involved. For instance, in *Bugdaycay v. Home Secretary* ([1987] AC 514), a deportation case in which the deportee's right to life was at risk if he were deported, Lord Bridge said that in such a case a decision would be subject to 'more rigorous examination' than if no such right was in issue. In *R. v. Ministry of Defence, ex parte Smith* ([1996] QB 517), in which homosexuals had been dismissed from the armed forces on the ground of their sexuality, Lord Bingham, MR, accepted that, in relation to an unreasonable decision, 'the more substantial the interference with human rights, the more the court will require by justification before it is satisfied that the decision is reasonable.' (But in that case the court did not hold the policy to be unlawful because of the sensitive nature of decisions to do with the defence of the realm. The court deferred to the executive, though expressing reservations about the continuance of the policy.) Although these are important and significant moves towards giving specially protected legal status to human rights, the protection given in these cases was relatively weak. Government must satisfy the court that it has strong justifications to legitimate interference with rights in the exercise of discretionary power. The courts stop short of outlawing the interference absolutely. Presumably, however, even this step would be incompatible with Griffith's preference for the political constitution (Griffith, 1979; see Chapter 1).

The courts then began to develop principles of constitutionalism and constitutional rights alongside these human rights protections, principles that could only be overridden by clear language in a statute. The right of all people, including those serving prison sentences, to communicate in confidence with their lawyers was held to be a 'constitutional right' so that a prison rule purporting to authorize the censoring of such correspondence was unlawful (R. v. Secretary of State for the Home Department, ex parte Leech (No. 2) [1994] QB 198). In R. v. The Lord Chancellor, ex parte Witham ([1998] QB 575) Laws J (who has been particularly active in developing principles of fundamental rights and constitutionalism) held that the Lord Chancellor could not unilaterally change the rules about the payment of court fees by those embarking on litigation so as to impose fees on those with no means to pay them. Such rules effectively denied 'a fundamental constitutional right of access to the courts'. If the Lord Chancellor wished to do so he would have to point to clear and express authority from Parliament in an Act. The retroactive lengthening of the minimum 'tariff' period that a person convicted of an offence must serve before being eligible for parole has been held to be unlawful as contrary to the rule of law, a constitutional principle (R. v. Secretary of State for the Home Department, ex parte Pierson [1998] AC 539). In that case Lord Steyn enunciated a general principle, that:

Parliament does not legislate in a vacuum. . . . Parliament legislates for a European liberal democracy based upon the principles and traditions of the common law . . . and . . . unless there is the clearest provision to the contrary, Parliament must be presumed not to legislate contrary to the rule of law. (at p. 575; see also Steyn, 1997; Jowell, 2000; Allan, 2001.)

A shift from a concept of an unfettered political Constitution to limited governmental power was perhaps made most explicit by Lord Hoffmann in R. v. Secretary of State for the Home Department, ex parte Simms ([2000] 2 AC 115). Lord Hoffmann observed that:

[T]he courts of the United Kingdom, though acknowledging the sovereignty of Parliament [will] apply principles of constitutionality little different from those which exist in countries where the power of the legislature is expressly limited by a constitutional document.

In R. v. Secretary of State for the Home Department, ex parte Daly ([2001] 3 All ER 433) Lord Cooke held that the common law by itself is a sufficient source of the 'fundamental right to confidential communication with a legal adviser' and said that 'some rights are inherent and fundamental to democratic civilized society.' This is a particularly significant point, since it rejects the legislative intent justification for judicial review and grounds the courts' powers explicitly in the common law. Only express words in a statute could override such 'fundamental rights'. The protection for constitutional rights under these dicta is stronger that the protection afforded under *Budgaycay* and *Smith*, for instance, requiring express statutory provision to legitimate interference with these rights.

Senior judges have expounded their commitment to constitutionalism in a number of extra-judicial writings, some of them published before the principles had started to surface in judicial decisions (see for instance Steyn, 1997, 1999). Laws (1993) suggested that a case (*Derbyshire County Council v. Times Newspapers* [1993] AC 534) which decided that a local authority did not have an interest in its governing reputation that would entitle it to sue for libel 'might prove to be an engine of change in the evolution of judicial review as a *constitutional safeguard for substantive fundamental rights*' (p. 68; emphasis added). He continued that the greater the intrusion proposed by a body possessing public power over the citizen where his fundamental rights were at stake, the greater must be the justification which the public authority must demonstrate. The unselfconscious assumption here is that fundamental rights exist (although the article was written before the passage of the Human Rights Act 1998) and that the judges are the right people to determine whether they have been breached.

Laws (1994) went on to develop a thesis that it was time for a 'fresh look at the quality of legislative power and its mediation to the people by the judges'. He proposed empowering the courts to make advisory declarations concerning the legality of forthcoming pieces of government legislation—and very provocatively wondered whether the sovereignty of Parliament was absolute where fundamental rights were concerned (see also Laws, 1995). This second point has not been pursued by Laws or other judges (see discussion of the democratic justification for judicial review, *supra*), and instead the doctrine of the constitutional statute, noted in Chapter 1 and considered below, places an obstacle in the path of parliamentary repeal of provisions of a constitutional nature by denying the possibility of implied repeal.

Laws' proposal for advisory declarations is of interest first, because the concept of an illegal act of Parliament is alien to our system, save in respect of European Community law, where the courts may disapply but not quash or set aside legislation that is incompatible with European Community law; and secondly, because such a jurisdiction would resemble in some ways the power of the Conseil constitutionnel in France to decide whether a proposed statute would be constitutional, which has been noted in Chapter 3. (Under the devolution legislation the Judicial Committee of the Privy Council has jurisdiction to determine on a reference from the relevant law officer whether an act of a devolved body is compatible with the empowering Act of Parliament. This device safeguards the UK Parliament's transfer of power and is not designed to limit the UK Parliament's powers: see Chapter 8.)

Developing his thoughts about constitutionalism Laws (1995) suggested that there are substantive principles which confine the scope within which discretionary decisions may be taken under statute and asks about 'the extent to which the concept of fundamental rights ought in principle to affect the reach and length of democratic power', i.e. the relationship between law and politics.

Sir Stephen Sedley, another Court of Appeal judge, has argued in favour of the control by judges of abuse of power, by whomever it is exercised, and suggests that 'the common law itself has both the capacity and the obligation to move in the next generation towards a principled constitutional order' (Sedley, 1994, 273). Clearly this approach treats the Constitution as a legal rather than a political one, contrary to Griffith's approach (see Chapter 1, and Griffith, 1979, 2001).

The coming into effect of the Human Rights Act and the devolution legislation have been influential in stimulating yet further interest in constitutionalism among lawyers. Lord Steyn (2002*b*):

A Bill of Rights cannot exist in a constitutional vacuum. It needs to fit into a constitutional structure of a democratic character. While we now have a written Bill of Rights, we have no written constitution as such. . . . I believe that we are inching towards becoming a constitutional state. . . . Our judges now speak not about subjects but about citizens or individuals. With devolution it is now beyond doubt that individuals have rights against the state and its agencies . . . the rule of law applies to all including the state.

And, he suggested, the Human Rights Act had invigorated the process of constitutionalization of public law. The phrase 'constitutional state' picks up on some academic literature about what is happening in other jurisdictions, such as Canada, Israel, and New Zealand (see Joseph, 1998, 2000; Barak, 1999; Weinrib, 1999).

The Human Rights Act 1998 (see Chapter 6) expressly empowers and requires the courts to protect human rights as set out in the European Convention on Human Rights (ECHR), unless Parliament has expressly authorized breach of those rights. That Act has expanded the ambit of what could be termed 'constitutional review'.

These articulations of constitutional and fundamental principles and rights by senior judges represent a departure from an earlier tradition of reluctance on the part of the judges to admit the political nature of the judicial review jurisdiction, or the existence of constitutional or democratic rights which might constrain the exercise of its sovereignty by Parliament or the implementation of its policies by government. Judicial review has until recently been largely about 'administrative law', carrying the implication, at least to the uninitiated, that administration is not political or constitutional. The principles also show that the common law is being actively developed by the judges and their role is not limited to identifying and applying principles that have always existed.

Constitutional statutes

A novel concept of a constitutional statute is in the process of development since the case of *Thoburn v. Sunderland City Council* ([2002] 3 WLR 247; it is known as the Metric Martyrs case). While previous decisions had been concerned with the exercises of administrative discretions and interpretation of statutory provisions but not with the sovereignty of the UK Parliament, this new concept establishes a hierarchy of Acts of Parliament. It represents a stronger principle of constitutionalism than previous decisions and grounds them firmly in the common law. In *Thoburn* traders objected to a regulation made under the European Communities Act 1972 to comply with European Community law, which required that goods be priced per kilogramme rather than in imperial measures. The regulation criminalized the use of imperial measures, save as supplementary indicators to metric units. One of the issues was whether the European Communities Act 1972 had been impliedly repealed by a subsequent Act of the UK Parliament, which had permitted the continued use of imperial measures but which had been overridden by the new regulation. On this point Laws LJ held that the common law had come to recognize that there are rights which should be classified as constitutional or fundamental, and that it follows that there is a hierarchy of Acts of Parliament, 'ordinary' statutes and 'constitutional' statutes. A constitutional statute, he held, is one which conditions the legal relationship between citizen and state in some general overarching manner, or enlarges or diminishes the scope of what we would now regard as fundamental constitutional rights. Laws LJ cited as examples Magna Carta 1297, the Bill of Rights of 1689, and the Human Rights Act, the Scotland Act, and the Government of Wales Act, all of 1998. The European Communities Act 1972, he held, was by force of common law such a constitutional statute. Unlike ordinary statutes, a constitutional statute could not be impliedly repealed by a subsequent inconsistent statutory provision, and the court would only treat such a 'constitutional statute' as having been amended or repealed by Act of Parliament if it was shown that Parliament actually intended to amend or repeal it. This could be shown by the use of express words in a later statute, for instance (paras. 62–3). Laws LJ considered that this position gave full weight to both the continuance of the legislative sovereignty of Parliament and the proper supremacy of Community law. (The other judge decided against the traders on different grounds.)

This is a substantial step forward in the development of the common law doctrine of constitutionalism. It is reminiscent of Eskridge and Ferejohn's (2001) concept of 'super-statutes' in US law, which 'penetrate normative and institutional culture in a deep way' (p. 1215) and which tend to trump ordinary legislation when there are clashes or inconsistencies, even when normal principles of construction would suggest the opposite (p. 1216). The facts of *Thoburn* show, however, how constitutional principles and their rationales can conflict. In that case the principle of primacy of European Community law was in conflict with the liberal principle going back to the *Case of Proclamations* that activity could not be criminalized except under the express authority of Parliament. The principle of primacy of European Community law which *Thoburn* upholds is certainly a 'fundamental' principle, as it is a condition of UK membership of the European Union that EC law should be given primacy in domestic courts. But it is not a liberal or democratic principle. Most of the constitutional principles to which the courts refer or which they have elaborated in recent years are rooted in principles of representative democracy or liberal principles—the subjection of decisions taken under the royal prerogative to judicial review if they are justiciable in the *CCSU* case, and other cases discussed above, are examples. In *Thoburn* Laws LJ gave precedence to the (non-democratic) constitutional statute over a (liberal democratic) common law principle (see Campbell and Young, 2002).

Justifications for the judicial development of principles of constitutionalism

The question arises, what justification is there for the courts to develop their own principles of constitutionalism in the ways we have been considering? If the UK were contemplating adopting a written Constitution it is likely that there would be broad consultation, possibly a constitutional convention and a referendum, before a Constitution was drafted and put into effect. And yet the courts have embarked on this exercise without such public involvement.

One contemporary justification for the development of constitutionalism might be that the courts are simply putting into effect or 'catching up with' a widespread political consensus about the particular constitutional rights and principles they elaborate. What they are doing is *substantively* right, even though the fact that it is they rather than politicians that are laying down these principles looks odd to those from civilian jurisdictions where the judges do not have this power. This justification fits well with the justification Nicol (2001) has put forward for the *Factortame* decisions (see Chapter 4). Nicol accepts that 'The "constitutional catch-up" justification represents in itself a good normative reason of principle to legitimize judicial modification of constitutional ground rules' (p. 264). However, the courts need to be wary about whether there is really a political consensus about the principles they are elaborating, particularly since the cases in which they do so are likely to involve political decisions that are inconsistent with them. Even if there is such a consensus, a question arises whether it is right for the courts to give effect to those principles rather than leave it to politicians who, on this assumption, share the consensus, to observe the principles in their decisions and legislation.

A further substantive justification of the courts' activity would be that the principles and values the courts are elaborating are consistent with international instruments to which the UK government is a party, so that they are giving effect to principles that the government accepts. Many decisions have indeed reflected such principles, though as we have seen in discussion of the *Thoburn* case, principles can clash.

We should bear in mind too when looking for justifications for this role that the development of principles of constitutionalism and requiring that they be observed is not an enterprise that is being undertaken unilaterally or solely by the courts. The government and Parliament have deliberately given the courts a constitutional role in relation to devolution and human rights, though seeking to retain the ultimate sovereignty of the Westminster Parliament (see Chapters 2 and 6). For instance, the devolution arrangements have resulted in courts in the UK having to determine 'devolution issues', issues about the powers of the devolved bodies and the compatibility of their arrangements with the devolution Acts, including the Human Rights Act and European Community law (see Chapter 13). These are essentially constitutional issues which the legislation in question has explicitly handed to the courts for decision. For instance, in *Starrs v. Ruxton* (2000 J.C. 208) the arrangements in Scotland for the appointing of temporary sheriffs—part-time judges—as, in effect, probationers with no security of tenure, were found by the Court of Session not to meet the requirements of judicial independence and impartiality laid down in Article 6 of the ECHR which the Scotland Act 1998 incorporated into Scots law. The independence of the judiciary and the rule of law that it underpins are among the most obvious requirements in a democratic Constitution. The decision led to revision of the arrangements for the appointment of temporary sheriffs in Scotland (and also of Assistant Recorders in England and Wales).

This kind of case raises essentially constitutional issues of the sort that would be decided by constitutional courts in countries with written Constitutions. Reforms such as devolution and the Human Rights Act have thus confirmed the process of the constitutionalization of government that was initiated by the courts independently of these reforms (see Steyn, 1999; Jowell, 2000). The government and Parliament have given their support to the courts' constitutional roles, but they have left it to the courts to formulate principles, for the statutes themselves do not include many explicit principles.

It may be that the question at the start of this section is phrased the wrong way round. A better way of putting it might be: why should not the courts develop principles of constitutionalism? The answer might be that there is no reason why they should not do so. The principles are broadly accepted by government in its ratification of international human rights instruments. But they must take care about it. This is a role the courts have performed over many years and they will continue to do so for as long as the common law basis of the system survives. Parliament has specifically given the courts powers to develop principles, in the devolution and human rights legislation. It is always open to Parliament to legislate to correct the decisions of the courts and override their principles and the values they rely on.

The Courts and Theories of Democracy, Citizenship, and Good Governance

The development of judicial review and constitutionalism then raise fundamental issues to do with democratic theory. A range of theories of democracy that have some currency in the United Kingdom were outlined in Chapter 2. The position of ministers who claim that it is undemocratic for the courts to require them to comply with the principles developed by the courts is, by implication, majoritarian and government-centred. Ministers, because they are Ministers and because they are members of and accountable to one or other House of Parliament, ought to be free in a democracy to make what decisions they wish and pursue what policies they wish, subject only to there being express legislative authorization if what they propose would be criminal or in breach of the ordinary law of the land without such authorization. This position acknowledges that Ministers should not break the ordinary law of the land without statutory authority, but it implies a very narrow view of the rule of law, and implies also that observation of the requirements of procedural propriety, rationality, and respect for the 'fundamental constitutional rights' which the courts have developed are not necessary in decision-making in a democracy. Democracy, on this view, has a very narrow meaning—Ministers who are accountable to Parliament should be legally free to do anything they want that is not contrary to the ordinary law, including statutes granting them special powers. But they are under no legally enforceable obligations to act fairly or reasonably. As long as they do not act in breach of the ordinary law, the only checks to which they should be subject are political—their accountability to Parliament and in due course the risk of losing office in the next election.

The theory implicit in the courts' principles, on the other hand, is richer and deeper than this majoritarian, government-centred, narrow view of what the reach of judicial review should be—which is admittedly something of a caricature. The courts' judicial review theory draws on principles of democracy, citizenship, and good governance which have been noted above in the discussion of the grounds for judicial review. First, it defers to the sovereignty of Parliament—which the Human Rights Act also retains—often treating this as a democratic doctrine. For instance, Laws LJ in his judgment in *International Transport Roth GmbH v. Home Office* ([2002] 3 WLR 344, paras. 69–87) referred repeatedly to deference to the democratic decision-maker, and drew together dicta from recent cases in which other judges had also spoken in such terms. (See Chapter 6 for further discussion.)

In my view the justification for this judicial deference to Parliament is not based in democracy but in good governance theory. I do not think that the courts are implying that whatever legislation a majority in Parliament passes is substantively democratic when they give effect to it. Constitutions based broadly on comity between institutions— as long as they are not corrupt—work best in the interest of citizens and in the general public interest, and the comity between the courts and Parliament is particularly important. It is to preserve this comity that the courts defer to Parliament, rather than because they are committed to the idea that whatever a majority in Parliament enacts is democratic until it is repealed. If comity were to be overstretched, either Parliament would limit the powers of the courts, or legislation would be introduced to limit the powers of the government. Appreciation of the risks to both sides if comity breaks down lies behind the deference of the courts to Acts of Parliament.

The *Venables* case, noted above, was one of a number in the mid-1990s in which the courts struck down decisions of Ministers, in particular of the Home Secretary, and this generated debate in the press and among politicians about the legitimacy of the judicial review activity of the courts. Le Sueur (1996) suggested that the controversy was caused not by increased judicial activism but by a new ministerial strategy of risk-taking, making decisions that their lawyers warned might be unlawful and then challenging the judges when those decisions were struck down: 'the public deference traditionally shown by politicians to judges and the law has ended. The gloves are off and the Queensbury Rules are to be ignored' (p. 11). Deference works both ways, but governmental deference to the courts was being withdrawn. If the conflicts of the mid-1990s were indeed due to a deliberate risk-taking challenging strategy, the strategy seems to have changed since the change of government in 1997. There have not been repeats of ministerial defiance of judges, despite the fact that Ministers have lost a number of important cases. Le Sueur rightly noted that every constitutional system relies for stability on tacit understandings between its formal institutions, and that in the long term the relationship between the judiciary and the executive could not be based on conflict (p. 26). It may be that a recognition of this on the part of both the courts and government has enabled peace to be restored.

Second, the courts' theory requires that *governmental* power should be limited or inhibited by legal accountability and not only by political accountability, so as to protect individuals affected by government action from unfair or arbitrary acts or breaches of human rights. This approach reflects a rights-based rather than a majoritarian theory of democracy and citizenship, one of limited government. It has been influenced by European Community law, in which legally enforceable individual rights against the member states are central (see Chapter 4). It imposes legal accountability alongside political accountability where decisions are contrary to the courts' principles of democracy, citizenship, and good governance, thus supplementing the political Constitution with legal checks.

In effect, the courts' view of democracy, citizenship, and good governance envisages joint or shared 'sovereignty'. A number of judges have spoken in these terms in the last decade or so. As Lord Bridge put it in 1991: 'In our society the rule of law rests upon twin foundations: the sovereignty of the Queen in Parliament in making the law and the sovereignty of the Queen's courts in interpreting and applying the law' (*X Ltd. v. Morgan-Grampian (Publishers) Ltd* ([1991] 1 AC 1, 48). Sir Stephen Sedley has put it as follows: 'it is in Parliament and the courts . . . that the sovereignties of the state reside' (Sedley, 1997, 26). And he has said that parliamentary sovereignty is giving way to 'a bipolar sovereignty of the Crown in Parliament and the Crown in the courts, to each of which the Crown's ministers are answerable—politically to Parliament, legally to the courts' (Sedley, 1995, 389; see also Allan, 2001, 14). This is part of a gradual process of erosion of the belief that one legal sovereign and a *Grundnorm* were essential to a nation state and its legal system (Austin, 1832; Kelsen, 1949; Goldsworthy, 1999), a process which we see also being eroded in European Community law, where member states have surrendered part of their sovereignty to the Union, but retain other parts of it (see MacCormick, 1999, and Chapter 2 *supra*).

However, this concept of democracy as rights-based with limited governmental power, and in particular of the role of the courts in a democracy, carries high risks for the judges—and for the public. Courts may interfere inadvisedly in public administration. The case of *Bromley London Borough Council v. Greater London Council* ([1983] 1 AC 768, HL) is a classic example. The House of Lords quashed the GLC cheap fares policy as being based on a misreading of the statutory provisions, but were accused of themselves misunderstanding transport policy in so doing. The courts are not experts in policy and public administration—hence Jowell's point that the courts should not step beyond their institutional capacity (Jowell, 2000). Acceptance of this approach is reflected in the judgments of Laws LJ in *International Transport Roth GmbH v. Secretary of State for the Home Department* ([2002] EWCA Civ 158, [2002] 3 WLR 344) and of Lord Nimmo Smith in *Adams v. Lord Advocate* (Court of Session, *Times*, 8 August 2002) in which a distinction was drawn between areas where the subject matter lies within the expertise of the courts (for instance, criminal justice, including sentencing and detention of individuals) and those which were more appropriate for decision by democratically elected and accountable bodies. If the courts step outside the area of their institutional competence, government may react by getting Parliament to legislate to oust the jurisdiction of the courts altogether. Such a step would undermine the rule of law. Government and public opinion may come to question the legitimacy of the judges exercising judicial review against Ministers and thus undermine the authority of the courts and the rule of law.

Procedurally there is much to be said for judicial decision-making: arguments are made and tested in open courts, decisions are reasoned and delivered publicly. But of course judges lack expertise and, often, legitimacy to make value-laden decisions. Many decisions are in fact highly political in the sense that they are about weighing up conflicting interests, as Lord Hope recognized, for instance, in *R. v. Director of Public Prosecutions, ex parte Kebilene* ([2000] 2 AC 326, at p. 381): 'The questions which the courts will have to decide in the application of these [fundamental] principles will involve questions of balance between competing interests and issues of proportionality.' The recognition of the political nature of some decisions was accepted by Lord Hope in that case as a justification for deference to the elected body.

A range of solutions has been advanced to the problems for the courts that their position on the review of administrative decisions and their models of constitutionalism and democracy raise. We have already noted Ewing's proposal (2000) that the common law should be replaced by statute and codes. Another would be to improve court procedures in judicial review cases so that the constitutional implications or the impact of a decision on public policy and administration could be ventilated in court and taken into account when a decision is made (Griffith, 1985; Woolf, 1990, ch. 4). Such a procedure would meet a requirement that in a democracy decision-makers should respond to the views of interested bodies. Another approach would be to provide judges dealing with public law cases with some form of training or experience of public administration; judges could benefit from discussions with administrators, visits to government departments and pressure groups (Woolf 1990, 115–20). This would reduce the extent to which they could be accused of meddling inappropriately in public administration or policy, although it could not of course guarantee that they never made controversial decisions.

A more radical solution to the risks posed for the judges would be the adoption by Parliament of an authoritative statement of Directive Principles of State Policy, such as are included in the Constitution of India (see Chapter 6). These would represent agreed principles for the exercise of the powers of government and the legislature, devolved bodies and local government, and all other state institutions, which could serve to guide the judiciary when determining cases where there are conflicts between what the government wishes to do and what seems to the courts to be fair and just. But even such an instrument would not remove all discretion and judgment from the courts.

Other solutions to the conflict inherent in relations between the courts and other institutions, and the legitimacy crises that such conflict may generate, involve reforms to the institutional position of the judiciary and their relationships with government and Parliament, which are discussed in Chapter 18.

Summary and Conclusions

The role of the judiciary has expanded in the last twenty years or so and it will continue to do so as a result of devolution, the Human Rights Act, and growing awareness of the constitutional importance of many cases that the courts are called upon to decide. Much of the increasing power of the judges has been granted them by Parliament, notably in relation to European law, human rights, and devolution. If relations between the UK government and the devolved bodies were to become strained with different parties in control at the centre and in Scotland or Wales—as will inevitably happen sooner or later—then it is likely that these relations would be put on a more formal statutory basis, and the role of the courts in resolving disputes between the different levels of government would be increased (see Chapters 13–15).

Under the common law system, and in the absence of a written Constitution, there is more scope than in other systems for the judges to take it upon themselves to develop concepts of democracy, good governance, and citizenship in their judgments, and thus to be instrumental in a shift from a political to a law-based Constitution. The courts in the UK have indeed been active in developing mechanisms of legal accountability for governmental bodies and those exercising public functions. The principles of judicial review reflect principles of good governance. In upholding human rights under the HRA, the courts have started to develop a legal concept of liberal citizenship. The principles of judicial review serve to protect the security and status of individuals and thus their social and economic rights. But the courts lack the framework and guidance that would be required if they were to develop a fuller concept of social citizenship. If such a concept is to develop the courts will have an important role both in elaborating it and giving it effect. A bill of social and economic rights or an authoritative statement of principles of state policy would assist them in doing so. Without such an instrument they may well develop the law in an incoherent way.

It will be suggested in later chapters that the judges are likely to expand their activities in developing concepts of democracy, citizenship, and good governance if, as seems likely, the political process continues to be ineffective in subjecting legislation to proper scrutiny and imposing due accountability on government. This will doubtless stimulate a debate about the institutional arrangements within which the judiciary operates, which is considered in Chapter 18.

PART II

CITIZEN-CENTRED REFORMS

6

Human Rights in the United Kingdom

One of the first bills to be introduced into the House of Commons after the general election in 1997 became the Human Rights Act 1998 (HRA). The Act came into force for the UK in October 2000. The HRA incorporates into UK law the principal provisions of the European Convention on Human Rights (ECHR—see Appendix) by requiring that they shall 'have effect' in various ways. The Act gives special legal protection to certain civil and political rights. In this chapter we shall outline the provisions of the ECHR and the Human Rights Act and consider their implications for democracy, citizenship, and good governance in the UK. We shall also look to possible future developments in the protection of rights, in particular social and economic rights (see generally Lester and Pannick, 1999; Clayton and Tomlinson, 2000; Fenwick, 2002; Feldman, 2002*a*).

The European Convention on Human Rights

First, the ECHR on which the Human Rights Act is based, needs some explanation. It is an international instrument which was adopted by many of the Western European democracies in 1950, was ratified by the UK in 1951, and came into force internationally in 1953. The British had played a major role in its drafting. At that time the focus was on preventing a recurrence of the abuses of civil and political rights that had taken place before and during the Second World War under the Nazi and fascist regimes, and preventing the spread of communism and the authoritarianism of the Soviet bloc, through protection of rights connected with a liberal democratic system. The British government did not expect that the Convention would have much effect in the UK as their assumption was that our law was fully compliant (Wicks, 2000). The Convention protects rights that had earlier been spelt out in the Universal Declaration of Human Rights of 1948. It does not, subject to few exceptions (property rights, a right to education) extend to social, economic, environmental, or cultural rights. The Convention provides for a right of individual petition to the European Court of Human Rights at Strasbourg (ECtHR), which states have the option to accept. The United Kingdom did not sign up to the individual right of petition until 1966. Until then cases could only be brought against the UK in the ECtHR by other states parties to the Convention, as in the case of *Ireland v. UK* ((1978) 2 EHRR 25) in which the Irish government complained that the interrogation techniques used by the UK security forces in Northern Ireland were in breach of ECHR protections against torture and inhuman and degrading treatment. Once the right of individual petition was accepted by the UK government, many cases were successfully brought against it by individual victims of breaches of the Convention rights.

Victims can complain to the ECtHR not only about breaches of their rights by the state and state bodies but also about breaches by private bodies. The state is responsible under the Convention if its legal system does not afford protection against breaches of these rights, whether by state or private bodies. For instance, UK law permitted employers to operate closed shops according to which only those who were members of a trade union could be employed and those who did not so belong could be dismissed; the ECtHR decided in the case of *Young, James and Webster v. UK* ((1982) 5 EHRR 201) that the UK was in breach of its obligations under the Convention as this represented a breach of the right of freedom of association (which includes a right not to associate) under Article 11. By way of further examples, UK law permitted the corporal punishment of children in school and this was held to be in breach of Article 3 as degrading treatment in *Costello-Roberts v. UK* ((1993) 19 EHRR 112, ECtHR); corporal punishment by parents or step-parents may also be in breach of Article 3 if it is unduly severe: *A. v. UK* ((1999) 27 EHRR 611, ECtHR).

The Human Rights Act 1998: a Sketch

As noted above the HRA enables articles of the Convention to have effect in the UK legal system. The UK's is a 'dualist' legal system, which means that international treaties such as the ECHR cannot give rise to rights or obligations that are enforceable or justiciable in our domestic courts, unless they are incorporated by statute into UK law (see for instance *Civilian War Claimants v. The King* [1932] AC 14). Thus until the Human Rights Act came into force the ECHR could not give rise directly to rights enforceable in UK courts, and complainants had first to exhaust remedies in the British courts before they could exercise the individual right of petition to Strasbourg. There was no obligation on parties to the Convention to incorporate its provisions into domestic law.

The HRA fills much of this gap by incorporating into United Kingdom law the main substantive provisions of the ECHR (Articles 2–12 and 14) and its first protocol (see Appendix). Thus they set out rights to life, freedom from torture or inhuman or degrading treatment, liberty and security of the person, a fair trial, respect for privacy and family life, freedom of speech and association, a right not to be discriminated against in the enjoyment of Convention rights, and so on. The articles of the first protocol that have been incorporated guarantee a right to peaceful enjoyment of one's possessions, and a right to education, respectively economic and social, rather than civil or political, rights. Article 13 of the ECHR is omitted. This requires that there be an effective remedy for breaches of the rights in the ECHR.

No exceptions are permitted to the rights to life, freedom from torture, prohibition of slavery, liberty and security, a fair trial and the prohibition of punishment without a breach of the law (Articles 2–7 ECHR). Exceptions are permitted to the exercise of rights of privacy, freedom of thought, freedom of expression, and freedom of association (Articles 8–11 ECHR). Where exceptions are permitted, typically, as in the free speech article, the exceptions must be 'prescribed by law and . . . necessary in a democratic society, in the interests of national security, . . . public safety, for the prevention of disorder or crime, for the protection of health or morals, for the protection of the reputation or rights or others . . .'. In effect this means that interference with rights is not justifiable if it is merely desirable rather than necessary, that the aim of the interference must be legitimate, and the interference must be proportionate.

Most of the Convention rights were already protected in UK law before they were incorporated in the 1998 Act, though they could be overridden by legislation or the exercise of administrative discretion. A right to privacy is the major exception, as it was not explicitly protected at common law—or in equity. But most Convention rights were regarded as liberties rather than rights in UK law. By incorporating the main substantive provisions of the ECHR into UK law the HRA transforms former liberties into rights, and this shifts the balance of power from the executive to the citizen and implies a rights-based concept of citizenship.

The HRA incorporates the Convention articles into UK law in subtle ways. In many countries—the United States is a particularly strong example—the provisions in Bills of Rights are protected against repeal or amendment by requirements for special majorities in the legislature or other procedural requirements. In New Zealand, by contrast, their Bill of Rights Act 1990 enjoys no such special procedural protection against repeal. The UK Act broadly follows the New Zealand approach.

By section 1 the 'Convention rights' 'are to have effect for the purposes of this Act'. The meaning of 'have effect' is elaborated in the following sections of the Act. It has a very special meaning. The Act adds, in effect, a human rights layer to existing UK law. First, a court or tribunal determining a question to do with a Convention right must take into account the decisions of the European Court of Human Rights at Strasbourg (ECtHR) and various other opinions and decisions of the organs of the Council of Europe, which is responsible for the Convention's observance in international law. Thus in the interpretation of statutes and regulations and in developing the common law the jurisprudence of the Council of Europe institutions will be influential but not binding. To give it binding force would be to delegate legislative power to an outside body. On the other hand, it is still open to a person who claims that his or her Convention rights have been breached to appeal to the ECtHR, and the UK courts will know that if they make a finding that goes against the jurisprudence of the ECtHR, a claimant will be likely to succeed there in the event of an appeal. They will therefore, in the absence of special circumstances, follow any clear and consistent case law of that court (see per Lord Slynn in *R. v. Secretary of State for the Environment, Transport and the Regions, ex parte Alconbury Developments and others* [2001] UKHL 23, para. 26).

Duty of compatible interpretation

By HRA section 3 UK legislation must be interpreted so far as possible in a way which is compatible with Convention rights (see Marshall, 1998). This provision has been treated by UK courts as requiring them, if they consider it to be necessary, to 'read in' to legislation additional words that are necessary to make the measure compatible with the Convention, or to 'read down' legislation by restricting the scope and effect of broad language to avoid incompatibility. They may not, however, themselves make new law on the matter. Their role is to interpret the law, not to legislate (per Lord Woolf, CJ in *Poplar Housing and Regeneration Community Association Ltd. v. Donoghue* [2001] 4 All ER 604, para. 75).

By way of example of how the courts have interpreted legislation to be compatible with Convention rights, in *R. v. A. (No. 2)* ([2001] 2 WLR 1546) the House of Lords construed a provision that prohibited the giving of evidence or cross-examination about any sexual behaviour of the complainant in a rape case except with the leave of the court as being subject to an *implied* provision that evidence or questioning which is required to secure a fair trial under Article 6 of the Convention should not be treated as inadmissible (1563H, para. 45), i.e. by reading in additional words.

These techniques of interpretation do not always enable the courts to find UK statutes to be compatible with Convention rights, however. There have been a number of cases in which the courts have held the legislation in question to be incompatible with Convention rights (see HRA section 4, *infra*) and have not been willing or able to give them very strained meanings so as to produce compatibility.

This section 2 rule of compatible interpretation alters the courts' approach to parliamentary sovereignty and the role of the courts in giving effect to the intention of Parliament (usually, in reality, the intention of the government expressed through an Act of Parliament) in an important respect. Hitherto the courts have been concerned to discover the meaning of the Act in question as it was intended by Parliament, relying on a number of presumptions, for instance that Parliament did not intend to legislate incompatibly with the UK's international obligations. But they would not give an entirely artificial or strained interpretation to legislation. Under the Human Rights Act, by contrast, the courts' function is to interpret legislation 'so far as possible' so as to give precedence to the Human Rights Act over another Act, even if they are satisfied that the Parliament which passed the other Act did not intend it to be compatible with the Convention rights.

Declarations of incompatibility and remedial orders

What if it is not possible to interpret UK primary legislation, i.e. Acts of Parliament and Orders in Council, compatibly with Convention rights? The courts cannot strike down or disapply the legislation. All the superior courts can do, by HRA section 4, is make a declaration of incompatibility (see Bamforth, 1998). Thus the HRA rejects the US approach under which the Supreme Court has the power to strike down legislation that is incompatible with the constitution (*Marbury v. Madison* 1 Cranch 137 (1803)) and preserves the legislative sovereignty of the UK Parliament in the special sense that the courts do not have the power unilaterally to disapply an Act of Parliament. We return to this point shortly. A declaration of incompatibility is not much of a comfort for the victim, who will know that an official has breached his or her rights but that the breach gives rise to no other remedy—though an application to the ECtHR would be likely to be successful in such a case. (On the other hand a declaration of incompatibility, if followed up by a remedial order, will be useful to potential subsequent 'victims', and pressure groups campaigning for the protection of certain rights will welcome such declarations for their value in future cases.)

The declaration of incompatibility does not meet the requirements of the unincorporated Article 13 of the ECHR, which requires that there be effective remedies for breaches. However, a declaration of incompatibility triggers a power on the part of the responsible minister, under HRA section 10, to introduce fast-track secondary legislation in Parliament—a remedial order—to remove the incompatibility. The first remedial order after the Act was passed was made to reverse the position that the burden of proof rests on patients to convince Mental Health Review Tribunals that their detention is no longer warranted rather than on those detaining them (*R. (H) v. Mental Health Review Tribunal, North and East London Region* [2001] EWCA, Civ. 415; [2002] QB 1, CA).

Although the HRA seeks to maintain the sovereignty of Parliament, the remedial order provision giving Ministers power to override legislation for incompatibility with Convention rights in fact negates this principle when applied to the removal of incompatibility in Acts passed after the HRA. This point may be illustrated by the following scenario. Parliament could deliberately pass an Act which in express terms overrides a Convention right. A court could then make a declaration of incompatibility under the HRA section 4. A Minister could then exercise the power under section 10 to remove the incompatibility by a remedial order. The HRA requires the Minister to lay a draft of the order before each House of Parliament for approval by a resolution in both Houses (see schedule 2), but if such an order comes into effect the reality is that a Minister, with simple resolutions of both Houses in favour of the order, has overridden an Act.

This ministerial power may be relatively constitutionally unobjectionable where the incompatibility with Convention rights was an oversight: an assumption that Parliament does not wish to legislate in breach of the UK's international relations or to place the government in breach of international law seems reasonable, and easy remedial action may be justified. But if, as in the above scenario, the incompatibility was deliberate on the Parliament's part, the remedial order provision effectively negates that Parliament's legislative supremacy by entitling Ministers to override its will. Simple affirmative resolutions by each of the two Houses of today's Parliament can effectively repeal formal Acts passed by a previous Parliament, a breach of the normal constitutional principle that the law, especially Acts, should only be changed by Act of Parliament.

The declaration of incompatibility and remedial order provisions preserve comity between the courts and Parliament by preventing the courts from challenging Parliament. But if the courts were to give effect to a remedial order instead of a prior statutory provision (as they would no doubt do) this comity may be undermined unless it so happens that opinion in Parliament is in favour of the court's decision, as it would have been when the remedial order was made, which will not necessarily be the case if majorities have changed in the meanwhile.

Vertical and horizontal effect

By HRA section 6 'it is unlawful for a public authority to act in a way which is incompatible with a Convention right' unless such action is authorized by primary legislation so that the authority could not have acted differently. 'Public authority' is not defined in the Act, save that it includes courts and tribunals, and private bodies when exercising functions of a public nature. Much governmental activity is carried on under discretionary powers, and if a discretion is exercised in breach of a Convention right the courts have the power under section 6 to find the decision to have been unlawful and to quash it or award some other remedy. Thus the HRA could well undermine the comity between the courts and the executive where ministerial decisions are found to be in breach of the Act. It will be remembered from the discussion in Chapter 2 that Griffith—and other commentators—take the view that it is inappropriate for the courts to make what are often highly politically sensitive decisions about whether the public interest in, for instance, national security, outweighs the individual's right to privacy. We shall return to this issue later.

There are two kinds of public authority under section 6. Standard ones such as Ministers, local authorities, and the police are bound by the Act in all that they do, whether it is a public function or a private one, such as purchasing supplies, contracting for the building of roads and so on. Functional public authorities are private bodies exercising some public functions, and they are only bound by the Act when performing public functions. This provision appears to secure that, like most Bills of Rights, the Act only has direct vertical effect, so that it only gives individuals rights against the state. (This is similar to the position of unimplemented directives in European Community law—see Chapter 6.) However, the position is not as simple as this. First, there is no clear concept in UK law of what is a 'public function', which matters if the body performing the function is private. Particular problems arise if activities once performed directly by public authorities are transferred to private bodies. If, for instance, housing or personal care were provided by a local authority, the 'customers' would have the protection for their Convention rights regardless of whether the provision of housing or care is regarded as a 'public function'. If, as is commonly the case under the government policy of using partnerships, privatization, and contracting out—networks—for the delivery of policy, the provision of housing or care is transferred to a private body, the customers lose their 'Convention rights' unless the service is regarded as a public function. Generally such services are not regarded as public functions (see *R. v. Leonard Cheshire Foundation* [2002] EWCA, Civ. 366, CA). But it is anomalous that, for instance, those whose housing or care are provided directly by standard public authorities are entitled to rely on Convention rights, and those receiving the same services from private bodies are not so entitled. This position is likely to lead to developments in private law to control exercises of power by private bodies which may adversely affect Convention rights (see further Oliver, 2000). As and when this happens the civil responsibility of the powerful towards the weak will be increased and a concept of civil citizenship will develop alongside civic citizenship (see Chapter 2).

Section 6 HRA provides that courts and tribunal are public authorities and it follows that they are acting unlawfully if they act in breach of Convention rights. This provision has given rise to debates about whether the Convention rights have full or direct horizontal effect—effect between private parties—in private law. The debate is unresolved at the time of writing. (Wade, 1998, 2000 argues that the Convention rights have direct horizontal effect; Hunt (1998) and Phillipson (1999) suggest that they will have some indirect horizontal effect; Buxton (2000) argues that they will have no horizontal effect.) The most likely development in my view is that the courts will develop the common law so as to make it compatible with Convention rights, but without applying the Convention rights horizontally explicitly and directly.

Horizontal effect has already started to develop in the law of privacy. Privacy is one right that received little protection before the HRA. The courts had found in the pre-HRA case of *Kaye v. Robertson* ([1991] FSR 62) that journalists entering a hospital room where a famous television actor was in a coma were not acting in breach of his right to privacy when reporting on his condition, because no such right existed. (See also *Malone v. Metropolitan Police Commissioner*, [1979] Ch 344, in which it was held not to be tortious or otherwise unlawful for the police to tap a telephone with the consent of the Post Office as there was no right to privacy on the part of a person whose telephone was tapped. This was held to be in breach of Article 8 of the ECHR and the British government introduced a bill to bring UK law into line with the ECHR—now the Interception of Communications Act, 1985.) The fact of the incorporation of Article 8 has led to the courts accepting not only a right to privacy as against public authorities, but also a common law right against private bodies, notably the press. The Court of Appeal indicated, in the case of *Douglas v. Hello Ltd* ([2001] 2 WLR 992, CA), that (per Sedley LJ) there exists a common law right to privacy which is breached where journalists take and publish photographs of a wedding without the consent of the parties, and that an effect of the Human Rights Act is to give rise to a 'horizontal' right to privacy as between an individual and the press. Hence one effect of the HRA has been to increase the protection that individuals enjoy against abuses by other private bodies or individuals, and the responsibilities of private bodies towards their fellow citizens, an illustration of the development of civil citizenship, as well as providing protection against interference with Convention rights by public authorities.

Remedies

A person claiming that a public authority has acted or proposes to act in breach of Convention rights may, if he is or would be a 'victim' of that act, bring proceedings against the authority in court or rely on Convention rights in his or her defence (HRA, section 7). The court may grant such relief or remedy within its powers as it considers just and appropriate, though damages may only be awarded if necessary to afford just satisfaction to the victim (HRA, section 8). This provision is supposed to meet the requirements of the unincorporated Article 13, but as we have noted the declaration of incompatibility where primary legislation cannot be interpreted compatibly with Convention rights would not meet the Article 13 requirement.

Parliamentary safeguards for human rights

By HRA, section 19 a Minister in charge of a bill in Parliament must make a statement either that in his view the bill is compatible with the Convention rights, or that although he is unable to make such a statement the government nevertheless wishes the House to proceed with the bill. If the second statement is made it is bound to generate opposition and put the two Houses and the public and press on notice of a possible breach of Convention rights. The intention of government was that this would provide effective political protection for rights, so that court enforced legal protection in the form of a right on the part of the courts to disapply provisions in Acts that are incompatible with Convention rights would be unnecessary. But it is by no means obvious that public opinion would be on the side of the persons whose rights are being interfered with under statute, especially if, as will often be the case, they are illegal immigrants, suspected paedophiles, drug dealers, and other social pariahs.

The government decided that a Minister could make a statement of compatibility if the proposed legislation was 'more likely than not' to withstand a challenge before the courts (Jack Straw, Home Secretary, HC Deb., 5 May 1999, col. 371). This became known as the 51 per cent rule. In practice such statements have almost always been made.

Parliament has itself established a Joint Committee on Human Rights of the two Houses which scrutinizes bills for compatibility with the Act. That Committee urged the government to make fuller statements of the reasoning behind the section 19 statement, and the government agreed to do so.

Derogation

Lastly, in the list of ways in which Convention rights 'have effect', the government may, by HRA section 1(2) and under the European Convention itself, derogate from the Convention in time of war or other public emergency threatening the life of the nation (Article 15, ECHR). The government did derogate from Article 5 (right to liberty and security) of the Convention on 18 December 2001 to allow for the detention of suspected foreign terrorists against whom there was insufficient evidence for prosecution, and who cannot be removed or deported from the UK, on the passage of the Anti-terrorism, Crime and Security Act 2001. Both the Joint Committee on Human Rights and the House of Commons Home Affairs Committee questioned the need for this derogation. A defect in the procedure was that the derogation order had to be considered before the proposed bill had itself been debated, so Parliament was being asked to consent to the derogation while the nature or extent of the measures to be taken in breach of Convention rights were still uncertain. The question arises whether derogation orders should be permitted to be made before the legislation authorizing the breach of Convention rights has been passed. In summer 2002 the Joint Committee on Human Rights started an inquiry into whether there was a continued justification for the terrorism derogation, and into the broader question of how procedures in Parliament and government could be improved to ensure adequate parliamentary scrutiny of derogation—not only under the ECHR but also under other instruments such as the International Covenant on Civil and Political Rights, in the light of experience with the Anti-Terrorism Act. It seems clear that the government is not subject to proper scrutiny when derogating from such international obligations, and a stronger formal procedure for parliamentary scrutiny against explicit criteria and consent should be put in place.

Democracy, Citizenship, and Good Governance under the Human Rights Act

With these sketches of the provisions of the ECHR and the HRA by way of background, we can now turn to consider their implications for our three themes of democracy, citizenship, and good governance, and the degree to which the HRA has contributed to the juridification and judicialization of the Constitution.

Majoritarianism v. human rights

The debate about the relationship between majoritarianism and the protection of human rights in a democracy was outlined in Chapter 2 and considered further in Chapter 5. On the one hand the argument has been put that democracy, if it is a good thing, must protect minorities against majorities and that this can only be done and should be done by entrenched bills of rights on the American model, which enable a Supreme Court to strike down legislation that breaches the Constitution and in particular breaches a bill of rights. On the other hand Waldron (1999) has argued that if a democratic system is about informed disagreements about fundamental matters such as individual rights—as opposed to being about self-seeking rivalry between self-interested factions—then it is right that *democratic*—political—processes resolve disagreements by majority vote rather than that judges in a supreme court do so, also by majority voting.

A difficulty in applying majoritarian v. human rights arguments to the United Kingdom, for instance, is to what extent it would be considered legitimate for a majority in a legislature to legislate to interfere with individual rights such as are protected in the European Convention and the Human Rights Act *without any particular procedure*—for instance, by simple majority voting on a resolution of Parliament. Waldron, who favours majoritarianism in principle, concedes that 'the legislative process may be made more complex and laborious' and that a 'slowing-down' device is not necessarily an affront to democracy; but only as long as such slowing down is not associated with the idea that there is something pathological about one side or the other in a disagreement of principle (pp. 305–6). The implication is that only the usual standing orders should apply to legislation that interferes with human rights and that—contrary to the position in the USA and other countries—requirements for special majorities in the Parliament, or joint sittings or referendums are inappropriate.

We have already noted in Chapter 5 that a new concept of a 'constitutional statute' appears to be evolving in the case law, so that legislation passed after the HRA came into effect and that is incompatible with the HRA would only be given effect by our courts if the later legislation made it plain that Parliament intended to repeal or override the provision of the HRA with which the later Act was incompatible. The use of express words would legitimate the court disapplying the HRA, but whether it would legitimate the incompatible legislation would again depend upon one's concept of democracy as majoritarian or including protection of human rights.

A further difficulty raised by the majoritarian argument is—which majority in which elected body should be able to derogate from human rights? Should all elected bodies with legislative power be free to do so? The position under the devolution legislation in the UK (see Chapters 13–15) is that the Scottish Parliament and the Northern Ireland Assembly, though they have broad legislative powers, are not competent to legislate contrary to the provisions of the European Convention (or the Human Rights Act). A justification for this is that the United Kingdom is a party to the European Convention and it would clearly not be acceptable in international law or to the British government if any state bodies, including the devolved bodies, were competent to act or legislate contrary to the Convention, as this would place the UK itself in breach and expose it to judgements by the ECtHR and awards of compensation and other remedies in favour of victims. This is in essence a functional rather than a democratic argument—the ECHR mechanisms cannot work if regional legislatures are free to depart from its standards. But what if devolution had taken place when the UK was not bound by international agreements to respect human rights, and its Parliament had not enacted a Human Rights Act? Would the British Parliament have been justified in democratic terms, when legislating for devolution, in limiting the competence of the devolved bodies to legislate in breach of human rights when it was not itself so constrained? Or would leaving them free to interfere with human rights have been only to extend to them the freedom enjoyed by the British Parliament and executive? If it would have been regarded as undemocratic to permit these bodies to use their legislative competence to interfere with human rights, it is hard to see why it should not also be regarded as undemocratic to allow the Westminster Parliament to do so.

Law, Politics, and the Human Rights Act

It will be recalled from our discussion in Chapter 1 that part of the debate about the balance between the political and the legal constitution initiated by Griffith (1979) concerns whether politicians or the courts are best qualified to make decisions where national security and other public interests are in conflict with the rights of an individual to freedom of association, privacy and the like. Griffith's strong preference is for politicians to make these decisions. The HRA is in a halfway house position in the political v. legal constitution debate, denying judges the power to disapply Acts of Parliament but requiring them to intervene where official decisions interfere with rights. This can clearly lead to conflict and sour relations between the courts and government, and undermine the culture of comity that pervades the Constitution.

The ECtHR has developed the doctrine of the 'margin of appreciation' as a way of leaving many sensitive decisions to the governments of the states parties to the ECHR. As we shall see the British courts have adopted a related doctrine, a doctrine of 'margin of discretion' or 'discretionary area of judgment' and deference to avoid quashing sensitive decisions of domestic bodies. The margin of appreciation doctrine belongs to public international law, not to domestic legal systems. Under the ECHR the primary duty to uphold Convention rights lies with the governments of member states, and the ECtHR plays a subsidiary role (*Handyside* case, (1976) 1 EHRR 737, at p. 753, ECtHR). Under Articles 8–11 ECHR a 'fair balance' has to be achieved between the rights of the individual and the general interests of the community (*Sporring v. Sweden* ((1982) 5 EHRR 35, p. 52, ECtHR). This is a matter of proportionality. The ECtHR accepts that the governments of member states are normally best placed to decide whether, for instance, a restriction on a human right is necessary in their society for the protection of national security and the other justifications for interferences set out in Articles 8–11 ECHR. Sometimes, therefore, the role of the ECtHR will be to ask only whether the government of the member state has acted in good faith, carefully and reasonably in the circumstances, thus giving it a wide margin within which to decide for itself what is necessary and proportionate to deal with a perceived threat to democracy, national security, and so on. In other cases the ECtHR will give the state only a narrow margin. The two approaches are illustrated in the *Sunday Times* case (1979) 2 EHRR 245, in which the question was whether the English laws of contempt of court which meant that the *Sunday Times* newspaper was not permitted to publish articles about the thalidomide tragedy while the litigation was not yet resolved were compatible with free speech under Article 10 ECHR. The minority of the judges in the ECtHR felt the court's decision need only be subjected to tests of good faith, care, and reasonableness, whereas the majority applied a more rigorous test, applied article 10 to the decision directly—and found that the interference with free speech was not justified (see Lester and Pannick, 1999, paras. 3.20–3.21; Fenwick, 2002, 34–7).

The British courts have been alert to the possible controversies that judicial decisions against Ministers and other decision-makers—particularly politicians—could generate. They have developed doctrines of proportionality and deference to democratically accountable decision-makers—the latter being similar to but not identical with the margin of appreciation doctrine—to justify non-interference with challenged decisions and actions (see generally Craig, 1999*a*, 2001; Jowell, 2000; Edwards, 2002; Lord Hope in *R. v. D.P.P., ex parte Kebilene* [2000] 2 AC 326, 380–1; Laws LJ in *International Transport Roth GmbH v. Home Secretary* [2002] 3 WLR 344, paras. 69–87).

The proportionality principle requires the domestic courts to ask whether the interference with a Convention right was authorized by law, whether it had a legitimate aim, whether the action in question furthers that aim, and whether there was a reasonable relationship of proportionality between the means employed and the legitimate objectives pursued by the contested limitation (*Fayed v. United Kingdom* (1994) 18 EHRR 393, 432, ECtHR). Would a less detrimental alternative have been possible? Only if the decision-maker can satisfy the court on each of these matters will the interference be justified (see *De Freitas v. Permanent Secretary of Ministry of Agriculture, Fisheries, Lands and Housing* [1998] 3 WLR 675, PC).

A doctrine of deference forms part of proportionality. Schiemann LJ put the position neatly in *R. (Isiko) v. Home Secretary* [2001] HRLR 295, 318–19: 'the courts should recognize that there is an area of judgement within which the judiciary will defer, on democratic grounds, to the considered opinion of the elected body or person whose decision is said to be incompatible'. This doctrine is however hard to apply. In some cases the test applied has been whether the decision-maker could reasonably have decided that the interference with the right was necessary, for instance *R. (Mahmood) v. Home Secretary* ([2001] 1 WLR 840). In *R. v. Home Secretary, ex parte Daly* ([2001] 3 All ER 433) a different test was applied. Lord Steyn stated that 'proportionality may require the reviewing court to *assess the balance* which the decision-maker has struck, not merely whether it is within the range of rational or reasonable decisions' (emphasis added). This comes close to reviewing the merits of the decision. These tests are still however being developed and it is not yet easy to predict how they will apply in a particular case.

The considerations which influence a court's decision to defer to the decision-maker or to intervene include the political sensitivity of the decision, the seriousness of the infringement of rights at stake, whether there has been a clear breach of international law, particularly in the context of human rights (see *R. (Abbasi) v. Secretary of State for the Foreign and Commonwealth Office and Secretary of State for the Home Department*, [2002] EWCA Civ., 6 November 2002, at para. 47), and whether the matter is one on which the courts have expertise, such as dealing with offenders, or a matter for which the executive has the primary constitutional responsibility. The matters on which the courts are most likely to defer include the defence of the realm and its borders (see Laws LJ in the *Roth* case, *supra*) or the making of a moral judgment, for instance about cruelty to animals and whether mounted fox hunting with dogs should be banned (*Adams and others v. Lord Advocate*, Lord Nimmo Smith, Court of Session, 31 July 2002; and see generally Clayton, 2001). In effect these tests promote a separation of powers and function between the judiciary and the executive, based on a range of judge-made principles: the desire to preserve comity between the courts, the executive, and Parliament; a notion that the courts may lack expertise in certain matters, and that the best mechanism of accountability for some sensitive political decisions is to be found in the democratic system rather than the courts. In other words, political and public accountability are more appropriate in sensitive cases than legal accountability. But the willingness of the courts to defer may be influenced by whether they are satisfied that political accountability systems are effective, and if it were to become obvious that they were not, then the courts may become readier to review decisions affecting human rights, even in highly sensitive cases (see *R. (Abbasi) v. Secretary of State for the Foreign and Commonwealth Office and Secretary of State for the Home Department*, [2002] EWCA, Civ., 6 November 2002). This would no doubt affect relations between courts and the executive and undermine comity.

Despite the courts' acceptance of the discretionary area of judgment and deference as justifications for non-intervention, they are at risk of using them as reasons to submit to, rather than merely respect, governmental or parliamentary decisions (see Edwards, 2002). In deferring too readily they would be abdicating their responsibilities under the Human Rights Act. This Act has built into it the potential for conflict between politicians and the courts and it requires that the courts should be ready to assert themselves against politicians, even if this will result in the undermining of comity. Comity and the separation of powers principles were influential in the case of *R. v. Secretary of State for the Environment, Transport and the Regions, ex parte Alconbury Developments and others*

([2001] UKHL 23, House of Lords). The case is complex, but for our purposes the issues were as follows. Objectors to the possible grant of planning permission for the development of land as a distribution centre complained that under the planning legislation the Secretary of State had power, which he was proposing to exercise, to make the decision on the application himself rather than leave it to an independent inspector to do so. The objectors claimed that a decision in favour of the development would be a breach of their civil rights, that the Secretary of State had an interest in the outcome of the decision since he and his department had made policy decisions about development, and thus that it would a breach of their right to 'a fair and public hearing ... by an independent and impartial tribunal' under ECHR Article 6 (see Appendix) for the Secretary of State to make the decision. The fact-finding in the case was done by an independent inspector. The Secretary of State agreed that he was not an independent or impartial tribunal, but claimed that the decision was a public interest and political one and separation of powers principles required that such decisions be made by him as a politically accountable Minister rather than by an independent body such as the courts or an inspector. He argued that the fact that there was recourse to the courts on a question of law met the requirements of Article 6.

The House of Lords found in the Secretary of State's favour, broadly on separation of powers and rule of law grounds. It was for Parliament and Ministers to make planning policy and apply it so long as the courts had the power—as they do—to secure that the appropriate procedures had been followed and that the decision was lawful. It was not necessary for the courts to have full jurisdiction to substitute their own views on the merits of the application. As long as the fact-finding process had been independent and fair, which it had been, and as long as the courts could review the legality of the decision (including incorrect assessment of fact), the requirements of Article 6 were met.

The case raised the question how one defines questions as political in the sense of properly belonging to politicians and being subjected to mechanisms of political accountability noted in Chapter 3, or as legal and properly belonging to the courts or tribunals and thus insulated from politics. These raise difficult issues of democracy and good governance theory. The *Alconbury* case firmly places political decisions as to the public interest in the hands of government, reserving to the courts decisions as to procedural propriety and legality.

Towards Rights-based Citizenship

The Convention and the Human Rights Act together give expression to an eclectic model of citizenship and, through citizenship, of democracy itself. They uphold the autonomy and dignity of individuals by protecting their interests in, for instance, their life, liberty and security of the person, privacy, and freedom of religion and conscience. However, the protection for these interests is not as wide as it might be. For instance the protections against discrimination in the Convention and the Act are limited to discrimination in the exercise of the Convention rights, and do not extend to discrimination in employment. Other UK and EU legislation does however give such protection, though it is limited in various ways.

The special protection given to freedom of thought and conscience, expression, assembly and association encourage and facilitate pluralism, criticism of government, accountability, and tolerance. Given the duty of our courts to have regard to the decisions of the ECtHR, their notions of citizenship and democracy and its links with Convention rights have been imported with the Act into UK law.

The Act improves the machinery from the citizen's point of view for obtaining a remedy for breach of a right by 'bringing rights home' and thus avoiding the necessity to pursue a remedy in the Strasbourg court. It enhances the idea of access to justice as an aspect of citizenship. This was one of the primary rationales for the Act put forward by the Labour Party in its pre-election Consultation Paper *Bringing Rights Home* (Straw and Boateng, 1996), which expressed concern about the weakening of the position of individual UK citizens in their inability to obtain remedies without going to Strasbourg.

The Human Rights Act and good governance

The arrangements in the Human Rights Act and the European Convention are also closely linked with concepts of good governance. The government's White Paper, *Rights Brought Home: The Human Rights Bill* (Cm. 3782), published with the Human Rights Bill in October 1997 noted, amongst other things, that the Bill 'stands alongside our decision to put the promotion of human rights at the forefront of our foreign policy', a reference to 'good governance' policy towards other countries. It was noted in Chapter 3 that good governance, at least as far as international relations and international aid are concerned, requires that proper provision be made for the protection of human rights, which in this context is taken to refer to civil and political rights. The Human Rights Act, by incorporating the substantive rights provisions of the Convention into UK law, indicates a governmental commitment to international good governance standards. Indeed, the provisions in the Act enabling ministers to introduce remedial orders to rectify incompatibilities between UK law and the Convention when a UK court has made a declaration of incompatibility or the ECtHR has found the UK to be in breach illustrate the importance attached to compliance by the British government.

A further issue to do with democracy, good governance, and human rights legislation is the extent to which protection of human rights needs to be 'properly sensitive to British legal and constitutional traditions'—cultural traditions. An important test of the success of the Human Rights Act will be its effect on the internal conduct and culture of government. Before the Human Rights Act came into force the government conducted an audit in each department to secure that their law and practice were compliant with the Act (see Croft, 2000, 2001). A Human Rights Unit was established in the Home Office as a resource on the basis of its experience in taking the legislation through Parliament. But it was mainly concerned to grade the degree of risk of activities being in breach of the Act, rather than seeing the Act as a vehicle for a new human rights culture and putting an awareness of human rights considerations at the centre of policy and decision-making in all parts of the government. The Home Office asked departments to prepare a plan of action for the implementation of the Act to ensure that new policies and legislative proposals would comply with Convention rights. Departments have viewed the Act variously—as a new layer to be grafted on to existing policies, as being more customer-orientated, as a new form of entitlement to benefit for their customers, or as linking in with open government, freedom of information, and data protection. The civil service in developing policy and preparing legislation is required by internal rules to carry out human rights assessments. If the process is effectively performed, judicial review of decisions for breach of human rights will be minimized, and bills and proposals for subordinate legislation would not attract criticism in Parliament for incompatibility with the Convention rights. So far, however, the culture in government is one of mere compliance, and it will take time for respect for rights to become embedded in the culture of public bodies—or private ones. (The main method of embedding a rights culture is through citizenship education in schools, which became part of the curriculum in 2001.)

Beyond the Human Rights Act

The Human Rights Act does not of course complete the business of developing human rights protection and concepts of citizenship, democracy, and good governance in the United Kingdom. The Convention articles are couched in very general terms and there is scope for a more detailed home-grown Bill or Charter of Rights to be developed, that would flesh out the protection of civil and political rights in the Convention. There is particular concern that the protections against discrimination are limited to the enjoyment of the Convention rights and there is no general provision against discrimination. However, both European Community law and UK law provide additional protection against discrimination, for instance in employment and services, on grounds not only of sex and race but sexual orientation, disability, religion, and age. But there is considerable scope for enhancing and generalizing protection against discrimination, for instance on grounds of sexual orientation in relation to the right to marry, to mention but one topical area. Rights not to be discriminated against could be extended beyond Convention rights to all civil rights and obligations. Those in favour of the political constitution (see Chapters 1 and 20) would prefer to see civil and political rights set out in detail in statutes so as to minimize the scope for the judiciary to make essentially political decisions as to whether particular interferences with rights are 'necessary in a democratic society in the interests of national security, public safety', and so on, as provided for in many of the Convention articles. But such an Act would constrain the freedom of action of politicians, in particular cases, which might be inconsistent with the principles behind the political Constitution.

At the time the Human Rights Act was passed the government resisted pressure for the establishment of a Human Rights Commission for the United Kingdom, preferring to allow the Act to settle down first, and concerned about how such a Commission would fit in with, for instance, the Commission for Racial Equality, the Equal Opportunities Commission, and the Disability Rights Commission.

The Northern Ireland Act established a Human Rights Commission for that province (see Chapter 14), and the Scottish executive plans to introduce legislation for a Scottish Human Rights Commission. The arguments for a Commission are, broadly, that it could actively promote a human rights culture and knowledge about human rights, not only in government but in civil society; it could bring test cases and give support to parties whose cases have important human rights implications; it could keep under review the operation of human rights legislation and consider whether further needs for human rights protection were emerging, for instance whether a more detailed, 'home grown' Bill of Rights was required (as the Northern Ireland Human Rights Commission is currently doing—see Chapter 14), and whether social, economic, environmental, or cultural rights should also receive legislative protection.

The Joint Committee on Human Rights undertook an inquiry into the issues in summer 2002. At the time of writing they have not completed their inquiry.

The government does not seem to be adopting a 'joined-up' approach to the subject: in late 2001 the government expressed the view that there were good arguments to move towards a single Equality Commission, but did not link this with proposals for a Human Rights Commission (*Towards Equality and Diversity: Implementing the Employment and Race Directive*, Cabinet Office, December 2001). It would clearly be anomalous if there were to be two Commissions with overlapping remits, and it would be illogical to pre-empt the question of a Human Rights Commission by establishing an Equality Commission before the Human Rights Commission issue was resolved.

Towards constitutional protection of social and economic rights?

It was noted in Chapter 2 that Marshall's definition of citizenship included social and economic rights as being necessary to enable all to participate effectively in society. Social and economic rights include, for instance, rights to housing, employment, health care, education, and a minimum income. Such rights are then substantive elements in a participatory democracy as well as means to ensure the dignity and autonomy of individuals. Yet they are not included in the Human Rights Act because they are not part of the ECHR; nor are they found in the Constitutions of older democracies such as the USA, France, and Germany. (They do find expression in some of the Constitutions of a number of newer democracies, for instance South Africa, and some Latin American countries, though the provisions for giving effect to them are different from those for civil and political rights: see Van Bueren, 2002.) In the UK these rights are given expression in ordinary statutes and statutory instruments and they do not have a specially protected legal status, unless they derive from European Community law, when the UK is bound to implement them.

The UK has ratified a number of international instruments for the protection of social and economic rights, including the Universal Declaration of Human Rights (1948), the International Covenant on Economic, Social and Cultural Rights (1966), and the European Social Charter of the Council of Europe (1961, and the1988 Additional Protocol) but they have not been incorporated into UK law. In 1997 the UK signed up to the social chapter of the Treaty on European Union, which contains commitments to improving working conditions in the Community. In 2000 the European Union proclaimed the European Union Charter of Fundamental Rights, an instrument which purports to set out the rights that already exist against community institutions and member states when acting in compliance with Community law (see Chapter 4). Although the Charter is not applicable in the UK outside the field of competence of the EU, it is likely to have an influence beyond those areas and thus bring into UK law statements of principles in the field of social and economic rights which would start to institutionalize or constitutionalize elements of social democracy.

The question arises whether, and if so how, social and economic rights could be further 'constitutionalized' by being included in the Human Rights Act or a new UK Bill of Rights. To an extent the existing social and economic rights that derive from European Community law—equal pay, paid holidays, parental leave rights, limits on working time, and so on—are already 'constitutional' in the particular sense that it is not open to the UK government or Parliament to repeal them unilaterally without putting itself in breach of European Community law and in danger of having to leave the Community. They are 'entrenched', a characteristic of constitutionality in many countries with written Constitutions.

Before considering the constitutionalization of social and economic rights further, it is worth reminding ourselves that domestic law in the UK does make extensive provision for the availability of some of the basic social and economic rights one would expect to find in a Charter of Social and Economic Rights. But these entitlements do not have special constitutional status, and the remedies in the case of a failure by a public authority to provide a particular individual with these services are generally 'public law' remedies, in the sense that at best a claimant could obtain an order from the higher courts that a public authority reconsider its decision whether or not to provide housing, health services, or education; or, in some few instances, notably cash benefits, an order from a tribunal that a particular benefit be paid or a service be provided, because the claimant has established his or her entitlement. There is at present no general right for an individual to obtain an order that a specific material entitlement be recognized and given effect to—no right to a house or flat in a particular area, no right to an operation now to cure an ailment. There is no equivalent in the UK to the administrative courts in Germany or France or the French Conseil d'Etat which have much more precise powers than courts, tribunals, or ombudsmen in the UK. However, some tribunals or ombudsmen in the UK have power to make specific orders, for instance that a child be admitted to a particular school.

A serious problem with incorporating international social and economic rights instruments and obligations into domestic law on similar lines to the way the Human Rights Act incorporates the European Convention on Human Rights articles is the justiciability and enforceability of such measures, since they are normally couched in broad general terms (see generally Van Bueren, 2002). This is why specific detailed legislation is required for such rights—but that kind of legislation is not normally found in charters of rights or constitutional statutes, as it may have to be frequently updated.

Generally the UK courts are reluctant to make decisions that have substantial implications for the allocation of resources. They tend to regard matters of public expenditure as non-justiciable. For instance in *R. v. Cambridge Health Authority, ex parte B.* ([1995] 2 All ER 129) the refusal of a health authority to give expensive treatment to a child suffering from leukemia was in issue. It was held that it was not for the court to decide between conflicting medical opinions or to decide how a health authority's limited budget should be allocated between opposing claims on its resources. On the other hand in *R. v. North and East Devon Health Authority, ex parte Coughlan* ([2000] 3 All ER 850) the Court of

Appeal, faced with a challenge to a decision to close a home for severely disabled people who had expected to remain there for their lives, quashed the closure decision on the basis that it was an interference with the residents' right to respect for their home, and it was unfair and an abuse of power, being in breach of a legitimate expectation, adding that 'the consequences to the health authority of requiring it to honour its promise are likely to be *financial only*' (para. 60, per Lord Woolf, MR, italics added).

This is not the place for an extensive discussion of the case law on justiciability and priorities in the expenditure of limited public resources, but these cases illustrate neatly the dilemmas facing many public authorities and the problems that would be faced by, and caused by, the courts if they were expected to adjudicate on such matters (see further McEldowney, 2000, 201–5).

Between detailed specific provisions for entitlements (which are relatively easily enforceable by the courts or administrative tribunals) and broadly drafted general rights to health care and other social rights (or, looked at through the other end of the telescope, duties on the state to provide health care and other social services) are gradations of legal entitlement. Ewing (1996) has opposed the entrenchment of a Bill of Rights and expressed a preference for treating civil and political, social and economic rights equally and protecting them by procedures such as scrutiny of legislation by a panel of judges and a constitutional committee in Parliament which could delay legislation for a year if it were contrary to stated principles. This is the approach adopted in Sweden, for instance. Given that a Joint Committee of the two Houses of Parliament scrutinizes legislation for compatibility with the European Convention rights incorporated under the HRA, it might be possible to extend that approach to a statute setting out social and economic rights, perhaps drawn from an international instrument. Such a provision would not necessarily involve the ordinary courts in judicial review of legislation alleged to be incompatible with the statement of social and economic rights.

An interpretive principle, modelled on the HRA, would be another possible position on the scale for the protection of social and economic rights. Lewis and Seneviratne have suggested that the European Social Charter should be incorporated into UK law and should be used as an interpretive instrument when social and economic rights statutes and regulations are in issue (see Lewis and Seneviratne, 1992; see also Ewing, 1999b). Ewing suggests that the courts could be required to interpret social legislation consistently with the requirements of the European Social Charter and related instruments, and the courts could have the power to declare legislation incompatible with those instruments, leaving it to the government and Parliament to decide whether to remove the incompatibility (Ewing, 2001c, 314). He also suggests that, as with the ECHR, the courts could develop the common law so as to impose duties of respect for social and economic rights on private bodies such as employers, through implied terms in employment contracts and, in the areas of tort and delict, through removing the courts' powers to grant injunctions restraining trade unions from acting as they are entitled to do under international instruments but not in UK domestic law.

Major advantages in incorporating international instruments into UK law, as opposed to drafting a home-grown instrument, from a political and practical point of view, are that the UK is already a party to these instruments and thus has agreed to these texts, whereas the exercise of devising a home-grown charter of social and economic rights could run up against disagreements about the content and the wording, and many contributors coming up with their own shopping lists which it would be difficult—though not impossible—to get consensus about. This is what happened with the European Charter of Fundamental Rights (see Chapter 4) which includes a number of rights which one would not normally expect to find in a domestic instrument, but which were important in the domestic law of various member states (for instance a right to free placement services). But at least that Charter is an agreed text, and if it were incorporated into our domestic law in ways similar to the ECHR there would be no room for rearguing the wording of the provisions. This consideration would drive politicians to decide yes or no whether such a Charter was needed and would shortcut wrangling about shopping lists.

Other countries, including countries whose legal systems are based on the Westminster system and the common law, have incorporated 'principles of state policy' or 'directive principles' in their Constitutions, which give constitutional status to social and economic rights. In effect the European Charter of Fundamental Freedoms is a set of directive principles for the EU. Part of the purpose of such principles is to embed them in the practices and culture of those in government. They have an educative function. The courts also give effect to these principles in various ways. The Indian Constitution includes Directive Principles of State Policy which, though not directly enforceable must be taken into account by decision-makers as material considerations. Decision makers will be subject to judicial review if they fail to take these into account (Sorabjee, 1994).

The South African Constitution—which was the product of widespread consultation—includes a comprehensive range of economic, social, and cultural rights. In *The Government of the Republic of South Africa and others v. Grootboom and others* (South African Constitutional Court, 4 October 2000) a number of women and children had been evicted from shacks on privately owned land and claimed that the government and the municipality were in breach of their constitutional rights of access to adequate housing and shelter (sections 26 and 28(1)(c) Constitution of the Republic of South Africa, 1996). The Constitutional Court asked whether the measures taken by the government and the municipality were reasonable, found that they were, and that the constitutional right had not been breached. However, they also decided that the state owed a duty of 'development and social welfare' to those who could not afford to find their own accommodation. In *Minister of Health v. Treatment Campaign* (CCT 8/02, 5 July 2002) the court required the government of South Africa to provide HIV treatment under the right to health care. These rights are, however, heavily qualified. Only 'access' to the rights is required, and only 'within available resources', and the government is bound only to provide the 'progressive realization' of those rights.

By implication social and economic rights, or perhaps more appropriately duties to secure the availability of social and economic provision or facilities, could be justiciable and court orders might be made if the state had acted unreasonably. An approach on these lines could be adopted by British courts if a general legal right to housing and so on were to be legislated for in a Bill of Social and Economic Rights.

Conclusions

The Human Rights Act has introduced a much more explicit concept of liberal democratic citizenship in the UK than had previously been the case. It constitutionalizes those rights by giving them a specially protected legal status. The addition of social and economic rights would add a social-democratic dimension to democracy and citizenship. The HRA is likely to lead to developments in private law, either through legislation or through the development of the common law—which is already taking place in the field of privacy—that subjects private bodies to responsibilities similar to those that lie on public authorities in their relationships with individuals and thus promotes a culture of civil citizenship.

The Act has juridified and judicialized relationships between the individual and state bodies in ways that could well bring the courts into conflict with the executive. But it has also led the courts to articulate explicitly the delineation of relations and lines of responsibility between the courts, and the executives and legislatures in the UK. The *Alconbury* decision in the House of Lords sets out principles for separating political from judicial decisions. As we have seen in Chapter 5, cases on the independence of the judiciary in Scotland have produced new arrangements for securing that temporary judges are not vulnerable to political pressures (see *Starrs v. Ruxton* (2000 JC 208—see Chapter 18)). Thus the HRA has constitutionalized the role of the judge in the sense of explicitly recognizing that constitutional principles are at stake in the appointment of judges and in their relationships with the executive, and requiring government to take corrective action if the arrangements do not accord with these principles.

The fact that the HRA does not permit the courts to disapply an Act of the Westminster Parliament should minimize the scope for conflict between Parliament and the courts, and promote the comity between those institutions, which many of our constitutional arrangements seek to preserve. However, the power of the courts to strike down executive decisions may well undermine good relations between them and lead in due course to the implementation of some of the changes in the court system that are discussed in Chapter 18.

There remain outstanding issues about the direction in which citizenship and democratic theory will develop, in particular whether it will move towards a social-democratic concept including entitlements to social and economic rights. Beyond those are the future development of cultural and environmental rights—the possibilities for the evolution of concepts of citizenship are infinite. Given that the role of the courts in the supervision of governmental—and network—activity is likely to continue to increase under the HRA and devolution legislation, there is a strong case for a bill or charter of social and economic rights, even of cultural and environmental rights, that would at the very least provide principles of interpretation and directive principles or principles of state policy to the courts—guidance as to the principles to be applied when governmental decisions and subordinate legislation are challenged—and thus secure that their decisions are more likely to be in line with public policy and less likely to be challenged as illegitimate and to undermine the relationship between government and judiciary.

7

Elections, Parties, and Referendums

In this chapter we shall consider the operation of the various electoral systems operating in the UK, and proposals for further reform, the related issue of party funding, especially for election campaigns, and referendums. Elections to legislatures and executive bodies are the essence of all representative democracies. The act of voting is part of the practice of citizenship, which requires political equality, and so all votes should be of equal value. Elections and the prospect of re-election for those in power should promote public accountability and good governance (see generally Rogaly, 1976; Bogdanor, 1981; Blackburn, 1995; *Report of the Independent Commission on the Voting System*, (The Jenkins report) Cm. 4090, October 1998; Morrison, 2001, ch. 7; Forman, 2002, ch. 14).

Important aspects of elections have been on the modernization agenda of the Labour party since it came to power in 1997. New—for the UK—electoral systems have been introduced for elections to the European Parliament, the Scottish Parliament, the Welsh Assembly, and the Greater London Assembly. These have involved the introduction of new controls on the financing of election campaigns, and the requirement for parties to register, which was formerly unnecessary. Overall there has been a dramatic juridification and a degree of judicialization of the activities of parties and of election campaigns in the last three years. In recent years a number of referendums has been held, which is something of a departure from the British tradition. Each of these developments has important implications for our themes of democracy, citizenship, and good governance.

Elections—General Issues

Legitimacy of elected bodies

A number of preliminary points needs to be made about the functions of elected bodies and persons before we proceed to consider the main electoral systems that operate in the UK and that could be adopted for the House of Commons and local authorities in Great Britain, if they were to change from the present first past the post system. The House of Commons, the Scottish Parliament, and the Northern Ireland Assembly are legislative bodies. An important aspect of their Members' functions is to give or withhold consent to legislation on behalf of their constituents—this is at the core of the idea of government by consent. As long as the electorate accepts the system as the channel through which their consent to government is given—or through which they may withhold it—election will serve to legitimate legislation and secure that the people cooperate in its application. If they do not perceive the elected body's consent as legitimating legislation, then, in extreme or sensitive situations, withholding of cooperation may result. The lessons of the community charge—a flat rate per capita 'poll tax' to finance local government—in the late 1980s and early 1990s illustrate the point. It was introduced in Scotland before the rest of Great Britain, at the instigation of the Conservative government. There were very few Conservative MPs sitting for Scottish constituencies, which were predominantly Labour. The tax was deeply resented as discriminatory, in that it was not operating (until a few years later) in the rest of Great Britain, and as unfair because the level of the tax was not related to means. Eventually the poll tax had to be repealed in 1992, both for Scotland and the rest of Great Britain, because of widespread refusals to pay and demonstrations against it across the country. The experience of this imposition of rules by a legislature in which Scotland's preferences were not reflected fuelled the pressure for devolution. (The other lesson to be drawn from the poll tax affair is that the electorate may reject legislation, even if it has been duly passed by a representative elected body, if it is perceived to be unfair. Legitimacy and illegitimacy depend on both procedure and substance.)

The House of Commons, the Scottish Parliament, and the Northern Ireland Assembly are also electoral colleges, from which executives are drawn. Elections can therefore serve to legitimate those executives. The executives are directly politically accountable to their legislatures, and via them indirectly accountable to the public, since the elected members in due course stand for re-election.

The Assembly for Wales has no primary legislative power. As we shall see in Chapter 14 the Assembly is technically itself a directly elected executive, but the reality is that it acts as an electoral college for membership of what in Wales is referred to as the Welsh Assembly Government (the WAG), which tends to be regarded as the real executive in Wales (and pressure is building up for the WAG to be regarded as a separate body from the Executive: see Chapter 14). To the extent that the Assembly approves secondary legislation proposed by the WAG, it does have legislative power.

Votes for representatives, delegates, or policies?

In practice voters tend to be governed in their voting decisions by their opinion of the parties or their leaders rather than the candidates or the list of candidates against whom they put their 'X' in the polling booth. Notable exceptions include journalist Martin Bell who was elected as an independent 'anti-sleaze' candidate to the House of Commons in 1997, standing against Neil Hamilton, the Conservative candidate, and Ken Livingstone (formerly Labour leader of the Greater London Council and an MP who had been elected as a Labour candidate but who lost the party whip when he announced he would stand as candidate for Mayor of London), who was elected the first mayor of London in 2000 standing as an independent.

According to traditional representative democratic theory as reflected in case law (*Bromley LBC v. Greater London Council*, [1983] 1 AC 768; *R. v. Waltham Forest Borough Council, ex parte Baxter*, [1988] 2 WLR 257) and the law and practice of Parliament (see

Chapter 9), elected persons are supposed to take personal responsibility for their acts and to exercise their own judgement as to what is in the public interest when deciding how to vote or what contribution to make to debates. This remains the legal position despite the fact that in practice voters normally vote for the party rather than the candidate. As representatives, not delegates, those elected are not supposed to take orders from either their parties or other external bodies. This raises difficult issues about what a member of an elected body should do if he or she gives up membership of the party on whose ticket they were elected and joins another party or sits as an independent. Should that person resign and stand for election again, or may they legitimately serve out the rest of their term, as in law they are entitled to do? We cannot explore those issues further here (see Cowley, 1996), but the relationship of an elected member with their party does raise issues as to the choice of electoral system. For instance, it is more convincing for a member elected on the first past the post system who received more votes—more 'Xs' against his or her name—than any other candidate to claim that he or she is entitled to exercise independent judgement, if necessary changing parties or refusing to follow the party line, than for a member elected on a closed party list to do so.

Turnout and the effective vote

If turnout in elections is low, the bodies in question may not have the necessary degree of legitimacy. This will be particularly problematic for legislative bodies, and less so for executive or administrative bodies such as local authorities. But even if turnout is high, if the results of the election do not reflect the votes of the electors sufficiently closely to give the results legitimacy, there will be a sense of alienation and injustice among the disenfranchised sections of the electorate, resulting in calls for an electoral system which more closely reflects voters' choices—and a downwards spiral in turnout.

Turnout in all elections in Britain compares unfavourably with turnout in other EU countries. The turnout in the UK for European Parliament elections in 1999 was 24 per cent, the lowest in the Community. Local government elections in 2000 had a turnout of 29.6 per cent. The average worldwide turnout in national elections since 1990 is 64 per cent: the turnout in the 2001 Westminster election was 59.4 per cent (Electoral Commission (2001) *Election 2001. The official results* (London: Politico's), 11–2). However, turnout has been falling in many Western democracies in recent years. The reasons may include the softening of the ideological divide between socialism and conservatism, and the weakening of class systems. As fewer voters remember the horrors of fascism and dictatorship before and during the Second World War and during the cold war, appreciation of the importance of voting may be weakening.

It is not clear why, apart from these considerations, turnout in UK elections in particular is low, or how it may be increased. It seems to depend on a range of matters:

- the level of trust in government (the British Social Attitudes survey, summer 2000, showed that 78 per cent of those who trust governments claimed to have voted in the 1997 election compared with only 62 per cent of those who almost never trust governments: see Bromley, Curtice, and Seyd, 2001);

- the nature of the competition between the parties;
- whether an individual's vote is likely to make a difference to the outcome of the election, especially if a historically large majority exists in the constituency for a particular party or if the electoral system gives a low effective vote (i.e. if the number of voters who are represented by a candidate for whom they voted is low);
- the style and content of national media coverage;
- decline in sense of civic duty among younger people; and
- the amount of effort that needs to be put into voting (Electoral Commission, 2001, 13).

MORI conducted surveys for the Electoral Commission around the 2001 election and found that civic duty and habit were among the main reasons people gave when asked why they were certain to vote, if they were. Some, especially young and ethnic minority non-voters, said they were not registered. Where sections of the population are increasingly mobile, failure to register affects turnout. A rolling register of voters has been introduced recently, which should make it easier for people who have moved to register to vote.

A major concern is that turnout may have been affected by disconnectedness between voters and politicians. Greater connectedness should improve turnout. Lowering the age for voting from 18 to 16 could help. Sixteen-year-olds tend to be more connected via their families and schools than 18-year-olds. It may be four or five years after reaching the voting age before a person has the opportunity to vote, and this is too late to acquire the habit of voting. Good habits inculcated young are likely to survive. (There are of course grounds of principle for lowering the voting age also, since 16-year-olds often pay taxes, have jobs, and so on.)

Compulsory voting—which is provided for in Australia, Belgium, Greece, Luxembourg, Lichtenstein, Turkey, and much of Latin America—is an additional provision that would increase turnout (see LeDuc et al., 2002). There are libertarian arguments against such a provision, but there are other civic duties which people are required to perform, including jury service, and one does not hear libertarian protests at that particular intrusion into life. Compulsory voting could produce high levels of spoiled and invalid votes, but that in itself is not a conclusive argument against it. A MORI poll at start of the 2001 election campaign found 49 per cent against and 47 per cent in favour of compulsory voting (Electoral Commission, 2001, 16) so its introduction is not as inconceivable as many would assume. However, as the Electoral Commission notes, compulsory voting would not on its own solve the apparent lack of engagement between potential voters and politics.

Turnout may also be increased by making the act of voting easier. The traditional method of voting has been by personal attendance at polling stations and marking 'X' on the ballot paper, which is followed by manual sorting and counting of the votes at town halls round the country. Recently voting by post has been made easier. In the general election in 2001, 1.4 million votes were cast by post, about twice as many as in 1997. In some local elections in 2002 voting was entirely by post. This increased turnout over the previous local elections in 2000 by 28 per cent on average, and up to 50 per cent in some areas (Electoral Commission, 2002). Other possibilities to encourage voting include digital TV voting, voting via the internet, telephone voting, and voting by text messaging on mobile phones (see generally Coleman, 2001). There were some experiments with these methods in the May 2002 local elections but they did not have a positive effect on turnout (Electoral Commission, 2002). Such methods bring with them dangers of unequal access by citizens to the technologies, and the pressurizing and personation of voters by members of their families and others, which could undermine the integrity of the system. These problems will have to be resolved or risks accepted if and when new technologies are introduced in the voting process.

Candidates for election: how representative should they be?

A major concern in recent years has been the disproportionately low number of women and members of the ethnic minorities that are elected into office (see generally Morrison, 2001; Ali and O'Cinneide, 2002). There are currently (summer 2002) only twelve black and Asian MPs, 1.8 per cent of the total, and only 118 women, 18 per cent of the total. Representation at all levels of elected bodies is well below the proportion of the population that is female or comes from ethnic minorities. This is in large part due to the difficulties that these candidates have in being selected by parties in winnable seats. The parties themselves may be consciously or unconsciously prejudiced when selecting candidates who do not fit the usual model of MP, councillor, member of the devolved bodies, or MEP—which has for long been white, male, and middle aged. To the extent that this is the case, it may suggest discrimination on the part of the political parties in their selection process, which is unfair to the individuals. On the other hand, party selection committees and bodies may also believe—and they may or may not be correct in this, depending on the actual constituency—that potential voters for the party will be less likely to vote for a female or ethnic minority candidate than for standard issue. The underrepresentation of women and members of ethnic minorities in elected bodies may undermine the legitimacy of those bodies in the eyes of women and ethnic minorities, and it may discourage turnout to the extent that it conveys the impression that the concerns and points of view of voters from these groups will not be considered by the elected body (see Mactaggart, 2000; Saggar, 2000).

In the early 1990s the Labour Party sought to increase the number of women candidates in winnable seats through the use of all-women shortlists. This was held to be unlawful discrimination in employment-related decisions by the Employment Tribunal in *Jepson and Dyas-Elliott v. Labour Party* ([1996] IRLR 116, ET). In *Triesman v. Ali* (*Times* Law Report, 7 February 2002, CA) it was held that the Labour Party is a club and is in breach of the Race Relations Act 1976 if it discriminates in matters of membership, and could be sued in the county court. The court did not treat candidate selection as employment-related, thus rejecting the approach in *Jepson* (see Ali and O'Cinneide, 2001, ch. 5). The Sex Discrimination (Election Candidates) Act 2002 has reversed the *Jepson* decision, and permits positive action measures to reduce inequality in the numbers of candidates elected for the particular party, but as its name suggests this measure only applies in relation to sex, not ethnic minorities. Ali and O'Cinneide (2002), in their consideration of the underrepresentation of ethnic minorities, propose that the parties themselves should take steps to promote ethnic minority candidates, especially on party lists, and that legislation is required to permit further positive action and to reduce uncertainty by clarifying the law. The point is not only that elected bodies on which substantial parts of the population are underrepresented may lack legitimacy in the eyes of the underrepresented sections of society, but also that the decisions of these bodies may be defective because those perspectives have not been taken into account.

Electoral Systems

There is a vast range of electoral systems in operation in democracies round the world. An electoral system that is appropriate for body w in country x may not be the right one for body y in country z. It may be that all the needs of a community cannot be met by any one electoral system, and so the least worst system has to be adopted. The working of electoral systems depends on the culture and traditions of the community in which the election is held. Thus, for instance, communities divided on class lines and those divided on ethnic or sectarian lines may require different electoral systems to secure a representative assembly with the legitimacy to enable it to function. Parties subscribing to an ideology may flourish more in one country than in another and the election system may need to balance ideologies against one another to secure good governance and accountability in that climate. The provisions relating to election campaigns, voting methods, and finances also need to be suited to the communities in which they operate and the electoral system. And, of course, elections, though essential, are not the only mechanisms for securing democracy, citizenship, and good governance in a community. Provisions for openness in government, the protection of human rights, judicial review, the design of executive institutions, and additional opportunities for citizen participation in government, are also relevant and can compensate for the limitations of a particular electoral system.

There are broadly three classes of electoral system—the first past the post or plurality system, which is used for House of Commons and local government elections in the UK; preferential voting systems, which are used in Northern Ireland; and true proportional representation systems. In fact these can be mixed—for instance elections to the Scottish Parliament and the Assembly for Wales are by a combination of first past the post and a party list system.

The term 'proportional representation' (PR), indicates that the purpose of elections is to secure that the parties win a proportion of seats in the elected body which corresponds closely with the level of their support, and thus to do justice between the parties. The principal objective of preferential voting systems, by contrast, is to give the voter a choice between candidates and to improve the level of the effective vote. In any system, it is suggested, voters should come before parties (see Jenkins, Cm. 4090, ch. 2). Important though the parties obviously are, we should not lose sight of the importance of the entitlements of citizenship, including equal and real rights to participate in and influence politics, by slipping into discussing the electoral system in terms of *parties* or *candidates* rather than *voters*. This should be borne in mind when weighing up the pros and cons of different systems.

Before the general election in 1997 the Labour Party and the Liberal Democrats had agreed that there would be a referendum on the introduction of an alternative to first past the post for elections to the Commons (Joint Consultative Committee on Constitutional Reform, 1997). The Labour government appointed an independent commission on the voting system for the House of Commons under the chairmanship of Lord Jenkins of Hillhead in December 1997 to recommend an alternative to be put before the electorate in a referendum. (We shall consider the realistic alternatives shortly.) That Commission reported in October 1998 (*Report of the Independent Commission on the Voting System,* (The Jenkins Report) Cm. 4090). It considered the various possible alternatives to the present first past the post system, and recommended a mixed system under which some MPs would be elected by alternative vote (AV), a preferential voting system, and additional members would be elected on open party lists (a propotional representation system) to compensate for the disproportionate results of the constituency alternative vote elections. (One member, Lord Alexander of Weedon, recommended that the constituency members be elected by first past the post instead of AV.) The Commission's recommendations were not considered to be acceptable alternatives to the present system that could be put a referendum, the agreement between Labour and the Liberal Democrats was not renewed when Charles Kennedy became leader of the Liberal Democrats, and it seems unlikely that there will be a referendum or that any change to the system for elections to the House of Commons will be made for the foreseeable future. Nevertheless, pressures for change will continue to be brought to bear on the government in the light of the low turnout, low effective vote, and disproportionality of the present system, and the use of alternative electoral systems in other elections in the UK.

A variety of electoral systems have been in operation in the UK since 1999: a pure closed list system for the European Parliament; an additional member system (AMS) for elections to the Scottish Parliament, the Welsh Assembly, and the London Assembly (this is also proposed for English regional assemblies); supplementary vote for election of the Mayor of London; single transferable vote (STV) for the Northern Ireland Assembly, local authorities, and European Parliament elections in Northern Ireland; and first past the post for the House of Commons and local authority elections outside Northern Ireland. It will be helpful to consider the pros and cons of these systems—reminding ourselves that no system is perfect—against the functions we have identified for elections and how they operate in the cultures and communities in the UK.

First past the post

The system used for the House of Commons (and for local authorities) is known as the 'first past the post', relative majority, or plurality, system (see Jenkins, 1998, ch. 3). There being no requirement that a member should have won over 50 per cent of the votes cast, the candidate with more votes than any others in a constituency is declared elected. Individual MPs are commonly elected on less than 50 per cent of the vote; and so over 50 per cent of votes in many constituencies are 'ineffective' in the sense that they do not produce a member for whom the elector has voted.

This system secures that the House of Commons consists entirely of members sitting for single member constituencies: this is something that no other electoral system can do. Attachment to the idea of the constituency MP is deeply embedded in the culture of Great Britain (see for instance Curtice and Seyd, 2000). First past the post emphasizes the importance of the individual voter and his or her direct relationship with one, identifiable, constituency MP, whereas in list systems the party is inserted between the voter and the representative and there is no direct relationship between a voter and a particular representative.

Under first past the post the national election results generally give an overall majority in the House of Commons to one party, but it will have won the support of fewer than 50 per cent of the voters. In every election since the Second World War a single party government has been formed by a party that received less than 50 per cent of the vote. The closest to a majority vote in the UK in a general election was the Conservative victory on 49.7 per cent of the vote in 1955. On two occasions the largest party in the House of Commons has received *fewer* votes than the runner up: in 1951 the Conservatives won with twenty-six more seats than Labour, having received 230,000 fewer votes; in February 1974 Labour won four more seats than the Conservatives with 230,000 fewer votes.

In the general election in 2001 Labour won 64 per cent of the seats in Great Britain (the mainland political parties do not field candidates in Northern Ireland) on 42 per cent of the votes cast. Fifty-eight per cent of those who voted had not voted for a Labour candidate. The turnout at that election was 59 per cent, so the vote for Labour represented only 25 percent of the electorate in Great Britain. Seventy-five per cent of the electorate and 58 per cent of those who voted had not voted for a Labour candidate. In that election the Conservatives won 26 per cent of the seats on 33 percent of the vote, and the Liberal Democrats won 8 per cent of the seats on 19 per cent of the vote (Electoral Commission, 2001, 220–1). These figures show a rather low effective vote, and must raise questions about the legitimacy of the government and of their legislation and policies which could rebound against the system. (This is not, however, something that seems to bother most of the electorate much.)

Under the first past the post system smaller parties with support fairly evenly distributed geographically have very little chance of winning seats. Labour, the Conservatives, and Plaid Cymru tend to have their voters concentrated in particular areas, and they have an advantage over parties with more widely distributed supporters. The Scottish National Party, the Liberal Democrats, and the Greens, whose support is not as concentrated in particular areas as those of Labour, the Conservatives, and Plaid Cymru, are unable to win seats in anything like due proportion to the level of their electoral support. This is a feature of first past the post. Reverting to the Democratic Audit Criterion 4 ('To what extent do the votes of all electors carry equal weight, and how closely does the composition of Parliament and the programme of the government reflect the choices actually made by the electorate?') the composition of Parliament does not closely reflect choices made by the electorate.

The working of the system, especially at Westminster, involves a sharp division between the party of the government and other parties, especially the largest non-government party, which will be the official opposition. This division, and the adversarial political style that goes with it, has the strength that the governing party is under constant pressure to justify its policies in Parliament—as long as the opposition party or parties are able to be effective in opposing. If a government has a small majority it is relatively easy for it to be dismissed at the next election, or even as a result of one or more by-election losses. The corollary of the fact that a party can win an election in the House of Commons on the votes of as few as 28 or 25 per cent of the electorate (as happened for Labour in October 1974 and in 2001), is that it may lose office on a small swing of votes from one election to another, possibly on the votes of a similar proportion of the electorate for another party. To the extent that removability of a government—electoral responsiveness—is itself a strong accountability mechanism this may be counted a positive aspect of the present system (though the counter-arguments are explored below). On the other hand, the legitimacy, or fairness to the voters (see below) of a system which could replace a government which had, say, 28 per cent of the vote in the previous election with a government that wins, say, 25 per cent of the vote in the subsequent one, is questionable. The first past the post system may also however produce very large majorities for the winning party and it will then require a large swing in the vote for that party to be defeated at an election.

Large majorities also mean that the government does not need to be responsive to pressure from other parties or even from its own backbenchers, as it is not at risk of losing votes. However much the ability of the House of Commons to scrutinize government is enhanced (on which see Chapter 9) its influence over government will be slight if the latter does not need to be responsive and chooses to rely on its large majority.

The fact that the House of Commons is dominated by the two main parties has produced what has recently been tagged a 'tribal' style of politics, which has contributed to the difficulties in reforming the House of Commons so as to reduce the power of the party whips over their members and the composition and chairs of select committees (Wright and Gamble, 2002; see discussion in Chapter 9). It also produces very adversarial politics, as parties see it as their main function to oppose the policies of other parties, almost on principle and regardless of their merits (Finer, 1975; Bogdanor, 1981).

This style of politics might be unobjectionable if the tribal loyalties and political style in the Commons mirrored the attitudes of the electorate; but it is increasingly evident that they do not do so. It is no longer the case that support for the two main parties reflects class divisions. Many middle-class voters voted Labour in 1997 and 2001, just as the votes of many working-class people brought Mrs Thatcher to power in 1979. Voters tend to vote for different parties from election to election, or even within elections: in the elections to the Scottish Parliament and the Welsh and Greater London Assemblies, there were substantial numbers of split votes, cast for a candidate of one party in the first past the post part of the election and for a different party list. An argument against first past the post then is that it encourages and produces tribal politics, with which the voters are not in sympathy. This may account to some extent for low turnout. The adversarial style promoted by first past the post leads to acrimonious relationships between the parties and tit-for-tat allegations of sleaze and impropriety against members of other parties. These are often petty or unfounded. The fact that they are made undermines public and press trust in politicians and politics, which further alienates the electorate.

This adversarial tradition at Westminster is not the only possible political style (King,

2001). In the devolved bodies in Scotland and Wales—where proportional systems are in operation—more collaborative political styles are emerging as a result of the fact that no one party has a majority in any of those bodies, so that cooperation or coalition with other parties becomes essential (see Chapters 13–15).

At local government level, first past the post has resulted in the same party remaining in control of some local authorities for many years, even decades, and this has been identified as the root cause of many problems of inefficiency and unresponsiveness, even corruption, in local government (see Chapter 16). As we shall see the government's response has not been a move to a different voting system. Instead it is introducing new executive arrangements in local government and subjecting local authorities to strong, central control and juridification. My own view is that many of the problems could be overcome by the introduction of STV—my preference—or AMS (on which see below).

Proportional representation systems: party lists and AMS

Proportionality between the parties can be achieved through the electoral system in a range of ways and a range of degrees. These include the exclusive use of party lists, which may be open or closed, and mixtures of the first past the post system or preferential voting (see below) and lists. Closed lists give the voter only the option of voting for one of a number of lists or not voting, and seats are awarded to the candidates in the order in which they are listed by their parties. Open lists give the voter the opportunity to express preferences between the names on the party list. Closed lists were used for the UK elections to the European Parliament in 1999, and a mixed system including closed lists is used for elections to the Scottish Parliament, the Assembly for Wales, and the London Assembly.

Many Western European countries use only party lists for their elections. These are true PR systems since their aim is to secure proportionality between the parties. Party list systems normally involve dividing the country into large regions instead of the usual small House of Commons constituencies. (Israel and the Netherlands are exceptions: the lists cover the whole country.) Thus for elections to the European Parliament the UK was divided into twelve regional 'constituencies'. Each regional constituency is allotted a certain number of seats, and the parties put up lists for the electorate to vote for. It may be permitted for candidates to stand as independents, but they are most unlikely to win seats. Exclusively list-based systems mean that there cannot be the direct relationship with the constituency which a member represents or between voters and an identifiable MP that is possible under first past the post. List systems give the party organizations that select the names of candidates to go on the lists considerable patronage and power. There is at present no statutory regulation of the ways in which parties draw up their lists and the order in which candidates are placed on them. (In Germany the parties are subject to statutory regulation in these matters.) If the party members were entitled to select candidates for the lists in their regions by secret ballot, this would spread the patronage and remove it from the leadership. The pure closed list system used for elections to the European Parliament in 1999 was criticized in the press because it gave the parties a great deal of power, both in placing candidates on the list and in determining the order in which they appeared on each list, and it gave the voters no choice but to vote for one party's list or another, to spoil the ballot paper, or not to vote. Analysis carried out in Scotland and Wales after the devolution elections in 1999 showed that closed lists were clearly less popular than open ones (Curtice and Seyd, 2000).

An alternative to a closed list system under which candidates take seats in the order in which their names appear on the list would be for candidates' names to be entered on the lists in random or alphabetical order, and for voters to be given the right to mark their preferences in order—open or partially open lists. Where open lists are used the voter may indicate the preferred candidate on the party list, and those who receive the most personal votes are elected. Partially open lists allow for a party or a personal vote and the allocation of the party vote by the party usually determines who gets elected, overriding the personal votes received by candidates further down the list (Seyd, 1998). This system has been mooted for future elections to the European Parliament, and it was proposed by the Royal Commission on Reform of the House of Lords (2000) for elections to a reformed second chamber (see Chapter 10). Open lists depend for their effectiveness on the size of the list. With a large list of twenty or so names it would not be easy for voters to express their preferences (if they know enough about the candidates to have any) with any accuracy, and the temptation would be for the party organizations to recommend 'slates' which could defeat the object of the exercise. Lists for elections to the European Parliament and the devolved bodies are relatively short and this should not be too much of a problem.

Overall pure party list systems give a high effective vote in the sense that voters are likely to find that at least one, and possibly several, of those elected is of the party for whose list they voted. This could encourage turnout, although this has not yet been shown to be the case. However, party lists do not enable there to be a personal relationship between the voter and the MP, and the House of Commons European Scrutiny Committee recommended for this reason that elections to the European Parliament should be by first past the post (HC 152, 2001–2). This would not however meet the European Community law requirements for uniform election systems.

An alternative to pure list systems is a mixed system with most candidates elected by first past the post and additional members elected from party lists (AMS). Elections to the Scottish Parliament and the Welsh Assembly are by such mixed systems. If—as is the most likely or least unlikely alternative to the present system—such a system were adopted for elections to the House of Commons, with some 20 per cent drawn from party lists, the low effective vote and disproportionate results of a pure first past the post system would be mitigated, the constituency MP would be retained, and the patronage of the parties in drawing up lists would be relatively small. The Jenkins Commission recommended top-up lists for 15–20 per cent of members in their proposals for an alternative to the present pure first past the post system, though as we have noted, their majority recommendation was that the constituency members should be elected by alternative vote rather than by first past the post (Jenkins, 1998, ch. 7). The possibility of securing the election of one or more candidates from a top-up list even if the constituency MP is unlikely to be of the voter's choice may encourage turnout. This system results in there being two classes of member (as there are in the Scottish Parliament and the Assembly for Wales) with different relationships with 'their' constituents.

Preferential voting: the single transferable vote and the alternative vote

It has already been noted that PR seeks fairness between the parties while preferential voting seeks a high effective vote for the voters and can limit the patronage of the parties. One form of preferential voting system, the single transferable vote (STV), is used for Assembly, local government, and European Parliament elections in Northern Ireland. The use of first past the post for the Stormont Parliament before 1972 had given rise to partisan one-party rule in the Province, a major factor in alienation of the Catholic population which led to the troubles of the last twenty years—a story that vividly brings home the dangers of an electoral system that does not promote public accountability and responsiveness in government and does not take account of the divides in the community—in this case ethnic and sectarian divides (Bogdanor 1999, ch. 3). STV is also used for elections to the Dail in the Republic of Ireland, and in Australian Senate elections. It is not only suited to communities that are divided on Northern Ireland lines. It is used by many organizations in the United Kingdom, including some trade unions and the Liberal Democrats, who use it for internal elections (see generally Bogdanor, 1981; Jenkins, 1998, ch. 6).

Although the system for returning officers counting votes under STV is complicated, for voters the system is simple. Briefly, each constituency returns several members, five— the number for Northern Ireland Assembly elections (see Chapter 14)—achieving an effective vote of 83.3 per cent. The ballot paper in an STV election contains the names of the candidates in alphabetical order, with a note of which party they stand for, if any. Each party may put up as many candidates as it wishes but in practice they will put up as many candidates as the number of seats they expect to win and possibly one more for luck. The voters mark the candidates they support in order of preference. When the count takes place the 'Droop' method is used to allocate seats. A quota for election of a candidate is worked out, being the number of votes cast divided by the number of seats available plus one. Thus the quota in a five-member constituency where 100,000 votes were cast would be 16,666. The first preference votes are counted first and any candidate reaching the quota is declared elected at this stage. Then the votes of the least popular candidates are transferred to the second choices of those electors (in the first past the post system those votes are wasted). The surplus votes of any winning candidates are also transferred at a fraction of their value to the second-choice candidate. Then the votes are counted again and any candidate reaching the quota is declared elected. This process of transferring votes continues until all the seats are filled (Rogaly, 1976, chs. 9 and 10; Bogdanor, 1981, Part V).

The single transferable vote has a number of disadvantages as against first past the post and AMS for the House of Commons. The principal problems are that there are no single constituency MPs, which runs against the cultural attachment to the present system in the UK. The multi-member constituencies under STV are large and this affects the ability of MPs to discharge their functions in the redress of constituents' grievances. On the other hand, these responsibilities diminish as regional and national Parliaments or assemblies are established. STV can also encourage candidates for the same party to campaign against each other. Whether this is a disadvantage of the system or not is debatable. Voters have a choice, for instance between a male or female, 'moderate' or 'extremist', candidate of their preferred party.

However, there are a number of compensating advantages in STV. The effective vote is high—about 83 per cent of voters in five-member constituencies will be represented by at least one MP for whom they have voted, as compared with well under 50 per cent in most UK constituencies at present. This may encourage people to turn out to vote. Proportionality under STV is also high; parties can expect to win seats proportionate within about 6 per cent to their support judged by first preferences (Bogdanor, 1981, 232–50). The contrasts with first past the post are stark. Under STV there would not be the problems about party patronage and the possible legal regulation of the parties that arise in list systems, especially closed lists. The system also gives incentives to the party organizations responsible for candidate selection to be responsive to the wishes of their supporters by putting up candidates whose views reflect those of local people. These may of course be either more moderate or more extreme and uncompromising than those of the party activists.

Another system of preferential voting is the alternative vote (AV) or a variation of it, the supplementary vote. The supplemetary vote was used for the election of the Mayor for London in 2000 (see Chapter 15). AV was recommended by the Jenkins Commission for the constituency members under their proposed mixed system alternative to first past the post for the House of Commons (Jenkins, 1998, ch. 7). Under this system only one candidate can be elected; voters express their preferences in order and if the voter's first preference is for an unpopular candidate, then that preference will be disregarded and the second preference counted instead. AV alone cannot produce proportionality between the parties in parliamentary elections and it cannot produce a Parliament which fairly reflects the support for the parties in the electorate. It does however raise the chances of electors having a member for whom they voted, though the vote might be a second or lower preference. This system, then, continues to make it difficult for supporters of smaller parties to elect their candidates. This is why Jenkins recommended topping it up with additional members from open lists.

These then are the realistically possible alternatives to first past the post if elections to the House of Commons were to be reformed. These alternatives have the advantages of increasing the effective vote and proportionality between the parties in the Commons, and they could increase turnout. But none of them is perfectly suited to the British culture and traditions—and nor in my view is first past the post.

Electoral systems and one-party or coalition government

A major implication of a change to a more proportional system would be the need to form coalition governments. It is unlikely that one party would have an overall majority in Parliament under an alternative system—unless the system were to be AMS with a very small percentage of top-up seats. Elections under AMS to the Scottish Parliament, the Welsh Assembly, and the London Assembly have produced hung assemblies with no single party having a majority. Systems designed to produce proportionality between the parties are likely to have this result. In Scotland and Wales this has produced coalitions: a 'programme for government' and a 'partnership agreement' respectively were reached between the participating parties.

On one view these arrangements have produced 'disproportionality of power' in that the Liberal Democrats, the minority party to both coalitions, have considerable power, more than might be expected from its electoral support. But then the Labour government at Westminster too might be regarded as having disproportionate power—100 per cent on 41 per cent of the UK vote. If there were a Labour-Liberal Democrat coalition at Westminster at present (which of course is not currently on any party's agenda), Labour plus the Liberal Democrats would have 100 per cent of the power on the basis of 59 per cent of the votes, which seems to me to be an improvement over 41 per cent. Unless a government of national unity is formed with all parties included, disproportionality of power is inevitable in any system.

A strongly held view against PR for the House of Commons in some circles is that the coalition government it would entail would be a bad thing and one-party government is to be preferred even if the voting system is unfair to voters for particular parties. Italy could be pointed to as a country that has moved to a mixed system with an element of first past the post to encourage the formation of one-party governments, after many years of unstable coalitions under party lists.

Let us consider the disadvantages that are alleged to flow from coalition as compared with single-party governments (see generally Jenkins, 1998, ch. 4). With members drawn from a wide range of parties, a government might take time to hammer out a programme after the election and this could be damaging to the country. The problems caused by delay in forming a new coalition government after an election are real—under the present system a Prime Minister is appointed generally within hours of the election result being known. But many countries live with transitional arrangements and caretaker governments—these problems are not insuperable or conclusive of the argument.

Coalition governments can be weak and unstable. Such has been the experience of Italy and the Netherlands in recent years, for instance. (On the other hand Italy's economy has been relatively successful despite her political problems.) It is clear that there are advantages in a system that encourages stable government by discouraging a proliferation and fragmentation of parties. But there are other ways of doing so apart from the choice of voting system, including, for example, the requirement (which is part of the present system) for candidates to pay deposits which are forfeit if a specified proportion of votes is not won. The formation of coalition governments, though more likely under PR than under first past the post, is by no means the inevitable result of proportional representation, and nor is a proliferation of small parties.

Nevertheless there is of course a possibility that coalition governments would have to be formed if the present discrimination against small parties and their supporters in the UK Parliament's electoral system were to end, whether naturally by a surge in support for those parties in particular areas, or by the introduction of another electoral system. But it is far from obvious that coalitions are to be avoided. It depends upon the coalition, especially its stability (see below).

Another argument against coalition is that the voters end up with a government for which they did not vote and a programme cobbled together by the coalition partners (like the programme for government and the partnership agreement of the Scottish and Welsh executives) that was not put to them. First, this is not necessarily a bad thing. And in any event it need not be the case. In the Federal Republic of Germany, for example, coalitions have been formed for most of the period since 1949 consisting of one or other of the main parties (the SPD or the CDU/CSU) and the FDP, the small 'centre party', or the Greens. But before each election the FDP (and latterly the Green Party) has indicated which of the other parties it would be prepared to join in a coalition, or what its terms would be for participation in a coalition, and voters therefore have known in advance what they were voting for or against. If the smaller parties in the United Kingdom announced before the election with which party they would be prepared to join in a coalition, or alternatively on what terms they would join a coalition with either of the main parties; or if the main parties were to indicate whether and on what terms they would be prepared to include the smaller parties in a coalition—then the electors would know what they were voting for (or against) when casting their votes.

As far as the objection to the programme 'cobbled together' by a coalition is concerned, the point is weaker than it seems. It implies that voters endorse the manifesto of the party they vote for so that it would be unfair to lumber them with another programme. But in practice voters do not by any means intend approval of every item in the manifesto of the party they vote for; and in some elections they have approved of very few of their own party's pledges and a substantial numbers of the pledges in the manifesto of the opposing party (Rose, 1976: 305–9).

The view that coalition government is undesirable, or, more accurately, more undesirable than single-party government, is often based on the argument that single-party governments are good because they are strong and effective whereas coalitions are bad because they are weak and indecisive. Again these assumptions need to be examined. A single-party government will not necessarily be either strong or effective. The Labour administrations from 1974 to 1979 did not succeed in beating inflation and revitalizing the economy; to this extent their policies were ineffective. And if strong government means decisive government, that administration was not strong either, for it changed policies quite drastically during the period, particularly in the late 1970s when, at the behest of the IMF, it reversed its policies of high public expenditure and embarked on a series of cuts. Equally it is very debatable whether the Conservative government in the 1980s and 1990s was effective: it managed to get most of its legislation (including the poll tax) through Parliament and if that is the measure of effectiveness then it succeeded. And if the Conservative governments under Mrs Thatcher are to be regarded as having been strong and decisive, there would by no means be agreement that this was an unmitigated blessing. Judgements about whether a government is good, strong, and decisive or stubborn and intransigent are highly subjective.

In truth the argument that single-party government is effective is bedevilled with the ambiguity of that term used in that context. And if strong government means determined government that does not give in to pressure or respond to criticism, it is not necessarily a desirable quality: it can come close to authoritarianism and a lack of accountability. Often effectiveness and strong government are good if one approves of the policies in question, and bad if one does not.

Even if it were the case that single-party governments can be counted on to be strong and effective, this can only be regarded as advantageous if the single-party government is also responsive and accountable. No one would seriously suggest that a strong, effective tyrant was a good thing. But the present electoral system does not promote responsive accountable government. Where a government has a safe majority there is very little to make it responsive to pressure from inside Parliament (see Chapter 9). Its own back-benchers may be able to exert some influence over its activities, and a government may succumb to such pressure in order to avoid the embarrassment of a backbench revolt; but these pressures will not generally do more than secure minor adjustments to government policy. They were not sufficient to deflect the Conservative government from introducing the community charge, privatizing the water industry, and implementing other unpopular legislation in the late 1980s and 1990s. The events of November 1990, which led to the replacement of Mrs Thatcher as Prime Minister by John Major were unusual: they reflected concern both in Cabinet and among Conservative backbenchers about the party's ability to win the next election, rather than a desire to improve the day-to-day accountability of the government to the House of Commons.

A taste of the effect of coalition government on ministerial responsiveness was had in the period of the Lib-Lab pact from 1977 to 1978. The Labour government had to pay heed to the wishes of the Liberals, who sustained the government in power by agreement until 1978 and thereafter on an ad hoc basis (Steel, 1980, chs. 4, 5, 6; Marsh, 1990). The fact that the government had to placate backbenchers of other parties during this period enhanced the influence of the House of Commons and hence the accountability and responsiveness of the government.

Marsh concluded that an arrangement such as the Lib-Lab pact 'needs to be buttressed by an enlarged framework of institutional and procedural changes' including stronger Commons committees (Marsh, 1990). But stronger committees cannot come into exist-ence from widespread wishful thinking alone. The decision of the House of Commons to retain the whips' patronage over appointments to select committees in July 2002 suggests that stronger committees will not emerge (see Chapter 9). One could add that better access to information (see Chapter 8) and more resources for parliamentary parties are needed to improve their contributions to the policy process (see below). Electoral reform alone would not solve the problems. But positive lessons about coalition government or pacts could be learned from the Lib-Lab pact and from experience in Scotland and Wales if and when a move to PR for the House of Commons is under consideration.

General conclusions about electoral systems

My own preference is for the introduction of AMS for elections to the House of Com-mons and STV for local authorities. These systems would produce bodies that more closely reflected the preferences of voters, coming closer to meeting the Democratic Audit Criterion 4. The small majorities or formation of coalitions that this would lead to should produce a more cooperative and less adversarial political style and a more responsive government, increase the influence of backbenchers and thus the effectiveness of their scrutiny functions, be fairer to voters, and reduce the rewards that parties currently reap from accusing members of other parties of sleaze. The coalitions that AMS would make necessary at Westminster would promote cooperation between the government at Westminster and the devolved bodies more than first past the post. The latter makes it likely that there will be a single party in control at the UK level that is different from the executives in the devolved levels and thus that there will be conflict between the two levels which could undermine cooperation. This could lead to central control of the devolved bodies through greater juridification.

At local government level the introduction of STV would prevent the same party from retaining control for many years and thus reduce the level of inefficiency, complacency, unresponsiveness, and even corruption in local government. This would enable the government to reduce the degree of central control over local government to some degree, though in my view no government committed to improving public services will risk relaxing its grip entirely (see Chapter 16).

However, in my view no system of proportional representation or preferential voting is likely to be introduced for the House of Commons for many years, if at all. It is not in the interests of the party in power, nor of the whips of the Conservative or Labour Party to give up the first past the post system. Those parties enjoy the tribal system that operates in the House of Commons (see Chapter 9) and the whips enjoy their power over their members. The implications of this reality are serious and will be considered in the chapters that follow. In sum, if first past the post is retained, turnout in elections to the House of Commons will continue to decline, and will do so more than if a proportional or preferential system were introduced; the legitimacy of government will become weaker; the adversarial party system will promote distrust and a culture of suspicion of politics; the scrutiny of legislation by the Commons will continue to be slapdash; and government will not be held to account effectively in the Commons; conflict between the government at Westminster and the devolved bodies will result in increasing juridification of relations between the different levels. This will give the judges greater power to adjudicate on disputes between the centre and devolved bodies.

As it becomes clear that there is an accountability vacuum in Parliament, the judges will become more willing than they currently are to impose legal accountability on government, and to expand their jurisdiction in judicial review as parties dissatisfied with poorly drafted, often unscrutinized legislation and poor-quality ministerial decisions turn to the courts. Judicial deference to political decision-makers may weaken. Increased judicialization will no doubt sour relations between the courts and the executive, but it may resolve senses of injustice on the part of litigants. There will be a shift from the political to a law-based Constitution. This is not necessarily a good thing, but in my view it is what will surely happen if the electoral system continues to produce adversarial politics and ineffective political accountability systems in Parliament and local government.

The Funding of Political Parties and Election Campaigns

We turn now from electoral systems to the provisions regarding the funding of political parties. The pattern of financial support for the parties from private sources has changed in the last decade or so, reflecting changes in the class system and the economy (in particular, union membership has dropped, and with it financial support for the Labour Party). Party policies have shifted, with Labour winning support for its policies from voters who would previously have supported the Conservatives, and this has contributed to the loss of financial support for the latter party.

Shortly after the 1997 general election the new Prime Minister, Tony Blair, asked the Committee on Standards in Public Life to review issues in relation to the funding of political parties, and to make recommendations as to any changes in present arrangements (see generally Hansard Society, 1981, 1991; Blackburn, 1995; Ewing, 2001b; Morrison, 2001, ch. 6; Forman, 2002, ch. 13). Concerns centred around a number of issues. The amount spent by the parties on election campaigns had spiralled in a kind of arms race. The parties were having increasing difficulty raising the funds they felt they needed to match their opponents' campaigns and to provide for their day-to-day operations between elections. Until recently the pattern had been for Labour to raise funds from individual members and affiliated trade unions and the Conservatives to raise funds from their members and companies. But both parties were experiencing difficulties raising sufficient funds from these sources, and their memberships had fallen. The Liberal Democrats relied heavily on contributions from their members. All parties had turned to wealthy individual donors for funds and had put on fund-raising events such as dinners and receptions attended by prominent politicians. Substantial funds had been raised by the Conservative Party from foreign or non-resident donors—about ten million pounds in the run up to the 1997 election.

All this had generated suspicion among the public, fuelled by the press and by politicians in other parties, that donations to the parties were buying access to politicians and, beyond access, influence over policy and particular decisions, or honours, notably peerages. A major scandal was the revelation that Bernie Ecclestone, a motor-racing tycoon, had made a one million pound donation to the Labour Party before the 1997 election. He had subsequently had a meeting with Tony Blair at which there had been discussion about the government's plans to stop tobacco advertising. Labour then announced that Formula One racing was to be exempted from the policy to ban tobacco advertising at sporting events. The inference that many commentators drew was that Labour was repaying a favour. The party then returned the donation, but public confidence in the integrity of the parties and government had been seriously damaged by that, and other, money-for-influence scandals. It was this which led Tony Blair to refer the matter to the Committee on Standards in Public Life.

We shall turn to the report of the Committee on Standards in Public Life and the government and parliamentary response to it shortly, but it is worth pointing out that there have been numerous further allegations of donations for favours since 1997, including concern about the award of a peerage to Michael Ashcroft, the Conservative Party treasurer and at that time a resident in Belize, who had made substantial donations to the party; the fact that the government awarded a contract for the provision of smallpox vaccine doses in April 2002 to a company which had made a donation to the Labour Party; and the fact that the Prime Minister recommended to the Romanian government that it should sell its state-owned steel industry to Mr Mittal, a Labour party donor, despite the fact that the British steel industry was in direct competition with the Romanian steel industry. These allegations of impropriety have all been strenuously denied by the government, and by the Conservative Party, but the fact of these repeated problems has given renewed momentum to pressure to free the parties from the need to rely on wealthy private donors, through some form of public funding or limitations on election spending.

The Committee on Standards in Public Life reported in October 1998. It rejected increased public funding (as we shall see there is a modest amount of such funding for parties), except for policy development work and the work of the parliamentary parties. The Committee proposed the establishment of an Electoral Commission with responsibility for enforcing proposed new provisions about the capping of party political election campaign spending, banning of donations from foreign sources, disclosure of donations above a certain figure, and a range of other matters (Fifth Report of the Committee on Standards in Public Life, *The Funding of Political Parties*, Cm. 4057, October 1998). The government accepted most of these recommendations (*The Funding of Political Parties in the United Kingdom: The Government's Proposals for Legislation in response to the Fifth Report of the Committee on Standards in Public Life*, Cm. 4413, July 1999), and the Political Parties, Elections and Referendums Act 2000 (PPERA) was passed and came into effect in time for the general election 2001.

PPERA is long and complex, and it is not our purpose to go into it in any detail (for discussion see Ewing, 2001*b*). It establishes an Electoral Commission with broad responsibilities in relation to elections (see below) and it introduces a detailed regulatory regime for political parties, an example of new 'hard law' juridification of political activity. The Act amends the previous rules about election expenditure, mostly found in the Representation of the People Act 1983, and introduces new provisions. It may be helpful to summarize briefly the law as it stands after the PPERA in relation to the funding of political parties and election campaigns for the House of Commons, before considering its general implications.

The Electoral Commission

The Electoral Commission established under PPERA has the responsibility for implementing and monitoring the new controls on political party funding and campaign expenditure imposed by PPERA, for proposing ways in which the electoral process and law could be modernized and—oddly—voter education. It will be convenient to consider it at this point, although not all of its activities are related to funding. It also has responsibilities in relation to referendums (see below). It has taken on responsibility for local government boundary reviews and in due course it will take on responsibility for making proposals for unitary local government where regional assemblies may be established (see Chapter 15), and parliamentary boundary reviews. The Commission is independent of the parties and Parliament. Its members—between five and nine in number—are appointed by the Queen on an address from the House of Commons, with the agreement of the Speaker, as chair of a new Speaker's Committee. The leaders of the political parties in the House must be consulted on appointments, though their agreement is not necessary. The majority of members of that committee are back-benchers chosen by the Speaker. The members of the Commission have substantial security of tenure. The Commission lays a report on its functions at the end of each financial year before the House of Commons. It also reports to the Speaker's Committee, which in turn reports to the House annually. And it reports to the Home Secretary—who has responsibility for elections—on issues relating to elections and referendums.

The Commission has some executive powers, for instance the making of payments under a scheme for the distribution of policy development grants to opposition parties, and funding in referendum campaigns; it also has legislative power in that it makes regulations prescribing the form and content of the annual accounts of the parties and the appointment of auditors of the parties' accounts. But major executive functions remain with the relevant Secretary of State, for instance, over the making of regulations on elections and the implementation of boundary review recommendations. Its functions are mainly supervisory and advisory. It is thus supposed to be immunized from political controversy. Overall the arrangements for the Electoral Commission are carefully designed to secure a non-partisan system of supervision, monitoring, and review of elections and election law, in line with principles of good governance, and maintaining the legitimacy of the system.

Election campaigns—candidates' and third-party expenditure

- There have long been limits on what may be spent by candidates in their constituencies. These are related to the number of registered voters, and the average is currently about £8,000.

- Candidates' agents must submit detailed accounts of expenditure and donations received for election campaigns.

- Third parties are not permitted to spend more than £500 in support of or in disparagement of a candidate. (This is the response to the finding by the European Court of Human Rights in the case of *Bowman v. UK* (1998) 26 EHRR 1 that the previous limit of £5 was an unjustifiable restriction on free speech. This is in contrast to the position in the United States where restrictions on the right to campaign for or against candidates are considered an unconstitutional breach of the right to free speech: *Buckley v. Valeo* (424 U.S.I.1976). The result is that money buys influence in American election campaigns, and can distort the outcome of campaigns. See Ewing, 1996.)

- Candidates receive certain benefits in kind: they may send out their election address free of postal charges to all electors; they are entitled to the free use of a room or rooms belonging to local authorities for election meetings.

These aspects of election law are generally considered to be working well. Lack of money does not prevent candidates from standing and there is no evidence that they are unable to campaign effectively when limited in these ways—though increases in spending on campaigning at constituency level have been shown to increase the vote for the party in the constituency (Johnston and Pattie, 1995). Much of the effective campaigning is done at national level. Some of the rules relating to accounts and donations are however onerous and technically difficult to operate and this is where the juridification of activity is most problematic.

Election campaigns—the national parties

The parties are entitled to free party election broadcasts, the length and number of which are determined by the television companies after consultation with the Electoral Commission. Apart from this, the national parties have no legal entitlements to benefits in cash or in kind for their election campaigns. Before the Act there were no limits on the amounts that could be spent by the national parties on election campaigns, no legal requirements that accounts of expenditure and donations be published, and no limits on the permissible sources of donations. PPERA has changed this in a number of ways.

- The amount that parties may spend on an election campaign for the House of Commons is subject to a statutory cap. For the 2001 election this was £24,000 per contested constituency or £15.8m. in the year before the poll (not an easy timespan to operate to since it is not usually known when an election will be held). The cap after 2001 is £30,000 per constituency or £20m. in the year before the poll. (The Electoral Commission Report on spending at the 2001 election showed that the Conservatives spent £12.8m. and Labour £11m. and the Liberal Democrats £1.4m.: Electoral Commission, 2002).

- Only permissible donations may be accepted. Impermissible ones will be forfeit by the Electoral Commission. Donations are permissible if they come from those who are registered to vote in the UK parliamentary elections or if they are made by companies registered in an EU country with business in the UK. Thus donations from foreign sources are banned. There is no cap on the size of donations.

- All donations over £5,000 must be notified to the Electoral Commission and the identity of the donor will be published.

- A person or organization other than a registered political party is required by law to register as a 'third party' if intending to spend over £10,000 in England (£5,000 in Scotland or Wales) in publishing material on behalf of a political party or a category of candidates. There is a limit of £800,000 on what a third party may spend in this way. In the 2001 election only ten third parties registered.

These are all new provisions, introduced largely on the recommendations of the Committee on Standards in Public Life. The principles of fairness and transparency behind them are broadly accepted. However, the Act has turned out to be extremely detailed. The regulations bring with them elaborate machinery for reporting, and onerous obligations for the parties. Grants of £700,000 were provided to parties to enable them to meet the new obligations in time for the first election, in 2001. PPERA is an example of intense juridifica-tion including a degree of judicialization of previously unregulated activity, with about seventy-five criminal offences which could be prosecuted by the Director of Public Pro-secutions, and the possibility of judicial review of the Electoral Commission's activities.

What alternatives could there have been to deal with the concerns about unequal funding and inappropriate influence by donors? Doing nothing would have been one but press and public opinion—the culture of suspicion of which O'Neill (2002) has complained—about money for favours made this impossible. (It is worth pointing out here that openness about donations to parties since the PPERA may have actually increased suspicion of parties. This cuts both ways. If it is the case that a donation has bought favourable treatment, then suspicion is a good thing. If the press and public draw unfounded adverse inferences from the fact that a donation has been made, it is a bad thing in that it undermines trust.) Regulating the honours system, including the award of peerages, would have been another way of counteracting concerns about donations. Or a much lighter touch system, based on trust. But trust in parties is not strong, either between the parties or in the press and the public. This is an area in which a relatively high degree of formal juridification and judicialization had become inevitable.

Public funding for parliamentary activity and research

As far as public funding is concerned, a distinction is drawn between the extra-parliamentary party political activity, such as conducting election campaigns and run-ning the constituency parties, and the activities of the party organizations in Parliament. There has been an injection of funds to enable the parties, including the opposition parties, to perform their parliamentary functions (see Sear, 2002, House of Commons SN/PC/1663).

- 'Short money' is paid to the opposition parties in the House of Commons, which may be spent only on parliamentary activity. Payment is made on a formula accord-ing to the number of seats won at the last election and the number of votes gained by the party. There are additional payments for travel and for the Leader of the Oppositions's Office. Allocations for 2002–3 are as follows: Conservatives £3,459,536; Liberal Democrats £1,174,410; the other parties received sums calcu-lated on the same formulae. (These grants are named after Edward Short who introduced them when he was Leader of the House in 1975.)

- 'Cranborne money' (named after Lord Cranborne, Leader of the House in 1996, who introduced it) has been paid for similar purposes to the opposition parties in the House of Lords since 1996. For 2002–3 the Conservatives' allocation is £230,556; Liberal Democrats receive £69,166.

- Under PPERA a new sum of £2m. annually is paid to opposition parties in Parlia-ment via the Electoral Commission as Policy Development Grants for the develop-ment of policies to include in their manifestos for British and European elections.

Additional public funding for the parties?

State support for the political parties at Westminster is relatively modest. Apart from the provisions noted above (and money provided for European Parliament election campaigns), there is no public funding for political parties in the UK. An increase in public funding was rejected by the Committee on Standards in Public Life in its 1998 report and by the government in its response. However, the issue was again under consideration in Spring 2002 because of continuing public concern about 'money for favours' where large donations are received by the parties, especially by the party of government, from individual or corporate donors. Examples of these donations have been noted above.

Public funding could take one or more of a number of forms (see generally Hansard Society, 1976, 1981, 1991; Report of the Committee on Financial Aid to Political Parties (the Houghton Report), Cmd. 6601, 1976; Ewing, 1987; Blackburn, 1995; Committee on Standards in Public Life, Cm. 4057, 1998). For instance, the state could match money raised by the parties privately, either pound for pound or in some other proportion; or tax on donations could be reclaimed by the parties; or taxpayers could nominate a sum from their tax to be paid to a party; or the parties could receive a sum per vote cast for them in the most recent election. Public funding could be limited to parties which field candidates in a certain number of seats, and to parties which win more than a certain number or proportion of votes. Total public funding overall or per party could be capped. There could be controls on how the funds may be spent, and duties to account for it.

But increased public funding for parties, especially for extra-parliamentary party organizations, is controversial. The arguments in favour of public funding are, briefly, as follows:

- The political parties are important in a democracy and they must be able to carry out their work of campaigning in elections and, when in opposition, providing effective opposition and preparing policy for when they may be elected into government. For various reasons they are unable to raise sufficient funds from private sources.

- The fact that substantial donations have to be disclosed acts as a deterrent for some potential donors who do not want to find themselves accused of trying to buy influence, and thus the parties' ability to raise sufficient funds for their needs privately is further restricted.

- Parties or MPs may find themselves under pressure from private financiers to support particular policies, as some Labour MPs were in the summer of 2002 when trade unions switched support from constituencies with whom they had been linked to others whose MPs were more sympathetic to the unions' causes. (The MPs concerned strenuously rejected any suggestion that unions were entitled to demand of 'their' sponsored MPs that they promote union policy.)

- As the parties are unable to raise sufficient funds in acceptable ways privately, public funding should be made available.

- Public confidence in the parties and in politics generally is undermined by publicity about private donations and fundraising, which are suspected of buying influence and favours, and this is especially damaging when the allegations are unfounded.

- Public confidence in politics can only be recovered by removing or reducing the pressure on political parties to seek and accept such donations by substituting public funding.

- Public confidence in the honours system is undermined if there are reasons to believe that honours are granted in return for political donations.

There are also arguments against public funding.

- It is wrong to compel taxpayers to make payments towards parties of whom they disapprove. (On the other hand we are all compelled to pay tax that will be spent on things of which we disapprove and we are expected to put up with it.)

- There are worthier priorities for public expenditure (but that would be a matter for the government and Parliament if there were to be legislation for public funding).

- The parties could become less engaged with their members and supporters if they relied on public funding, thus reducing civic engagement and encouraging the trend towards disconnectedness in the electorate, since this would result in fewer people being involved in party political activity and fund-raising activities.

- The parties could become less responsive to public opinion if they did not have to rely on individuals to provide their financial needs and this would be unhealthy for democracy and lead to the ossification of policies and possible further reductions in turnout.

- It would be more difficult for new parties to emerge if they were competing with parties in receipt of public funding.

- Public funding may be wasted—there is little evidence that poster advertising, for instance, influences voters in favour of the party advertising: some posters might have the reverse effect (the Conservatives' 'Demon Eyes' advertisement in the run up to the 1997 election is an example).

- Once public funding is introduced, the parties will treat it as a milch cow and vote to increase the funding as and when they are under pressure, the costs will escalate and the parties will, indeed, become less responsive to voters as they come to rely on them less for their finance.

My own view is that the priority is to try to neutralize the atmosphere of distrust and suspicion that surrounds the parties, by enabling them to function and to oppose, develop policies and campaign with adequate funds at hand and without having to rely on large donations from private sources. Some public funding would on balance be desirable, and most of the substantial disadvantages could be overcome. Funding could be linked in part to the number of votes won by the party in the previous election, in part to party membership, and in part to privately raised funds. There could be an overall cap on the amounts in public funding payable to the parties. Parties would be required to publish their accounts, including of course accounts of how public funding has been spent. Increases in funding should require either primary legislation or a proposal from the Electoral Commission in order to prevent MPs from treating public funding as a bottomless purse available to their parties. Conditions of this kind would encourage parties to be responsive to the voters, to keep up their membership, and to raise funds for themselves, while also enabling them to perform the functions expected of them in a democracy.

Referendums

There has been an increase in the use of advisory referendums in the UK over the last thirty years or so (see generally Bogdanor, 1981; Fifth Report of the Committee on Standards in Public Life, Cm. 4057, 1998; Commission on the Conduct of Referendums, 1996; Morrison, 2001). A referendum was held in 1975 on whether the United Kingdom should continue its membership of the European Community. Referendums were held in 1978 and again in 1998 on devolution to Scotland and Wales, and in 1998 on devolution to Northern Ireland. Referendums were held on whether there should be a Mayor for London, and in 2001 on whether new mayoral executive models should be adopted by local authorities. There have to date been no binding referendums, and these would be regarded as severely undermining principles of governmental responsibility.

The traditional argument against referendums is that they represent abrogations by a government of its duty to decide what policies to adopt. The EC referendum in 1975 was held largely because the Labour government of the time was divided about continuing membership (Bogdanor, 1981). However, as that referendum shows, a referendum cannot excise fundamental disagreements from the system permanently. As Bogdanor has observed of the referendum: 'It can articulate a submerged consensus, but it cannot create one' (1981, 91). Resort to referendums may undermine governmental responsibility by enabling a government to blame the voters if a policy that was submitted to a referendum turns out to be mistaken or unpopular. And when voting in a referendum people may be expressing their disillusionment with the present government, rather than their views about the referendum question.

The arguments in favour of advisory referendums include the following. Even if a government considers that a certain policy is right, it should not impose it upon an unwilling community. If it did so, those affected might withhold cooperation with the policy in question and regard it as illegitimate. A referendum can give legitimacy to a controversial policy. There are many matters, especially where a decision either way will not be wrong or disastrous, which the people can and should decide for themselves.

Assuming that further referendums will be held from time to time—for instance on the adoption of the euro as the currency for the UK or on the introduction of a proportional electoral system for the House of Commons, a number of issues need to be resolved about the conduct of referendums. For instance: who should be responsible for framing the question? Do there need to be safeguards against biased or tendentious questions? What, if any, public funding should be available to protagonists for the two sides in a referendum? Should there be limits on the amount that may be spent by protagonists?

To date there has been specific legislation about each of the referendums that has been held. The independent Commission on the Conduct of Referendums proposed in 1996 that there should be a generic Referendum Act. Part VII of the PPERA goes some way in this direction. It requires participants in campaigns to register with the Electoral Commission, and makes provision for the payment of grants to one campaigner for each of the options in the referendum, up to a limit of £600,000. It regulates and imposes limits on expenditure on referendum campaigns. It also regulates the publication of promotional material by the government or other public bodies in the 28 days before the poll. And it makes provisions for the counting of the votes.

There are at present statutory provisions for polls under the Government of Wales Act 1998, section 36, and provisions for polls or referendums to be held in local government. But there is still no generic legislation about when referendums may be held, how they may be triggered, or the criteria for the framing of referendum questions—though the Electoral Commission may give an opinion on whether a proposed question is intelligible. So an Act would have to be passed authorizing each referendum.

The Future Reform Agenda—Unfinished Business

We have already noted a number of outstanding matters on which legislation could be brought forward in the near future. Some are highly politically contentious—a proportional or preferential voting system for the House of Commons and in local government, for instance. In its election manifesto for 2001 the Labour Party indicated that it would review the experience of proportional representation systems before considering changes for the House of Commons. On the initiative of the Constitution Unit an Independent Commission to Review Britain's Experience of PR Voting Systems was established in summer 2002 to review the experience of PR voting systems in elections to the devolved bodies, the Greater London Assembly and the European Parliament, to consider elections to the second chamber and the House of Commons, and to produce an interim report in spring 2003, and a final report by the end of 2003. It is not known whether the government too is carrying out a review, as promised in the manifesto. It is clear that the issue of PR for the House of Commons will not go away, though as I have already indicated any proposal for PR is most unlikely to be accepted and implemented.

Electoral Commission projects

Other matters under consideration for future reform are managerial, though likely also to be controversial if they disturb the status quo to the disadvantage of any vested interests. The Electoral Commission (2001) identified, among other issues to be explored, a possible code of practice on campaign spending, a code on political advertising, and a review of the operation of the PPERA. Given that the legal position on campaign spending is complex, a code of practice could well promote consistency and transparency and would be consistent with principles of good governance. Political advertising and party election broadcasts are currently not subject to formal statutory or even non-statutory regulation, save that political advertising on television is prohibited. (The allocation of time to the parties for party election broadcasts is determined by the broadcasters themselves, after non-binding consultation with the Electoral Commission.) These are areas where there are strong arguments for increased juridification, if only by codes implemented by the Electoral Commission or some other body, rather than by the courts, and few would defend the present highly informal system in principle.

Fixed-term Parliaments?

A major issue is whether we should move to a fixed-term Parliament, of say four years. This is unlikely to be on the political agenda of any government since it benefits from the fact that the Prime Minister—not necessarily in consultation with the Cabinet—may decide when an election shall be held, which will normally be at the most propitious time for his or her party. The present legal position is that an election must be held no later than five years after the previous one, but Parliament may be dissolved at any time before then. By convention there must be a dissolution and an election if the government loses a vote of confidence in the House of Commons—as last happened in 1979.

The Scottish Parliament and the Assembly for Wales, and the European Parliament, serve for fixed four-year terms—though in the case of the Scottish Parliament there is provision for early dissolution, but with the body elected after an early dissolution that takes place more than six months before the expiry of the four-year term serving only for the unexpired term of the dissolved body, so that there is no incentive on the incumbent administration to engineer an early dissolution. It is hard, in my view impossible, to think of any principled justifications for the position in the UK Parliament and it seems contrary to any principles of good governance for a government to be able to choose the date of its own judgement by the electorate.

Conclusions

Reforms connected with elections and referendums in the last few years offer a number of lessons that are relevant to our themes. There has been a progressive juridification of the administration of elections and the operation of parties, in response to public pressure and the growing culture of suspicion in the country. Whatever view one takes of the desirability of the political rather than the legal constitution, this trend has been unstoppable.

Second, the electoral system and the level of turnout raise fundamental issues to do with concepts of democracy and citizenship. How representative of the views of electors should elected bodies be? What steps if any should be taken to increase voters' participation in elections? The answer to these questions seems to point towards the introduction of a more proportional electoral system for elections to the House of Commons, based either on an element of party lists or preferential voting. There is concern that the coalition government which would probably result from a more proportional electoral system might be weak and ineffective in a way that would be damaging to both good government and good governance. In my view these fears are exaggerated and coalition government commanding the support of a majority of the electorate would be better for the country than single-party government with minority support in the electorate. It would promote a more responsive and collaborative style of politics and enable good relations to be maintained between the different levels of government. These issues demonstrate how balances have to be sought in reconciling what may be the conflicting demands of the three desiderata of democracy, citizenship, and good governance in the system.

8

Freedom of Information

The United Kingdom is joining the ranks of Western democracies with Freedom of Information Acts very late. Its Freedom of Information Act 2000 (FOIA) comes fully into effect only in 2005. There has for long been freedom of information legislation in comparable common law systems (Australia, Canada, and New Zealand all introduced FOI in 1982), in the USA since 1966, and, among our partners in the European Union, in Denmark, Finland, France, Greece, Netherlands, Norway, Sweden, and Austria. In this chapter we consider the present position in relation to access to official information, and the position as it will be when the FOIA comes into force, together with the arguments for 'open government' in the sense of government that willingly gives access to information in its possession. (There is another sense to the term 'open government', namely government which is open to public participation and debate in its decision-making, and responsive to citizens: see Birkinshaw, 2001a. This is considered at various points in other chapters.) This is a large and technical subject and we shall focus only on some general issues and the main provisions of the FOIA (see further Birkinshaw, 1991, 2001a; Birkinshaw and Parkin, 1999; Austin, 2000; Wadham, Griffiths, and Rigby, 2001).

The importance of openness in the sense of public access to official information is recognized by international organizations. The UN General Assembly passed a resolution in 1946 affirming that 'Freedom of information is a fundamental human right and is the touchstone for all the freedoms to which the United Nations is consecrated' (Resolution 59(2), 14 December 1946). The United Nations Declaration of Human Rights (Article 19), the International Covenant on Civil and Political Rights (Article 19(2)), and the European Convention on Human Rights (Article 10) declare the right of everyone to receive and impart information and ideas. This does not however impose a duty on those in possession of information to disclose it. The Committee of Ministers of the Council of Europe has adopted a recommendation on access to information held by public authorities (Council of Europe R(81) 19, 25 November 1981). The Council of Ministers of the European Union issued a Decision of 20 December 1993 (93/731/EC) approving a code of conduct concerning public access to council and Commission documents.

Why is Open Government a Good Thing?

Before we consider the 2000 FOIA, let us remind ourselves why openness in government is supposed to be desirable. Citizenship is not only about holding the state to account and securing the rights and performing the obligations of citizenship. It is also about opportunities to participate in governmental and other decisions. The value of public participation is much less if undertaken from a position of ignorance than of informed understanding of the business of government. Thus access to information encourages and facilitates deliberative democracy: effective deliberation by citizens in public affairs requires that they have access to information, and open access means equality of access—equality being another aspect of citizenship and democracy. It is worth noting here that the National Audit Office study *Government on the Web* (1999) showed that Web provision has produced dramatic increases in the numbers of people accessing consultation documents and responding to agencies' invitations to comment.

Access to official information also has developmental and educative functions in that it enables citizens to understand what government is about and to make mature judgements and contributions. It can thus legitimate governmental decisions in the minds of citizens.

Open government also provides protection against corruption and other forms of wrongdoing in government by undermining secrecy. These are good-governance issues. But openness does not necessarily on its own promote trust or limit deception. What is revealed in an open government system may not be the truth. As O'Neill (2002) has suggested: 'Transparency certainly destroys secrecy: but it may not limit the deception and deliberate misinformation that undermine relations of trust. If we want to restore trust we need to reduce deception and lies rather than secrecy.' Open government needs to be supplemented by other measures and processes such as enforceable codes of conduct, and social and cultural pressures, if it is to engender deserved trust and trustworthy behaviour by public officials.

The need to make government genuinely accountable is central to the United Kingdom political system, indeed to the political systems of all democracies. Sir Richard Scott, in his *Report on the Export of Dual-Use Goods to Iraq etc.* (1995–6, HC 115) expressed the view that the giving of information to Parliament was more important to the effectiveness of the conventions of ministerial responsibility even than any requirement of ministerial resignation.

Access to information is important for many reasons besides imposing accountability on government and enabling individuals to participate in political debate and decision-making. It enables individuals to make informed decisions about their own welfare or that of their families: it is a matter of individual autonomy and security as against state paternalism. Much information is held by government and regulatory bodies about matters such as environmental pollution, health, and safety, and if this is withheld from those affected by dangers they are deprived of the opportunity to protect themselves that the regulatory agency was set up to promote in the first place. On this approach individuals are rights-bearers as well as citizens in a political community.

Public bodies hold large amounts of information about individuals. Access by the individuals concerned to this information is important so that they can have an opportunity to correct any inaccuracies that might affect their treatment by the state: the right to correct information is one way of protecting social and economic citizenship rights (see Chapters 2 and 6) since publicly held personal information forms the basis for state bodies to determine such matters as rights to welfare benefits, housing, education, rights to vote, and to receive grants of various kinds. It also serves to protect the dignity, security, and status of individuals in their relations with public bodies.

There is general agreement, even among those in favour of freedom of information, that some categories of information should not be disclosed to the general public. These include certain information relating to defence and the security services, foreign relations, the investigation and detection of crime, advice given by civil servants and Ministers and thus to Cabinet discussions, sensitive commercial information, and personal information, which should not be made available to third parties. It does not of course follow that all such information should be kept secret or that there should be no processes of accountability in respect of these matters, and much needs to be done to enhance the accountability of the security services, the Foreign Office, and other organs operating in sensitive areas (The security services are on a statutory footing since 1989: Security Service Act of that year; see Leigh and Lustgarten, 1989; Ewing and Gearty, 1990, ch. 6; Norton-Taylor, 1990).

Access to Information in the UK—until 2005

The FOIA, passed in 2000, is not due to come into effect fully until January 2005. Since November 2002 publication schemes for central government information under the Act are coming into effect (see below), and schemes for local government must be in force by February 2003. For the time being however there is no comprehensive FOI regime in the United Kingdom. Instead there is a piecemeal set of arrangements, some statutory and some in the form of 'soft law' codes. The statutory provisions for access to official information in the UK are very limited, but they are supplemented by a system of administratively provided for access. For instance, Green Papers are commonly published before firm policy decisions are taken and these provide useful information for interested members of the public. Royal Commissions, committees of inquiry, and various other bodies are set up to report on matters of concern and their reports are published. The Central Office of Information publishes statistics and large quantities of other information. Administrative directions have been issued from time to time to encourage the disclosure of information.

The Code of Practice on Access to Government Information

The *Open Government* White Paper of 1993 proposed a *Code of Practice on Access to Government Information*, which was published and came into effect in 1994, and was updated in 1997. The code applies to all government departments, agencies, and authorities subject to the jurisdiction of the Parliamentary Commissioner for Administration (the ombudsman). It requires them to publish facts and analysis which the government considers relevant in framing major policy proposals and decisions and to release factual information on request. The Code covers a very broad range of information, wider in some respects than the FOIA. It sets out exceptions for defence, national security, and other usual matters, but also for internal discussion and advice, policy analysis, information relating to immigration and nationality, effective management of the economy, and other topics, most of which—and more—are also found in the FOIA. Under this system complaints of refusal of access to information are dealt with by the PCA, who may find such refusal to amount to maladministration. His findings are not legally binding in the sense of compelling the body in question to disclose the information, but the normal practice in relation to the PCA's findings has been that the Select Committee on Public Administration (the PASC, formerly the Select Committee on the PCA) will bring political pressure to bear on a reluctant minister to comply with the PCA's recommendations, and this proves to be generally effective (see Tomkins, 1998, ch. 3 for analysis of the PCA's decisions dealing with Code requests).

There is also some legislation requiring disclosure of governmental information or access to records. The Data Protection Act 1984 gave 'data subjects' a right of access to all automated personal records, whether held by government, public bodies, or private persons who are data controllers. These rights were extended in 1998 to non-automated records to meet European Community law requirements. The rights are subject to exemptions for areas such as national security, defence, and crime prevention. The last important measure on freedom of information before the FOIA was the Public Interest Disclosure Act 1998—known as the Whistleblower's Charter. The Act is concerned with employees' rights and provides that an employee is not to be subjected to a detriment— i.e. victimized—if he makes a disclosure to a responsible person of information revealing wrongdoing. If the employee is subjected to a detriment, he will be entitled to seek compensation before an Employment Tribunal. There are exceptions for information concerning national security and the like. There is also a number of environmental Acts and regulations which provide for access to information on pollution, health and safety risks, pesticides, and so on.

To summarize, until the implementation of the FOIA openness in government is provided for largely by 'soft law' in the form of codes, the Citizen's Charter, and other informal arrangements, supplemented by some statutory, legally enforceable provisions or legal protections for those who disclose information. These provisions for openness add up to a rule that information held by central government should be made available to the public unless refusal is based on a specific reason. Under the Code of Practice the general rule is that information will be disclosed. But access is not legally enforceable.

The government's performance under this largely extra-legal regime has been considered by the PCA and PASC. The PCA reported in November 2001 that the Home Secretary had refused to disclose to him the number of times that Ministers in his department had made a declaration of interest to colleagues under the *Ministerial Code* (see Chapter 11). He noted that this appeared to be the first occasion on which a government department had refused to accept the conclusions of the PCA on a question of disclosure of information under the Code of Practice (PCA, Fourth Report 2001–2, HC 353, 2001–2). He noted that 'there is no valid reason under the Code of Practice on Access to Government Information why this information should not be released, and that there is a public interest in making it available' and he regretted that Ministers had not agreed to the release of the information. In June 2002 the PASC started an inquiry into the government's open-government performance, including a particular matter associated with the PCA's report, the refusal of the Home Office to release information about an alleged telephone conversation between Peter Mandelson MP and Mike O'Brien MP about the passport application of the Hinduja brothers some years earlier, following up the reports by the PCA on the matter (HC 353, 2001–2, HC 844, 2001–2). At the time of writing it is clear that the informal regime operating, pending the coming into force of the FOIA, shields government from some embarrassment and accountability. A question is, however, to what extent the FOIA will in due course expose the government to full accountability.

Openness in local government

There is greater provision for public or individual access to information held by local authorities than to that held by central government and its agencies. Local authorities were not governed by the Official Secrets Act 1911, which criminalized all unauthorized disclosures of official information (although the common law of confidentiality applies in principle to disclosures of their information as it does in central government: see Austin, 2000). Secrecy in local government has been eroded by a series of statutes passed in the last thirty years which have opened up the town halls to a much greater extent than Whitehall. The FOIA will supplement, but not replace, them (see Leigh, 2000, ch. 3). For instance, since the Local Government Act 1933 the accounts of local authorities have been open to inspection and audit, and the authorities must supply community charge payers with information about how the council's revenue is spent. By the Public Bodies (Admission to Meetings) Act 1960 council meetings are required to be open to the press and the public. Under this measure (introduced as a private member's bill by Margaret Thatcher MP) the minutes of council and committee meetings must also be published. By the 1972 Local Government Act, as amended, council committee and sub-committee meetings must be open to the press and the public. The Local Government (Access to Information) Act 1985 improved public rights of access to local authority papers that are being submitted to meetings of the council or to committees, save where specific confidential matters are in question. The categories of exempt information include personal and financial information about council employees, tenants, and social service clients. The Proper Officer (see Chapter 16) in the authority is charged with deciding upon exempt information, but there is no statutory appeal or complaint mechanism if his or her decisions are challenged. Judicial review would sometimes be available. Government circulars and the General Principles of Conduct for Local Authorities (see Chapter 16) also require openness. Overall, then, local government is subject to a broad freedom of information regime even without the FOIA. But since the introduction of separate executive arrangements in local authorities under the Local Government Act 2000 (see Chapter 16) there is concern that the arrangements for openness will be eroded since the 'cabinet' is not formally a committee of the council. This problem will however be resolved once the FOIA 2000 comes into effect fully in 2005 since it applies to local authorities as well as other public authorities.

The Freedom of Information Act 2000

One of the commitments in the Labour Party manifesto of 1997 was the introduction of a Freedom of Information Act. Similar commitments had been included in earlier election manifestos over the years, but Labour governments had not implemented them. The Cabinet Office White Paper which preceded the publication of the Bill, *Your Right to Know* (1997), was very liberal in the scope of freedom of and access to information which was proposed (see Birkinshaw, 1998). When the Freedom of Information bill was eventually introduced into Parliament by the Home Secretary, eighteen months later, however, it was less liberal as far as exemptions are concerned, substituting 'public interest' and 'prejudice' tests for the 'substantial harm' test originally proposed to justify refusals of access to information. A draft bill was among the first that was subjected to pre-legislative scrutiny in Parliament, and as a result a number of rather minor changes were made.

The Act is not concerned solely with the provision of information on request. Public authorities covered by the Act are required to draw up publication schemes for the automatic and routine publication of information, in stages from November 2002, for approval by the Information Commissioner (Mr Richard Thomas). He will also be charged with promoting good practice by public authorities in relation to disclosure of information.

The FOIA will undoubtedly increase rights of access to information held by public authorities very substantially. However, under the FOIA a person will need to know or suspect that information exists before a request for it can be made. The Act does not provide for automatic disclosure of much information, though the Information Commissioner is responsible for encouraging voluntary disclosures under publication schemes. The restrictions on disclosure, both under the Act and under other provisions, are still therefore of importance. A number of other legal provisions will continue to restrict access to information, including rules relating to the protection of information received in confidence and of privacy.

A very brief summary of what is a detailed and complex Act will serve to bring out the main points. As has already been noted it will not be fully implemented until January 2005, but once in force it will be retrospective in relation to information that came into existence earlier.

The prima facie right to access

The Act will replace the *Code of Practice on Access to Government Information*, which was introduced in 1994 and under which a person complaining of a breach of the Code's provisions for access to information held by the government could complain to his MP who could refer the matter to the Parliamentary Commissioner for Administration. The broad principles on access to information under the Act are similar to those in the Code, and it extends to many more organizations than the Code, which only bound central government.

But the exemptions in the FOIA are broader. Under the Act any person will be able to request information from a public authority, and will be entitled (subject to specific exemptions and exceptions) to have that information communicated to him if the authority holds it. 'Public authority' includes government departments, the Houses of Parliament, devolved bodies, local authorities, the NHS, maintained schools and universities, police authorities and the police, and a large number of other public bodies listed in the First Schedule to the Act, including the ombudsmen, and regulatory and advisory bodies. The Secretary of State may bring further bodies within the scope of the Act as exercising functions of a public nature or exercising functions of a public authority under contract. There are however a number of exceptions to this general right.

There is no requirement under the FOIA that the person requesting information has any particular interest in receiving the information, and thus the press and pressure groups will be able to take advantage of its provisions. This could result in turn in the role of the MP in extracting information through parliamentary questions becoming less important, and involve a shift of emphasis from parliamentary to public accountability. On the other hand, in Australia, New Zealand, and Canada, MPs have come to exploit their FOI rights. They and their researchers put in monthly requests for the latest crime figures, trade figures, and so on. FOI can be more useful than answers to parliamentary questions, because it gives the requester the raw information rather than the aggregated or sanitized version that is often given in answer to Parliamentary Questions. The FOI regime undermines to an extent the claims that used to be made by Ministers that ministerial control over access to information is part of the doctrine of individual ministerial responsibility, and thus it represents a lessening of the centrality of ministerial responsibility and thus of Parliament in our constitutional arrangements. It is noteworthy that the Act specifically protects information the disclosure of which would prejudice the effective conduct of public affairs in that it would, for instance, prejudice the maintenance of the convention of collective ministerial responsibility. The Act does not mention individual responsibility. That particular justification for secrecy has thus been abandoned.

Absolute exemptions from the duty to disclose information

Section 2 and Part II of FOIA provide for some absolute exemption, though they do not themselves forbid disclosure, which remains technically discretionary. Some exemptions are class based, so that all information in the class is exempt. Other exemptions are prejudice based and information is exempt only if disclosure would cause prejudice. As noted earlier, the original test in the White Paper *Your Right to Know* had been 'substantial harm', a heavier burden for the public authority to discharge when refusing access than 'prejudice to the public interest', the test introduced by the FOIA.

The exemptions include information that is accessible to the applicant by other means, information supplied by or relating to bodies dealing with security matters, court records, parliamentary privilege, information prejudicial to the conduct of public affairs held by the House of Commons or the House of Lords, some personal information, information provided in confidence and other information the disclosure of which is prohibited by other legislation, Community law, or contempt of court rules.

Qualified or public interest exemptions

Section 2 and Part II deal with requests where the prima facie right of access under the Act is subject to an exemption that permits the department to decide to refuse access on public interest grounds. The exemption applies to many kinds of information, some class based, some prejudice based. They include national security, defence, international relations, relations within the UK, the economy, criminal and other investigations, law enforcement, audit functions, formulation of government policy, prejudice to the effective conduct of public affairs other than that held by either House of Parliament, communications with the Queen, health and safety, environmental information, personal information about a third party, legal professional privilege, and commercial interests.

In these cases there is a duty on the part of the body holding the information to disclose it unless satisfied that the public interest in maintaining the exemption outweighs the public interest in disclosure. Many FOI regimes have a test of this kind (for instance, Australia, New Zealand, and Ireland).

Environmental information is covered by separate regulations (FOIA, section 74) to implement the United Nations Convention on Access to Information, Public Participation in Decision-making, and Access to Justice in Environmental Matters (the Aarhus Convention) to which the UK is a party.

Appeals and the ministerial veto

A person who has requested information but has been denied it will be able to complain to the Information Commissioner, and if the Commissioner finds the complaint to be well founded, he or she will specify the steps to be taken by the authority to meet the request. If the public authority does not comply, the Commissioner may issue an enforcement notice, and failure to comply may be referred to the court and dealt with as if it were a contempt of court. Either side may appeal from the Commissioner's decision, to the Information Tribunal and from there to the Court on a point of law.

Where access is refused, the requester can argue, including on appeal, that the information does not fall within the exemption relied upon by the public authority. Where the information falls within an absolute exemption the Information Commissioner has no power to order its disclosure in the public interest, though he may decide that the alleged prejudice does not exist. Where the exemption is claimed on a public interest ground the Information Commissioner can decide whether any alleged prejudice exists, and if not he may order disclosure. He may also decide whether on balance the public interest favours disclosure.

A Cabinet Minister may override—veto—the Information Commissioner's decision notice or enforcement notice in relation to any exempt information held by central government (and the Welsh Assembly and other designated public authorities). By way of safeguard a copy of the override certificate must be laid before each House of Parliament, but there is no provision for parliamentary approval or veto. This override power may apply to public authorities specially designated by the Secretary of State, but it will not apply to information held by the public authorities listed in schedule 1 to the Act, for instance, which are not part of central government. A decision to issue an override certificate will be subject to judicial review, and the Information Commissioner will be entitled to institute judicial review proceedings.

General Comments and Assessment

Having outlined the way in which the FOIA will work, let us summarize its positive aspects. It will mark a radical move in favour of openness in government, despite the broad exceptions it contains. It is significant that it contains a presumption in favour of the communication of information on request, and the burden rests on the public authority to justify non-disclosure on one of the grounds set out in the Act. The FOIA, taken with other legislation requiring openness in government sketched in above, reflects acceptance in principle of a number of the justifications for rights of access to information considered in the early part of this chapter—the importance of openness on good governance grounds, to promote accountability and provide protection against corruption and wrongdoing in government; the protection of individuals as consumers of public services; the promotion of individual autonomy in the ability to make decisions about one's life with full information, and protection of individuals from the dissemination of inaccurate information about them. And, lastly, the facilitating of effective citizen participation in public affairs, from a position of knowledge.

On the other hand, the FOIA may be criticized on a number of grounds. The Act falls short of what the White Paper had promised, and what advocates of Freedom of Information were hoping for, in a number of ways. The exemptions in the Act—and in other legislation, for instance on the environment and public health—are substantial and leave control over large tracts of information, much of it exactly the information that the public and press would need to have access to in order to hold government to account, in the hands of Ministers. The public interest exceptions could be used to prevent the public from finding out about health and safety and environmental risks, for instance, to their own detriment.

In giving complainants access to the Information Tribunal and then to the courts, the Act increases the juridification and judicialization of public administration, and this may be seen as a shift from political forms of accountability to legal forms. However, the FOIA preserves the political Constitution by empowering a minister to override an order for disclosure by the Information Commissioner. In this respect the Freedom of Information Act 2000 provides an interesting contrast with the Human Rights Act, which does not allow ministerial override of human rights unless expressly authorized by an Act of Parliament. Thus in some respects the FOIA gives greater protection to political decision-makers than the HRA. While under the HRA the courts do have the power to override political decisions, though the power will be used sparingly in deference to democratic-ally accountable decision-makers, under the FOIA a minister has the power to override the Information Commissioner's decision to require the disclosure of information, his over-ride certificate to be laid before each House of Parliament. Although the minister may be subject to judicial review, in principle this provision favours the political Constitution. The shift to legal accountability where a ministerial override is not exercised recognizes that much public activity is carried out by bodies which are not, even indirectly, politically accountable—quangos (see Chapter 17) are an obvious example.

Like the HRA, the FOIA juridifies many decisions that would formerly have been made by politicians or by officials on their behalf in the exercise of unregulated discretion. But it goes beyond the soft law juridification that the *Code of Practice on Government Information* effected, by constructing a new statutory framework in which the PCA no longer has jurisdiction to require the disclosure of information, but instead the Information Commissioner will have the power to require disclosure. The system will also be judicialized with the right of appeal to the Information Tribunal and the courts, and the possibility of judicial review of a ministerial override.

We have noted that the position until the Freedom of Information Act comes into effect is that recommendations of the PCA, though not legally binding, are backed up by the select committee to which the PCA reports, currently by the PASC, and this political mechanism has generally—though not always—been effective. Thus under the FOIA there will be a shift from political to legal accountability, from weak to strong juridifica-tion and, where there is access to the courts, a degree of judicialization of political decisions to refuse access.

Despite the positive aspects of moves towards openness in government, the fact remains that the original White Paper proposals on Freedom of Information were far more liberal than what has emerged in the FOIA. In the eighteen months between publication of the White Paper and the draft bill the government and the civil service had managed to water down the provisions considerably. This suggests that Freedom of Information is not welcome in many parts of government. Just as there is concern about the depth of human rights culture in government (see Chapter 6) so there is little sign as yet of a genuine culture of openness in government.

PART III

INSTITUTIONAL REFORMS

9

Parliament: The House
of Commons

In this chapter and the next we are concerned with the project to 'modernize' Parliament. This chapter will focus on the general role of Parliament and its nature, and the attempts to reform the House of Commons since 1997, and before then. The next chapter concentrates on the House of Lords and reaches some general conclusions about the reform of Parliament.

A range of commissions and bodies have made detailed recommendations for reform of the scrutiny roles of the House of Commons and the Lords in recent years (see for instance, Hansard Society Commission on the Legislative Process, 1992; Commission to Strengthen Parliament, 2000; Hansard Society Commission on Parliamentary Scrutiny, 2001; and see generally Miers and Page, 1990; Morrison, 2001, ch. 11; Forman, 2002, chs. 10, 11). Parliamentary committees too have come up with proposals from time to time to strengthen the ability of the House of Commons to hold government to account, notably the Procedure Committee, the Liaison Committee, the old Treasury and Civil Service Committee, the current Public Administration Committee, and the Modernization Committee that was established in 1997. The main concerns have been to improve the scrutiny of legislation, for instance through scrutiny of draft bills and carry-over of bills so as to reduce time pressures in the scrutiny process, and improving the capacity of select committees to hold government to account. A number of significant reforms to select committees were introduced in 1979, when a newly elected Conservative government implemented reforms that had been recommended by the Procedure Committee in the previous Parliament (*First Report from the Select Committee on Procedure*, 1977–8, HC 588-I to II; see Drewry, 1989). But these reforms, designed to release the tight grip of the party whips over the work of the committees were, as we shall see, frustrated by the whips.

In the run-up to the 1997 general election the Joint Consultative Committee of the Labour Party and the Liberal Democrats agreed on the need to modernize Parliament: 'Renewing Parliament is key to the wider modernization of our country's system of government' (Joint Consultative Committee Report, para. 64). The priorities were securing effective scrutiny of legislation and draft bills, making Prime Minister's Question Time a more genuine and serious means of holding the government to account, improving the scrutiny of European Community legislation, strengthening the ability of MPs to make government accountable, and enhancing the role of the select committees. The Labour Party was committed in its 1997 election manifesto to removing the hereditary peers from the House of Lords as a first step towards reforming the second chamber. However, progress in achieving the necessary consensus and government support to implement reforms and make them work has been very laboured, and many widely accepted proposals have been frustrated by governments and their supporters in the House of Commons. This is largely due to the very nature of Parliament, especially of the House of Commons.

What is Parliament?

Before considering specific modernizing measures, it will be helpful to consider briefly what Parliament is, since this will shed light on the difficulties experienced in the reform process. Strictly *a* Parliament is a meeting at which discussion takes place, and the word could be taken to refer to the persons who attend those meetings—'the Lords Temporal and Spiritual, and Commons in this present Parliament assembled', to quote from the words of enactment of statutes—though when the UK Parliament is acting as the legislature the Queen's assent is required. The two Houses of Parliament of the UK are collections of individuals and they are there to achieve consensus, if they can, and to legislate accordingly. Neither House has a recognized corporate legal personality (though there are statutory corporate bodies which contract for them), so they are not themselves, from a legal point of view, institutions. (Though the House of Lords, acting in its judicial capacity, is a Court of Record.) This means that much of what the two Houses do is invisible to the courts save where the product is an Act of Parliament. This invisibility accounts in turn for the fact that much political activity is outside the jurisdiction of the courts. This invisibility is buttressed by Article 9 of the Bill of Rights 1689 which provides that the freedom of speech and debates and proceeding in Parliament shall not be called in question in any court or place outside Parliament. And parliamentary privilege, which is asserted by the two Houses, according to which they have 'exclusive cognisance' of their proceedings, is accepted as part of the law by the courts (see generally Erskine May, 1997; Leopold, 1998).

Legal categories are not of course everything, but from a social or cultural point of view too 'Parliament' is hardly an institution at all, as opposed to a collection of its members. The House of Commons in particular, immediately after a general election, has no speaker, no organization (though it has support staff), and no committees. Without organization it is impossible to exercise power (Galbraith, 1983). Some weeks after an election the House of Commons does have an organization, consisting of a speaker or presiding officer and committees. Procedures for its operation are in place, and so it looks, from a social or cultural point of view, like a powerful, organized institution. But what happens in the interval between a general election and committees and procedures being put in place is crucial to understanding this chamber: the House of Commons' members will have been captured by their parties, one of which is the party of government. These are essentially tribal groupings, to borrow an analogy of Cook (2002; see also Wright and Gamble, 2002). These groups are organized in advance of the election, and are well placed to manipulate the organization of members in their own party interests. A major difference between the two Houses is that the House of Lords is less dominated by these groupings than the Commons.

To pursue Cook's analogy, the primary sense of loyalty of party members is to their tribespeople. The majority party in the House is that of the government of the day. Each tribe has a leader, with the authority to appoint front-benchers to government or opposition portfolios, and they have party rules and whips. The whips agree between themselves, guided by conventions and some parliamentary party rules, the distribution of chairs of House of Commons committees, and these are then approved by the members of the House in their capacities, normally, as tribespersons—or not, as happened after the 2001 election, when members rebelled at the non-appointment of two previous chairs to select committees (see below). By the time the committees are nominated and appointed, it is too late for 'the House' in the sense of the collective body of Members to assert an independent corporate existence. Its Members have been captured. The House and its Members' capacity to determine its own future has largely gone (see Winetrobe, 1998).

Kennon (2000) has commented that 'A common misunderstanding is that the House has the ability to reform itself . . . [O]nly changes acceptable to the Government of the day are put into effect.' This explains why the dominant tribe, government and its whips and backbenchers, and on occasions opposition parties, have blocked a number of reforms that the Modernization Committee and other select committees have proposed: many reforms, though clearly beneficial to the public interest, are not in the interests of either the government or the tribal party system itself. However, with persistence, as we shall see, the select committees, especially if chaired by persons with independence deriving from the fact that their appointment to government posts in the future is unlikely, have extracted some concessions from the government.

Even when the House of Commons claims to act in a corporate capacity (as when it votes on recommendations of its Standards and Privileges Committee for instance, when it is sometimes said that 'The House has spoken') this is in fact a mystification. As the Hansard Commission recognized in *The Challenge for Parliament* (2001) Parliament lacks a corporate ethos which promotes collective functions such as imposing accountability on government (p. xi). Any corporate identity or spirit the House may sometimes have is easily overridden by party loyalties and discipline. Any attempt to promote a corporate House of Commons, as opposed to party, spirit is resisted by the parties, who, in the case of Labour and the Conservatives, have a stake in the tribal system, and are jealous of surrendering their status and power either to one or other chamber of Parliament or, often, to other arrangements such as civil society's own participatory processes. What actually happens in our constitutional arrangements, then, is that the executive acts through its majority in the House of Commons. This is what Hailsham's 'elective dictatorship' (1976, 1978) was about. And, given a large majority, a government does not need to be responsive to members of the House, however 'modern' the procedures for scrutiny are.

The Modernization of the House of Commons

Shortly after the 1997 election a Modernization Committee was established in the House of Commons, chaired by the Leader of the House, Anne Taylor. (The Leader has a schizophrenic, even make-believe, position in our constitution. He or she is both the voice of the Commons in the Cabinet and the representative of the government in the House.) Taylor was succeeded by Margaret Beckett and then, after the 2001 election, by former Foreign Secretary, Robin Cook, who has been more strongly committed than his predecessors to the modernization project. A number of reforms have been introduced on the recommendations of the Committee, though significant ones have also been rejected.

There have been five strands to this modernization process. First, the removal of some of the more archaic aspects of Commons' style, for instance the use of the opera hat to make points of order during a division, making the order paper more comprehensible and user-friendly, and generally eliminating out-of-date rules (see for instance Fourth Report of the Select Committee on Modernization of the House of Commons, *Conduct in the Chamber*, HC 600, 1997–8). Secondly, making Parliament, and the Palace of Westminster, and other parliamentary buildings, more accessible to the public, with a new Visitor's centre and guides who focus on the current role of the House rather than its history and the architecture of the building, and a user-friendly House of Commons website on which Acts and Select Committee Reports can be found. Thirdly, making the life of MPs more convenient and family-friendly, for instance by reforming sitting hours to enable MPs to get home after work at reasonable times and to go to their constituencies, and allowing deferred divisions so that voting could take place on a number of divisions after Prime Minister's questions. The Modernization Committee recommended in its report *A Reform Programme* (HC 1168, 2001–2), that the Commons calendar should be announced a year in advance to enable MPs to plan their time. (This was accepted by the House of Commons in October 2002.) (There have in fact been projects to improve MPs' working conditions going back many years, such as the new offices and facilities at Portcullis House and improved use of IT.) Fourth, enabling the government to get its legislation through Parliament, for instance by permitting the carry-over of bills from one session to the next, and facilitating the timetabling of the legislative process.

Important though these reforms are, they do not themselves improve the ability of Parliament to perform its core functions of scrutiny of government policy, administration, and legislation. Indeed, the timetabling of bills may actually reduce the scrutiny of legislation. These reforms were not what the Joint Consultative Committee's report was about, nor what the proposals of the Commission to Strengthen Parliament or the Hansard Society Commission were mainly concerned with. Reform of this core function is the fifth strand in the modernization process, and it has proved far more difficult to make progress on than modernizing procedures, improving public access, improving working conditions, and facilitating the passage of the government's legislation. Improving parliamentary scrutiny of legislation and policy is inconvenient for government, and without government support such improvements are virtually impossible. Save where some scandal precipitates action, as the Arms to Iraq affair did in 1993–6 (on which more below), or where a new government is elected after a period in opposition during which proposals for reforms were well prepared by committees of the House, as was the case when the new select committee system was introduced in 1979, governments will usually block improvements to the scrutiny capabilities of the Commons if they consider that they will make life more difficult. This appears to be an immutable fact of parliamentary life. Better scrutiny involves undermining the tight hold that parties, especially the government party, have over backbenchers; and it imposes additional burdens on MPs, which runs counter to the other modernizing moves to improve their working conditions.

Reforming the legislative process

The legislative process is full of procedural technicalities that we cannot go into in any detail here, though a few of the technicalities will be mentioned to bring out the complexities of reform (see Kennon, 2000. See generally Miers and Page, 1990; Hansard Society Commission on the Legislative Process, 1992; Erskine May, 1997). Most of the reforms that have been approved since 1997 under the modernization project have been designed to enable the government to secure the passage of its legislation more smoothly. Some experiments with improving the quality of scrutiny of legislation have been tried, however.

The Modernization Committee recommended a package of improvements to the legislative process in 1997 that were initially accepted by the government; but they were not implemented because the government changed its mind about their desirability and did not bring forward new standing orders to give effect to them. Only the government may propose changes to House of Commons standing orders with any chance of success. Instead, the Modernization Committee's proposals have been implemented partially and on an ad hoc basis. In October 2002 the House of Commons agreed to the recommendations in HC 1168, 2001–2 (HC Deb., 29 October 2002, col. 801). In summary, the following reforms to the legislative process have been agreed to by the House of Commons and the government as a result of the modernization process.

Full explanatory notes to bills and Acts are routinely provided. Pre-legislative scrutiny has been piloted. A number of bills—six in 1998—were published in draft and considered by committees which reported on them before they were presented to the House. For instance the Financial Service and Markets bill was examined by a joint committee whose recommendations for bringing the proposals on penalties for market abuse into compliance with the Convention rights incorporated into UK law by the Human Rights Act were accepted by the government (see First Report of the Joint Committee on the Draft Financial Services and Markets Bill, HC 50, HL 328, 1998–9; Second Report HC 465, HL 66, 1998–9). The draft Local Government Organization and Standards Bill (1998–9) was also examined by a joint committee. And a draft Freedom of Information Bill (1998–9) was examined by separate committees in each House. Only one bill was subject to pre-legislative scrutiny in the 1999–2000 session. Three bills were published in draft for consultation early in the 2002–3 session, on housing, reform of the law on corruption, and management of nuclear liabilities. There are likely to be six draft bills in all in the 2002–3 session. There will however be difficulties in finding the resources in the time of parliamentary counsel to produce draft bills in good time when pressures will naturally be towards prioritizing bills that are passing through the legislative process in both Houses. In its Second Report, (HC 1168, 2001–2) *A Reform Programme* the Modernization Committee recommended that the government continue to increase with each session the publication of bills in draft and that where this was not possible the government should submit a detailed statement of policy for pre-legislative scrutiny.

There has been some ad hoc carry-over of bills from one session to the next. One bill (the Financial Services and Markets Bill) was carried over from one session to the next in 1998. In October 2002 the House of Commons accepted the recommendation of the Modernization Committee in HC 1168 that standing orders be amended to permit carry-over, though for no more than one extra session. The House of Lords agreed to automatic carry-over in its procedural reforms in the summer of 2002, and at the time of writing it is not clear how Commons and Lords carry-over will work in tandem (Second Report of the Modernization Committee, *A Reform Programme*, HC 1168, 2001–2). However, carry-over deprives the Opposition of one of its most powerful weapons against government, delay, and it is not certain that the opposition parties in the House of Commons will agree to carry-over motions.

The programming/timetabling of bills has become institutionalized. Seventeen bills were programmed by agreement between the parties in the 1997–8 session. But after 1998, bills were guillotined regularly as the Conservative opposition started obstructing non-contentious bills, so that the timetabling of bills has become a matter of course under new standing orders since the 2000–1 session. The promise of modernization in 1997 was that the programming of bills would improve scrutiny, but in practice timetabling has not done so. In its Report HC 1168, 2001–2, the Modernization Committee recommended that there should be more flexibility over programming motions if carry-over is adopted and that the Opposition should be willing to engage constructively in agreeing to such motions and this was agreed in the House of Commons in October 2002.

A number of steps has been taken to enable changes in the law to be made by order rather than by primary legislation. For instance, the Regulatory Reform Act 2001 seeks to break the legislative logjam by providing for orders that remove a regulatory burden to go through by order rather than by primary legislation. The remedial order provisions of the Human Rights Act enable incompatibilities to be removed by order (see Chapter 6).

Overall, however, progress on improving the legislative process is painfully slow and very hard for outsiders to track. A commitment is made to some reform and then it does not happen and the reasons are seldom transparent.

A problem is that what is called the scrutiny of bills can be used to serve three purposes: to scrutinize the government's proposals with a view to improving the bill; to draw attention to weaknesses in the bill; and simply to oppose and harass ministers (see Feldman, 2002*b*, 328–42; Second Report of the Select Committee on Procedure, *Public Bill Procedure*, 1984–5, HC 49, para. 30). The second and third tend to be partisan exercises, while the first is hard to perform in an adversarial institution like the House of Commons, and in the absence of developed and formally recognized criteria for the scrutiny process. Feldman suggests that scrutiny should involve testing provisions of a measure against certain standards, which are independent of the terms or subject matter of the measure itself, and can and should be applied consistently to all measures which are scrutinized. Such standards should be chosen and applied so as to be largely unaffected by political, or at any rate party political, considerations (Feldman, 2002*b*, 328). This concept of scrutiny is, then, a process of a different kind from the giving or refusing of consent to legislation on party lines, which is the core function of the Commons in the legislative process. Unlike scrutiny, the process of giving consent involves politicians reaching decisions where often highly contested political values and objectives of legislation are at stake, rather than reaching conclusions about whether certain objective and specially important standards are met in the legislation.

The Human Rights Act (see Chapter 6) provides some criteria for scrutiny of legislation, and the Joint Committee on Human Rights performs the task of scrutiny for compatibility with Convention rights well. But in the absence of a written Constitution there are few 'hard-edged' criteria on which there is consensus between the parties and against which the process of scrutiny of bills can take place in the Commons. The standing committees in the House of Commons set up to deal with particular bills after second reading (at which the policy of the bill is debated) debate them without specific terms of reference setting out criteria. They are in practice largely concerned with the technical drafting and workability of a bill, and opposition members are concerned to draw attention to weaknesses and harass ministers. On the floor of the House, in its second reading and report stage debates, political and non-political issues, such as constitutionality and compatibility with Convention rights, tend to be confused, the latter being subordinated to the former.

Here the absence of a written Constitution and the political nature of British arrangements mean that the constitutional implications of bills may not be fully appreciated—or admitted—by the House of Commons or the government. This is illustrated by the passage of the European Communities Act 1972, which enabled the UK to join the Community (see Chapter 4). Nicol (2001) has considered the different approaches of the Irish Parliament, operating under a written Constitution, and the British Parliament, operating without one, to the process of joining the European Community. Many members of the British Parliament were unaware of the implications of the step for its own sovereignty, whereas members of the Irish Parliament were compelled by the Irish Constitution to face up to the implications, and the Irish Parliament authorized entry into the Community with its eyes open (see Chapter 4).

The long and the short of it is that the House of Commons does not scrutinize legislation with the thoroughness or detachment that are necessary to secure well-drafted, workable legislation that is compatible with our international obligations and safeguards our constitutional principles. Many provisions in bills are not scrutinized at all in the standing committee or any other stage of the legislative process. The job of scrutiny of legislation is generally better done by the House of Lords (see Chapter 10). In practice the main point of the legislative process in the House of Commons is to give (or refuse) consent on behalf of the electorate to the government's proposed legislation, inserting only those amendments to government bills to which the government is prepared to agree.

The select committees

In 2000 to 2001 concerns about ministerial responsibility and accountability to the House of Commons via the select committees escalated, despite the resolutions on ministerial responsibility that the two Houses had passed in 1997 and their incorporation in the *Ministerial Code* and other steps (see Chapter 11). The departmentally related select committees had been put in place in 1979 (Drewry, 1989). They were supposed to be more effective and independent of the whips than the previous system, with members sitting on the committees for the whole of the Parliament and appointments to them removed from the whips. Committee members are appointed by the House of Commons following selection and nomination by the Committee of Selection. However a convention has developed that the members of the two main parties in the Committee of Selection decide which of their parties' nominees go forward for approval and they consult the whips on appointments. Thus over the years the whips have managed to retain control over nominations and this undermines the effectiveness of the committees.

Various proposals have been made over the years for increasing the independence of these committees from the whips and making them more effective. The Liaison Committee (First Report *Shifting the Balance: Select Committees and the Executive*, HC 300, 1999–2000) proposed that the influence of the whips in the selection of Committee members should be removed through the creation at the start of a new Parliament of a Select Committee Panel to which a Chairman and two Deputies would be appointed at an early stage. They would work in a non-partisan way to put forward nominations for Committee membership. The government rejected these proposals out of hand. The Committee also proposed that more time should be given on the floor of the House and in Westminster Hall to debating select committee reports and that select committees should follow up progress in their recommendations, and this has been accepted.

The independence of the select committees from the whips surfaced as an issue again in the summer of 2001 when, after the general election, two prominent and popular select committee chairs from the 1997–2001 Parliament were not renominated to those chairs by the Labour whips. The House—acting for once in a non-tribal, corporate spirit—voted down the nominations, the whips relented, and the two former chairs were reappointed. This led the new Leader of the House and chair of the Modernization Committee, Robin Cook, to undertake to bring forward proposals for the reform of the select committees.

In its report (*Select Committees*, First Report of the Select Committee on Modernization of the House of Commons, 2001–2, HC 221) the Modernization Committee recommended, among other things, that nomination to committee membership be independent of the whips and parties, to meet the concerns about committee chairs the previous autumn, that specialist and administrative support for the committees be increased, that additional salaries should be paid to chairs of the principal investigative committees. The Committee also proposed a statement of eleven core tasks for these committees and recommended that each committee should produce an annual report showing how it has met each core task. The report and the response of the Liaison Committee (Second Report from the Liaison Committee, HC 692, 2001–2 *Select Committees: Modernization Proposals*) were debated in the Commons in May 2002 and most of the Modernization

Committee's proposals were accepted in principle; the payment of additional salaries to committee chairs was to be referred to the Review Body on Senior Salaries. But the proposal to remove the whips' ultimate control of appointments to committees was rejected (HC Deb., 14 May 2002, cols. 648–730). The vote on this and the other proposals was supposed to be free, but a complaint was made that in fact government whips had been encouraging members of the Parliamentary Labour Party to vote against the independent appointment of committee members, flying in the fact of the proposals brought forward by the Leader of the House. The whips had been spreading misleading rumours about the implications of removing the whips' patronage. They suggested for instance that certain named maverick or independent-minded Labour MPs would be on the selection panel, that this would be a bad thing, and that the PLP's own arrangements should govern these appointments, via the whips. Given that it was the row over the whips' decision not to reappoint two respected chairs of committees that precipitated the commitment of the Leader of the House and the Modernization Committee to bring forward proposals for reform, this outcome is particularly disturbing. What had happened in the meantime, of course, was that the tribal system had reasserted itself, and overcame the initial enthusiasm of MPs for independent appointments to committee chairs. The reforms approved have in fact increased the patronage of the whips, since the appointment to or removal from the position of chair of a committee may, if subsequent resolutions so decide, carry with it implications for his or her salary.

The core tasks approved for these committees are:

- to consider major policy initiatives;
- to consider the government's response to major emerging issues;
- to propose changes where evidence persuades the Committee that present policy requires amendment;
- to conduct pre-legislative scrutiny of draft bills;
- to examine and report on main Estimates, annual expenditure plans, and annual resource accounts;
- to monitor performance against targets in the public service agreements;
- to take evidence from each responsible departmental Minister at least annually;
- to take evidence from independent regulators and inspectorates;
- to consider the reports of Executive Agencies;
- to consider, and if appropriate report on, major appointments made by a Secretary of State or other senior Ministers; and
- to examine treaties within their subject areas.

These core tasks reflect a number of debates that had been taking place about the role of the committees over the previous few years. The Treasury Committee, in its report *HM Treasury*, (see discussion in Chapter 11) recommended both external review of departments' performance against their Public Service Agreement targets by a body such as the National Audit Office, accountable to Parliament, and greater select committee involvement in scrutinizing the Treasury, which was considered to be far too interventionist. The

Hansard Commission Report *The Challenge for Parliament* had put forward a number of proposals that were picked up by the Modernization Committee, including the suggestion that the House should establish itself at the 'apex' of the system of accountability, partly by considering reports from inspectorates and other bodies charged, in effect, with imposing accountability on public and private bodies. The significance of the commitment to pre-legislative scrutiny of draft bills, also recommended by the Hansard Society Commission and the Commission to Strengthen Parliament, has already been noted. A new specialist scrutiny unit is being established to assist the committees, a significant increase in the support and potentially in the influence of the committees.

Notwithstanding the influence of the whips over the composition of the select committees, these committees do produce large numbers of reports, many of them critical of government policy or of the way in which government is conducted, and the government has agreed that it should respond to them, normally within two months of their publication. Some of these reports are debated in Westminster Hall, the 'parallel' chamber. Some of these committees have shown great persistence in pressing the government to be more accountable to Parliament. The Public Administration Select Committee successfully pressed the Prime Minister to agree to incorporate the resolutions on ministerial responsibility in the *Ministerial Code* and to acknowledge his responsibility for its operation. It was under sustained select committee pressure that the Prime Minister eventually agreed to meet the Liaison Committee twice a year (see Chapter 12). They have also been pressing Ministers to give full answers to parliamentary questions (which the government has agreed to: HC 136, 2002–3, Appendix) to improve the financial scrutiny of quangos, and many other machinery of government and good-governance issues on which they have had some successes, but normally only after repeated pressure.

A positive view of progress in Commons reform?

The rejection of the proposals to free the select committees from the whips is perhaps not surprising, given the party domination of the Commons. The Leader of the House, Robin Cook, nevertheless was optimistic about progress when he gave his Hansard Society lecture *Parliament and the People: Modernization of the House of Commons* in May 2002, shortly after the House of Commons' vote. He felt that the rest of the reforms to the select committees were important, as was the Prime Minister's agreement to appear before the Liaison Committee twice a year. Cook attributed the refusal of a majority of MPs to agree to a new independent Committee of Selection for membership of the select committees to the tribal tradition in the House, which he saw as being outdated and not reflecting the way in which electors see the parties and the House. The implication is that MPs, or at least party whips, are unable to countenance or imagine scrutiny not based on tribal conflict. The trouble is that MPs are both parliamentarians and party politicians. This chimes with the point made earlier, that the House has no real sense of corporate identity and is in reality a collection of MPs with party loyalties which easily displace any sense of a common purpose in the House itself. Cook was also upbeat about the possibility of proposals that are found in HC 1168, noted above, to modernize the legislative process (carry-over, scrutiny of draft bills) and changes to the working day being implemented.

All this is fine so are as it goes, but it does not in truth go very far. Over and again the interests of the parties block reform of House of Commons procedures which would enhance scrutiny of legislation and of the policies and administration of the government and increase government's willingness to respond positively to criticism. It seems to be impossible to overcome this hurdle, and as we shall see this opens up questions about how else government may be held to account, in particular by the introduction of a different system of election that could enhance the influence of backbench MPs (see Chapter 7), and in the second chamber, and in the courts.

Politicians of all parties express concern at the fall in turnout at elections (Chapter 7) and the lack of interest among the public in Parliament and in politics generally. There is also widespread agreement that the decline in the status of parliamentarians and ministers should be reversed. But there is little agreement about the reasons for these problems or how they might be resolved. Cook is right that the tribal system in the Commons does not go down well with the electorate, in which there is much less party loyalty than used to exist. This is in part attributable to the facts that the electorate is less divided on class lines than it used to be, the parties are less ideologically committed than, say, twenty years ago, and thus they are not associated with predictable policy positions related to principled stances. In the absence of the introduction of a system of proportional representation in the House of Commons, which would change the politics of the House (see Chapter 7, on electoral systems, and Chapter 13 on the use of proportional representation in the Scottish Parliament), the remedy if any lies with the parties and there is no prospect of the House itself achieving procedural or other reforms that could change matters without the consent of the government.

Much of the blame for public apathy and scepticism about Parliament was being attributed to the press in the summer of 2002 (see for instance Cook, 2002). The press tends to focus on 'Westminster village' issues, often to do with 'spin' which do not greatly interest the public and are, in truth, not very significant. In June 2002, for instance, the village issue was whether the Prime Minister had sought to attract attention by walking from Downing Street to the Palace of Westminster during the lying-in-state of the Queen Mother, and whether he had put pressure on Black Rod, who was in charge of the arrangements. These are hardly important matters when compared with improvements in public services, security, human rights, war with Iraq, and so on. O'Neill too attributes some of the culture of suspicion about politics to newspaper editors and journalists who are not held accountable in the ways that politicians are but who indulge some of the time in 'smears, sneers and jeers, names, shames and blames'. She expresses concern at the fact that we cannot be sure that we can trust what the press reports. 'How can we tell whether and when we are on the receiving end of hype and spin, or misinformation and disinformation?' (O'Neill, 2002, ch. 5).

O'Neill's approach to the unaccountable press and the damage it may do to trust in politicians is that there should be mechanisms for checking on what the press reports, while at the same time protecting its freedom. 'Freedom of the press does not also require a licence to deceive.' She puts forward the following possibilities for consideration. Owners, editors, and journalists could be required to declare financial and other interests, including conflicts of interest, and to distinguish comment from reporting; penalties could be imposed for recirculating rumours others publish without providing and checking the evidence;

chequebook journalism could be reduced by requiring publication of information about who was paid how much for what contribution to the story. 'Our present culture of suspicion cannot be dispelled by making everyone except the media trustworthy' (O'Neill, 2002).

Cook suggested that three things needed to be done to improve the standing of MPs and of Parliament.

- MPs must have space to respond to events as individuals not as tribal members because the voters' respect goes to individuals not party managers.
- The media must be less obsessed with combat and more mature.
- The House of Commons must be seen to belong to the modern age and get rid of its archaic image.

The problems here are that the government and its party whips will not give MPs space that makes the government's life more uncomfortable; the press cannot be transformed by exhortation; many in the Commons are attached to its archaism.

Standards of Conduct in the House of Commons

In the mid-1990s a succession of scandals about 'sleaze' in the House of Commons erupted, which had obvious good-governance implications, raising problems about trustworthiness, accountability, and openness in the House. Given that this led to the establishing of the Committee of Standards in Public Life and the juridification not only of the regulation of standards of conduct in the House of Commons but also of standards in many of the other institutions with which we are concerned in this book, we shall consider the issue at some length.

Some Members of Parliament had been accepting sums of money in return for asking parliamentary questions (see First Report of the Committee of Privileges, *Complaint concerning an article in the 'Sunday Times' of 10 July 1994 relating to the conduct of members*, HC 351, 1994–5). The most notorious of these was the case of Neil Hamilton MP who had accepted cash and other benefits from Mohammed Al Fayed, proprietor of Harrods (The Report of the Parliamentary Commissioner for Standards on these matters is at HC 30, 1997–8; see also Oliver, 1997, Rush, 1998). This was probably in breach of the House's own rules, according to which bribery is a 'high crime and misdemeanour'. (The taking of cash by MPs for asking parliamentary questions was not criminal under the Prevention of Corruption Acts, and in any event, as we have noted, the courts have no jurisdiction over parliamentary proceedings.) The rules or principles with which MPs should comply were unclear and there was no effective machinery or procedure in the House of Commons for dealing with these issues.

Other concerns at that time were about sponsorship and consultancy arrangements between MPs and outside bodies, from which MPs often stood to make substantial sums of money. There was evidence that some MPs believed that as long as their relationships with outside bodies were not unlawful and their interests were registered, any kinds of arrangement were permissible. The notion that MPs' first duty was to the public interest was giving way in some quarters to the idea that the office of MP was property that could be exploited to the personal advantage of the MP (Mancuso, 1993).

It was pressure from the press and the public for sleaze in the House of Commons to be dealt with that resulted in the appointment of the Committee on Standards in Public Life in 1994 (see Chapter 3). The Committee made a number of proposals for reform of the mechanisms to uphold high standards of conduct in the Commons in its First Report (Cm. 2850, 1995). Most of these were implemented fully by the House. It adopted a Code of Conduct based on the Seven Principles of Public Life elaborated by the Committee together with Notes of Guidance (HC 688, 1995–6, approved 24 July 1996; see Chapter 3). The House also resolved on a ban on paid advocacy, on rather stricter lines than the Committee had proposed. (In 2002 the rules on paid advocacy were relaxed when the Code of Conduct was modified to deal with a number of difficulties experienced in its operation.) A Parliamentary Commissioner for Standards (PCS) was appointed to advise MPs on the rules and to investigate complaints of breaches. Rules on the registration and disclosure of interests and avoiding conflicts of interest were tightened up. (The registration requirements were amended in 2002 to bring them into line with requirements of the Political Parties, Elections and Referendums Act 2000.) The House's Committee for Privileges was replaced by a Select Committee for Standards and Privileges. MPs' salaries were substantially increased to reduce the temptation to enter into financial arrangements with outside bodies that could compromise MPs' independence from sectional interests.

Procedural problems

The reformed system put an end to the taking of cash for asking questions, but it soon ran into a series of problems, mostly to do with the procedures for investigating complaints against MPs and for imposing penalties. Complaints may be of failure to register interests, of unjustifiable claims for allowances or misuse of allowances, for instance. The House of Commons itself ultimately decides on guilt and on what penalties if any to impose where a member has acted in breach of the code or of the rules relating to registration of interests. Members of the House, including members of its Standards and Privileges Committee, are not independent or impartial. Many members will have interests in the outcome of the investigation of a complaint against an MP, which may be politically embarrassing to the party to which the MP under investigation belongs. While some penalties for breach of the rules have no legal effect—reprimand, for instance—some of the penalties affect the legal rights and interests of MPs quite seriously—their salary may be withheld, or they may be suspended from the House for a period. Such penalties are enforceable by the House itself and its officers. There can be no appeal against findings and penalties to the courts or any other external, independent body.

The procedures for dealing with complaints against MPs may therefore be in breach of Article 6 of the ECHR (see Appendix), which requires access to an independent and impartial tribunal in the determination of a person's civil rights and obligations, or of criminal charges. The European Court of Human Rights does not consider Parliaments to be exempt from the Convention requirement of access to a court under Article 6 (*Demicoli v. Malta* (1991) 14 EHRR 47). Although the Westminster Parliament is not bound by the

Human Rights Act, section 6 of which specifically excludes the two Houses from the duty to act compatibly with the Convention rights (see Chapter 6), the United Kingdom is bound in international law to secure that its laws, including its procedures, meet the requirements of the Convention. The European Court of Human Rights could well decide, if the question should arise before them, that the lack of access to an independent and impartial tribunal by MPs accused of breach of parliamentary standards, where the allegation is criminal in essence (such as taking bribes) or may result in punishments that interfere with the civil rights of MPs, for instance rights to their pay and access to the House, amounts to a breach of Article 6. The implication of such a finding by the ECtHR would be that jurisdiction over such complaints should be transferred to a court or some other independent tribunal or that there should be appeal to such a body against findings by the House itself or its Committee.

The role of the Parliamentary Commissioner for Standards has also raised problems. It has been understood in different ways. On one view, which was fostered by the second PCS, Elizabeth Filkin, the role was to investigate complaints of impropriety and to reassure the public that standards of conduct in the House were being upheld. The House of Commons, on the other hand, views the PCS' role as an internal one, advising MPs and assisting the House. This latter view seems to have prevailed since the appointment of the third person to hold that office, Philip Mawer, in 2002. But the House of Commons has been inconsistent about the role, claiming that the position of the PCS, as 'a person of independent standing' as recommended by the Committee on Standards in Public Life, introduces an independent element into the investigation of complaints which should reassure both those under investigation and the public about the integrity of the process, and meets any requirement of fairness in procedure. However, the PCS is not institutionally independent of the House or of the Standards and Privileges Committee, and he has no authority in relation to findings of guilt or penalties. The office is non-statutory. The PCS is an officer or servant of the House, he reports to the committee, not to the public, his findings of fact are not binding on the Committee, the Committee makes recommendations to the House about the facts of particular complaints and the penalties if any that should be imposed, and the House itself ultimately decides on guilt and penalties. The procedure adopted by the PCS is generally investigatory, not adversarial in the manner of a trial, though he may engage counsel to advise, and MPs may take legal advice while under investigation, as was the case in the Hamilton and Vaz investigations.

Some of those under investigation by the PCS have refused to cooperate fully in investigations, complaining that the procedures adopted by the PCS have been unfair. The Report of the Committee on Standards and Privileges (Fifth Report, HC 605, 2001–2) on a complaint against Keith Vaz MP, a junior Minister, found some of the charges against him to be well founded and recommended his suspension from the House for a month. The report contained special criticism of his uncooperative approach to the PCS. In response Vaz accepted the report, but stated that he thought the procedure had been unfair. Neil Hamilton too complained about the procedures of the PCS and the select committee, challenging them as unfair. There have also been concerns that the Committee and the House have been reluctant to make findings against members of the government, as was the case in relation to Hamilton, when the investigation started, and Vaz.

The procedures for dealing with parliamentary privilege and conduct have been considered by a number of parliamentary bodies (see Report of the Joint Committee on Parliamentary Privilege, HL 43, HC 214 (1998–9); Fifth Report of the Committee on Standards and Privileges, HC 267 (2000–1)) and the matter has been revisited by the Committee on Standards in Public Life (Sixth Report, Cm. 4557, 2000; Eighth Report Cm. 5663, 2002). There is general agreement that allegations of criminal conduct, bribery of an MP, or acceptance of a bribe by an MP in particular, should be referred to the police and not dealt with in Parliament (see Law Com. 248, *Legislating the Criminal Code: Corruption,* 1998; Committee on Standards and Privileges of the House of Commons, Fifth Report, Session 2000–1, HC 267; Committee on Standards in Public Life, Sixth Report, 2000). The government agreed to bring forward legislation to criminalize bribery of a MP in the run up to the 2001 election (see Home Office, *Raising Standards and Upholding Integrity: The Prevention of Corruption,* Cm. 4759, June 2000). At the start of the 2002–3 parliamentary session the draft bill was published for consultation.

Even if cases of bribery were transferred to the criminal courts, problems would remain over parliamentary procedures for investigating other complaints which might lead to penalties such as suspension from the House or loss of salary. The reports referred to above have sought ways of bringing the procedures for investigation of complaints by the PCS or committees of the House into line with requirements of fairness. For instance, the Committee on Standards in Public Life recommended in its Eighth Report (Cm. 5663, 2002) that the Parliamentary Commissioner for Standards should have a non-renewable fixed term appointment and should be given direct powers to call for witnesses and papers, that no one party should have a majority on the Committee on Standards and Privileges, and no Parliamentary Private Secretaries should serve as members. They also proposed that an investigatory Panel with an independent Chair should hear evidence to help the Committee decide on the most serious and contested cases. However, in my view it is not possible for internal proceedings to meet proper standards of fairness as required by Article 6. An independent, external element is essential. In short the problem is that the House of Commons and its members are highly political and partisan, and complaints about MPs are often politically motivated. The Standards and Privileges Committee is vulnerable to accusations of whitewash if it rejects findings of guilt by the PCS, and of accusations of unfairness if it accepts them. Its members do not themselves have the time to hear all the evidence and arguments in contested cases, and yet they do not hold themselves bound by findings of guilt by the PCS, who does have the time to do so. The PCS cannot be expected to follow full trial-like procedures in investigation. The PCS, even if appointed for a fixed term, would be neither independent nor external; nor would the Panel proposed by the Committee on Standards in Public Life. The Committee on Standards and Privileges would not be bound by the findings of the PCS or the Panel and it would not itself be independent and impartial.

The system was criticized by the Council of Europe's Group of States against Corruption (GRECO) project in 1999. It expressed concern at the continuing self-regulation pursued by the UK Parliament. It proposed that MPs should not be exempt from the law for corruption offences, that the registration of interests system should be tightened up, that the PCS and his powers should be put on a statutory basis with the power to compel the production of information and attendance, and that codes of conduct should also be put on a statutory basis (GRECO *First Evaluation Round: Evaluation Report on the United Kingdom,* Council of Europe, 2001; see Doig, 2002).

Overall one is driven to the conclusion that a system of self-regulation in this highly political field will not be workable. While initial investigation and reporting by the PCS— or by a subcommittee of the Standards and Privileges Committee itself—may be appropriate in cases where the member accepts that he or she has acted improperly or where the complaint is of a minor or accidental infraction, if the system is to be fair to members and command the respect of the public and the press, a right of access by a member accused of misconduct to an independent external and non-political body will be required.

However, in my view there is no prospect of the House of Commons willingly giving jurisdiction over such disciplinary matters that affect the civil rights and obligations of MPs to a properly independent body until the ECtHR makes a finding against them.

Summary and Conclusions on the 'Modernization' of the House of Commons

There have been genuine efforts to enhance the capacity of the House of Commons to exercise an effective scrutiny role in relation to legislation and government policy and administration over at least forty years. Some of these efforts have been stimulated by the sense of powerlessness of a government in waiting—an opposition party that hopes to win the next election and reverse the pattern of government immunity from parliamentary attack which it has suffered for the previous years. This was the stimulus for the select committee reforms in 1979, and for the modernization project which started in 1997. However shortly after an opposition party wins power its sense of the inadequacy of parliamentary scrutiny withers and the priorities of government—to govern with as little uninvited interference as possible and implement its policies—dominate (see Kennon, 2000).

The lesson must be that if reform is not implemented very promptly after a change of government, it becomes increasingly difficult and often impossible to achieve reforms that will more than marginally enhance the role of the House of Commons in holding government to account. No amount of attributing the paralysis to press preoccupations with personalities and stories rather than issues, or exhorting MPs to act differently and whips to change their spots will, in my view, achieve much progress in enhancing the effectiveness of the scrutiny functions of the House of Commons, especially if the government has a safe majority. The political reality is that no government will permit the House of Commons to act autonomously as a scrutineer unless under great political pressure to do so, including political scandal. Unless the party system can be circumvented, which can only be through fundamental shifts in electoral behaviour, facilitated above all by proportional representation for House of Commons elections (see Chapter 7)—which no government will support—the Commons is culturally incapable of performing the scrutiny role our Constitution allocates to it effectively.

This political reality raises the question: if the Commons cannot do this, can or should any other body do so? Clearly on good-governance grounds this function must be discharged somewhere or somehow in the system. This is where the conflict between those committed to the political Constitution (see Chapters 1 and 20) and the law-based Constitution becomes particularly acute. In a customary and common law Constitution such as that of the UK, the courts have it in their power to assume a role as scrutinizers of government and its policies, through judicial review. As we have seen in Chapter 5, the UK courts have developed the jurisdiction in judicial review in radical ways in the last forty years or so. However, they have been fairly deferential to ministers and to Parliament where sensitive policy decisions are in issue (save where they affect identifiable individuals adversely) and they have been reluctant to intervene, on separation of powers grounds, in cases where they believe that the proper channel of accountability is via the House of Commons. Save where European Community law is at issue the courts will not at present countenance striking down legislation of the Westminster Parliament, however badly drafted or undemocratic or 'unconstitutional' or incompatible with human rights and our international obligations it might be. At most the courts require clear and express words to authorize interference with fundamental or constitutional rights (see Chapters 1, 5, and 6). But as it becomes clearer that the Commons are not able themselves to scrutinize government effectively, and if the second chamber is unable to do so—see next chapter—the balance is likely to tip towards judicial intervention, despite the damage this might do to the comity between the courts on the one hand, and Parliament and the government on the other. The continuance of the political Constitution depends in large part on the acceptance by our politicians, including backbenchers in the government party, of their responsibility to hold government to account, a responsibility which in practice is subordinated in the House of Commons to party interests.

There have also been major concerns about standards of conduct in the House of Commons, and public trust has been undermined by instances of taking cash for questions in the 1990s. Mancuso's research established that there was a wide range of ethical standards in the House, some very lax. The response to public concern about sleaze has been reaffirmation of the Burkean view of the role of the MP and a strict insistence on altruistic and public-spirited standards. Reforms have led to increased juridification in the regulation of conduct in the House of Commons, but so far judicialization has been resisted. However, if proper standards of fairness to those against whom complaints are made were to be met, some form of judicialization would be necessary. In my view however the House of Commons will not agree to this unless and until the ECtHR requires it, because of its sensitivities about its privilege of self-regulation.

While the new system for regulating conduct in the House of Commons seems to have put an end to the major abuses of the 1990s, it will take time for the culture of suspicion about MPs to dissipate. Further concerns about misuse of parliamentary allowances could easily arise as and when information about this becomes available under the Freedom of Information Act from 2004. The widespread cynicism about the unwillingness of MPs to act independently of the party whips and their ability to be effective scrutinizers of government policy and legislation will make it harder for the public to regain confidence in the integrity of MPs. Meanwhile the unfairness of the disciplinary system means that as and when serious and contested complaints about an MP's conduct arise, proceedings are likely to be acrimonious and protracted, and this will do further damage to the House of Commons' reputation.

10

Parliament: The Second Chamber

In this chapter we turn to the second chamber of the UK Parliament, the House of Lords. The Preamble to the Parliament Act 1911 made clear that the measure was intended to be temporary. (The Act removed the requirement for consent of the second chamber to money bills, and provided that House of Commons bills could receive the royal assent after two years without the consent of the House of Lords.) The stated long-term aim was to create a new second chamber whose composition was not based on the hereditary principle. Attempts were made to secure inter-party agreement in 1918 (Cd. 9038, 1918), 1948 (Cmd. 7390, 1948), and 1968 (White Paper on House of Lords Reform, Cmnd. 3799, 1968; see Morgan, 1975), but they failed and, until 1997, the electoral mandate or groundswell of public pressure for further reform did not materialize. Instead the only significant reforms to the second chamber were the reduction of the period of delay of legislation to one year by the Parliament Act 1949 and the introduction of life peerages by the Life Peerages Act 1958. The House of Lords remained therefore a partly hereditary, partly appointed body with no claim to democratic legitimacy.

The Labour government's commitments to modernize the Constitution on taking office in 1997 included the removal of the hereditary peers from the House of Lords. A 'democratic and representative' second chamber was to replace the House, but the government had no developed model for such a chamber (Labour Party, *Manifesto*, 1997). In this chapter we shall outline the present position and the recommendations of the Royal Commission on Reform of the House of Lords (of which I was a member), which reported in January 2000, the differences of view about the role, functions and composition of the second chamber, and the theories of constitutionalism, democracy, citizenship, and accountability that lie behind the different views. We shall try to look to the future and consider the implications of the various possible options for the further reform of the House (see generally Dickson and Carmichael, 1999; Patterson and Mughan (eds), 1999; Richard and Welfare, 1999; Forman, 2002, ch. 10; Russell, 2000).

Composition of the Second Chamber

The government's original proposal for the modernization of the Lords focused on its composition—all hereditary members of the second chamber should be removed. But during the passage of the House of Lords bill in 1998 an agreement was struck between the Labour and Conservative parties in the House of Lords that 10 per cent of the hereditary peers plus the deputy speakers and the Earl Marshal and the Lord Great Chamberlain should remain. The amendment to the bill making this provision was moved by the former speaker of the House of Commons, cross-bencher Lord Weatherill, though the deal was struck between the Lord Chancellor and Lord Cranborne, the leader of the Conservatives in the second chamber (Morrison, 2001, ch. 5). These remaining hereditary members are thus known as 'Weatherill peers'. The Conservatives' stated objection to the removal of all hereditary members was in part that it was mistaken to remove them when there was no longer-term policy on how the second chamber should be composed—whether by election, or a mixture of election and appointment—and they threatened to oppose this and other government legislation unless a proportion of the hereditary peers was retained as security for further reform. Seventy-five Weatherill peers were elected by the then hereditary peers in the Lords in proportion to the party balance between them and the independents at that time. Thus they were predominantly, i.e. 52, Conservative. A further 15 hereditary peers who had held office in the Lords—as deputy speakers—were elected by all members of the House. So there are still ninety-two places for hereditary peers in the chamber, including two 'ex officio' hereditary Great Officers of State.

The overall membership of the chamber numbers nearly 700. There is no cap on the size of the second chamber and the numbers fluctuate according to the number of new appointments that are made and the numbers who die. Of these some 575 are life peers, twenty-six are bishops of the Church of England (who serve until retirement and are not life peers), and nearly thirty are Lords of Appeal in Ordinary (Law Lords) and retired Law Lords—and the hereditaries. Most of the members of the House are affiliated to one of the parties. As of September 2002, some 219 took the Conservative whip, 192 took the Labour whip, and 65 took the Liberal Democrat whip. There were 181 cross-benchers, including the Law Lords, retired Law Lords, and deputy speakers. There were eight others, mostly of small parties. And there are 26 archbishops and bishops of the Church of England, who sit on the bishops' benches. The Law Lords seldom take part in the business of the House save in the Appellate Committee (see Chapter 18) and other proceedings of a judicial nature including privilege. A Law Lord chairs Sub-Committee E (Law and Institutions) of the European Union Committee, a successful and important subcommittee.

Thus no one party has a majority in the Lords and the support of independent members may need to be won in highly contentious matters. It is said that this means that parties cannot rely on party discipline and loyalty, but need to rely on argument and evidence to win their points. The government's White Paper *Modernizing Parliament: Reforming the House of Lords* (Cm. 4184, 1999) gave the Royal Commission a strong steer that there should continue to be no single-party majority in the Lords, that party-aligned membership should be in proportion to votes cast in the most recent general election, and that a proportion of members should be cross-benchers.

Most appointments to the House of Lords are formally made by the Queen in the exercise of royal prerogative powers on the recommendation of the Prime Minister. The appointment is by way of the award of a life peerage which carries with it the right to a seat in the House of Lords for life. There is no statutory regulation of the nomination or appointment process. It is not possible for a life peer to resign the peerage, though it is possible to take leave of absence.

The Prime Minister agreed in 1999 to accept the recommendations made by the political parties for 'their' life peers. The way in which the parties select their members is not regulated. There is, for instance, no merit criterion—despite the fact that a peerage is supposed to be an honour—and no requirement that the parties take account of needs for gender or ethnic balance or of other needs of the House, such as for certain 'voices' to be heard, or for particular kinds of expertise or experience. Nominations are vetted by the Political Honours Scrutiny Committee for propriety only. The parties are in practice largely concerned to reward their own activists and donors with peerages, and to provide for their own needs for spokespersons and committee members in the House of Lords. They have therefore a good deal of unregulated patronage.

The Prime Minister reserves the right to determine how many members each party shall have and thus the party balance, and how many members there shall be in the House overall. The appointment of bishops is made by the Crown on the recommendation of the Prime Minister, who receives nominations from the Church of England; the most senior twenty-six sit in the House of Lords until they retire. They are not peers. Law Lords are appointed by the Prime Minister, who usually takes the advice of the Lord Chancellor (see Chapter 18) and like all life peers they remain members of the House for life. Other independent members were appointed for the first time in 2001 on the recommendation of a non-statutory Appointments Commission, the Prime Minister having determined how many should be appointed. These appointments had been flagged as 'people's peers', but those appointed were for the most part people who could well have been appointed directly by the Prime Minister anyway, people of distinction and seniority. The Prime Minister reserves the right to appoint other independents, for instance the retiring Chief of the Defence Staff, retiring Cabinet Secretary, and former speakers of the House of Commons without reference to the Appointments Commission.

The award of a life peerage was originally considered to be an honour carrying no obligations of attendance in the House of Lords. Members may claim an allowance per day for attendance, plus an allowance towards expenses. A distinction between a 'working peers list' and an honours list grew up in the 1980s and in practice nowadays most appointees are regarded as 'working peers'. The parties will only nominate those who undertake to be active in the House in the work of the chamber or in committees. The Appointments Commission also required those it nominated as cross-benchers to be 'working peers', though in practice not all of the Commission's appointees have been active members of the House. They were chosen with the needs of the House, for particular expertise, for example, in mind. Since the first batch of appointments was recommended by the Appointments Commission in 2001 there have, at the time of writing, been no further appointments of cross-benchers, reflecting perhaps embarrassment at the way in which the Commission operated.

The House of Lords differs in many respects from other second chambers. To recap, it is very large, its members are unelected, appointed by the head of the executive, under a system that is not regulated by statute or a constitution—there being no written constitution—they are part time and not salaried, membership is for life (save for the Bishops) and is linked to an honour (see generally Patterson and Mughan, 1999; Russell, 2000). The fact that its members are not elected means that the House lacks legitimacy if it refuses consent to the government's legislation. On the other hand the same fact coupled with membership for life and the distinction of many of those appointed means that the members of the House are relatively independent of party and non-partisan, the operation of the whip system is weak, and the quality of the work of the Chamber is often high.

The Role and Functions of the Second Chamber

A second chamber in a federation where a Senate was part of the deal to protect the interests of the federating states has a different history and function from a second chamber in a non-federal system such as the UK. A second chamber in a country with a written constitution may have explicit roles in relation to the Constitution spelt out in the basic law, which the Westminster Parliament does not have.

At one time all Lords Spiritual and Temporal sat in the Lords and they gave or refused consent to legislation on their own behalf. But this has not been the position for many years. A major difference between the two Houses is, then, that the House of Lords does not give or refuse consent to legislation or scrutinize government policy on behalf of anyone. It is not a representative assembly in the sense that the Commons is. Instead, the House performs a function of scrutiny of legislation and government policy in a non-representative but often expert and independent capacity. This de facto role sits uncomfortably with the fact that most members of the House are party-aligned, but the contradictions of this position are mitigated to an extent by the fact that the conditions of membership of the House enable its members to act in a relatively independent, non-partisan way as compared with the House of Commons.

The House of Lords has in principle the same powers as the House of Commons, but these powers are subject to the House of Commons' financial privilege, to conventions relating to manifesto commitments, and to the Parliament Acts. Thus the second chamber may amend and give or refuse consent to all proposed statutes except money bills. But according to the Salisbury convention a 'manifesto bill' foreshadowed in the governing party's most recent election manifesto and passed by the House of Commons should not be opposed by the second chamber on second or third reading. This convention has prevented conflict between the two Houses.

In the event of a disagreement between the two Houses on legislation, a bill first introduced in the Commons may be passed under the Parliament Acts 1911 and 1949 without the consent of the Lords thirteen months after its second reading in the Commons. But the Lords may still veto an Act to prolong the life of Parliament beyond the normal maximum of five years.

The House holds the government to account in broadly similar ways to the House of Commons. It passed a resolution on ministerial responsibility at the same time as the

Commons in 1997 (see Chapter 11). Its select committees are highly regarded, though it does not have a system of departmentally related select committees like the Commons. And its scrutiny of legislation both via specialist select committees and on the floor of the House is of a high quality. In May 2002 it accepted an important role in the scrutiny of draft bills as part of a package of procedural reforms.

The House of Lords has assumed roles as a constitutional council or watchdog, as general purpose scrutinizer of legislation on technical and 'workability' grounds and of government policy, and as a forum for discussion of matters of public concern. The life peers in particular are able to bring experience in government, the House of Commons, and other walks of life to their activities in the House, and this combination of knowledge and wide experience gives authority to the debates in the House.

The Lords complements the Commons in holding government to account. In fact its scrutiny of bills and of European Community legislation and many of its committee activities and debates are considered to be of a higher quality than the Commons' activity. This is partly because of its membership and the relatively non-partisan conditions in which it operates. But also the purpose of much scrutiny is clearer in the Lords. While the standing committees in the House of Commons and the House of Lords when engaging in line-by-line scrutiny of bills 'debate' them at large and deal with proposed amendments, the orders of reference of the legislative scrutiny committees in the House of Lords, its select committees, and Joint Committees of the two Houses, are specific and make much clearer the constitutional aspects of scrutiny than the terms of reference of standing committees in the Commons. The Delegated Powers and Regulatory Reform Committee of the House of Lords scrutinizes bills for, among other things, the inappropriate delegation of powers. The Constitution Committee, established in 2001 in response to recommendations of the Royal Commission (see below), has made important recommendations about the process of constitutional change and proposed that the publication of bills in draft should be the norm, that constitutional issues should be dealt with in a more integrated approach, securing that a culture of knowledge and understanding of constitutional matters is developed, and it has indicated a willingness to cooperate with House of Commons Committees on constitutional issues (Fourth Report of the House of Lords Select Committee on the Constitution, *Changing the Constitution: The Process of Constitutional Change*, HL 69, 2001–2). In late 2002 it embarked on systematic scrutiny of bills and draft bills for constitutional implications, engaging a legal adviser to assist with the work.

The European Union Committee, which has six subcommittees, identifies some thirty or forty items of EU business each year for in-depth study and analysis (see Chapter 4). It thus complements the Commons' European Scrutiny Committee which, via its advisers, rapidly sifts all proposals under consideration in the Council of Ministers and recommends to the European Standing Committees of the Commons which should be subject to debate or consideration. The combined activities of the House of Commons and House of Lords committees produce one of the most highly developed systems in the EU for considering proposed European legislation and other proposals and for ensuring that Ministers are aware of the balance of opinion within Parliament before they commit the UK to any significant new position (Royal Commission, para. 8.12). These committees do not normally take votes and they do not divide on party lines. As we noted in Chapter 4, two members of the House of Lords have been appointed as Alternates to two House of Commons Representatives to the Convention on the future of Europe, and they may participate in a House of Commons Standing Committee that was established in June 2002, charged with monitoring the work of the Convention and reporting back to Parliament on it.

There are also important and effective Joint Committees of the two Houses in which scrutiny of proposed legislation on defined constitution-related criteria takes place. The Joint Committee on Human Rights scrutinizes bills for compatibility with the Human Rights Act and generally inquires into human rights issues, again in a non-partisan spirit. On the government's attempts to rush through a number of authoritarian provisions in the wake of the 11 September 2001 bombing of the World Trade Centre in New York the Committee commented:

Parliament should take a long view, and resist the temptation to grant powers to governments which compromise the rights and liberties of individuals. The situation which may appear to justify the granting of such powers are temporary—the loss of freedom is often permanent . . . Too many ill-conceived measures litter the statute book as a result of such rushed legislation in the past. (Second Report of the Joint Select Committee on Human Rights, HC 372, HL 37, 2001–2, para. 76.)

The House made a number of important amendments in its scrutiny of the Terrorism Bill.

The terms of reference of the Joint Committee on Statutory Instruments require it to review the vires, drafting, and certain technical aspects of Statutory Instruments, but not their merits and to determine whether the instrument—secondary legislation—imposes a charge on the revenue, is excluded from judicial review, has retrospective effect, or might be *ultra vires*.

The main problem with the House of Lords, then, is the composition of the House, which many find difficult to reconcile with democratic principles. The actual role and functions of the House are not considered to be undemocratic, though there are some who would prefer a single chamber Parliament and assume that the House of Commons could itself perform the scrutiny and constitutional watchdog functions of the second chamber. Given the highly partisan nature of the Commons it is not in my view credible to suggest that they would be capable of the objectivity necessary for performing these functions, and nor would they have the expertise to perform them.

The Recommendations of the Royal Commission on Reform of the House of Lords

With this background summary of the position of the House of Lords in mind, let us now turn to the principal recommendations of the Royal Commission and the issues they raise (Cm. 4534, 2000). There were 132 recommendations in all, many of a detailed nature. We shall focus on those which relate to our themes. The Royal Commission considered the role and functions of the second chamber first and then made recommendations as to composition and other issues which would enable it to fulfil that role and perform the functions they had identified for it. It is worth noting at this point that many commentators have assumed that a wholly elected second chamber could perform all the functions that it is agreed the second chamber should perform. This is arguably not the case—election does not necessarily qualify those elected to perform many of the functions of the second chamber, notably those which require non-partisan and expert consideration. Election makes a non-partisan approach difficult to sustain. We shall return later to the question whether these functions are intrinsically parliamentary functions.

The Royal Commission considered that the second chamber should bring a range of perspectives to bear on the development of public policy, be broadly representative of British society so that there is a voice in Parliament for regional, vocational, ethnic, professional, cultural, or religious aspects of people's personalities, that it should play a vital role as one of the main checks and balances in the Constitution, complementing the Commons in doing so, and it should provide a voice for the nations and regions of the UK. Its powers should continue to include, as now, a delaying power under the Parliament Acts, but its power to veto statutory instruments should be replaced by a delaying power so that the second chamber's rejection of an SI could be overridden by an affirmative vote in the Commons. Its role in protecting the Constitution should be enhanced through a Constitutional Committee (one was set up in 2001) and a Human Rights Committee (a Joint Committee was set up in 2001). Its other powers and activities should continue broadly as at present, though better support facilities should be provided (such support was agreed to in May 2002).

On the question of composition, the Royal Commission proposed that membership of the second chamber should be separated from the peerage, though existing life peers should be entitled to retain their seats if they wished. The remaining hereditary members should be removed. Some members of the reformed second chamber should be elected to represent the nations and regions on a proportional basis, either 65, 87, or 195 in number, and they should serve for either three electoral cycles—between twelve and fifteen years in practice—or for fixed twelve-year terms. It is worth noting at this point that many of the submissions received by the Royal Commission urged that the reformed second chamber should be substantially or wholly elected, but also expressed hostility to the dominance of the parties in the Commons. The fact of the matter is that elected members would inevitably stand for parties and the party battle would be reflected in a House of elected members as it is in the Commons.

The Royal Commission recommended that the rest of the members should be appointed by an independent statutory Appointments Commission, and the Prime Minister's power to determine the party balance and the overall size of the chamber should cease. The Appointments Commission would appoint party-aligned members to produce proportionality between the parties in accordance with shares of the vote in the most recent general election. It would also appoint independents, who should be about 20 per cent of the total. The parties wold be entitled to put forward nominations, but the Appointments Commission would make its own decisions on appointment. The

Commission would work to guidelines so as to move towards due representation of ethnic minorities and at least 30 per cent women members and 30 per cent men members. It would identify the needs of the house in terms of expertise and provide voices for a range of sections of society—a chamber broadly representative of British society. This would include representatives from other Christian denominations and other faiths. The number of Lords Spiritual should be reduced. Appointments would be on merit. The House would derive its legitimacy and authority from the facts that a proportion of members was elected, that party-aligned membership overall was proportionate to votes in general elections, and from the merit criterion for appointment and the fact that the membership overall gave voices to a wider spectrum of society than is possible in the House of Commons.

Responses to the Royal Commission's Recommendations

The general press and public reaction to these proposals was that the elected element was far too small. There was little interest in the recommendations as to the role, functions and powers of a reformed second chamber, though these were broadly supported. Almost all comments focused on composition. The two Houses debated the proposals in March 2000 and it was clear that there was no cross-party consensus in favour of the report or indeed in favour of any other set of proposals.

In November 2001 the Lord Chancellor published a White Paper, *The House of Lords: Completing the Reform* (Cm. 5291) proposing a house of some 600 members, of whom 120 would be elected and 330 would be appointed on the nomination of the parties. There would be 120 independent members, appointed by an independent Appointments Commission, sixteen bishops, and the Law Lords and retired Law Lords up to seventy or seventy-five years of age. The strong sense in the Commons was that only a substantially elected House would be acceptable, and these proposals were rejected on that ground. Opinion in the House of Lords was divided over the balance of elected and appointed members, although there was stronger support for a preponderance of appointed members than in the Commons. The public consultation on the White Paper proposals showed that most respondents favoured a substantially or wholly elected House (*Analysis of Consultation Responses*, Lord Chancellor's Department, May 2002). After the Commons debate on the White Paper, the Conservative Party committed itself to a house of three hundred members, 80 per cent of whom would be elected by first past the post system (see Chapter 7), 20 per cent would be appointed cross-benchers. The Liberal Democrats put in a bid for an 80 per cent elected chamber, elections to be by proportional representation (see Chapter 7), the remaining twenty per cent to be appointed cross-benchers.

After the Commons debate the Public Administration Select Committee (PASC) undertook a short but extensive inquiry into the issue of House of Lords reform to try to establish whether there was a basis for agreement on which reform of the second chamber could proceed (Fifth Report of the PASC, 2001–2, *The Second Chamber: Continuing the*

Reform, HC 494). They accepted that a mixed House, with different streams of member-ship feeding into it, able to play the role of a standing civic forum as well as a processor of legislation, would give the second chamber a distinctive and valuable place in the political system, complementing the House of Commons in the task of scrutiny and account-ability and so adding value to the political system as a whole (Report, para. 7). Their conclusion was that there could be a consensus on a reformed chamber consisting of 60 per cent of members elected by STV or fully open regional lists (see Chapter 7) to represent the nations and regions. Of the remaining 40 per cent, half should be nomin-ated by the political parties, and the proportions of nominated members should reflect the votes won in the most recent second chamber election. The remainder should be independent, non-aligned members (recommendation (c)). Appointments should be by a statutory Appointments Commission, which would take the final decision as to appointments of party-aligned members. In other words parties would not have the absolute right to nominate members. If the government was unable to accept this rec-ommendation, there should be no element of party nominees in the reformed chamber and its composition should consist of 70 per cent directly elected members and 30 per cent independent appointees.

Following disagreement on the matter within government, in July 2002 a Joint Com-mittee of the two Houses was established to try to produce agreed proposals for reform (HC Deb., 13 May 2002, col. 516; HL Deb., 13 May 2002, col. 13). In December 2002 the joint Committee recommended that, after debate on the report, there should be votes in each House on seven options: a second chamber that was fully appointed, fully elected, fifty per cent elected and fifty per cent appointed, or with appointment and election in ratios of 80:20, 60:40, 40:60 or 20:80. Members should be free to vote in favour of as many options as they considered acceptable. Thereafter the Joint Committee would resume its deliberations and seek to develop, in their second report, a single set of proposals for reform (First Report from the Joint Committee on House of Lords Reform, HL 17, HC 171, 2002–03). At the time of going to press these votes had not taken place.

Reform of the Working Practices of the House

An aspect of the House of Lords which the Royal Commission hoped could survive any reform of the chamber was its open procedures, which give considerable freedom to individual members. This is in marked contrast with the House of Commons, where the strong party system and a history of obstructionist tactics by Irish Nationalist MPs led to the rights of individual MPs being progressively restricted to ensure that the govern-ment's business would be processed. In the Lords the Speaker—the Lord Chancellor—has no authority over the House. The Leader of the House, though a member of the government, merely advises the House matters of procedure and traditionally seeks consensus on these matters, and has no authority over it either. The members of the House themselves have responsibility for maintaining order, and in the relatively non-partisan, high-trust atmosphere of the chamber this mechanism has proved effective. Any member may raise any point and there is no formally enforceable timetable. Government business does not have priority. There is, however, a convention that all government business should be considered within a reasonable time.

These open procedures have come under pressure from the increased workload of the House in recent years. The Royal Commission recognized that this had led to, and would continue to lead to, peers being subject to guidance which restricts the freedom of members in various ways—for instance by limiting the number of Questions for Written Answer that a peer could table and the number of Starred (Oral) Questions, and limiting Question Time to thirty minutes. Nevertheless the Royal Commission hoped that any restrictions on the rights of members should preserve the open character of the chamber's procedures (Royal Commission Report, 2000, ch. 16).

The Leader of the House after the 2001 election, Lord Williams of Mostyn, set up a cross-party working group on the working practices of the House, which brought forward a number of proposals for improving the scrutiny of legislation and government policy by the House while preserving the rights of members. In July 2002 the House of Lords agreed to a number of important improvements to its working practices, recommended in the *Report from the Leader's Group appointed to consider how the working practices of the House can be improved, and to make recommendations* (HL 111, 2001–2; see also Fifth Report of the Select Committee on the Procedure of the House, HL 148, 2001–2). The principal reforms were a commitment to pre-legislative scrutiny for almost all major government bills published in draft. The House also approved taking the committee stage of more bills off the floor of the House, carry-over of bills where pre-legislative scrutiny had taken place, more sensible working hours with the House rising at 10 p.m., compensated for by sittings in September, a new ad hoc committee for Finance bills that would look at issues to do with taxation (other than those within the financial privilege of the Commons such as rates of tax), and a new select committee to scrutinize statutory instruments on the merits. These had all been agreed by the cross-party working party and were presented to the House by Lord Williams as ways of securing that Parliament as a whole could perform its scrutiny role well, utilizing the expertise in the House, and emphasizing that although the members of the House were part time, it was a full-time House (see HL Deb., 21 May 2002, cols. 642–725). They also substantially preserve the freedom of members and the open and informally regulated procedures in the House. The government, however, rejected the proposal that Finance bills should be scrutinized in the House of Lords, maintaining that this would trespass on the Commons' privileges.

The reforms to the working practices of the House will lead to a significant increase in the Committee work of the House, with the potential for a pre-legislative scrutiny committee, a Grand Committee, and a Committee of the Whole House all meeting on the same day, in addition to the other committees. This will make it necessary for the legislative timetable to be carefully planned to avoid Ministers, opposition spokespersons, and others having conflicting demands for their time and presence in the House. It will also be necessary to increase the rooms available for committee work and the support for the committees.

Overall, however, more and smoother progress has been made by the House of Lords in modernizing its working practices than by the House of Commons. This may be put down to the consensual, non-partisan approach to these matters in the Lords. This is made possible by the composition of the House, and it seems unlikely that a House with a substantially elected element would be able to reach agreement on procedural reforms in the same way.

Issues for Democracy, Citizenship, and Good Governance in the Reform of the Second Chamber

Let us now try to tease out the assumptions behind the various positions taken on reform of the second chamber and the different models of democracy and citizenship and attitudes to good governance that inform them. There is broad agreement about the role, functions, and powers of the second chamber. These are functions that need to be performed in a democracy. The House of Commons is incapable of performing some of them, notably the constitutional scrutiny and watchdog, civic forum, and deliberative assembly roles, because of its party-dominated nature, the absence of voices for many sections of society, and the limited range of expertise of its members.

The function of scrutiny of legislation for compatibility with the Constitution and international obligations is performed in other countries by various bodies—by chambers of the Parliament, but also by courts or constitutional councils. In the USA, for instance, the Supreme Court may strike down legislation that is incompatible with the Constitution (*Marbury v. Madison*, 1 Cranch 137 (1803)). In France the Conseil d'etat scrutinizes bills and other proposed laws before they are introduced into Parliament and rejects them or requires amendment if they are badly drafted or defective in various ways (see Bell, 1992; Massot, 2001). The French Conseil constitutionnel examines bills before they are promulgated for their constitutionality and if the Conseil d'etat has rejected them the Conseil constitutionnel is likely to declare them unconstitutional. Procedures for the scrutiny of proposed laws for the quality of their drafting and their constitutionality are part of the system of good governance in these democracies. It need not be done exclusively by an elected chamber of the legislature. It is not considered anti-democratic in such countries for these non-parliamentary, unelected bodies to play such roles.

A difference between almost all other countries and the UK that has a bearing on the role of the second chamber is that the UK does not have a written Constitution in the sense of an authoritative text against which a bill can be measured for compatibility with the Constitution. Thus adoption of the US or French models, which rely on a Supreme Court or a constitutional council or council of state, would be problematic. The UK's system of government is nevertheless regarded as being subject to constitutional conventions and principles that are common to other democracies, such as the independence of the judiciary, compliance with international standards of respect for human rights and good governance, and responsible government (see discussion in Chapters 1–3, and Birch, 1964). While government in the UK is not limited by a written Constitution in the ways that governments in most other democracies are, these principles imply at the least a theory of *inhibited* government, government subject to non-legal, conventional, and moral constraints in its activities, in a majoritarian, liberal democracy.

Many of the functions of the House of Lords positively promote this model of democracy. It has a distinctive role that is performed in other countries by non-parliamentary institutions. Set against the Parliament Acts and the power of the government to insist on its legislation on the consent of the Commons alone, the UK's arrangements represent a middle way between raw majoritarianism and formally constitutionally limited government. (As we noted in Chapter 6 the same model is also reflected in the Human Rights Act.) The most important point is that these essential legislative scrutiny functions should be well performed and this means performed by people with the necessary expertise and experience and, importantly, people working in conditions that promote an objective approach and do not subject the scrutineers to pressures to defer to the judgement of others or party political pressures.

The other functions of the House of Lords, scrutiny of government policy and administration and the debate of matters of public interest, are generally well done in that chamber. An important point about them is that a member of the government is normally present when these matters are debated in the chamber and responds to points raised, and the government is expected to respond in good time to the reports of the select committees of the House. There is thus an inbuilt response procedure in the House which imposes a stronger form of accountability than is imposed where policy and administration are criticized by the press or by other outside bodies, whether in the voluntary or commercial sector.

The Royal Commission's recommendations envisaged that the membership of the chamber would become more representative of a broad range of 'voices' in society through the Appointments Commission they proposed, thus enhancing the capacity of the reformed second chamber to be a forum for public participation, via its members, in the development of policy and holding government to account. Citizens' voices would be heard directly and not mediated through the parties. The Royal Commission rejected proposals that these voices should reach the second chamber by nomination from organizations such as professional bodies, trade unions, and so on as being unworkable in practice and likely to give rise to conflict and disagreement about which bodies should have nomination rights and whether such nominees were in the second chamber to promote the interests of their nominating body—which would not be compatible with the functions of that chamber— or to contribute their perspectives and expertise to the activities of the chamber. The experience in the Republic of Ireland has been that the parties have taken over the members nominated by such groups and this too would not be compatible with the scheme of the Royal Commission recommendations. In effect, as the PASC noted (Fifth Report, 2001–2, HC 494) arrangements on the lines of the Royal Commission's proposals would add an explicit 'civic forum' role for the second chamber (see Chapter 14 on the use of civic forums in the devolved areas). This would increase the participatory and deliberative democracy elements in the Constitution, running alongside the representative arrangements in the House of Commons, the devolved bodies, and local government. It would strengthen the socio-cultural dimension in our constitutional arrangements, whereas a wholly or substantially elected second chamber would reinforce the political Constitution.

The fact that the Royal Commission's proposals as to composition were strongly resisted by the political parties, who insisted for the most part either that the second chamber should be wholly or very substantially elected or, if members were to be appointed, that the parties not the Appointment Commission should appoint party-aligned members, reflects a sub-conscious resistance to anything other than party-dominated, tribal, representative democracy. (We shall see in our consideration of devolution that civic forums have been established in Scotland and Northern Ireland. There too they are not taken very seriously by the political parties.) As Wright and Gamble (2002) have put it, party is an important channel for citizens' voices to be heard, but not the only one. Parties 'need to occupy enough political territory to do their job, but not so much that they crowd out other forms of civic expression. . . . Thinking about what a "civic" chamber might look like, instead of merely assuming that the only means of civic expression was through a party system would at least acknowledge that there was a problem' (p. 124). Their comment on debates about reform of the composition of the House of Lords was that: 'All good democrats promptly announced that direct election was the only basis upon which a reformed second chamber could be constructed . . . this ignored the fact that party list elections were in practice the same as appointment, and that a revising second chamber dominated by party control in the image of the Commons risked diminishing real scrutiny and accountability' (p. 123).

In sum, a substantially or wholly elected House or a House most of whose members were in effect nominated by the parties would become tribal, like the House of Commons, and thus in my view it would become less able to perform the functions which it currently performs rather well.

On the other hand it is clear that a chamber of Parliament that is not elected, or substantially elected, could not have the legitimacy necessary to give authority to its rejection of the policy or legislation of the government of the day. At issue, in other words, is the conceptualization of the second chamber as a chamber of Parliament in the image of the senates of other democracies, or as a council of state, constitutional council and civic forum, as well as a legislative chamber, which is in effect what the House of Lords has become and what it would be if the Royal Commission's recommendations or something close to them were put into effect.

At present (January 2003) the most likely outcome of the deliberations of the Joint Committee on reform of the House of Lords and the votes on its proposals in the two Houses is a substantially elected chamber whose party-aligned members would be partly elected and partly appointed automatically on the nomination of the parties, subject to vetting only for propriety, by the Appointments Commission. This would represent a rejection of the concept of the chamber as a constitutional watchdog and civic forum, an institution that could contribute a participatory and deliberative dimension to democracy and citizenship in the UK. An opportunity to develop a socio-cultural dimension would be missed. Such a model would also give immense patronage and power to the parties which could be open to abuse, for instance in rewarding party donors or in finding a resting place for MPs who were no longer able to contribute in the House of Commons. Such a system would not produce sufficient numbers of people qualified to perform the specialist functions, which it seems to be generally agreed the second chamber should perform. It would increase the level of tribalism in the second chamber since most members would owe their appointment to the parties and would be likely to be strongly politically partisan. And, given that appointment would not be on merit or on the basis of criteria spelling out the needs of the chamber for voices from various otherwise unrepresented or underrepresented sections of society to have an input into its deliberations, it would undermine the capacity of the chamber to fulfil its functions. Although the fact that a substantial element of the House would be elected should add to its legitimacy, the quality of its work would be likely to be lower than at present.

Looking ahead, if I am right in predicting that the ability of the second chamber to perform its functions will be damaged by future likely reforms, more ill-thought-out legislation will find its way on to the statute book and there will be increasing recourse to courts by litigants who are aggrieved by the law. The courts' inhibitions against stretching the interpretation of legislation or even reading down or reading in provisions that would make statutory provisions more conforming to liberal-democratic norms will be undermined, and the courts will become more interventionist. The courts' reluctance to strike down legislation, based on a desire to preserve comity with Parliament and the executive, will also be undermined, especially if the press and the public become concerned about the quality of legislation and less respectful of Parliament and the executive. As laws come on to the statute book that are incompatible with the European Convention on Human Rights and other international obligations both chambers will come under increasing pressure and criticism.

In due course, as the European Court of Justice and the European Court of Human Rights are—inevitably—called upon to intervene in UK government action and legislation that may breach European Community law and the Convention, there will be pressure for the establishment of other, extra-parliamentary, independent, pre-legislative scrutiny mechanisms and institutions to subject bills, statutory instruments, and Orders in Council to scrutiny for compliance with European Community law and the ECHR.

A further difficulty, and one which the Royal Commission sought to avoid in its proposals but which many members of the House of Commons in its debates on reform of the second chamber seemed not to be concerned about, could be that a wholly or substantially elected second chamber—especially if elected by proportional representation—would have a claim to legitimacy equal to or even superior to that of the Commons. This could lead to deadlock in conflicts between the two Houses in which even the power to delay legislation for a year might seem an unreasonable fetter on the second chamber if public opinion were on its side.

There are, then, advantages in having a second chamber which does not have the same democratic legitimacy as the Commons, and this suggests some merit in a chamber that is not entirely or even substantially elected. If the second chamber were entirely elected, whether on the same electoral system as the House of Commons or on some form of proportional representation, then there could be clashes between the two chambers, since each could lay claim to an electoral mandate and democratic legitimacy, and a substantially elected chamber could not perform the functions expected of it as well as the present House of Lords does.

A question for consideration is: would attitudes to reform of the House of Lords be changed if it were re-named 'The Council of State'?

Conclusions on the Reform of Parliament

The account in this and the previous chapter of reforms and attempts at reform of the two Houses of the Westminster Parliament shows how difficult it is to achieve coherent change. Progress is made, if at all, on an incremental basis, often with no clear view of where the reform is heading and what the ultimate shape of the institution will be. This is typical of the British political system—devolution too has been a step-by-step process lacking coherence.

The actual reforms to the two Houses of Parliament that have been achieved in recent years and those that are likely to be made in the near future bring out the clash between different democratic models. Some reformers seek to widen the representative character of Parliament and to strengthen its ability to hold government to account against explicit constitutional criteria, extending representation beyond the two main parties through proportional representation. Others seek to retain, even extend, the dominance of the two-party system and the executive in Parliament. Yet others prefer a forum where voices other than those of the parties can be heard. A model of constrained government and deliberative and participatory democracy, which lay behind many of the proposals of the Royal Commission does not chime with the Commons', nor with majority public, opinion.

Despite recent reforms, it seems most unlikely that the House of Commons will be able to strengthen its own scrutiny function in relation to government for as long as the electoral system produces disproportionately large majorities. It is increasingly obvious that alternatives will need to be found to subject administrative bodies including executive agencies (see Chapter 12) and quangos (see Chapter 17) to account. It is also likely that further reform of the second chamber, though it may increase the representative element in the chamber, will actually weaken its ability to perform a scrutiny—as opposed to consent-giving—role. We have already noted the likelihood of increased judicial review of public administration, including review of the quality of legislation if Parliament cannot perform this role. It would not be surprising if pressure mounted for an independent external agency like the French Conseil d'etat or Conseil constitution-nel—perhaps a development of the Judicial Committee of the Privy Council—to pre-vet legislation (as is already possible for legislation of the Scottish Parliament and the Northern Ireland Assembly). In other words, if Parliament cannot be made to hold government to account effectively—and in my view it cannot now and it will continue to be unable to do so under the first past the post system, which it will not agree to give up—we shall come to realize that there are alternatives that could be made to work well and in due course they will develop. But this will involve moves away from the political Constitution towards the legal Constitution.

11

Government: Ministers

In this chapter and the next we are concerned with issues to do with reform of 'Her Majesty's Government'—the government of the United Kingdom. The government includes the Cabinet and other Ministers—the political arm of the executive—and civil servants, the professional, largely non-political arm. The latter are considered in the next chapter. Other executive bodies include the executives of the devolved bodies, which are discussed in Chapters 13–15, local authorities, discussed in Chapter 16, and non-departmental public bodies or quasi-autonomous non-governmental organizations—Quangos—discussed in Chapter 17.

The executive undergoes frequent reshaping as new departments are created and old ones are wound up or split, and as responsibilities are transferred from one department to another. The Prime Minister and the Cabinet Office are growing in importance as Prime Ministers seek to ensure that government policies are put into practical effect by the civil service and other bodies. We shall not however be concerned with these, often ephemeral, issues in this chapter. Rather we shall be focusing on general issues to do with the different forms of accountability that operate in government, the relationships between Ministers and Parliament, and concerns about possible undermining of standards of conduct in government as a result of the development of governance via network arrangements.

The Crown and the State

First, a few background observations about the legal position of the government. The government of the United Kingdom is conducted in the name of the Crown (see generally Sunkin and Payne, 1999). This is a rather mysterious legal concept, roughly but not entirely equivalent to the concept of 'the state' in many European countries (Dyson, 1980). In UK law, however, 'the state' is an almost unknown concept, save in the context of international law. The courts have had to interpret the use of the phrase 'the state' or 'interests of the state' when used in a statute in a number of cases. For instance in *Chandler v. DPP* ([1964] AC 763) the question was whether demonstrators who had planned a sit-in in a military airbase would have entered it 'for a purpose prejudicial to the . . . interests of the state.' It was held that 'the state' meant the organized community (per Lord Reid and Lord Hodson) or 'the organs of government of a national community' (per Lord Devlin and Lord Pearce); and that 'the interests of the state' meant such interests according to the policies of the state as they in fact were, not the interests as, it might be argued by demonstrators, they ought to be (per Lord Devlin and Lord Pearce). In *R. v. Ponting* ([1985] *Crim. L.R.* 318), it was held that 'the interests of the state' under the Official Secrets Act 1911 were those interests as defined by the government of the day, not by the defendant or a jury. But these cases do not add up to a developed concept of the meaning or purpose of the state in our legal system.

What civil law countries regard as the state is split in the UK between a mixture of Crown bodies, bodies that are the creatures of statute such as the devolved bodies, local authorities, and quangos. There are in addition many other bodies created, for instance, by royal charter or as companies, whose status as 'state bodies' (or, to use the terminology of the Human Rights Act and other recent legislation such as the Freedom of Information Act, 'public authorities') is unclear. In most European democracies, for instance—Ireland is a notable exception—universities are regarded as state institutions and university lecturers are civil servants. In the United Kingdom most universities have royal charters, with some of their powers confirmed by statute, but their staff are not civil servants and they are not generally regarded as state bodies.

While we shall not dwell on the difficulty in distinguishing state bodies or public authorities or functions from other bodies and functions in this book, it is worth pointing out at this stage that the absence in UK law of a developed, or indeed even a minimalist, concept of state may be more suited to modern conditions than the Continental approach. Many European countries have, or have had until recently, a clear and developed sense of the state, its role, its prerogatives, its powers, duties, and privileges (Allison, 1999; Bell, 1992). Given the increasing use in the UK and in other European democracies of networks to deliver public policies (see Chapter 1) and the privatization of many enterprises in the last twenty years or so, the concept of 'state' and associated concepts such as public services (see Freedland and Sciarra, 1998) are becoming increasingly imprecise and hard to apply, and it may be that the common law's virtual ignorance of the concepts makes it easier for our legal and constitutional system to adapt to these changes than many Continental systems are able to.

The legal status of the Crown and the royal prerogative

The Crown is the governmental aspect of the monarch's powers. In law the Crown has corporate personality separate from the person of the monarch, and separate from the Ministers and civil servants who act in the name of the Crown. The Crown's legal personality is a matter of common law—the Crown's existence and its powers are not owed to a written Constitution (there is none) nor to any statute, although such matters as the succession are regulated by statute. Much of the government's power derives from the royal prerogative. There is a debate among lawyers about whether these powers are only the 'special preeminence which the King hath over and above all other persons, and out of the ordinary course of the common law, in right of his royal dignity' (Blackstone, 1765–9, 239), which would cover only such special powers as defence, declaring and waging war, making treaties, dissolving Parliament, awarding honours, granting pardons and so on, or whether it is the residue of non-statutory discretionary or arbitrary authority power of the Crown (Dicey, 1885, 1959 edn, 424) which would include the 'special pre-eminence' referred to above, as well as the power to own and dispose of property and to make contracts, which derive from the fact of the corporate personality of the Crown. On any account these powers derive from the common law and not from statute nor, as would be the case if the UK had a written Constitution, from a basic law.

The *special* common law powers of the Crown belong formally to the monarch, but by convention they are exercisable only on the advice of the relevant Minister. To this extent it might be said that the UK has a monarchical Constitution—many governmental powers are inherent, do not derive from statute, and are not subject to parliamentary control. The royal prerogative is or includes (depending which definition is adopted) the residue of what was until the late seventeenth century almost absolute monarchical power. Much of this power has been removed from the monarch by statute and either abolished or formally transferred to Parliament or Ministers. For instance, in the Bill of Rights of 1689 it was provided that the powers of suspending and dispensing with laws which the King had been exercising were unlawful, and that there should be no taxation without the consent of Parliament (see discussion of *Cheney v. Conn* in Chapter 5)—a provision designed to remove from the King the power to raise revenues without statutory authorization.

Most of the substantive royal prerogative powers exist in other countries—all governments need power to conduct foreign relations, to organize and dispose of the armed forces and the civil service, to select Ministers and dismiss them or receive their resignations. In the UK however, these powers may generally be exercised without the prior or subsequent consent of Parliament. Thus, for instance, the power of disposition of the armed forces may be exercised by the government unilaterally, and treaties may be entered into and commitments made to the European Union, without the consent of Parliament.

These powers are not completely unregulated, but the regulation is generally political and indirect rather than formal or statutory. For instance, the power to make dispositions of the royal forces is exercised against the provisions of the Bill of Rights 1689, which prevents the maintenance of an army in peacetime without the consent of Parliament. Nowadays this consent is given every five years in an Army Act and, indirectly, annually in the appropriation of funds for the army, without which of course an army cannot be maintained. Thus a government will not act in the face of known strong opposition from Parliament which could, at least in theory, retaliate by refusing to renew the Army Act or to grant funds without government concessions on its right to be consulted. As far as treaties are concerned, we have seen in Chapter 4 that there are particular safeguards against undertaking treaty obligations in the European Union. Generally treaties cannot have effect in domestic law in the UK unless incorporated by statute. In this respect the UK's dualist system differs from most European countries' monist systems, under which treaty obligations can give rise to rights that are enforceable in their courts. However, by a convention known as the Ponsonby rule, treaties requiring ratification are laid before Parliament for twenty-one sitting days prior to ratification or mutual notification by the parties of the completion of constitutional or other internal procedures, with a commitment that time will be found for debate if demanded. These are just examples of the ways in which prerogative powers are regulated either by law or by convention, but it remains the case that the protections against arbitrary or unreasonable use of prerogative powers by government are less developed than those against abuse of statutory powers. This became an issue in the summer and autumn of 2002 as the government moved towards committing forces to a war against Iraq. The disposition of forces and a possible declaration of war did not require, by law, parliamentary consent, nor even a parliamentary debate. This was a matter for the unjuridified political Constitution.

It is then a peculiarity of the royal prerogative that generally no particular procedures are prescribed in law for its exercise—no requirements of prior consultation, consent of Parliament, and so on—and it leaves considerable powers in the hands of, for instance, the Prime Minister or even, exceptionally, of the Queen. For instance, given that there are not fixed-term Parliaments in the UK (see Chapter 7) the Prime Minister advises the Queen of his choice of an election date. By convention the Queen acts on the advice of the Prime Minister, but there may be a residual right on the part of the monarch to refuse a dissolution if, for instance, there has been a very recent general election. The power to decide upon a date for the dissolution of Parliament could be replaced by a provision, which would remove discretionary power from the system, for fixed-term Parliaments which would come to an end by effluxion of time. Alternatively, early dissolution could be ordered subject to non-discretionary criteria such as loss of a vote of confidence by the government or a resolution of both Houses of Parliament (see Chapter 7). But such a change would require an Act of Parliament and no government is likely to want such a change, given the advantages of the present system to the Prime Minister of the day (see generally Brazier, 1998).

The Queen has discretion in the choice of a new Prime Minister after an election, though that choice is regulated to a considerable degree by convention. However, where there is a hung Parliament after an election and the incumbent Prime Minister is unable to command the support of a majority in the House of Commons and resigns, the Queen may have to make a choice between asking the leader of the largest or next largest party to form a government, or seeking some other person who may be able to command the support of a majority formed from two or more parties, not including the largest party. The making of such a choice may be very controversial and the monarch is likely to be exposed to allegations of partisanship from disappointed parties. An alternative mechanism for selecting a Prime Minister would be for the House of Commons to elect the Prime Minister—as happens with the First Minister in the Scottish Parliament and the Taioseach in the Irish Parliament—thus removing any discretion from the Queen as Head of State, though she would still formally make the appointment. Such a change need not require legislation. The House of Commons could itself resolve that it should be invited by the Queen to elect a Prime Minister, and the Queen would likely accede to the request when a new Prime Minister has to be found.

Other prerogative powers—the right to declare war or to enter into treaties, for instance—could either be abolished and replaced by statutory powers, or subjected to regulation. For instance, it could be a requirement that before a government enters into a treaty obligation, resolutions of the House of Commons and the Lords are required, possibly after a select committee of one or other of the Houses of Parliament has had an opportunity to report on the treaty. It would not be desirable for all treaties to be subjected to a requirement of such scrutiny, however, since many of them—double tax treaties, for instance—are highly technical but non-controversial. But requiring parliamentary consent to ratification of a treaty would provide protection against the arbitrary exercise of the treaty-making power. This change in practice could be achieved by statute—though no government is likely to wish to introduce legislation reducing its own powers—or it could be achieved, again, by House of Commons and House of Lords resolutions, in the same way as the rules of ministerial responsibility were changed by a combination of parliamentary resolutions and government concessions after 1997 (see Chapter 9). The power to declare war or to commit the armed forces overseas could also be subjected to prior or subsequent parliamentary approval. Such measures would subject the government to at least some direct democratic accountability, which is lacking except incidentally at present.

The *Carltona* principle

The Crown is in some respects a single, undifferentiated, entity. Thus a civil servant's decision, made in the Minister's name, is treated as the Minister's own decision (*Carltona v. Commissioner of Works* ([1943] 2 All ER 560, CA). If a Minister consults his civil servants before reaching a decision, he is treated as consulting himself and he does not need to inform third parties who will be affected by his eventual decision about this process (*Bushell v. Secretary of State for the Environment* [1981] AC 75). This doctrine serves to secure that Ministers are both legally and politically accountable for everything that happens in their departments. It can however be used by Ministers as a shield from, rather than to expose them to, parliamentary scrutiny. The doctrine secures that Ministers, and Ministers alone, are generally answerable in Parliament for what happens in their departments, and although civil servants are permitted to appear before select committees they do so, under rules that are set out in what is now known as *Departmental Evidence and Response to Select Committees* (Cabinet Office 1997, formerly the Osmotherly Rules) on behalf of and at the direction of their Minister. The Minister reserves the right to refuse to allow them to answer questions and to decide whether or not to answer them himself (see Chapter 12). Ministers have been pressed by select committees to permit the chief executives of executive agencies to reply on their own behalf to questions from select committee members but, save that the chief executives are personally responsible as accounting officers for financial matters, Ministers have refused to concede this point to the select committees (see Chapter 12).

The *Carltona* doctrine also serves to protect the anonymity of civil servants, though this is being increasingly eroded. For instance, the names of permanent secretaries to government departments and of chief executives of executive agencies are well known, as are their views. However, anonymity remains an important general principle for the higher echelons of the service as it enables civil servants to serve under successive governments of different political hues without being associated with particular policies. Further down the hierarchy, however, anonymity is being progressively removed and replaced by transparency: for instance under the Citizen's Charter initiative 'customers' are entitled to know the names of the front line staff with whom they were dealing (see Chapters 2 and 12).

The Ram doctrine

Much of the organization of government itself is conducted under prerogative or common law powers rather than statute. The Treasury and many other departments of state are recognized at common law and are not creatures of statute or royal charter, and the civil service itself is managed largely under prerogative powers (see the *CCSU* case, discussed below). This means, for instance, that no Act of Parliament, nor even a statutory instrument, is necessary when the terms and conditions of service of civil servants are changed with or without consultation with the civil service unions. The executive agencies were set up by government fiat without reference to Parliament in the late 1980s (see below and Chapter 12). This ability of government in the name of the Crown to reorganize the civil service without reference to Parliament has been one of the factors in the growing pressure for a Civil Service Act (see next chapter).

The fact that the Crown has corporate personality and thus general legal capacities of ordinary people is known as the Ram doctrine (after Treasury Counsel, Granville Ram, whose advice on the matter was taken in 1945). This doctrine enables government to organize and reorganize the civil service, substantially without reference to Parliament and without the need for legislation. Legislation is not legally necessary to authorize an extension of the existing powers of a particular government department unless such an extension is precluded by a previous statute. If such extended powers involve an annual charge extended over a period of years, legislation, though not required by law, is required by the established practice. Where a new office is created, such as a new parliamentary secretaryship, legislation is not legally necessary (unless this would take the number of Ministers of the Crown receiving salaries and sitting in the Commons beyond the statutory limit under the Ministerial and Other Salaries Act 1975 which is designed to limit spending on salaries and the number of Ministers in the House). Overall, therefore, the Prime Minister, who has responsibility for the organization of the bureaucracy, has considerable freedom as to how government departments are organized. The machinery for holding the Prime Minister to account for these decisions in Parliament is weak. As we shall see however the Prime Minister agreed in 2002 to meet the Liaison Committee of the House twice a year, and this will afford an opportunity to parliamentarians to question arrangements relating to departments if they wish to do so.

The Crown and the courts: the *CCSU* case

A distinction is made in law between the Crown, and Ministers of the Crown. While the Crown itself, being a kind of alter ego of the monarch, cannot be subject to court orders, Ministers of the Crown may be, and they may find themselves in contempt of court, for instance, if they disobey a court order (*M. v. Home Office* [1994] 1 AC 377; see also the Privy Council decision *Gairy v. Attorney General of Grenada* [2001] 3 WLR 779). In recent years the activity of the Crown and its Ministers has been increasingly judicialized, via judicial review—in other words, they have been subjected to legal accountability (see

Chapters 3, 5, and 6). As we have noted, this jurisdiction has the potential to undermine the comity between the courts and the executive which has become a feature of UK constitutional arrangements. This is not the place to go into the judicialization of government in any detail (judicial review was considered in Chapter 5), but there has been a marked change from a position, at the end of the Second World War, where the government was subject to very little judicial control, to the current position that it is broadly subject to the same legal accountability as other public bodies. First, the Crown Proceedings Act 1947 broadly permitted the Crown to be sued in tort and for breach of contract where previously this could only be done on sufferance—by petition of right. (The Act left in place however a number of important Crown immunities and special provisions relating to Crown land.) Since then the courts have extended their control over the Crown in further important ways.

In the case of *Council of Civil Service Unions v. Minister for the Civil Service* ([1985] AC 374—the *CCSU* case) the Appellate Committee of the House of Lords expanded the scope of judicial review of government decisions into exercises of the royal prerogative. The Prime Minister as Minister for the Civil Service had ordered a change in the terms and conditions of employment of civil servants employed at the Government Communications Headquarters at Cheltenham, a body that monitors communications for security purposes. At a time of industrial strife the government was concerned that the civil service unions to which the employees belonged would call for industrial action which could in turn jeopardize the country's security. The Prime Minister therefore ordered that they should no longer be members of these unions and offered to permit them to form and join a staff association instead and to pay them a sum in compensation. Those who refused to accept these terms would be transferred to other jobs or dismissed.

The unions and their members were not able to argue that the order was an interference with their rights of freedom of association, since no such rights in UK law existed at the time. It was not until the Human Rights Act came into force that such rights could have been relied on, though the exceptions to the rights in article 11(2) of the European Convention on Human Rights might well have provided the government with its justification (see Appendix for the text of Article 11, and Chapter 6 for discussion of the Human Rights Act). Instead of relying on a non-existent right (as opposed to an unprotectable residual freedom) of association, the unions contended that they had a legitimate expectation based on previous practice that they would be consulted before changes in the terms and conditions of service of their members were imposed, that the decision should therefore be quashed, and consultation should take place before another decision was made.

The government's response was that the power to manage the civil service derived from the royal prerogative—which the court accepted to be the case—and that the courts could only consider whether a prerogative power existed and could not impose obligations of, for instance, fairness, before such powers were exercised. This had been the position of the courts in previous cases. However, in this case the House of Lords decided that the test for whether a power was judicially reviewable was the nature of the power rather than its source. The mere fact that a power derived from the prerogative did not necessarily result in its being unreviewable. In principle decisions relating to the terms and conditions of service of civil servants were reviewable. This was a major departure from the previous position of the courts and extended the reach of legal accountability significantly.

In the *CCSU* case the House of Lords decided that judicial review should not be available if the particular decision under challenge was not justiciable. In effect they respected the political Constitution and deferred to government in some sensitive areas. In this case the government was alleging that for them to have consulted the unions before the decision was taken would have provoked industrial action at GCHQ, which would in turn have been damaging to national security. In the view of the House of Lords this made an otherwise reviewable decision not suitable for judicial review—not justiciable. Other decisions taken under the royal prerogative, which the court indicated would be non-justiciable, included treaty making and foreign affairs. Despite the outcome of the *CCSU* case—the unions lost because of the national security issue—the decision of the court that the prerogative is in principle reviewable and that were it not for the national security issue the government should have consulted the unions before imposing these changes was a major step forward in the judicialization of government action, including the actual conduct of government, and a step away from the political Constitution.

The question of justiciability of foreign relations decisions was raised in *R. (Abbasi) v. Secretary of State for the Foreign and Commonwealth Office and Secretary of State for the Home Department* ([2002] EWCA, Civ., 6 November 2002). Two British citizens were being held without trial or access to lawyers by the United States in detention, at the American naval base in Guantanamo Bay in Cuba on suspicion of terrorism, in the aftermath of the attack on 11 September 2001 on the World Trade Centre in New York. They complained that the British government was not putting sufficient pressure on the US Government to bring them to trial or to release them. In the event, the Court of Appeal decided that no order should be granted to compel the Foreign Secretary to make representations to the United States government or to take other appropriate action, as this would have an impact on the conduct of foreign policy at a particularly delicate time (para. 107); and in any event the Foreign Secretary was considering the claimants' request for assistance and taking steps to assist them. However, the Master of the Rolls, Lord Phillips, giving the decision of the court, made a number of important observations about the reviewability—justiciability—of decisions in the field of foreign affairs. He noted that the court did not need a statutory context to be free to express a view in relation to what it conceived to be a clear breach of international law. (In this case the USA appeared to be acting in breach of international human rights law and fundamental principles: paras. 57, 64.) The court rejected the submission made on behalf of the government that there was no scope for judicial review of a refusal to render diplomatic assistance to a British subject who is suffering violation of a fundamental right such as the right to freedom and access to a court as a result of the conduct of a foreign state. The court found that the British government had given rise to a legitimate expectation in the minds of citizens that they would receive diplomatic protection when there was evidence of miscarriage or denial of justice, and he stated that in a suitable case the court might make an order that this expectation be met by requiring the Foreign Secretary to consider a claimant's request for diplomatic protection if, for example, the court were satisfied that the government's exercise of its discretion in these matters was irrational or contrary to legitimate expectations (at para.106). Although the claimants lost the case, it nevertheless represents a step forward in extending the availability of judicial review into sensitive areas of foreign relations (but not foreign policy), and in the finding that the government can generate legitimate expectations, which the courts might protect, when it becomes a party to international instruments for the protection of individuals.

A further milestone in the process of subjection of the Crown to legal accountability was the case of *M. v. Home Office* ([1994] 1 AC 377). A court ordered that an immigrant should not be deported pending a full hearing of his case, since he feared that he would be murdered if returned to his country. The Home Office ignored the order and deported the immigrant, M., who was not heard of again and was presumably murdered, as he had warned would happen. The question then was whether the Home Secretary was in contempt of court for disobeying the order. His argument was that the Crown was not bound by court orders and obeyed the court only as a matter of grace. The House of Lords agreed that the Crown itself was not bound by court orders but found that a Minister of the Crown was so bound, and found the Secretary of State to have been in contempt. *M. v. Home Office* was, then, a major further step in the judicialization of government activity. It has not in practice damaged relations between the courts and the executive, no doubt because the government's reliance on the argument that the Crown deferred to the court as a matter of grace only, though based in historical precedent, was not consistent with elementary good governance principles or the rule of law. And this was an area in which political accountability was of no effect.

Regulation inside government

We have already noted that the Crown's running of the machinery of government is carried on under the royal prerogative and is not subject to statutory regulation. (This has raised the question whether a Civil Service Act is required, which will be discussed in the next chapter.) But in recent years this management function has become increasingly regulated and juridified. Reference has already been made to the document *Departmental Evidence and Responses to Select Committees*, and we noted a number of codes of practice to which government subjects itself in Chapter 2. Further examples will be noted in this chapter. In fact these are just the tip of an extensive iceberg of regulation inside government, a phenomenon which was discussed with audit and inspection in Chapter 3 (Daintith and Page, 1999; Scott, 1999; Hood et al., 1999). Some of this internal regulation is effected by Orders in Council, by which for instance the civil service is regulated. These resemble in many respects statutory instruments, except that they are not required to be laid before Parliament, they are not subject to prior parliamentary scrutiny, and they are not subject to affirmative or negative resolution. They count as primary legislation under the royal prerogative, but the accountability mechanisms in respect of them are in fact even weaker than the very weak procedures covering ordinary delegated legislation.

Much of the internal regulation of government is effected by ministerial fiat and administrative means—the introduction of the executive agencies in the civil service, discussed in the next chapter, is an example. In contrast, in mainland Europe this kind of regulation is rooted in rules that are recognized as having legal effect, and which are challengeable or enforceable in administrative tribunals or courts. Although this is not the case to any great extent in the UK, the jurisdiction of the UK courts in judicial review has developed in recent years, subjecting ministers to legal accountability for many of their decisions, including, since the *CCSU* decision, those made in the process of the running of the government machine itself. But for the most part the internal regulation of government, though juridified in various ways, is not judicialized.

The Treasury and Public Service Agreements

The Treasury, the most powerful of the government departments, has been an important driver for joined-up government (see next chapter) in recent years. The Treasury is in theory only one among a number of government departments. In practice it has come to exercise a pervasive influence on and within all departments, and indeed on local author-ities, regional development agencies, and devolved bodies. It is able to do this through its power of the purse, or, in Daintith's terms (1979), *dominium*. Another way of expressing it is that the power to allocate resources is a lever of power. But, pursuing this analogy, concerns are expressed about the elusiveness of the transmission mechanism. Not only does this lever give the Treasury control, as part of the system of regulation within government, of how much money departments receive and the right to scrutinize how they spend it, but in recent years the Treasury has used public service agreements (PSAs) with other departments and other public bodies as levers to seek to achieve its and the government's objectives (see Chapter 3).

PSAs may be central or local, i.e. between the Treasury and government departments, or between government departments and local authorities. They are agreements between funders and the bodies delivering public services as to the quality and level of service to be delivered. By way of illustration, the government committed itself in its White Paper *Strong Local Leadership—Quality Public Services* (December 2001) to 'put in place a national PSA for local government informed by the priorities defined through the CLP [central local partnership] which draws together all the relevant outcome targets; and devolve these targets to local services through best value and local PSAs' (para. 3.13). The devolved versions would be Local Public Service Agreements. The government proposed also 'in partnership with local government and other stake-holders' to put in place defined standards and clear criteria against which performance can be assessed for each defined standard (para 3.14). However, the technique has led to the Treasury being accused of micro-management, which is less effective than local delivery.

The House of Commons Treasury Committee found in 2001 that the use of Public Service Agreements had substantially increased the Treasury's influence over the affairs of spending departments, to the point where it was too powerful and ought itself to be subject to greater accountability, for instance in the setting and assessment of public service agreement targets (Third Report of the Treasury Committee, 2000–1, *HM Treasury*, HC 7303). In good governance terms, there was a lack of appropriate accountability, and effectiveness was being undermined. The Committee also felt that the influence of the Treasury meant that it imposed policies on its 'client' departments and other bodies without sufficient prior consultation and sometimes in ill-thoughtout ways, a further breach of good-governance principles.

In his spending-review announcements in July 2002 the Chancellor of the Exchequer emphasized the government's determination to secure the desired results in improvements in public services through a combination of regulation and rewards: 'In each area of service delivery, from housing to education, from policing to defence, we are tying new resources to reform and results, and developing a modern way for efficient public services, which includes setting demanding national targets; monitoring performance by independent and open audit and inspection; giving front-line staff the power and flexibility to deliver; extending choice; rewarding success; and turning round failing services' (HC Deb., 15 July 2002, col. 22).

In June 2002 the chief economic adviser to the Treasury, Ed Balls, indicated in a lecture entitled 'The New Localism' (reported in *The Times*, 15 July 2002) that the Treasury was more committed than hitherto to devolution and local discretion. He admitted that there was sometimes a tension between the desire to devolve flexibility and encourage local innovation, and the fact that often it was Ministers at the centre who remain accountable to Parliament and the public for fiscal stability, tax, value for money, and performance. He cited the controversial public-private partnership for the London Underground, where the government was insisting on its terms despite opposition from the London Mayor, as an example of the government's need to retain control of projects for which it was paying. Other examples would be concern that increases in public spending on education, health, and employment might not produce the desired improvements in the quality of public services. Balls outlined a new model entitled 'constrained discretion' under which the centre will set standards and ensure accountability, but there would be local flexibility and discretion, as with competition, financial regulation and regional policy. The accountability mechanism would be independent inspection and independently audited reports by the service providers. This 'constrained discretion' model does not fit well with the use of targets under the PSAs, and it seems likely that the tensions between disaggregating and decentralizing processes and centralizing, joined-up government—see next chapter—will continue.

Ministers and Parliament: individual ministerial responsibility

We now turn to relationships between Ministers and Parliament, and in particular the conventions of individual ministerial responsibility to Parliament (see Marshall 1984, 1989; Woodhouse, 1997a, b). The salient characteristic of the Westminster system is the parliamentary executive. By convention all Ministers have to be members of one or other of the two Houses of Parliament, and the Prime Minister and the Chancellor of the Exchequer must be members of the House of Commons. The presence of Ministers in the Houses of Parliament enables Parliament to impose duties of accountability and ministerial responsibility on them. But the operation of these conventions has altered over the years and this has raised issues in turn about exactly what the conventions making up individual responsibility require, who owns the rules, and how effective Parliament can hope to be in holding Ministers to account. These questions in turn raise issues as to whether alternative or supplementary accountability mechanisms are required, such as an expansion of the jurisdiction of the courts over political matters—the issue at the heart of the debate about the political or legal nature of the Constitution—or whether and how Parliament can be reformed so as to enable it to hold Ministers to account adequately (see discussion in Chapters 9 and 10).

A growing concern since at least the Second World War, and one which has grown further as a result of the growth of executive agencies in the 1990s (see Chapter 12), is whether accountability could be separated from responsibility. Much of the debate about accountability and responsibility has concerned the duties of Ministers to Parliament, and this serves to illustrate the points well. A Minister may be under a duty to explain or give information to Parliament about something that has been done by another person and which it was not the Minister's job to do. For instance, Ministers are supposed to answer questions about what has been done in their departments (except, in some circumstance, in executive agencies—see next chapter). Ministers may also have to pass on information about the activities of bodies over whom they have little or no control, such as police forces and quangos (see Chapter 17). If something has gone wrong and the Minister himself was not at fault, he will not be regarded as culpable, and his obligation will be limited to giving the account and, so far as it is in his power to do so, putting things right. The point was made by the then Home Secretary, Sir David Maxwell Fyfe, in a classic statement in the Crichel Down affair in 1954:

where action is taken by a civil servant of which the Minister disapproves and has no prior knowledge, and the conduct of the official is reprehensible, then there is no obligation on the part of the Minister to defend what he believes to be wrong. . . . But, of course he remains constitutionally responsible to Parliament for the fact that something has gone wrong, and he alone can tell Parliament what has occurred and render an account of his stewardship. (HC Deb., 20 July 1954, vol. 530, col. 1286.)

One point to note in this account of ministerial accountability is the claim that *only* the Minister can give the account to Parliament. Accountability can sometimes be used as a shield in the sense that it may be claimed to involve a monopoly of the right to give information, precluding others from revealing iniquity.

In the Crichel Down affair the Minister was seeking in effect to separate accountability—the duty to explain what had happened and justify it—from responsibility for what happens. This distinction has been relied on by Ministers in many instances since then as they seek to avoid having to take the blame themselves when things had gone wrong. By responsibility Ministers understand the job or set of functions that a person has to do, and the idea that he or she may be expected to take the blame in some way if mistakes are made. Thus if an official for whom a Minister is accountable does wrong in the course of his or her job, it would be the official who was responsible and would take the blame, and the Minister would merely give an account of what had happened and might, if he considers it to be part of his job to do so, undertake to put things right.

A problem here is that there is no broadly understood job specification for a Minister, and it is not easy to draw the line between an official doing wrong and a Minister failing in his or her job. This has become an issue particularly since the formation of executive agencies which, though formally within a Department, are semi-autonomous, operating under 'framework documents' which spell out the respective functions of the Minister and the chief executive of the agency. An attempt was made by the government to define a Minister's job in broad terms in the White Paper, *Taking Forward Continuity and Change* (Cm. 2748, 1995, 28):

The Minister is responsible for the policies of the Department, for the framework through which those policies are delivered, for the resources allocated, for such implementation decisions as the [Framework Document] may require to be referred or agreed with him and for his response to major failures or expressions of Parliamentary or public concern.

This is a useful working definition of 'responsibility' and serves to bring out the distinction between accountability and responsibility quite well.

A (non-legal) duty on the part of Ministers to account to Parliament was explicitly acknowledged by the government in *Civil Servants and Ministers: Duties and Responsibilities* (Cmnd. 9841 1986, para. 11) but it was not clear until recently whether the duty was imposed by Parliament or voluntarily undertaken by the government. The matter was clarified as a result of the Arms to Iraq affair (see Tomkins, 1998). Two men were prosecuted for illegally exporting arms. It transpired during the trial that the government in fact knew about the exports and had consented to them. The government had knowingly allowed the men to be put at risk of a wrongful conviction. A senior judge, Sir Richard Scott, then Vice-Chancellor—head of the Chancery Division of the High Court—was commissioned by the Prime Minister, John Major, to inquire into the whole affair. He produced a very critical *Report on the Export of Dual-Use Goods to Iraq* (1995–6, HC 115). The report was open to criticism for being far too long and lacking an executive summary, but Sir Richard made a number of very plain and explicit criticisms of Ministers and civil servants in it. When the Report was published the government—which had had an advance copy of the report—produced a press pack which put a pro-government spin on the Report's findings. The Report was debated in the House of Commons, Ministers claimed that it had in fact exonerated them from various allegations including misleading Parliament, which was not true, and the Conservative majority in the Commons voted to save them from having to resign and, in effect, let them off. But concern about this outcome led to pressure for the duties of Ministers and the Prime Minister to Parliament to be clarified.

This story brought out the relative weakness in political accountability mechanisms as opposed to legally enforceable rules in the UK's version of the Westminster system. There was no legal sanction against any of the Ministers or civil servants implicated in the Scott report, neither they nor MPs were bound by Scott's findings of fact, and being politically aligned they could reject or ignore findings of fact for arbitrary political reasons. There is in such matters no authoritative binding fact-finding machinery to deal with what might be seriously improper activity by Ministers and civil servants, and this can only undermine public confidence in the system as a whole (Oliver, 1996).

The Arms to Iraq saga resulted in pressure building up from select committees in the House and from the press and the public for the conventions of individual ministerial responsibility to be clarified, and for it to be made clear that the obligations of the convention were imposed on Ministers by Parliament and were not, for instance, solely voluntary and self-imposed and therefore capable of being suspended, by Ministers or the Prime Minister. The upshot was that in the last days of the 1992–7 Parliament resolutions were passed in both Houses restating the conventions (HC Deb., 19 Mar. 1997, cols. 1046–7; HL Deb., 20 Mar. 1997, cols. 1055–62). The House of Commons resolution reads as follows:

That, in the opinion of this House, the following principles should govern the conduct of Ministers of the Crown in relation to Parliament:
   (1)   Ministers have a duty to Parliament to account, and be held to account, for the policies, decisions and actions of their Departments and Next Steps Agencies;
   (2)   It is of paramount importance that Ministers give accurate and truthful information to Parliament, correcting any inadvertent error at the earliest opportunity. Ministers who knowingly mislead Parliament will be expected to offer their resignation to the Prime Minister;
   (3)   Ministers should be as open as possible with Parliament, refusing to provide information only when disclosure would not be in the public interest, which should be decided in accordance with relevant statute and the Government's Code of Practice on Access to Government Information (second edition, January 1997);
   (4)   Similarly, Ministers should require civil servants who give evidence before Parliamentary Committees on their behalf and under their directions to be as helpful as possible in providing accurate, truthful and full information in accordance with the duties and responsibilities of civil servants as set out in the Civil Service Code (January 1996).

(The House of Lords resolution was slightly differently phrased. For discussion of the background to the passing of these resolutions, see Woodhouse, 1997b.) An important aspect of the adoption of the resolutions is that it illustrates the trend towards the juridification of the political process that has taken place over the last twenty years or so, stopping short of judicialization but clarifying what were previously unarticulated and often inconsistent understandings and expectations.

   It is worth noting that these resolutions focus on the duty to account and say nothing about what a Minister should do if something has gone wrong in his department. Sir Richard Scott did not think that a duty to resign—which the convention had once required—was as important as the duty to provide information. But party influence is strong in this area, and in all but the most exceptional cases Ministers can not only avoid resignation if criticized, but they may not have to change policy. They can generally placate Parliament by undertaking to make amends or ensure that similar criticisms do not arise in future if the issue is one of administration rather than policy.

   There has as yet been no evaluation of whether the resolutions on ministerial responsibility have in practice made any difference to ministerial accountability, but it is worth noting that the then Speaker of the House of Commons, Betty Boothroyd MP, protested from time to time in the 1997–2001 Parliament about the unwillingness of Ministers to be accountable to Parliament in various ways. For instance, many policy statements were (and still are) made outside Parliament, to the press, or the BBC on the *Today* programme. Her objection was that Parliament's role was downgraded if Ministers could avoid facing the House. (A similar experience in Scotland led the presiding officer of the Scottish Parliament in January 2001 to refuse to allow a Minister to make a statement which he had already made to the press.) On the other hand it is understandable that Ministers should wish to obtain media coverage of their statements, and one of the problems has been that the working hours of Parliament did not fit well with the needs of the media. This led the Modernization Committee to recommend, and the House of Commons to accept, a change in House of Commons' sitting hours so that ministerial statements made in Parliament could catch radio and television—and press—coverage (see Chapter 9). And in December 2001 the government undertook, in response to pressure from the Public Administration Select Committee (PASC), that Ministers would be required to make policy announcements first to Parliament. The PASC expressed the hope that this new approach would 'help to tackle one of the main sources of public cynicism about politicians—the accusations of media manipulation, leak and spin that have been levelled at recent governments of both parties' (PASC Second Report, HC 439, 2001–2, para. 5).

The Prime Minister's accountability to the House of Commons

There has been a longstanding series of disagreements about the Prime Minister's role in relation to ministerial conduct and his own accountability to the Commons. We can see how hard it is to achieve change in increasing accountability to Parliament from the following brief account of rather a protracted battle, still not fully won, to secure that the resolutions on ministerial accountability are put into practice and that the Prime Minister accepts responsibility for the proper operation of government and observance of the rules.

Generally it is the departmental Minister responsible for matters who has to answer questions and is responsible to Parliament. The Prime Minister does not himself have responsibilities for matters for which other departmental Ministers are accountable. The Prime Minister is Minister for the Civil Service, and has responsibility for various departments and teams from time to time, such as the Cabinet Office, the Office for Public Services Reform, and the Forward Strategy Unit, but in the past he has been reluctant even to answer questions about these, leaving it to junior Ministers in those departments or offices to do so. Yet he will often have been involved in decisions, especially those having implications for general government policy.

The Prime Minister does, however, have sole responsibility for the *Ministerial Code*, which is revised by each new PM and, since 1992, has been republished after each general election. This code includes the rules—for the most part conventional rather than legal—that regulate the operation of the Cabinet and the conduct of Ministers. They cover matters such as divesting of interests, standards of conduct for Ministers, the agenda for Cabinet meetings, and so on. Until recently the Code said very little about the Prime Minister's own role and responsibilities.

The Committee on Standards in Public Life and the PASC and its predecessors have been pressing for the Prime Minister's responsibility to Parliament to be sharpened up and made explicit in the *Ministerial Code*. (For a useful summary of the Committee on Standards in Public Life's recommendations in its first seven reports and a note of responses to them and which of them have been accepted, see Committee on Standards in Public Life, *The First Seven Reports. A Review of Progress*, 2001.) In its first report (Cm. 2850, 1995) the Committee on Standards in Public Life made a number of recommendations for improvement of the *Code*, including that it should stress that it was for the

Prime Minister to determine whether a Minister had acted in conformity with the code in particular circumstances (para. 13) and that he should draw out of the *Code* the ethical principles and rules which it contained to form a free-standing code of conduct or a separate section within a new code. The Committee's proposals as to how essential principles could be spelt out were incorporated into the revised version of the *Code* that was published in July 1997 after the general election, and which incorporated the resolutions on ministerial responsibility. The 1997 *Code* did not however adopt the recommendations of the Committee as to the Prime Minister's role in relation to ministerial conduct and in its Sixth Report, *Reinforcing Standards* (2000), the Committee urged that the position should be further clarified (Recommendation 13).

The PASC recommended in 2001 various ways in which Prime Ministerial accountability for the conduct of Cabinet government could be enhanced (HC 235, 2000–1) so as to close the gap that had become obvious between the resolutions on ministerial responsibility and the actual putting into practice of those obligations. The PASC proposed that each new Prime Minister should be required to lay his version of the *Ministerial Code* before Parliament for debate and approval of the parts of it affecting the relations between Ministers and Parliament. They wanted the remit of the Parliamentary Commissioner for Standards to be expanded to include advising ministers on their responsibilities under the *Code*. And they wanted the Parliamentary Commissioner for Administration to have the power to investigate allegations of breach of the *Code* by ministers. They also wanted an annual meeting between the Prime Minister and the Liaison Committee, using the government's Annual Report (initiated by Tony Blair soon after he took office in 1997) as its basis, and at this meeting the Prime Minister's responsibilities under the *Code* might be discussed, among other matters. The Prime Minister's duty to account to Parliament in this way ought to be included in the *Code*. The Committee's view was that: 'The responsibility of Ministers to Parliament is enhanced, not diminished or diverted, if it is reinforced by the Prime Minister's responsibility for ensuring that the provisions of the *Ministerial Code* are met' (Third Report of the Select Committee on Public Administration, *The Ministerial Code: Improving the Rule Book*, HC 235, 2000–1, para. 22). Except for its recommendation that the Prime Minister should meet the Liaison Committee, all of these proposals were rejected by the Prime Minister.

Tony Blair initially refused to justify his record to MPs, despite the recommendations by the PASC and the Liaison Committee. His position was that this would break the convention set by his predecessors, that Prime Ministers do not appear before select committees, and it would blur ministerial accountability if he strayed into his Cabinet colleagues' responsibilities. This was regarded by the Liaison Committee in its response as sophistry. Eventually, after rejecting these proposals on various grounds, and under sustained pressure from the Liaison Committee and the PASC (see HC 439, 2001–2), the Prime Minister agreed in a written answer in early 2002 to meet the Liaison Committee twice a year, and to incorporate the resolution on individual responsibility and any updating of it that might be necessary into the *Ministerial Code* relating to parliamentary accountability (HC Deb., 26 April 2002, col. 465W). Thus the expectations of Parliament and of the Prime Minister, who in effect polices compliance with the *Code* and is the ultimate judge of the standards of behaviour expected of a Minister and of compliance with the requirement of the *Ministerial Code*, are in conformity with one another on this point. But it was only after a sustained campaign by the select committees that even these concessions were made on the Prime Minister's responsibilities and his accountability to Parliament. The first meeting took place on 16 July 2002 and appeared to improve relations between the Prime Minister and the Liaison Committee, countering the atmosphere of suspicion that had been developing about the use of spin and special advisers (see next chapter).

The resolutions on ministerial responsibility and the Prime Minister's acceptance of his responsibility to Parliament for compliance with them by Ministers have set in place a stronger and more explicit framework for Parliament to hold Ministers to account. However, there is still no effective coercive machinery for *compelling* Ministers to answer questions in Parliament, or for enforcing the attendance of civil servants before select committees, or their answering of questions. (It would in fact be difficult to devise coercive machinery, save by way of the criminalization of refusals of witnesses to attend or answer questions in Parliament, which is the mechanism provided under the Scotland Act 1998, section 25 in relation to the Scottish Parliament.) The PASC has been pressing for full answers to be given to parliamentary questions and gradually the government is accepting its responsibilities (see for instance HC, 464, 1086, 2001–2, and HC 136, 2002–3).

The Public Service Ethos and Standards of Conduct in Government

As in other aspects of the Constitution, concerns have arisen increasingly in recent years about the standards of conduct of Ministers and civil servants, and the mechanisms by which conduct may be regulated, and standards may be set and enforced—good-governance issues. This is in part due to the increasing use of incentives and targets for public employees which can undermine the public service ethos (see next chapter). The undermining of the public service ethos is also exacerbated by the breaking down of the public–private divide and the proliferation of cooperative relationships between government, charities, and other voluntary sector non-governmental organizations and commercial enterprises—networks. This is because bodies seeking to enter into partnership and other relationships with government engage in lobbying of Ministers, political advisers, and civil servants. Some government projects are sponsored by commercial interests. Sponsorship can raise questions as to whether the public interest is being subordinated to the interests of the sponsor. Some of the contacts between the private sector and government are informal in nature, opening up the possibility of at least the appearance of unregulated patronage, cronyism, and secret deals.

In its Sixth Report, *Reinforcing Standards*, the Committee on Standards in Public Life noted this relatively new concern about privileged access to Ministers. It observed that 'The ministerial code is silent on the specific issue of contacts with lobbyists' (Cm. 4557-I, 2000, para 7.32) and recommended that the basic facts about official meetings with external interests should be recorded in their office diaries, which should be retained. The

Ministerial Code should be supplemented accordingly (ibid. recommendation 27). This recommendation is implemented in the *Code* issued in July 2001, which requires that the basic facts of formal meetings between Ministers and outside interest groups should be recorded (at para. 63). New guidance for civil servants and special advisers on contacts with outside groups has been issued, requiring them to make a record of basic facts including the people involved and the general subject under discussion in any contact in which interests attempt to influence policy and decisions.

A question has also arisen whether the public service ethos needs to be spelt out and given legal force, not only in relation to government but also the devolved bodies, local authorities, and quangos (see Chapter 2). The PASC has recommended the adoption of a Public Service Code which would be approved by Parliament and apply to all bodies providing public services (see Chapter 2; Seventh Report of the Select Committee on Public Administration, *The Public Service Ethos*, HC 263, 2001–2). As far as central government is concerned the recommendation was that the code should be included in a Civil Service Bill (HC 263, 2001–2002; see next chapter). The government rejected the proposal for a public service code (HC 61, 2002–3).

Conclusions

The legal position of the Crown is peculiar in the UK and gives government many powers which are not subject to formal requirements of parliamentary approval or scrutiny, or to judicial scrutiny. Although placing the Crown and the royal prerogative powers on a statutory or constitutional footing is not on the realistic political agenda at the time of writing, it could come onto the agenda if public disquiet about, for instance, the ability of the government to commit troops to a war against Iraq or some other major issue were not satisfactorily soothed by the government. Although accountability for the management of government itself is imposed largely through political mechanisms and internal regulation rather than through the courts, the actual machinery of government is becoming increasingly juridified with the proliferation of detailed codes. Accountability to Parliament for the management of government has been improved with the resolutions on ministerial responsibility, clarification of the *Ministerial Code*, and the government's agreement that parliamentary questions should be fully answered. This has been largely due to reaction against the outcome of the Arms to Iraq affair, the persistence of select committees, and pressure from the Committee on Standards in Public Life. So political mechanisms can be effective. But no sooner has one concern about accountability been resolved than others arise: problems with micro-management by the Treasury and the use of Public Service Agreements illustrate both how Parliament needs to be alert to emerging problems, and how good governance involves weighing up effectiveness against accountability in the search for a proper balance between the two.

12
Government: The Civil Service

In this chapter we turn our attention from the elected, ministerial arm of the executive to its supporting bureaucracy. We shall consider accountability issues in the relationships between ministers and civil servants and political advisers and the proposal for a Civil Service Act to resolve some of the difficulties—a measure that would represent a shift away from the political Constitution to a law-based system.

The civil service is the permanent professional arm of the executive (see generally Hennessy, 1990; Drewry and Butcher, 1991). Since the late 1980s there has been a transformation in the organization and management of the civil service, through the adoption of New Public Management techniques. Before turning to consider these we shall outline the main elements of the previous arrangements, to bring out the significance of the reforms. The civil service had, since the Northcote–Trevelyan reforms of the nineteenth century, been organized in a hierarchical, merit-based, procedure-oriented way. Recruitment was competitive, and the emphasis was more on inputs and processes within the system than on outputs or outcomes. The service was imbued with the public service ethos (see Chapman, 1988).

Although these values continued until the late 1980s to be regarded as fundamental, and are still so regarded, there was frustration in successive governments at failures to deliver the policies that ministers had decided upon, and some of the blame was directed at the civil service and the way it was organized. From the late 1980s the focus shifted from inputs and internal processes to outputs and outcomes, and this has been achieved through the importation into the public service of private-sector techniques known as New Public Management. This was also influenced by public choice theory which assumes that everyone, including public servants, is a utility maximizer, concerned primarily with advancing his or her own interests, an assumption that runs counter to those of the public service ethos (see generally Hood, 1991; Rhodes, 1991, 1994; Stewart and Walsh, 1992; Oliver and Drewry, 1996).

New Public Management in the Civil Service

We noted in Chapter 3 that one of the principles of good governance is maximizing effectiveness. This objective has had the greatest impact in importing into the public sector New Public Management (NPM). The term refers to the development of a set of theories and techniques in the last fifteen years or so which are supposed to improve the effectiveness and efficiency of organizations. NPM is not one coherent theory. The main characteristics of the approach include an acknowledgement that public services should be 'managed' and not simply 'administered' and that management requires a particular set of skills separate from policy-making or administration. NPM influence has meant that, as Owen Hughes has put it: 'The rigid, hierarchical, bureaucratic form of public administration, which has predominated for most of the twentieth century is changing to a flexible, market-based form of public management' (Hughes, 1998).

The features of the private sector that NPM has brought into the public sector include emphasis on the discipline of competition and market forces, reduction in security of employment, performance-related pay, the use of performance indicators, annual plans, targets and so on, audit, and attention to the 'customer' whose patronage is to be wooed. Rhodes summed it up as follows:

a focus on management, not policy, and on performance, appraisal and efficiency; the disaggrega-tion of public bureaucracies into agencies which deal with each other on a use-pay basis; the use of quasi-markets and contracting out to foster competition; cost-cutting; and a style of manage-ment which emphasises, amongst other things, output targets, limited term contracts, monetary incentives and freedom to manage. (Rhodes, 1991, 1.)

Equity, personal loyalty and mutual confidence in the public service were displaced by these values—a shift to a 'low trust' approach to management. A 'high trust' approach, by contrast, would involve negotiation, consultation and communication within the service, a participative management style, rewarding success rather than punishing failure, and encouraging a sense of teamwork (Fox, 1974; Faulkner, 1998).

Harmon and Mayer (1986) identified three families of values in public sector organiza-tions, each of which is affected by NPM:

Sigma-type values: match values to defined tasks. These values promote frugality and avoidance of waste and incompetence. This entails specifying goals and measuring success in meeting them. NPM relies closely on these values.

Theta-type values: honesty, fairness, and mutuality. This requires the avoidance of bias, inequity, abuse of office. These were reflected in the traditional civil service arrangements and are clearly 'good-governance' values. They are consistent with Sigma values to the extent that honesty and avoidance of corruption prevent waste, but they may clash with them to the extent that cost considerations which are central to NPM may outweigh mutuality and fairness.

Lambda-type values: reliability, robustness, adaptivity. These good-governance values were important in traditional public service arrangements. They are also important in NPM, but they may conflict with sigma values of cost-cutting, and tight definition of functions which could undermine flexibility and reliability.

These sets of values may conflict with one another, and thus the design of organizations needs to take account of how they are to be prioritized. As Hood (1991) puts it: 'a central concern with *honesty* and the avoidance of policy distortion in public administration may have different design implications from a central concern with *frugality*; and a central concern with *resilience* may also have different design implications. If NPM is a design for putting frugality at centre stage, it may at the limit be less capable of ensuring honesty and resilience in public administration' (p. 15). Some of these concerns have indeed surfaced in the implementation of NPM in the civil service.

From NPM to Next Steps agencies

NPM theory has been highly influential in reforms to the civil service in the last fifteen years or so, and led to the devolution of responsibility to managers and Executive Agencies from 1988 (see Prime Minister's Efficiency Unit, *Improving Management in Government: The Next Steps*, 1988; *The Financing and Accountability of Next Steps Agencies*, 1989, Cm. 914). The idea bore some resemblance to recommendations in the Fulton Report of 1968 (Cmnd. 3638), which had drawn on arrangements in Sweden as a model. The ultimate objective was that the central civil service should be reduced in size to 'a relatively small core engaged in the function of servicing ministers and managing departments, who will be the "sponsors" of particular government policies and services' (Efficiency Unit 1988, at para. 44). This is now in effect the Senior Civil Service. These arrangements were implemented—for the most part without legislation and relying on the royal prerogative—on a rolling programme from 1989. By 2000 the process was more or less complete.

The bodies charged with these hived-off functions are known as Executive Agencies (often referred to as 'Next Steps' agencies after the Efficiency Unit report). Staff in these agencies remain civil servants. Within the diversity of the agencies, they are said to be unified by the five fundamental civil service values of impartiality, integrity, objectivity, selection and promotion on merit, and accountability through Ministers to Parliament (see *The Civil Service: Continuity and Change*, Cm. 2627, 1994, paras 1.3, 2.7). These are system values which should promote good governance. (These same values were also adopted in the Fifth Report of the Treasury and Civil Service Committee, *The Role of the Civil Service*, HC 27, 1993–4, para. 72; and see *The Civil Service: Taking Forward Continuity and Change* Cm. 2748, 1995, para. 2.2.) Many of these agencies are formally within their parent ministerial departments (though some non-ministerial departments—the Board of Inland Revenue and the Commissioner of Customs and Excise, for instance— are run 'on Next Steps lines').

The agencies have at their heads professional managers with authority over their budgets and organizations, who are to concentrate their efforts on the effectiveness and quality of their service delivery. They are under a duty to get value for money from assets and to run their offices on profit and loss account lines, they are expected to improve their service to 'customers', and many operate under PSAs (see Chapter 11).

It is helpful to highlight the good-governance implications of these new arrangements. The relationship between the government department and the agency is more transparent than former relationships in departments could be. The agencies operate through published framework documents and PSAs, which specify the policy that the agencies are to implement and set explicit targets. These documents state clearly who is responsible for doing what, and set out the ways in which the performance of the agency is to be measured (TCSC HC 481 1989–90, paras. 14–24; and Oliver and Drewry, 1996, ch. 7). The framework documents may be supplemented by annual performance agreements which detail the requirements of the Agency, and commonly there are also corporate plans. The overall objective is 'to improve performance, efficiency and effectiveness by switching the focus of attention away from process towards results' (*Next Steps* report, at para.1), a characteristic of NPM theory. Thus civil service activity is far more regulated— juridified—than before these reforms were made.

Good governance should require stability and a non-partisan approach to machinery of government issues. The Next Step reforms won cross-party support, being seen as 'a piece of transferable technology' (Hennessy in HC 481 1989–90, Appendix I) which if carefully managed should improve efficiency and effectiveness for governments of any party. The TCSC gave them its blessing in 1990, expressing the view that the process was crucial for governments of whatever political colour, and should help to transform the civil service into a more efficient deliverer of public services (TCSC HC 481 1989–90). The Next Steps principles were regarded as politically neutral and the Committee saw itself as having a unique involvement in monitoring these agencies. It should be a simple matter for an incoming government with different policies from those of its predecessor to change the terms of the framework document (TCSC HC 481 1989–90, para. 20). By the time of the general election in 1997 these arrangements commanded cross-party consensus and the transition to a new government with a new set of policies did not prove problematic.

However, the juridification that NPM has introduced into government can have negative effects on the public service ethos. The use of targets, performance indicators, and performance-related pay can have a distorting effect on the exercise of judgement by officials. If a hospital is supposed to be reducing waiting lists, the temptation may be for doctors to allow that consideration to influence the way they prioritize patient care rather than their clinical judgement, or for management to manipulate waiting lists, as has happened in the NHS (see Comptroller and Auditor General's Report *Inpatient and outpatient waiting in the NHS*, HC 221, 2001–2 and *Inappropriate Adjustments to NHS Waiting Lists*, HC 452, 2001–2; Forty-sixth Report from the Committee of Public Accounts *Inappropriate Adjustments to NHS Waiting Lists*, HC 517, 2001–2). The professional ethos of the doctor—and in equivalent situations in the civil service, of the official—should lead him or her to resist making distorted judgements, but the incentives in such arrangements are perverse. The criteria for accountability and the measures of economy, efficiency, and effectiveness that NPM imposes do not necessarily promote public service or professional values and they introduce a culture of suspicion, even mild corruption, into public services.

There has been very little public or parliamentary participation in making these NPM changes. For the most part the reforms have not required legislation. This is a sharp contrast with the way in which the equivalent reforms were introduced in New Zealand, for instance. But the Government Trading Act 1990 expanded the powers of Ministers to set up large parts of Whitehall on company lines with trading funds. And the Civil Service (Management Functions) Act 1992 required all agencies with 2000 or more staff to be ready to implement their own pay and grading structures and this requirement was extended to other agencies. Agency chief executives are appointed as agency accounting officers and are thus directly and personally accountable (albeit in some cases jointly so, with the department's Permanent Secretary) to Parliament for the agency's expenditure.

There are clearly conflicts between the public service ethos and the public choice assumptions that underlie much of NPM, in the notion that employees in fact pursue only their own interests, and incentives and disincentives need to be devised that will mean that their own interests coincide with the objectives of government policy. In New Zealand the emphasis in the State Sector Act 1988, which introduced the agency arrangements, was broader, embracing both efficiency and the standards and conditions of work of employees. The objectives included, for instance, to ensure that employees in the State services are imbued with the spirit of service to the community, promote efficiency in the State services, to ensure the responsible management of the State services, to maintain appropriate standards of integrity and conduct among employees in the State services, to ensure that every employer in the State services is a good employer, to promote equal employment opportunities in the State services, and to provide for the negotiation of conditions of employment in the State services (on New Zealand NPM reforms see Wistrich, 1992; Boston et al., 1996; Palmer, 1987).

By contrast with the New Zealand approach the Next Step arrangements appear to place a low value on the role of staff in the agencies. They are under pressure to increase their productivity on pain of penalties for failure to do so, they are on performance-related pay, they have to apply for their next job, and they are not on an automatic promotion or pay scale ladder. In late 2001 the Prime Minister began to seek to reassure public service workers that they were valued by the government despite the fact that it was looking for improved performance and reforms that many of the workers themselves opposed and considered to be contrary to the spirit of public service.

Accountability for agencies

In recent years Ministers have claimed that they are responsible—and therefore obliged to take the blame if things go wrong—only for their policies, and that others, notably the chief executives of agencies in their departments, are responsible for operational or administrative matters. Ministers accept a duty to give an account to Parliament of operational matters—indeed they assert the exclusive right to give such an account and deny civil servants the right to do so save on their behalf and at their direction (see *Departmental Evidence and Response to Select Committees*, 1997). They also accept that they are under a duty to put things right if they have gone wrong. But they will not accept blame for operational matters.

There is no clear line between the personal responsibility (in the sense of 'job'—see Chapter 11) of Ministers and their mere duty to account—explain—to Parliament what has happened in their departments. This factor undermines accountability. There is no ministerial job specification. The Minister-made distinction between policy and operational or administrative matters is hard to apply in practice, since policy can be made at all kinds of level, and operational matters may be very policy laden. The Treasury and Civil Service Committee in its Fifth Report (1993–4, HC 27-I, *The Role of the Civil*

Service), proposed a more useful distinction than one between policy and administration to base the accountability of Executive Agencies, a more tangible distinction between decisions made by the Minister or parent Department, for which the Minister is responsible, and decisions made by the Agency, for which he is accountable.

A question when the agencies were being established from 1989 was whether the chief executives would be directly accountable to Parliament, or whether they would be in the same position as Permanent Secretaries and other civil servants in departments, answering in Parliament on behalf of and on instruction from their Minister under *Departmental Evidence and Response to Select Committees* (formerly the Osmotherly rules). The *Next Steps* report on which the Executive Agency arrangements were based was not specific on the forms of accountability, except that it proposed that in hearings by the Public Accounts Committee the Departmental Accounting Officer (who would normally be the Permanent Secretary in the Department) should be accompanied by the manager of the agency. The Accounting Officer would answer questions about the framework within which the agency operated while the manager would answer questions about operations within the framework (Annex A, at para. 7). At that time the TCSC (a predecessor of the PASC) expressed regret that the government had paid insufficient attention to the role of Parliament in holding these agencies accountable (1988 Cm. 524; TCSC HC 348 1988–9; 1989 Cm. 841; 1989 Cm. 914; HC Deb. 21 Dec. 1989, Written Answers, cols. 367–8; TCSC HC 481 1989–90). They felt that 'giving managers a sense of personal responsibility for improvement is a key step in securing the cultural change in the Civil Service, which is essential to the success of the Next Steps' (TCSC HC 494 1987–8, para 39).

The position where an individual MP raises questions about the conduct of these agencies is not entirely clear. The government's position remains that 'It is ministers who are accountable to Parliament for all that their Departments do including the work of executive agencies' (*The Civil Service: Continuity and Change*, 1994, p. xx). Agency framework documents make provision for responsibility, and the position varies from agency to agency. Broadly, if the Secretary of State receives a question about an agency in the department, he or she has to decide whether it is a matter to do with strategy or resources, in which case he or she deals with it, or an operational matter in which case it is passed on to the Chief Executive. The Chief Executive's reply is placed in the House of Commons library so that it is accessible both to all MPs and to the public. If the MP asking the question is dissatisfied with the Chief Executive's reply, he or she may table a further question to the Minister, who will press the Chief Executive on the matter and in due course give a ministerial reply that is published in Hansard. (The original practice was that the chief executive would be the named author of written answers, but Ministers took back responsibility under pressure from Parliament by agreeing that these replies should be ministerial.)

The problems which remain in identifying the extent of a Minister's responsibility for these agencies are illustrated by the failures of the Child Support Agency in 1994–5 (see *Investigation of Complaints against the Child Support Agency*, Parliamentary Commissioner for Administration, HC 1994–5 135, iii; Harlow, 1999). The CSA was an agency in the Department of Social Security. It had been set up in a hurry with insufficient trained staff. The workload had been heavier than anticipated and consequently there were unacceptable backlogs. Very many complaints about the way parents were treated by the Agency were made to MPs, who referred a lot of them to the Parliamentary Commissioner for Administration. The issue was the extent to which the Minister had a duty to take action where there were problems in the operational aspects of the work of an agency due to inadequate planning. In effect, what was the minister's job? The Select Committee for the Parliamentary Commissioner for Administration (predecessor of the PASC) took evidence from the junior Minister in the Department, and he accepted that he was 'responsible' when things went wrong; but the problem was in deciding how much a Minister could rely on civil servants to establish an agency satisfactorily. The report's conclusions about the Minister's responsibility—his job—insisted that it extends into administrative arrangement:

We consider that Ministers were too easily satisfied with the assurances given by officials . . . Ministers should have reacted more quickly to the situation as problems became apparent. They should have sought assurances that, were pressures to arise from other sources, lessons had been learned in relation to backlog, volume of complaints, dealing with correspondence, training of staff. We expect the questioning of agency officials by Ministers to be searching and robust and for Ministers to be briefed accordingly. We are in no doubt that maladministration in the CSA cannot be divorced from the responsibility of Ministers for the framework within which it operated. (Third Report from the Select Committee on the Parliamentary Commissioner for Administration, HC 199, 1994–5: para. 27.)

The implication is clear. Ministers are responsible not only for policy (in the sense that the formulation of policy is their job), but also for securing that the implementation of their policy, including operational matters, is properly organized, funded, etc. It is part of their job to secure that these matters are attended to and they will be to blame if they do not do so.

The saga of the Prison Service provides another illuminating example of the problems over accountability for executive agencies (see Barker, 1998). After the escape of prisoners from the high-security Parkhurst prison in January 1995 the Home Secretary, Michael Howard, maintained that he was not responsible for operational matters such as ensuring security at prisons, and that since nothing had gone wrong with the things he was responsible for—the things it was his job to do—he had no duty to resign (HC Debs., col. 40, 10 Jan. 1995). Among the facts that emerged from the subsequent Learmont inquiry into prison security (Learmont Report, *Review of Prison Service Security in England and Wales and the Escape from Parkhurst Prison on Tuesday 3rd January 1995*, Cm. 3020 (1995)) was that the Director General of the Prison Service, Derek Lewis (who was dismissed by the Home Secretary when the report was published) had been regularly distracted from his operational duties by constant ministerial interventions. Despite his denials, the evidence suggested that the Home Secretary had involved himself in the operational issues which he said were not part of his job. The Learmont Report called for the relationship between the Home Office and the Prison Service to be reviewed 'with a view to giving the Prison Service Agency the greater operational independence that Agency status was meant to confer' (Learmont Report, para. 3.87. See also Fry, 1997; Woodhouse, 1997*a*).

The point for us is that in the absence of a job specification the boundaries of a Minister's functions are uncertain. The Home Secretary had, on the findings of the Report, stepped into the operational area—for which he claimed not to be responsible—and yet he was able to escape having to admit that he had done so or that it was wrong for him to do so by denying that operational matters fell within his responsibility or job specification, and thus he avoided having to apologize or resign, or undertake not to intervene in future. (However, the Home Office settled out of court the action brought by Lewis for breach of his contract with the Secretary of State.)

After the general election in May 1997 the new Home Secretary, Jack Straw, in effect wrote a partial job specification for himself, and announced that 'as a first step towards restoring proper ministerial responsibility' all parliamentary questions about the Prison Service would be answered by Ministers and not by the Director-General, adding that 'I regard it as essential that Ministers should answer personally to the House for what is done in our prisons and not leave the matter to their civil servants' (HC Debs., 19 May 1997, col. 396). Part of his job, then, was to receive and answer questions, although he did not state what his job was in relation to intervention in the Service.

The Prison Service saga raised issues about the position taken by the minister that civil servants—the Director-General of the Prison Service in this case—should not answer directly and for themselves to Parliament for what happens in their agencies. The House of Commons and other commentators, including Lewis himself (1997), have pressed for chief executives to be permitted to answer on their own behalf for these matters and to answer questions about the implementation of the policy set out in their framework documents. Both the former Conservative government and the Labour administration that has been in power since 1997 have steadfastly rejected these proposals. More radical proposals have been made for the separation of some executive agencies, including the Prison Service, as freestanding statutory corporations whose chief executives would be directly accountable as quangos (see Chapter 17) to Parliament and perhaps to other independent agencies (Foster and Plowden, 1996; Lewis, 1997, 170–94, 230–4). A problem here would be what authority Parliament would have over the chief executives if it should be found that they have been in some way to blame or open to criticism. The House itself could not dismiss or discipline the chief executive and could at most put pressure on the Minister to do so. Another difficulty in the eyes of Ministers would be knowing where to draw the line at what the chief executives were permitted to say about the policy which they are supposed to be implementing. Under present arrangements they are not permitted to give anything other than the ministerial view of the policy or to refer the questioner to the Minister. If these executives were in charge of statutory independent bodies, they would be likely to feel free to criticize the policy they are charged with, especially if defects in the policy were giving rise to the problems which they might be unfairly criticized for.

Steps since Next Steps

Since the introduction of the Next Steps initiative the civil service has been through a series of radical changes, many of which challenge some of the social-democratic assumptions of the welfare state after the Second World War. In the early 1990s the government embarked on a series of reviews of the functions of the civil service. They required market testing of much of the work of the agencies, to ascertain whether a better service or better value for money could be obtained if it were transferred to the private sector (*Competing for Quality*, 1991; the *Government's Guide to Market Testing*, 1993). This process was followed up by the passage of the Deregulation and Contracting Out Act 1994 which facilitated the contracting out of activities for which Ministers are legally responsible. Next the government moved to a 'prior options' policy (see *Continuity and Change*, 1994, ch. 2; *Taking Forward Continuity and Change*, 1995, para. 3.7) which required departments to consider whether a function needed to be done at all, and if so, whether it was a job for which the government should take responsibility. If the answer to this question was 'yes', then consideration must be given to whether the function should actually be carried out by the government, or by some other body. In effect this policy required Ministers and departments to consider what the 'irreducible core' of government might be, with a view to privatizing or contracting out the rest (Rhodes 1994; Fry, 1997, 697). After a Senior Management Review in 1995 a Senior Civil Service was formed.

Running in parallel with these reforms, since 1992, has been the Private Finance Initiative (see Chancellor of the Exchequer, *Autumn Statement* 12 November 1992, HC Debs, vol. 208, col. 996; *Private Opportunity, Public Benefit—Progressing the Private Finance Initiative*, 1995; Freedland 1998; Elsenaar, 1999). The stated aim of this policy is to improve the efficiency and quality of public services by procuring their provision by the private sector (although critics argued that its real purpose was to reduce the public sector borrowing requirement and transfer risk to the private sector). PFI involves contractual arrangements with commercial enterprises for, for instance, the building of hospitals and their maintenance and the provision of ancillary services—a strong example of the use of networks to deliver public policy (see Chapter 1). On the change of government in 1997, the new Chancellor of the Exchequer endorsed PFI policy as one of a number of possible 'public/private partnerships' on the basis that such arrangements enable the private sector to 'bring a wide range of managerial, commercial and creative skills to the provision of public services, offering potentially huge benefits for the government' (*Partnerships for Prosperity*, November 1997).

More recently the government, particularly the Treasury, has moved on to use public service agreements (PSAs) which award resources to departments and others funded by government (see for example discussion in Chapters 1, 11 and 16) on condition that certain targets are reached, and on pain of refusal of funding if those targets are not met. Funding is on a three-year rolling allocation rather than, as previously, annual allocation.

An effect of the executive agency initiative and related NPM changes has been to 'disaggregate' the civil service by separating out activities, introducing flexible pay arrangements in place of the former uniform system, and focusing the energies of the agencies on achieving their own targets rather than advancing the strategic objectives of the department within which they operate or of government as a whole. (Devolution is a further example of the disaggregation of a formerly strongly centralized state: see Chapters 13 to 15.) This disaggregating process runs in some respects counter to the government's other commitment since 1999 to 'joined-up' and 'integrated' government.

This gives priority to achieving the overall strategic objectives of government, which may mean cooperation between departments and agencies—even between devolved bodies, local authorities, and the centre—and working across institutional boundaries within government (see the White Paper *Modernizing Government*, Cm. 4310, 1999). For instance, NHS hospitals and local government social service departments ought to be able to cooperate so that patients can be discharged from hospital to make room for new patients, but this imposes burdens on the social service departments of local authorities which they may be unable or reluctant to bear (Flynn, 1999). One mechanism for the pursuit of joined-up government has been the establishment of a number of cross-cutting 'joining up' units in Whitehall, such as the Social Exclusion Unit, the Women's Unit, the Performance and Innovation Unit, and the crime-reduction programme. Joined-up government undermines departmental identities and power, but it also means the exercise of tight control over departments and devolved bodies from the centre—particularly from the Treasury—to ensure that they do not undermine joined-up government. Joined-up government also runs counter to the accountability mechanisms in Parliament. The system of departmentally related rather than subject-related select committees shadowing departments does not make it easy for the House of Commons to monitor the wisdom or success of failure of the joined-up government policy.

Generally the disaggregation of governmental activity through NPM, taken with the use of networks to delivery policy and the shift from government to governance that this implies mean that the Westminster system does not match the reality of governing.

The Citizen's Charter and *Service First*

The Next Steps arrangements and the steps outlined above that have been taken since the executive agencies were introduced have been designed to deal with 'supply side' problems in the provision of public services. In 1991 the Conservative government launched the Citizen's Charter (Cm. 1599, 1991) which sought to deal with 'demand side' issues (see Chapter 2). The Charter's focus was on 'empowering' recipients of public services by treating them as consumers who were entitled to a degree of choice as to where the service should be obtained, and to information about the levels of service they were entitled to and about how they could complain if those levels were not achieved. The Charter did not give customers new legally enforceable rights, but by making more transparent what they were entitled to and consequently what Next Steps agency staff and others governed by the Charter were supposed to be providing, it increased the incentives on services to be efficient and effective in their work. Apart from requirements for the publication of standards—usually to do with the time within which services had to be provided rather than with their substantive quality—the Charter also proposed to increase the number of channels through which complaints could be pursued informally, whether via publicized internal complaints procedures or in other ways. The Charter introduced incentives to staff at local offices to optimize their levels of service by providing 'Chartermarks' as awards for high standards of service, and by publishing league tables so that provision in different areas could be compared. The Charter also promised improved inspection and audit, with inspectors being independent of the service inspected and a lay element to be introduced (though the latter was in fact quickly dropped). Performance indicators would be introduced to make audit more effective. By 1997 most areas of public service provision both in central government and in local authorities were covered by a charter—for instance, the patient's charter, the jobseeker's charter, the Benefits Agency Customer Charter, the taxpayer's charter, and so on.

The Citizen's Charter raised a number of issues to do with good governance and citizenship. It was criticized at the time it was launched as implying that citizenship was about consumerism rather than the equitable distribution of services, collective services, and political participation, and as a gimmick which might fool people into expecting better-quality services when all they were getting was the right to complain (see Barron and Scott, 1992). The criticism illustrates some ambiguities about concepts of liberal or social-democratic citizenship. Consumerism tends to be associated with liberalism rather than social democracy. But social democrats prioritize social and economic rights, which is what the Citizen's Charter was partly about.

The Labour government elected in 1997 retained this consumer focus, and the package of reforms proposed by the White Paper *Modernising Government* (Cm. 4310, 1999) included consumer-oriented measures, such as: ensuring that public services are available twenty-four hours a day, seven days a week; all dealings with government to be delivered electronically by 2008; and making sure that users, not providers, are the focus by match-ing services more closely to people's lives and delivering high-quality and efficient public services.There were also concerns that the performance indicators and targets might distort judgements and encourage 'creative compliance'—for instance by giving an incen-tive to NHS hospitals to cut waiting lists by establishing lists of people waiting to get on waiting lists. The science of setting targets and standards and auditing them went through and continues to undergo rapid development to keep pace with this kind of creative compliance. Nevertheless, the charter idea proved remarkably durable and adaptable. Similar initiatives have been taken in many European countries.

The initial emphasis in the charter arrangements was on the three Es, economy, effi-ciency, and effectiveness rather than on high-quality services. Labour refocused on issues of quality and participation, both by 'customers' and employees. The initiative was relaunched as *Service First—The New Charter Programme* in 1998 (see also the White Paper *Modernising Government*, Cm. 4310; and see Scott, 1999; Drewry, 2002). The char-ter values were extended to nine principles of service delivery. The original value for money principle is now 'best value for taxpayers'; the principle of choice and consultation is now an exhortation to consult and involve and to encourage access and promotion of choice by, for instance, flexible opening hours. The original requirement to provide courteous and helpful service is now a requirement to treat all fairly. In addition there are new duties to innovate and improve and to work with other providers—reflections respectively of government commitments to business models of continuous improve-ment and joined-up government. Overall *Service First* represents a (slight) shift away from the three Es and consumerism and towards quality, participation, and consultation—for employees as well as users—a shift in the concepts of good govern-ance and citizenship. It also marks a greater concern on the part of government to exert central control over service-providers and thus political responsibility for standards. As

Scott puts it, *Service First* 'reorients the accountability structures of the Charter programme away from the "downward" accountability to consumers to complement this
with the "upwards" accountability to regulatory units and elected politicians and the
"outwards" accountability to other stakeholders (such as users groups and employees)'
(Scott, 1999, 602).

It remains remarkable, however, that these mechanisms do not give rise to any legally
enforceable rights for consumers, and the UK remains very different from many mainland European countries who have adopted charters, but with legal force (Deakin, 1994).
In this respect, as in many others, the political Constitution remains the preferred choice
of British government as against law-based administration.

Civil Servants and Ministers

As we noted in the previous chapter the civil service forms part of the Crown, and
technically it has no separate existence from the government of the day. Generally, the
duty of the individual civil servant is first and foremost to the Minister of the Crown who
is in charge of the department in which he or she is serving. The rider to this rule is that
accounting officers—the permanent secretary in departments and chief executives in
Next Steps agencies as agency accounting officers—have personal responsibility for the
financing and expenditure of their departments, for which they are accountable to the
Comptroller and Auditor General and the National Audit Office and to the Public
Accounts Committee of the House of Commons.

The basic rule raises a number of questions. First the points raised by the *Ponting* case
(see Chapter 1): what if a Minister is acting improperly in some way? Does, or should, a
civil servant have a right or a duty to bring the matter to the attention of the public or
Parliament? Does a civil servant owe any loyalty to the general public? What if a Minister
uses civil servants for party political purposes? The legal position since the *Ponting* case is
in effect that it is not for civil servants to take in public a different view of the public
interest from that of their Minister. Given this position, the question arises whether the
political process can provide for cases such as these where civil servants are concerned
about the propriety, as opposed to the wisdom, of their Minister's activities, or whether
some other process of accountability should be introduced.

The nature of the problem is illustrated by the Westland affair (see Oliver and Austin,
1987; Fourth Report from the Defence Committee 1985–6: *Westland plc: The Government's Decision-Making*, HC 519). The Head of Information at the Department of Trade
and Industry had disclosed, on instructions from the Secretary of State in that department, the contents of a confidential letter from the Solicitor-General to the Secretary of
State for Defence. (The Secretary of State for Trade and Industry eventually resigned over
the matter.) She had doubts about the propriety of this action and had tried to contact
her Permanent Secretary to clear it with him, but had been unable to do so and had gone
ahead and made the disclosure. The circumstances of this disclosure were investigated by
the Defence Committee (Defence Committee HC 519 1985–6). The Prime Minister

refused to allow the civil servants involved to give evidence to the Committee, on the ground that to do so would have major implications for the conduct of the government and for relations between Ministers and their private offices, so the Head of the Civil Service appeared instead. In the absence of full evidence the Select Committee had difficulty in ascertaining the facts against which to make judgements about proprieties and form a view as to whether any further mechanism for accountability was required. The Committee criticized the Ministers involved for failing to accept that they had a duty to account fully to Parliament, for leaving their civil servants in the lurch, and for refusing to allow them to testify to it. The civil servants who had master-minded the leak were also criticized for adopting a method of disclosure that was improper, authorized or not. They were further criticized for not owning up to leaking the document when the Prime Minister had asked Sir Robert Armstrong, the Head of the Home Civil Service, to investigate the circumstances of the leak.

Under pressure from the TCSC the government eventually agreed that civil servants who had been unable to resolve such a matter through their permanent secretary should have a right to appeal to the Head of the Home Civil Service if they alleged illegality, impropriety, or maladministration on the part of a Minister, and the government gave an assurance that such complaints would not damage a civil servant's career prospects unless they were frivolous or vexatious (TCSC CH 617 1989–90, at paras. 16–18). The Civil Service Pay and Conditions of Service Code now includes this provision. Ultimately however the civil servant may have to resign or be moved to another department if he is not satisfied with the outcome of these internal procedures. The Head of the Civil Service is hardly in a position to remonstrate with the Minister, or authorize the Civil Servant to refuse to comply with instructions. Nor can he or she lawfully disclose these matters to a Select Committee, or an MP, or the press. The *Ministerial Code* (2001) now makes plain that Ministers must uphold the political impartiality of the Civil Service, and not ask civil servants to act in any way which would conflict with the Civil Service Code (*Ministerial Code*, 2001, para 1 (ix), 58). If a civil servant considers that he is being asked to act improperly and is not satisfied with the result of departmental processes, he may report the matter to the Civil Service Commissioners (see Civil Service Code, para. 12) who oversee senior civil service appointments and lay down the procedures for them. But it is not the function of the Civil Service Commissioners to discipline Ministers: only the Prime Minister has this power.

The question remains whether any further outside recourse is needed for where impropriety in government is alleged. If a Public Standards Commissioner were appointed, as was being urged by the PASC and the outgoing Parliamentary Commissioner for Standards, Elizabeth Filkin in 2002, then his or her remit could extend to dealing with complaints about impropriety by Ministers in their relations with civil servants. A Civil Service Ombudsman could be appointed, reporting to the PASC, who could take up cases that the government was not prepared to deal with to the satisfaction of that Committee. This would introduce a measure of independence into the process of holding ministers and civil servants accountable for their methods of operation.

Special Advisers

Since at least 1974 it has been permissible for governments to appoint a number of special advisers. These are either people with specialist expertise in their field, or people who can add a political dimension—a political 'reality check'—to advice available to Ministers (see *Ministerial Code*, para. 50). However, it is confusing that those employed for their expertise and those employed on politically partisan and media-related activities are not dealt with separately, since the latter are more highly political than experts. They also have roles that are supposed to be complementary to those of members of the Government Information Service but which in fact can cause conflicts between the two.

The availability of political advisers protects the political neutrality of the permanent civil service by distinguishing the sources of political advice and support that Ministers receive. The fact that this point is fairly widely accepted brings out the fact that Ministers, the political arm of the executive, are highly political beings. And government is not simply about objective determination of what policy would best promote the public interest, but is ultimately about values and ideologies. The status of political advisers has however become increasingly controversial in recent years, in ways which we shall note shortly.

Special advisers work with specific ministers. There is a legal maximum of eighty. Formally they are civil servants—albeit temporary ones—paid for out of public funds, and subject to discipline by the Permanent Secretary in the Department. They are governed by the Civil Service Code, subject to certain exemptions, and by the Seven Principles of Public Life (see Chapter 3). They are, however, in many respects in a quite different position from career civil servants. Their posts are not advertised and they are not recruited on competitive merit. Their appointment is normally within the personal gift of a Minister. In practice only the Minister can dismiss a special adviser, and the permanent secretary's position of authority over these appointees is very ambiguous. Special advisers lose their jobs when the Minister leaves his post. Generally they have no authority over career civil servants, though a controversial provision for up to three special advisers to have authority over civil servants was introduced in the Civil Service Order in Council of 3 May 1997 (which, being an Order in Council, did not, incidentally, have to be laid before Parliament). One of these is the Director of Communications (Alistair Campbell at the time of writing) who has authority over the chief executive of the Central Office of Information in her role as government chief adviser on market and communications and information campaigns (see further Fourth Report of the Select Committee on Public Administration, *Special Advisers: Boon or Bane?* HC 293, 13 March 2001, 2000–1 and *These Unfortunate Events*, HC 303, 2001–2).

There is, since 2001, a special contract with special advisers and a *Code of Conduct for Special Advisers*. The code for the most part brings together statements from the previous model contract for special advisers, but it contains two new provisions. Article 22 invites any civil servant who believes that action by a special adviser is in excess of authority or breaches the Civil Service Code to raise the matter immediately with the Secretary to the Cabinet or the First Civil Service Commissioner. Secondly, the code adds to the sorts of work a special adviser may do, 'representing the views of their Minister to the media'. This goes beyond the basic role of special advisers under the Civil Service Order in Council, which is to provide advice to the Minister (see Daintith, 2002), and it legitimates a role as 'spin doctors' (see below).

This code runs counter to the usual assumption that government Ministers act on their own responsibility and are primarily accountable to Parliament, by emphasizing at a number of points the importance of relations with the Party (and a capital P is used throughout the code where Party is mentioned). By Party is meant the extra-parliamentary party. The code stresses the importance of checking facts and research from a Party political viewpoint (para. 3. ii), and of policies which reflect the political viewpoint of the Minister's Party (para. 3. iii). Many more examples could be given of the institutionalization of the extra-parliamentary party in the system via political advisers. Some reference is also made in the code to 'Party MPs' and while it is no doubt sensible for government to be attuned to the parliamentary party's responses to its policies and MPs' reactions to government, this has traditionally been done by the whips, junior Ministers, parliamentary private secretaries, and the parliamentary party organizations rather then special advisers.

The political adviser's role in securing that the extra-parliamentary Party's interests are incorporated into government policy is reminiscent, at an extreme, of the institutional-ization of the 'leading role' of the Communist Party in the former Soviet Union and the Warsaw pact states, and it runs counter to the UK model of representative democracy. The relationship between the extra-parliamentary Party and the Labour government in the 1970s and the parliamentary Labour Party in the early 1980s, in which the party sought the right to bind its MPs to the party manifesto, the right to write the manifesto, and the right to subject MPs to automatic reselection by their constituency parties—a theory of intra-party democracy—was at odds with representative democracy theory as commonly understood in the UK, and it was part of the reason for the marginalization of Labour at that period (Oliver, 1981). While it would be an exaggeration to draw a direct analogy between those controversies and the existence of special advisers, the overt Party-based partisanship that these positions appear to legitimate does not fit at all well with the traditional UK model of a non-partisan bureaucracy supporting elected politicians. A contrast may be drawn here with the position in many other European countries, includ-ing Germany, which have no problem with the partisanship of some top civil servants. The possibility of introducing Continental-style ministerial *cabinets* was mooted by the Treasury and Civil Service Committee in the 1980s but this was not taken up.

The rows about special advisers that have erupted in recent times include the email sent by Jo Moore, special adviser to Stephen Byers, Secretary of State for Transport, Environment and the Regions, on the day of the Al-Qa'ida bombing of the World Trade Centre in New York, 11 September 2001, noting that this was a good day to get out anything the government wanted to bury. This happened after the *Code of Conduct for Special Advisers* had come into effect (Daintith, 2002). She was disciplined by her per-manent secretary as a civil servant, but few people were happy with this outcome. The permanent secretary took the view that he could not dismiss her (and that this was not in any event a sufficiently serious matter for dismissal) and, in due course was of the view that she had not really been a civil servant at all. The status of these appointees is very ambiguous. It emerged later that Moore had previously asked a civil servant to disclose adverse information about the Transport Commissioner for London, who opposed the government's proposed public–private partnership for the London Underground, to discredit him. The civil servant had refused and had then been moved from his job. Eventually Moore resigned, and the row about her email and her conduct generally contributed to the resignation of the Secretary of State, Stephen Byers, some months later. She had also been in conflict with the head of information in the Department. The communications section of the Department felt her position to be unfair and some members had maliciously leaked information about her to the press. This was condemned by the PASC in its report on the matter (HC 303, 2001–2), but it illustrates the fact that good governance depends on clarity and fairness in relations, trust, and ethical behaviour on all sides. Another special adviser, in the Department of Transport, had sought information from the Labour Party in June 2002 about members of the Paddington Rail crash survivors group, in particular whether they were Conservative supporters. He had left the service by the time the request became known, and he apologized, as did his former Minister.

The concerns that these and other incidents raise are about the fact that appointments are not made on objectively assessed merit and about the link that these advisers commonly promote with the extra-parliamentary Party, noted above; the lack of clarity about whether they are civil servants or not, and who has authority over them; the personal nature of the relationship between the adviser and the Minister, which makes disciplinary proceedings by the permanent secretary difficult; the quality of these advisers and the ethos they bring to the job; and the ethics implied by the very existence of these appointments, including the fact that the advisers are specifically entitled to act for the party political advantage of the government at public expense, which ordinary civil servants may not do. These advisers have access to governmental information and to Ministers for that purpose. And up to three of them have authority over civil servants, which could put the latter in a position of conflict between their professional responsibilities, their duties as employees to take instructions from those in authority over them, and—as the Moore saga shows—their career prospects. There is little real accountability for them. Ministers refuse to allow these special advisers to appear before select committees and they have proved reluctant to take responsibility for their actions in Parliament. Despite the terms of their contracts and the code, their position does not seem to comply with three of the Seven Principles of Public Life (see Chapter 3)—objectivity, accountability, and leadership

Spin and the press

There was a series of conflicts between incoming 'spin doctors' and the Government Information Service after the formation of the Labour government in 1997. However, in 2002 the press became increasingly critical of the government's use of special advisers for the purposes of 'spin'—public relations activity—to the extent that it has undermined public confidence in what the government says. This has not arisen only from specific scandals such as those mentioned above. News management—for instance, releasing bad news on days when public attention is focused elsewhere—has increased public scepticism about government generally. The same information about increased expenditure on public services tends to be announced on several occasions, giving the often misleading impression that increases are cumulative. It was being alleged in the summer of 2002 that presentation was becoming more important than substance.

One reaction of the government was to blame the press for undermining confidence in the government (see Cook, 2002, and discussion in Chapter 3). This diagnosis of the problem however cannot produce a prescription for a remedy. The press cannot be prevented from expressing its scepticism about government or from concentrating on the personality-based politics of the Westminster village to the exclusion of substantive policy. O'Neill has offered some suggestions for making the press more accountable for any misreporting and cultivating a culture of suspicion, by requiring them, for instance, to separate reporting from comment and to disclose their interests and payments to informants (O'Neill, 2002, ch. 5; see Chapter 3) but there is no immediate prospect of such reforms being implemented.

The Prime Minister admitted in his meeting with the Liaison Committee on 16 July 2002 that the government had been mistaken in relying so heavily on spin and that it had only belatedly realized that announcements of policy and targets were only expressions of intention and did not mean that they would actually be delivered, and that this had contributed to misunderstandings (Liaison Committee, *Minutes of Evidence*, 16 July 2002). From the summer of 2002 government Ministers were taking care to make policy statements first to Parliament, the Prime Minister had taken to holding press conferences, and the first of his promised biannual meetings with the Liaison Committee had taken place. The government appeared to be reducing its reliance on spin-doctors and speaking directly to Parliament and the press.

Is reform possible?

There have been a number of efforts to come up with proposals for reforming the political adviser system, by the Committee on Standards in Public Life, the PASC, and others. The House of Lords debated the issue and the question whether a Civil Service Act should be passed in May 2002 (HL Deb., 1 May 2002, cols. 691–731). The Committee on Standards in Public Life, in its inquiry, received evidence from the first Civil Service Commissioner, responsible for upholding the impartiality of the civil service, that the use of special advisers was blurring the boundaries with the executive, which was confusing to civil servants. She called for senior special advisers to be deprived of their position of authority over civil servants.

The PASC in its report on the Jo Moore saga, *These Unfortunate Events* (HC 303, 2001–2) found that the use of codes of conduct and the systems in departments were incapable of dealing with special adviser problems if, as was the case with Jo Moore and the Secretary of State, there was a close political relationship between the Minister, who appoints the adviser, and the adviser, which makes it impossible in practice for the permanent secretary to discipline or dismiss the adviser, whatever the formal rules. Their recommendation was that the government should clarify the system for managing special advisers to make clear the roles of the Permanent Secretary, Ministers, and the Prime Minister, especially in relation to disciplinary matters. It should be made simpler for civil servants to voice their grievances and concerns.

At the time of writing it seems likely that the Civil Service Code will be amended to provide guidance to civil servants on how to report on the behaviour of special advisers if they force them to bend or break the rules on impartiality. The Cabinet Office announced in July 2002 that training for special advisers would be directed to improving their understanding of their relationship with civil service press officers, and that guidance would be produced to clarify the relationship between special advisers and members of the Government Information Service. However it is doubtful if the role of these advisers, other than those who can give expert advice, can be made to work compatibly with the conventions that political activity in government is the province of Ministers accountable to Parliament, and civil servants should be politically neutral. Special advisers are in effect politicians who are neither members of Parliament nor accountable to it. This is why the public is uncomfortable about them. There is at present no satisfactory method of accountability for or control over such people in the Westminster model.

In sum, special advisers are not true civil servants, and they should be recognized as belonging to a separate category that would need to be created for them with its own management structure and disciplinary arrangements. These advisers should be paid for by Ministers from a different source from the civil service vote, and be regarded as the alter ego of ministers, in the way that civil servants were until relatively recently. Ministers should be expected to take direct personal responsibility for all that they do and to answer to Parliament for them. There should be a resolution in each House of Parliament setting out the relationship and the conventions that govern it, in addition to any provision in a Civil Service Act.

A Civil Service Act for the UK?

In recent years there have been many proposals for a Civil Service Act that would put the service on a statutory basis and thus subject it to greater parliamentary scrutiny (see for instance, Committee on Standards in Public Life, Sixth Report, *Reinforcing Standards*, Cm. 4557, 2000, and Government Response, Cm. 4817; Lewis, 1998; Hennessy, 1996). The government has committed itself to introducing such a measure (see *The Government's Response to the Report from the House of Lords Select Committee on the Public Service*, Cm. 4000, July 1998) but no time-scale has been agreed, though it is agreed that there should be consultation before any legislation is brought forward. The PASC has called for a Royal Commission on the matter (Seventh Report, HC 94, 2000–1). The issue was debated in the House of Lords in May 2002 (HL Deb., 1 May 2002, cols. 691–731).

For the most part proposals for a Civil Service Act have been directed to clarifying, for instance, the rules relating to the relationship between Ministers and civil servants and the steps open to civil servants who may believe that they are being asked to act in contravention of the civil service code or otherwise in an unethical way, and the position of special advisers. As far as central government is concerned the recommendation was that the civil service code should be included in a Civil Service Bill (HC 263, 2001–2).

As we have seen, the trend in recent years has been for these matters to be resolved, usually only after sustained pressure by the select committees of the House of Commons and the Committee on Standards in Public Life, by issuing non-statutory codes or amending the Civil Service Order in Council without reference to Parliament. A Civil Service Act could put these codes and statements of principles and the core values of the civil service on a more formal basis by requiring parliamentary approval of them after debate, and make provision for a body such as a the Civil Service Commissioners or a Commissioner for Public Ethics and Standards to handle complaints about breaches of the codes, and report to Parliament on matters that have been investigated and the operation of the system overall (see for instance Treasury and Civil Service Committee *Report on the Role of the Civil Service*, HC 27, 1993–4; see also House of Lords Select Committee on Public Service, HL 2, 1997–8).

But the case for a Civil Service Act is broader than that. The passage of a bill through Parliament would give opportunities for parliamentary confirmation of the basic principles that should govern the civil service—a permanent, professional service appointed on merit—and relations between ministers, civil servants, and special advisers. An Act would give stronger legal protections to those principles. An Act would also secure parliamentary input into the arrangements, including provisions for how structural changes may be made in the future, for parliamentary approval of changes that affect the fundamental principles (it has already been noted that the executive agencies were introduced with no prior reference to Parliament), and for reporting to Parliament on the operation of codes and of the service as a whole. Provision could be made about the status and authority of special advisers. And, most importantly, legislation putting the whole service on a statutory footing, as it is in most democracies (including our close constitutional relatives, Australia and New Zealand) would make clear that the civil service is not the property of the government of the day. It would impose a duty on the Prime Minister and departmental ministers to accept accountability to Parliament for the management and operation of the service, and thus clarify the extent to which civil servants are to be regarded as acting solely at the direction of government, or in a wider public interest. It could make provisions as to how such an interest might be safeguarded, for instance by annual reports to Parliament from the Head of the Civil Service or a statutory, independent Civil Service Commission responsible for the general standards of the service. As O'Neill has argued, 'if we want a culture of public service, professionals and public servants must in the end be free to serve the public rather than their paymasters' (2002, Ch. 3).

An objection to a Civil Service Act might be that it would lead to judicial review of decisions relating to the management of the civil service, thus judicializing it. This need not be the case, if alternative mechanisms to judicial review are in place to deal with concerns about breaches of the requirements of the Act, such as parliamentary committees or a Public Service Ombudsman, and if government were responsive to concerns about the management of the service.

This is not the place for any detailed proposals for the content of a Civil Service Act, but experience in comparable countries shows that statutory regulation should not be disproportionately detailed. Wide consultation is required before legislation is brought forward, and the Committee on Standards in Public Life recommendation for a Royal Commission—which could report within a year—should be accepted. A Royal Commission could secure that the options are properly explored, drawing on experience in other Westminster-based countries and countries in Europe, so that a reasonable balance between over- and under-regulation is achieved and the fundamentals of the service and its relationship with the political arm of the executive and with Parliament are made explicit and protected against unilateral, unchecked change by government.

Conclusions

NPM has raised a number of issues about the accountability of Ministers for the civil service. Management techniques that have been introduced to enable government to have its policies implemented effectively have added new dimensions to the concept of citizenship, but they have also raised good-governance problems over accountability and ethics.

The civil service and special advisers are still very much part of the political Constitution. Though not regulated by statute they have become increasingly juridified in recent years. But concerns remain about the adequacy of using ad hoc codes to regulate them and about the reluctance of government to respond to parliamentary concerns about its running of the service. Some of these problems could be eased by a Civil Service Act. Though this would formalize the juridification of the civil service it need not undermine the political Constitution by increasing judicial review to any significant extent. An Act could enhance Parliament's ability to hold government to account by putting in place clear rules and criteria that government should observe in its management of the civil service and placing special advisers on a proper constitutional basis.

13

Devolution: General Principles

In 1998 a process of devolution of power to institutions based in Scotland, Wales, and Northern Ireland and to an extent the regions of England—including London—began. These arrangements are still very young and it is too early to reach mature judgements about them, but we can draw from them some indications of the ways in which concepts of democracy, citizenship, and good governance are developing. The devolution legislation has produced more highly juridified political and administrative processes than operate at UK level, and this raises issues as to how rules governing political behaviour can be enforced, as to the implications of involving the courts in disputes about breaches of norms, and the relative advantages and disadvantages of non-judicial mechanisms for resolving disputes where rules governing inter-institutional relationships have been breached.

As we shall see the devolution process has been asymmetrical in that the nature and degree of devolution have been different in different parts of the UK. The reasons for the asymmetry are that the arrangements have been tailored to respond to the varying pressures from and needs of Scotland, Northern Ireland, and Wales. The asymmetry means that the legal and political relationships between each of the devolved bodies and UK wide institutions vary considerably. The UK government has powers and responsibilities over a wider range of matters in Wales than in Scotland or Northern Ireland. The Westminster Parliament is the sole primary legislature for Wales, but though it retains the power by virtue of its legislative supremacy to legislate for Northern Ireland and Scotland in respect of devolved matters without the consent of their legislatures it will not normally do so. The matters devolved are different as between those two countries. As we shall see these asymmetries generate tensions and pressures for further changes. Some of these tensions may be creative, but others may damage relations between the countries which make up the Union and between them and the United Kingdom itself.

The devolution arrangements are also internally asymmetric, that is, the arrangements within or between the devolved bodies vary considerably. For instance, the statutory provisions as to the formation of executives, and committee structures are different for each executive body—the Scottish executive, the Welsh Assembly (which is technically an executive body within which there is a 'Welsh Assembly Government' or WAG), and the Northern Ireland executive (which is strictly a *sui generis* committee of the Northern Ireland Assembly). The Scottish Parliament, the Northern Ireland Assembly, and the Assembly for Wales each adopt their own standing orders, and standards of conduct are regulated in different ways in each of the areas. This kind of asymmetry need not generate tensions with other institutions in the way in which asymmetries in relations between the devolved institutions and the UK level institutions do, though of course each may learn from the different experiences and arrangements of the others.

The United Kingdom has traditionally been regarded as a unitary state. In reality it is a 'union' state (Rokkan and Urwin, 1982), the product of successive unions, first between England and Wales, then in 1707 between England and Wales and Scotland which produced a united Great Britain, and finally a union in 1800 between Great Britain and Ireland, later to become a union between Great Britain and Northern Ireland. But it was only in the 1990s that this reality came to be widely appreciated. Bulpitt (1983) has observed that the union rests on twin claims of *contract* between the constituent parts of the union and *solidarity*. Devolution over the last four years or so has been a process of renegotiating the contracts between Scotland, Wales, Northern Ireland, and England on one hand, and the UK on the other (though the role of England in any such renegotiation has been minimal thus far because of the traditional equation of England with the UK).

Until 1999 government in the UK was highly centralized. Apart from the fifty years of devolution in Northern Ireland in the mid-twentieth century, local government was the only elected tier below Westminster; it has only executive powers, and as we shall see (Chapter 16) the autonomy of local authorities has been progressively eroded in the years since 1980. There have for many years been national outposts of central government in the form of the Scottish Office, the Welsh Office, and the Northern Ireland Office, each with Secretaries of State responsible for them, but there was no system for imposing local public or political accountability on these outposts. Since 1994 there have been regional outposts of central government in England, Government Offices in the Regions (but no Secretary of State for England or its regions). But there is no machinery for holding these outposts to account locally in England.

Among the implications of this degree of centralization had been that government was accountable to the national public and not to local, national, or regional publics. This in turn meant that effectiveness in government was measured largely in nationwide terms rather than in terms of the effectiveness of policies on, for example, employment, economic development, environmental protection, in solving local or regional problems.

The unitary, centralized system also discouraged senses of 'multiple citizenship' (Heater 1990, ch. 9), in the population. There were until 1999 almost no political institutions apart from those at the centre and local authorities that provided opportunities for political experimentation or fostered a sense of belonging to a range of communities, some local, some functional. There was confusion, especially among the English, between Britishness and Englishness. Many English people thought of England as being a synonym for Britain. The Scots and Welsh, and members of the two communities in Northern Ireland, on the other hand, have strong senses of national identity, sometimes alongside and sometimes to the exclusion of, a sense of Britishness. But these identities could find almost no expression in formal political arrangements.

Before outlining the devolution arrangements in this and the next two chapters, let us sketch in the cases for and against devolution, the forms that devolution could take, and the broad arguments around the various options.

Arguments for Devolution

The centralization of power in the UK became a political issue from the late 1960s; it continued to be so throughout the 1970s. It was the growth of nationalism as reflected in swings to the Scottish National Party and Plaid Cymru in election results in Scotland and Wales that put the issue on the political agenda. In response to this pressure, in 1969 the Royal Commission on the Constitution was set up by the Labour government to 'examine the present functions of the central legislature and government in relation to the several countries, nations and regions of the United Kingdom' and other related issues. Its Report—the Kilbrandon Report, named after the Commission's chair at the time of publication—was published in 1973 (Cmnd. 5460).

The Report's recommendations for 'devolution' did not bear fruit; but given the resurgence of interest in decentralization in the 1990s, its findings are instructive. The Commission ascribed the rise in interest in decentralization of government to popular dissatisfaction with the remoteness and unresponsiveness of Westminster and Whitehall to the needs of the remoter parts of the country, and the ineffectiveness of government attempts to deal with the problems of those areas (Cmnd. 5460, 1973, chs. 8 and 9). This issue would nowadays be regarded as one of good governance. In Scotland and Wales the desire for greater participation in the development of policy was bolstered by the fact of nationhood (Cmnd. 5460, 1973 ch. 10) but, the Commission felt, there was a general demand from people in England too to 'win back power from London' (Cmnd. 5460, 1973, paras. 1–7).

Subsidiarity

The findings of the Kilbrandon Commission in effect recognized the importance of the principle of subsidiarity which has become a guiding principle in the European Union (see Chapter 4). This principle is not only a consideration in relations between member states and the Community; it also plays a part within some member states, particularly Germany, where the Länder are guaranteed the right to regulate on their own responsibility all the affairs of the local community within the limits set by law (Article 28 of the German Basic Law). Article 91a of the German Basic Law provides that the Federation shall participate in the discharge of certain responsibilities of the Länder, provided that such responsibilities are important to society as a whole and that federal participation is necessary for the improvement of living conditions. Otherwise, by implication, the federal government may not interfere in Land government.

The principle of subsidiarity has been influential in the discussions about decentralisation to national and regional governments in the United Kingdom. It also appears in consideration of local government (see Chapter 16)—there is no reason why the levels of government to which functions may be devolved in accordance with the subsidiarity principle should be limited to central and national or regional levels. But we have to bear in mind that the principle is easier to state than to apply: it does not provide us with the means for deciding whether any particular function—education, for example—is better performed at central, regional, or local level. Many of the functions of government have a range of aspects, some of which can be performed more effectively at one level than another—in effect the functions are shared between different levels. For example, the raising of revenue to finance education could arguably be best done by central government, the setting of standards by subnational or regional government, the actual provision of schools might be better left to the localities, and their management might be devolved to the schools themselves.

In a country without a written Constitution that protects the autonomy of regions or nations against encroachment from the centre, the mere allocation of functions to a lower tier of government rather than to the centre cannot prevent the centre taking an interest in and eventually seeking to control how the functions are discharged. This is particularly the case if the central government provides most of the money and thus has a legitimate interest in how it is spent. In the UK system it is legally possible for central government to use its majority in Parliament to pass legislation enabling it to intervene in the decisions and actions of devolved bodies or local government, thus undermining subsidiarity. Without some constitutional protection in the form of entrenchment, for example (see Chapters 1 and 20) or strong political resistance in the devolved areas, a commitment on the part of a government to subsidiarity cannot be guaranteed any formal or strict permanence or stability, since a later government could always go back on it.

There are further governance-related arguments in favour of decentralization. In general terms the case rests on the belief that bringing government closer to the people allows it to be more responsive, accountable, efficient and effective, and enables people to participate as citizens should in decisions that affect their lives. This is the way the case is put in the *Modernising Government* White Paper (Cm. 4310, 1999) which states that the objectives of devolution to regional and local bodies in England are to provide more responsive government and initiate a process of democratic renewal. Modernization is aimed at increasing quality and efficiency in service provision and joining up government.

Options for Reform

There were, and are, a limited number of broad options for resolving the problems identified by the Kilbrandon Commission and other commentators, and decentralizing power: the two extremes would be separatism for Scotland, even for Wales, England, and Northern Ireland, or maintenance of the pre-1999 centralized system on the basis that, though imperfect, it was better than any of the alternatives. As far as separation is concerned, there is considerable, though fluctuating, support for independence for Scotland. In Northern Ireland the nationalists and republicans want separation in the sense of breaking away from the United Kingdom and uniting with the Republic of Ireland, while the unionists and loyalists favour remaining in the United Kingdom. There appears to be some support for independence in Wales, but little pressure in England for separation from the rest of the United Kingdom.

Between separation and the pre-1999 centralized system a range of decentralizing possibilities exists. A strictly federal arrangement would involve establishing national or regional legislatures with some exclusive competences, and limiting the powers of the Westminster Parliament to legislate in those areas. This kind of limitation of the West-minster Parliament's powers would not necessarily be recognized and given effect by the courts as it would be contrary to the common law doctrine of the sovereignty of Parlia-ment (see Chapter 2). It would involve institutionalized subsidiarity, and would necessi-tate the elaboration of the principles underlying subsidiarity in order to provide due protection for the devolved bodies against encroachment by the centre. Such an arrange-ment would be symmetrical if all members of the federation had the same legislative powers and the Westminster Parliament's powers were the same in relation to each of the members of the federation. A strictly federal arrangement is not on the serious political agenda in the United Kingdom, though in 1999 some arguments in its favour were beginning to be heard (see Olowofoyeku, 1999).

A quasi-federal solution—what the Kilbrandon Commission called 'devolution'—could take a number of forms. Devolution differs from a federal arrangement in that it does not limit the powers of the Parliament at Westminster and entrench the powers of the national and regional Assemblies. It is 'a delegation of central government powers which would leave overriding control in the hands of Parliament' (Cmnd. 5460, 1973, para. 543.) A commitment could have been made by the UK to 'devolution all round'; instead it has been made only to Scotland, Wales, and Northern Ireland. A choice could be made between uniform or 'symmetrical' decentralization on the same model to all the nations and regions; or 'asymmetrical', lopsided decentralization under which some nations or regions enjoy a range of powers that is greater or less than the range enjoyed by others—the latter was chosen.

Devolution could involve granting legislative and executive or only executive power to the nations and regions, and doing either symmetrically or asymmetrically. As we shall see the United Kingdom has adopted a mixed asymmetrical set of devolution measures drawing on a range of the models sketched above.

A number of objections has been taken to the whole idea of devolution. Some of them figured strongly in the Conservative Party's manifesto for the 1997 general election:

The development of new assemblies in Scotland and Wales would create strains which could well pull apart the Union . . . In a world where people want security, nothing would be more danger-ous than to unravel a constitution that binds our nation together and the institutions that bring us stability.

Thus there is concern that decentralization, especially to Scotland and Wales, could contribute to a problem of 'balkanization' if in due course the smaller nations of Europe were to seek and obtain independence. (On the other hand devolution to Scotland could serve to keep the Union together by providing outlets for national preferences and defus-ing some of the resentment about the power of the centre.) Heater expressed the fear that 'multiple citizenship' (the sense of belonging to a multiplicity of political communities such as Scotland, the United Kingdom, the European Community) 'could not, naturally, be achieved if present nation-states disintegrated into their smaller component parts.'

But he speculated that an alternative, more desirable development than balkanization would be a reduction in the powers of governments of member states in the Community, with some of that power being devolved downwards to provincial administration and some transferred upwards to the supranational community (Heater 1990: 326–7).

The Background and Common Features of the Devolution Arrangements

Having outlined some of the options and the general issues raised by devolution, let us return to the arrangements that have been put in place since 1998. The first point to make is that the UK is not creating a federal system in the classical sense: the Westminster Parliament retains the right to amend the devolution Acts. Classical federalism implies that the federal level has limited power to alter the powers and institutional arrangements of the states or provinces and, correspondingly, that the states' and provinces' constitutional position is protected against encroachment from the centre (Wheare, 1960, 1963). Secondly, a central feature of the legal arrangements for devolution in the UK has been that the Westminster Parliament retains the power to legislate even in devolved fields, which is also inconsistent with formal federalism. However, conventions are evolving that inhibit the Westminster Parliament from legislating for Scotland on devolved matters without the consent of the Scottish Parliament (see discussion of the Sewel convention, below). Although a similar convention exists for the Northern Ireland Assembly (see *Devolution Guidance Note 8: Post-Devolution Primary Legislation Affecting Northern Ireland*), it has not been used in the same way as in Scotland: in 2000 the Westminster Parliament legislated to give the Secretary of State for Northern Ireland the power to suspend devolution (At the time of going to press (January 2003) devolution to Northern Iceland is suspended).

A major question will be whether a system of *informal* federalism in which the UK Parliament refrains from legislating on devolved matters without the consent of the devolved legislatures will, or should, evolve to mitigate the formal legal position that the UK Parliament retains its legislative supremacy. It would be easy to assume that such a development would be a good thing and in line with concepts of democracy. However, it should not be forgotten that during the period of home rule in Northern Ireland from 1922 to 1972 the government and Parliament in London operated a convention that they would not intervene in the running of the Province. The Northern Ireland Parliament and its executive and some local authorities exercised their powers in a highly discriminatory and sectarian way, which contributed to the resurgence of troubles since the late 1960s and the conflict between the two communities. One lesson from this is that the arrangements for devolved bodies, whether in the UK or in a true federal state, need to contain safeguards against abuse of power by the devolved bodies or member states. In effect devolved areas need their own written (in the sense of limiting) Constitutions, and the Devolution Acts in the UK provide such Constitutions. The convention that the Westminster Parliament will not exercise its sovereignty in relation to devolved matters without the consent of those legislatures should not give rise to the kinds of abuse that were perpetrated in Northern Ireland before the Stormont Parliament was dissolved, because protection against abuse by the devolved legislatures and executives are built into the devolution legislation. But the fact that the Westminster Parliament retains the legal power to intervene provides additional protection against abuses of power and interferences with rights (though of course the Westminster Parliament's intervention could itself be an abuse or undermine rights in the devolved areas).

The political pressures for devolution were different in Scotland, Wales, and Northern Ireland. There was strong interest in Scotland in devolution or even separatism in the 1960s and early 1970s, as well as in the 1990s. In Scotland there is a strong sense of national identity, a distinctively Scottish civil society, and a separate legal system; Scotland had its own Parliament until 1707. The largest party in Scotland for many years has been Labour. The fact that there was a Conservative government in office in the United Kingdom from 1979 to 1997, which introduced policies which were not in line with the wishes of the majority of Scots—including the early introduction of the unpopular poll tax which had eventually to be abolished throughout Great Britain in face of civil unrest—fuelled discontent with the system, and thus support for devolution.

These factors alone might not have been sufficient to lead the Labour Party to a commitment to devolve power to Scotland—Labour has been traditionally a highly centrist party. But from the 1970s the Scottish National Party began to increase its electoral support, largely at the expense of the Labour Party. Fear of losing yet more support was a factor in Labour's decision to adopt the policy of devolution in the late 1970s (the Scotland Act and the Wales Act 1978 were repealed after failing to achieve the required level of support in referendums in 1979—see Chapter 14). The same concern lay behind the renewed commitment to devolution which formed part of Labour's election manifesto in 1997. Before the general election in that year Labour had reached an agreement on constitutional reform with the Liberal Democrats (*Report of the Joint Consultative Committee on Constitutional Reform*, 1997). That party has a longstanding commitment to devolution, which formed part of that agreement.

There was much less political pressure for devolution in Wales than in Scotland. There is a strong national cultural identity in Wales, but the principality does not have a separate legal system nor, before devolution, was there a deeply and widely felt sense of a separate political identity as Scotland has. Nevertheless there are strong arguments based on subsidiarity in favour of devolution to Wales.

The case for devolution to Northern Ireland is different again. The Stormont Parliament had had to be suspended in 1972. Thereafter it was widely agreed that direct rule was not satisfactory and that a way had to be found to devolve power in a way that would command the support of both communities, and secure that the interests and rights of both communities were protected, and that a peaceful way could be found to resolve the conflict between the nationalists and republicans, who seek union with the Republic of Ireland, and the unionists and loyalists who wish to remain in the United Kingdom. Devolution became possible with the Belfast Agreement on Good Friday in 1998 (see Chapter 14).

Thus the option of maintaining the status quo was rejected by the UK government elected in 1997 for a range of reasons. A new Scottish Parliament, a Northern Ireland

Assembly, and a Welsh Assembly were established. Steps have also been taken to devolve functions to regionally based institutions in England—in line with the agreement between Labour and the Liberal Democrats. In the rest of this chapter we consider some of the common features of these very asymmetrical arrangements. In the following two chapters the particular arrangements for each part of the UK will be discussed, together with the implications for the UK as a whole.

Maintaining the sovereignty of the UK Parliament

The Scotland Act and the Northern Ireland Act expressly preserve the legislative sovereignty of the Westminster Parliament. This is not strictly necessary according to orthodox constitutional doctrine. The Government of Wales Act does not grant primary legislative power to the Assembly for Wales and Westminster therefore retains that power in any event. Although, as we shall see, extensive legislative competence is devolved to the Scottish Parliament and the Northern Ireland Assembly, the United Kingdom Parliament may legislate on any devolved matter, and its legislation will 'trump' that passed by the devolved legislatures. It has already been noted that it is for this reason that the arrangements are not 'federal', for federalism normally implies that the devolved bodies' areas of competence are protected from incursions by the federal parliament. It is doubtful whether, without a written Constitution radically altering the present system, a statute purporting to limit the competence of the United Kingdom Parliament to legislate contrary to measures passed by the devolved legislatures would be given effect by the courts.

But quite apart from this consideration, the continued legislative supremacy of the Westminster Parliament was considered by the Labour government that was formed after the election in 1997 to be justified on democratic, constitutional, and good-governance grounds. If devolution were to limit the powers of the UK Parliament, the courts would need to have the power to disapply an Act of the Westminster Parliament that exceeded those limits by, for instance, encroaching on the powers of devolved bodies. Such a power would bring the courts and the devolved bodies into conflict with the United Kingdom legislature and executive, representing a radical departure from the traditions of the political Constitution and of deference by the courts to the UK Parliament and executive on sensitive political issues. It would surely raise to the top of the political agenda the question whether a Supreme Court on United States lines or some other institution such as the German Bundesverfassungsgericht or the French Conseil constitutionnel would be required to resolve such constitutional issues (see discussion in Chapter 18).

Quite apart from any questions about the desirability or otherwise of such arrangements, it is unsurprising—and typical of the UK incremental and pragmatic tradition—that no such powers for the courts were included in the devolution arrangements. In my view it is unlikely that such possibilities will reach the top of the political agenda in the UK unless a crisis arises which requires such solutions to be considered. This is partly because of the dominance of the executive over the UK Parliament and the reality that a UK government would not be willing to give up its powers to legislate, through Parliament, on any subject matter unless there were pressing political pressures to do so. It is also attributable to the strong UK (though perhaps not Scottish) political and cultural tradition that controversial matters ought to be resolved through the political process rather than through the courts, not only because that process introduces democratic accountability (which American-style judicial review does not), but also because of a concern to maintain good relations between the courts, Parliament, and the executive.

Limited competence of the devolved bodies

All of the devolved bodies have limited competence, though the limitations are asymmetrical. The competences they do have derive from their parent statute, and this has raised the issue whether their powers are only 'delegated' or 'conferred' by the Westminster Parliament and the UK executive, so that their legislation is delegated or secondary legislation, in essence similar to statutory instruments made by UK Ministers; or whether power has been 'devolved' in the sense that Westminster's own powers to legislate have been *transferred* to the devolved bodies so that the Acts of the Scottish Parliament and the Northern Ireland Assembly are to be regarded as primary rather than secondary legislation (Burrows, 2000, ch. 3; Hadfield, 2000). The difference has considerable symbolic as well as legal importance, as it affects the socio-political status of the devolved legislatures radically. This is a politically controversial issue, especially for Scotland, since it will affect the attitude of the UK government to the devolved bodies, which could be troublesome if different parties were in power in Westminster and Edinburgh.

None of the devolved bodies has the power to act contrary to European Community law or the European Convention on Human Rights. There is therefore a contrast between Acts of the Westminster Parliament, which are classified as 'primary legislation' by the Human Rights Act, and Acts of the devolved legislatures which are not in the class of primary of legislation under that Act, but for these purposes are treated as subordinate or secondary legislation. The UK courts may disapply secondary legislation that is incompatible with Convention rights, but not primary legislation, and it may disapply Acts of the Scottish Parliament or the Northern Ireland Assembly. These provisions are essential to protect the UK—the responsible body in European Community and international law—from being exposed by the devolved bodies, against its wishes, to liability for breach of its obligations in European Community law or for breach of the requirements of the ECHR in the Strasbourg court. The competence of the devolved bodies is also limited in many other areas (see discussion of the devolution arrangements in each country in Chapter 14), but Acts passed within those other areas of competence may nevertheless be regarded or treated as primary legislation under the 'devolving' acts.

A consequence of the limited competence of the devolved bodies is that both the legislatures and the executives may be subject to judicial review on the ground that they have exceeded their competences. This puts these legislatures in a very different position from that of the Westminster Parliament, and places a considerable responsibility on the courts which might be called upon to adjudicate in disputes about competence. Lord Rodger in the Scottish Court of Appeal, in *Whaley v. Lord Watson* ([2000] S.C.125, p. 348) observed of the Scottish Parliament that 'It is a body which, like any other statutory body, must work within the scope of [its] power. If it does not do so, then in an appropriate case the court may be asked to intervene and will require to do so.' This implies that Acts of the Scottish Parliament are secondary, though primary devolved, legislation. The *Whaley v. Lord Watson* case shows that the creation of legislatures of limited competence in the devolution Acts is a significant departure from the traditional position that political matters are best left to the politicians, a view which still prevails at Westminster and Whitehall and which was explicitly maintained, as we have noted, in the preservation of the legislative supremacy of the United Kingdom legislature in the devolution Acts. However, Lord Nimmo Smith in *Adams v. Lord Advocate* (Court of Session, Outer House, *The Times*, 8 August 2002) noted that Acts of the Scottish Parliament had far more in common with public general statutes of the UK Parliament than with subordinate legislation as it was commonly understood. Consequently there was no room for the imposition of common law judicial review concepts such as principles of procedural impropriety or unreasonableness (see Chapter 5) on the Parliament. Instead the courts should consider whether legislation was within the discretionary area of judgement of the Parliament, the same approach as is adopted in Human Rights cases where a declaration of incompatibility may be made in relation to Acts of the UK Parliament (see *R. v. DPP, ex parte Kebilene*, [2000] AC 326, per Lord Hope and *Stott v. Brown* 2000–2 SC (PC) 43; *International Transport Roth GmbH v. Secretary of State for the Home Department*, [2002] EWCA 158; [2002] 3 WLR 344, paras. 69–87, per Laws LJ; and Chapter 6). In *Adams* the Protection of Wild Mammals (Scotland) Act 2002, which banned mounted fox-hunting with dogs, was held not to be in breach of the Human Rights Act protection of the Convention right to property because it was open to the Parliament to strike the right balance by controlling the use of property in accordance with the general interest in the prevention of cruelty to animals, without paying compensation. Nor was it in breach of the right not to be discriminated against without objective justification.

If an Act of the Scottish Parliament or the Northern Ireland Assembly, or subordinate legislation by the Scottish, Northern Irish, or Welsh executives is found by a court to be outside competence, the court may refuse to give effect to the relevant provision. It may—though it need not—then make an order removing or limiting the retrospective effect of that judgment or suspending the effect of its decision to allow the defect to be corrected (see further Craig and Walters, 1999).

Under the devolution legislation there will inevitably be disputes between the devolved bodies and the Westminster Parliament or the UK government on the competences of the devolved bodies. There will also be disputes between individuals and the devolved bodies where individuals object to decisions or acts of devolved executives or legislation passed by the Scottish Parliament or the Welsh or Northern Ireland Assemblies. The devolution legislation provides that bills before the devolved legislatures may be referred to the Judicial Committee of the Privy Council for pre-enactment review and a decision on their compatibility with the devolution legislation. Once legislation has been passed challenges to it may be raised in any court. The lower courts may refer 'devolution issues' to higher courts, and the Appellate Committee of the House of Lords should normally refer a devolution issue to the Judicial Committee. The point of this last provision is that devolution issues may raise clashes between legislation passed by the Westminster Parliament and legislation passed by the devolved bodies, and it would be inappropriate for the Lords of Appeal in Ordinary sitting as the Appellate Committee of the House of Lords to be adjudicating on legislation that had been passed—or rejected under the Parliament Acts—by that House. Further, as the Appellate Committee has no jurisdiction over Scottish criminal appeals, a devolution issue raising a criminal matter might be found not to fall within the jurisdiction of the Appellate Committee. There is thus a bifurcated appeal and referral system—to the Appellate Committee of the House of Lords or to the Judicial Committee of the Privy Council—under the devolution legislation.

Inter-institutional relations

A strong feature of the devolution arrangements is the informality of the arrangements for intergovernmental relations (see generally Burrows, 2000, ch. 5; Hazell, 2000*b*). The UK government deliberately rejected formal arrangements of the kind used in federations such as Canada, which has a large Department of Intergovernmental Affairs. Instead a Joint Ministerial Committee has been established, on which the UK government and the devolved administrations are members. This committee is at the apex of the political machinery, but for the most part intergovernmental relations are conducted between officials or bilaterally between Ministers of the UK and devolved executives. The terms of reference of the JMC are to consider non-devolved matters which impinge on devolved areas and vice versa, to consider common issues of concern across all devolved areas, to keep the arrangements for liaison under review, and to consider disputes between the administrations. The JMC meets either in plenary session, at least once a year, which the Prime Minister and the Deputy Prime Minister and their equivalents in the devolved administrations attend, or in functional format. There are four ministerial subcommittees: on Health and Poverty; Economy; Knowledge; and the European Union, where particular departmental UK Ministers and their equivalents in the devolved administrations meet. Hazell summarized the working of JMC on health after a year as having settled down, after initial suspicion on the part of the devolved administrations that they were being brought together to be lectured by the UK government on how to use the extra funding for the NHS, into a genuine forum for the exchange of information and best practice (Hazell, 2000*b*, 166). There are many other contacts at ministerial and officer level and bilaterally.

The UK government and the devolved executives have agreed on a series of *Memorandums of Understanding* (the most recent as of September 2002 was Cm. 5240, December 2001) and a number of Supplementary Agreements (Concordats). These agreements seek to avoid potential conflicts between institutions (Cornes, 2000; Hazell, 2000*b*; Rawlings, 2000; Poirier, 2001; Scott, 2001). These agreements were not submitted for prior discussion or approval to the devolved bodies or to the Westminster Parliament but were reached through discussion between civil servants and politicians at the different levels. The Scottish Parliament endorsed them on 7 October 1999. The House of Commons Procedure Committee endorsed them in its report on *The Procedural Consequences of Devolution* (4th report 1998–9, HC 185, May 1999, para. 23). The *MoU* also bind the executives to encourage their respective legislatures to respect each others' areas of primary responsibility (paras. 14–15).

The *MoU* deal with the continuing legislative supremacy of the Westminster

Parliament by providing that 'the UK Government will proceed in accordance with the convention that the UK Parliament would not normally legislate with regard to devolved matters except with the agreement of the devolved legislature' (*Memorandum of Understanding*, 2001, para. 13). This agreement, known also as the Sewel Convention as it was formulated by Lord Sewel in a House of Lords debate (HL Deb., 21 July 1998, vol. 592, col. 791; see Winetrobe, 2001*a*), has, unexpectedly, been quite frequently resorted to. For instance, between its establishment in May 1999 and March 2002, thirty Sewel motions had been passed by the Scottish Parliament covering thirty bills of the Westminster Parliament. (Some bills require more than one Sewel motion and a motion may cover more than one bill.) During that period the Scottish Parliament passed thirty-six Acts. There have been almost as many Westminster Acts for Scotland since devolution as Acts of the Scottish Parliament (see Page and Batey, 2002).

The practice in Scotland is for the Scottish executive to produce a memorandum describing the purpose and effect of the provisions of the bill for which consent is sought, and a motion is lodged seeking the Parliament's approval. The Parliamentary Bureau decides whether time should be given for debate, but the expectation is that the motion will be passed without debate, and in practice the executive has been reluctant to allow debate. This has led to consideration whether the Scottish Parliament's participation should go further and whether the Westminster bills should be subjected to formal detailed scrutiny by committees of the Scottish Parliament, for instance as to whether it is 'sensible and proper' (a phrase used by Donald Dewar, First Minister at S.P. O.R. 16 June, col. 403) for Westminster to legislate in devolved areas of responsibility.

The four overarching Concordats published with the *MoU* cover Co-ordination of EU Policy Issues, Financial Assistance to Industry, International Relations and Statistics, and the JMC. These devices, again, are designed to preserve good relations and an atmosphere of trust between the centre and devolved bodies, and to minimize conflict. As Hazell observes (2000*b*, 158) they set out principles of good administration and negotiation—no surprises, proper consultation, confidentiality in the exchange of information, respect and understanding for each other's positions, clear definitions of roles and responsibilities. The concordats and the *MoU* are designed to minimize the need to resort to litigation or legislation, by laying down procedures for avoiding and resolving disputes. They are themselves expressed not to be legally binding.

The preference for informal and non-legal mechanisms based on trust and cooperation for regulating intergovernmental relations and resolving disputes in the devolution arrangements provides a strong illustration of the UK concept of good governance and its reliance on 'soft law' or 'quasi-legislation'—forms of juridification—rather than positive law and judicial review—judicialization. But whether the spirit of trust and cooperation would survive if different parties were in control in Westminster and the devolved bodies (as is bound to happen at some stage) must be questionable. If the use of concordats turned out to be ineffective in securing cooperation, it is likely that relations would have to be regulated by statute, opening up possibilities for judicialization that current arrangements seek to avoid. In other words devolution will, in due course, lead to a further shift from the political to a law-based Constitution.

Finance

Only the Scottish Parliament has revenue-raising powers under the devolution arrangements—a power to vary the rate of income tax by up to three pence in the pound. To date this power has not been used. The devolved bodies rely almost entirely on grants from central government. The devolution Acts provide for the establishment of a Consolidated Fund in each country, and the relevant Secretary of State makes payments into these Funds out of money provided by Parliament of 'such amounts as he shall determine'. The amounts to be paid are therefore not statutorily determined. In effect, the practice which had evolved before devolution, of the making of payments to the three Secretaries of State, as part of what has been called 'regulation inside government' (see Hood et al., 1999) has been adapted for devolution, and it has not been regarded as necessary to place the making of payments on a detailed statutory basis. This is a further example of the preference in the UK system for non-legal mechanisms.

None of the devolved bodies has significant borrowing powers, and capital expenditure has to be funded from the current budget or public–private partnerships. One of the side effects of this non-statutory regime of funding by central government is that, unlike the position in many federal states—Germany and Spain for instance—disputes about the level of funding are not taken to the courts. They are to be resolved by consultation with the Treasury (see *Statement of Funding Policy*, HM Treasury, 2002; Bell and Christie, 2001, 136–9).

This reliance on funding from the UK Treasury raises important issues about the accountability and responsibility of the devolved bodies. With no independent revenue-raising power (unlike local authorities) they may blame their failings on inadequate funding by central government, and central government may blame those failings on poor management by the devolved bodies.

The allocation of the block grant to the devolved bodies by the Treasury is governed largely by the Barnett formula (see generally Bell and Christie, 2001). This formula was produced in 1976 by the then Chief Secretary to the Treasury, Joel Barnett. It is population-based, not needs-based. Its starting point was the then level of spending in England, Wales, and Scotland. That level of spending had evolved over the years and was not based on any particular formula, though spending levels were supposed to be based on needs in each area. There has not, however, been a needs assessment for the four countries for over twenty years. The Barnett formula provided that in future for each change of £85 of spending in England on comparable services to those in Scotland and Wales, there would be £10 increase in Scotland and £5 increase in Wales. To this formula Northern Ireland spending was added on the basis that for each additional £100 spent in Great Britain, an additional £2.75 would be spent in Northern Ireland. These calculations are roughly related to the relative size of populations in the four countries. In other words decisions about the level of spending in England drive the level of spending in the other parts of the realm. But the devolved bodies are not required to spend the sums granted to them in the same ways as they are spent in England, as is illustrated by the decisions of the Scottish executive to abolish tuition fees for university students, to improve the salaries of teachers, and to fund the personal care of the elderly. These commitments have to be met from the overall Scottish budget, so that economies will have to be made elsewhere.

The Barnett formula is non-legal. It has been described as a 'non-statutory policy rule based on a mutual understanding between parties within the policy network, the implementation of which is subject to both sides observing behavioural "rules of the game"' (Thain and Wright, 1995). Because it is non-legal, there appears to be no scope for judicial review of the Treasury's decisions about grant allocations. This provides a further useful example of the system relying on political mechanisms rather than the law and judicial review for its operation.

The net effect of the Barnett formula has been that more is spent per capita in Scotland, Wales, and Northern Ireland than in England. The Treasury estimated that in 1995–6 expenditure per capita in Scotland was 32 per cent higher than in England, in Wales it was 25 per cent higher, and in Northern Ireland it was 32 per cent higher (Treasury Committee, *The Barnett Formula: The Government's Response*, Appendix 2, para. 9, HC 619, 10 March 1998).

There has been some convergence in the level of spending in the four countries as public expenditure on health and other areas has increased under the Labour government's Comprehensive Spending Review. The Barnett formula operates to give lower proportionate rises to areas that enjoy higher levels of per capita spending than those with lower levels of such spending. As public expenditure increases (as it is assumed that it will) the rate of convergence between the different regions also increases. Ultimately, Bell argues, the formula will equalize per capita public spending throughout the UK, but levels will not be related to need (Bell, 2001). Nor are the present levels. The regions of the north of England fare the worst, and London fares best. Scotland and Northern Ireland do next best to London, and Wales does better than all but one English region and better than England overall (Bell and Christie, 2001, 139–42).

There is scope for some funding to be allocated outside the Barnett formula. This is what happened when the Welsh executive claimed in 2000 that the additional money needed to match the £1.3 billion European union structural funds awarded for Wales and based on measures of need should not be found from their own budget but should be provided by the UK Treasury. Eventually the money was found by the Chancellor of the Exchequer, who produced an assigned budget with a 5.4 per cent increase in real terms over three years from 2000–1 to 2003–4, a 1 per cent greater increase for Wales than for Scotland. This included sums outside the Barnett formula to provide Public Expenditure Survey cover for the European funds (see Hazell, 2000b, 175–7; Osmond, 2000, 45–7; Bell and Christie, 2001, 147–50).

It is estimated that by about 2004 there will have been sufficient convergence in the spending in each of the four countries for a new needs assessment to be politically possible. There will by then be discontent on all sides with the Barnett formula. The executives in Scotland, Wales, and Northern Ireland will participate in the devising of possible new formulae. What will be missing however is any democratic voice for the English regions (except London) or for England itself, separate from the UK Treasury, when a new set of funding and spending arrangements is made (see the discussion of England's position in Chapter 15).

The Barnett formula has come in for criticism from a number of quarters, and an issue is whether, when eventually a new needs assessment is carried out for the four countries of the UK and, within England, the regions, a statutory and therefore more juridified, system for the allocation of funds will replace the present informal arrangements. There are strong arguments in favour of a more transparent and democratically legitimate formula for allocating funds than the present one, but a major issue would be whether recourse could be had to the courts in the event of allocations being alleged to fall outside the legislative provisions. Such disputes would in turn raise issues about the suitability of the courts to adjudicate upon them. The record of the courts in the few judicial review cases involving financial matters (for instance, *Bromley LBC v. GLC* [1983] 1 AC 768, HL in which the House of Lords found the GLC policy to subsidize fares on London Transport to be unlawful) suggests that the courts might not be qualified to deal with what could be highly politically controversial and value-laden determinations, or that they would not wish to take on this jurisdiction and would prefer to defer to Parliament or the government. The point illustrates the ways in which degrees of juridification raise different issues: judicialization in the sense of opening up the possibility of judicial review raises different issues from juridification that introduces transparency linked to some enforcement mechanism other than judicial review.

The Barnett formula gives the constituent parts of the UK no formal or institutionalized political clout or leverage in relation to resources. Yet, as Coulson has noted: 'The main argument for regional government is that an elected regional Assembly will be able to ensure that its region gets a fair share of the resources available' (Coulson 1989: 3). But the writings on this subject pay very little attention to how the required clout can be contrived. The present system does not even recognize the need for clout. No doubt the UK government would not want the devolved bodies to be in a position to exert pressure on the Treasury. Yet the mechanisms for extracting money from central government (or from the European Community) need to be effective, for less prosperous regions are not able to bring their standards up without equalization schemes of some kind.

On this point the Spanish model is instructive. Decentralisation to the 'autonomous communities' is progressive. There is a special Council for the Fiscal and Financial Policy of the Autonomous Communities, composed of the Finance Ministers from the communities together with the state Finance Minister and the Minister for Public Administration. This consultative body looks at coordination of policy in regard to public investment, costs of services, the distribution of resources to the regions, etc. There is also elaborate provision for the regions to retain a greater share of revenue as their responsibilities increase and for an Inter-regional Compensation Fund to ensure adequate finances for the disparate regions. The rights of regional assemblies to control their own budgets and the responsibilities of their finance departments are also provided for (Donaghy and Newton, 1987: 105–6; Heywood, 2000).

As and when the Barnett formula does come to be re-examined, the nations and regions will assuredly seek to exercise some kind of political pressure in their own interests. This is not something to which much thought seems to have been given. Whether the regional and national members that are likely to be elected to the reformed second chamber (see Chapters 10 and 15) would provide channels for such pressure is hard to predict.

The Secretaries of State

The Secretaries of State for Scotland, Wales, and Northern Ireland remained in place after devolution. Their roles, according to the *MoU*, were to promote the devolution settlement, to ensure effective working relations between the UK government and the devolved administrations, and to help resolve any disputes. It is through them that payments into the Consolidated Fund of each devolved body are made, and they explain the basis of estimated payments. By 2002, however, it was being reported in the press that the Secretary of State for Scotland did not have sufficient work for a full-time appointment. The Secretary of State for Wales has to attend to needs, for instance, for the Westminster Parliament and government to reach agreement with the Welsh Assembly about primary legislation passed for Wales. But the merger of these two posts might be desirable. The Secretary of State for Northern Ireland on the other hand has responsibility for major matters in the reserved domain including justice and security, and has had to take on responsibility for the province during periods of suspension, and spends much time on the province, and it would not be practicable for that post to be merged with another.

Regulation of conduct and procedure

Finally, in this summary of the most significant common features of the devolution arrangements, the provisions for the regulation of conduct of members of the devolved Parliament and Assemblies, and for the regulation of their procedures are formalized in a break from the tradition at Westminster (Chapter 9).

It is clearly central to notions of good governance that elected representatives and others holding public offices should be under an effective regime that secures integrity, openness, and observance of the Seven Principles of Public Life compiled by the Committee on Standards in Public Life (First Report, Cm. 2850, 1995). The main point here is the contrast between the current arrangements at Westminster and those for the Scottish Parliament, the Northern Ireland Assembly, and the Assembly for Wales. The two Houses of Parliament at Westminster are self-regulating and enjoy parliamentary privilege. The courts will not investigate their procedures (see *Edinburgh and Dalkeith Railway v. Wauchope* (1842) 8 Cl and F 710; Article 9, Bill of Rights 1689). Their requirements for the registration and declaration of interests are self-imposed. The rules about conduct are their own creation, as is the machinery for their enforcement. The Scottish Parliament, the Northern Ireland Assembly, and the Assembly for Wales, by contrast, do not enjoy parliamentary privilege, although there are some statutory protections against challenges to the validity of acts on procedural grounds. They are subject to statutory regulation, and breaches of those statutory rules are criminal offences. Each has a duty to adopt its own standing orders, but they are also subject to extensive statutory regulation in a range of ways. They have standards committees. The Scottish Parliament is obliged by section 39 of the Scotland Act to compile and publish a register of Members' interests. Members must declare their interests before taking part in proceedings relating to the interest, members may be prevented from participating in proceedings in the Parliament where they have interests, members may be prohibited from advocating or initiating matters on behalf of any third party for consideration. Any member of the Parliament who contravenes these requirements is guilty of an offence (Scotland Act, section 39; see Burrows, 2000, 39–45). Decisions of the Scottish Parliament on these matters are subject to judicial review, which is not the case in relation to decisions of the Westminster Parliament (*Whaley v. Lord Watson*, 2000 SC 125).

There are similar provisions for the Northern Ireland Assembly in section 43 of the Northern Ireland Act 1998 and for the Welsh Assembly in section 72 of the Government of Wales Act 1998. Further, the Prevention of Corruption Acts 1889–1916 apply to these bodies, with the result that the giving or offering of a bribe to a member is a criminal offence (Scotland Act, section 43; Government of Wales Act, section 79). This is not the case in the Westminster Parliament, though the Committee on Standards in Public Life, the Law Commission for England and Wales, the Joint Committee on Parliamentary Privilege, and the Home Office have proposed criminalizing such bribery (see Chapter 9).

The devolved bodies have made their own arrangements for maintaining standards in quite interesting ways (Gay, 2002*a, b*). In Northern Ireland the ombudsman has also been appointed the Commissioner for Standards for the Assembly and the advantage is that he has his own resources and so some independence. There has in fact been very little concern about standards in Northern Ireland, and the complaints have been mostly of misuse of Assembly stationery. Again devolution raises important issues to do with the peculiarity of the position of the Westminster Parliament in relation to the courts and its reliance on self-regulation to uphold standards.

14

Devolution: Scotland, Northern Ireland, and Wales

Having considered some of the common points about devolution in the previous chapter, we consider here the particular arrangements for Scotland, Northern Ireland, and Wales.

Scotland

The Scotland Act 1998 was the culmination of a period of pressure for devolution dating back to the 1960s—it was this pressure which had led to the appointment of the a Royal Commission on the Constitution in 1969 (see generally Bogdanor, 1999; Burrows, 2000; Morrison, 2001; Forman, 2002). After the Report of the Royal Commission (Cmnd. 5460, 1973—the Kilbrandon Report) was published the Labour government in 1974 prepared legislation for devolution to Scotland (and Wales). Acts for devolution to Scotland and Wales were passed in 1978, but they were not to be brought into effect unless 40 per cent of the electorate in each country voted in favour in a referendum. The Scottish referendum failed to produce the necessary per cent, though over 50 per cent of those who voted favoured the bringing into effect of the Act, and the Act was repealed in 1979. (The referendum in Wales also did not produce a sufficient per cent of the electorate in support.)

In the wake of the Scottish referendum a Campaign for a Scottish Assembly, a cross-party organization, was formed. The Campaign did not have a high profile before the 1987 general election. After the election however it sprang back into life and set up a committee to produce a report, *A Claim of Right for Scotland*, which was launched in July 1988. It recommended that a Constitutional Convention should be established to draw up a scheme for a Scottish Assembly or Parliament. The Scottish Constitutional Convention's aim was 'to reach agreement on how Scotland ought to be governed' (Scottish Constitutional Convention 1989, 1). Although it had no official status, its members included 80 per cent of Scotland's MPs and MEPs, members from the Regional and Island Councils and most District Councils, and representatives from the churches, business, industry, the unions, and from the Labour Party, the Social and Liberal Democrats, the Social Democratic Party, the Green Party, and the Communist Party. The Conservatives and Scottish National Party refused to take part, the former because it opposed any devolution, and the latter because the Convention was not able to discuss independence as an option.

The SCC proposed that a Parliament should be established for Scotland, with legislative powers (SCC, 1990). The SCC took as its starting point the *Claim of Right* referred to above which acknowledged 'the sovereign right of the Scottish people to determine the form of government best suited to their needs'. Following the Conservatives' victory in the 1992 election, the SCC produced more detailed plans for devolution to Scotland in November 1995, *Scotland's Parliament. Scotland's Right*. This envisaged a Scottish Parliament having sole or shared responsibility for all matters, save any expressly reserved to the United Kingdom Parliament (for instance, defence, foreign affairs, economic, and fiscal matters), representation for the Scottish Parliament in Council of Ministers delegations to the European Union, and a Bill or Charter of Rights. A partly proportional system of election was proposed, an assigned budget using the Barnett formula, power over public expenditure in Scotland, and power to vary the basic rate of income tax by three pence in the pound.

In the general election in 1997 Labour's manifesto promised a referendum on their proposals for a Scottish Parliament, which were roughly in line with the SCC's 1995 proposals. In September 1997 a (non-binding) referendum on devolution was held in Scotland, with a separate option on the question of tax-varying powers. The turnout was 60.2 per cent. There was no threshold—a majority of those voting would be taken as justification for devolution. The vote in favour of devolution was 74.3 per cent, and in favour of a tax-varying power the majority was 63.5 per cent. Forty-five per cent of the electorate was in favour of devolution. The Scotland Bill was passed in 1998. Devolution to Scotland, then, came about differently from the processes in Wales and Northern Ireland. Lessons may be learned from this for English regions or England itself (see Chapter 15).

There was a strong (though not universal—the Conservative party and the SNP were not parties to the SCC) consensus in Scotland, including the Labour Party, trade unions, and many institutions of civil society, not only in favour of devolution in principle, but also in favour of a particular scheme of devolution that could be acceptable to a broadly sympathetic UK government. The policy of devolution was in the Labour manifesto and this served to ease the passage of the bill. The use of a referendum which produced a positive result before the actual bill was introduced made it even more politically difficult for the opposition at Westminster (which faced a huge government majority), even in the House of Lords, to oppose it credibly or to allege that it was undemocratic. The role played by the SCC may be seen as an example of a participative and deliberative democratic process feeding into public policy successfully. It provides evidence also of a flourishing civil society in Scotland—social capital—the contribution of which continues to be influential under the devolution arrangements.

Scotland's Parliament

The Scottish Parliament has in principle full—or residual—legislative competence (Scotland Act 1998, section 29), but that competence is subject to certain specified exceptions. In this respect the arrangements for Scotland, and for Northern Ireland (see below), follow the model for the Stormont Parliament in Northern Ireland from 1922 to 1972 and many former colonial Constitutions, a model which was recommended by the Constitution Unit in its report on *Scotland's Parliament* (1996a, chs. 3, 4). The case for general legislative competence subject to specific reservations and exceptions is based on a concept of good governance that requires as much transparency and simplicity as possible in order to minimize litigation and disputes between the devolved legislatures and their executives and United Kingdom bodies.

The Scottish Parliament may not legislate in relation to matters reserved to the Westminster Parliament (section 29(2)(b)). These reserved matters are extensive. They include basic constitutional matters, foreign affairs, defence and national security, immigration and nationality, many aspects of financial and economic policy, regulation of markets, and employment and social security (see Scotland Act, schedule 5). Given the complexity of the reserved matters there must be a case for simplification by the transfer of further powers to the Scottish Parliament (see Burrows, 2000, ch. 7).

The Scottish Parliament does not have the legislative competence to remove the Lord Advocate from his position as head of the system of criminal prosecution and investigation of deaths (section 29(2)(e)). Senior judges in the Court of Session have more formal protection from removal than those in England and Wales: the Scotland Act provides by section 95 that they may be removed from office only on grounds of unfitness or misbehaviour, on a recommendation from the First Minister, if the Parliament, on a motion from the First Minister, resolves that such a recommendation be made. Before this procedure can be put in train however a tribunal of three chaired by a member of the Judicial Committee of the Privy Council must be appointed to investigate the grounds for removal. These aspects of the system of justice in Scotland thus enjoy formal and procedural constitutional protection which does not have a parallel in relation to the United Kingdom (see further Himsworth, 1999).

It is also outside the Scottish Parliament's competence to legislate incompatibly with certain basic laws. These include the provisions for freedom of trade in the Acts of Union between Scotland and England of 1706 and 1707 (an acknowledgement of the importance of the history of the Union to Scotland and the preservation of good relations between the UK and Scotland). Nor may the Scottish Parliament legislate incompatibly with parts of the European Communities Act 1972 (Scotland Act section 29 (2)(c) and schedule 4), a provision designed to enable the UK to comply with its European Community obligations and thus to facilitate good governance within the Community. The Scottish Parliament may not legislate for a country or territory outside Scotland (section 29(2)(a)), a measure which preserves the status of the UK in international relations and preserves good relations with other countries. It may not legislate incompatibly with Convention rights (section 29(2)(d)), a provision which protects the civil and political rights of people in Scotland against incursions by the Parliament—as does the Human Rights Act 1998, which applies throughout the UK. This measure is primarily designed to protect the UK government from being found in breach of its obligations under the European Convention on Human Rights in the Strasbourg Court, but incidentally it gives additional protection to these aspects of citizenship in Scotland (and in Northern Ireland and Wales), which are not enjoyed in England, or elsewhere in the UK when the legislation of the Westminster Parliament is in issue.

Unlike the Assemblies in Northern Ireland and Wales, the Scottish Parliament has a revenue-raising power in that it can legislate to vary the rate of income tax by up to three pence in the pound. Apart from that power the Parliament relies on funding from the UK government under the Barnett formula (see previous chapter) and any other funding awarded outside that formula.

In summary on the question of legislative competence, issues of good governance played a large part in determining its scope. But the arrangements illustrate the different degrees of trust in different levels of the system. The retention of power at Westminster which is not subject to legal limitation or judicial review suggests a high degree of faith and confidence in political mechanisms for securing wise and good governance at UK level, while some of the limitations on the Scottish Parliament and Executive reveal a lack of such trust and confidence.

Election of Members of the Scottish Parliament (MSPs) is by a form of proportional representation (see Chapter 7). Each voter has two votes, one for a constituency member (73 in all) and one for a party list based on regions (56 in all). The number of Scottish seats in the House of Commons is likely to be reduced by the year 2005 because of the over-representation of Scotland at Westminster. When this happens the number of seats in the Scottish Parliament is also likely to be reduced, to about 57 constituency seats, and 44 regional seats, to maintain the statutory ratio of 73:56. The disproportionality in terms of seats won on votes cast between the parties on the election of constituency members is mitigated by the places awarded to those on the party lists. The first election to the Scottish Parliament in 1999 produced a hung Parliament with no single party having a majority. Of the 129 seats in the Parliament, Scottish Labour won 56, the SNP 35, Conservatives 18, Scottish Liberal Democrats 17, and others 3. A 'Partnership for Scotland Agreement' was entered into between the Labour members and the Liberal Democrats— in effect a coalition agreement. This arrangement highlights the implication of proportional representation, that one party is unlikely to gain an overall majority—which seemed to take the Labour Party by surprise—and that cooperation between parties is then necessary.

A Consultative Steering Group was set up by the UK government in 1997, in advance of the legislation, to draw up detailed proposals for how the new Parliament should operate. Its chair was the then Minister of State for Scotland, Henry McLeish MP, and its members included a range of people from aspects of Scottish public and legal life. Activists were keen for the Parliament to adopt effective procedures that would be quite different from those used at Westminster. Indeed the vision of those who had campaigned for the Parliament was of a different kind of Parliament. The CSG in its Report *Shaping Scotland's Parliament* (Scottish Office, December 1998) adopted four key principles, which the Parliament has sought to follow. They are:

- the Scottish Parliament should embody and reflect the sharing of power between the people of Scotland, the legislators and the Scottish Executive (power-sharing);

- the Scottish Executive should be accountable to the Scottish Parliament and the Parliament and Executive should be accountable to the people of Scotland (accountability);

- the Scottish Parliament should be accessible, open, responsive, and develop procedures which make possible a participative approach to the development, consideration, and scrutiny of policy and legislation (participation); and

- the Scottish Parliament in its operation and its appointments should recognize the need to promote equal opportunities for all (equal opportunities) (p. 3).

Winetrobe examined the performance of the Parliament in its first year and concluded generally that the Parliament had started to synthesize this 'new politics' with a more adversarial, less consensual approach 'to produce a lively and very productive assembly embracing genuine debate and disagreement within an ethos of collegiality unknown at Westminster' (Winetrobe, 2001*b*, 2).

The Parliament's committees have much more varied remits than those at Westminster, and in particular they deal both with the scrutiny of legislation, which is done by standing committees at Westminster, and with the scrutiny of the executive, a matter for departmental select committees at Westminster.

The Parliament has a Parliamentary Bureau—a Business Committee—which performs some of the functions that fall to the 'usual channels' at Westminster. The Bureau consists of the Presiding Officer—the rough equivalent of the Speaker in the House of Commons—and representatives of the main political parties. It proposes the daily and weekly business programme of the Parliament, the establishment, composition and remit of committees, and timetables for debates. Despite the hope that this Bureau would loosen the grip of the Executive over the Parliament and operate openly, in practice it has operated in secret and, Winetrobe concludes, it had been 'more a formalization of Westminster-style "usual channels"' than had been hoped (Winetrobe, 2001*b*, 2).

There have been attempts on the part of the Parliament, and in particular by the presiding officer, Sir David (otherwise Lord) Steel, to assert the authority of the Parliament as against the executive and to demand that it be treated as central to the political system. So in March 2001 the presiding officer used his casting vote against the executive, thus inflicting its first defeat, on the ground that he was representing the will of the Parliament, not the executive. On another occasion he refused to allow a Minister to make a statement to the Parliament on a matter which the Minister had already leaked to the press. He expressed the view that the Minister had failed in his duty to treat Parliament courteously (*The Times*, 15 March, 2001).

In its first year it was already evident that the additional legislative time that a devolved Parliament creates was paying dividends both in enabling specific Scottish measures instigated by the executive to be enacted, and in the field of law reform: the Abolition of Feudal Tenure (Scotland) Act 2000 and the Adults with Incapacity (Scotland) Act 2000 were both Scottish Law Commission bills which would not have been found time for at Westminster. Time was also available which would not have been found at Westminster for Members' bills (the equivalent of private Members' bills at Westminster), which have proved to be among the most contentious legislative proposals of the Parliament. Committees can also initiate their own bills.

The Scottish executive

The Scottish executive is in many respects modelled on the UK executive. It is formed from members of the Scottish Parliament, and its Ministers are accountable to the Parliament and its committees (of which they are not members). Officials of the executive are civil servants. Ministers of the Scottish executive have powers that have been transferred to them by UK Ministers (including the powers formerly exercised by the Secretary of State for Scotland) and any additional powers granted to them by the UK or the Scottish Parliament. The First Minister is nominated by the Parliament and is appointed by the Queen, a provision designed to secure that the First Minister is accountable to that Parliament. Standing orders of the Parliament provide for the election of the First Minister by the MSPs, with special provisions according to the number of candidates standing for election. The First Minister submits the names of Ministers to the Queen for appointment, having obtained the approval of the Parliament. There is no standing order provision for the scrutiny of the list of names or of individual nominations and in practice the First Minister's proposals have been approved by the Parliament. The Lord Advocate and the Solicitor-General are law officers of ministerial rank.

As we have noted, after the first elections to the Parliament in 1999 no single party had a majority and Labour, the largest party, entered into a Partnership for Scotland Agreement with the Scottish Liberal Democrats (on coalition government see Chapter 7) which provided for the Deputy First Minister to be a member of the Liberal Democrats and for other Liberal Democrat members of the executive and included agreement on a large number of substantive policies. A *Ministerial Code* has been produced and a *Guide to Collective Decision-making* in the coalition.

A Civic Forum

A spin off of the devolution legislation in Scotland has been the establishment of a voluntary Scottish Civic Forum. This, again, illustrates the flourishing civil society in Scotland and the value of the social capital that goes with it. The Civic Forum's vision is that it:

will help break the mould of old-fashioned politics. It will increase participation, find new ways to open up dialogue, raise awareness and stimulate debate on the many challenges facing Scotland. It will have a vital role in creating a more open and broadly based political culture. (see www.civicforum.org.uk/aboutus/whatisscf/introwhat issscf.html)

The forum was awarded a core funding grant of £300,000 over three years, and it won funding from the Joseph Rowntree Charitable Trust for an *Audit of Public Participation* (2002). Generally the Forum seeks to create a more open and broadly based political culture in Scotland. It encourages its members to respond to consultations by the Scottish executive. However, there is disagreement about whether the Civic Forum does in fact open up participation or seeks to provide an institutionalized role for the more organized professional pressure groups.

Overall the signs are that devolution has become embedded in the Scottish political system and that it is widely supported by civil society. It was modelled in large part on the proposals of the Scottish Constitutional Convention, an organization of which many of the political parties, trade unions, churches, and other civil organizations were members.

The Scottish polity is supported, in other words by senses of Scottish identity and citizen-ship and a developed sense in the community of democracy as involving engagement in public life.

Northern Ireland

Devolution in Northern Ireland was suspended by the Secretary of State for Northern Ireland in October 2002 after revelations of IRA spying in the Assembly and Executive and a consequent collapse of trust between the parties. At the time of going to press – January 2003 – it is not known whether or when devolution will be restored. Elections to the Assembly are due to be held in May 2003. The discussion that follows assumes that devolution is in operation. The background to devolution in Northern Ireland is of course very different from that in Scotland (see generally Bogdanor, 1999; Boyle and Hadden, 1999; Burrows, 2000; Wilford and Wilson, 2000, 2001a, 2001b; Morrison, 2001; Forman, 2002; Wilford, 2001). Northern Ireland had its own legislative assembly from 1922 to 1972, when it was suspended because of sectarian violence in the Province. In the aftermath of the suspension of the Stormont Parliament the UK Parliament passed the Northern Ireland Constitution Act 1973, which, among other things, replaced the guaran-tee in the Ireland Act 1949, that neither Northern Ireland nor any part of it would cease to be a part of the UK without the consent of the Northern Ireland Parliament, with a provision that the consent of the majority of the people of Northern Ireland voting in a poll would be required for the Province to cease to be a part of the UK. This consent principle was reiterated in the Belfast Agreement of 1998 (see below). No border poll has yet been held since devolution took place from 1998.

Under the Northern Ireland Constitution Act 1973 devolution was restored for a period of five months in 1974. Thereafter Northern Ireland was subject to direct rule from Whitehall until 1999. Under direct rule, legislation for Northern Ireland was not for the most part passed as Acts of the Westminster Parliament, as was the case for Scottish legislation pre-devolution, but by Orders in Council. Those that were modelled on legis-lation for England and Wales were commonly laid before Parliament subject to a negative resolution procedure. Others were subject to affirmative resolution.

Given the complexities of the issues in Northern Ireland and the conflict between the nationalist and unionist communities, the Scottish model of a Constitutional Convention could not be emulated. There was a constitutional convention in Northern Ireland in 1975, and during the period of direct rule the people and many of the parties in Northern Ireland were involved in repeated attempts to achieve agreement on devolution or the future of the province. Agreement for devolution and its terms was eventually reached only after protracted negotiations involving the UK and Irish governments and many of the parties in the province, and support from the United States.

The major problem in Northern Ireland, which has not afflicted the other countries to which power has been devolved, is intercommunal violence and the absence of trust between the two communities. The political parties are divided on nationalist–unionist lines. Each community and its parties are suspicious and mistrustful of the others. There is also considerable mistrust between the parties representing each community. The provisions for devolution have therefore included mechanisms and procedures, designed both to prevent abuse of power by one party or section of the population against another, and to promote trust. In particular the legal protection of human rights is stronger in Northern Ireland than in Great Britain, in recognition of the fact that the conflict between the two communities was considered to stem in part from the history of abuse of power and discrimination against the nationalist or Catholic community by the Unionist majority, which had subscribed to a majoritarian democratic theory during the life of the Stormont Parliament. Thus, for instance, discrimination on grounds of religion, origin-ally in employment and extended to the provision of goods and services, is unlawful in Northern Ireland, which is not the case in the rest of the UK.

The arrangements in Northern Ireland are far more juridified than those in Scotland or Wales, with the Northern Ireland Act and subordinate legislation setting out in consider-able detail procedures and powers, for example on the composition of the executive (see below), which it has not been necessary to set out in the other devolution legislation. This illustrates the point that was made earlier, that the political Constitution depends on a high level of trust and comity between institutions and on the part of the population, without which the pressure for statutory regulation of politics becomes irresistible. Legis-lation (the Northern Ireland Act 2000) has also had to provide for the eventuality of suspension of devolution—which took place for several months in 2000 (and again for two twenty-four-hour periods in 2001 and from October 2002). In effect there is an alternative system of government under the Secretary of State for Northern Ireland on stand-by in the Province.

The period since the Belfast Agreement on Good Friday in 1998, outlined below, has been very eventful in Northern Ireland, and in the account that follows our focus will be on institutional arrangements and their working rather than on the complex political events. But some account will be given of some of these, and of the input of the voluntary sector, to put the institutions in context.

The Belfast Agreement

In the spring of 1998 agreement was at last achieved on the terms on which devolution to Northern Ireland would take place, in the Belfast or 'Good Friday' Agreement (Cm. 3883, April 1998; see generally Bogdanor, 1999; Burrows, 2000; Hazell (ed), 2000a; Hadfield, 2001; Morrison, 2001; Wilford, 2001). There are three strands to the agreement. Strand 1 deals with the internal government of Northern Ireland. Strand 2 deals with North–South relations. Strand 3 deals with relations between the UK and the Republic of Ireland. A referendum was held in May 1998 on the proposals in the Belfast Agreement in Northern Ireland, and a substantial majority supported the agreement. A referendum was also held in the Republic of Ireland on amendments to the Constitution of the Republic to give effect to parts of the overall agreement. In Northern Ireland 71 per cent of the votes cast were in favour of the agreement, 29 per cent against. In the Republic 95 per cent of those voting were in favour of the proposed amendments to the Constitution.

The key principle in the Belfast Agreement is protection of both communities by power-sharing, a consociational approach. The protections for the two communities in the agreement include the use of the single transferable vote in elections of the 108 members of the Northern Ireland Assembly, which secures that all substantial parties are represented. (STV has been used for all elections in Northern Ireland other than for the Westminster Parliament since 1972; see Chapter 7 for an explanation of STV.) All parties, and a diarchy of the First Minister and the Deputy First Minister, in the Assembly are to be represented in its committees and in the executive, in proportion to their party strengths in the Assembly. Members of the executive committee, committee chairs, and deputies are selected by the d'Hondt method. The remaining committee places are allocated by a different formula, although still aiming for proportionality. Important decisions by the Assembly on matters such as the election of the First Minister and Deputy First Minister, the Presiding Officer (also known as the Speaker) of the Assembly, and the approval of standing orders and the annual budget are taken by qualified majority voting. Further protections for the two communities are noted below.

An important provision of the Belfast Agreement was the recognition of a right to self-determination. The Northern Ireland Act 1998, which implements the agreement, provides by section 1 and schedule 1 that:

(1) It is hereby declared that Northern Ireland in its entirety remains part of the United Kingdom and shall not cease to be so without the consent of a majority of the people of Northern Ireland voting in a poll held for the purposes of this section . . .

(2) But if the wish expressed by a majority in such a poll is that Northern Ireland should cease to be part of the United Kingdom and form part of a united Ireland, the Secretary of State shall lay before Parliament such proposals to give effect to that wish as may be agreed between Her Majesty's Government in the United Kingdom and the Government of Ireland.

The agreement thus holds out the possibility of a united Ireland being brought about peacefully in accordance with the majority wish, with a commitment on the part of the government of the United Kingdom to give effect to that wish in agreement with the government of the Republic.

The decommissioning of illegal arms was a major issue between the communities and their representatives in Northern Ireland. A decision to establish an Independent International Commission on Decommissioning had been announced in November 1995. In May 2000 the IRA announced that it was ready to begin a process that would 'completely and verifiably' put its arms beyond use. The UK Prime Minister and the Irish Taoiseach then announced the appointment of a team to inspect IRA weapons dumps. However, no decommissioning by the IRA took place until late October 2001.

The Belfast Agreement provided for the creation of 'an interlocking network of committees' (Hazell, 2000b, 154) creating links North–South, East–West, and across what are commonly referred to in the UK as the British Isles (terms such as 'these isles' or 'the islands of Great Britain and Ireland' being preferred by Ireland and republicans in Northern Ireland). There are three very different elements to the network. First, a North–South Ministerial Council, to bring together Ministers from the Northern Ireland Executive and the Irish government, to develop consultation, cooperation, and action on matters of mutual interest, including through implementation on an all-island and cross-border basis (see Northern Ireland Act 1998, s. 52; Belfast Agreement, article 2(i)). The Council is to meet in plenary format twice a year and in specific sectoral formats on a regular and frequent basis with each side represented by the appropriate Minister. At its first meeting, in December 1999, it was attended by the entire cabinet of the Irish Republic and all ten Ministers from Northern Ireland and the First Minister and Deputy First Minister. They agreed to establish six cross-border implementation bodies to harmonize North–South policy on inland waterways, the promotion of the Irish and Ulster Scots languages, food safety, acquaculture and marine matters, trade and business development, and special EU programmes (see Hadfield, 2001).

From late 2000 until October 2001, the First Minister, David Trimble, refused to nom-inate Sinn Fein Ministers to attend these ministerial meetings, as a sanction for the failure of the IRA to fulfil the Belfast Agreement commitment to decommissioning of illegal arms. On an application for judicial review by two of the Sinn Fein Ministers it was held that Trimble's refusal was unlawful, on the ground that nominations to attend these meetings should be made on grounds of suitability of the nominee and not for political objectives (see *In the matter of Bairbre de Brun and Martin McGuinness for judicial review*, [2001] NIEHC 9, paras. 42–54). After an act of decommissioning by the IRA took place in October 2001 the First Minister resumed nominating Sinn Fein Ministers to attend meetings of this Council.

The second element in the network was a British–Irish Council (BIC), known infor-mally as 'the Council of the Isles' and modelled to some extent on the Nordic Council. Its membership comprises representatives of the UK and Irish governments, and of devolved institutions in the United Kingdom, together with representatives of the Isle of Man and the Channel Islands (Belfast Agreement, Cm. 3883, Strand 3, para. 2). England is not separately represented. The purpose of the BIC is 'to promote the harmonious and mutually beneficial development of the totality of relationships among the peoples of these islands'. Its inaugural meeting was held on 17 December 1999 and a number of issues for early discussion were agreed (drugs, social inclusion, the environment, trans-port, and the knowledge economy) sharing the responsibilities as lead administrations between the Irish government, the Scottish executive and Welsh cabinet, the UK govern-ment, the Northern Ireland executive, and Jersey. Meetings that had been arranged in 2001 were cancelled because of the problems encountered in the peace process, notably the suspension of devolution. Some ministerial meetings took place and work was done at officer level. BIC meetings took place in Jersey in June 2002 and in Edinburgh in November 2002. Generally, however, this has not been an active or productive arrangement.

The third element is a standing British–Irish Intergovernmental Conference, to sub-sume the Anglo–Irish Intergovernmental Council and the Intergovernmental Conference that had been established under the Anglo–Irish Agreement of 1985. The conference is concerned with non-devolved matters (devolved matters are for the North–South Minis-terial Council) and it meets at summit level as required and in meetings to be co-chaired by the Irish Foreign Minister and the UK Secretary of State for Northern Ireland. Its main interests are rights, justice, prisons, policing.

The Northern Ireland Assembly

Once the Belfast Agreement was reached the Northern Ireland (Elections) Act 1998 was passed by the Westminster Parliament and provided for elections to a new Northern Ireland shadow Assembly. It had no legislative or executive power but its purpose was to make preparations for the functioning of a fully fledged Assembly once the proposed Northern Ireland Act was passed and brought into force. Elections to the shadow Assembly took place in June 1998 and the Assembly had its first plenary meeting in July of that year.

Elections were by the single transferable vote, a system with which voters in Northern Ireland are familiar as it has been used there in local government and for European Parliament elections. It is also used for general elections in the Republic of Ireland. It secures reasonable proportionality between the parties and the two communities in the Assembly. However, unlike the alternative vote, it provides no incentive for individual candidates to moderate their views and policies to attract votes from moderate voters. Horowitz (2001) suggests that STV was a bad choice for Northern Ireland because it allows candidates to be elected on small, core votes (14 per cent of the first preferences in six-member constituencies such as those used in the Assembly elections) and thus provides little disincentive for extremist electoral behaviour.

The election of the shadow Assembly was followed by the passing of the Northern Ireland Act 1998, which was implemented on 2 December 1999 with the devolution of power to the executive and assembly. The Assembly was suspended from 11 February 2000 and direct rule was reimposed, because the relations between the main parties had broken down over the failure of the IRA to decommission weapons. Devolution was reinstated on 11 May of that year. It was suspended again briefly for two periods of twenty-four hours in August and September 2001 for technical reasons, to avoid the calling of a general election while the First Minister had resigned over the failure of decommissioning and no replacement had been elected. The UK government was not ready to trust the resolution of the dispute over the leadership and the decommissioning to the electorate at this stage (see *Robinson v. Secretary of State for Northern Ireland*, [2002] UKHL 32, in which the Appellate Committee of the House of Lords upheld the decision of the Secretary of State not to call an election. Lord Bingham emphasized the importance of the political Constitution in the British tradition, stating that 'Where constitutional arrangements retain scope for the exercise of political judgment they permit a flexible response to differing and unpredictable events in a way which the application of strict rules would preclude' (at para. 12)). On 23 September 2001 the Independent International Commission on Decommissioning announced that there had been an event of decommissioning and thereafter devolution was reinstated by Order and David Trimble was restored as First Minister. (As we have noted, devolution was suspended again in October 2002.)

The legislative powers of the Assembly follow broadly the Scottish model, which in turn followed the model used for the Northern Ireland Parliament from 1922 to 1972. General, residual legislative competence was transferred to the assembly, but certain matters are reserved, excepted, or entrenched (Northern Ireland Act 1998, sections 4, 5–8, schedules 2, 3). Entrenched matters include the European Communities Act 1972, the Human Rights Act 1998, and parts of the Northern Ireland Act itself. Excepted matters are listed in schedule 2 of the Act and include the range of subjects that are referred to as 'reserved' in the case of Scotland (the Crown, UK elections, international relations—subject to relations with the Republic of Ireland—and international obligations, defence, nationality, and immigration, for example). It is not anticipated that these would ever be transferred to the Northern Ireland Assembly. Reserved matters are those on which the Assembly may legislate subject to the consent of the Secretary of State and the Westminster Parliament—i.e. some of them may be transferred in due course. They include navigation, civil aviation, domicile law, public order law, the police, civil defence, consumer safety, for example.

The Assembly does not have competence to legislate incompatibly with the Convention rights or with Community law, for a territory outside Northern Ireland, or—and in this respect the arrangements differ for those for the rest of the UK—if 'it discriminates against any person or class of person on the ground of religious belief or political opinion' (section 6(2)(e)).

The Assembly has a Business Committee chaired by the Presiding Officer and including members of all parties prepared to participate in committee work, and party whips. It conducts discussion over the arrangement of business and facilities for members. Until the suspension of devolution in October 2002 it was believed to function well, and relations between its members were good—to the extent that it attracted attention from other countries, including Canada, as a possible model.

There are ten statutory committees (also known as departmental committees) in the Assembly each shadowing a department of the executive, and also being responsible for scrutiny of legislation in the committee stage. They advise on the formulation of policy, and they can initiate legislation, though this power has not so far been used. The chairs of the committees are nominated by their parties and the d'Hondt method is used for the allocation of chairs to committees. Each committee has eleven members, and the membership is broadly proportional to the balance of parties, except that the Northern Ireland Unionist Party members and the UK Unionist Party (which were originally the same party) refuse to participate in the Assembly's committee system.

There are also six standing committees, including the Committee of the Centre, which monitors half of the functions of the Office of the First Minister and Deputy First Minister (OFMDFM). That Committee does not however scrutinize the external functions of the office in relation to the Republic of Ireland, the rest of the United Kingdom, and the rest of Europe. The OFMDFM is not accountable to any committee for these matters, only to the Assembly as a plenary body. Nor do the statutory committees scrutinize Strand Two aspects of the Belfast Agreement, including the six cross-border bodies. There are then serious gaps in the accountability arrangements.

Most committee meetings are held in public. Relations between the party members in the committees, particularly between the Democratic Unionist Party and Sinn Fein, were significantly more cordial than they appeared to be in plenary sessions. Overall the Committees have not been very enterprising, but their reports are usually debated at plenary meetings of the Assembly (Wilford and Wilson, 2001b, 24).

There are serious problems about the ability of the committees in the Assembly to hold the executive to account. The majority of seats on each committee are held by members of the four parties forming the executive (see below), and it is rare for the committees to criticize ministers. When the committees have on occasions disagreed with a Minister, they have been ignored (as in a dispute over whether maternity hospital provision should be sited in East or West Belfast: at Westminster Ministers are expected at least to respond to select or scrutiny committee reports) or their report has been rejected—with reasons (as when a committee recommended a 'no fees' policy for university students which the Minister showed would be of most benefit to the middle-class students and was not consistent with the agreed policy of 'targeting social need'). These two examples show that, as at Westminster, it is possible for Ministers to ignore or reject committee recommendations and Assembly motions with impunity. By early 2002 the Assembly plenary sessions had been reduced owing to paucity of executive business.

The Northern Ireland executive

The arrangements for the election of the First Minister and the Deputy First Minister (both have coequal powers) and for the allocation of ministerial portfolios are set out in detail in the Act, and are designed to ensure power-sharing in the government. Ministerial portfolios are allocated on the d'Hondt formula, a complicated method of allocation that secures that all parties with more than 10 per cent of the members of the 108 strong Assembly are entitled to ministerial posts. Thus there are five members of the Ulster Unionist Party in the executive (the First Minister, three executive committee members, and one junior Minister), five SDLP members (the Deputy First Minister, three executive committee members, and one junior Minister), and two Democratic Unionist Party and two Sinn Fein executive committee members. The Executive's first agreed Programme for Government, *Making a Difference*, was approved by the Assembly in March 2001, and its budget was agreed by the Assembly after revision in December 2000.

The First Minister and the Deputy First Minister and their office have become an important 'executive within the executive', as we have noted subject to committee scrutiny only in relation to their internal functions by the Committee of the Centre. They have an interdependent and equal relationship and this has been crucial to the progress of devolution.

The Ministers in the executive run their departments rather autonomously. The executive Committee itself meets relatively infrequently. Neither individual Ministers nor the executive can be dismissed or forced to resign by the Assembly. The Assembly can only force an early election if two-thirds of its members agree. It is not possible for parties to agree to get together to form an administration in advance of an election. The d'Hondt arrangements in effect institutionalize an atomized executive which is not subject to the normal pressures for collective responsibility found in a Westminster system. This has been referred to as 'institutionalized sectarianism' (Wilford and Wilson, 2001b, 70). In practice, however, the executive has tended to avoid internal conflict by keeping politics out of its decisions and seeking consensus (Wilford and Wilson, 2001b, 66). This is encouraged by the need to get Assembly approval of the Programme for Government. But there have been suggestions that the d'Hondt-based arrangements should be replaced by a 'voluntary cross-community' coalition.

A Civic Forum

Strand One of the Belfast Agreement provides for the establishment of a Civic Forum. The idea came from the Northern Ireland Women's Coalition, which predated—and took part in negotiations for—the Belfast Agreement, and is committed to securing that the voice of civil society is heard in government. The NIWC has two members in the Assembly. Its original proposal was for an Assembly comprising an elected chamber, and 'a civic chamber comprised of business, trade union, community and voluntary sector interests indirectly elected through electoral colleges' (Northern Ireland Women's Coalition Policy Document www.niwc.org/files/policystrand2.htm). In fact what emerged was the Civic Forum.

The Northern Ireland Act section 56 requires the First Minister and Deputy First Minister to make arrangements, with the approval of the Assembly, for obtaining from the Forum its views on social, economic, and cultural matters. The expenses of the Forum are to be defrayed out of public funds. The Forum consists of a chair and some sixty members nominated by consortia of business interests, agriculture and fishery interests, trade unions, voluntary sector bodies, the churches, and cultural and other bodies. It has a gender balance, a community background balance, a geographic spread, and an age balance. Membership is for three-year terms and is staggered.

The Civic Forum was represented by the then Deputy First Minister, Seamus Mallon, as an expression of Northern Ireland's inclusive democracy. It can be seen as an example of an institutionalized extra-parliamentary, and therefore non-party, deliberative democracy mechanism, which was regarded as necessary by those in favour because of the expected shortcomings and exclusiveness of the Assembly and the executive. However, the Forum has experienced problems. Anti-agreement Unionists criticized it for the fact that members of the Orange Order are not included. Some members of the Assembly resented its consultative status. This attitude implies a belief that elected politicians should have a monopoly of influence and power in government, illustrating the potential for conflict between representative and participative democratic mechanisms where elected representatives are not committed to participation outside politics. Others, supportive of the Forum, are concerned that it may not have the resources to enable it to fulfil an important role in improving government and involving groups with specialist knowledge in the consultation and scrutiny activities in the Province (Wilford and Wilson, 2001b, 55–7). It is too early to reach any conclusions about these matters, but the Forum did respond to the Executive's first draft Programme for Government. Its projects as of September 2002 were anti-poverty, lifelong learning, towards a plural society, and creating a more sustainable Northern Ireland.

Towards a Bill of Rights for Northern Ireland?

It has already been noted that protection of human rights has a high priority in the devolution arrangements in Northern Ireland. The Northern Ireland Act Part VII provides for the establishment of a Human Rights Commission. Its function is to keep under review the adequacy and effectiveness in Northern Ireland of law and practice relating to the protection of human rights. There is no equivalent body in other parts of the United

Kingdom (see Chapter 6). It has powers, among other things, to advise the executive, the Secretary of State for Northern Ireland, and the Assembly of measures which ought to be taken to protect human rights, advise the Assembly on whether bills are compatible with human rights, and it may give assistance to individuals and bring proceedings involving human rights issues.

The Commission published a report in November 2001 proposing that the Assembly should establish a standing committee on human rights and equality with a mandate to examine and report on all human rights and equality issues that are within the competence of the Assembly, including the compatibility of bills with relevant human rights standards. This proposal has not been accepted by the Assembly and each assembly committee deals with human rights and equality issues separately.

The Belfast Agreement on Northern Ireland empowered the Secretary of State for Northern Ireland to seek advice from the Northern Ireland Human Rights Commission on what should be contained in a Bill of Rights for the Province. The consultation was to 'reflect the particular circumstances of the province, drawing as appropriate on international instruments and experience, these additional rights to reflect the principles of mutual respect for the identity and ethos of both communities and parity or esteem, and—taken together with the ECHR—to constitute a Bill of Rights for Northern Ireland' (Belfast Agreement, Cm. 3883, April 1998, para. 4). These terms of reference have raised intepretive questions. The Commission proposed a Bill that would include the civil and political rights normally found in such instruments, but also rights to the highest achievable standards of physical and mental health and well-being, the right to a standard of living sufficient for that person and those in dependent relationships with him or her, the right to adequate housing, the right to contribute to the economic and social life of society, including the right of access to work and the right to choose and practice a trade or profession, and the right to a healthy and sustainable environment (Northern Ireland Human Rights Commission, *Making a Bill of Rights for Northern Ireland*, 2001, Appendix I). The Commission proposed that such a Bill of Rights should be enforceable along the same lines as the Human Rights Act, especially the principle of compliant interpretation in section 3 of that Act (see Chapter 6). It would not be possible to give effect to such a bill by disapplying an Act of the Westminster Parliament, but it would be possible for the courts to disapply an Act or part of an Act of the Northern Ireland Assembly to give effect to a charter of this kind. But it was not envisaged that the Bill of Rights would actually give rise to new rights as opposed to ensuring that existing legislation and administrative discretions were used compatibly with the rights, and possibly that breaches or interferences with the rights might be defences to governmental decisions—for instance decisions to demolish existing public sector housing without making adequate alternative provision.

Though there was consensus in favour of some of these proposals the NIHRC document was badly received in some quarters, for a range of reasons—some of them to do with the atmosphere of mistrust between the parties in the Province. McCrudden (2001, 383) thought that it was 'sloppy, rushed, internally inconsistent, technically unconvincing and lacking any coherent vision'. In the light of the negative responses to its proposals, the NIHRC decided to undertake a further phase in work on the project, involving public meetings about certain key issues that had been raised and were controversial, such as the meaning of 'identity and ethos of both communities', the extent to which equality of treatment and of opportunity should be secured, protection of social and economic rights, and enforcement. But there is concern that it will not be possible to deliver political consensus around a coherent set of proposals. A point that emerges from this experience is that the *process* by which such a document is produced affects its legitimacy, and can lead either to the production of something that is open to serious criticism on the lines given by McCrudden and which does not command popular support or, if the right process is followed, to a high-quality instrument that commands widespread public support. A broadly based consultation exercise such as was adopted prior to the adoption of the Canadian Charter of Rights and Freedoms (Part I of the Constitution Act, 1982) could generate public interest and commitment to the document: in Canada there were nationally televised hearings by a joint parliamentary committee, with over one thousand individuals and three hundred groups petitioning for changes and additions to the draft Charter, resulting in the committee successfully proposing some 65 substantial amendments to the government's draft. In effect the Canadian people took up the Charter (Penner, 1996), something that has not happened in Northern Ireland.

Observations

As we have noted, the Northern Ireland executive and the Assembly experienced severe difficulties and interruptions in their first three years of operation. But by the first quarter of 2002 there appeared to be an air of stability in the Northern Ireland executive and Assembly. A revised *Programme for Government* and budget were agreed to. The Assembly and the settlement of which it forms part appeared to have the support of both communities in Northern Ireland (though unionist/loyalist support may no longer be strong). Neither side appeared to wish to bring it down, despite the continuing hot spots of conflict between the two communities. However, as noted at the start of this section, trust between the two communities collapsed after it was revealed that the IRA had infiltrated the Assembly and executive offices and obtained confidential information from them.

But, as Morison and others have argued (Morison, 2001) the formal governmental institutions in Northern Ireland, together with the Civic Forum, give only a very partial picture of how governance actually operates in the Province. During the period of direct rule, an active and effective voluntary sector developed which took on many of the functions of participation, consultation, policy development, and service delivery which would have fallen to a Northern Ireland based-government, had it existed. That sector continues to flourish, and indeed its existence chimes well with the trend from government in the top-down sense towards governance via networks and partnerships, which is developing in all parts of the UK, and beyond. That sector could also have a positive role in the development of the required consensus for the introduction of a charter of social and economic, as well as civil and political, rights in the province.

Wales

Unlike Scotland and Northern Ireland, Wales' devolution arrangements do not involve the Assembly for Wales having primary legislative power. The model is of 'executive devolution' or what Rawlings (2001) terms 'quasi-legislative devolution'. The background to devolution in Wales was different again from that to Scottish or Northern Ireland devolution (see generally Rawlings, 1998; Bogdanor, 1999; Burrows, 2000; Morrison, 2001; Forman, 2002). The principal political pressures for devolution in Wales came from Plaid Cymru (the Welsh nationalist party) and the Liberal Democrats. There was no equivalent to the Scottish Constitutional Convention in Wales, and no broad-based organization in civil society to formulate principles for devolution to Wales (see Constitution Unit, 1996b). There were, however, increasing concerns about the lack of accountability of the Welsh Department and of the increasing number and powers of Quangos (see Chapter 17) in the principality. The crucial commitment to devolution came from the Labour Party in its pre-1997 election manifesto.

In putting together its detailed proposals the Labour government did not have a blueprint from a constitutional convention on which to base the scheme. There was no majority in the Welsh electorate in favour of devolution. In the referendum on devolution that was held in Wales shortly after the referendum in Scotland in 1997 the turnout was 51 per cent, of whom 50.3 per cent voted in favour of a Welsh Assembly—some 26 per cent of the electorate. The justification for devolution in Wales then could not be popular demand, but rather, as it was put in the White Paper, *A Voice for Wales* (Cm. 3718, July 1997) the need to remedy a democratic deficit, and the belief that a more responsive elected body wold be better placed to promote economic prosperity and quality of life in Wales (at para. 1.4). After the referendum the bill for the establishment of a National Assembly for Wales was introduced and in due course passed. The Secretary of State for Wales established a National Assembly Advisory Group in late 1997 to plan for devolution, in particular for Assembly processes and procedures, and to focus on principles of inclusiveness. Its members were drawn from the parties, local government, business, and the voluntary sector.

Despite the fact that there had been no strong pressure from civil society for devolution in Wales, it is now unthinkable that the Government of Wales Act 1998 could be repealed without being replaced by other measures acceptable in Wales. An issue that could arise once regional government spreads in England will be whether Wales will move in the direction of Scotland's arrangements, with its own legislature, or whether it will move closer to the regional government model in England. The Assembly and the belief that decisions for the principality should be made there are rooted in the politics and culture of the place. But as we shall see there is already a move for the revision of the arrangements, and a question arises whether that would have been necessary so soon after devolution if a constitutional convention in Wales had played a part in thinking through and developing plans for the devolution arrangements.

The National Assembly for Wales

The provisions for Wales are different in important respects from those for Scotland and Northern Ireland (see generally Rawlings, 1998, 2001; Bogdanor, 1999, ch. 5; Burrows, 2000, chs. 3.4; Osmond, 2000; Ward, 2000; Forman, 2002, ch. 5). The Welsh Assembly has legislative competence only in respect of subordinate legislation—statutory instruments and regulations, for instance. Devolution is primarily executive—the powers formerly exercised by the Secretary of State for Wales have been devolved to the Assembly. The Assembly has no revenue-raising powers and it is financed by block grant under the Barnett formula and by other grants—to match EU funding for instance—outside the Barnett formula (see previous chapter).

The extent of the Assembly's secondary legislative power will depend upon the terms of enabling Acts passed by Westminster from time to time. It may be that the UK government will draft bills for the Westminster Parliament to pass that grant broad powers of secondary legislation in order to maximize the room for manoeuvre of the Welsh executive and Assembly. This approach would have an important impact in England too, since the same delegated powers would be exercisable for England by Ministers of the UK government in Whitehall as will be exercisable in Cardiff by the Welsh assembly and its executive, and this will highlight the fact that England has no voice or representation separate from the UK.

Election to the Welsh Assembly was by a system similar to that used in Scotland, though the proportions of constituency members and list members differed. Forty constituency members were elected on the first past the post system, and an additional 20 were elected from party lists in 1999. The first elections produced a hung Assembly, the largest party, Labour, having 28 of the 60 seats. Labour decided at first to govern as a minority administration. The Assembly's business committee took up the role of finding consensus—without votes—on the Assembly's business.

The Welsh Executive Committee

The Assembly is—formally at least—essentially an executive body. It has taken on the functions formerly exercised by the Secretary of State for Wales. The Government of Wales Act 1998 lays down complex arrangements for the exercise of these executive functions. It is required by the Act to operate through an Executive Committee consisting of the First Secretary, elected by the Assembly, and seven Assembly Secretaries appointed by the First Secretary. There is a subject committee for each of the Secretaries, of which the Secretary is a member but not the chair. Committee chairs are allocated in accordance with the balance of the parties in the Assembly. There are also a subordinate legislation scrutiny committee, an Audit Committee, and regional committees.

In practice however the Executive Committee acts as a Cabinet or government and is known as the Welsh Assembly Government (WAG). A division of function between the government and the Assembly has developed, despite the legal position that the Assembly itself is a corporate body responsible for executive functions in Wales. The arrangements have moved towards a 'parliamentary' system with the Assembly 'Secretaries' calling themselves Ministers, a developing separation of powers between the Ministers and the rest of the Assembly, and the Presiding Officer having his own budget to run the Assembly. The committees have been primarily concerned with generating information and developing policy; they do not hold the executive to account, nor do they make policy or scrutinize secondary legislation. The function of holding the executive to account has, Osmond (2000) suggests, been more effectively performed in plenary sessions of the Assembly.

The first First Secretary of the Assembly was Alun Michael, the favoured candidate of the UK Labour Party. Resentment in the Assembly at the virtual imposition on them by the Labour Party of their First Secretary (nowadays known as First Minister) boiled over when a vote of no confidence in him was tabled, ostensibly over the question of finding match funding from public moneys—from the Treasury—for EU Structural Funds, to be drawn down over a seven-year period. Michael resigned before the vote was taken. In the event the UK government found the money. The Assembly then elected their own choice of leader, Rhodri Morgan. He encouraged an informal arrangement with Plaid Cymru which led to an agreement in support of the Labour Party's policy document, *A Better Wales*, which set out policies which included many that had been negotiated with Plaid Cymru (see Osmond, 2000, 43–5). This focuses on three guiding themes for the Assembly: sustainable development, tackling social disadvantage, and equal opportunities.

In October 2000 Morgan reached a formal Partnership Agreement with the Liberal Democrats, which gave them two 'Cabinet' posts. The agreement also included an important commitment to secure the independence of the Office of the Presiding Officer, which represents a move away from the Assembly as a corporate executive body towards a parliamentary system, since such independence is necessary if there is to be a separation between the executive and scrutiny functions of the Assembly.

Since the Assembly for Wales came into being, a number of distinctive policies for Wales, quite different from those in England, have been developed. School league tables have been abolished; a new means-tested 'learning grant' of up to £15,000 per person per year for students in higher and further education has been introduced; school milk for infants has been introduced; additional money has been provided for school building; free prescription charges have been extended to the under 25-year-olds; and bus passes have been introduced for the elderly.

But all has not been positive in Wales. There have been a series of destabilizing disputes between the parties. Allegations of fraud against the Welsh Liberal Democrat leader forced him to stand down as Deputy First Minister when the police decided to investigate. There have also been disputes about the use of the Welsh language, the in-migration of non-Welsh-speaking people into Welsh-speaking communities, and concern about the limitations on the powers of the Assembly (Osmond, 2001). The difficulties in influencing Westminster legislation that will apply to Wales and in securing legislation for Wales only at Westminster have fuelled pressure for the Welsh Assembly to be given primary legislative powers.

Partnership arrangements

There is no civic forum in Wales, unlike Scotland, Northern Ireland, and London. However, section 113 of the Government of Wales Act requires the Assembly to establish a Partnership Council for Wales consisting of Assembly Members and members of local authorities. The Assembly must also have regard to the interests of the voluntary sector and business in Wales (Government of Wales Act, sections 114, 115). Partnership councils have been established for each of these sectors and they provide forums for them to give advice and make representations to the Assembly about matters affecting them. In the case of the voluntary sector and business, the partnership councils were established following consultation. Membership comprises Assembly Members of all parties and representatives from the sector (see Cm. 5511, ch. 7).

The future

In the light of experience in its first two years the Assembly set up a review group in 2001, chaired by the Presiding Officer of the Assembly, which reported in February 2002. On its recommendation an independent commission on the Assembly's powers and electoral arrangements was appointed, chaired by Lord Ivor Richard, to report after the elections in 2003; in some respects this resembles a—rather belated—constitutional convention for Wales. Under the terms of the partnership agreement between Labour and the Liberal Democrats the Commission will look at the Assembly's electoral arrangements as well as its power. The review group also proposed the separation of the legislative and scrutiny function from the executive; and rejection of the status of the Assembly as a corporate executive body. The scrutiny powers of backbench members needed to be protected to enable them to hold the executive to account. It was also proposed that the Assembly should be better able to influence primary legislation passed at Westminster. The policy development role of the subject committees needed to be enhanced. These matters are all then on the agenda for possible change in the near future, probably after the election in 2003.

It seems inevitable that the Government of Wales Act 1998 will be amended in quite radical ways in the next few years. Reforms are likely to include the grant of some primary legislative powers. These could not be as extensive as those in Scotland and Northern Ireland, which, unlike Wales, have retained their own separate legal systems since the Acts of Union. It is not currently on the agenda for there to be different laws relating to the family, contract, tort, and property in Wales from those in England. Arrangements for the passage of legislation by the Westminster Parliament for Wales will need to be tidied up pending the transfer of primary legislative power to Wales.

15

Devolution: England and the United Kingdom

In this chapter we consider the position of England in relation to devolution, starting with London. We also consider some of the implications of devolution for the United Kingdom as a whole.

London

London is the only part of England with anything like an elected layer of regional government (see generally Morrison, 2001; Tomaney, 2001; Forman, 2002). Arrangements for the governance of London are a hybrid, falling between regional and local government, but it will be convenient to treat them in this chapter, alongside consideration of English regions. London is not generally regarded as a model for devolution to the other regions of England, since the office of Mayor is normally linked with the governance of cities or towns rather than of mixed urban and rural areas such as the regions.

The Greater London Council was abolished under the Conservative government in 1986, partly in response to the Labour-controlled Council's very vocal and high-profile opposition to many of the policies of the Conservatives (for instance, County Hall, across the Thames from the House of Commons, with its banners advertising unemployment figures in London, was a provocation and an irritant to the government). The abolition of the GLC left London with no strategic level of government. The boroughs were responsible for local service delivery; many of the functions of the former GLC were transferred up to central government or down to the boroughs (education for instance) or were suspended (strategic planning is an example).

In a Green paper *New Leadership for London* published in 1997 and followed up by a White Paper *A Mayor and Assembly for London: The Government's Proposals for Modernising the Governance of London* (Cm. 3897, March 1998)—note the recurrence of the 'modernizing' theme—the government developed its proposals for an elected Greater London Authority, with an elected Mayor. The GLA would prepare and take action on plans to tackle issues which affect the whole of London or cross several London boundaries. A referendum was held on the proposals in May 1998 and on a very low turnout a majority voted in favour of the plans. The Greater London Authority Act 1999 was passed to establish the Authority, which consists of the Assembly and its staff and the Mayor, and set out their functions in considerable detail. The government's wish was influenced by public opinion in the light of the responses generated by the Green Paper, that the system should be internally non-confrontational (relations between the London Mayor and the government, especially over the London Underground, have been confrontational), and inclusive of a wide range of interests, and that the Mayor and Assembly should work through networks and partnerships with the business community, voluntary bodies, and the boroughs.

Separate elections for the Mayor and for the Assembly take place on the same day every four years. The election for Mayor is by supplementary vote, a preferential voting system under which voters are limited to two preferences. If no candidate gains an overall majority of first preference votes, the top two candidates go through to a second round of counting in which the second preferences of all the other candidates' votes are reallocated to one of the top two candidates (if they are for one of those candidates) until one wins, either gaining a majority or plurality at the end of counting. The Greater London Assembly has 25 members elected on an AMS system (See Chapter 7), 14 for areas and 11 top-up members. In the first elections in May 2000 the turnout was 32 per cent. In the Assembly election the Conservatives and Labour each won 9 seats, the Liberal Democrats 4, and the Green Party 3. A Programme for Government was then agreed to.

The Mayor

The Mayor has the executive power in these arrangements, and he is accountable to the Assembly. He has appointed an 'advisory Cabinet' consisting of some of the elected members of the Assembly and others brought in from outside. But the arrangements do not follow the local government Leader and Cabinet model or Mayor and Executive models (see Chapter 16). It is closer to the local government Mayor and Council Manager model, though there is no obligation to appoint a council manager in London. The Mayor must develop and present strategic plans in relation to a wide range of matters. These strategies may require action by a range of independent organizations, and provide examples of the use of networks to deliver policy. The Mayor also produces strategies for four functional bodies—the London Fire and Emergency Planning Authority, Transport for London, the London Development Agency, and the Metropolitan Police Authority. He appoints the board of these bodies, and they are bound to implement his strategies. The boroughs will have responsibility for planning within his framework. He has a coordination role in improving the environment and air quality and other issues such as waste and noise, and in encouraging local initiatives. He may delegate responsibility to the Deputy Mayor, Transport for London, and the London Development Agency.

The Mayor's accountability to the electorate is secured by election. Between elections he is accountable to the Assembly in a range of ways. He must present his strategy and his budget to the Assembly for approval. He must also submit a report to it before its monthly meetings, setting out decisions he has taken, with reasons, and responding to any formal proposals made by the Assembly. He attends the Assembly's meetings and is subject to questioning. He is required to produce an annual report and this is followed by a 'State of London' debate. A 'People's Question Time' must be held twice a year.

As is well known the first London Mayor, elected in 2000, was Ken Livingstone MP, who stood as an independent against Labour and other candidates. He had taken the Labour whip in the House of Commons, but it was withdrawn when he decided to stand against the Labour candidate in the mayoral election. He had been chair of the Greater London Council from 1981 until its abolition in 1986. Livingstone's election (and the election of Mayors in local government: see Chapter 16) suggests that the parties may find themselves circumvented in these elections by prominent and popular local personalities. We have already noted that similar weakening of central party control has taken place in elections to the Scottish Parliament and the Assembly in Wales. There has been some ambivalence about this on the part of the parties. The reforms to the executive structures in local government were introduced by the Labour government partly to weaken the grip of the parties, and yet the party has found it hard to loosen its grip on the nomination process for candidates in these higher-level elections.

The election of Livingstone brings out the governance-related tensions in the devolution arrangements in similar ways to what happened in Wales, discussed in the previous chapter. The Labour leadership considered it natural, indeed essential, that a candidate acceptable to the Labour government should stand for Labour in London. It was clear that public opinion, including Labour public opinion, did not favour the various candidates mooted for Labour and in the event Livingstone won by a margin of 11 per cent over the runner-up, the Conservative candidate Steven Norris (51.6 per cent of the first and second preferences as against 41.2 per cent). The Labour Party was finding it hard to reconcile its own centrist tendencies—considered by some commentators to be 'control freakery'—with the electorate's wishes.

The Mayor receives no single block grant from central government. He receives some fixed grants from the centre and a share of non-domestic rates, and he raises additional money by precepting on the London boroughs' council tax and from fees and charges.

The limitations on the Mayor's functions are illustrated by his relationship with London Underground Ltd. This is a wholly owned subsidiary of London Transport, and is a state-owned industry with statutory powers and duties. Its operations are in the hands of a public-sector operating company 'New London Underground'. Responsibility for maintaining and improving the infrastructure is being transferred to three privately owned companies under a public-private partnership—PPP—arrangement. The Mayor's role in this set-up is that his transport strategy will be implemented through an executive body, Transport for London. Control over London Underground could only be transferred to Transport for London once the PPP for its management was in place. The Mayor sets the general level and structure of fares to be charged by London Underground and the general structure of services provided. But he had no part in the negotiations for the PPP contracts and his ability to affect the obligations of London Underground and of the infrastructure companies will be limited by the terms of the PPP agreement for up to thirty years. Disputes, for example on pricing, will be resolved by a statutory public-private partnership agreement arbiter appointed by the relevant Minister—at the time of writing (January 2003) the Secretary of State for the Office of the Deputy Prime Minister. The Mayor's other transport-related strategies include congestion charging for those entering central London and bus routes.

The Mayor also has powers of general competence; these have enabled him to take a number of initiatives, for instance setting up a 'Partnership Register' for same-sex relationships. He has acted as 'champion' for London in relations with the government, claiming in 2001 that Londoners were subsidizing the rest of the country and that more of 'their' money should be returned to London. This generated objections from the neighbouring South East regional development agency and regional assembly. Thus the beginnings of healthy, if irritating to some, political debate and engagement may be one of the outcomes of this—and potentially other—initiatives in regional government.

The Assembly

The Greater London Assembly has 25 members elected on an AMS system, 14 for areas and 11 top-up members drawn from closed party lists. It has no legislative power, not even the secondary legislative power devolved to the Welsh Assembly. Its main purpose is to promote economic development and wealth creation, social development and the improvement of the environment in Greater London, to keep the activity of the Mayor and the Authority's staff under review, and to prepare reports on matters within the competence of the Mayor and the Assembly. The Mayor is required to respond to the Assembly's proposals.

The Assembly has, then, a mainly scrutiny role in relation to the Mayor. He consults it on his strategic plans, though he is not bound to obtain its consent. It may approve his budget, or reject it by a two-thirds majority. (It rejected the first budget presented to it by the Mayor through the combined votes of Labour and Conservative groups and negotiated it down by £23 million.) It has the power to investigate and question the Mayor on progress in the implementation of his strategic plans.

The Assembly may appoint committees and delegate functions to them—or to a single Assembly member or a member of staff of the Authority. The committees must reflect the political balance on the Assembly as a whole. Members of the Assembly may be appointed by the Mayor to the police and fire authorities and they may sit on various other London-wide bodies.

Bogdanor has commented that 'The London mayor and authority will be part of a weak upper tier of local government rather than an embryonic regional authority' (Bogdanor, 1999, 274). But as and when elected regional bodies are put in place in England it is clear that London will not form part of another region, but it, and its Mayor and Assembly, will be the regional body for London. While the London model could not be used for other regions, the asymmetry need not be the cause of uncreative tension between regions or between regions and central government. The aspects of the asymmetry in the devolution arrangements to Scotland, Wales, and Northern Ireland that are likely to cause difficulties are the Westminster and the West Lothian questions (see below) rather than asymmetries internal to national or regional devolved bodies or to their relations with the UK government.

Regional Devolution in England

England's regions (apart from London) have until recently been left out of plans for the devolution of legislative or executive power to locally elected bodies (see generally Bogdanor, 1999; Tomaney 2000, 2001; Tomaney and Hetherington, 2001; Morrison, 2001; Sandford and McQuail, 2001; Forman, 2002). (England itself has also been left out of devolution arrangements, and this is discussed below.) Regional devolution in England has been an issue for some twenty years, with advocates of elected regional government regarding it as essential to develop regional political power centres which would have power to adopt and pursue policies best suited to meet local needs and could bring pressure to bear on central government to do more to meet the needs of the least advantaged regions. In 1993 the Liberal Democrats proposed in their policy paper on constitutional reform, *Here We Stand*, devolution to regional Assemblies, the aim being to enhance local economies through more responsive decision-making, the extension of democratic participation, and a fairer system for the distribution of political and economic power. These Assemblies would replace existing bodies such as quangos and central government agencies and outposts in the regions with democratically accountable regional Assemblies and executives. In 1995 Labour produced a paper *A Choice for England*, basing its case for regional government on its view that 'over-centralized government is not only undemocratic but inefficient too.' The paper proposed first the establishment of indirectly elected Regional Chambers of local authority representatives and, in due course, directly elected Regional Chambers. Each would seek to involve business, community and trade union representation in its activities. These proposals were expanded in Labour's 1996 paper, *New Voice for England's Regions*. The agreement between the Labour Party and the Liberal Democrats before the 1997 election contained a commitment to regional government in England. The Conservatives, however, were opposed to elected regional government. It was not until the election of the Labour government in 1997 that the question started to move, slowly, up the government's agenda.

'Top-down' decentralization to the regions

We shall consider proposals for the delegation or devolution of powers to elected regional bodies in due course, but first let us summarize other developments in regional dimensions to government in England over the last decade or so. Senses of regional identity can find expression in a variety of ways—cultural, linguistic, political, and so on. Though senses of cultural identity are strong in some parts of England, they have not—until recently—found political expression or been reflected in regionally based political structures or institutions. Nor is there much consensus about where regional boundaries are or should be. This has made it difficult for regionally based voices to emerge and thus for those in favour of regionally elected government to find a forum for their campaigns. It has been the policy of the Labour government since 1997 to move towards uniform boundaries for regional bodies, and hence the boundaries of the eight RDAs (see below) were used to provide the basis for the regional list elections to the European Parliament in June 1999 and for the regional chambers and Assemblies (see below). As the White Paper *Modernising Government* (1999, Cm. 4310) put it, the government is committed to working to align the boundaries of public bodies to increase efficiency and underline its philosophy of 'joined up government' (p. 33). The regions are the North East, the North West, Yorkshire, the South West, West Midlands, East Midlands, Eastern, and South East.

In 1994 the Conservative government established ten Government Offices for the Regions (GORs), integrating the regional activities of the then Departments of the Environment, Trade and Industry, Transport, and Employment. These are kinds of 'one stop shops'—regional outposts—of government departments outside Whitehall. But these integrated offices are not in any way locally or regionally accountable. Under the Regional Development Agencies Act 1998 eight Regional Development Agencies (RDAs) were established; they became operational in April 1999. Each has a board of thirteen members and a chair. Half of the members of the board are drawn from business and one-third from local authorities. Their chairs and members are formally appointed by Ministers and they are formally accountable to their Minister—in the Department of Trade and Industry—and through them to Parliament. In essence they are quangos, non-departmental public bodies with business-led boards that reflect regional interests including local government (see Chapter 17). Their purpose is to improve competitiveness and to provide for effective coordination of economic development in the regions. Their budgets were initially small, amounting to less than one per cent of government expenditure in the region, but by 2003 it is estimated that they will reach £1.7 billion under the Spending Review. They have been handed responsibility for Regional Selective Assistance from the GORs, and they have, since April 2002, the flexibility to allocate the extra resources from the 2000 spending review to the priorities for the region which they have identified. But they are subject to government-imposed targets in areas such as economic development, regeneration, and skills development. The government views them as 'strategic drivers of economic development and regeneration in the English regions' (Cm. 5511, para. 2.10). These have all been centrally directed top-down decentralizing arrangements.

Towards 'bottom-up' devolution

The policy of the Labour government since 1997 has been to encourage the establishment of voluntary, non-statutory, locally based regional chambers or Assemblies—a 'bottom-up' process. They are intended by the government to build up the voice of the regions (though as we have noted the boundaries used by the government are artificial). These chambers or Assemblies are composed of voluntary groupings of local councillors and representatives of others with interests in the economic, social, and environmental issues in the region. Their numbers range from 40 to 120, and 70 per cent of the members are drawn from local authorities in the region. They are primarily intended as mechanisms through which Regional Development Agencies can take account of regional views and to which they should give an account of themselves and their activities.

Once established a chamber may apply to the Secretary of State for 'designation'. Once designated these bodies prefer to call themselves 'Assemblies' rather than chambers. The process of designation started in May 1999 and within about a year Assemblies had been designated in most of the English regions. The conditions for designation were that the local authority element should reflect the regional, local, and political balance and type of authority; that the non-local authority element should be open to representatives of the main regional economic development partners with an interest in the work of the RDAs; that the local authority element should be dominant, but that the overall size of the Assembly should enable the wide range of non-local authority interests to be represented; and that all the regional partners should have the opportunity to contribute to the debates of the Assembly and for their views to be reflected in its public statements (*Building Partnerships for Prosperity*, DETR, 1997). The significance of designation is that the Assemblies become recognized regional planning bodies; they produce draft regional planning guidance, which includes regional transport strategies and waste strategies, to be approved and issued by the government. The Assemblies are primarily financed by local authorities, though they do receive earmarked government funding of £15 million over three years to enable them to improve regional input into the RDAs and to develop their own position as the strategic focal point for the regions (Cm. 5511, ch. 2).

The Constitutions of the Assemblies designated under the 1997 Act may vary. By way of example the Constitution of the East Midlands Regional Assembly that was established in December 1998 has as its purpose to be 'the pre-eminent voice for the East Midlands region', working with the RDA and other regional partners to promote the delivery of the region's agreed visions. Its strategy is to boost the social, economic, and environmental quality of life for the people of the region. Its members consist of seventy local authority representatives nominated by the East Midlands Region Local Government Association, eight business representatives, four trade union representatives, and others from the voluntary sector, faith communities, environmental groups, education providers, and other sectors. It depends for its budget on contributions from member organizations, though membership of the Assembly does not depend upon financial contributions. A twelve-member steering group mirroring the membership body representation on the Assembly is in effect the Executive Committee. There are also policy forums and task groups. The Assembly itself meets three times a year, plus special meetings. The Assembly shall normally operate on the basis of consensus, but voting if required is to be by show of hands and simple majority.

It is noteworthy that the main focus of activities of these Assemblies and the RDAs is economic development and related issues. Membership of the Assemblies reflects the networks through which policy is increasingly delivered (see Chapter 1) and the parties are not dominant.

The governance arrangements in these institutions are very loose. The relationship between the Assemblies and RDAs is far from clear. The Assemblies are supposed to be responsible for holding the RDAs to account and they have been given grants by central government to enable them to acquire the research capacity to do so. The RDAs are under statutory duties to consult the Assemblies, but they are primarily accountable to their appointing ministers and to Parliament rather than to the Assemblies, and the Assemblies have no formal powers over them. But, despite the lack of formal powers, a determined assembly may be in a position to pressurize its RDA to amend its strategy, as happened in the East of England Assembly in 2001 (Tomaney, 2001, 117–18). Accountability lines between, for instance, central government and the Government Offices for the Regions, the RDAs, regional Assemblies, and local authorities are unclear or absent. The ambiguities in these relationships have been met pragmatically. A number of concordats has been signed to define relations between the RDAs, Regional Chambers, and Government Offices for the Regions. Some concordats have been signed with non-governmental bodies, for example between RDAs and the TUC. This soft law juridification has been seen as a partial solution to tensions in relationships. Overall, however, the system lacks coherence and clarity of rationale.

The establishment of the RDAs and regional chambers and Assemblies, and the different treatment of Scotland and Wales, stimulated pressure for elected Assemblies in some of the regions. Constitutional Conventions have been established by local activists in some regions. The most active have been in the North East and Yorkshire. These Conventions typically include a majority of elected representatives from the region—councillors, MPs, and MEPs—plus representatives from business, trade unions, education, and the voluntary sector. Some have been chaired by diocesan Church of England bishops. The Conventions establish working groups to bring forward proposals as to whether there is a case for an elected regional assembly, what powers, budget and form of governance might be most appropriate for such an assembly, and relations with other regional bodies—the RDA and Government Offices for the Region—and with central government, the two Houses of Parliament, and European Union institutions. An umbrella group, the Campaign for the English Regions, was established in 2001.

The government's proposals

In May 2002 the government published its plans for devolution of powers to elected Assemblies in the regions (*Your Region, Your Choice: Revitalising the English Regions*, Cm. 5511). The government introduced a bill to allow the holding of referendums on regional government in England in the 2002–3 session. The stated rationales for elected regional Assemblies set out in the White Paper are that centralist policy is not the best answer to tackle regional disparities and respond to the challenges of the modern knowledge economy; a more effective approach is to give real economic power to the regions to enable them to improve regional prosperity (Cm. 5511, para. 6); elected Assemblies will ensure regional accountability of public bodies, including quangos.

The main elements of the proposals are as follows. When the Secretary of State is satisfied after informal soundings that there is demand for an elected regional assembly in a region, a referendum will be held on the issue. Before a referendum is held the Boundary Commission for England will bring forward proposals for unitary, single-tier local authorities in the region. If the result of the referendum is in favour of such an assembly, one will be established by the Secretary of State. Election to it will be by AMS, broadly on the model in Scotland and Wales, with two-thirds of members elected by first past the post, and the remainder from party lists (see Chapter 7). There will be a 5 per cent threshold for seats from lists. Elections will be held every four years (Cm. 5511, ch. 6).

Local government will become unitary. Thus the proposals leave the decision whether there should be an elected assembly—and therefore whether there should be single-tier, unitary, local government—in the hands of people in the region. The government antici- pates that the first referendum may be held during the current Parliament and the first regional assembly could be operational soon after the next general election.

Under the proposals the Assemblies' executive powers will be largely those currently exercised by the government, through the GORs and regional quangos. They will be 'broad and shallow' rather than 'narrow and deep' (Sandford, 2002) and they are cer- tainly wider than expected. The Assemblies will also have 'influencing' functions, involving rights to be consulted by and to give advice to certain bodies, to appoint to certain bodies, and to make proposals to the Highways Authority and the Strategic Rail Authority. The RDA in the region will be accountable to the assembly rather than, as at present, the government. Sandford suggests that this is 'a very peculiar hotch-potch of responsibilities' which are not clearly related to the rationales for devolution.

Regional devolution is not intended to remove powers from local authorities or to increase the size of the bureaucracy to any great extent. Each assembly will have a staff of about 200, excluding those working for the RDA, mostly drawn from the GOR. Each assembly will have a chief executive, a chief finance officer, and a monitoring officer. There will be up to three political advisers, and a majority group could not use its position to take all three posts. There is thus ambiguity here about an executive–assembly split. Local authorities will continue to focus on local service delivery and community leadership. The code of conduct regime that applies to local authorities (see Chapter 16) will broadly be applied to the regional bodies, the monitoring officer of each assembly should establish and maintain a register of interests, and participation in assembly proceedings should be prohibited unless relevant interests are disclosed.

The Assemblies will have responsibility for some ten joining-up strategies for strength- ening the region, and ensuring that relevant stakeholders are engaged in developing and delivering these strategies, and a range of executive and influencing function. The strat- egies will cover sustainable development, economic development, skills and employment, spatial planning, transport, waste, housing, health improvement, culture, and biodiversity (Cm. 5511, ch. 4). The Assemblies will be expected to work in partnerships with business, trade unions, the voluntary and community sectors, local authorities, and other key partners to steer the formulation of their overarching strategy and its implementation. The government will issue guidance to them on how best to do this. Each elected assembly will set out its key objectives in a small number of high-level targets, which it will agree with central government (Cm. 5511, para. 13, and chs. 4, 5, and 7). These targets will include improving the region's economic performance. Assemblies will be expected to monitor their performance against these targets and produce an annual report for the region's electorate on their progress.

The Assemblies will be funded primarily by government grant, and they will have freedom to spend their grants as they judge best. This is a more flexible arrangement than that for Greater London. Thus the Barnett formula (see Chapter 13) will not be extended to the regions. The government estimates that an elected assembly in the North East would be responsible for around £350 million a year, and one in the North West for around £730 million a year (Cm. 5511, ch. 5). The Assemblies will also have a say in further public expenditure by the government—in the regions. Additional funding by way of rewards will be available if an assembly meets or exceeds its targets. They will also be able to precept on local authorities' council tax, subject to a capping regime (Cm. 5511, ch. 5). And they will have borrowing powers that will replace those of the RDAs.

Assemblies will operate on the executive/assembly model similar to that operating in Scotland and, in practice, in Wales (see Chapter 14), and in most local authorities (see Chapter 16). The Leader and Cabinet will be chosen by the full assembly. The assembly could replace the executive at any time by a simple majority vote (Cm. 5511, ch. 7). The executive will propose its budget to the assembly, which will approve, amend, or reject it. Thus executive and scrutiny functions will be split. Assemblies will have between 25 and 35 members, and executives of up to six members. The government's proposals are to continue involvement of business, trade unions, voluntary organiza- tions, and environmental groups, for instance through their co-option onto assembly scrutiny committees or executive policy development committees, or as policy advisers, or through consultative forums. The civic forums in Scotland, Northern Ireland, and London and the partnership arrangements in Wales could provide models for the involvement of 'stakeholders' in policy in the regions (Cm. 5511, ch. 7). This participa- tory model will operate in parallel with the representative model in these arrangements.

Members of the assembly, executive, and the chair will be full-time and paid. Other members will probably be working three days per week and they will receive a salary of about two-thirds of that for the executive members and assembly chair.

The powers devolved to the regional Assemblies will be fewer than those enjoyed by the Welsh Assembly—for instance there will be no power to make secondary legislation, and power will be limited to the matters noted above, which are far narrower than those enjoyed by the Welsh Assembly. The arrangements for the regions are also different from those for London—with its elected Mayor and more limited competence.

The proposals mean that regions will have to overcome considerable obstacles before elected Assemblies can be put in place, particularly the need to persuade the electorate of the wisdom of reorganizing local government on a unitary basis, to be determined not by the region but by the Electoral Commission (which will by then have absorbed the Local Government Commission. It is far from clear what this will involve). Assemblies will be subject to considerable central control, particularly via 'reward' funding and the need to agree strategies with government. Their powers will be far more limited than those of the Welsh Assembly. There are no proposals for immediate 'rolling devolution' in the sense of further powers being devolved to the bodies as and when they request them and are ready to undertake them.

Overall the system will be highly asymmetrical, but given that the regional Assemblies will not have either primary or secondary legislative power this will not directly affect the operation of the legislative process in Parliament. Nor will it solve—or exacerbate—the West Lothian question (see below). But it is to be expected that, as has happened in Wales, government will have to consult regional Assemblies before introducing legislation which has regional implications, and it may find itself under pressure to introduce legislation to deal with problems which the regional Assemblies and their executives consider require legislation.

The United Kingdom

Devolution, it has often been said, is a process not an event (Davies, 1999). The process is a continuing one, especially in the English regions, and relations between the constituent parts of the UK are developing as all parties adjust to the new political dynamics that devolution has created. Already, and inevitably, some particular problems are attracting controversy. These stem largely from the parliamentary asymmetry of the arrangements and the neglect of the interests of England.

The West Lothian question

During the devolution debates in the 1970s Tam Dalyell, the Member of Parliament for West Lothian, repeatedly asked what came to be known as 'the West Lothian question' (SCC 1989, at paras. 2.2, 8.6–8): ought Scottish MPs at Westminster to have the right to participate in the legislative process where the Act in question will not apply to Scotland because of devolution? (In fact the way the question was put was: why should Scottish MPs continue to vote on English domestic matters when English MPs can no longer vote on such matters in Scotland? This formulation seems to imply an inappropriate 'two wrongs can make a right' approach, that it would be acceptable for Scottish MPs to vote on English matters as long as English MPs could vote on Scottish ones, which must be wrong. In fact the question was intended to highlight the instability of partial, asymmetrical devolution.)

This is a matter of good governance. The House of Commons consents or refuses consent on behalf of the people to legislation that will affect them, not to legislation that affects other people. There would be outrage if deputies from the French Parliament, for instance, sat in the House of Commons and voted on legislation that only affected the UK. The fact that before devolution English, Welsh, and Northern Ireland MPs partici-pated in legislation which applied only to Scotland (for instance, the poll tax which was introduced in Scotland before England) was often resented in Scotland. There is likely to be resentment of Scottish influence at Westminster on English issues, which will under-mine good relations between the people of the countries that make up the union. This could be generated if, for instance, Scottish MPs at Westminster voted in favour of a ban on fox-hunting in England or in England and Wales. (Fox-hunting with hounds has been outlawed in Scotland by the Scottish Parliament.)

At present (September 2002) it is unlikely that the votes of Scottish MPs could make a difference to legislation in the Westminster Parliament as the Labour government has a large majority. But the time could come when a majority of English and Welsh MPs at Westminster were not Labour, but there was a Labour government in office relying on the votes of Scottish MPs for its majority. When legislation for England and Wales is passed against the opposition of a majority of English and Welsh MPs on the strength of Scottish Labour MPs' votes the West Lothian issue will become critical.

The devolution legislation has not tackled this problem. (Under the Scotland Act 1978, section 66, there was to be a 14-day 'cooling off period' between two divisions on the second reading of a bill whenever the votes of Scottish MPs made a decisive difference in a Commons division. This provision could well have been unworkable in practice, but at least the West Lothian question was acknowledged to create a problem and some attempt was made to resolve it. No such attempt has been made in the devolution legislation this time round.)

It would be a constitutional novelty to legislate to limit the voting and speaking rights of certain classes of MPs at Westminster. If the matter were not dealt with by legislation but left to convention, then it might be hoped that a convention would grow up to the effect that Scottish MPs would not vote on matters affecting only the rest of the United Kingdom. But it is difficult to imagine, for example, a Labour government with a majority of forty in the House of Commons, including fifty Scottish MPs, accepting the defeat of a measure affecting England and Wales when it could call upon its Scottish supporters to push it through. Without some formal or informal regulation of the right of Scottish MPs to vote in the Commons on matters that do not apply to Scotland, the risk of deteriorating relations between Scotland and the rest of Great Britain will be high.

Lord Irvine, the Labour Lord Chancellor, is reported to have said that the best answer to the West Lothian question is to stop asking it (to which William Hague, the Conservative leader, is said to have replied that the best way to find an answer is to stop asking Lord Irvine: see Hazell, 2001, 275). It may be that Lord Irvine's is also the answer to the English and Welsh question, to which we now turn, that the government prefers. Hazell (2001) implies an alternative answer, that the Westminster Parliament itself could resolve the questions by acting as a proxy English Parliament—at least for the next few years, until—as in my view is bound to happen—different majorities are present in the English and UK memberships of the House of Commons.

The English (and Welsh) question

As we have seen the UK Parliament is the only primary legislature for England and Wales. But Wales has its own executive. The asymmetry of devolution means that England as a country has been left entirely out of institutional arrangements (see Hadfield, 2002). It has been subsumed in the UK government and Parliament, and assumed not to have a separate existence or interests and claims separate and different from those of the UK. It has neither its own legislature, nor its own executive institutions. Wales, too, has no separate legislature. Instead the UK institutions, Parliament and government, exercise functions not only for the United Kingdom as a whole in matters of defence, foreign affairs, tax, and the many other non-devolved matters (and even, as we have seen, in relation to some devolved matters with the consent of the Scottish Parliament or the Northern Ireland Assembly) but also for England and Wales. Unlike Scotland, Northern Ireland, and Wales, England has no separate voice in government, in either of the two Houses of Parliament, or in Europe. There is no Secretary of State for England. And MPs and Ministers sitting for non-English and non-Welsh constituencies may participate in making decisions that will apply only to England or Wales.

The blind spot which has left England out of account in devolution raises a number of issues. There is a strong possibility that the UK government and Parliament will operate on the assumption that what is good for the whole of the United Kingdom is good for England or England and Wales. With no voice of its own, England will find that its interests are neglected by central government and Parliament in deference to the organized pressures from the other countries. It is unlikely that the converse will happen, i.e. that the UK government will operate on an assumption that what is good for England or for England and Wales is good for the whole of the UK, when in fact it might be bad for the rest of the UK, or that the UK government gives preferential treatment to England and England and Wales, since the other countries have their own voices and champions to counteract any such pro-English tendencies in UK institutions.

As devolution takes place to elected Assemblies in the English regions in the next few years, the absence of a voice for England as a whole may be mitigated by the collective voices of its regions. But they will not be concerned with the interests of England as a whole, only with their own interests, which may very well conflict with one another. Each region may plead for additional resources for itself, drawing comparisons with other regions and with Scotland, Wales, and Northern Ireland, but no institution would be able legitimately to argue the case for England as a whole as against Scotland, Wales, and Northern Ireland. For the UK government to do so would be seen as partisan, given that it is supposed to be promoting the interests of the UK as a whole. These inequalities are not, it is suggested, consistent with principles of good governance, transparency, and equality.

Unease about the position of England has led to consideration whether there should be a separate English Parliament, or whether the Westminster Parliament should, for some purposes, act as a Parliament for England within the Parliament for the UK. In 1998 William Hague, Leader of the Conservative opposition, proposed an English Grand Committee in the House of Commons, or even an English Parliament. In 1999 some Conservative commentators and MPs started to propose an English Parliament, or devolution to England, as responses to the privileged position enjoyed by Scotland and Wales under the devolution settlement that was then being put in place, and concern about the West Lothian Question. In the run up to the 2001 general election William Hague stated that if elected 'English votes on English laws will be one of my first priorities. In the opening days of the next Conservative government there will be a change to the procedures of the House of Commons. We will make English votes on English laws a reality' (speech at Magdalen College, Oxford, noted in Hazell, 2001, 276).

A separate English Parliament is not however on the serious political agenda of any of the parties at present, for a number of reasons. It would bring the UK closer to a federal or quasi-federal system: but England contains about 85 per cent of the population of the United Kingdom, and no federation or quasi-federation has been successful with such an imbalance in size between its members. If the majority of members of an English Parliament were of a different party from the Westminster government, it would necessitate a separate government for England. If present moves towards regional devolution are to continue, the result would be too many layers of government—local government, regional government, English government, and the UK government—and of course the European Union institutions. An English Parliament and government would only be feasible if there were no regional layer. While there is some political momentum for English regions, there is no such momentum in 2003 for an English Parliament and government. None of the parties, nor public opinion, is prepared for such radical changes.

The question then arises whether England can be accommodated in other ways in the constitutional arrangements of the UK. One possibility might be for the Westminster Parliament itself to develop its English activities in order to compensate for the fact that England does not have its own legislature. It is already doing so in various ways (see generally Hazell, 2001). Steps are being taken in the House of Commons, and further steps are being mooted, to deal with specifically English and Welsh issues. For instance, many select committees, including of course those that deal with issues that can only relate to England and Wales, are dominated by English or English and Welsh MPs—this is a natural consequence of the fact that membership reflects the balance of seats in the House. But their composition reflects the balance of the membership of the whole House, not of English or English and Welsh members—despite the fact that the government has a majority of English and Welsh members. There is a Standing Committee on Regional Affairs, charged with considering 'any matter relating to regional affairs in England which may be referred to it' (note the focus on English regions, not on England). Its members all sit for English constituencies, but they reflect the balance of the parties in the whole House. There have been proposals for an English-and-Welsh-MPs-only stage in the legislative process, for instance an English Grand Committee on the lines of the previous Scottish Grand Committee, which took the second reading of Scottish bills before devolution, and for the committee stage also to be taken by that Committee (see for instance the Report of the Commission to Strengthen Parliament, 2000, chaired by Lord Norton of Louth and set up by the Conservative leader, William Hague). Logically this should be an English and Welsh Grand Committee. A variant on this would be a Second Reading Committee of some English MPs and a standing committee of English MPs to take the committee stage (see the Procedure Committee's report on *The Procedural Consequences of Devolution*, HC 185, 1999). No such reform has as yet been introduced.

Overall there is clearly scope for the Westminster Parliament to take on a special role in relation to English and Welsh issues and legislation that apply only to those countries (unless and until the Welsh Assembly itself acquires legislative power on a par with that of the Scottish Parliament). At present however moves in that direction have been modest.

There are other ways in which institutional arrangements could take account of the separate interests of England. Hadfield (2002) suggests, for instance, an English Human Rights Commission (Northern Ireland has its own Human Rights Commission and the Scottish Parliament is likely to legislate for one in the near future), separate English representation at the British–Irish Council, and a Secretary of State for Constitutional Affairs into which the territorial Secretaries of State would merge as Under Secretaries, with a separate one for England.

At present people in England and Wales do not seem unduly bothered by these questions (Curtice, 2001, 232–4). The UK's constitutional arrangements are full of anomalies and the traditional way of dealing with them is to ignore them for as long a possible and, if it becomes necessary to do so, to make pragmatic, incremental adjust- ments to defuse tensions. As the Barnett formula continues to move towards convergence of expenditure per capita in the four countries of the union, that particular irritant may become less irritating. However, if the time should come when there is a different major- ity of English or English and Welsh MPs at Westminster from the majority for the government, the issues will become crucial and decisions about how to deal with this aspect of asymmetry will have to be made. Telling people to stop asking awkward questions will not work forever.

A role in devolution for the second chamber?

In federal and confederal states the second chamber—often a Senate—normally has roles in protecting the states' interests, and also as a constitutional watchdog. It has already been noted that devolution in the UK is nowhere near a classic federal system. At most it is 'quasi-federal'. But could and should the nations and regions be repre- sented in the second chamber? As we have seen (Chapter 10), the proposals for reform of the second chamber envisage a directly elected element based on the nations and regions. Let us explore briefly the implications of such a system. (There is little support for indirectly elected representatives, i.e. representatives chosen by or from the Scottish Parliament, the Northern Ireland Assembly, the Assembly for Wales, and any English regional bodies.)

The argument for directly elected national and regional representation in the second chamber has focused mainly on the idea that any legislative body should be elected in order to give it legitimacy. The arguments around that issue have been explored in Chapter 10. If there were to be such representatives in the second chamber, they would not only be concerned with the kind of scrutiny of policy and legislation that the House of Lords as currently composed exercises. Representation of the nations and regions would open up possibilities for their representatives to exert political pressure on the UK government, by bargaining and withdrawal of cooperation in order to extract advantages for their electorates.

Devolution is likely to result in the devolved bodies and their electorates increasing their demands on the centre not only for money and possibly increased powers, but also for a say in the United Kingdom government's policy on non-devolved matters, such as Europe, tax, and social security and, for England and Wales, regional policy. It is to be expected that national and regional representatives in the second chamber might use their presence there to bargain with the government about these matters, using the delaying power of the chamber as a lever.

Reflections on Devolution

Devolution has introduced a principle of subsidiarity into the UK Constitution, though in a very pragmatic way. It has enabled decisions to be made in the devolved areas that are more responsive to local opinion and needs than was possible under a centralized system. It has promoted cross-party collaboration and a less adversarial style of politics than operates at Westminster. Experience in the devolved bodies may offer lessons for the Westminster Parliament, especially about the scope for committees to scrutinize government and the relative effectiveness of plenary as opposed to committee session, and the regulation of standards of conduct.

Devolution has not meant a formal move towards federalism—quite the reverse—because of the continuing sovereignty of the Westminster Parliament. However, informal quasi-federal conventions—for instance the *Memorandum of Understanding*, concordats, and the Sewel convention—are developing to protect the devolved bodies against unilateral interference from the centre. It is doubtful whether these soft law mechanisms will be effective if different parties are in control in Westminster and devolved bodies. Thus devolution opens up many possibilities of future conflicts and tensions between the devolved bodies and those at UK level. It has also opened up divisions within the political parties, notably the Labour Party which had assumed that devolution to different parts of the country would not lead to loosening of the party's control over its national and regional organs. A culture of devolution has not yet taken root in that party itself.

The devolution legislation has already produced more highly juridified political and administrative processes than operate at UK level, and this has necessitated the beginnings of a constitutional court in the form of the Judicial Committee of the Privy Council. However, the devolution arrangements also maintain to a considerable degree the tradition of the 'political Constitution', notably in maintaining Westminster's sovereignty, and in relation to finance and intergovernmental relations. These relationships depend very much upon trust and comity between the levels of government, and they may not work if there are different parties in control at Westminster and one or more of the devolved bodies. If and when this happens, the relationships between the centre and devolved bodies are likely to become increasingly juridified and the courts will be given the function of resolving issues between the levels of government. The shift away from the political Constitution will accelerate.

The enjoyment of citizenship rights in the sense of the opportunity to elect the bodies that will make laws and executive decisions has become uneven across the UK as a result of the asymmetry of devolution. Voters in Scotland and Northern Ireland have greater opportunities to influence these processes than voters in Wales, and voters in England have even less opportunity than those in Wales to do so, since MPs and Ministers from outside England or England and Wales influence policies that will apply only to England or England and Wales. Devolution has also resulted in variable citizenship entitlements, notably to social and economic rights as, for instance, university fees for undergraduate courses have been abolished in Scotland.

The financial arrangements for devolution (based on the Barnett formula) do not pass tests of openness or transparency, rationality or equity. But reform of finance will raise issues as to how a more juridified system can be subject to independent supervision. These are not matters in which the courts would want to be involved, and nor would governments generally wish the courts to have jurisdiction in disputes in these matters.

The devolution arrangements have provided the opportunity for some interesting experiments in participatory democracy and citizenship, notably in the civic forums, but is it too early to reach any judgements about their importance. There is no reason why similar experiments should not undertaken in England.

The use of proportional representation brings about a shift to a less confrontational and more consensual form of government than operates at Westminster. As yet Westminster does not seem inclined to switch to proportional representation, but the fact that the electorate is becoming accustomed to proportional systems may shift public opinion in favour.

The asymmetry in the system is generating pressures for further change, notably in Wales where the fact that the Assembly has no primary legislative power is increasingly seen as second-class devolution, and in some of the regions of England which are starting to build up support for devolution to elected Assemblies on a par with Wales. But it seems most unlikely that the regions would ever be granted primary legislative power, and thus regional Assemblies cannot provide an answer to the West Lothian and English questions. These raise issues of democracy and good governance that, despite the attempts of the government to ignore them, will not go away.

The people in England are not at present particularly interested in these questions, but it is inevitable that they will become interested if Conservative fortunes revive in England or the Labour Party were to win an election with a small majority that meant they had to rely on Scottish, Welsh, or Northern Ireland MPs to push through legislation for England. Then the English question and the sovereignty of the Westminster Parliament in a quasi-federal state will become highly political issues.

16

Local Government

In England local authorities are the only elected tier below the UK Parliament and executive. Scotland, Wales, and Northern Ireland have their elected Parliament and assemblies between Westminster and local government. Throughout the United Kingdom local authorities are creatures of statute and they have only the powers granted to them by the relevant legislature. They have little discretion in raising their own revenue and they rely substantially on grants from central government. Their status in the Constitution is therefore precarious, for Parliament may alter their powers or even abolish them (as was done with the Greater London Council and metropolitan county councils by the Local Government Act 1985).

This layer of the system of government in England and Wales has been subjected to repeated reforms since the end of the Second World War. Reforms have affected the finance, functions and structure of local government, and, most recently, the operation of political processes within authorities, and standards of conduct. The 1980s and 1990s in particular saw a series of important measures that radically affected the powers of local authorities. These raised issues about the proper constitutional role of this tier and whether there are or should be limits to central government interference in local government.

Rationales for Local Government

Given the history of efforts over the last 150 years to improve local government and to find the right balance in central–local relations we should have a picture of the rationales that are advanced for this tier. (For brief histories of local government and the rationales for it see the Kilbrandon Report, Cmnd. 5460, ch. 7, at paras. 189–98; Loughlin, 1996, ch. 1; Leigh, 2000, ch. 1). First, the value of political pluralism as a safeguard against abuse of power. The over-concentration of power at the centre paves the way for abuse, and so the existence of other institutions, responsible for the provision of public services and possibly under different political control, acts as a counterweight against abuse by the centre. The positive side of this is that pluralism enhances democratic accountability. It can give voters the opportunity to see different ideologies and policy priorities in operation, and can provide a more informed basis for voter choice at local, regional, and national level.

Second, the value of the responsiveness that comes from the responsibility for service delivery being operated locally, possibly experimentally, a version of the 'subsidiarity' principal recognized in European Community law (Chapter 4) and in the European Charter of Local Self-Government (see below). At one time the assumption might have been that services should be delivered by local authorities, but the trend recently has been for the local authority to be legally responsible for seeing that services are available—for procuring them: they are not necessarily responsible for actually delivering them. In fact this idea has a longer pedigree than is sometimes realized, since John Stuart Mill stated that 'the business of the elective body is not to do the work, but to see that it is properly done' (Mill, 1975, 369 (first published in 1861), quoted in Leigh, 2000, 8). This is linked to the 'diversity and difference' argument for subsidiarity, that bringing power and decisions closer to the people who will be affected by them secures improvements in the quality of decisions and greater flexibility: services can be delivered more efficiently and effectively at a local level.

Third, local government should have leadership, educational and developmental roles, acting as a training-ground for citizenship (see Chapter 2) and as the promoter of local community development. This is coming to be recognized as a significant role for local government, and not one that central government can perform. Citizen involvement in local government provides experiential education in democracy and political skills, both for the voters and for the politician (Mill, 1975). Participation in local government can encourage citizen assertiveness and efficacy and thus forms part of the civic culture. Local government can also be developmental in the related sense of promoting community well-being, particularly in relation to environmental, economic, and social issues. This role for local government has been explicitly recognized under the Local Government Act 2000, Part I. The role can involve experimentation and 'social learning'. The ways in which communities and cities are run, and the climate of social relations there (for instance between people from different ethnic backgrounds), can be powerfully affected by 'social capital' built up over very long periods. Social capital consists of networks of trust and capabilities for taking collective action to manage social problems without being wholly reliant on government efforts but which can be fostered by local government activity (see Sixth Report of the Select Committee on Public Administration, *Innovations in Citizen Participation in Government*, HC 373, 2000–1).

Lastly, local government has a role as community champion and advocate for local people. This is a role noted in the government's White Paper on regional devolution in England (Cm. 5511; see Chapter 15), which envisages that local authorities would have a voice in regional affairs, promoting their own areas' interests in the region.

Each of these arguments for local government implies that local authorities and local communities should enjoy a real degree of autonomy, both financially and in the making of choices between possible policy options. However, as we shall see, the autonomy of local government has been substantially restricted since the 1980s, and government policy to return some autonomy since 2000 is still subject to central government intervention in the case of poor performance.

The importance of local government is recognized by the international community. The Council of Europe's European Charter of Local Self-Government, 1985 (Treaty Series No. 122) aims to protect local authorities from encroachment by central government by ensuring that they have their own adequate financial resources and providing that financial equalization processes are not to be used to diminish the decision-making powers of local authorities (Article 9). Nor should their powers be undermined by administrative action by central government (Articles 4 and 8). Authorities should have powers of general competence (Article 4) to promote the welfare of their inhabitants. They should have freedom of choice as to the manner of provision of services and in their internal organization (Article 6). They should also have the power to determine the rate of their own taxes (Article 9). The United Kingdom ratified the Charter in 1998. The Charter is not however directly enforceable in UK law and it is far from clear that arrangements in England and Wales actually meet the requirements of the Treaty.

Reforming Local Government

Local government—including the government and governance of London—has been the subject of a large number of successive reforming Acts of Parliament for at least three decades. This is not the place to go into these in any detail. Landmarks in the last twenty years have been the abolition of the Greater London Council and the metropolitan counties in 1985 and the introduction in 1988 of the community charge—the poll tax—followed quickly by its abolition and replacement by the council tax.

Central government is commonly concerned to deliver its own policies through local authorities—primary and secondary education and care in the community are examples—and yet those authorities may be of a different political colour from central government, they may have different political agendas, and they may have a different—probably better—understanding than central government of local needs and possibilities. The interests of central government will often override the pluralistic case for local government, and it is here that the constitutional vulnerability of this layer of government is most obvious. There was a period of acute conflict between the Conservative government and a number of Labour councils after the 1979 election. There is also scope for conflicting political agendas between the centre and the locality *within* political parties, as there was, for instance, between Liverpool City Council and the Labour Party in the 1980s (and as there is, to a degree, between the Labour government at Westminster and Labour members of administrations in Wales and Scotland). Many conflicts were dealt with by central government in the 1980s and 1990s by legislation which transferred the functions or services formerly performed by local authorities to the private or voluntary sector, immunized from political control through detailed regulation, and imposed tight controls on local authorities' remaining functions and their spending. Thus, for instance, schools were removed from direct management by local education authorities and are now locally managed by heads and governing bodies; the school curriculum is centrally prescribed. As a result local education authorities' legal responsibilities include the supply of special educational needs and appointments, but they are no longer responsible, as used to be the case, for the day-to-day management of primary or secondary education in their areas. Under the Local Government Act 2000 local authorities have been encouraged to enter into partnerships with voluntary sector and private enterprises to deliver policy and services (see below). Contracts are made by local authorities with commercial or charitable care homes for the care of those in need, and their standards are legally regulated. The housing stock of many local authorities has been transferred to housing associations, or sold to sitting tenants at a discount. Many other former local authority functions are contracted out to the commercial private sector.

A regime of compulsory competitive tendering (CCT) was introduced by the Conservative government to force local authorities to consider contracting out work previously done by their direct labour force to the private sector on cheaper terms. CCT was replaced by a 'Best Value' regime introduced by Labour in 1998, discussed below. But although local authorities are freer under the 'Best Value' regime to employ their own workforces to provide public services, it is still the case that many functions such as refuse collection are performed for local authorities under contract by private firms.

Fifty per cent of local government money comes from central government, and another 25 per cent comes via central government from the National Non-domestic Rate. Only about 25 per cent is raised locally from the council tax. The exercise of local authority functions and the way in which their block grant from central government is spent are strictly regulated by law and by guidance in government policy documents. Authorities may bid for special project funding, the grant for which may not be spent on other things, or for funding for local strategic partnerships (LSPs). Councils' ability to raise their own revenue through local taxes—the council tax—has been restricted by the setting of the business rate nationally, and the power of central government to cap council taxes.

Loughlin (1996, ch. 1) has interpreted the trend in legislation in the last thirty years or so as being away from a facilitative approach to local authority activity and towards an instrumental one: legislation in this period—until the 2000 Local Government Act—was concerned with achieving central government's policies and ends locally. Local authorities had become agents of central government. The system was one of local administration, not local government. This period represented a departure from earlier legislation, which had been designed to enable local authorities to achieve their own policies for their localities. At an extreme it could have been envisaged that local authorities' function was no more than to meet once a year to authorize contracts with private providers giving effect to central government policy and to pay the bills.

The Local Government Act 2000 seeks to give effect to a commitment on the part of government to a new positive role for local government, in promoting the 'general wellbeing' if their areas, though with elaborate accompanying safeguards against abuse of power, and continuation of local government's reliance on funding from central government rather than freedom to raise revenue from its own tax base—fiscal autonomy. The breakdown of trust between central and local government caused by political polarization in the 1980s has not been forgotten by central government.

The well-being power

The White Paper, *Modern Local Government—In Touch with the People* (Cm. 4014, 1998) which preceded the Local Government Act 2000 committed the government to enshrining in law a new role for the local authority as the elected leader of their local community, with responsibility for the well-being and sustainable development of its area. Councils are to work in partnership—i.e. to network (see Chapter 1)—with other public, private, and voluntary organizations and with local people to promote the economic, social, and environmental well-being of their areas (Cm. 4014, 1998, para. 22).

The 2000 Act, Part I, gives local authorities their new community development and well-being functions, seeing their role less as providers and deliverers of services than facilitators or enablers (see Leigh, 2000, ch. 10). As Lord Whitty for the government put it when the bill was at second reading in the House of Lords: 'Community leadership means generating support for change and working with others to deliver that change. It means managing, negotiating differences, coordinating and facilitating action by others' (HL Deb., vol. 607, col. 1022). Under the Act authorities must prepare a community strategy and consult widely on it (s. 4) and they must have regard to this strategy when exercising their well-being powers. These are very broadly drawn (though they may not be used to raise taxation indirectly).

The Local Government Association has defined this role in community planning as follows: 'A multi-organizational, community-based process, initiated by the council, for creating a shared vision of community identified priorities leading to a programme of actions which demonstrate the commitment and support of the organizations and groups involved' (DETR, *Preparing Community Strategies: Government Guidance to Local Authorities*, 2000, 11). This is a clear example of an explicit vision of participatory democracy operating alongside representative democracy. It also illustrates the way in which governance in the sense of the involvement of non-governmental bodies in the delivery of public policy and public services has come to be formally recognized in this, as in other, fields. This new role for local authorities is promoted by a range of techniques, including consultation and participation, partnerships, and 'Best Value'.

Consultation and participation

The LGA 2000 instructs authorities to consult on the economic and social well-being of their areas and, in some circumstances, to hold referendums on the future form of local government and particular policies, for instance on the size of the budget. Participation is a prerequisite of funding under various regeneration budgets. Partnerships—which form part of the well-being approach (see further below)—have to demonstrate that they have consulted local interests.

In accordance with the policy in the 2000 Act, by summer 2001 local referendums had been held by a number of councils in England to seek citizens' view on raising local budgets and council taxes. In Milton Keynes in 1999 there was a 41 per cent response in a referendum on budget options, with citizens voting for a 10 per cent increase in local council tax. In early 2001 a similar budget referendum in Bristol produced a lower response rate and a different decision, with voters rejecting options for raising council taxes and going for a standstill budget, which the council explained would entail dismissing some teachers.

The extension of consultation and participation in local government raises issues as to the right balance between consultation and council responsibility, between participatory and representative democracy. As elected representatives, councillors have a duty to make hard choices and take responsibility for them, and they should not place this responsibility on voters who may be less well informed of the consequences of different choices. But consultation should not be regarded as just a hoop to jump through. Both the council and citizens can learn from the process, and prior consultation serves to legitimate decisions. However, it has been recognized that consultation can be onerous and the Select Committee on Public Administration in its *Innovations in Citizen Participation* report (HC 373, 2000–1) recommended that the government consider introducing legislation to replace the current multiplicity of individual statutory obligations to consult by one overarching framework.

There is also considerable local apathy about consultation and referendums, possibly because of the negative view of councils held by much of the public or because people realize that they have relatively little power. Members of certain groups (such as young people, single parents, and ethnic minorities) tend not to take part in participation opportunities, and unless these groups are targeted, participation may in practice reinforce exclusion rather than lead to more democracy. Given widespread concern in government and Parliament about the fall in turnout at the 2001 general election (see Chapter 7), the need to reconnect the people with politics has moved up the agenda and this kind of consultation and participation at local government level should be pursued as possible means of reconnection. However, the emphasis on local government as promoting participation seems to have weakened as new executive structures become more topical (see below).

Service delivery: partnerships, 'Best Value', Public Service Agreements—and take-overs

The new positive role for local government envisages innovations in methods of service delivery. The well-being power is linked to a range of techniques, many of which rely on networks in the sense of cooperation between government and local government and, more prominently, local authorities and private or voluntary sector institutions.

Arrangements include the use of Local Strategic Partnerships (LSPs) by local government (see *Strong Local Leadership—Quality Public Services*, Cm. 5237, 2001). A LSP is a single body based in the local authority area that brings together different parts of the public sector (for instance, the local authority, the local NHS bodies, the local police, the Employment Service and the Benefits Agency offices in the area) and the private, business, community, and voluntary sector, so that different initiatives and services support each other and work together (see *Local Strategic Partnerships—Government Guidance Summary*, DETR, March 2001).

These arrangements are regarded as 'the key element in developing integrated approaches to local service delivery, and to tackling policy priorities in a joined-up way' (para. 2.31, *Strong Local Leadership*). The government uses various levers to encourage effective partnerships, including 'budgetary mechanisms', Public Service Agreements, line management systems to provide staff with incentives to achieve partnership objectives, and organizational incentives, i.e. local public service agreement rewards (see *Strong Local Leadership*, para. 2.42).

The advance in these arrangements over previous privatization and contracting-out techniques is that the government envisages long-term relationships developing between authorities and their partners. The presupposition is that authorities and private-sector organizations will enter into partnering or partnership arrangements that move beyond the traditional 'supply for service' contract to arrangements where the skills and experiences of both come together to achieve continuous improvement in the delivery of services (DTLR, *Working Together: Effective partnering between local government and business for service delivery*, December 2001, ch. 2). The arrangements may be partly or wholly contractual, or they may be effected by memorandums of understanding or partnering protocols.

A second technique for the improved delivery of services is the move to 'Best Value' principles. These involve an externally audited regime (conducted by the Audit Commission) based on the setting of priorities in consultation with local people. The new regime shifts the focus from the cost of services, which was the focus of the previous compulsory competitive tendering (CCT) regime, designed primarily as a cost-cutting measure, to overall service quality or effectiveness, using partnerships with private and voluntary sector bodies—networks—and encouraging local experimentation.

This new statutory duty of 'Best Value', set out in section 3 of the Local Government Act 1999, requires local authorities to 'secure continuous improvement in the way in which their functions are exercised, having regard to a combination of economy, efficiency and effectiveness.' (See the Green Paper, *Modernising Local Government: Improving Local Services through Best Value*, March 1998; White Paper, *Modern Local Government: In Touch with the People*, Cm. 1404, 1998; white paper *Strong Local Leadership—Quality Public Services*, Cm. 5237, December 2001, ch. 7; Leigh, 2000, ch. 10; Martin, 2000.) This means balancing costs and quality in consultation with local people—possibly through referendums—and identifying the most appropriate method of service delivery, whether public, private, voluntary, or in partnership.

Local Public Service Agreements between a local authority and the government (see Chapters 3, 11, and 12 on Public Service Agreements as accountability mechanisms) encourage councils to stretch their performance beyond what could be achieved under the 'Best Value' regime, in particular 'areas of activity' (e.g. increasing the percentage of children of certain ages reaching expected standards of literacy, increasing bus use, and reducing fly tips) in return for additional finance and freedoms and flexibilities—i.e. release from some regulation (*Strong Local Leadership*, para. 1.5). The government will expect authorities seeking to enter into Local Public Service Agreements to be acting in partnership with other local bodies. The government offers a cash reward of 2½ per cent of the year's net budget for achieving the 'stretching' targets in full, and a scaled-down grant for achieving a large part of the improvement. Authorities are to conduct regular reviews to secure the improvement of their performance, and to produce annual performance plans. These plans are subject to audit by the Audit Commission, and performance indicators are devised and monitored by local authorities themselves, and by the Audit Commission and central government. Councils will be assessed on a 'scorecard'

(*Strong Local Leadership*, para. 3.19) in four categories: high-performing, striving, coasting, and poor-performing. High-performing councils will be released from some of the controls and regulations imposed by central government, such as the ringfencing of grants and the capping of council-tax increases (paras 3.25–3.30). Poor-performing councils will receive 'a directed approach to support and capacity building and government intervention where this is necessary to tackle corporate or service weaknesses' (para. 3.37). A 'beacon council' scheme gives recognition to councils which are achieving well in certain specified services such as adoption, fostering business growth, and neighbourhood renewal. They are entitled to use a beacon council logo for a period, and they are encouraged to disseminate good practice through 'showcases' (exhibitions), open days, and the like (see Beacon Council Scheme documents on the DTLR website). These arrangements explicitly encourage networking. They suggest mistrust on the part of government of the ability or willingness of local authorities to reach high standards without highly controlling sticks and carrots being wielded by government to focus their efforts.

The Local Government Bill 2002 will give councils new freedoms over their activities and finances. The government Spending Review in 2002 will match extra money for local authorities, using detailed reform proposals, long-term targets, national standards, and audit with a 'new localism' in public service delivery (Balls, 2002).

These arrangements, then, replace some of the detailed direct regulation of local government that was imposed under Conservative governments with incentives and the development of networks to induce local authorities to stretch their performance and cooperate with others to improve local services. Martin (2000) suggests that the policy represents a drive towards more 'citizen-centred' services with a focus on cross-cutting issues such as community safety and regeneration, adopting a community-based approach, and a devolution of responsibility and discretion to local authorities from the highly centralized CCT technique which it replaces. It is too early to reach conclusions about the effectiveness of the system, but the Audit Commission argues that overall services are improving, although it has identified many failings. In its first report it found that 2 per cent of services were 'three star'—the top rating; 35 per cent were 'two star'; 55 per cent were 'one star', meaning only fair; and 8 per cent were 'no star' or poor (Audit Commission, *Changing Gear: Best Value Annual Statement 2001*; Pratchett, 2002; see also Audit Commission, *Comprehensive Performance Assessment*, 12 Dec. 2002).

Partnerships, 'Best Value', and Public Service Agreements are all facilitative mechanisms for good service delivery. But under the Public Spending Review of July 2002 the Chancellor of the Exchequer emphasized the government's willingness to take and exercise powers to intervene directly in failing councils or failing council services:

Poor performing schools will be subject to takeover by new leadership or by a neighbouring school, or closed and reopened as a new school. Failing local education authorities will be subject to takeover by high-performing authorities. . . . Poor-performing social services and housing departments will have new directorates and senior managers. Poor-performing local authorities will first be subject to a recovery plan to tackle bad performance and, if that is insufficient, subject to new managers or takeover of functions. (HC Deb., 15 July 2002, cols. 25, 26)

The purpose is to secure that the additional funding for services the government was making available is not wasted and that services are in fact improved.

The Office of the Deputy Prime Minister followed this up with the publication of a consultation paper in August 2002 (*Tackling Poor Performance in Local Government*) in which it proposed a Recovery Plan to be required of all failing councils, a Partnership or Improvement Board to support recovery plans, External Support where the government does not believe that a council can produce or implement a Recovery Plan under which external contractors would be employed to develop and start the implementation of the plan, and Interim Management Teams to be appointed to undertake specific functions for the council if the government believes a council is not able to take forward a recovery plan, even with external support. After consultation the government proposed to use the Audit Commission's *Comprehensive Performance Assessment* (2002) as the basis of dialogue with local authorities leading to action on the above basis where appropriate (Office of the Deputy Prime Minister, *Response to Consultation Exercise*, 13 December 2002).

New Executive Arrangements in Local Government

Until recently local authorities have been run on a committee system in which members of all parties sat on decision-making committees. This worked reasonably well when local authorities were relatively unpoliticized, and cooperation between members was not made difficult by adversarialism and competitiveness. This was the position in many local authorities until the 1970s. In 1967 the Maud Committee found that only 50 per cent of authorities had been under party control (*Report of the Committee on the Management of Local Government*. London: HMSO). By 1986, the Widdicombe Committee found, the party system in local government was 'widely accepted' (Widdicombe 1986, Cmnd. 9797, para. 2.43). Today the political reality is that most local authorities are under the control of one party, and in very many areas the same party retains control for many years. This has undermined the committee system. The ruling party meet in caucus informally before the official council or committee meetings, to agree what decisions they support, and opposition parties meet in caucus to decide on their party line. One party domination is likely to remain the norm unless the electoral system for local government is changed to a proportional system, or unless it becomes a realistic possibility that independent, non-party people who stand for election as Mayors (see below) can win. (In fact two out of seven Mayors elected in May 2002 stood as independents.) Generally, however, for the majority party the prospect of loss of a majority at the next election is remote and hence public accountability is relatively weak.

The committee system attracted a range of criticisms. The absence of a separation of function between the de facto controlling party and opposition parties meant that political scrutiny and accountability were weak. Opposition councillors spent their time on committees on which they could have little influence, rather than on scrutiny and holding the majority to account and acting as 'champions' and representatives of their wards. In the relatively rare hung councils where no one party had a majority, decision-making was hampered by the fact that deals had to be struck between coalition partners. This meant that responsibility was blurred. And in such councils frequently the officers acquired substantial de facto power.

These concerns about the accountability and effectiveness of decision-making in local government led the government to lay the foundations for adoption of alternative executive arrangements, in which an executive is separated from the whole council, in the Local Government Act 2000. This measure requires county, county borough, district, and London borough councils to consider which of three possible new executive arrangements they wish to adopt. (Parish and community councils are exempted, and small shire districts can opt for alternative arrangements.) Theoretically these new arrangements will sharpen accountability and increase the capacity of opposition party groups to scrutinize the work of the executive. The new arrangements are currently being phased in and it will be some time before their effectiveness can be assessed.

Under the new provisions councils have to consult their citizens as to their preferred executive model, and submit their plans to the Secretary of State. Their proposals must set out the functions for which the executive will be responsible (some functions may remain for the whole council) and the overview and scrutiny committees and details of transitional arrangements. If they propose to adopt a Mayor and Executive or Mayor and Council Manager model (see below) a binding referendum must be held. If the Leader and Cabinet model is proposed no referendum is necessary—this is in effect the default model. There are three options for the new executive arrangements.

The Leader and Cabinet system

Under the Leader and Cabinet system the full council elects a Leader who then either appoints an executive drawn from the council (the strong Leader model) or heads an executive appointed by and drawn from the council (the weak Leader model). The executive and the committees may be drawn from one party. Membership of the executive is likely to be a full-time, salaried occupation.

This Cabinet model is the closest to the previous system, and it formalizes the influence of the majority party in the council. In fact it may well increase the power of the majority party—both the party caucus of council members and the local party organizations, for the Leader and members of the executive will be even more dependent on their parties than hitherto if they stand to lose their livelihoods as a result of decisions taken, in reality, by the parties. To counteract the opacity that could result from this change the executive is obliged to record its decisions and the reasons for them, and a 'proper officer' of the council has the legal responsibility to see that this is done.

The change is supposed to improve the capacity of 'backbench' council members to scrutinise decision-making. Thus the legislation provides for the establishment of overview and scrutiny committees. These are modelled on select committees of the House of Commons. Like them, their membership will reflect the balance of the parties on the council, so they will be dominated by the executive's party. But members of the executive will be disqualified from membership of these committees. Their role is to scrutinize the discharge of executive functions and to make reports and recommendations to the authority or the executive about the discharge of their functions and on matters which affect the area or its inhabitants. Given that opposition parties are generally more suited to scrutinize decisions than members of the party of the executive there must be a question mark over how critical these committees, with a majority of members of the party of the executive, will be willing to be.

The unofficial networks in the system—the influence of party over councillors—could easily subvert the reforms. The Labour Party sought to prevent this by producing new model standing orders for Labour Party groups, which prohibit the whipping of members on scrutiny and overview committees (Leigh, 2000, 236n). It is not known how effective this will be, or how the other parties will deal with the whipping issue.

As far as the legal position of individual councillors and the whipping system and party discipline is concerned, the courts have sought a subtle balance between allowing parties to put pressure on councillors to influence their voting, while also maintaining that it is the legal—common law—duty of each councillor to consider the issues involved and reach his or her own decision (see Leigh, 2000, ch. 6). In *R. v. Waltham Forest Borough Council ex parte Baxter* ([1988] 2 WLR 257) for instance, the Court of Appeal held that the existence of party whips did not invalidate decision-making by the council, though party rules requiring a councillor to resign his seat if he wished to oppose the party group would be objectionable as interfering with the councillor's independent exercise of judgement. On this approach, if a party group removed a Leader of a council or (if the weak Leader model were in operation) if the group removed members of the executive, for not following the party line, they might be acting unlawfully, especially since the decision would also deprive the members of their livelihood. This common law principle follows the Burkean model of the independent representative. It is reflected and reinforced in the model principles for good conduct approved by Parliament in spring 2001, that govern the conduct of members. These include a duty of personal judgement (see further below).

These new arrangements have been criticized for reducing the influence of members of opposition parties, since, not being members of decision-making committees, they no longer have any input into actual decision-making and only have a scrutiny role after decisions have been taken. They have less access to relevant information than under the previous committee-based system and it is suggested that their commitment to the work may be less because they have no direct input into decision-making (Cole, 2001).

Some Liberal Democrat-controlled local authorities have established Area Committees, as permitted under the Local Government Act 2000. These consist of all the councillors for the area, and they are the main decision-making bodies of the Council for the area on a day-by-day basis, so that the Executive is in effect the strategic body for the Council. These Area Committees can be more aware of and responsive to the needs and wishes of those living and working in the area than the full Council can be, and these committees may permit councillors of all parties to participate in local decisions.

Mayor and Executive model

Under the 'Mayor and Executive' (commonly referred to as 'Mayor and Cabinet') model a directly elected Mayor appoints an executive of two or more councillors. The executive and the committees may be drawn from one party only. The Mayor is expected to be full time and will be paid. In Lewisham, for instance, the Mayor's special responsibility allowance is £56,800, and other members of the executive receive more modest but not insignificant payments.

This model is broadly based on the practice in urban areas in the USA, France, Italy, and Germany. This is close to the model adopted for Greater London (see Chapter 15). The theory behind it is that a powerful position of Mayor—and an attractive salary—will attract high calibre candidates and should generate greater public interest and thus higher turnout in elections than the old committee-based system. The Mayor should derive authority to enable him or her to push forward a programme from the fact of election. On this model the Mayor formulates his or her policy framework proposals and budget and submits them for approval to the whole council, which may propose amendments or reject them, normally by a two-thirds majority. The Mayor's proposed appointments of a chief executive and chief officers would be subject to agreement by the full council.

The main concerns under this system are that the scrutiny committees will not in practice make information available to all councillors and the public, and that the considerable power concentrated in the hands of the Mayor may open up opportunities for corruption and patronage. The arrangements for promoting high standards of conduct—see below—may be crucial here.

A number of referendums on the introduction of elected Mayors were held in 2001 and 2002. Out of a total of eleven Mayors elected in May and October 2002, five were independent, four were Labour, one was Conservative, and one was a Liberal Democrat. If a pattern of election of independents were to emerge, this would present yet another example of the public looking for alternatives to party control in constitutional arrangements—examples noted in previous chapters include the election of an independent Mayor for London, the unpopularity of Labour's choice for the London Mayoral candidate, the unpopularity of Labour's choices of leaders for the Assembly for Wales and in Scotland, and the formation of coalitions in Wales and Scotland.

Mayor and Council Manager model

Under the Mayor and Council Manager model (which has not so far been adopted by any local authority) the council would be managed by a directly elected Mayor and a Council Manager appointed by the council. The Mayor would be responsible for overall political leadership and proposing the broad policy framework of the council and the budget. The full council would be responsible for approving the policy framework and the budget, and members could propose amendments. The Council Manager would develop and implement policy and the budget under the guidance of the Mayor. The Mayor would have less power under this model than under the elected Mayor and Executive model, and the Council Manager would have very considerable power. There is a much greater separation between the council and the Mayor here and thus the power of the parties might be reduced.

The role of the Department for Transport, Local Government, and the Regions

The Department for Transport, Local Government, and the Regions has issued a large number of 'guidance' documents for local authorities on the adoption of new executive arrangements. The Department has also made elaborate regulations on the subject. As of March 2002, for instance, nineteen statutory instruments had been made, on topics ranging from the making of standing orders through the conduct of referendums to Members' allowances to terms of office and casual vacancies. These SIs and guidance documents provide strong examples of the increasingly elaborate juridification of government that has taken place over the last two decades, for the reasons outlined in Chapter 1—politicization and loss of trust—together with awareness of dislike of party political activism on the part of many voters.

Good Governance in Local Government: The Hull Experience

The Audit Commission (AC) has power under section 19 Local Government Act 1999 to recommend government intervention in local authorities that are failing. The Commission recommended in July 2002 that the government intervene in Kingston upon Hull City Council because of failures in its corporate governance (Audit Commission, July 2002). The intervention options are: imposing a timetable and action plans, bringing in management consultants, establishing a supervisory board, or bringing in new management. The AC report illustrates a number of points about good governance generally and in local government in particular.

Hull City Council had not been short of money—it had sold off a share of its telephone business for £263 million in 1999 and was regarded as the richest council in the country at that time. The AC found that Hull had misspent this windfall. Unlike many local authorities, then, Hull's problems did not stem from underfunding.

The city had been under the control of one party (Labour) for sixty years until the elections in 2002 produced a hung council. The Liberal Democrats then took over with the support of independents. A point here is that single-party rule over many years can lead to complacency and inefficiency, lax procedures, and poor relationships between members and officials. The use of the first past the post system in council elections makes one-party rule over long periods more possible than a proportional system would do.

The AC found a large number of failings in the corporate governance of the council, as is reflected in their many recommendations. These included that the council should reach a unified strategy in relation to housing and the provision of other services to residents, and make internal improvements to the effectiveness of its leadership, management systems, and culture. To act effectively in providing community leadership, the council needed to promote public debate about various problem areas and encourage tenant groups to take a greater part in decision-making about housing. It needed to implement e-government measures, securing benefits for service users, to reform management and clarify relations between officers and between officers and members, to improve corporate controls and thus risk management, to build leadership capacity, and become involved in national networks in order to increase its awareness of good practice.

The AC report on Hull shows that councils can fail; electoral accountability alone may not be a sufficient guarantee of good governance and good performance by councils; much depends on the electoral system used and whether a ruling group feels under threat of losing its control; leadership and comity between those involved in government are essential to good governance; public participation and involvement are important.

Standards of Conduct in Local Government

Local government is one area of public life in which there has for long been, and still is believed to be, corruption (see discussion in Chapter 3). This has resulted in a climate of suspicion of local government, loss of trust, and a succession of statutory provisions, regulations and codes of conduct, resulting in elaborate juridification of political activity in local government. Corruption of various kinds has been a feature in particular of relations between developers and the council to whom they apply for planning permission. In December 1993 in a survey of fraud and corruption in local government the Audit Commission warned that the creation of an anti-fraud culture and environment had been 'rendered more demanding and complex by recent changes to the nature and operation of local government services. Many of these changes, such as the delegation of financial and management responsibilities, while contributing to improved quality of services, have increased the risks of fraud and corruption occurring' (quoted in Doig and Wilson, 1998). Doig and Wilson comment that 'The belief that public office may be used to pursue personal ambition and the perks of the job, that risks may be taken with public funds and that the ends justify the means has turned the public service ethos on its head' (p. 274).

There have been a number of prosecutions of councillors and those who have offered bribes under the Prevention of Corruption Acts. The criminal law is supplemented by rules about the disclosure of interests by councillors. There have also been other examples of serious political misconduct on the part of councillors, and in some cases of council officers, most notably recently the scandal about the policy of 'homes for votes' in Westminster council culminating in the House of Lords decision in *Porter v. Magill* ([2001] UKHL 67; [2002] 2 WLR 37, HL). In that case Dame Shirley Porter, leader of Westminster Council, and her deputy leader had promoted a policy to sell council-owned property in marginal wards to new residents who, as owner occupiers, would be likely to vote Conservative. It was held that it is unlawful for councillors to promote and implement a policy directed to the pursuit of party political electoral advantage and not to the achievement of proper housing objectives; the two councillors in question knew that it was unlawful, and they were therefore guilty of willful misconduct under section 20 of the Local Government Finance Act 1982; they were required to make good the consequent loss to the council. The loss in that case was over £26 million. (Surcharge has since been abolished.) It will be remembered from discussion in Chapter 3 of the scandal in New

South Wales in 1988 about the appointment of a retired MP to a lucrative public post (Philp, 1997) that there are differing approaches to politics and ethics. On one view— rejected in that case—politics must necessarily involve the exercise of patronage and other forms of partiality. On another view the partial exercise of official functions consti- tutes a breach of trust. The decision in *Porter v. Magill* reasserts the principle of trust and altruism in politics. There are, then, statutory provisions about standards of conduct in local government, and some breaches attract criminal penalties and obligations to make good any losses. But large parts of the regulation of standards in local government are not primarily the concern of the courts, and reliance is placed on 'soft law', internal mechanisms.

As a response to concerns about standards of conduct in local government, in 1985 the government appointed a Committee of Inquiry into the Conduct of Local Authority Business under David Widdicombe QC. The Committee considered a number of then controversial activities by local government. These included the publication of politically partisan propaganda, allegations of improper indoctrination in schools, the practice of 'twin tracking' (by which an officer employed by council A would be given paid leave by that council to enable him or her to sit as an elected councillor on council B, where both were controlled by the same political party), preferential treatment of political sympa- thizers in housing allocations and appointments, and refusals to contract with those whose opinions the council disapproved of. The Committee produced its interim report on *Local Authority Publicity* in 1986, in which it recommended legislation to prohibit local authority publicity of a party political nature. The government responded by secur- ing the passage of the Local Government Act 1986 which prohibited the publication of 'any material which, in whole or in part, appears to be designed to affect public support for a political party' (for a discussion see Gyford et al., 284–8). This marked the beginning of a period of increasing legal regulation of the political activity of local government. (The original Act had to be amended by the Local Government Act 1988 to achieve the government's purpose. This illustrates the difficulties inevitably experienced in trying to reduce constitutional conventions to the form of statutory rules and the inadequacy of parliamentary scrutiny of bills.)

In its main report (Cmnd. 9797, 1986) the Widdicombe Committee found many of the allegations about improper politicization in local government at that time to be exagger- ated, but recommended nevertheless that steps should be taken to protect the older conventions about non-partisan, neutral local government administration by depoliticis- ing some aspects of local government activity (see Gyford et al., 1990, especially ch. 8). The Government accepted some of the Committee's recommendations (see Cm. 433, 1988) and introduced legislation in the 1988–9 session of Parliament to deal with the problems. The use of patronage for political purposes was stopped by the provision that all appointments are to be made on merit, which implied that it would be unlawful to take account of a person's political activities or affiliations in reaching decisions about appointments (Local Government and Housing Act 1989, s. 7). An important exception to this general rule was that a maximum of three appointments may be made for the purpose of providing political assistance to members of political groups in the authority, provided that no such appointments may be made unless each of the three largest groups is to have such an adviser (s. 9). This then has been another area where there has been increased juridification of political activity, including the definition and regulation of political groups.

The Committee on Standards in Public Life has also examined the question whether the arrangements for securing standards of conduct in local government were appropriate. In its Third Report, *Standards of Conduct in Local Government in England, Scotland and Wales*, Cm. 3702, 1997, the Committee recommended major reforms in the ethical framework for councillors and officers. These were largely accepted by the government in *Modern Local Government: In Touch with the People* (Cm. 1014, 1998, ch. 6). The Local Government Act 2000 contains new provisions about standards in local government. The former National Code of Local Government Conduct has been replaced by locally adopted codes, each containing General Principles of Conduct common to the codes of all councils which have been approved by the Secretary of State and endorsed by Parliament. The General Principles are: selflessness, honesty and integrity, objectivity, accountability, openness, personal judgement, respect for others, duty to uphold the law, stewardship, and leadership. The Committee on Standards in Public Life's view was that councils needed to 'own' their codes and that they were more likely to adhere to codes which they had themselves adopted than codes imposed on them, and so councils are required to adopt their own codes. In practice though the codes they adopt are based on the model approved by Parliament in the Local Authorities (Model Code of Conduct) Order 2001 (SI 3575). All councillors must agree to abide by their council's code, failing which they will be legally disqualified from membership of the authority.

There are to be local Standards Committees for all authorities except parish councils, composed of a combination of councillors and independent members, with advisory, training, and monitoring functions. This arrangement was recommended by the Committee on Standards in Public Life (Third Report, Cm. 3702, 1997, recommendations 27–30).

Each council establishes and maintains a public register of Members' interests; a Monitoring Officer will keep the register up to date. Failure to register is no longer a criminal offence. Disciplinary arrangements will be via an internal council Standards Committee for each council with one or two independent members and supported by the council's Monitoring Officer. The Standards Committee may reprimand councillors, subject to an appeal to the Standards Board for England. This Board may receive complaints from the public, from councillors, or from the Monitoring Officer. It may refer the matter back to the council for a report, pass the complaint to the police, the auditor or the Commissioner for Local Administration where appropriate, or commission an external report by an independent panel. The panel has the power to make a judgement on the matter and to give a public censure, or to suspend or disqualify for up to five years the person against whom the complaint was made. There is an appeal to a National Board or Tribunal and the possibility of judicial review of either the decision of the Standards Board or of the National Board or Tribunal. This is a very elaborate structure.

Many councillors, especially in town or parish councils, find the duties of disclosure unduly intrusive in their private lives, and a number resigned from their councils in the spring of 2002, when the code provisions came into effect. Their comment was that their councils often had minute budgets of only a few thousand pounds and that the duty to register interests was disproportionate given the very small scope for them to benefit themselves or those they knew financially in their positions.

There is also a code of conduct for council employees under the 2000 Act, which is part of the terms and conditions of their employment. The Local Government Association has produced a Model Employee's Code which has been approved by the Secretary of State and endorsed by Parliament. It is to be enforced through the staff disciplinary procedures, and employment law. The rule that certain posts are 'politically restricted', i.e. that certain employees may not engage in political activity, which was introduced in response to the Widdicombe Report, has been retained, though the threshold salary level will be increased.

There has then been a strong trend towards the juridification of conduct in local government in the last twenty years or so. In 2002 the Public Administration Select Committee (HC 263, 2001–2) recommended further juridification in the form of a statutorily backed Public Service Code which would set out in simple and explicit terms the requirements of the public service ethos (see Chapter 3). Principles on which the code would be based include quality requirements. Public services should 'match in quality the best private-sector equivalents, including standards of customer care', for instance. They would be made binding not only on local authorities and other public bodies providing public services but also, via contractual terms, on private sector bodies contracting with local authorities and others for the provision of such services. The government rejected these proposals in November 2002 (HC 61, 2002–3).

From Politics to Juridification in Local Government

Loughlin (1996, 2000*b*) has shown how the relationship between central and local government was an informal network-based one until the reforms that were introduced by statute in the 1980s and 1990s. Local authorities derived, and still derive, their powers from statute, but until the 1980s these were predominantly facilitative rather than regulatory (though many powers were exercisable only with ministerial consent. Some of these controls were removed by the Local Government, Planning and Land Act 1980). Central government was in practice content to leave it to local authorities, using their statutory powers, to determine how best to discharge their functions locally. This altered with the period of confrontation between central and local government after the general election of 1979. The Conservative government was intent on changing the functions, operations, and finances of local government and this was resisted by many Labour-controlled, and other, authorities. The network broke down and a highly regulated set of relationships was put in place. Local authorities' powers and functions were reduced in ways alluded to above—the local management of schools, and removal of discretion over council housing, and the transfer of the housing stock to housing associations or to tenants who exercised the right to buy, are only two examples of many. Authorities' discretion in the spending of their grants from government and other income was progressively removed by capping. The result has been steadily increasing juridification of the relationship between central and local government and of local government activity generally, through statutes, statutory instruments, codes, circulars, and guidance in White Papers.

The regulatory character of local government legislation has given rise to litigation between central and local government (e.g. *R. v. Secretary of State for the Environment, ex parte Brent LBC* [1982] QB 593, a dispute about the determination of the level of grant from central government to the local authority), and between local authorities (e.g. *Bromley LBC v. Greater London Council* [1983] 1 AC 768: Bromley challenged the size of the GLC precept on it on the grounds that its 'fare's fair' transport policy was *ultra vires*. The challenge was upheld on the grounds that the policy was not 'economic' as required by the Act. A revised scheme was later approved by the Divisional Court). The courts have been called upon to adjudicate on issues which would formerly have been resolved without recourse to law and the courts, and they have attracted considerable criticism for the ways in which they have dealt with these cases. This was particularly the case in *Bromley v. GLC*, when the quashing of the GLC precept suggested that the judges did not understand the issues raised by transport policy and were too willing to take the side of ratepayers as against the general public interest and the interests of travellers.

On occasions the courts have refused to intervene, recognizing that the relationships are best regarded as informal networks rather than rights-based relationships, and that the issues are, often, non-justiciable. Thus in *Nottinghamshire CC v. Secretary of State for the Environment* ([1986] AC 240) the House of Lords overruled a Court of Appeal decision to quash the Secretary of State's expenditure target powers, exhorting local authorities to 'bite on the bullet and not seek to persuade the courts to absolve them from compliance with the Secretary of State's guidance' (per Lord Templeman). Loughlin comments that the decision articulated the values of the traditional framework relationship between central and local government recognizing that central–local relations were essentially an internal-rule game (2000*b*, 153). However, he notes, the court failed to recognize that the framework was disintegrating, and something else needed to be put in its place. The legislation on local government that has been passed since 1997 is seeking to replace the old system, but in an eclectic and very controlling way.

Summary and Conclusions

The legal status of local government in England and Wales does not meet the requirements of the European Charter on Local Government: local authorities do not have adequate financial resources of their own—some 75 per cent comes from or via central government. Their powers are undermined by administrative action by central government, for instance various powers to take over local authority functions or substitute new administrations. They have limited freedom of choice as to the manner of provision of services. These provisions undermine the pluralistic and responsiveness rationales for local government. On the other hand local authorities have broadened powers of general competence—to promote general well-being—under the 2000 Act reforms, and some increased freedom of choice, within prescribed possible options, over their internal organization. But they will continue to rely substantially on central government grants. In sum, since the early 1980s, even to an extent before then, there has been increasing legal regulation of local government activity and government-imposed limits on their fiscal autonomy, to the point where the system has become substantially one of local adminis- tration rather than local government. Governmental powers to control and regulate local government represent a major undermining of local democracy and they demonstrate a lack of faith on the part of the government in election as a means of securing good local government. But this lack of confidence is understandable.

Election has not provided the degree of accountability that is necessary to secure a high degree of responsiveness, efficiency, and openness in local authority operations. This is partly because party support tends to be geographically concentrated, so that in many areas there is little prospect of the majority party losing control—as has been the case in Hull, for example. Turnout has been low (see Chapter 7). A change to a proportional election system—STV would be most appropriate in my view—would make coalition arrangements more likely and this prospect could increase interest in elections and thus turnout (see Chapter 7). However, the introduction of PR would be unlikely, on its own, to expose local authorities to sufficient pressure to perform effectively and openly to justify removal of much of the regulation to which they have been subjected in recent years. (In any event, PR in local government is not supported by Labour or the Conservative Party, and it is unlikely to be introduced in the foreseeable future.)

If local authorities were less reliant on block grants and other grants from central government and had to raise larger proportions of their revenue from their own tax base, their electorates might become more interested in this area of activity, and turnout and local accountability might increase. But from the government's point of view this and the deregulation of local authorities would be a high-risk strategy: public services for which local authorities are responsible might well not improve if local authorities were given additional freedoms, and the government, committed to improving public services, would take part of the blame. In any event the most needy local authorities would not be in a position to raise a significant proportion of the finance they need from their own areas. I consider it most unlikely that local authorities will be freed unconditionally from the strict regulation and financial control to which they are subject by any government, of whatever party.

The Labour government's legislation since 1997 has sought to create a new, 'modern' role for local government as providing leadership for the local community and promot- ing sustainable development. But these arrangements hardly reduce the juridification of relationships between central and local government. The tradition of informal network- ing and trust between central and local government that enabled the previous loose framework system to work until the late 1970s has not been reinstated. The arrangements under the 2000 Act do however enable the government to reduce the level of regulation of successful authorities, though on strict conditions, an indication that as trust is recreated by authorities a more informal network relationship may become possible again.

The reforms to local government have sought to promote democratic mechanisms in a range of ways. The hope is that the new executive structures will sharpen up account- ability and provide greater transparency, thereby increasing local interest in local government and leading to increased turnout. This may be seen as an aspect of the policy to 'reconnect' government with the electorate, which became a particularly obvious necessity after the low turnout in the 2001 general election. Without proportional representation, however, the reconnection is likely to be limited. The reforms also seek to develop, in parallel with representative democracy, local participatory and consultative democratic processes. The provisions for referendums are an example, but so too are the well-being powers which will involve local individuals and organizations both voluntary and commercial in the delivery of services and debates about how they may be improved. This approach in turn is a development in the concept of citizenship beyond the limited function of voting to more active involvement by individuals and the voluntary sector in the local communities. It remains to be seen how effective this will be in practice.

There is considerable scepticism about the extent to which new executive arrangements will in fact sharpen up the scrutiny of local government decision-making and improve the accountability of decision-makers. The alternative, changing to a system of proportional representation, would make it more likely that party control would change at elections and that coalitions would be more frequent and this could serve to sharpen accountability to the electorate. This option is not on the realistic political agenda for local government, no doubt in part because the introduction of PR at this level would make the arguments against first past the post for the House of Commons less convincing and the government is not ready for a commitment to a change for the Commons. (PR was introduced for Scotland partly because this was what the Scottish Constitutional Convention desired, and for Northern Ireland because of the particular problems in the province, so the granting of proportional elections to those bodies—and to Wales—did not necessarily imply that it would be appropriate for the House of Commons.)

Overall, the fact that local authorities are elected is coming to be of minor significance. The ways in which they are controlled by the setting of objectives, targets, and standards, the auditing of their performance and publication of league tables, and possible takeovers are mirrored in many unelected bodies, including quangos (see Chapter 17), parties to partnership agreements, executive agencies, and many other bodies delivering public services. Local government is but one layer of many institutions that are being subjected to a process of homogenisation of the ways in which public-sector bodies are expected to work and the ways in which public services are expected to be delivered. The rationales for local government that were set out at the start of this chapter have not been regarded as persuasive by governments concerned to raise standards of public service and to take responsibility for the effectiveness upon themselves rather than leave it to the electorate.

17

Quangos

In this chapter we consider the position of the many public bodies which are not subject to direction by elected bodies such as Ministers, Parliament, the devolved bodies, or local authorities. They include several bodies which we have encountered in previous chapters, for instance the Committee on Standards in Public Life, the Royal Commission on House of Lords Reform, the Civil Service Commissioners, the Electoral Commission, the Audit Commission, the Information Commissioner, Regional Development Agencies, and the Standards Board for England. These bodies, commonly referred to as quangos (for quasi-autonomous non-governmental organizations) are very diverse (see Barker, 1982). There are many of them and they spend a large amount of public money each year. As of April 2000 there were 297 executive non-departmental public bodies (NDPBs), and 536 advisory ones. The number fluctuates, particularly the number of advisory bodies, which may be appointed for a particular purpose and disbanded once their job is complete. But in addition to the NDPBs there is a large number of other quangos.

A difficulty in this area is trying to define or even recognize a quango when one sees one. They are rather more difficult than elephants in this respect. The government's annual publication *Public Bodies* includes a list of quangos and their functions, though the list is not claimed to be exhaustive (see Weir and Hall, 1994). The Select Committee on Public Administration in its report *Mapping the Quango State* (2001) adopted as a definition 'all bodies responsible for developing, managing or delivering public services or policies, or for performing public functions, under governing bodies with a plural membership of wholly or largely appointed or self-appointing persons' (para. 5). This definition included Task Forces and local public spending bodies.

The fact that it is difficult to define these bodies need not detain us too long. For our purposes the point is that they are bodies which are supposed to be acting in the public interest and are publicly funded, and they are not elected nor directly politically accountable. It is these characteristics which cause problems in our constitutional system since, in the absence of accountability directly to Parliament or to Parliament via Ministers, there is a concern that they cannot be trusted to act in the public interest and not to abuse their powers. In other liberal constitutional systems where bodies are not accountable to Ministers or to Parliament alternative or supplementary accountability mechanisms have been developed. These include—to use the terminology of accountability adopted in Chapter 3, legal accountability, via judicial review, which involves treating the 'rules' which these bodies are supposed to observe as legal rather than political or administrative rules; accountability to auditors—the National Audit Office or the ombudsman, for instance; requirements of openness towards 'stakeholders'; and opportunities for participation in decision-making on the part of those affected by the activities of these bodies and their representative organizations—a form of public accountability.

Classifying Quangos

Quangos may be classified in various ways. The usual classification is: public corporations and nationalized industries; health bodies; and non-departmental public bodies (NDPBs). NDPBs are of four types: executive, advisory, tribunals, and Boards of Visitors to penal establishments. (In fact tribunals are rather different from the other three groups because they act judicially and the case for them being immunized from political and some public pressures is particularly strong: they are better treated as courts. Their decisions are normally appealable to the courts or subject to judicial review by the Administrative Court, so that legal accountability is in place. Their administration is normally the responsibility of the Court Service, an Executive Agency in the Lord Chancellor's Department, so that a mechanism of accountability is available on that side of their operations.)

It can be difficult to classify a particular body as a quango rather than, for instance, an ad hoc committee or working party. Certain bodies which might be thought to fall into this category are not regarded as quangos. For instance executive agencies (see Chapter 12) are technically in government departments, and their staff are civil servants, for whom Ministers are accountable to Parliament. They are not therefore regarded as quangos, whose staff are normally not civil servants and for whom Ministers are not accountable to Parliament. There are, however, exceptions to every rule, and the staff of the Health and Safety Executive and the Advisory, Conciliation and Arbitration Service are civil servants, but these are non-departmental public bodies, no Minister is accountable for them to Parliament, and thus they fall into the category of quangos. A private body that is charged with performing some task for the government, as some charities are (for instance, the National Society for the Prevention of Cruelty to Children has statutory powers to institute prosecutions for cruelty to children; housing associations often work closely with local authorities) would not be regarded as a quango. Nor are private contractors running prisons, for instance, or engaged under a public-private partnership or a private finance initiative arrangement, regarded as quangos.

The points we can draw from this are, first, that there is no real system in the quango arrangements, second, that there is no firm line between the public and the private spheres, and third, that it is broadly agreed that a body that is public (not a simple concept), if it is not covered by the conventions of Ministerial responsibility to Parliament or some other form of strong democratic accountability, needs to be made accountable in some other way or ways for its activity.

Quangos are not of only marginal importance in our constitutional arrangements. Overall it has been estimated that there are some 105,000 people appointed to quangos—plus their employed staff. There are over 1,000 NDPBs and boards of visitors, plus over 4,000 local spending bodies. Quangos have been estimated to spend over £18 billion per annum of funds voted by Parliament. Their accountability is thus of great importance (Select Committee on Public Administration, Sixth Report, 1998–9, HC 209, *Quangos*).

Rationales for Quangos

Before considering the problems raised by quangos we need to bear in mind why they exist. Quangos have been deliberately set up or left at arm's length from government to protect them and their activity from political interference, or to enable them to function effectively outside a department or a local authority. The need for them to be immunized from political interference may be dictated by the nature of their activity. The funding of universities and research, for instance, or the regulation of health and safety, or of utilities, or of AS and A-level examinations may require an absence of political interference in order to promote public confidence that the function will be discharged objectively and not for partisan or party political advantage or in breach of the laid down criteria for the function.

Quangos are often performing highly specialized functions, whereas government departments have a wide range of responsibilities. An organization may be more effective if it is composed of members and staff with the required expertise operating in the way best suited to the task, rather than in a complex government department. This is particularly the case with advisory bodies such as the Law Commissions and the Royal Commission on Environmental Pollution and with executive bodies like regulators. Quangos, if their workloads and staff complement are small, can be less bureaucratic in the ways in which they operate and have smaller bureaucracies than would be possible inside government departments. They are often effective and economical providers of services. They can be set up rapidly to solve a problem (as was the Committee on Standards in Public Life in 1995).

Quangos can also contribute positively to the democracy of the system, despite the fact that they are unelected and are immunized from party politics. Some quangos are designed so as to involve large numbers of 'ordinary people', non-politicians and non-professionals, in public life. Some tribunals include lay members working with a legally qualified chairman—employment tribunals and the Value Added Tax tribunal are examples. Some quangos are required to have, or choose to have, users' committees or advisory boards. In their introduction to *How to Make Quangos Democratic* (1997), Flinders et al. pinpoint participation and accountability (see below) as two paramount principles. The reference to such arrangements as forming part of a democratization programme illustrates how democracy is coming to be accepted as more complex than a requirement that elected people should be responsible for government.

The quango arrangements raise issues to do with democratic accountability, governance, and citizenship. In some circles there is a sense of indignation that quangos exist and have supplanted Parliament and government. Lord Smith of Clifton, in a House of Lords debate on the relationship between Parliament and the executive, spoke of 'a myriad of persons and agencies that have mushroomed over the past 20 years or so. These comprise what I have called the *demi-monde* of government. They are sometimes accorded the more sanitized term of "policy networks". They are part of the British state that is characterized as tentacular government' (HL Deb., 18 July 2001, vol. 626, col. 1514). But it is generally accepted that quangos are inevitable and can be positively desirable in an advanced Western system, and the main issue is to 'democratize' them in a range of ways. This will form the focus of much of the discussion in the rest of this chapter.

Accountability

The ways in which quangos, like other bodies, are or could be held accountable, can be classified in various ways. Sir Leo Pliatzky in his report on *The Governance of Public Bodies* (Cm. 3557, 1997) identified five ways in which such bodies are accountable: upward accountability, responsiveness, openness, complaints procedures, and consultative arrangements. To these should of course be added legal accountability, in that the terms of reference and the powers of these bodies set the limits to their powers, and excess of power or abuse of power—including breach of human rights requirements—may be judicially reviewed or may even give rise to liability in damages.

The government looked into ways in which the accountability of quangos to Parliament could be improved in 1998, largely being concerned with the roles of Select Committees in relation to them. They recognized that the effectiveness of ministerial accountability could be reinforced when MPs and Select Committees scrutinise the work of quangos and ask effective questions (*Quangos: opening the doors*, Cabinet Office, 1998, para. 5). The Select Committee on Public Administration then produced a series of reports on quangos in the 1997–2001 Parliament (see for instance the Sixth Report of 1998–9 *Quangos*, HC 209 and the Fifth Report of 2000–1 *Mapping the Quango State*, HC 367) and these elicited some positive responses from government, regarding appointments, for instance. But the *Quangos* report found that the job of monitoring quangos and holding them to account is far too great for a Select Committee—and in any event many quangos are not 'sponsored' by a government department but operate locally or regionally (see below), and thus fall outside the scope of accountability to Parliament. The *Mapping the Quango State* report (discussed at some length below) highlighted ways in which quangos could be made accountable other than via the House of Commons Select Committees.

The Hansard Society Commission on Parliamentary Scrutiny, in its report *The Challenge for Parliament* (2001), acknowledged that bodies such as the utility regulators, inspectorates such as Ofsted (responsible for school inspections), and the Information Commissioner are usually formally accountable by statute through Ministers to Parliament via the publication of annual reports and appearance before Select Committees. But they noted that in practice neither House gives much priority to scrutinizing the work of these quangos. Their proposed solution was to increase the resources of the Select Committees substantially to enable them to scrutinize the work of these bodies (Hansard Society, paras. 1.25–1.37, and recommendations 18 and 19). This is not, however, one of the core functions of the Select Committees under the 2002 reforms (see Chapter 9).

Many quangos *substitute* for parliamentary scrutiny of the activities for which they have responsibility. They are only notionally complementing parliamentary scrutiny, since in practice Parliament does not concern itself with these matters.

In *The Challenge for Parliament* (2001) the Hansard Society Commission, urging that Parliament should place itself at the apex of the Constitution, recognized that alongside Parliament there exists 'an array of independent regulators, commissions and inspectors responsible for monitoring the delivery of government services'—all of these are quangos. Parliament should, the Hansard Commission suggested, provide a framework for their activity and use their investigations as the basis on which to hold Ministers to account (Hansard Commission, ch. 8). This is now one of the core functions of the Select Committees. The issue therefore is not only about holding quangos to account, but using the work of some quangos as a resource to enable Parliament to hold government to account. There is some formal recognition of the role that Parliament can play in this way, in the arrangements for the Commission for Health Care and Improvement, formed in 2002, to inspect NHS hospitals and report directly to Parliament, rather than to the Minister who would in turn report to Parliament, which has been the usual arrangement for inspectorates and regulators.

As far as finance is concerned concerns were expressed in many quarters from the mid-1990s about the lack of proper audit and control over some quangos. In 1998 the government undertook to impose rigorous financial management and policy reviews of NDPBs at least every five years, though this was subject to the consideration whether the full rigour of these reviews should apply to advisory NDPBs or whether a lighter touch might be applied to them. In response to concerns about accountability the remit of the Comptroller and Auditor-General was expanded in 2002 under the Government Resources and Accounts Act 2000, and the current position is that he is the auditor or has inspection rights over all executive non-departmental public bodies (see Sharman Report, *Holding to Account*, 2001; Cm. 5456, 2002). Formerly many of them had been subject only to audit by auditors appointed by their sponsoring Minister or auditors appointed by the bodies themselves.

Quangos and ombudsmen

The Parliamentary Commissioner for Administration's jurisdiction extends to many quangos. This arrangement has the advantage for Parliament that the PCA reports to Parliament and that relationship lends authority to the PCA's findings so that those about whom critical findings are made almost always comply with the PCA's recommendations as to how amends may be made.

At present not all quangos are subject to the jurisdiction of the PCA. The government proposed in 1998 (*Quangos: Opening the Doors*) that all executive quangos should be brought within the PCA's remit unless there were exceptional reasons for not doing so or they were already within the remit of another ombudsman. In its review of the ombudsman system in 2000 (see Cabinet Office *Review of the Public Sector Ombudsmen in England*, 2000; Seneviratne, 2000), the government proposed that the jurisdictional line should be drawn where a service is 'largely publicly funded, provides a service to the public and operates within a detailed specification by a public authority to a demanding performance requirement' (para. 5.9). This would in practice catch many executive quangos. The recommendation has not as yet been implemented.

Propriety and the Public Service Ethos

Propriety, or a sense of the values and behaviour appropriate to the public sector, is an issue in these bodies in relation to conduct, appointments, and financial matters. Mrs Thatcher as Prime Minister encouraged the appointment of people with a 'can do' approach to their work, and this included people committed to Conservative policy or donors to the Conservative Party. This had laid the government open to the allegation that appointments were being politicized and were not being made on merit. (Under the Labour government from 1997 such allegations persisted, and the term 'cronyism' was coined.) There was a series of scandals in the 1990s including fraud and mis-spending in the Welsh Development Agency and other quangos, and corruption and wrongdoing in local government.

In response to concerns about abuse of power by quangos in the early 1990s the government took steps to impose—administratively and not by statute—safeguards against abuse (see *The Governance of Public Bodies: A progress report*, 1997, Cm. 3557). These have taken the form of *Codes of Best Practice for Board Members of Public Bodies*, together with *Guidance*, which sets out public service values, the role of the chairman and responsibility of board members, handling conflicts of interest, openness and responsiveness, and accountability for public funds. All NDPBs should adopt a code of practice taking into account the *Guidance* and they should also adopt a code of conduct for their staff. However, this is not a statutory requirement, and although most NHS and Department of Health bodies implement these requirements others do not. Since 1999 registers of interests have been established for advisory bodies. The Freedom of Information Act and the Public Interest Disclosure Act (also known as the Whistleblower's Act) also provide some security against abuse of power by these bodies. The Committee on Standards in Public Life has been keeping up pressure on government to implement its recommendations on propriety, most of which have in fact by now been implemented. The proposals have been detailed and we shall briefly summarize the position below. (For a useful summary of progress on implementing recommendations up to September 2001 see Committee on Standards in Public Life *The First Seven Reports. A Review of Progress*, September 2001.)

The provisions about propriety noted so far have been introduced on a piecemeal basis, and there is at present no definitive code setting out the public-service ethos which all bodies providing public services, quangos among them, should subscribe to. The PASC recommended in 2002 that such a code should be produced (see Chapters 3 and 12). It would be approved by Parliament as part of a statutory framework, perhaps included in a Civil Service or Public Service Act, and it would bind not only public bodies providing public services but also contractors and private bodies doing so, who would be required to include in their contractual obligations the ethos duties (Seventh Report of the Select Committee on Public Administration, *The Public Service Ethos*, HC 263, 2001–2). The government, however, rejected these proposals (See HC 61, 2002–3).

Appointments

Appointees to quangos have been referred to—unfairly in my view—by one commentator as 'a kind of nomenklatura of fixers, henchmen and renegades' (Lord Smith of Clifton again, HL Deb., 18 July 2001, vol. 626, col. 1515). The comment indicates that there is a degree of public hostility to these bodies and their appointees.

The normal position in relation to appointments to NDPBs has been that Ministers in the sponsoring departments make the appointment under statutory powers. Many appointments are part time and they are either paid at a modest daily rate or unpaid. The terms of appointment to quangos vary, but generally these are for fixed terms, with the possibility of renewal. The sponsoring Minister may remove appointees either at will or for cause.

The Committee on Standards in Public Life investigated public appointments including appointments to quangos in its first and fourth reports (Cm. 2850, 1995, and 1997). It revisited some issues in its sixth report (Cm. 4557, 2000). In its first report the Committee noted that there was concern about the making of appointments to quangos, especially fears that they were not always made on merit and that political considerations were influential. The Committee agreed that these appointments should always be made on merit, but accepted that the overall composition of boards should represent an appropriate mix of relevant skills and background. This range should be clearly and publicly set out in job specifications. They felt that Ministers should continue to make board appointments to Executive NDPBs and NHS bodies, but an independent Public Appointments Commissioner should be appointed to regulate, monitor, and report on the public appointments process. The Commissioner should also recommend best practice and departments should have to justify any departures from it. There should be advisory panels to secure formal and impartial assessment of candidates, including an independent element. All candidates whom Ministers consider for all appointments should have been approved as suitable by an advisory panel (Committee on Standards in Public Life, first report, recommendations 33, 34). The first independent Commissioner for Public Appointments (CPA—another quango), Sir Leonard Peach, was appointed in December 1995. He was succeeded by Dame Rennie Fritchie in March 1999. The CPA issues a *Code of Practice for Public Appointment Procedures* which she updates periodically, and which sets out seven principles for public appointments: Ministerial responsibility for appointments, merit, independent scrutiny, equal opportunities, probity, openness and transparency, and proportionality. The Commissioner reports annually to Parliament.

The Committee on Standards in Public Life revisited the matter of appointments in its fourth report (1997). They emphasized that Departments and NDPBs should apply the principle of proportionality to the appointments procedures, though proportionality should not be an excuse for sloppy procedures. The CPA reported some concern that the code was being applied too mechanistically and was thus imposing unnecessary burdens in the form of advertising of posts, for instance. But the system was working well.

In its Sixth Report (Cm. 4557, 2000) the Committee on Standards in Public Life welcomed the forthcoming review of the operation of the system by the CPA, and her proposal to consider whether it would be appropriate to introduce a special category of appointments designated 'expert' to which different appointment rules should apply. The CPA also proposed to develop measures to improve the balance of representation on boards of public bodies and suggested she consider how to improve the range of candidates from which public appointees are drawn and how the concept of 'merit' can be reconciled with the need for a balanced and appropriately qualified representation. (We may note here that similar considerations of the need to define 'merit' and to balance the criterion of appointment on merit with achieving a balanced set of appointments has surfaced in debates about judicial appointments: see Chapter 18.)

The PASC in its report on *Quangos* (HC 209, 1998–9) noted that many people accept membership of the Board of a quango as a matter of public service, but they noted also that some of these appointments are well paid, and some confer benefits such as access to information, useful contacts and influence where the body is advising a Minister. They recognized concerns that Ministers may take the opportunity to appoint friends or political allies or, where an appointment is made by the Board itself, to limit the field for appointment to a narrow circle. The fact that such suspicions existed, whether well-founded or not, raised question marks over the legitimacy of the appointments and of the activity of the body itself. Further, the fact of the matter was, they felt, that appointees do tend to come from a limited segment of the population. The PASC revisited the issues in March 2002 in an inquiry into public appointments and patronage and questioned the CPA about progress in encouraging a wide range of applicants and securing that the merit principle is followed. She has taken a very proactive approach, encouraging a wide range of people especially women and members of ethnic minorities to apply for public appointments. In particular the question was raised whether it is sufficient to have a CPA monitoring the appointment process as opposed to an Appointments Commission which would actually make Public Appointments (see HC 686, 2001–2, Minutes of Evidence. There is already such a Commission for NHS Appointments). Such a move from Ministerial appointment is not currently high on the agenda. (At the time of writing the PASC has not yet published its report on public appointments and patronage.)

Some good governance points emerge from these reforms to the public appointments system. The existence of the Committee on Standards in Public Life has served to keep problems over public appointments in the public eye and has placed the government under pressure to respond when it might not otherwise have taken steps to meet concerns about appointments. The creation of the CPA as an independent monitoring body has had a positive effect in improving practice in departments by making the principles that should govern these appointments explicit. The CPA has brought forward proposals for improving the system as and when complaints about, for instance, proportionality, bureaucracy, delay in making appointments, and so on have surfaced. The non-statutory system of monitoring is flexible and enables concerns to be met reasonably promptly. However, many of the concerns about proportionality, bureaucracy, and delay flow from over-mechanistic and overstrict application of the principles and guidelines by civil servants fearful of being accused of breaking the guidelines. This has been a side effect of the loss of trust that flowed from the highly partisan adversarial period in politics in the 1980s and 1990s, which produced a distrustful press and political atmosphere and have led, inevitably, to juridification.

Connecting Quangos with the Public

In a House of Lords debate in 2001 on the relationship between Parliament and the executive—including quangos (HL Deb., 18 July 2001, vol. 626, cols. 1480–1553)—Baroness Williams commented that 'We must . . . recognize that the extraordinary proliferation of quangos, regulators, commissioners, and the like, over the domestic field for which Parliament was once responsible has created a feeling of distance between the electors and Parliament which is . . . serious' (col. 1481). The comment was made in the context of a debate about improving the accountability of government and other bodies to Parliament. However, it would be mistaken to assume that the problem of disconnection would be solved, or will be solved, by reassertion of parliamentary accountability. Other ways of reconnecting should be considered, as the *Quangos* report recommended (at paras. 49–54). Democratic alternatives or complements to parliamentary accountability include an increase in various forms of openness and consultation.

The authors of the Democratic Audit paper, *EGOTRIP* (1994, 30–1), Weir and Hall, proposed that consultation by quangos of the groups affected by their activities—their stakeholders—should be formalized. Comments and evidence received in response to consultation exercises should be published; there should be a general requirement that reasons should be given for decisions, and reasons would be expected to respond to points that had emerged from consultation. However, neither Parliament nor government has acted on this proposal. No formal systematic consultation requirements have been imposed. Some quangos do have statutory obligations to publicize proposals and consult—the Gas and Electricity Markets Authority under the Utilities Act 2000 for example. In judicial review the courts have developed requirements to give reasons for decisions which have an adverse impact on individuals in some situations, for instance if a decision casts a slur on their character (*Al Fayed* case) or it is aberrant (*Cunnigham* case: see Chapter 5). But these requirements are piecemeal only and there is as yet no general legally enforceable duty to give reasons for decisions.

The informal position on consultation in the UK may be compared with the American one. Under the US Administrative Procedure Act 1946, where agencies roughly equivalent to British quangos are making rules (as our regulators do, for instance) a formal procedure of notice and comment must be followed. The proposed rules have to be published in draft and comments are invited, there may be hearings and eventually the rules will be formally promulgated. The American system is highly formalized and there is little support for the adoption of a similar system in the United Kingdom, though the procedures of the Gas and Electricity Markets Authority noted above represent a step in that direction. The arguments against it are broadly based on proportionality—the delay and expense incurred by following formal procedures could well outweigh benefits from a more formal procedure on these lines. But the comparison does serve to highlight the extreme informality, by contrast, of the British arrangements (see Prosser, 1997, ch. 3; Ziamou, 1999).

In 1998 the government made, in *Quangos: Opening the Doors*, a range of recommendations as to how quangos should be more transparent and accessible. Advisory and executive quangos are expected to produce and make publicly available Annual Reports; where practicable an annual open meeting should be held; they should release summary reports of meetings; and they should invite evidence from members of the public on matters of public concern, possibly via the internet. They should consult their users on a wide range of issues by means of questionnaires, public meetings, or other forms of consultation, though proportionately to the size and resources of the body; these bodies should put much more information about themselves in the public domain, especially about their role and achievements. The government itself undertook to establish a central NDPB website containing summary information on all bodies, which would be linked to the bodies' own websites; the annual publication, *Public Bodies* which lists and describes quangos, would be put on the internet.

There are then a range of ways in which the operations of quangos could be made more open and participative and might thus reconnect with the public. It is not part of the purpose of this chapter to recommend particular mechanisms, but rather to point up that these pressures for change reflect public opinion and the views of politicians as to what democracy involves, and what is required to promote good governance where political accountability is weak.

Local and English regional quangos

Many executive and advisory quangos operate at local or regional rather than UK level. But not all of these are accountable to or have links with local or regional elected bodies. Regional development agencies (RDAs—see Chapter 15) and Regional Arts Boards (RABs) clearly also impact upon local government.

The Select Committee on Public Accounts (PASC) considered this aspect of quangos in its report *Mapping the Quango State* (HC 367, 2000–1). They felt that the need for local authorities to have an input into quango activity that affected their area was reinforced by the new leadership role that they have been given under the Local Government Act 2000 (see Chapter 16). But they found that local government was poorly represented on executive and advisory NDPBs and Task Forces. By contrast, local authorities do have a high profile on RDAs as well as being leading partners in regional chambers. And since 1999 all governing bodies of further education institutions are required to have at least three members nominated by local authorities. Health authorities, NHS trusts, and primary care groups are to be obliged to consult local authorities on major changes in policy, and their managers may be obliged to attend local authority scrutiny committees, if asked, twice a year. The PASC welcomed this new trend and recommended that a systematic drive should be made to improve the links between quangos at all levels and local authorities, supported by formal requirements if necessary. This was not with a view to giving local authorities a role in holding NDPBs and other local public bodies to account, but with a view to improving coordination and cooperation between local authorities and quangos—joined-up government in other words—and on the basis that the local authority's input and its knowledge of local needs could improve the quality of work of these quangos.

There has been a proliferation of regionally based quangos—including of course the RDAs, appointed by Ministers, and regional chambers established regionally, since 1997. All this notwithstanding the government committed itself in *Quangos: Opening the Doors* (1998, Cabinet Office) to reducing the number of NDPBs and ensuring that 'a new NDPB will only be set up where it can be demonstrated that this is the most cost-effective and appropriate means of carrying out the given function' (at para. 14). The PASC report noted that the policies towards quangos of central government departments, each pursuing their own objectives and initiatives, were uncoordinated and cumulatively damaging to local democracy, in so far as they undermined the powers and functions of local government (at para. 15). They were also concerned that these developments were not 'bedded down in democratic arrangements' and urged that in due course directly elected regional assemblies in England would have a role in imposing accountability on regional and local quangos and even on 'the quango state as a whole', implying that even national quangos might be called to account for the regional or local impact of their work.

A Democratic Audit of quango arrangements

In its report, *Mapping the Quango State* (HC 367, 2000–1), the PASC adapted the criteria developed by the Democratic Audit in its report, *Political Power and Democratic Control in Britain* (1999), to audit the accountability and openness of non-departmental public bodies. This PASC report is particularly interesting as an example of Parliament using a formula or methodology—in this case developed by the Democratic Audit (see Chapter 2)—to audit a particular area of policy, and as an example of the way in which academic research can produce toolkits and methodologies for use by Parliament and indeed other bodies. We shall therefore consider it at some length.

The criteria for the PASC audit of quangos included, for executive NDPBs:

1. Are they required to publish annual reports?
2. Are they required to publish annual accounts?
3. Are they subject to a full audit by the National Audit Office?
4. Are they under the jurisdiction of the Parliamentary Ombudsman or other Ombudsman?
5. Do they have their own complaints procedures?
6. Are they required to observe the Code of Practice on Access to Government Information?
7. Do they possess a register of Members' interests?
8. Are they required to allow the public to inspect a register of Members' interests?
9. Are they subject to a public right to attend board or committee meetings?
10. Are they required to release public reports of meetings?

11. Are they subject to a public right to inspect agendas of meetings?

12. Are they subject to a public right to see minutes of meetings?

13. Are they required to hold public meetings?

14. Do they maintain an Internet website?

15. Have they recently been subject to a quinquennial review?

The criteria adopted for advisory NDPBs were:

1. Are they required to publish annual reports?

2. Are they required to lay their annual reports before Parliament?

3. Are they required to allow the public to inspect a register of Members' interests?

4. Are they subject to a public right to inspect agendas of meetings?

5. Are they subject to a public right to see minutes of meetings?

6. Are they required to hold public meetings?

7. Are they required to observe the Code of Practice on Access to Government Information?

8. Are they required to consult outside interests?

9. Are they required to consult the general public?

10. Are they required to publish their advice to government?

11. Are they under the jurisdiction of the Parliamentary Ombudsman or other Ombudsmen?

12. Is the Government required to consult the NDPB before legislating in its area of interest?

13. Is the Government required to respond publicly to the NDPB's advice?

The PASC found that, by comparison with 1997, the proportion of executive NDPBs required to comply with these accountability measures had increased. Overall, though, the Committee found that they still complied with only just over half of these measures (52 per cent). The large increase in the proportion of executive NDPBs now subject to the jurisdiction of the Ombudsman—from 49 to 76 per cent—and progress in instituting complaints procedures (present for 74 per cent of all executive NDPBs) were, the PASC felt, gratifying. Over three-quarters of these bodies maintained a website, but the Committee saw no reason why they cannot all do so (para. 33).

However, the PASC were disappointed at the low priority attached to public access to executive NDPBs. 'There are more black holes than examples of open governance' (para. 34). There had been very slow progress since 1997 on the government's expressed wish that these bodies should hold more open annual meetings and other public meetings (which the Committee had also recommended in its *Quangos* report: the increase had been from 12 per cent to 17 per cent overall in 2000).

The PASC believed that more attention should be given to the important role that advisory NDPBs play within government (para. 35). They did not doubt the value of the disinterested and professional service that members of such committees give to the public, but public confidence in the advice these bodies give on sensitive issues was very low. An ICM poll for the Joseph Rowntree Reform Trust had recently asked respondents whether they trusted government Ministers and their advisory committees (quangos) to tell the truth about the safety of nuclear installations, medicines, GM foods and crops, and British beef and food in general. In every case, more people replied 'No' than 'Yes'. Positive responses ranged from a low of 18 per cent in the case of nuclear installations to 37 per cent on medicines. The report observed that the representation of industrial interests and the inclusion of expert members with close links with such interests on these advisory bodies prompted damaging suspicions which were exacerbated by the closed nature of many of them. In the view of the Select Committee, the government should seek to dispel popular suspicions by creating a very open regime for such bodies, allowing peer review and public access so far as possible, and making registers of Members' interests a statutory requirement rather than (as now) a largely voluntary arrangement (para. 36). In principle, they believed that public bodies should be at least as open as is required of local authorities under the Local Government Act 2000. The proportion of advisory NDPBs required to comply with the criteria for accountability, consultation, and openness adopted by the Committee had not risen significantly since 1997. The average rate of compliance across all the criteria for advisory NDPBs was only 11 per cent (para. 36).

There had however been substantial progress on public access to registers of interests. Some 212 (42 per cent) of advisory NDPBs gave the public access to registers, whereas in 1997 only 21 bodies (3 per cent) did so, but it was not clear from departmental responses whether this was because of a statutory requirement rather than an extension of voluntary arrangements. A higher proportion of advisory NDPBs were publishing annual reports—up from 6 per cent in 1997 to 29 per cent—but it remained unsatisfactory that about three-quarters of advisory bodies were still not required to publish annual reports or to observe the open government code (para. 37).

The position on other indicators of openness and access to the public was found to be even more unsatisfactory. Only 2 per cent were required to allow the public to see the agendas of their meetings. Only 1 per cent were required to hold public meetings; 3 per cent were required to consult the general public.

Some advisory NDPBs 'topped up' statutory requirements through voluntary practice. For example, 11 per cent voluntarily consulted the general public; another 5 per cent held public meetings. There was, the Committee felt, a clear need to restore public confidence in advisory committees and a need for a systematic review of what could be done to open up these bodies to public and peer group scrutiny.

The Select Committee concluded that the quango state was 'a permanent and dynamic aspect of modern government in the United Kingdom'. They felt it was time for an urgent government review of the principles and practice of appointed governance in the United Kingdom. None has so far taken place.

Lessons from Overseas

Lessons in accountability of quangos could be learned from overseas (see Barker in Flinders et al., 1997). In Sweden, for instance, there is not the distinction that we have between bodies for which Ministers are accountable to Parliament, which would not be regarded as quangos in the UK, and other public bodies. There is no system of individual Ministerial responsibility for departments or agencies in Sweden. All public bodies (including their equivalents of our executive agencies) are both directly accountable to the Parliament and subjected to an extensive freedom of information regime, a comprehensive ombudsman system, and a range of forms of audit including administrative audit and promotion of good administrative practice via the Swedish National Agency for Administrative Development. (It is worth noting here that the PASC in its *Quangos* report considered that 'there may be a need for a system of administrative audit of quangos which can ensure that they conform to common standards': HC 209, 1998–9, para. 104.) Swedish agencies normally have advisory boards on which are represented consumers of the services and others, including those working in the agency. Swedish arrangements could provide some useful models for the reform of quangos in the UK.

An important point of contrast with the British system though is that in Sweden, with a more highly developed system of administrative law than the UK, many of the controls of public administration are legal in nature—and they treat as law a range of rules that in the UK would be regarded as 'soft law' codes or guidance which would not be enforceable by a court or tribunal. A central function of the ombudsman in Sweden is to secure that public administration is conducted in accordance with law, which is not the function of the British ombudsman. Instead the British tradition is to minimize the legal regulation of public administration and to impose instead political and administrative controls. A probable development in the United Kingdom, if effective non-legal controls are not developed, will be an increase in legal controls and in the development of administrative law (see Oliver and Drewry, 1996, ch. 9) through judicial review, the operation of the Human Rights Act and the Freedom of Information Act, and through additional statutory provisions, for instance, for audit. (For further information about the Swedish system see Elder, 1970; Richardson, 1982; Lundvik, 1983; McDonald, 1992a, 1992b).

In Australia, a system closer to the British one than Sweden's, the Administrative Review Council is an independent advisory body charged with ensuring that administrative law and practice, which govern quangos as well as other public bodies, develops in a principled way. A British version of this might be the establishment of a Council on Executive and Advisory Quangos, modelled to a degree on the Council on Tribunals, whose function would be to keep under review the constitution and working of tribunals and to make reports on them and to consider matters that are referred to it and to report to the Lord Chancellor (as a Minister of Justice) on them. A body of this kind charged with keeping the arrangements for quangos under review could secure that problems were placed on the political agenda and they could possibly meet some of the criticisms of the system, performing the role envisaged by the PASC (HC 209, 1998–9, para. 104, *supra).* which in many respects resembles the function of the Swedish National Agency for Administrative Development.

Conclusions

Quangos provide a useful example of how unelected bodies discharging public functions can make a positive contribution to the democracy of a system in a way that Ministers and other elected or directly politically accountable bodies cannot do. But the extent to which they can do so depends on getting the systems for appointment, accountability, openness, and participation right. The resurgence of interest in quangos after the 2001 general election was due partly to alarm at the degree of disconnection between citizens and the state that the low turnout in the election suggested. But longstanding concern about the accountability of these bodies against a background of assumptions that political accountability is the 'default' position has tended to make it difficult to develop alternatives to political accountability. A welcome feature of the literature on quangos in the last few years has been acknowledgement that alternatives to political accountability can not only secure high standards from these bodies, but also, via consultation with and involvement of non-politicians, and openness, make positive contributions to a democratic system.

The lessons that can be drawn from quangos could be easily transferable to the political sphere. While it would be inappropriate to treat Ministers and their departments and executive agencies in the same way as quangos, the fact is that they are, in practice, quasi-autonomous in the sense that their parliamentary accountability for their policies and actions is not as effective as it should be and Ministers tend to take a 'hands off' approach to them (see Chapter 12). There is no reason why departments of government, local authorities, and bodies which fall within the ambit of Ministerial and other forms of political accountability and responsibility should not also be subjected to the kinds of democratic and good-governance safeguards which are appropriate for quangos. Many of these safeguards have, of course, applied for many years to government departments. Some of the reforms to quangos (on audit, ombudsmen, propriety, and appointments, for instance) are designed to bring them into line with departments.

A suggestion that Ministers, like quango members, should be appointed on 'Nolan principles' and on merit might be entertaining, but is not on the political agenda. However, arguments in favour of openness and participation apply equally to government as to quangos. The publication of annual reports, extensive and open consultation, publication of responses to consultation exercises, the giving of reasons for decisions, including responses to points put in consultation, could all enhance the accountability of Ministers and their departments. If an Administrative Review Council were set up, it could make useful contributions to bodies other than quangos.

18

The Judiciary

The courts have an important role in any democracy, being charged with: the application and interpretation of legislation—giving effect to democratically passed laws; the resolution of disputes between private parties or between individuals and the state—which may involve upholding civil and political rights and other rights given constitutional protections; upholding the rule of law; and, in common law systems, developing the law and themselves acting from time to time as architects of the Constitution (see Chapter 5). As we have noted in other chapters the courts are by no means the only constitutional architects in the system, and Parliament and the executive also assume architectural roles, as they have done in the last few years with the introduction of devolution, the Human Rights Act, freedom of information, and parliamentary, local government, and civil service reform.

The role of the judges in relation to judicial review and the development of a theory of constitutionalism has been considered in Chapter 5. In this chapter we shall be considering the relationships between the courts on the one hand and Parliament and the executive on the other hand, and the institutional arrangements within which the courts operate. The role of the courts in relation to European Community law was considered in Chapter 4.

Relationships between the Judiciary, Parliament, and the Executive

The United Kingdom's judicial system differs from many others in that, although there is no separation of powers between Parliament and the Executive—quite the reverse, as the two are substantially fused—there is a near separation between the judiciary and the other two branches of government. The separation is not however complete. The Lord Chancellor is in effect the Minister for Justice and (many) Constitutional Affairs, he is a judge and head of the judiciary, and he presides in the House of Lords. The members of the highest court for the United Kingdom, the Appellate Committee of the House of Lords, are all members of that chamber and when he sits in that Committee the Lord Chancellor presides. The Judicial Committee of the Privy Council, which deals with devolution issues under the devolution legislation and some other UK appeals, for instance, from decisions of the General Medical Council and other professional bodies, is technically part of the executive (see Le Sueur, 2001).

The lack of separation between these higher echelons of the judiciary and the other branches has become a particular issue in the last five years or so, as it may be incompatible with Article 6 of the European Convention on Human Rights' requirement of access to 'an independent and impartial tribunal' in the determination of civil and criminal cases. This requires a separation of personnel between those exercising judicial functions and those exercising legislative or executive functions. The ECtHR decided in *Procola v. Luxembourg* ([1995] 22 EHRR 193), that the Luxembourg Conseil d'Etat was not an independent and impartial tribunal for the purposes of Article 6 ECHR, since its members had an advisory function in relation to the passage of legislation—a role similar to that of the Conseil d'etat in France (see Chapter 10). In the case of *McGonnell v. UK* (8 BHRC 56, *The Times* 22 February 2000) the ECtHR decided that it was incompatible with the requirements of Article 6 that the Deputy Bailiff of Guernsey, who was the sole judge in the case in issue, should also be President of their Parliament (the States of Deliberation) when it adopted the legislation in issue in the case. The ECtHR held that:

[A]ny direct involvement in the passage of legislation, or of executive rules, was likely to be sufficient to cast doubt on the judicial impartiality of a person subsequently called on to determine a dispute over whether reasons existed to permit a variation from the wording of the legislation or rules at issue.

These findings have implications both for the Lord Chancellor, who presides in the House of Lords, and for the Lords of Appeal in Ordinary, who, as well as sitting in the Appellate Committee, may also sit in the Lords when it is exercising its legislative functions.

In the Scottish case of *Starrs v. Ruxton* (2000 JC 208) it was held that a temporary sheriff in Scotland was not sufficiently independent for the purposes of Article 6. Lord Reed observed that the Human Rights Act had effected a:

very important shift in thinking about the constitution. It is fundamental to that shift that human rights are no longer dependent solely on convention, by which I mean values, customs and practices of the constitution which are not legally enforceable. Although the Convention protects rights which reflect democratic values and underpin democratic institutions, the Convention guarantees the protection of those rights through legal processes, rather than political processes. . . . It would be inconsistent with the whole approach of the Convention if the independence of those courts rested upon convention rather than law. (p. 250E.)

These cases demonstrate how the pressure towards a constitution based on law rather than politics is coming from the ECtHR as well as internally.

The role of the courts has become much more potentially controversial with devolution (see Chapters 13, 14, and 15), the process of reforming the second chamber (see Chapter 10), and the coming into effect of the Human Rights Act 1998 (see Chapter 6). Most devolution issues so far have been about the application of the Human Rights Act to the Scottish Executive and Parliament, and generally the courts in Scotland and the UK have been willing to defer to elected bodies' judgement of the balance between Convention rights and public interests, save where issues to do with special areas of judicial expertise such as criminal justice and the detention of individuals have been at stake. Some devolution issues, however, do not raise human rights issues but issues of the technical competence of the devolved bodies as against the UK government and legislation of the Westminster Parliament. The use of concordats and the Sewel Convention serve to reduce the areas of possible conflict here, but as and when such issues are taken to the courts the legitimacy of the members of these courts is likely to be subject to scrutiny. Here the fact that by convention two members of the Appellate Committee are drawn from Scotland and in practice one is from Northern Ireland goes some way to meet these points.

As judicial review expands, judges are more likely to find themselves exposed to allegations that they are not independent of the executive or of Parliament, either because of the method of their appointment (see below) or, in the case of the Lord Chancellor, because he is also a member of the executive, and in the case of the Lord Chancellor and the Law Lords, that they are members of the second chamber. Questions are likely to be raised about who the judges are, how they are appointed, and how consistent with democratic principles it is for them to have the power to challenge government in judicial review, or to disapply legislation that is incompatible with European Community law, or declare statutes to be incompatible with human rights or, in the case of the devolved bodies, with devolution legislation.

As the judges' role in the Constitution becomes more high profile they may need to be in a position to formulate and put their own collective views about their responsibilities and their place in the Constitution. In many jurisdictions there is constitutional provision for a judicial council of some kind. In Spain the Constitution establishes a General Council of Judicial Power, and in the US judges have their own Judicial Conference of the United States. Such bodies are reasonably well-resourced and influential and they enable judges to communicate their collective views. In the UK there is no such institution. The Judges Council, an informal body, represents the views of judges in England and Wales, but the Law Lords are not part of this. The Lord Chancellor sometimes claims to be 'the voice of the judges at court' but he does not make arrangements for their views to be made known to him and to pass them on and given his position in the executive he is not in a position to do so formally (see Le Sueur and Cornes, 2001, 56; Steyn, 2002a).

These concerns about the constitutional position of the judges have given rise to proposals for reforming the institutional arrangements for their independence, appointments, and relations with Parliament and the executive.

Independence and impartiality: what do they mean?

Before considering the present position and possible reforms in a little more detail let us remind ourselves why a separation between the judiciary and the other branches, and independence and impartiality, are supposed to be good things. A central principle in any liberal democracy is that judges should be independent of the other branches and impartial as between state institutions and the citizen and, of course, between private parties. This is necessary to protect the integrity of the judicial process and the arrangements for the resolution of disputes, and to secure the legitimacy of the courts in the eyes of the public and, of particular importance, of litigants. It is often assumed that this requires that they should not be members of another branch of government—that there should be separation of personnel between the judiciary and other branches.

The importance of the independence and impartiality of the judiciary is recognized as a fundamental principle by the United Nations (see *Basic Principles on the Independence of the Judiciary*, General Assembly Resolution 40/31 and 40/149, 1985) and in the European Convention on Human Rights, Article 6.

Independence involves both the collective independence of the judiciary and the individual independence of each judge from outside pressures, particularly from government and Parliament; to put it another way the bench, unlike other state bodies, is not to be subjected to political forms of accountability. This in turn requires security of judicial tenure, financial security, and institutional independence with respect to the administration of the courts (*Valente v. The Queen* (1986) 24 DLR 4th 161, Supreme Court of Canada; see also Shetreet, 1976; Green, 1985). However, respect for judicial independence does not necessarily preclude other forms of (non-political) accountability. The courts are accountable to the public in that they sit in public and give reasoned decisions; decisions of the lower courts are subject to appeal up the judicial hierarchy; and it is open to the government to introduce legislation in Parliament to alter the law as laid down by the courts.

In the UK, the judges of the superior courts, including the Lords of Appeal in Ordinary, enjoy security of tenure and high salaries, which provide protection against pressure from the other branches. Once appointed they may not be removed before retirement save on an address from both Houses of Parliament (Supreme Court Act 1981, s. 11(3), Appellate Jurisdiction Act 1876, s. 6). No such address has been made since the nineteenth century. Their salaries are charged on the Consolidated Fund, which means that they may be increased by administrative action but they are immune from challenge or reduction at the instance of backbenchers and may only be reduced by Act of Parliament.

Independence is not the same as impartiality, but the two are clearly closely related. Impartiality means that judges should so far as possible be neutral between different groups of litigants and between religions and ideologies, and that they should not be influenced by personal considerations in their treatment of individual litigants. Without impartiality the legal process would come into disrepute and lose its legitimacy, and some laws could become unenforceable in practice. Griffith (1991, 1993) has suggested that judges are not impartial in the sense that they are influenced by their own political views and assumptions, often being hostile to trade union and working-class interests. It is probably inevitable that judges, like other decision-makers, start off with a set of preconceptions, but consciousness of that factor, which has been stimulated by Griffith's work, serves to some extent to alert judges to this possibility and to make them reason out their decisions and avoid allowing irrational prejudices and unarticulated assumptions to influence them as much as they would do if they were not alert to this problem. Part of the problem has been that Parliament has not provided judges with authoritative statements of explicit values to inform their decision-making. But the Human Rights Act has provided a partial set of such values. The adoption by Parliament of a statement of directive principles of state policy (see discussion in Chapter 6) or reference to the European Union Charter of Fundamental Rights could provide the judges with the values that would enable them not to make decisions that are too subjective.

The impartiality of judges in particular cases is secured in a number of ways. The principles of the common law disqualify judges for bias from hearing cases. Complaints of bias may be dealt with by the appeal system (see Jones, 1999; Olowofoyeku, 2000; *R. v. Bow Street Metropolitan Stipendiary Magistrate, ex parte Pinochet Ugarte (No. 2)* [2000] 1 AC 119; *R. v. Gough* [1993] 2 All ER 724; *Locabail (UK) Ltd. v. Bayfield Properties* [2000] 1 All ER 65). Ewing (2000) has pointed out that parties may not know whether a judge is biased in the sense of having an interest in the outcome of a case, because judges do not have to register their interests. MPs and local councillors and others have to do so, and Ewing proposes that judges be obliged to enter some of their interests in a register. This would indeed increase openness. Many judges draw parties' attention to any interests they or their spouses have that might be affected by the case. Normally the parties make no objection to judges hearing cases if they or their spouses have minor shareholdings or the like that might be affected. The ethos of the judiciary is strongly against judges allowing their material interests to affect their judgment. It is far from clear what effect a public register of judges' interests would have on public trust in them. It could add to the culture of suspicion which O'Neill (2002) has identified as undermining trust.

Constitutional conventions protect judges from parliamentary pressure. There are strict parliamentary rules about the criticizing of a judge's conduct or of judges generally, which is only permitted on a debate on a substantive motion calling for dismissal. Comments may be made by backbench MPs about a decision or a sentence once it has been delivered, but the *sub judice* rule requires that no comments be made about a case in the Commons until after the decision has been made. There is therefore virtually no scope for parliamentary supervision of judges. In principle, it is suggested, this approach is a wise one. Some commentators have expressed the view that the rules about comments by Members of Parliament on cases and judges are unduly restrictive and that judges sitting without juries would not be influenced by comments made in Parliament. But there would be a risk that parties to cases and members of the public might believe that judges had been so influenced and were therefore not exercising their own judgments but deferring to politicians. That would be inconsistent with the duty of a judge, and this in my view justifies the strictness of the present rules.

On the other hand there are various open channels of communication between senior judges and politicians, notably in Parliament. Lord Bingham, the senior Law Lord, Lord Phillips, the Master of the Rolls, and Lord Woolf, the Lord Chief Justice of England and Wales, gave evidence to the Joint Committee on Human Rights, and other judges gave evidence to the committee on the draft Freedom of Information Bill. A concern about the possible removal of the Law Lords from the House of Lords to a separate Supreme Court (see below) is that parliamentarians and judges become distant from each other and do not exchange views, and that trust and confidence between these institutions would suffer from lack of direct communication. The strongly independent traditions of the judiciary also serve to promote their independence and impartiality.

The current arrangements for protecting the independence and impartiality of the judiciary seem to work reasonably well, despite the fact that they do not embody a separation of powers. But we should also note that a strict separation of powers between the judiciary and the other branches of government would not necessarily of itself secure the correct balance of power between them. Separation is not a panacea. As Lord Simon put it:

It is no use separating your executive if it has powers over the individual which are considered inordinate. The executive's powers should be balanced by that of the legislative and adjudicature. That is threatened by advocacy of a system purely based on separation of powers. It is a balance of powers that will vouchsafe liberty of the subject and individual rights. (HL Deb., 17 February 1999, col. 719)

The position of recent Lord Chancellors has been that the independence of the judiciary need not extend beyond their appointment and security of tenure, their freedom from executive pressure in the ways in which they deal with individual cases, and the immediate 'penumbra' of listing of cases. Other matters affecting the judiciary, including securing that the cost of the administration of justice (including legal aid, fees paid to lawyers out of public funds, and the level of court fees) is affordable, are increasingly considered to be rightly the business of the executive rather than the judges. Indeed, the executive aspects of the Lord Chancellor's role have assumed increasing importance in the last twenty years or so (see for instance Stevens, 1993; Woodhouse, 1998, 2001). The switch in focus in the Lord Chancellor's Department from supporting the judges and acting as a buffer or link between the government and the judges—the view that prevailed until the 1980s—to asserting executive control over much of the administration of justice, has produced some high-profile conflicts in recent years, including the issue with Mr Justice Wood (see below; see also Woodhouse, 1998, 2001). This trend has produced a loss of confidence in the Lord Chancellor on the part of some judges and the press, which has contributed to the case for reform of the position of Lord Chancellor itself. As Woodhouse put it:

[T]he executive role of the Lord Chancellor continues to dominate and to include the implementation of policies which challenge judicial views of their role in the administration of justice. Disagreements about who should run the courts are therefore likely to continue. These seriously weaken the Lord Chancellor's constitutional role, as a bulwark or buffer between the executive and the judiciary and cast doubt on his position as head of the judiciary. (1998, 630)

The nub of the problem is that the Lord Chancellor has become increasingly political and there is no bulwark between him and the judges. Let us now consider, therefore, the relationship between the Lord Chancellor and the judges, before turning to consider how the office of Lord Chancellor might be reformed.

The Lord Chancellor

The Lord Chancellor is a constitutional anomaly. He is a member of the Cabinet, he presides in the House of Lords, and he is himself a judge and the head of the judiciary in England and Wales. He is responsible for a major government department. The job has increased enormously in the last forty years. In 1960 the Lord Chancellor's Department— then an Office—was staffed by thirteen lawyers and some clerks and typists. Now it has a staff of over 10,000 and an annual budget of £2.5bn. It has changed from what was little more than a small private office to a major spending department of government. The Department is responsible not only for the appointment of judges and the administration of the courts (which is undertaken by the Court Service, an executive agency within the Department), but for freedom of information, data protection, human rights, and law reform. Lord Chancellor Irvine sees his department as a Ministry of Justice and Constitutional Affairs, similar to its counterparts in Australia, Canada, and New Zealand.

The Lord Chancellor is personally responsible for large numbers of judicial appointments (though the appointment to the most senior positions is made by the Queen on the advice of the Prime Minister, who in turn consults the Lord Chancellor). In 1960 there were fifty-six members of the higher judiciary, now there are 155. Every year the Lord Chancellor is responsible for more than 700 full-time and part-time judicial appointments. He also appoints Queen's Counsel. Lord Chancellors are also increasingly high-profile political figures, and have been since the 1960s.

The constitutional position of the Lord Chancellor, straddling the executive, Parliament, and the judiciary, and acting independently and on his own responsibility, clearly has the potential to undermine the independence of the system and its legitimacy in the eyes of the public. The protections against this are largely governed by constitutional political conventions—by the operation of a political Constitution. The Lord Chancellor is not supposed to intervene in particular cases in which he or the government have an interest. In making appointments the Lord Chancellor acts on his own responsibility and does not consult Cabinet colleagues. He is not supposed to take political considerations into account when making judicial appointments, which should be made on merit only.

These conventions have been breaking down in recent years. So far it is not suggested that breaches have been due to conscious abuse of power as opposed to administrative concerns. But they do reveal a lack of awareness of the existence and content of conventions and of the constitutional implications of breaches. For instance, in 1994 Mr Justice Wood objected to being put under pressure by Lord Chancellor Mackay—who asked him to 'consider his position', a thinly veiled suggestion that he might resign—in the procedures he was following in the Employment Appeal Tribunal, the Lord Chancellor being concerned that costs were being incurred for his Department unnecessarily. This resulted in a debate in the House of Lords in which the Lord Chancellor was criticized for this pressurising of a judge (HL Deb., 21 March 1994, vol. 553, cols. 497–9, and 27 April 1994, cols. 751–804; see Oliver, 1994; and Purchas, 1994).

The potential for the Lord Chancellor's position to undermine the reputation for independence and thus the legitimacy of the judiciary arose again in the run up to the 2001 general election. Lord Chancellor Irvine had written to known lawyer supporters of the Labour government inviting them to a fundraising dinner for the Party. The press queried whether a lawyer's willingness to contribute to Labour funds might not affect the question whether he or she was favourably considered for a judicial appointment or appointment as a Queen's Counsel. Lord Irvine's response was that he was a politician and that part of his job as a Minister was fundraising. Lord Macnally for the Liberal Democrats put down a question in the House of Lords about this. His view was that this was not a resigning matter, but that Lord Irvine should have acknowledged that he had made an error of judgement, and apologize. In reality it was not seriously believed that the Lord Chancellor's decisions about judicial appointments or awards of silk were affected by whether a candidate supported Labour, but it was predictable and understandable that the press reacted as they did, and the incident added to pressure for the roles of the Lord Chancellor to be separated and for the appointment of judges and QCs not to be in the hands of an active politician.

Lord Chancellors do not in practice sit very often on cases as they do not have the time to do so, but when they do there may be a breach of the requirement for an independent and impartial tribunal, or an appearance of lack of impartiality. This would surface as a particular problem if the Lord Chancellor were to exercise his right to sit as a judge in cases in the Appellate Committee of the House of Lords, where the government had an interest or a Minister was a party. This happened in the case of *Pepper v. Hart* ([1993] AC 593). In that case one issue was the possible increase in the cost of legal aid if the courts were to be willing to consult Hansard to determine the intentions of Parliament when a statutory provision was ambiguous or obscure or where the literal meaning would lead to absurdity. The Lord Chancellor, Lord Mackay, whose own department would be affected by increased legal aid costs if lawyers were entitled to rely on statements made in Parliament in support of their interpretation of legislation, sat on the case. He based his minority decision in favour of the government on the additional costs for his department which would be incurred if the decision went in favour of the taxpayer on this point.

Lord Chancellor Irvine's position is that he is free to decide whether he himself will sit on a particular case, though he has undertaken that he would not do so if the government were involved. He does not acknowledge that there is any rule or principle against his so sitting. However, Lord Chancellor Irvine sat in *DPP v. Jones* ([1999] 2 AC 240) on criminal liability for trespass to the highway by an assembly of people aiming to get to Stonehenge. It was held that the defendants were not guilty in this case, but Lord Irvine held that an offence would have been committed if the assembly was not consistent with the primary use of the highway for passing and repassing. The participation of the Lord Chancellor in a decision one implication of which was that an assembly of people demonstrating against government policy could be criminal clearly raises questions about possible conflicts of interest and impartiality.

The Lord Chancellor's relationship with his fellow judges, especially members of the appellate committee of the House of Lords, could also give rise to problems. Lord Chancellor Irvine normally delegates to the senior Law Lord (whom he appoints, not necessarily by seniority) the right to decide who shall sit on cases, but he reserves the right to decide for himself which cases he will sit on, and to make the selection of other judges himself when he is proposing to sit and indeed in other cases too (see HL Deb., October 1998, vol. 593, W.A. 137; Oliver, 1999; Steyn, 2002a). The scope for at least the appearance—and indeed the practice—of political interference in the composition of a court is obvious here. Lord Steyn has proposed that the Lord Chancellor should not be regarded as the Head of the Judiciary but that the Lord Chief Justice of England and Wales should have that position (Steyn, 1997, 2002a). The Lord Chancellor has not accepted this proposal. Such an arrangement would go some way to meet the problem, but it is suggested that more radical solutions, such as separating out the roles of the Lord Chancellor, are required.

Modernizing the office of Lord Chancellor?

There are a number of ways in which the office of Lord Chancellor could be reformed to meet the criticisms made of it. Woodhouse proposes that the executive responsibilities of the office should be transferred to a Minister of Justice in the House of Commons. Proposals for a Ministry of Justice go back to the Haldane Report on the Machinery of Government of 1918 (Cd. 9230; see Drewry, 1983) and even before then—Bentham was in favour of a Ministry of Justice. The main objection has been concern that the independence of the judiciary would be imperilled if a Minister in the House of Commons had responsibility for appointments. But this problem could be met by a Judicial Appointments Commission (see below) or by retaining a Minister in the House of Lords—possibly the Lord Chancellor—with responsibility for appointments. Under Woodhouse's proposals the Lord Chancellor could continue to preside in the House of Lords, but an independent Appointments Commission would be responsible for making recommendations for judicial appointments. The advantages of transferring executive responsibilities to a House of Commons Minister would be that there would be full parliamentary accountability for the large budget of the department, the potential for full debate about politically charged issues within the ministerial remit such as freedom of information, human rights, and data protection, and proper political scrutiny of the efficiency with which the system of justice was being administered.

Lord Alexander of Weedon (2001) has proposed the transfer only of the Lord Chancellor's more political executive functions—for instance for legal aid, and political law reform—to a Minister of Justice in the House of Commons, so that the Lord Chancellor retains responsibility for court administration, non-political law reform, and judicial appointments. This proposal would preserve the role of the Lord Chancellor as the judges' voice at court, arguing against policies and legislation that might be contrary to the rule of law and respect for the independence and impartiality of the judiciary. A problem here is that Cabinet meetings are confidential and it is impossible to know whether this is in fact a role played by Lord Chancellors—though a number of them claim that it is.

The Appointment of Judges

Mention has already been made of the fact that the Lord Chancellor is responsible for the appointment of judges, and the concerns this generates about possible undermining of their independence. There are further issues around appointment provisions, including the criteria for appointment, how reflective the judiciary should be of the population as a whole, and institutional arrangements for appointments. These are important good-governance issues.

Criteria for appointment

A question that has been raised on a number of occasions in recent years is the extent to which the judiciary should be representative or 'reflective' of the population at large. The judiciary is predominantly male and there are very few members from the ethnic minorities. Recently Lord Chancellors have expressed their concern to increase the numbers of women and members of ethnic minorities on the bench so that its composition should more fairly reflect the balance within the population; but these efforts are hampered by the fact that the senior members of the bar, from whom most appointments are made, are predominantly white and male. However, the ethnic minorities are disproportionately highly represented among junior members of the Bar in relation to their proportion of the population generally, and in due course this should result in more appointments of ethnic minority judges. Solicitors became eligible for appointment to the bench under the Courts and Legal Services Act 1990, and the wider catchment for appointments should result in a slightly more representative bench. But it is likely to be some years before the legal profession from which judges are appointed is itself more representative of the population at large and thus before the bench can be expected to be fully reflective of it.

Concerns about the unrepresentativeness of the bench have spawned a debate about what the criteria for appointment should be as to age, experience, success in practice, and personal qualities—the ability to work fast, patience, and so on. Ewing (2000) has suggested that we move to a career judiciary as in the civil law jurisdictions in Europe. The judges would be recruited on merit straight from university and trained for judging and would then have a career path up the court structure. This method would over time produce a more representative balance between men, women, and members of ethnic minorities. Such a step is not however on the active agenda in the UK at present, or indeed in any of the common law jurisdictions. The tradition of recruiting judges from among experienced practitioners is deeply embedded. It is widely considered that this background and the relatively flat career and salary structure of the UK judiciary are more likely to promote the culture of judicial independence and thus provide a constitutional safeguard against executive interference than an arrangement in which entrants start young and earn promotion up a career and salary structure. Also the high status that judges undoubtedly enjoy and respect for the rule of law in the UK rely to an extent on the seniority and successful prior careers of those appointed.

As a matter of practice the Lord Chancellor has until recently only appointed people to the bench in their forties, although the formal requirements are for seven to ten years' experience, which can be achieved well before that age. Given that in recent years the proportion of women entering the legal professions has been around 50 per cent and the proportion of those from the ethnic minorities has grown, a higher proportion of appointments from those groups could be made if the age for appointment were lower. In April 2002 the Lord Chancellor announced that he would lower the age at which appointments were made, thus making it more possible that women and lawyers from the ethnic minorities would be appointed. This may be the start of a longer judicial career structure, as early appointees would be appointed to the lower courts and might have the opportunity to move up the ladder.

The current practice is to appoint to the bench on professional merit, but the concept of 'merit' is more fluid than might at first appear. Sir Thomas Legg (2001), former permanent secretary in the Lord Chancellor's department, draws a distinction between maximal and minimal merit. The former is the traditional civil service approach, which assumes that there is one candidate who will have greater merit than all others and that that candidate must be appointed. This is the policy adopted by the Lord Chancellor: he will appoint the candidate who appears to him best-qualified, regardless of gender, ethnic origin, marital status, sexual orientation, political affiliation, religion, etc.

On the other, 'minimal merit', approach all candidates who reach a minimal standard are treated as equally eligible, and the appointing authority may exercise discretion in choosing between them. This approach would permit the appointments to be made so as to secure the kind of people the authority wants to see on the bench and gives scope for positive action to secure a judiciary which is reflective of society.

A question arises why one might want the bench to represent or reflect the community. If the fact that there are few women and members of ethnic minorities on the bench were to mean that those people were being denied equality of opportunity, i.e. they were being discriminated against in the appointment system, that would clearly be unacceptable, because it would be unjust to them. Two kinds of discrimination are possible—as to the process for appointment and as to the criteria for appointment. While the process purports to be even-handed, there have been suggestions that in practice it favours those who are known to the existing judges and other senior practitioners who are consulted, including QCs, and that it thus favours barristers as against solicitors and members of certain barristers' chambers as against others (Malleson and Banda, 2000, 39). Appointments to the lower ranks of the judiciary—deputy district judge, for instance, do follow an open process that is close to that for appointments to other occupations. But the criticisms noted above may still be levelled at appointments to recorderships and the circuit bench, and upwards. The higher the appointment the more closed the appointment system (McGlynn, 1998, ch. 7) and thus the more difficult for those with low visibility to be appointed (Hale, 2001, 497).

The criteria for appointment to the High Court include success in practice, particularly in advocacy, and particularly achieving high earnings, before appointment to the bench. Success in practice is taken to guarantee independence, status, and incorruptibility. Hale (2001) and Ewing (2000) question how relevant to this success in practice should be. Hale also notes that these criteria can disadvantage women who may have had career breaks for children or may not be willing to put in the long hours necessary for high earnings and effective networking. Other 'non-standard issue' may also be prejudiced by these criteria.

The argument for representativeness is not however usually about doing justice to the candidates, but about producing the kind of bench the country needs. What does representativeness—or, as Legg (2001) prefers, reflectiveness—have to do with meeting the country's needs? On one view it is irrelevant and runs the risk of undermining the maximal merit principle and thus lowering the quality of the bench. On another view we need a different sort of judiciary, one which judges in different ways, and this can only be achieved by reforming the appointment process and criteria. Hale (2001) suggests that our stereotypical judge is essentially male in character and style, with an emphasis on authority and decisiveness, to the point of pushyness, aggessiveness, and being unyielding—essentially male characteristics. She suggests that gender-based stereotypes are also embedded in the attitudes of male judges, and she rejects the commonly held idea that background, gender, and experience should not make a difference to what judges decide. She argues instead that appointments to the bench should be of people who can counteract the deeply embedded stereotypes that affect judges—in other words that they should include people who will not hold to these stereotypes, including women and members of minorities who are not often appointed at present. She concludes on this point that: 'a generally more diverse bench, with a wider range of backgrounds, experience and perspectives on life, might well be expected to bring about some collective change in empathy and understanding for the diverse backgrounds, experience and perspective of those whose cases come before them' (p. 501).

Hale's final argument for a more representative bench is that an unrepresentative or unreflective bench lacks democratic legitimacy and does not command public confidence. Genn's research (1999, 502) suggests a popular perception of judges as out of touch. Hale argues that 'In a democratic society in which we are all equal citizens, it is wrong in principle for [the authority of the courts] to be wielded by such a very unrepresentative section of the population', and she urges that positive efforts be made to recruit from a wider range of possible candidates than at present—more women, more members of religious and ethnic minorities, more varied social and educational backgrounds, more varied professional backgrounds—for democratic reasons.

The present system of judicial appointments undoubtedly produces a high-quality bench. It has been defended by successive Lord Chancellors. But quite apart from arguments for reflectiveness there are powerful arguments based on both principle and practicality for reforming and formalizing the appointment of judges: the closed nature of the system undermines its legitimacy in the eyes of the public, and indeed of the professions, notably solicitors. As the catchment area extends to the solicitors' profession the present highly personalized system will not be able to cope. And under the present system there can be no guarantee that Ministers responsible for the judiciary will not allow political considerations to influence them.

There needs to be more openness about the criteria for appointment. There should be public discussion about the characteristics sought in judges and in the bench as a whole. While it is in my view essential that the concept of maximum merit should continue to govern appointments, that concept itself needs exploring along the lines suggested by Hale. The notion that one candidate from a field will be the best assumes that the criteria are clear and uniform. In most selections a range of qualities have to be weighed against one another and it cannot truly be said that one candidate is the best. The principal quality is being a good lawyer, of course, but alongside that the ability to control a court, good judgement, decisiveness, the ability to work fast and under pressure, patience, and good communication skills are all important in judges.

Parliamentary confirmation hearings?

Concerns about the present system for appointing judges have opened up a debate about ways of reforming it. Concerns are not limited to the possible politicization of appointments should the Lord Chancellor's position be changed. The objectives of a reformed system would be to make the criteria and processes for appointment more open, and to increase the legitimacy of the judges. The main issues are whether there should be parliamentary confirmation of senior judicial appointments, and how open the system should be.

While the legitimacy of the courts in the eyes of the government might be secured through a political input, for instance approval by a select committee of the House of Commons, such input might undermine the legitimacy of the court in the eyes of private litigants in cases brought against the government. It has sometimes been suggested (see Ewing, 2000) that those considered for appointment to the highest judicial offices should be subject to hearings by such a committee—or a committee of the House of Lords (the new Constitution Committee, for instance) or a joint committee (the Joint Committee on Human Rights or an equivalent). Hearings by such a committee might follow the US Senate hearings model for appointments to the US Supreme Court. But these would create a number of problems in the United Kingdom.

First, what criteria should the hearings committee apply in deciding on confirmation? If the criteria were expertise and experience—is this judge a good lawyer, has he or she had experience of judging?—then a committee of Parliament would be likely to be no better qualified than any other body—and less well qualified than, for instance, a Judicial Appointments Commission—to make the decision. It is more likely that the confirmation hearings would be most concerned with the judge's beliefs and politics. This is what Ewing envisages. These ought not in my view to be relevant in the UK. First, it might not in fact legitimate the judges if, for instance, the majority in Parliament did not reflect a majority of the electorate, which is commonly the case under the present electoral arrangements (See Chapter 7). Second, the legitimacy of those appointed for their political values might be questioned after a new government with different values was elected. This might in turn lead to a reduction in the security of tenure of judges. Our system has operated on the basis that judges will listen to the arguments both ways and give a reasoned decision; they should be careful to approach issues of law with an open mind and not allow their own prejudices to influence them. This is a counsel of perfection, but generally it works. Accountability, up to the top level, is imposed via appeal up the court system. And if the government or Parliament should disagree with a legal principle developed by the courts then in our system it is open to them to secure the passage of legislation to change the rule.

Even if the criteria for confirmation hearings were spelled out in detail in statute, the members of a parliamentary committee holding such hearings would be unlikely to keep to their briefs. Almost inevitably they would ask questions about the appointee's attitudes to, for instance, the law relating to abortion, homosexuality, animal rights, or asylum-seekers or other issues of controversy at the time, the balance of interests between the individual and the state or the community where, for instance, the possible extension of liability for failures in the provision of public services are concerned, and whether or when public interests should outweigh the interests of individuals. Such questioning would raise a number of difficulties. It might be unfair to expect judges to deal with purely hypothetical problems, especially without the benefit of argument both ways and a specific set of facts to apply a finding to. Litigants in future cases might feel that they would not receive an open-minded and fair hearing if the judge in question had already expressed a view under pressure to a committee of politicians on an issue, especially if his job and livelihood hang on his reply. One argument put in favour of confirmation hearings before parliamentary committees is that judges appointed after such a procedure will then enjoy a sense of their own legitimacy when criticized by government for their decisions. This of course can work both ways. That sense of legitimacy might be interpreted by those they find against as arrogance.

The balance of opinion at present in the UK seems—rightly in my view—to be against subjecting judicial appointments—at any level—to parliamentary approval, and in favour of either retaining the status quo—appointment by the Lord Chancellor or by the Prime Minister—or transferring the function of appointment or at least of selection to a Judicial Appointments Commission.

A Judicial Appointments Commission?

The present position in England and Wales is that there is no formality in the system for applying for appointment to the High Court (the procedure for lower appointments is more formal) although the Lord Chancellor invites applications periodically and publishes a booklet and an entry on the website, entitled *The Lord Chancellor's Policies and Procedures on Judicial Appointments*, in which he sets out the criteria for appointments. The system of selection involves the informal and confidential 'sounding out' of various people, including senior members of the judiciary, about possible appointments. Opinions about candidates are not revealed to them, although factual information that emerges during the process is disclosed if requested, so that errors may be corrected (see further McGlynn, 1998).

The process is open to a number of criticisims for its lack of transparency. However, Sir Leonard Peach, the then Commissioner for Public Appointments, reviewed the system in 1999 (Peach, 1999) and pronounced it in the covering letter to his report to be 'as good as any which I have seen in the public sector'. He did, however, recommend some improvements including, inter alia, the appointment of an independent lay commissioner to oversee and monitor the process. The first appointment of an adviser to the Lord Chancellor on the judicial appointments process, Sir Colin Campbell, was made in 2001. The appointments process has been opened up in additional ways in recent years. The Lord Chancellor now makes an annual report to Parliament on judicial appointments, so a greater degree of political and public accountability is being introduced into the system. The Home Affairs Committee has looked in to the appointments process (but not actual appointments) and reported on it.

There are a range of ways in which judicial appointments can be made and the necessary protections provided for judicial independence. Many countries use judicial appointments commissions of various kinds (Skordali, 1991; Malleson, 1997, 1999; Thomas and Malleson, 1997). In some jurisdictions commissions with responsibility for judicial appointments, including discipline and promotion have proved open to infiltration by political influences, which would be unacceptable in the UK (Thomas and Malleson, 1997). In many states of the USA (but not at federal level) and in Canada merit commissions are involved in appointments. The composition of commissions varies but generally they include senior judges and lay members.

Proposals have been made from time to time for a Judicial Appointments Commission for England and Wales or for the UK. (A Commission is being introduced in Scotland.) Lord Lester of Herne Hill QC made one such proposal in debates on the devolution legislation (see HL Deb., 2 November 1998, col. 41). And a Commission was Labour policy in 1997 (*Manifesto. A New Agenda for Democracy: Labour's proposals for constitutional reform*, p. 40). The Liberal Democrats have a long-standing commitment to a Commission (see also Institute of Public Policy Research, 1991).

The main arguments in favour of a Judicial Appointments Commission for the UK are first, to avoid abuse of the system by a Lord Chancellor at some future date, and second, to secure the legitimacy of the appointees. As the powers of judges and their involvement in controversial cases increase with the Human Rights Act and devolution, their legitimacy is likely to be called in question and it would be right to preempt this possibility by introducing a system of appointment that would give them greater legitimacy. Removing the appointment of most judges—except in a formal sense—from the Lord Chancellor, and limiting his power over appointments to choosing between a small number of possible candidates in the more high-profile appointments, would protect the judges from having their legitimacy challenged on grounds of political influence. Placing the nomination process in the hands of an independent and high-status Commission containing not only some judges but also independent members of established independent reputations should enhance the legitimacy of the courts, when ruling against the government in particular. And formalizing the criteria and the process for appointment could (depending how they were formulated) secure that candidates were not discriminated against and that a suitably qualified and reflective bench overall was produced.

The jurisdiction closest to ours which might provide a model for judicial appointments is South Africa. Their Judicial Service Commission makes recommendations for the appointment of judges. Judges of the Constitutional Court are nominated by the President (the English or UK equivalent would be the Prime Minister) from a list produced by the Judicial Service Commission. The Commission holds hearings for senior appointments in public, but it makes its decision on whether to recommend appointments in private. Malleson (1999) concludes that public questioning of potential appointees in South Africa has been restrained and helpful in reinforcing the Commission's reputation for making non-discriminatory appointments. She also concludes that Commissions in a number of countries have been able to secure a more reflective bench with closer to proportionate numbers of women appointees, that appointees are as competent as those appointed previously, and that they generate increased public confidence in the appointments process and thus in the judiciary (Malleson, 1997, 1999). However, an Appointments Commission must be designed so as to avoid politicization, which has been a problem in Ireland and the USA and some European jurisdictions, for instance. There should not be excessive control of membership of the Commission by elected politicians. A wide range of people should be on the appointing bodies and on the Commissions. And the judicial system should be free of a culture of partisan politics — which is the position in the UK.

Provisions for the dismissal of judges are as important as the procedures for appointment. Judges of the High Court, the Court of Appeal, and the House of Lords enjoy very considerable security from dismissal (Supreme Court Act 1981, section 11), but Recorders are appointed only for a three-year period and they have no right to be reappointed. Magistrates may be removed by the Lord Chancellor at any time. Scotland, and England and Wales, have for many years used part-time sheriffs and recorders and assistant recorders, but as we have already noted, the practice was held to be contrary to Article 6 of the European Convention on Human Rights in the *Starrs v. Ruxton* case (2000 JC 208) in Scotland. The objection was that these judges were appointed by the Lord Advocate, a member of the Scottish executive, from year to year and had no guarantee of work, leaving open the possibility that the Lord Advocate might stop giving them work, or decide not to reappoint them if they decided cases in ways that he disapproved of. As a result of this case the systems in Scotland and England and Wales have been reformed so that these appointees have greater security of tenure and a guarantee of work.

A Judicial Appointments Commission could be given functions in relation to the renewal of appointments or removal of members of the lower judiciary: these should be subject to procedural requirements, limited grounds and safeguards such as a duty on the Commission to report to Parliament. This, it is suggested, would be preferable to the present arrangement which is open to political abuse (although there are few suggestions that it is in practice abused in that way) and may not be compliant with Article 6 ECHR.

A New Supreme Court?

Technically the High Court and the Court of Appeal are 'the Supreme Court' of England and Wales. But the usual sense of 'Supreme Court', as used for instance in the United States, is of the highest or 'top' court in the system. It is this sense of the term that we shall discuss here. The Appellate Committee of the House of Lords is the highest court for most cases and hears certain appeals from the High Court and the Court of Appeal in England and Wales and from higher courts in Scotland (in civil cases only) and Northern Ireland. The Committee sits in a committee room in the House of Lords, where the only facilities for the litigants and their lawyers are the benches in the corridor. The Law Lords themselves have cramped offices in the Palace of Westminster. The Judicial Committee of the Privy Council hears some appeals and references on devolution issues, sitting in Downing Street. The position on the court hierarchy is more complex in the UK than in, for instance, the USA or Australia, in that the European Court of Justice is the 'top court' as far as issues of European Community law are concerned, and the European Court of Human Rights plays a major role in the interpretation of the ECHR, though its decisions are not binding on courts in the UK (HRA section 2; see Chapter 6).

Supreme Courts are of various kinds. In federal systems their jurisdiction is limited to broadly constitutional issues, particularly to regulating the relationships between the federal level and the states or provinces in the federation. The United States Supreme Court is the paradigm example. That court assumed the jurisdiction to strike down legislation and acts and decisions that were contrary to the US Constitution in the case of *Marbury v. Madison* (1 Cranch 137 (1803)) and this kind of judicial review is now regarded as central to that country's constitutional arrangements. The United Kingdom does not have a written Constitution in the American sense of an instrument that, among other things, delineates and thus limits the legislative capacities of the Parliament (see Chapter 1). There is thus no authoritative source from which the UK courts could deduce a power to strike down legislation or acts of the Westminster Parliament or executive for incompatibility with the Constitution. However, they do have the power to disapply legislation that is incompatible with European Community law (see Chapter 4) and the power to make a declaration of incompatibility of a UK statute with Convention rights comes close to striking it down (see Chapter 6). Further, the devolution legislation specifically provides for the supremacy of legislation of the UK Parliament as against laws of the devolved bodies (see Chapters 13–15). This is in sharp contrast with the American Congress whose powers are limited so as to protect the states from federal encroachment. However, there is a need in the UK system to resolve 'devolution issues', which are currently within the jurisdiction of the ordinary courts or, ultimately, the Judicial Committee of the Privy Council—which has become a quasi-constitutional court (see Chapter 13, and Le Sueur, 2001).

Supreme courts or equivalents like the Conseil constitutionnel in France (see Brown and Bell, 1998), may also operate in unitary states, and their function is to adjudicate on the compatibility of acts and other laws and actions with the Constitution. There is no equivalent British jurisdiction.

There is at present no real pressure to establish a *purely* constitutional court for the United Kingdom, in the sense of a court that would have jurisdiction only in relation to constitutional matters such as devolution issues and human rights. In any event, in the absence of a written Constitution, is it not easy to define constitutional issues in the UK. There is, however, growing pressure for a top court with broader jurisdiction, extending not only to constitutional issues but also certain aspects of criminal law, private law, and administrative law—a new Supreme Court that would, broadly, take the place of the Appellate Committee of the House of Lords and the Judicial Committee of the Privy Council.

The arguments in favour of a new Supreme Court may be elaborated, briefly, as follows (see generally Dickson and Carmichael, 1999; Le Sueur and Cornes, 2001). Despite the fact that the independence and impartiality of the Appellate Committee of the House of Lords—our top court—from Parliament and government are effectively secured by the combination of legal rules, conventions, and traditions noted above, the arrangements do not look right to the uninitiated outsider, and the court could lose its legitimacy and authority if public opinion came to view it as inappropriate. It has already been noted that the present arrangements run the risk of incompatibility with Article 6 ECHR (the requirement for courts to be independent and impartial) since the Law Lords have both legislative and judicial functions.

In practice the degree of participation in the legislative and scrutiny activity of the House by the Law Lords is not great. The Senior Law Lord, Lord Bingham, set out the principles by which the Law Lords would be bound in future in June 2000, in response to a suggestion by the Royal Commission on Reform of the House of Lords that if the House were to continue to exercise judicial functions the conventions should be clarified (Cm. 4534, 2000, recommendation 26). These general principles are that the Lords of Appeal in Ordinary do not think it appropriate to engage in matters where there is a strong element of party political controversy; and they bear in mind that they might render themselves ineligible to sit judicially if they were to express an opinion on a matter which might later be relevant to an appeal to the House (HL Deb., 22 June 2000, vol. 614, col. 419). The effect of these principles is that the Law Lords' role in the legislative business of the second chamber and in general debates there is much reduced (see Steyn, 2002a,b), rendering their membership increasingly anomalous and reducing some of the perceived benefits of having Law Lords in the chamber, such as their ability to bring their expertise to bear in debates, committee work etc., and their contact with the political world.

A second argument in favour of a new Supreme Court is that it is anomalous and confusing that, under the devolution arrangements, there is a double apex to the appeal system, the Appellate Committee of the House of Lords and the Judicial Committee of the Privy Council. A single Supreme Court with jurisdiction over these matters would be preferable and more transparent. The reason for the 'double apex' was that the Appellate Committee of the House of Lords is a committee of the second chamber of the Westminster Parliament; it should not have jurisdiction over devolution issues which might well raise questions about the interpretation of legislation which its parent chamber had participated in passing. Hence jurisdiction in respect of devolution issues was given to the Judicial Committee of the Privy Council. But most of the senior members of the JCPC are the Lords of Appeal in Ordinary—in other words the JCPC panel hearing a devolution issue case will be largely made up of the same people as would sit on the Appellate Committee, though in different capacities. Also, the Privy Council is formally a part of the UK executive so that similar points against its hearing devolution issues where the interests of the UK executive might clash with those of the claimants could arise.

These arguments for a new Supreme Court are largely negative—based on the defects in the institutional design of the present system, which has become outdated. But the case for a new Supreme Court, separate from the House of Lords and taking over the work of the Appellate Committee of the House of Lords and much of the work of the Privy Council, may be put positively. With a Supreme Court the system would be transparent and the relationships of separation between judges in the highest court and the executive and Parliament would be institutionalized and readily understandable. A separate institution, in its own building and clearly set apart from Parliament and the executive would generate confidence in the courts generally. Further, the fact of the matter is that there will be a great deal more 'constitutional' litigation in the light of devolution and the Human Rights Act 1998 than there has been in the past. Lord Bingham (2000) has identified an important function of the present Appellate Committee as being to rule on disputed questions of constitutional significance, giving 'constitutional' a broad meaning to embrace any issue which would probably be governed by a written Constitution if we had one. This function is analogous to the functions of the Supreme Court of Canada or the High Court of Australia. The point was made in Chapters 1 and 5 that the courts are starting to recognize in their decisions that there is a set of constitutional principles and constitutional issues which might have been regarded as merely part of 'administrative law' before the recent spate of constitutional reform. The issues that will be raised under this legislation may be extremely politically charged or morally controversial and it will be essential that the courts dealing with these cases have the strongest possible legitimacy and are properly constituted, housed, and serviced and that the system for appointment of judges who exercise these jurisdictions should be open and publicly and politically acceptable.

In the British system, where there is no written Constitution and the boundaries between constitutional law and other law is uncertain, it would not be workable to establish a specifically and exclusively constitutional court. It has already been noted that the present 'top courts' have important functions in developing the whole of the law, including the criminal law, private law, family law, and administrative law. Lord Bingham, the Senior Law Lord (2002), proposes a separate Supreme Court that would deal with issues across broad areas of the law as the Appellate Committee does now, running alongside the Judicial Committee, whose jurisdictions in relation to devolution issues and appeals from Commonwealth countries will continue. This would not involve American-style power to strike down legislation of the UK Parliament. The gains he sees in a separate supreme court 'lie in regularization and rationalization of the constitutional position of the supreme courts and (it would be hoped) improved facilities leading to a clear enhancement of its operational efficiency' (p. 8). He rejects amalgamating the Appellate Committee and the Judicial Committee, partly because of the implications for Commonwealth countries who still resort to the Judicial Committee as their final court of appeal. He also rejects a separate specialist constitutional court, since it is impossible to define constitutional matters, or a Luxembourg-style court that would deal only with references on points of law.

In sum, the balance of the arguments seem to me to be strongly in favour of the establishment of a new Supreme Court for the UK to replace the Appellate Committee of the House of Lords and some parts of the jurisdiction of the Judicial Committee of the Privy Council. The only objections of any merit are pragmatic in nature, namely the cost of providing a new building and finding legislative time for the measure. A new Supreme Court should inherit the United Kingdom wide, Northern Irish, Scottish, and English and Welsh jurisdictions of the present courts. The jurisdiction of the Judicial Committee in relation to the professional disciplinary proceedings should be transferred to another body, possibly the High Court. Members of the Supreme Court should be appointed formally by the Queen on the recommendation of an independent Judicial Appointments Commission. If hearings before appointment of judges of the new Supreme Court were considered appropriate in order to maintain public confidence in the appointment system and the appointees, the JAC could hold hearings, as the Judicial Services Commission in South Africa does when making equivalent appointments. The new Supreme Court should have its own accommodation and its members should not be members of the second chamber. No member of the government should be eligible to sit in the Supreme Court. The JAC's procedures for appointment should be transparent. The JAC should publish its criteria for making appointments and these criteria should be open for discussion.

Summary and Conclusions

The increasing activity of the courts in judicial review raises issues of legitimacy, accountability, openness, and the relations with other branches of government—all aspects of good governance. The position of the Lord Chancellor is becoming increasingly untenable and it undermines the legitimacy of the courts. Protection of public confidence in the system requires that the independence of the courts be more securely and transparently guaranteed than under the present informal arrangements, which rely heavily on conventions. This requires a Judicial Appointments Commission to take responsibility for judicial appointments and for opening up the criteria for appointment and the appointment process. A new Supreme Court should replace the Appellate Committee of the House of Lords and much of the jurisdiction of the Judicial Committee of the Privy Council.

Given the importance of the system of justice—and its enormous budget—there should be a Minister of Justice in the House of Commons with responsibility for the system. This would improve accountability for these matters, without undermining the legitimacy of the courts. The Lord Chancellor could remain as a Minister in the House of Lords with responsibility for matters which should be insulated from intense party political debate, including the appointment of the Judicial Services Commission, the formal making of judicial appointments, and the running of the courts, but he should no longer sit as a judge or be the head of the judiciary.

PART IV

CONCLUSIONS

19

Modernization Reviewed: Towards Democracy, Citizenship, and Good Governance?

We started our exploration of the reform of the UK Constitution in Chapter 1 with references to the commitment of the Labour government that was elected in 1997 to modernize the UK's system of government. We also noted that the modernization project, and indeed the longer-standing reform project that goes back to the Conservative governments from 1979 to 1997, have not been guided by a vision of democracy or a master plan. Modernization has taken three main forms: first, the removal of some rather arcane traditions and practices, which gave a dated air to the system. The use of the opera hat in the House of Commons to make points of order is the obvious example. The removal of most of the hereditary peers from the second chamber could be regarded as another. Secondly, modernization has meant improving working conditions in the House of Commons and other institutions, and provisions for the delivery of public services, to meet contemporary needs and realities. The introduction of more family-friendly hours in the House of Commons, the provision of up-to-date accommodation for MPs in Portcullis House, and the round-the-clock availability of some public services are examples. Thirdly, and this has been the focus of most of the discussion in previous chapters, modernization has been about responding to pressures from sections of the electorate, and from outside the UK, to make government at all levels more accountable, responsive, and effective, to involve those affected by government policy in decisions and policy-making, and to open up the system, providing opportunities for participation in the political process outside the party system. This has resulted in a major set of reforming measures, both citizen-focused (human rights, elections, freedom of information) and institutional (in Parliament, devolution, local government). We summarize these aspects of change in this chapter, focusing on the implications for democracy, citizenship, and good governance. Two charts at the end of the chapter summarize the implications for good-governance principles, especially for juridification, of the reforms. In the next and final chapter we turn to the question to what extent a concept of constitutionalism is penetrating or replacing the political constitution.

Developing Democracy

Many of the reforms that have been discussed in previous chapters have affected the theory and practice of democracy in the UK. The doctrine of the legislative supremacy of the UK Parliament is evolving, the nature of representation is changing, and channels for participatory and deliberative democracy are opening up. The relationships between these three aspects of democracy and their relationship in turn with the concept of citizenship and good governance principles are complex.

Sovereignty

The doctrine of the legislative sovereignty of Parliament—essentially a legal doctrine but with important political implications—is undergoing subtle change as a result of UK membership of the European Community, the Human Rights Act, and devolution. It will be helpful to draw together the points about sovereignty that have emerged from previous chapters. European Community law requires the British government and the courts to implement European Community law and to give primacy to it over domestic law. Since the *Factortame* and *Equal Opportunities Commission* cases it has been clear that the legislative supremacy of the Westminster Parliament is substantively limited by UK membership of the European Community, and that British courts will disapply any legislation that they find to be incompatible with European Community law.

In some countries in the EU, for example France, Austria, and Spain, it is explicitly acknowledged that a duality of sovereignty is developing, with European Community institutions and member states interacting (Schwarze, 2001). Bell (2002) suggests that there is in Europe a *network* of norms rather than a Kelsenian *hierarchy*, both within states –especially federal states—and between member states (p. 192). (This point about the replacement of hierarchy by networks is interesting, because it is mirrored in the development of networks and collaborative governance arrangements in government and public administration in the UK.) The rational or philosophical basis for such an interpretation of how the UK Constitution is developing is hotly contested and will no doubt surface in the courts from time to time, as it already is in the academic literature (see for instance Goldsworthy, 1999; MacCormick, 1999; Waldron, 1999). This aspect of democracy and democratic theory will continue to evolve in response to developments in the EU. One thing that a European Constitution could do is delineate and therefore protect the areas of sovereignty of member states and clarify the rules of this network.

While the Human Rights Act preserves the formal sovereignty of the Westminster Parliament, in practice both the UK government and the Westminster Parliament are subject to a number of political, procedural, and legal constraints as a result of the Act, some statutory, some self-generated, and some imposed by the courts. A model of inhibited parliamentary sovereignty is emerging. The HRA itself, by section 19, in terms imposes particular constraints on government Ministers when introducing legislation in Parliament, as they are required to apply their minds to whether their proposals are compatible with Convention rights, to state whether they consider the bill to be so compatible, and if not, to state that nevertheless the government wishes to proceed with it. These provisions are designed to draw attention to the issue of human rights compatibility in Parliament and to generate debate about the legal and political issues the proposed legislation raises, thus erecting obstacles, though surmountable ones, in the way of a government intent on interfering with these rights. The Joint Committee on Human Rights which the two Houses have established also places political hurdles in the way of a government seeking Parliament's consent to legislation that is or may be in breach of Convention rights, since the Committee's findings and reports may create or focus parliamentary opposition to possibly incompatible legislation. There is also clearly scope for the House of Lords Constitution Committee to focus attention on these issues. Thus statutory and political mechanisms combine to make it harder for Parliament to exercise its sovereignty where civil and political rights may be damaged by proposed legislation.

The power of Ministers under section 10 HRA to introduce remedial orders in the case of legislation that is incompatible with Convention rights enables them to repeal such legislation and replace it by compatible measures without having to go through the full legislative process. In this respect, perhaps paradoxically, ministerial power is increased by the Act and parliamentary sovereignty is reduced. Once a remedial order has been introduced, only resolutions of the two Houses are required for it to come into effect. This provision could be seen as extending the power of 'Parliament' to legislate by making it easier for it to do so. But in fact section 10 substitutes for 'the Queen in Parliament', the legal sovereign (which may normally only legislate by Acts passed after three readings in each House of Parliament and royal assent), a legislative body consisting of a Minister who lays a remedial order before Parliament and the two Houses operating by simple resolution. The remedial order provision undermines the legislative supremacy of the Parliament which earlier passed the incompatible legislation, exposing an Act to possible repeal or amendment by order where previously this could only be done by another Act. Apart from the fact that this undermines the pre-HRA doctrine of parliamentary supremacy, the HRA implies that democracy requires that a Parliament that legislates contrary to Convention rights is liable to have its laws overruled at the instigation of a Minister, by simple resolution in the two Houses, thus in turn modifying the concept of democracy as raw majoritarianism where these rights are concerned and substituting a concept of democracy as majoritarianism constrained by respect for civil and political rights.

The courts too have been given, by Parliament, new powers to impose constraints on Parliament where Convention rights are in issue, being under duties of compatible interpretation under section 2 HRA, which modifies the earlier doctrine of implied repeal by requiring that only if a statute cannot be read down or if words cannot be read in, should the courts give effect to a provision that is incompatible with Convention rights.

The devolution Acts preserve the formal legislative supremacy of the UK Parliament, but where devolution issues arise this is in practice exercised subject to a number of new legal and political constraints. Acceptance of the fact that the Scottish Parliament, and by analogy the Northern Ireland Assembly, exercise primary, not delegated, legislative power (see for instance *Adams v. Lord Advocate*, Court of Session, Outer House, P557/02, *The Times*, 8 August 2002) suggests that the UK Parliament is in practice sharing its sovereignty with those legislatures, though retaining the legal right to 'trump' their legislation.

The political climate has been changed by the devolution arrangements, and both the government and Parliament are inhibited by political pressures from the devolved areas in their ability to legislate on matters within the competence of the devolved legislatures without their consent—an inhibition which finds expression in the Sewel convention, for instance. (In fact, as we have seen, so far this convention has not been much of an inhibition for the Westminster Parliament, but it is possible that the Scottish executive and Parliament will subject Sewel motions and Westminster bills to greater scrutiny before that Parliament consents to the Westminster Parliament legislating on devolved matters, and thus a dialogue will have to take place between UK institutions and Scottish ones.) In relation to Northern Ireland the UK Parliament and government are further politically constrained by their relations with the Republic of Ireland.

Under the recently elaborated doctrine of the 'constitutional statute' in *Thoburn v. Sunderland City Council* ([2002] 3 WLR 247) there is scope for the courts to impose common law constraints on Westminster legislation which is incompatible with the devolution Acts by developing a principle that such a provision will only be given effect if it is shown that the Westminster Parliament actually intended to override the devolution Acts, or even Acts of the devolved legislatures, for instance by the use of express words in a later statute. Such a principle would give effect to the policy of modernization that has given primary legislative power to those legislatures, and it would 'constitutionalize' devolution.

It is clear that the simple hierarchy of laws in the UK that existed before it joined the European Community, before the HRA, and before devolution is being replaced by a far more complex system or network of norms as positive laws emanating from the European Community are given effect in the UK, as principles of compatible interpretation penetrate our law, and as relations between the UK Parliament and the devolved legislatures develop. As the UK courts draw on values and principles found in instruments such as the European Charter of Fundamental Rights (as they surely will) and on the jurisprudence of other comparable jurisdictions, they will develop the common law to include substantive legal principles and principles of interpretation that will influence their interpretation of Acts of the Westminster Parliament.

The HRA, the devolution legislation, and British membership of the European Community inevitably raise a number of questions about the justifications for a doctrine which has purported to grant legislative supremacy to the UK Parliament. If the devolved legislatures are subject to legal restrictions on broadly constitutional grounds as to the legislation they may pass for their own jurisdictions, then the question arises why the UK Parliament, when legislating for England and Wales (or indeed for the UK) should not also be formally bound by the same substantive constraints, or at least inhibitions? Part of the answer might be that the UK government, having control of Parliament, would not permit Parliament to pass legislation that could put the government in breach of its European Community obligations or its obligations under the ECHR or other international instruments. This, it could be argued, provides sufficient protection for the government against UK law being found to be in breach of European Community law or international law, and for the people of England and Wales (or indeed the people of the UK) against legislation being passed by the Westminster Parliament that is incompatible with their Convention rights. This justification for the legislative supremacy of the UK Parliament relies on arguments for a political rather than a legal Constitution. It is not based on a concept of democracy but on contractarian and functional justifications. It does not entail an argument that it would be undemocratic for the UK government or Parliament to be unable to legislate contrary to the UK's international or European community law obligations. Frankly, it is rather weak.

In practice, the formal preservation of the legislative supremacy of the UK Parliament is regarded as necessary for the maintenance of good relations between the courts and the other branches of government in England and Wales and indeed, where UK matters are at issue, of good relations between the government and Parliament, and the courts in Scotland and Northern Ireland. In my view this is a powerful argument. These are essentially good-governance issues rather than aspects of a positive democratic theory. In practice in the UK the understanding of the justifications of parliamentary sovereignty are based in a culture of comity, trust, and cooperation with both external and internal bodies, rather than in democratic theories. However, that culture could be damaged if different parties were in control in the UK and devolved levels and this could place the courts in a position where comity could not be preserved.

The HRA, the devolution legislation, and membership of the EC/EU have given rise to a heightened awareness in Parliament and government, and in the courts, of the *constitutional* dimensions of legislation and government policy, where previously the Constitution was, as Griffith observed, 'what happened' and Parliament was subject to no normative restrictions or inhibitions (see Chapter 20). These developments in the practical and political conditions in which parliamentary sovereignty is exercised in the UK represent radical departures from earlier practice. They affect our understanding of Parliament's position in the Constitution. It is no longer at the apex of a simple hierarchy of strictly legal norms. Instead a more subtle and varied network of relationships between laws or rules of different kinds and from different sources is developing. At the highest, Parliament is at the centre of a web rather than at the apex of a pyramid.

As the doctrine of the legislative supremacy of the UK Parliament is modified to give way to EC/EU membership, the HRA and the devolution legislation, the common assumption that it is the fundamental democratic doctrine in the UK and that the essence of democracy in the UK, is majoritarianism, is being undermined. A new concept of UK democracy as being based in constitutionalism will take its place (see Chapter 20), and what remains of the doctrine of the legislative supremacy of Parliament will come to be recognized as based in cultural concerns for comity between state institutions rather than in democratic theory.

Representation and representative democracy

The point was made in Chapter 2 that parallel theories of democracy operate in the UK, both representative and participatory. The practice and the concept of representative democracy in the UK are changing since proportional representation has been introduced at various levels. The devolved bodies in Scotland and Wales, and in London, operate under additional member electoral systems in which, while most members are elected on the first past the post system, others are elected on party lists to compensate the parties for the disproportionate results of the first past the post elections. Most proposals for reform of the House of Lords envisage that the elected element would be elected by party lists, open or closed. Elections to the European Parliament are by closed party lists. In Northern Ireland the single transferable vote is used.

These systems all affect the operation of the practice and the theory of representative democracy in various ways. As far as practice is concerned, turnout could increase if voters knew that the results of the election were likely to reflect their own candidate or party preferences to a greater degree than the first past the post system can. It is too early to know if increased turnout will flow from proportional representation, though the elections to the Northern Ireland Assembly, the Scottish Parliament, and the Assembly for Wales in 2003 may give some indication. The use of proportional systems can increase the effective vote, thus getting closer to meeting one of the criteria for a democracy (see Democratic Audit Criterion 4) that all votes should have equal value: whereas under first past the post votes for minority parties have a low value, under a proportional system the difference in value between votes for large and small parties is smaller.

First past the post gives electors an identifiable representative. Systems that use party lists mean that a number of MPs, possibly from several parties, represent the electors in the area or constituency. But lists do not produce a particular representative with responsibility for the area and its constituents and a direct relationship with each voter. Party lists institutionalize the power of party organizations by giving them patronage, in effect the right to give seats to candidates of the party's choosing. They do not give the voters an opportunity to choose between candidates of a party, as STV—a preferential system—does. Thus the use of a pure party list system, as for European Parliament elections, represents a shift from a theory of representative democracy which emphasizes the importance of the votes of individuals for individual candidates who, if elected, have a direct relationship with their voters, to a theory in which the party comes between voters and those who have been elected. Mixed systems, such as are used for elections to the Scottish Parliament and the Assembly for Wales do retain individual constituency members, but they produce two classes of representative, those serving a constituency and their party and those, in practice, serving only the party. The place of party in the system is, therefore, becoming institutionalized and more powerful.

Representative democracy, at least in Great Britain, has been based, though indirectly, on party since the extension of the suffrage in the nineteenth century. But these recent developments increase and legitimate the influence of parties, raising questions about relations between the extra-parliamentary party organizations and their elected members. As we have seen, these issues have in turn led the courts, for instance, and the Committee on Standards in Public Life in its Seven Principals of Public Life, to reassert the traditional representative theory, that those elected are to exercise their own judgement and should not be mandated by outside interests, whether their own parties or other bodies such as sponsors and trade unions. The relationships between party and elected representatives raise fundamental questions of political ethics and representation. As the use of proportional representation systems increases the power of the parties, counterbalancing measures to facilitate public participation in political debate, and decision-making outside the parties will be necessary to enable the public to feel connected to politics and to counteract the potential for abuse of their power and patronage by the parties.

Devolution has produced competition within the national parties, particularly Labour, whose desire at UK level to impose their own choice of leader in Scotland and Wales was rejected by the parties in those countries. This particular effect of devolution was not anticipated by the national Labour Party and took it by surprise. The experience brings out the fact that the interests and perspectives of the sub-national party organizations may be different from those of the 'parent' UK party. Under devolution, then, representative democracy operates at more than one level and serves to loosen the hold of the centre and central party organizations over the activities of the devolved bodies.

Proportional representation has produced coalitions of various kinds in the devolved bodies in Scotland, Wales, and London. (The system and the situation in Northern Ireland are different from those in other bodies where proportional electoral systems are in use and coalitions have been formed, and it would be hard to draw lessons for the rest of the UK from this aspect of Northern Ireland experience.) Coalition is a relatively novel practice in the UK, and if the coalitions in Scotland and Wales are successful or prove popular with their voters, the assumptions that operate at Westminster, that the voters do not like coalitions and that single-party government is best, may be undermined, and pressures for a proportional system for the House of Commons may build up. In my view, however, it would have to build up to an irresistible degree before it produced a response in the form of legislation for PR, since the vested interests in the present system (both Labour and the Conservatives) are so great. In reality there is no prospect of proportional representation being introduced for elections to the House of Commons for the foreseeable future, and the continuance of the present system and the adversarial political culture it promotes will lead to increasing public disconnection from politics and undermine the political Constitution and lead to increased judicialization of the system in ways that have been noted in earlier discussion and will be elaborated in this and the next chapter.

At the same time as proportional systems that give considerable power to the parties are taking root in the devolved bodies, there appears to be increasing public alienation from politics at UK level—manifested, for instance, in falling turnout in elections—and from the parties themselves, or at least from the parties as they operate in the House of Commons. Evidence received by the Royal Commission on Reform of the House of Lords indicated that while there was strong support for an elected element in a reformed second chamber, the parties themselves were disliked and the relatively non-partisan culture of the House of Lords was appreciated. In practice it is impossible for any electoral system to do anything other than produce predominantly party-aligned representatives. The tribalism of House of Commons does not seem to play well with the public. But no electoral system will produce non-party members in any number. Elections and parties go together and only by making it possible for non-party or non-partisan people to participate in decision-making outside elected bodies could the dissatisfaction of many members of the public with the party system be met.

Women and ethnic minorities are under-represented in all elected bodies in the UK.

This factor is not inconsistent with the theory of representation, which requires elected representatives to exercise their own judgement on behalf of their constituents. Representation does not mean representativeness in the sense of reflectiveness of the population by sex, ethnic background, or indeed age, disability, or other characteristics. But under-representation or under-reflectiveness of certain sections of society could account in part for low electoral turnout, to the extent that members of ethnic minorities and women were unable to identify with elected bodies. It could also undermine the legitimacy of decisions taken by elected bodies that were perceived to be discriminatory, for instance against women or members of ethnic minorities. Thus the procedures for the selection of candidates for election is a significant aspect of the practice of representative democracy. This is not however regulated by law (save that the Sex Discrimination (Election Candidates) Act 2002 permits—but does not require—positive action measures to reduce inequality in the number of female members elected for a party).

Overall, then, the traditional theory and practice of representative democracy are called in question by the introduction of systems other than first past the post in the UK and as yet there is no coherent or, in my view, satisfactory, theory of representation that can explain both how representative democracy works and in what sense or senses elections are democratic. At UK level elections produce an adversarial political style that will not be suited to a situation in which other parties are in control at devolved level than the party in power in Westminster. This will make the continuation of the culture of comity and the political Constitution difficult to maintain.

Participatory democracy

Representative democracy tends to concentrate formal public participation in government on voting in elections and standing for election, and exercising any influence on policy through the parties. This characteristic of the representative system serves to place those who wish to contribute effectively and to have their concerns responded to, and who are not members of one of the major parties, in a weak position as compared with party activists and supporters of the major parties. There is no reason to suppose that the contributions of those who wish to contribute independently of the parties are any less valuable than the contributions that pass through the parties. Participatory democracy can then provide opportunities for the public to contribute to politics and government outside the parties. Participatory democracy and citizenship are closely linked.

Many statutory provisions facilitate non-party-mediated participation in decision-making: planning inquiries are a strong example. Further, the courts have developed common law rights for those who are likely to be affected by decisions to be consulted or heard before decisions are taken. Some formal institutional arrangements have been put in place to promote non-party public participation, for instance the civic forums in Northern Ireland and Scotland. Some quangos have members or boards drawn from a range of interests and groups whose voices should be heard in the decision-making of these bodies. If a reformed second chamber were to contain in its membership people chosen for their ability to give voices to points of view which should be heard but which do not emerge via elections, then that would be a further example of a shift to a more deliberative or participatory democratic system.

The regional chambers operating in preparation for the eventual establishment of elected regional assemblies in England provide further examples of participatory institutions that are not party dominated. Their members are drawn from a range of interests in the region. This characteristic of regional governance will be replaced by party once elections to new regional chambers are held. But the government proposes that there should continue to be forums where non-party voices are heard, for instance by the co-option of business, trade union, voluntary organization, and environmental group members onto scrutiny or executive policy development committees, or as policy advisers, or through consultative forums.

Public, or at least civil society, non-party based, participation in the delivery of policy is promoted by the use of partnerships—networks—at various levels. The proposed regional assemblies for England will be expected to work in partnerships with business, trade unions, the voluntary and community sectors, local authorities and other key partners to steer the formulation of their overarching strategy and its implementation. Local authorities, too are expected to work with partners, and they have responsibilities for promoting community well-being and to encourage participation by voters and civil society in their areas.

Advisory referendums were held on an ad hoc basis before devolution legislation was introduced, and one is promised on the question whether the UK should join the European currency. There is as yet no generic referendum legislation in the UK, though the Political Parties, Elections and Referendums Act introduces the beginning of a framework for future referendums to be held.

Thus there has been a proliferation of non-party-based participatory arrangements alongside representative democracy in recent years. There are, however, weaknesses in some of these participatory processes. They may be captured by sectional interests: some regard the civic forums as merely providing voices for professional and trade associations—though this need not be a bad thing—rather than for disinterested people with special expertise or perspectives to contribute, or 'ordinary people'. There is clear scope for leadership and responsibility to be undermined in a participatory system, unless it is made clear whose job it is ultimately to make executive decisions and to take the blame if they go wrong, and be under a duty to put things right. This will normally be the elected representative body (though quangos too have executive functions) rather than the consultative or other participatory body or group. The strong tradition in the UK in favour of responsible government in the sense of public decision-making by identifiable bodies who will act prudently, take the blame if things go wrong, and put them right, inevitably limits the scope for formal, decision-making participatory democracy in the UK.

In many ways representative and participatory arrangements function comfortably alongside one another. But there is clear scope for conflict between them and the theories that underlie them. Participatory mechanisms can be seen as threatening by representative institutions, particularly by the parties. This is no doubt why the parties insisted in response to the government's proposals for reform of the House of Lords (Cm. 5291,

2001) that in a reformed House of Lords any party-aligned nominated members should be appointed by the parties themselves and not by an independent appointments commission. The Public Administration Select Committee expressed concern about the unregulated patronage that such arrangements for party appointment to the House of Lords would entail, and proposed that a better alternative to party appointment would be appointment by an appointments commission, which could receive nominations from the parties.

There is some evidence that the political parties and elected bodies do not take participatory processes and bodies seriously, unless they are required to do so by law—as with planning inquiries—or unless they consider that it is in their own interests to do so. Thus the civic forums in Scotland and Northern Ireland are not highly regarded by politicians. Unsurprisingly, since their own position is at stake, the preference of those in control— the political parties—at present is for elected institutions.

Despite the fact that participatory arrangements are not taken seriously and that they are not well theorized in the UK, deliberative and participatory mechanisms are becoming increasingly important as a result of the proliferation of networks, partnerships, and other cooperative relationships for the delivery of services and policy. Morison (1998) suggests that these networks and relationships raise issues of accountability and participatory and deliberative democracy that the liberal constitutional reform agenda, with its emphasis on representative democracy and its neglect of participatory democracy outside the representative system, does not address. He goes so far as to suggest that, because it is blind to these issues, the constitutional reform movement, with its ideas of restraining big government and reviving the role of Parliament, has missed the point (1998, p. 525). He suggests that promoting deliberative democratic processes is necessary to mitigate the problem that elected bodies lack the moral resources required to generate and sustain legitimate collective solutions. A deliberative approach is concerned with preference building: 'It is an interactive as opposed to aggregative approach that sees society as an essentially social construct where preferences are endogenously produced and empowerment comes from participation in collective decision-making.' Although there are a range of versions of deliberative or discursive democracy, they all put emphasis on the fairness of the debate, and the need to extend it beyond elected bodies and parties where interests are aggregated and thus focuses not on institutions but on process. I would not go as far as Morison on this, but it would indeed be foolish to ignore these issues and assume that proportional representation, an elected second chamber, more devolution, and a Supreme Court are a panacea for all constitutional ills and would necessarily produce good government and good governance.

Overall, the theory and practice of democracy in the UK are shifting from a majoritarian parliamentary system to a system of limited government, from legislative supremacy to legislative power shared by Parliament, the EU, and devolved bodies, from direct individual representation to representation explicitly mediated by parties, from government and Parliament strongly legitimated by the process of election to government, and Parliament lacking that legitimacy because of a low turnout and a low effective vote, to a system where legitimacy has to be won through success in meeting the needs of the people, through openness, and responsiveness through participatory arrangements.

Citizenship in the UK

Many of the reforms to the British Constitution that have been discussed in earlier chapters have affected the concept and content of citizenship in the UK. They have built up the liberal content of the relationship between the individual and the state. In developing the grounds for judicial review in the last forty years or so, the courts have been strengthening the position of individuals in their relationships with the state, requiring procedural fairness where individuals' interests are affected by an official decision, rationality on the part of decision-makers, and legality. Under the influence of European Community law and the jurisprudence of the European Court of Human Rights, the UK courts have moved towards requiring that government acts proportionately when implementing public policy that interferes with the rights or interests of individuals. Under the Human Rights Act public authorities are expressly required to respect the civil and political rights of individuals. Thus the relationship between the individual and the state has become judicialized and more strongly rights-based under the Human Rights Act 1998 than it was before that Act came into effect.

Many social and economic rights are also protected by law in the UK. To that extent the concept of citizenship as reflected in the law is both liberal and social democratic. Some aspects of government policy, such as the Citizen's Charter and the Best Value and *Service First* initiatives, elaborate on social and economic rights and thus on social-democratic citizenship, which is coming to include the concept of the citizen as a consumer with access to good-quality public services and channels for complaint if standards are not met. But these arrangements are administrative and they do not themselves give rise to rights that are enforceable in the courts. This strand of citizenship is less secure than rights based on legal guarantees, since it depends on passing and easily changeable government policy, and less secure still than guarantees which are constitutionalized in the sense of being strongly legally protected against change.

Citizenship is coming to entail legal responsibilities beyond the civic duties to pay tax, do jury service, and the like. Social obligations backed up by law include the duties of parents to send their children to school, parental responsibility for the criminal behaviour of children, and personal obligations to find work or train for employment. What was regarded as a citizenship of unconditional entitlement from the 1950s until the 1990s (Dahrendorf, 1988) has been modified, with the imposition of conditions on some entitlements to social benefits, the conditions being designed to discourage a culture of dependency and to encourage individuals to take responsibility for themselves and their families, by requiring unemployed people to undergo training as a condition of receipt of benefits, for instance. A model or paradigm of the autonomous, rights-bearing, complaining, but dutiful and responsible citizen of a responsive state has replaced the previously dominant model of the passive, vulnerable, claimant citizen of a protective, providential, and supportive state.

With devolution, some of the content of citizenship has become variable, and this raises issues as to the extent to which citizenship requires equality. Rights to vote for legislatures or executives, and to stand for election to those bodies, are exercisable below the national level, but asymmetrically. The use of proportional representation in Scotland, Northern Ireland, and Wales increases the effective vote as compared with first past the post as it is used for the Westminster Parliament. But the voting systems are different in each of these areas. In devolved areas, then, citizens have greater influence over the policies of their governments than citizens in England; and in Scotland and Northern Ireland citizens have greater influence over the legislation that affects them than citizens in Wales and England. As a result, different social and economic rights may be enjoyed in Scotland, Wales, Northern Ireland, and the rest of the UK: the abolition of university tuition fees for students from Scotland is an example. This means that citizenship entitlements vary from place to place in the UK, as citizens exercise their citizenship rights to make their own collective decisions about entitlements. Thus devolution produces inequality of citizenship rights within the UK. Citizenship has become asymmetrical. The point illustrates the contradictions in the concept of citizenship as equality, since local decision-making inevitably opens up the possibility of variable entitlements.

Civil society—in particular 'a democratic society' in the words of the Democratic Audit (Weir and Beetham, 1999)—is important in a democracy. Devolution should promote a lively political culture in the devolved areas and encourage political activists to engage in local political activity, to promote economic development and quality public services. It is already clear that many Scottish politicians prefer to put their energies into Scottish politics rather than UK politics. As and when regional assemblies are established, it is to be expected that new political energies will be released in England too.

Senses of identity are important social and cultural features of citizenship. There have long been multiple identities in the UK, as people think of themselves as, for instance, Scots, British, perhaps European. Those who have come to the UK from other countries will think of themselves a having those identities too. Devolution promotes senses of multiple identity and multiple citizenship (Heater, 1990). While Scottish and Welsh identities are fairly well-developed there is as yet no strong sense of English identity among many of the population. Those who have migrated to England are more likely to consider themselves British than English.

Towards European citizenship?

UK membership of the European Community and Union has introduced a concept of 'citizenship of the European Union'. Whether this is true 'citizenship' depends upon how citizenship is defined. On one view citizenship only exists where there is a 'demos' (Weiler, 1995) and only in relation to a state. It is clear that there is as yet no European demos, and nor is there a European state. The status is best regarded, then, as extended UK (and other member-state) citizenship and as a *sui generis* form of quasi-citizenship.

Citizens of member states of the European Union enjoy some civil and political rights in relation to the EU: they have rights to vote in elections to the European Parliament for representatives of the people of Europe, not of the member states from which they are elected. Voters have, via the parties, a relationship with their MEPs and the European Parliament, which is not mediated by their governments. Citizens of the European Union (and, though to a lesser extent, third-country nationals) have legal rights under European

Community law, which are enforceable against member states in the domestic courts of the member states and through the European Court of Justice. They have rights against the European Union and Community institutions, which may be enforced through the European Court of Justice. The ECJ's case law casts individuals in the role of citizen enforcers, with access to the courts, thus having a role in securing that member states and European institutions implement Community law and that the Community is based soundly in the rule of law.

The European Commission's *European Governance* White Paper, while not a legal document, writes in terms of 'civil society' and 'giving voice to the concerns of citizens' in a context which clearly assumes that civil society and citizens have important roles in relation to the Community and not solely in relation to their own states or the states in which they operate or reside. The 'social partners' across the EU have a role in EU policy-making, so that directives made by the Council on the basis of 'framework agreements' reached between them are binding in Community law. The White Paper assumes the existence and importance of a democratic society, one of the elements of citizenship required by the Democratic Audit (see Chapter 2).

These aspects of European Community law extend the concept of citizenship beyond the relationship between nationals and their state to a 'commonwealth'-based concept. Citizenship, like democracy, is coming to be the result of a complex network of norms, some domestic, some European, with the domestic rights to social and economic provision varying, with devolution, in different parts of the UK. Citizenship is an increasingly multi-layered and asymmetrical concept.

The future of citizenship

The UK has been moving away from a nationality-based citizenship model for some years. Since the formation of the Republic of Ireland, Irish nationals living in the UK have not been regarded as 'aliens' and have had the right to vote in UK elections. Commonwealth citizens also enjoy that right (though they may not have the status of European citizenship). Many people living in the UK, including citizens of member states of the European Union, have many of the same civil and political, social and economic rights and responsibilities as British citizens. In principle the Human Rights Act gives protection to everyone regardless of nationality or residential status. The trend towards opening up citizenship in the sense of civil and political, social and economic rights in the UK seems likely to continue, separating out the right to come and go from the country, which is at the core of nationality, from other rights and duties usually associated with citizenship.

There is a substantial agenda for the future development of citizenship in the UK. Work on developing a Bill of Rights for Northern Ireland could move the special legal protection of social and economic rights up the political agenda in the rest of the UK. European Community directives, mainly concerning rights in employment, already provide protection for some social and economic rights; these are in effect entrenched or 'constitutionalized', since the UK government cannot derogate from them without putting itself in breach of European Community law. No doubt further directives to protect social and economic rights will be promulgated by the Council of Ministers in the next few years, and implemented in the UK. The European Charter of Fundamental Rights, though regarded as declaratory only by the UK government, crystallizes a number of social and economic rights as well as civil and political ones which are binding on the European Community institutions and on member states when exercising Community competences.

The inequality of treatment of civil and political rights on the one hand (which have specially protected status under the HRA) and social and economic ones on the other (which have no such protection and many aspects of which are protected administratively rather than by statutory provisions) has led to suggestions that a new Charter of Social and Economic Rights should be adopted for the UK that would place those rights on at least an equal footing with civil and political rights, and thus constitutionalize them. We have considered in Chapter 6 how this might be done. One method would be to impose on Parliament and the legislatures in Scotland and Northern Ireland the same inhibitions against passing legislation that is incompatible with a charter of social and economic rights or a statement of Directive Principles of State Policy as the Human Rights Act imposes, i.e. requirements of ministerial statements as to the compatibility of a bill or statutory instrument with social and economic rights, scrutiny of legislation for compatibility with a charter, and reference of bills of the devolved legislatures to the Judicial Committee of the Privy Council or some other body for a determination as to their compatibility with such a charter. The courts and government could be placed under the same duties of compatible interpretation of social and economic rights as there are in respect of civil and political rights under the Human Rights Act and it could be made unlawful for public authorities to act incompatibly with those rights unless specifically authorized by statute to do so. Beyond that, however, it would not be possible to give exactly the same legal protection to social and economic rights as is given to civil and political rights.

An alternative method of achieving equal protection of social and economic, civil and political rights would be to repeal the Human Rights Act, in its place to formulate a charter of rights which would include civil and political, social and economic rights, and to put in place parliamentary procedures along the lines of those operating in Parliament under the Human Rights Act to protect those rights—scrutiny of bills by a Joint Committee on Rights, the power to make remedial orders, and so on. However, it is not on any realistic political agenda for the Human Rights Act to be repealed, and overall its seems unlikely that social and economic rights will be given the same protection as civil and political rights in the UK.

There is, however, considerable scope for the protection of social and economic rights to be enhanced in the UK and for the concept of citizenship to be developed more strongly towards a social-democratic one which could be constitutionalized in a number of ways, even if those rights did not enjoy the same protections as civil and political rights.

Good Governance

It will be remembered that principles of good governance include openness, accountability, effectiveness, public participation, legitimacy, trust, reliability, an absence of corruption, and respect for human rights. Clearly there is a great deal of overlap between these principles. There is, however, a far clearer concept of good governance than of democracy and citizenship and there is broad consensus about what good governance requires. The ways in which principles of good governance have been explicitly promoted in reforms in the period with which we have been concerned and the points they raise, are summarized at the end of this chapter in two charts, one summarizing how principles of good governance are reflected in recent reforms, and the other noting the implications of particular reforms for juridification, which is the main way in which accountability, the central principle of good governance, has been increased. Here we are primarily concerned with issues of accountability, and of juridification and trust.

Accountability

Many of the reforms in the period with which we have been concerned have been directed to improving—usually by increasing—the accountability of public bodies in each of the four ways noted in Chapter 3. Public accountability has been increased by a, rather unconvincing, commitment to freedom of information, by the use of proportional representation for elections to the devolved bodies, which is far more sensitive to shifts in public opinion than first past the post can be, and devices such as the Citizen's Charter and other mechanisms through which individuals in receipt of public services can make their needs known and complain if they are not met. In local government the preference has been for tight central administrative and audit-channelled control rather than improving the responsiveness of local government through the electoral system.

Political accountability has not greatly improved in the House of Commons despite the efforts of the Modernization and Public Administration Committees, in the face of government resistance and obstruction from the party whips. The fact that the electoral system has been producing large government majorities which can be unresponsive to the House of Commons does not help. This is very depressing. Political accountability has improved in the devolved areas where executive decisions are scrutinized in the elected bodies, though the ambiguity of the position in Wales is currently under review. Local authorities are under increasingly tight political acccountability duties to central government. Quangos remain relatively unaccountable politically and alternative mechanisms of accountability are developing.

Legal accountability—judicialization—has greatly increased under the Human Rights Act and the devolution legislation, and the courts have themselves developed the grounds for judicial review to impose stronger accountability, for instance in the development of proportionality as a ground for review and doctrines of fundamental and constitutional rights, constitutionalism, and constitutional statutes.

Audit and administrative accountability have been major growth areas, and are seen as alternatives to political or legal accountability. There has been a proliferation of codes, guidance, targets, performance indicators, and the like, to the extent that the level of freely given trust in the system has decreased dramatically. This has been in part due to incidents of seriously untrustworthy conduct by politicians and some other public officers, but it is also a response to a growing culture of suspicion in society at large—see below.

Juridification and trust

As the second chart at the end of this chapter shows, a strong trend towards juridification of government has been taking place in the period with which we have been concerned. Some of the pressures in the direction of legal regulation have come from outside the UK—from membership of the European Union and the fact that the country is party to the European Convention on Human Rights. (There has not been the space here to look at other external pressures but the obligations imposed by the World Trade Organization and other international organizations have reduced the freedom of activity of politicians in many areas.) Other pressures for the juridification of the Constitution have come from within.

Devolution inevitably means the statutory establishment of new institutions. There was no assumption that these new bodies could operate on the basis of trust and adherence to a public service ethos, and so the organization and proceedings of the executives, assemblies, and Parliament are tightly regulated. It is significant that the Scottish Constitutional Convention itself sought considerable legal regulation of its proposed Parliament for Scotland. In Northern Ireland the arrangements were designed to overcome the lack of trust between the two communities, and drew on experience with the unregulated Stormont Parliament from 1922 to 1972. The absence of statutory regulation of procedures and standards of conduct in the UK Parliament and government is now exceptional in the UK. It can be accounted for by their historical development and the culture of trust that has existed to a considerable extent until recently.

O'Neill (2002) has argued that legislation for legal protection of human rights and devolution, for instance, has been passed in part as a response to a culture of suspicion that has developed in the UK. This culture is fostered by the competitive atmosphere in which politics is conducted under the adversarial two-party system, and by the press. Her view is that human rights and democracy are not the basis of trust, but rather that trust is the basis for human rights and democracy. 'I think we may undermine professional performance and standards in public life by excessive regulation, and that we may condone and even encourage deception in our zeal for transparency' (O'Neill, 2002, ch. 5). Some of the reforms that have been introduced or that are under consideration are supposed to reduce regulation, though not explicitly because of the implications of juridification for trust. The Committee on Standards in Public Life has urged proportionality in the procedures for making public appointments on the grounds of cost and bureaucracy; under the *Strong Local Leadership* proposals successful local authorities will be relieved of some regulation and enjoy additional freedoms.

This does not, however, add up to a willingness on the part of government to relax its hold and trust those with whom it deals. Let us remind ourselves of the reasons for this. First, it is a fact that there have been examples of seriously corrupt conduct, cynical abuses of power, and partisanship by public bodies, notably local authorities, in recent decades which are not compatible with principles of public service such as those listed in the Seven Principles of Public Life. Trust, once forfeited, is hard to win back. Only some of these transgressions can be dealt with by the criminal law or other coercive measures such as disqualification from office. Some of the reluctance of government to trust local authorities, for instance, flows from their record of inefficiency, complacency, and unresponsiveness which would not be suitable for criminal or other judicial control. Judicialization is a response to some of these problems.

An alternative or parallel approach to juridification to solve these problems would be to sharpen up the political checks in the system so as to provide effective deterrents against abuses and punishments for them. The electoral system has not provided an effective check in local government, where in many areas the same party has retained control for years and this has led to complacency, inefficiency, and abuses of power. The introduction of proportional representation in local government would undermine the security of controlling parties and expose them to competition that should provide the incentives for them to improve their performance and win back trust and confidence.

The adversarial, tribal political system is responsible in large part for the culture of suspicion to which O'Neill referred. Her concern was with misplaced suspicion. No one would suggest a public body or office holder acting improperly should be trusted. O'Neill's assumption, with which I agree, is that most allegations of 'sleaze' against public bodies or individuals either have no basis in fact or are grossly exaggerated; most elected representatives, public servants, and other public office holders act in a spirit of public service and altruism. But the electoral system, again, encourages each party to undermine the public's trust in the others. At each election only one party can hope to win, and the winner wins all the spoils. The others receive nothing. There is no real possibility of the parties sharing power. The opposition has to pull out all the stops to undermine the party in power and win power for itself. A powerful weapon in the hands of an opposition, especially where large sections of the public support the controlling party's substantive policies or where the opposition has few policies of its own but wants power nonetheless, is to cultivate public mistrust and suspicion of the governing party, to make allegations of sleaze, to gain publicity for this in the press, even where there are no real grounds for such suspicion. A natural reaction on the part of the governing party is to retaliate in kind.

If a more cooperative spirit could be fostered between parties, in other words, if the electoral system offered rewards for cooperation rather than competition, then the incentives to promote mistrust of other parties would be reduced. The adversarial system at Westminster and in local government is not an unavoidable feature of a Western democracy. There is not the same degree of antipathy between the parties in Scotland and Wales as there is at Westminster. And in many European democracies antipathy is moderated by the exigencies of the electoral process and the need for cooperation and compromise (see King, 2001).

The introduction of proportional representation in the form of AMS for the House of Commons, and in local government in the form of STV, would have benefits beyond the promotion of trust and trustworthiness and the erosion of the culture of suspicion. It should make it possible to reduce the juridification of government and public administration. In the House of Commons it should enhance the ability of committees to scrutinize legislation and hold the government to account, it should increase the influence of backbenchers and undermine the power of the party whips. In local government it should increase the responsiveness of those in control to scrutiny and to their electors. However, because PR would undermine the power of the two main parties, it is most unlikely to be introduced. Thus the trend to juridification—which is in part a symptom of the culture of suspicion and mistrust and in part a response to adversarial politics— will continue and trust will be further damaged by the adversarial political style which first past the post promotes. But it will also, in my view, lead to judicialization and further undermining of the political Constitution, to which we turn in the next chapter.

Chart 1: *Constitutional reform and good governance*

Principle of good governance	Promotion of the principle	Comments
Openness (The natural tendency of public bodies is towards secrecy, although administrative requirements for openness have improved matters over the years, and local authorities have been under obligations of openness for some time.)	The Freedom of Information Act, 2000.	There are many exemptions to the right of access to information. The 'prejudice' rather than 'substantial harm' test for non-disclosure of some information favours government excessively and undermines openness. The ministerial override and the use of the Information Commissioner instead of the courts protect the relationship between the government and the courts, though judicial review of the override is possible. The courts are likely to defer to government on this.
	Requirement for publication of information about party funding and election expenditure.	See comments about trust, below.
	Committee on Standards in Public Life requirements for openness, for instance in public appointments, declarations of interest and registration of interests, mostly enforced by soft law mechanisms—except in local government.	See comments on trust, below. Over-prescriptiveness can be costly.
	Publication of the Ministerial Code, inclusion in it of resolution on ministerial responsibility, possibility of questioning the PM about his custodianship of the code by the Liaison Committee.	PM resistance to including the resolutions and meeting the Liaison Committee to protect secrecy of internal workings of cabinet and government demonstrates absence of culture of openness in government. PM's reliance on 'convention' to justify not meeting the Liaison Committee abandoned.
Accountability (see also discussion of democracy and juridification, above and in *Chart 2*)	*Public accountability*—see Openness above—promotes accountability to the general public by providing the information on which accountability rests.	
	The Citizen's Charter and other provisions for choice and	

(cont'd over)

Chart 1: continued

Principle of good governance	Promotion of the principle	Comments
Accountability: continued	complaints promote accountability to those in receipt of or needing public services.	
	Under first past the post electoral system accountability to the public is weaker than under PR.	
	Political accountability—some improvements to government accountability to Parliament, for instance in the resolutions on ministerial responsibility, new core roles for select committees, the Joint Committee on Human Rights, the House of Lords' Constitution Committee.	The capacity of the House of Commons to hold government to account and to scrutinize its proposed legislation is severely restricted by party discipline and the power of the whips.
	Devolution—subsidiarity—means that decision-making in Scotland, Northern Ireland, Wales and London, and potentially English regions is subject to local accountability.	England and, so far, English regions, have been left out of the arrangements. Scottish MPs can influence legislation for England and Wales—inappropriate accountability.
	In local government, government policy implies that accountability through election alone does not impose sufficient accountability to secure effectiveness and that strict regulation of what used to be political activity and accountability to central government are required.	The tight control exercised by central government over local government calls in question their commitment to local political accountability. The question whether good-governance provisions such as audit and administrative accountability and strict regulation of standards of conduct, and openness can substitute for or complement electoral mechanisms is also an issue in relation to quangos and the EU.
	In quangos, duties to report to Parliament, government, or devolved bodies impose light touch accountability. Provisions for openness in appointments and as to interests and the use of appointed boards in which affected interests have 'voices'—a form of participatory democracy—provide accountability through juridification.	There are problems in insulating these bodies from inappropriate political or partisan pressures and yet securing due accountability. Lessons may be learned from Sweden here.

(cont'd over)

Chart 1: *continued*

Principle of good governance	Promotion of the principle	Comments
Accountability: continued	*Audit and administrative accountability*—use of codes of conduct, frameworks agreements, performance indicators, PSAs, etc., provides the criteria for imposing accountability in non-political matters.	See discussion of juridification in next chart. Use of soft law keeps the courts out of the system and thus avoids confrontation and mistrust between courts and bodies subject to these requirements. Ill-designed performance indicators and targets can generate (mild) corruption. These techniques can be used to give government tight control over activity thus undermining pluralism and independence for local government, devolved bodies and others. Micro-management undermines effectiveness and responsibility. Over-regulation is inefficient. Those imposing these rules may not themselves be duly accountable—e.g. the Treasury. See second chart.
	Legal accountability/ judicialization —Greatly increased under the devolution legislation and the Human Rights Act. Judicial review requirement that reasons are given for decisions. Judicial review requirement of consultation before decisions are made should secure better-quality and so more effective decisions.	Judicial deference to Ministers on matters in which the judges have no expertise promotes effectiveness, in the sense that judicial intervention may be ill-advised and make government unworkable. But the judges may expand their review functions if political mechanisms remain ineffective.
Effectiveness	Adversarial politics under the first past the post system may produce ineffective policies and poorly drafted legislation. The House of Lords is better at the scrutiny of legislation, on objective criteria, than the House of Commons.	Weakness in political mechanisms are likely to lead to an expansion of judicial review or to the institution of extra-parliamentary scrutiny, for instance by a new council of state.
	Effectiveness is supposed to be improved by the use of codes, targets, etc.	See comments under accountability, above.
	Executive agency arrangements should promote effectiveness by clarification of outputs, standards, etc.	Over-regulation can lead to unnecessary bureaucracy, increase costs, and stifle initiative. A balance is required. Disaggregation of administration by executive agency arrangements makes joined-up government more difficult.

(cont'd over)

Chart 1: continued

Principle of good governance	Promotion of the principle	Comments
Public participation	See discussion of democracy and citizenship. Some statutory provisions require public participation, e.g. in planning inquiries. Civic forums in Scotland and Northern Ireland seek to promote public participation.	Public participation is not taken seriously by elected politicians unless they are required to do so by statute.
Legitimacy	Use of proportional representation for elections to Scottish Parliament and Northern Ireland and Welsh Assemblies should give legitimacy.	Turnout in elections for House of Commons, European Parliament, and local authorities is low and this may affect legitimacy. First past the post may not produce a government that is accepted as legitimate because of the underrepresentation of smaller parties. PR in House of Commons elections could improve legitimacy. The House of Commons may lack legitimacy because of the underrepresentation of women and members of ethnic minorities. List systems increase the power of the parties, STV does not. Not known what effect of PR will be on turnout. Alternative participatory opportunities needed for non-party sections of society. No move towards PR for the House of Commons. Questioning of the legitimacy of the judiciary with their increasing powers over legislation (EU, HRA, devolution) and ministerial decision-making may lead to reform of the appointment system.
Trust (which includes, in the UK context, comity between institutions, cooperation, and goodwill)	Openness and accountability—see above—should promote trust or defuse suspicion.	But information can generate a culture of suspicion. Inappropriate regulation, e.g. unrealistic targets, can encourage untrustworthy behaviour and undermine trust.

(cont'd over)

Chart 1: continued

Principle of good governance	Promotion of the principle	Comments
Trust: continued	Proposals for a Civil Service Act and a statutory statement of the Public Service Ethos should improve standards and generate trust.	Legislation alone cannot create an ethos if institutional arrangements (e.g. special advisers) and incentives (e.g. under NPM) in the system are incompatible with the ethos.
	The use of *Concordats*, etc., to regulate relations between the UK and devolved bodies should promote trust between them.	This may not work where different political parties are in control at UK and devolved levels. This could lead to pressure for stricter statutory regulation—juridification—and possibly judicialization of parliamentary proceedings and of relations between institutions.
	Clarification of standards of conduct in House of Commons and Parliamentary Commissioner for Standards should improve conduct and thus generate trust.	Petty tit-for-tat complaints by MPs of breach of code of conduct or registration of interest rules generate mistrust, suspicion, and bad relations between parties.
	Judicial deference to Parliament's legislation promotes trust.	The courts may feel justified in expanding judicial review to statutes if the political accountability mechanisms remain ineffective.
	Judicial deference to parliamentary self-regulation should promote trust and cooperation between Parliament and courts.	Procedures for dealing with contested complaints are unfair. Strong case for transferring jurisdiction over complaints that could lead to suspension or loss of salary to a court or a new independent judicial body. But parliamentary self-regulation, especially in relation to disciplinary matters, can be procedurally unfair to those accused of misconduct. Judicial procedures would be fairer.
	Judicial deference to Ministers should promote trust between judges and government.	Deference may be given at the price of unfairness to those complaining of ministerial decisions. When judges challenge Ministers on highly controversial issues, Ministers may resort to a strategy of challenging the legitimacy of the judges. Trust then breaks down.

(cont'd over)

Chart 1: continued

Principle of good governance	Promotion of the principle	Comments
Trust: continued	The workability of deference depends on self-restraint on the part of Ministers and voluntary compliance with the law on their part. This in turn depends on the effectiveness of political accountability and pressures on Ministers.	Absence of trust generates pressure for more juridification which in turn can undermine trust and increase costs and bureaucracy.
Reliability	See accountability, effectiveness, and trust, above. The judicial development of a doctrine of legitimate expectations promotes trust and reliability.	The strong tradition of responsible, in the sense of prudent, government favours reliability. But responsiveness to volatile public opinion can undermine it unduly.
Absence of corruption	The government has promised to bring forward legislation for the criminalization of bribery of MPs. See openness, accountability, and trust, above.	Absence of corruption is largely a cultural matter and it can be undermined if a culture of suspicion increases, for instance because of adversarial politics.
Respect for human rights	The Human Rights Act protects civil and political rights.	No special protection for social and economic rights (other than the right to property under the HRA). No Constitutional statement in the UK of Directive Principles of State Policy protecting such rights.

Chart 2: The juridification of political decision-making—a summary

Subject area	Form of juridification. Judicialization?	Comment
Membership of EU	Under the European Communities Act 1972 and European Community law the UK courts must disapply UK laws or ministerial decisions that are incompatible with European law. Strongest form of judicialization	This is a necessary aspect of membership of the EU, justified in contractarian and functional, not democratic, terms.
Judicial review—general (see also other subject areas in this chart)	The courts will not strike down Acts of the Westminster Parliament (save for incompatibility with EU law)—no judicialization. Judicialization of some political decision-making if principles of legality, procedural propriety, rationality (including breach of legitimate expectations), and in some cases proportionality are broken.	Strong preference on the part of judges—and Parliament and government—for the political Constitution. The basis is comity, not democracy. The same grounds for judicial review apply for non-political decision-making, e.g. by police, quangos, inferior courts. But the courts defer to Ministers where highly politically sensitive issues are at stake, unless the matters are within the expertise or province of the courts, such as criminal justice.
Human Rights Act	Strong juridification and judicialization of decision-making. The HRA provides that any public authority (i.e. including Ministers, members of the devolved executives, the devolved legislatures, local authorities as well as non-politicians such as quangos) but not Parliament acts unlawfully if they act incompatibly with Convention rights and the courts may grant remedies. The courts thus have power to decide whether breach of a Convention right was justified on any of the grounds specified in the Convention—necessity in a democratic society in various public interests.	The HRA would be regarded by the courts as a Constitutional statute if this concept takes root, and it would then be amendable by Parliament only by express words or other clearly expressed intention. The courts have power to strike down some highly political decisions but they defer to political decision-makers by allowing them a margin of discretion and thus uphold to some extent the political Constitution.

(cont'd over)

Chart 2: continued

Subject area	Form of juridification. Judicialization?	Comment
Human Rights Act: continued	The courts may not strike down or disapply a statutory provision that can only be interpreted incompatibly with Convention rights.	The Human Rights Act in terms prevents judicialization here. The declaration of incompatibility places the issue in the political arena. HRA substantially undermines the political Constitution except in relation to parliamentary sovereignty, and substitutes a law-based, possibly 'Constitutionalized' system (see below).
Elections, etc.	Conduct of election campaigns, election expenditure, and election funding heavily juridified under the Political Parties, Elections and Referendums Act 2000. Regulatory body is the Election Commission. Little scope for judicialization.	
	Election date for House of Commons elections determined by the Prime Minister—only regulation is the five-year rule. No conventions or other juridification of PM's decision. Minimal juridification here, no judicialization. Statutory provisions for dates for elections to devolved bodies and local authorities—strict juridification here. In practice little if any judicialization of this subject.	Strong case for statutory regulation—juridification—for instance by fixed four-year parliamentary terms. There would be little if any scope for judicialization in such a system.
Open government	Statutory requirements under FOIA 2000 from 2005 for rights of access to official information. Judicialization minimised by use of Information Commissioner. Pending FOIA rights of access are required by a Code enforced by the Parliamentary Commissioner for Information.	Ministerial override of Information Commissioner in some circumstances protects the political Constitution. Political actors protected from judicial control but subject to extensive juridification and constraints on their freedom not to disclose information.
Parliament	HRA specifically excludes Parliament from the duty to Act compatibly with Convention rights.	Protects the political Constitution.
	Parliamentary privilege prevents the judicialization of Parliament's proceedings.	Arrangements promote the political Constitution.

(cont'd over)

Chart 2: continued

Subject area	Form of juridification. Judicialization?	Comment
Parliament: continued	Parliamentary proceedings and conduct are regulated by recent new registration of interest and code of conduct requirements enforced by the two Houses—self-regulatory juridification. The whips have a strong influence on how the self-regulatory function is exercised.	Weak juridification and no judicialization of parliamentary procedures. Strong argument in favour of judicialising disciplinary procedures by putting them on a statutory basis and giving a court or an independent judicial body jurisdiction to meet the fair trial requirements of Article 6 ECHR and in any event to be fair to those accused.
	Scrutiny of legislation by standing committees subject to little juridification—no explicit criteria. Some select committees, e.g. Joint Committee on Human Rights, HL Constitution Committee, and Delegated Powers and Regulatory Reform Committee are guided by specific criteria.	Open to strong criticism for failing to meet the needs of the country for legislation to be properly scrutinised. Likely to lead to increased willingness of judges to read in or read down legislation that has not been properly scrutinised to uphold Constitutional principles and make it workable and fair.
	Scrutiny of government policy improving but whips dominate proceedings in the HC and government reluctant to respond to criticism.	Failing to meet the needs of the country for government to be held to account effectively. PR would improve matters but it will not be introduced. Likely to lead to increased judicialization as judges and the public realize how ineffective Parliament is.
Government	Organization and conduct of government not on a statutory basis. Organizational powers derive from the royal prerogative and are regulated by Constitutional conventions. Ministerial code lays down rules, and PM is responsible for enforcing them. Juridification has increased in recent years. Little judicialization.	Political Constitution preserved from judicial intervention.
	Many substantive powers derive from the royal prerogative and are not subject to parliamentary approval. Judicial review has been extended to cover decisions taken under the prerogative that are justiciable.	This may be a judicial response to weak political accountability of government for these powers. But judges defer to Ministers in highly sensitive matters. Balancing of deference and the courts' functions of protecting human rights under the HRA may lead to increased judicialization.

(cont'd over)

Chart 2: continued

Subject area	Form of juridification. Judicialization?	Comment
The Civil Service	Not on a statutory basis. Regulated by Orders in Council and numerous codes governing minister/civil service relations. Highly juridified. Very little judicialization, save that the *CCSU* case required expectations of consultation of civil service unions to be met unless national security at issue.	Political Constitution preserved from judicial intervention but freedom of action of politicians constrained by juridification. A Civil Service Act would increase juridification but would not be likely to increase judicialization much.
Devolution	Statutory basis. Highly juridified and, through the possibility of judicial review, judicialized (though legislative procedures enjoy statutory protection akin to parliamentary privilege). Detailed statutory provisions as to formation of executives in Scotland and Northern Ireland, regulation of conduct, registration of interests, committee system, etc.	Strong contrast between the level of juridification and judicialization of UK Parliament and government and devolved bodies. Political Constitution not as strong here as at UK level.
	Relations between devolved bodies and UK Parliament and government regulated by *Memorandums of Understanding* and *Concordats*. No judicialization.	Political Constitution tradition extended to devolution in these areas.
	Barnett formula for funding the devolved bodies is non-statutory, weakly juridified, not judicialized.	In some federal countries funding is prescribed by statute and is highly judicialized. Political Constitution free of judicialization preferred for devolution in UK.
Local government	Statutory basis. All aspects, including executive arrangements, conduct, finance, standards of service, contracting out, etc. heavily juridified by statute, guidance, codes, etc. Strong central control via public service agreements, Best Value, *Service First*, beacon status, conditional funding, etc.	Political checks are ineffective because of the working of the electoral system and low turnout. As a result juridification and judicialization are likely to continue, even increase. Not yet known whether elected Mayors will be more accountable. Juridification unlikely to be reduced by any government in my view.
	Subject to judicial review— extensive judicialization.	judicialization has resulted in some inappropriate decisions, e.g. in *Bromley v. GLC*, because the courts do not understand some aspects of local government.

(cont'd over)

Chart 2: continued

Subject area	Form of juridification. Judicialization?	Comment
Quangos	Unelected, thus outside the political Constitution. Legal basis varies—some statutory, some chartered, some companies, etc. Appointments usually made by Ministers, dismissible by Ministers. Most report to Ministers or Parliament. Increasingly juridified by codes regulating appointments, conduct, auditing, reporting, etc. Judicially reviewable so some judicialization.	Not much of the political Constitution here.
The judiciary-institutional arrangements	Mostly statutory basis. Self-regulating to a considerable degree. Appointments becoming juridified by Lord Chancellor's published policies. Conventions protect against political interference.	No-go area for the political Constitution. Some pressure for more open appointment systems which could politicize it.

20

The Political Constitution in Transition?

We now return to one of the questions that have run through discussion of constitutional reform in the previous parts of this book: what is happening to the political Constitution and what will happen to it in future?

It will be remembered that Griffith, in his lecture in 1979, argued that 'the constitution is no more and no less than what happens' and that political decisions should be taken by politicians, not judges. He argued from and for a highly positivist interpretation of the Constitution, with no 'oughts' or moral content. He accepted that this does not prevent people from arguing from moral or self-interested positions about what the Constitution ought to be and what the law ought to provide, but his interpretation was that the Constitution was the result of the settlement of various conflicts between classes and interests over the years and had no moral or normative content.

Griffith's particular concern at that time was that a Bill of Rights would take away from politicians the right to make decisions about whether public interests in, for instance, national security, should outweigh the rights of individuals, transferring that power to the judges. That has happened with the Human Rights Act, in which Parliament deliberately gave the judges a function in relation to ministerial and other governmental decisions that might be incompatible with human rights. Griffith felt that decisions about conflicting interests are essentially political and that the law is not and cannot be a substitute for politics. Giving decision-making powers to judges does not change a political decision to a non-political one, it just transfers a political decision-making function from a politician to a judge. Thus, he argued, political decisions should be taken by politicians. This was not necessarily because politicians were any cleverer or had greater expertise than judges (though they might), but because they are removable and judges are not. It was not by attempting to restrict the legal powers of government that we would defeat authoritarianism, he argued, but by insisting on open government. And he was against any further judicialization of the administrative process. He did not express a view about juridification of politics short of judicialization, however. His main concern was about judicial power. Waldron too (1999) has argued that political decisions should only be taken by politicians, that they should not be constrained in their powers and that Constitutions should not give special protection to specific values.

Cultural Aspects of the Political Constitution

Griffith was mainly concerned with judicialization rather than with other forms of juridification of political decision-making, though those forms may well constrain political decision-makers to a considerable extent and very effectively. As we have seen in Chapter 19, there has been a strong process of juridification of politics in the last twenty years or so. Despite this increase in juridification, the political, in the sense of non-judicialized, Constitution survives in the UK where in other Western democracies legal regulation could well have been introduced. This is due to the political culture of the UK. Comparative examples will serve to bring out this characteristic of UK arrangements.

- *The maintenance of the sovereignty of the Westminster Parliament under the Human Rights Act and the devolution legislation.* Most other Constitutions limit the legislative competence of their Parliaments and/or impose procedural constraints on changes in certain constitutional laws, and provide for a Supreme Court or a Constitutional Council to prevent the passage of unconstitutional legislation.

- *The formation and conduct of cabinet government.* This is not regulated by law at UK level. The devolution Acts make provision for this in Scotland and Northern Ireland. The Constitutions of many countries also make provision for this.

- *Reliance on the Sewel convention to regulate the use of its residual legislative power by Westminster on devolved matters.* In federal systems and systems with constitutionally protected local or regional government, the Constitution or legislation set out in detail the central legislature's relations with lower tiers. This is not the case in the UK.

- *Reliance on the non-statutory Barnett formula for the funding of devolved bodies and England.* In many federal states these matters are regulated by statute. Not in the UK.

- *Self-regulation in the Houses of Parliament.* The devolution legislation lays down detailed provisions in some matters. The Westminster Parliament remains self-regulating.

- *The extensive use of codes of conduct at all levels of government.* These would be regarded as law and subject to administrative court or tribunal jurisdiction in may civil law jurisdictions.

My point is that the continuing strong preference for political rather than legal and judicial control mechanisms in many aspects of the UK Constitution marks it out from many Western democracies. The survival of the UK's political Constitution suggests that law and politics can coexist effectively. Loughlin (2000, 6) argues that peaceful coexistence is most likely to occur only when it is acknowledged that law forms an intrinsic part of politics. It may be that the judges in the UK realize that their interventions in political matters are themselves political, and that they lack the legitimacy and expertise of the executive and Parliament, and so they hold back from challenging primary legislation or highly politically sensitive decisions. This accounts for their professions of deference to democratically accountable decision-makers in recent cases. However, this tradition, even instinct, of deference, may be undermined where human rights are at stake, since the role given to the courts by Parliament in the HRA is not entirely consistent with deference.

The advantages of this culture of continuing reliance on informal political mechanisms rather than on legal measures and adjudication by courts and tribunals are that it enables relationships between the courts and Parliament and the executive to be based on comity, and it avoids detailed legal regulation of government activity and the conflict between institutions that such regulation can produce; it presumes and fosters trust and co-operation between institutions; and it protects the courts from becoming over-politicized. Griffith's argument in favour of the system was based on a belief that political account-ability mechanisms were more appropriate than judicial ones, and that they were effective in practice. At that time, however, there had already been breakdowns in comity between government and the courts in a series of controversial decisions by the courts against the Labour government's policies, which had formed much of the material on which Griffith based the first edition of *The Politics of the Judiciary* in 1978. Griffith's argument was not, presumably, dependent on the existence of such a culture.

There are, however, a number of disadvantages in the preference for the political Constitution in the UK, notably a lack of openness and transparency when the current culture of suspicion demands more open and formal controls on power; and the fact that in practice the trust and cooperation on which the arrangements rely are open to abuse. Further, in my view political accountability mechanisms are not in reality as effective as they should be in the UK's political Constitution, largely because of the working of the electoral system and the consequent hold of the two main parties in Parliament and many local authorities (see Chapter 19).

The political Constitution depends heavily upon a culture of self-restraint on the part of constitutional actors. If that culture should disintegrate, then the remaining advantages of the arrangements would disappear and the case for a law-based Constitu-tion with more judicialization would become the stronger. We have already suggested that the culture could suffer, for example, if different parties were in power in Westmin-ster and Scotland or Wales or in many of the larger local authorities. Particularly if one or more of these levels of government were controlled by radical single-party adminis-trations set on policies that were not compatible with those pursued at one or more other levels, it is to be expected that the UK Parliament and executive would feel justified by their electoral success in imposing their own policies on the devolved bodies or local authorities, exercising the legislative supremacy of the Westminster Parliament to do so, even if the devolved bodies did not consent. The Sewel convention would be discarded. That this is a real possibility is borne out by experience in the 1980s, when local authorities under Labour control opposed the Conservative govern-ment's policies, and the government then secured legislation to limit the freedom of action of local authorities and impose tight regulation of political activity at that level. If PR were in operation at Westminster and in local government, then a more con-sensual political style would enable confrontations to be avoided or settled without recourse to controlling legislation. Given that proportional representation will not, in my view, be introduced for the House of Commons or local government, it seems inevitable that such conflicts and confrontations will arise sooner or later. The upshot of such inevitable conflicts will be that the political Constitution will be further undermined. Once it and the trust on which it depends have gone, it will not be restored. Among the results is bound to be increased judicial activism and the juridification and judicialization of politics.

Towards Constitutionalization?

We have noted in previous chapters that UK judges have recently been elaborating some fundamental constitutional rights and principles, and setting out their concepts of democracy, and we have considered the issues this raises as to the source of this judicial power and its legitimacy. In the event of the increased judicial activism that I envisage developing as a result of conflict between different levels of government, these principles are likely to take on even greater importance. Even the doctrine of the legislative supremacy of the Westminster Parliament may be called in question.

The courts may well find that they have support from other quarters in doing so. It is not only the courts that have begun to elaborate constitutional principles according to which government should be conducted. Parliament has done so too, in legislation such as the European Communities Act (e.g. giving effect to principles of primacy of European Community law and direct effect), the Human Rights Act (protection of civil and political rights subject only to express statutory derogation), and the devolution legislation (e.g. subsidiarity, maintenance of parliamentary sovereignty, proportionality in elections). And so have other bodies, both in the international community and within the UK. Many of the values and principles that are now regarded as 'constitutional' and form part of the law in the UK are given expression in international instruments such as the ECHR. Constitutional principles are also expressed in codes and other non-legal texts elaborated by other public bodies in the UK which have been adopted to guide government at many levels. The Committee on Standards in Public Life's Seven Principles of Public Life, the parliamentary resolutions on ministerial responsibility, the law and practice of Parliament forbidding bribery of MPs, the Sewel convention, the restrictions on parliamentary comment about particular cases which are *sub judice*, the Code of Conduct of Civil Servants: all express constitutional principles.

The courts and constitutionalism

Thus many constitutional actors besides judges have been elaborating constitutional principles in recent years. In acknowledging the existence of, and elaborating, principles of fundamental and constitutional rights, constitutionalism and, latterly, constitutional statutes, the courts are reflecting, even catching up with, constitutional principles that are fairly widely relied upon in the UK, and in the wider democratic world. They have not been engaging only in unilateral, freelance constitutionalization. But the existence, indeed the proliferation, of these constitutional values and rules sits uncomfortably with Griffith's rejection of any moral content to the Constitution.

The courts may feel the need to call in reinforcements in their support when their constitutionalizing activity brings them into conflict with government or Parliament. International instruments, such as the ECHR, the International Covenant on Civil and

Political Rights, and the European Charter of Fundamental Rights will inevitably be invoked by the courts to buttress their findings, for they supply some of the priority values, approved by the UK government, that are otherwise missing in the UK legal system.

What kind of constitutionalism—liberal or . . . ?

An assumption is often made that 'constitutionalism' is necessarily 'liberal constitutionalism' rather than 'social-democratic constitutionalism'. It is the fact that much of the case law on constitutionalism and the constitutional legislation that has been passed in the last six years or so, and many of the other measures of an administrative or 'soft law' kind that have been taken, promote liberal principles. The prime example is the Human Rights Act. However, much of what has been happening in the UK's constitutional arrangements has been ambiguous. The Citizen's Charter and 'Best Value' initiatives treat individuals as consumers, an approach that is consistent with liberal (in the economic sense) concepts of citizenship. But they are consumers of public services, and the emphasis on the entitlements of individuals to social and economic benefits which are promoted by the 'Best Value' policy is also consistent with social citizenship and social-democratic theory. The difference between liberal-economic and social-democratic theory here is a matter of enforcement mechanisms rather than values. On both liberal and social-democratic principles citizens ought to receive social and economic 'rights' from the state. On the liberal approach citizens should have power as consumers to press their claims; on the social democratic approach citizens should use the political process to press their claims, but not as individuals—rather, as members of the political community. The latter approach assumes that the political community is effective in pressing claims, but is prepared to be tolerant of political unresponsiveness, even if it leaves individuals unprovided for. The liberal approach places less faith in politics and is less tolerant of the possibility that individuals will not be provided for if the political process does not meet their needs. It thus treats individuals as rights bearers who can press their own claims, whether through elections and via their MPs, or in the courts, or through internal complaints procedures and other means. Devices such as these bridge what has been a divide between liberal-economic and social-democratic theory.

Some constitutional measures are suggestive of parallel concepts of liberal and social-democratic constitutionalism. While the Human Rights Act promotes a liberal concept of constitutionalism, much of European Community law is 'constitutional' in the UK in the sense that it is binding on the government and laws or policies that are incompatible with European Community law are disapplied by the courts. This constitutional law is in many respects of a social-democratic kind. For instance, the entrenchment of rights not to be discriminated against on grounds of sex or nationality in employment, and many employment protection rules such as the Working Time Directive and other social policies of the EU, are social in nature, though their ultimate aim is the promotion of an economic and political community. The European Charter of Fundamental Rights—which applies only to the exercise of European competences, whether by the institutions of the EU or by member states—includes both the usual civil and political rights and an array of employment-related social and economic rights. To the extent that constitutionalism is about giving specially protected legal and political status to certain provisions, in the UK both 'liberal' and 'social' provisions enjoy that status to a degree, and there is clearly scope for further constitutionalization of social and economic rights.

Future Prospects for the Political Constitution

There are growing pressures for more aspects of the UK system to be put on a statutory basis which would reduce the freedom of action of politicians and thus the reach of the political Constitution—notably an Act to regulate the exercise of some royal prerogative powers, a Civil Service Act, an Act to regulate standards of conduct in public life and further devolution legislation. There could be further statutory provision, for instance for the joint ministerial council under the *MoU* on devolution, or for the financial calculations of Exchequer payments to devolved bodies in lieu of the Barnett formula. Statutory provisions in these areas would put in place frameworks that regulate political activity, but without necessarily opening up new possibilities of judicialization. Judicial review is not the only form that juridification can take, or the only alternative to the political Constitution.

The extent to which constitutional arrangements are put on a statutory basis will depend to some extent on whether Parliament can itself act as a policeman or watchdog over government action and legislation. As I have already indicated, in my view the House of Commons is not capable of reforming its scrutiny of legislation or of government so as to perform these functions adequately because of the party system and the operation of the electoral system. The Joint Committee on Human Rights and the House of Lords Constitution Committee are taking responsibility respectively for scrutinizing legislation for compatibility with human rights provisions and generally with constitutional principles, but there should be more safeguards in the political Constitution than the activity of such committees.

A written Constitution for the UK?

In the 1990s there was a flurry of interest in the question whether the UK should adopt a written Constitution (see Liberal Democrats, 1990; Macdonald, 1990; Institute of Public Policy Research, 1991; Oliver, 1991, ch. 11, 1992). While this an important and fascinating issue, it is not high on the realistic political agenda and we shall not spend much time on it (cf. Brazier, 2001). But it is worth noting that a resurgence of interest in the matter could take place if it were felt that only a written Constitution could protect the UK from unwelcome encroachment by the European Union: a written Constitution for the UK could require formal amendments to be made, perhaps after a referendum, if the powers of UK institutions would be reduced by changes in the European Community or the European Union. Germany, Denmark, and Ireland have all needed constitutional amendments before changes in the Community can be implemented.

Second, a written Constitution could become necessary, or at least it could be pressed for, if relations between the UK government and the UK Parliament on the one hand and the devolved bodies on the other hand became strained. In effect a written Constitution would then represent a new bargain between the countries in the UK and the UK itself. The necessity for it would be caused by a breakdown in comity and trust between the different levels of government. It would further undermine the political Constitution and put in its place a law-based Constitution with provision for judicial review—US style.

We noted in Chapter 1 that a written Constitution would probably have to be the source of power in the state, rather than an attempt to write down the existing system or a desired system without entrenching it in any way. It would probably entail setting up an American-style Supreme Court or a French-style constitutional council or council of state, that could review legislation or decisions that were alleged to be in breach of the Constitution. This would further undermine the political Constitution.

Conclusions

The process of judicialization of politics and the establishment of the constitutional state that are taking place in the UK have also been trends in other parts of the world since the Second World War (see Vallinder, 1994; Shapiro and Stone, 1994; Barak, 1999; Weinrib, 1999). Weinrib, for instance, argues that Canada with its Charter has been transformed from a legislative to a constitutional state. It may be, then, that the preference for a political Constitution expressed by Griffith and others is out of line—however regrettably—with actual developments in other comparable jurisdictions. It does not of course follow that the UK should follow their example. What is interesting is that the United Kingdom has sought a third or middle way, retaining the legislative supremacy of the Westminster *Parliament* alongside devolution and the Human Rights Act, but subjecting *government* to legal constraints against breaches of human rights that are not plainly authorized by Parliament. It is hard to see how a devolutionary arrangement could have been made that did not provide for judicial resolution of conflicts between the levels of government. The political Constitution becomes more difficult, even impossible, in a devolved or federal system.

Discussions of constitutionalism tend to oppose two views about the relationship between politics and law, or perhaps more accurately, about the relationship between politicians and the courts. The real question is about balance. What is being sought currently in the UK, in a blind-leading-the-blind, Heath Robinson, incremental way, is a balance which takes into account the inevitable increase in the role of the law and the courts and the legal regulation of political activity that comes with membership of the European Union and devolution, and the problems that will inevitably arise if the courts are seeking to limit the freedom of action of those who are elected. A difficulty is that the lawyers who argue for a new constitutionalism are primarily focused on limiting the power of the executive as ruler rather than on seeing a Constitution—which could well include restrictions on the power of the state to interfere with certain activities of individuals and protections against discrimination against minorities—as, in Loughlin's words, an instrument of collective self-rule (Loughlin, 2000a, 191). In effect the courts' concept of democracy is diverging from that held by many politicians.

The middle way that is evolving, then, is based on recognition that the courts have an important, rather political role, in giving effect to constitutionally significant legislation and in developing the common law. They need to realize that there are contested concepts of democracy in issue and to beware of making decisions that neglect this point and do not face up to the fact that they may be making controversial political choices. My own sense is that the judges are learning to do this, and that the traditions of comity, trust, and cooperation between institutions, and of discriminating deference on the part of judges to politicians where statutes permit, can, if they endure, secure the continuation of a strongly political Constitution. However, if the judiciary is operating in a culture where comity, trust, and cooperation have been damaged—whether by insensitivity on their part or on the part of politicians, or because of political polarization affecting relations between the levels of government—they will inevitably be drawn into highly contentious decision-making and this will undermine the judicial system. The appointment of judges would become more political, there would be pressure for either a Supreme Court whose members would be politically appointed or some other body or bodies such as a council of state to determine questions of constitutionality. Ultimately the political Constitution would be replaced by a law-based, law-dominated one.

Much responsibility lies, then, with politicians under the UK's strongly political Constitution. Under the present electoral system the government is under little pressure to be responsive to Parliament. The prospects of the House of Commons being able to improve its scrutiny of legislation and its willingness to hold government to account are, in 2003, rather depressing. The House of Lords is relatively good at these jobs but whether a reformed second chamber would be as good or better is in the air. In my view a substantially elected second chamber could not do them well. If politicians prove unable to perform the roles which justify the political Constitution, then inevitably some of those roles will pass to the judges.

However constitutional arrangements develop, the genie of constitutionalism is out of the bottle. The once-taboo subject is now being discussed, not only in the courts and academic circles but in Parliament and even in the press. The interest in constitutionalism will be kept alive as and when reforms that have not yet been implemented rise up the political agenda, such as proportional representation for the House of Commons, further reform of the House of Lords, regional government in England, further devolution to Wales, and adjustments to the arrangements in Scotland and Northern Ireland.

And finally . . . two futures

In my view the UK Constitution is at a cross-roads, and the choice of road will dictate the destination. I suspect that our leaders cannot read the pointers, and a metaphorical coin will be tossed to determine which direction is taken.

Along one of those roads lies a dynamic, effective, legitimate, responsive, decentralized political system commanding broad public support and trust, holding government to account and securing high-quality legislation, with a low level of juridification and effective political and legal provisions for the protection of civil and political, social and economic rights. Running parallel with it is a participatory lane.

The landmarks along the road to that system will be:

- the introduction of an additional member system for elections to the House of

Commons and some form of PR for local authorities; a House of Commons elected in that way will be able to hold government to account and a government will have to adopt a responsive, collaborative, less competitive style;

- reform of the Second Chamber, with a small elected element, other members appointed on merit by an independent Appointments Commission, including independents who will hold the balance; that chamber will be able to complement the House of Commons in scrutinizing legislation and holding government to account; and

- a statute incorporating a statement of Directive Principles of State Policy including social and economic rights; this will underpin citizenship and legitimate the courts' judicial review activity.

Along the other road—which is the road we are currently travelling along—will lie a weak political system lacking legitimacy, a public that is mistrustful of its politicians and their adversarial style, a Parliament that is incompetent at holding government to account, an unresponsive government, and a highly centralized, juridified, over-regulated, inefficient system of public administration. The Scottish Parliament, the Northern Ireland Assembly (with any luck) and the Welsh Assembly will have greater legitimacy than bodies at Westminster. Participatory mechanisms will be ineffective in the face of a strongly tribal political culture at Westminster. The system will be heavily judicialized.

There will be few progressive landmarks along that road. There will be a series of statutes imposing more and more central control on state activity, and there will be a series of decisions by the courts expanding the reach of judicial review, which they will feel justified in taking because they will know that the public is disaffected from Parliament, that Parliament cannot hold the government to account, that it is not representative or reflective of the population:

- the courts will decide to treat the European Union Charter of Fundamental Rights as a source of values that they can use in developing the common law and interpreting Acts of Parliament and subordinate legislation; and

- the courts will decide to increase the scope of judicial review to enable them to disapply provisions in Acts of Parliament that were passed in the face of objections by the Joint Committee on Human Rights or the Constitution Committee of the House of Lords, unless there is an express provision in the Act in question that it is to take effect notwithstanding the defects identified by either of those committees.

There will be other landmarks on that road, and several battles will be fought along the way. Possibilities include the introduction of a substantially or wholly elected second chamber that will reduce Parliament's ability to scrutinize legislation and hold government to account; this will reinforce the courts' claim to do so; steps may be taken to reduce the security of tenure or the independence of the judiciary in the face of its decisions against Ministers.

Whichever of the two roads is taken, there may be other landmarks, but they will not be as significant for the UK Constitution as the major ones noted above: increasing the powers of the Assembly for Wales; the unification of the island of Ireland; the establishment of English regional assemblies; revision of the Barnett formula; increasing the powers and fiscal autonomy of local authorities.

The second road, it seems to me, is the one our politicians at Westminster will take. The first, which would make the continuation of the political Constitution possible, would have been the better one.

Appendix

Articles from the European Convention on Human Rights that have been incorporated into UK law by the Human Rights Act 1998 (taken from Schedule 1 to the Act).

SCHEDULE I

THE ARTICLES

Part I
The Convention Rights and Freedoms

Article 2
Right to life

1. Everyone's right of life shall be protected by law. No one shall be deprived of his life intentionally save in the execution of a sentence of a court following his conviction of a crime for which this penalty is provided by law.

2. Deprivation of life shall not be regarded as inflicted in contravention of this Article when it results from the use of force which is no more than absolutely necessary:

    (a) in defence of any person from unlawful violence;

    (b) in order to effect a lawful arrest or to prevent the escape of a person lawfully detained;

    (c) in action lawfully taken for the purpose of quelling a riot or insurrection.

Article 3
Prohibition of torture

No one shall be subjected to torture or to inhuman or degrading treatment or punishment.

Article 4
Prohibition of slavery and forced labour

1. No one shall be held in slavery or servitude.

2. No one shall be required to perform forced or compulsory labour.

3. For the purpose of this Article the term 'forced or compulsory labour' shall not include:

(a) any work required to be done in the ordinary course of detention imposed according to the provisions of Article 5 of this Convention or during conditional release from such detention;

(b) any service of a military character or, in case of conscientious objectors in countries where they are recognized, service exacted instead of compulsory military service;

(c) any service exacted in case of an emergency or calamity threatening the life or well-being of the community;

(d) any work or service which forms part of normal civic obligations.

Article 5
Right to liberty and security

1. Everyone has the right to liberty and security of person. No one shall be deprived of his liberty save in the following cases and in accordance with a procedure prescribed by law:

    (a) the lawful detention of a person after conviction by a competent court;

    (b) the lawful arrest or detention of a person for non-compliance with the lawful order of a court or in order to secure the fulfilment of any obligation prescribed by law;

    (c) the lawful arrest or detention of a person effected for the purpose of bringing him before the competent legal authority on reasonable suspicion of having committed an offence or when it is reasonably considered necessary to prevent his committing an offence or fleeing after having done so;

    (d) the detention of a minor by lawful order for the purpose of educational supervision or his lawful detention for the purpose of bringing him before the competent legal authority;

    (e) the lawful detention of persons for the prevention of the spreading of infectious diseases, of persons of unsound mind, alcoholics or drug addicts or vagrants;

    (f) the lawful arrest or detention of a person to prevent his effecting an unauthorized entry into the country or of a person against whom action is being taken with a view to deportation or extradition.

2. Everyone who is arrested shall be informed promptly, in a language which he understands, of the reasons for his arrest and of any charge against him.

3. Everyone arrested or detained in accordance with the provisions of paragraph 1(c) of this Article shall be brought promptly before a judge or other officer authorised by law to exercise judicial power and shall be entitled to trial within a reasonable time or to release pending trial. Release may be conditioned by guarantees to appear for trial.

4. Everyone who is deprived of his liberty by arrest or detention shall be entitled to take proceedings by which the lawfulness of his detention shall be decided speedily by a court and his release ordered if the detention is not lawful.

5. Everyone who has been the victim of arrest or detention in contravention of provisions of the Article shall have an enforceable right to compensation.

Article 6
Right to a fair trial

1. In the determination of his civil rights and obligations or of any criminal charge against him, everyone is entitled to a fair and public hearing within a reasonable time by an independent and impartial tribunal established by law. Judgment shall be pronounced publicly but the press and public may be excluded from all or part of the trial in the interests of morals, public order, or national security in a democratic society, where the interests of juveniles or the protection of the private life of the parties so require, or to the extent strictly necessary in the opinion of the court in special circumstances where publicity would prejudice the interests of justice.

2. Everyone charged with a criminal offence shall be presumed innocent until proved guilty according to law.

3. Everyone charged with a criminal offence has the following minimum rights:

   (a) to be informed promptly, in a language which he understands and in detail, of the nature and cause of the accusation against him;

   (b) to have adequate time and facilities for the preparation of his defence;

   (c) to defend himself in person or through legal assistance of his own choosing or, if he has not sufficient means to pay for legal assistance, to be given it free when the interests of justice so require;

   (d) to examine or have examined witnesses against him and to obtain the attendance and examination of witnesses on his behalf under the same conditions as witnesses against him;

   (e) to have the free assistance of an interpreter if he cannot understand or speak the language used in court.

Article 7
No punishment without law

1. No one shall be held guilty of any criminal offence on account of any act or omission which did not constitute a criminal offence under national or international law at the time when it was committed. Nor shall a heavier penalty be imposed than the one that was applicable at the time the criminal offence was committed.

2. There shall be no interference by a public authority with the exercise of this right except such as is in accordance with the law and is necessary in a democratic society in the interests of national security, public safety or the economic well-being of the country, for the prevention of disorder or crime, for the protection of health or morals, or for the protection of the rights and freedoms of others.

Article 8
Right to respect for private and family life

1. Everyone has the right to respect for his private and family life, his home and his correspondence.

2. There shall be no interference by a public authority with the exercise of this right except such as is in accordance with the law and is necessary in a democratic society in the interests of national security, public safety, or the economic well-being of the country, for the prevention of disorder or crime, for the protection of health or morals, or for the protection of the rights and freedoms of others.

Article 9
Freedom of thought, conscience, and religion

1. Everyone has the right to freedom of thought, conscience and religion; this right includes freedom to change his religion or belief and freedom, either alone or in community with others and in public or private, to manifest his religion or belief, in worship, teaching, practice and observance.

2. Freedom to manifest one's religion or beliefs shall be subject only to such limitations as are prescribed by law and are necessary in a democratic society in the interests of public safety, for the protection of public order, health or morals, or for the protection of the rights and freedoms of others.

Article 10
Freedom of expression

1. Everyone has the right to freedom of expression. This right shall include freedom to hold opinions and to receive and impart information and ideas without interference by public authority and regardless of frontiers. This Article shall not prevent States from requiring the licensing of broadcasting, television, or cinema enterprises.

2. The exercise of these freedoms, since it carries with it duties and responsibilities, may be subject to such formalities, conditions, restrictions, or penalties as are prescribed by law and are necessary in a democratic society, in the interests of national security, territorial integrity, or public safety, for the prevention of the reputation or rights of others, for preventing the disclosure of information received in confidence, or for maintaining the authority and impartiality of the judiciary.

Article 11
Freedom of assembly and association

1. Everyone has the right to freedom of peaceful assembly and to freedom of association with others, including the right to form and to join trade unions for the protection of his interests.

2. No restrictions shall be placed on the exercise of these rights other than such as are prescribed by law and are necessary in a democratic society in the interests of national security or public safety, for the prevention of disorder or crime, for the protection of

health or morals, or for the protection of the rights and freedoms of others. This Article shall not prevent the imposition of lawful restrictions on the exercise of these rights by members of the armed forces, of the police, or of the administration of the State.

Article 12
Right to marry

Men and women of marriageable age have the right to marry and to found a family, according to the national laws governing the exercise of this right.

Article 14
Prohibition of discrimination

The enjoyment of the rights and freedoms set forth in this Convention shall be secured without discrimination on any ground such as sex, race, colour, language, religion, political or other opinion, national or social origin, association with a national minority, property, birth, or other status.

Article 16
Restrictions on political activity of aliens

Nothing in Articles 10, 11, and 14 shall be regarded as preventing the High Contracting Parties from imposing restriction on the political activity of aliens.

Article 17
Prohibition of abuse of rights

Nothing in this Convention may be interpreted as implying for any State, group or person any right to engage in any activity or perform any act aimed at the destruction of any of the rights and freedoms set forth herein or at their limitation to a greater extent than is provided for in the Convention.

Article 18
Limitation on use of restrictions on rights

The restrictions permitted under this Convention to the said rights and freedoms shall not be applied for any purpose other than those for which they have been prescribed.

Part II
The First Protocol

Article 1
Protection of property

1. Every natural or legal person is entitled to the peaceful enjoyment of his possessions. No one shall be deprived of his possessions except in the public interest and subject to the conditions provided for by law and by the general principles of international law.

2. The preceding provisions shall not, however, in any way impair the right of a State to enforce such laws as it deems necessary to control the use of property in accordance

with the general interest or to secure the payment of taxes or other contributions or penalties.

Article 2
Right to education

No person shall be denied the right to education. In the exercise of any functions which it assumes in relation to education and to teaching, the State shall respect the right of parents to ensure such education and teaching in conformity with their own religious and philosophical convictions.

Article 3
Right to free elections

The High Contracting Parties undertake to hold free elections at reasonable intervals by secret ballot, under conditions which will ensure the free expression of the opinion of the people in the choice of the legislature.

Part III
The Sixth Protocol

Article 1
Abolition of the death penalty

The death penalty shall be abolished. No one shall be condemned to such penalty or executed.

Article 2
Death penalty in time of war

A State may make provision in its law for the death penalty in respect of acts committed in time of war or of imminent threat of war; such penalty shall be applied only in the instances laid down in the law and in accordance with its provisions. The State shall communicate to the Secretary-General of the Council of Europe the relevant provisions of the law.

List of Official Publications

(in approximate chronological order)

1918

Bryce, Viscount (1918), *Report of the Conference Chaired by Viscount Bryce*, Cd. 9038. London, HMSO.

Report of the Machinery of Government Committee (The Haldane Report), Cd. 9230. London, HMSO, 1918.

1967

Maud, Sir John (1967), *Report of the Committee on the Management of Local Government*. London, HMSO.

1968

Report of the Committee on the Civil Service (The Fulton Report), Cmnd. 3638. London, 1968.

House of Lords Reform, Cmnd. 3799. London, 1968.

1973

Report on the Royal Commission on the Constitution 1969–73 (The Kilbrandon Report), Cmnd. 5460. London, 1973.

1977

First Report from the Select Committee on Procedure, 1977–8, HC 588-I to II.

1978

House of Lords Select Committee on a Bill of Rights (1978). *Report* (House of Lords Paper 176 (1977–8). London, HMSO.

1980

Report on Non-departmental Bodies (The Pliatzky Report), Cmnd. 7797. London, 1980.

Alternatives to Domestic Rates, Cmnd. 8449. London, 1981.

1985

Fourth Report from the Defence Committee 1985–6: *Westland plc: The Government's Decision-Making*, HC 519. London, HMSO.

1986

Local Authority Publicity (Interim Report of the Committee of Inquiry into the Conduct of Local Authority Business). London, 1986.

Report of the Committee of Inquiry into the Conduct of Local Authority Business (The Widdicombe Report), Cmnd. 9797. London, 1986.

1988

The Conduct of Local Authority Business: The Government Response to the Report of the Widdicombe Committee of Inquiry, Cm. 433. London, 1988.

Efficiency Unit (1988). *Improving Management in Government: The Next Steps*. London, HMSO.

Eighth Report from the Treasury and Civil Service Committee 1987–8: *Civil Service Management Reform: The Next Steps*, HC 494. London, HMSO.

Developments in the Next Steps Programme. The Government Reply to the Eighth Report from the Treasury and Civil Service Committee, Session 1988–9 HC 348, Cm. 524. London, 1988.

First Report from the Agriculture Committee 1988–9, HC 108. London, HMSO.

1989

Select Committee on Procedure 1989–90: *The Working of the Select Committee System*, HC 19–I. London, HMSO.

Eighth Report from the Treasury and Civil Service Committee 1989–90: *Progress in the Next Steps Initiative*, HC 481. London, HMSO.

The Financing and Accountability of Next Steps Agencies, Cm. 914. London, 1989.

House of Lords Select Committee on the European Communities, Twenty-seventh Report 1989–90.

1991

Making the Most of Next Steps (Fraser Report), May 1991. London, HMSO.

The Citizen's Charter (1991), Cm. 1599. London, HMSO.

Competing for Quality: Buying Better Public Services, 1991, Cm. 1730. London, HMSO.

1992

Citizen's Charter Indicators. Charting a Course, Audit Commission. London, 1992.

1993

Open Government, Cm. 2290, 1993.

1994

Parliamentary Commissioner for Administration, *Investigation of Complaints against the Child Support Agency*, HC 135, 1994–5.

Third Report from the Select Committee on the Parliamentary Commissioner for Administration, HC 199, 1994–5.

Code of Practice on Access to Government Information, Cabinet Office, 1994.

1995

Sir Richard Scott, *Report on the Export of Dual-Use Goods to Iraq*, HC 115, 1995–6.

Committee on Standards in Public Life, First Report, Cm. 2850, 1995.

Review of Prison Service Security in England and Wales and the Escape from Parkhurst Prison on Tuesday, 3 January 1995 (The Learmont Report), Cm. 3020.

First Report from the Committee of Privileges, *Complaint concerning an article in the 'Sunday Times' of 10 July 1994 relating to the conduct of members*, HC 351, 1994–5.

1996

Public Service Committee, 3rd Report 1996–7, HC 78 *The Citizen's Charter*.

1997

The Governance of Public Bodies: A Progress Report, Cm. 3557, 1997.

Committee on Standards in Public Life, Third Report, *Standards of Conduct in Local Government in England, Scotland and Wales*, Cm. 3702, 1997.

A Voice for Wales, Cm. 3718, July 1997.

Rights Brought Home: The Human Rights Bill, Cm. 3782, October 1997.

Fourth Report of the Committee on Standards in Public Life, *Review of Standards of Conduct in Executive NDPBs, NHS Trusts and Local Public Spending Bodies*, 1997. London, Stationery Office.

Your Right to Know: The Government's Proposals for a Freedom of Information Act, Cm. 3818, 1997.

Building Partnerships for Prosperity, DETR, 1997.

Departmental Evidence and Response to Select Committees, Cabinet Office, 1997.

Good Governance. The IMF's Role. Washington: International Monetary Fund, August 1997.

Green Paper, *New Leadership for London*, Department for the Environment, Transport and the Regions, 1997.

First Report from the Committee on Standards and Privileges, *Complaints from Mr Mohamed Al Fayed, The Guardian and others against 25 members and former members*, HC 30, 1997–98.

1998

Modern Local Government: In Touch with the People, Cm. 1014, July 1998.

The Belfast Agreement: An Agreement reached at the Multi-Party Talks on Northern Ireland, Cm. 3883, April 1998.

A Mayor and Assembly for London: The Government's Proposals for Modernizing the Governance of London, Cm. 3897, March 1998.

Sixth Report from the Select Committee on Public Administration, HC 209, 1998–9, *Quangos*.

Service First—The New Charter Programme, 1998, Cabinet Office.

Quangos: Opening the Doors, 1998, Cabinet Office.

Fifth Report of the Committee on Standards in Public Life, *The Funding of Political Parties*, Cm. 4057, October 1998.

Report of the Independent Commission on the Voting System (The Jenkins Report), Cm. 4090, October 1998.

Implementation of the Best Value Framework, Government Response to the Select Committee on Environment, Transport and Regional Affairs, Cm. 4092, October 1998.

Treasury Committee, *The Barnett Formula: The Government's Response,* HC 619, 10 March 1998.

Consultative Steering Group on the Scottish Parliament, *Shaping Scotland's Parliament,* Scottish Office, December 1998.

Green Paper, *Modernizing Local Government: Improving Local Services through Best Value,* March 1998.

Public Services for the Future: Modernization, Reform, Accountability. Public Service Agreements 1999–2002, Cm. 4181, December 1998.

Joint Committee on Parliamentary Privilege, *Report,* HL Paper 43–1 and HC 214–1 (1998–9).

Law Commission, *Legislating the Criminal Code: Corruption,* Law Com. No. 248, 1998.

1999

Modernizing Parliament: Reforming the House of Lords, Cm. 4184, 1999.

Modernizing Government, Cm. 4310, March 1999.

House of Lords Select Committee on the European Union, 8th Report, *EU Charter of Fundamental Rights,* HL 67, 1999–2000.

The Funding of Political Parties in the United Kingdom: The Government's Proposals for legislation in response to the Fifth Report of the Committee on Standards in Public Life, Cm. 4413, July 1999.

National Audit Office, *Government on the Web* (1999).

Sir Leonard Peach, *An Independent Scrutiny of the Appointment Processes of Judges and Queen's Counsel in England and Wales. A Report to the Lord Chancellor by Sir Leonard Peach,* December 1999.

House of Commons Procedure Committee Report, *The Procedural Consequences of Devolution* (4th report 1998–9, HC 185, May 1999).

Liaison Committee 1999–2000: First Report *Shifting the Balance: Select Committees and the Executive,* HC 300.

Opinion of the Economic and Social Committee, *The Role and Contribution of Civil Society Organizations in the Building of Europe,* OJ C329, 17.11.99.

2000

Second Report from the Select Committee on Public Administration, *Ministerial Accountability and Parliamentary Questions,* HC 61, 2000–1.

Select Committee on Public Administration Third Report, *The Ministerial Code: Improving the Rule Book,* HC 235, 2000–1.

Royal Commission on the Reform of the House of Lords, *A House for the Future,* Cm. 4534, 2000.

Home Office, *Raising Standards and Upholding Integrity: The Prevention of Corruption,* Cm. 4759, June 2000.

Committee of the Regions (EU), *New forms of governance: Europe, a framework for citizens' initiatives* (CdR 186/2000).

Sixth Report from the Public Administration Committee, *Review of Audit and Accountability for Central Government,* HC 260, 2000–1.

Fourth Report from the Select Committee on Public Administration, *Special Advisers: Boon or Bane?,* HC 293, 2000–1.

Report from the National Audit Office, *Measuring the Performance of Government Departments,* HC 301, 2000–1.

DETR, *Preparing Community Strategies: Government Guidance to Local Authorities,* 2000.

Committee on Standards in Public Life, Sixth Report, *Reinforcing Standards,* Cm. 4557, 2000.

The Government's Response to Sixth Report of the Committee on Standards in Public Life, Reinforcing Standards, Cm. 4817, July 2000.

2001

Third Report from the Treasury Committee, 2000–1, *HM Treasury*, HC 73-I, 1 February 2001.

Fifth Report from the Select Committee on Public Administration, *Mapping the Quango State* HC 367, 30 March 2001, 2000–1.

Sixth Report from the Select Committee on Public Administration, *Innovations in Citizen Participation in Government*, HC 373, 2000–1.

Select Committee on Public Administration Second Report, *The Ministerial Code: Improving the Rule Book: The Government's Response to the Committee's Third Report of Session 2000–01*, HC 439, 2001–2.

Holding to Account: The Review of Audit and Accountability for Central Government (the Sharman Report), Cabinet Office, February 2001.

House of Commons Select Committee on Public Administration, Seventh Report, *Making Government Work: The Emerging Issues*, HC 94, 2000–1, 10 April 2001.

Guidance to Officials on Drafting Answers to Parliamentary Questions, Cabinet Office, 2001 as amended (see Annex A, HC 136, 2002–3).

Second Report from the Liaison Committee, *Select Committees: Modernization Proposals*, HC 692, 2001–2.

First Report from the Select Committee on Modernization of the House of Commons, *Select Committees*, HC 221, 2001–2.

Northern Ireland Human Rights Commission, *Making a Bill of Rights for Northern Ireland*, September, 2001.

Electoral Commission (2001) *Election 2001. The Official Results*. London, Politico's.

Ministerial Code, Cabinet Office, July 2001.

Commission of the European Communities White Paper, *European Governance*, COM (2001) 428, Brussels, 25.7.2001.

Committee on Standards in Public Life, *The First Seven Reports. A Review of Progress*, 2001.

The House of Lords. Completing the Reform, Cm. 5291, November 2001.

Code of Conduct for Special Advisers, Cabinet Office, 2001.

Fourth Report from the Select Committee on Public Administration, *Ministerial Accountability and Parliamentary Questions: The Government Response*, HC 464, 2000–1.

Working Together: Effective partnering between local government and business for service delivery, Department for Transport, Local Government and the Regions, December 2001.

Treaty of Nice, Cm. 5090, 2001.

Strong Local Leadership—Quality Public Services, Cm. 5237, December 2001.

First Report from the Public Administration Select Committee, *Public Participation: Issues and Innovations: The Government's Response to the Committee's Sixth Report of Session 2000–2001*, HC 334, 2001–2.

Parliamentary Commissioner for Administration, Fourth Report, HC 353, 2001–2002.

Memorandum of Understanding, Cm. 5240, December 2001.

United Nations Economic and Social Commission for Asia and Pacific (no date), *What is Good Governance? www.unescap.org/huset/gg/governance.htm.*

2002

Fifth Report from the House of Commons Public Administration Select Committee, 2001–2, *The Second Chamber: Continuing the Reform*, HC 494, 2001–2.

First Report from the Select Committee on the Modernization of the House of Commons, HC 224-I, 2001–2.

Fifth Report from the House of Commons Committee on Standards and Privileges, *Complaints against Mr Keith Vaz*, HC 605, 2001–2.

Audit and Accountability in Central Government. The Government's Response to Lord Sharman's Report 'Holding to Account', Cm. 5456, March 2002.

Your Region, Your Choice. Revitalizing the English Regions, Cm. 5511, May 2002.

The House of Lords. Completing the Reform—Analysis of Consultation Responses, Lord Chancellor's Department, May 2002.

Government Response to the Fifth Report from the Select Committee on Public Administration Select Committee, 2001–2, *The Second Chamber: Continuing the Reform*, HC 494, HC 794, 2001–2.

Statement of Funding Policy, HM Treasury, 2002.

Electoral Commission (2002), *Modernizing Elections. A Strategic Evaluation of the 2002 Election Pilot Schemes*, London, Electoral Commission.

Select Committee on Report by the Group Appointed to Consider How the Working Practices of the House can be Improved and to make Recommendations, *Report from the Leader's Group appointed to consider how the working practices of the House can be improved, and to make recommendations*, HL 111, 2001–2.

Seventh Report from the Select Committee on Public Administration, *The Public Service Ethos*, HC 263, 2001–2.

Fourth Report from the House of Lords Select Committee on the Constitution, *Changing the Constitution: The Process of Constitutional Change*, HL 69, 2001–2.

Eighth Report from the Select Committee on Public Administration, *These Unfortunate Events*, HC 303, 2001–2.

Ninth Report from the Select Committee on Public Administration, *Ministerial Accountability and Parliamentary Questions*, HC 1086, 2001–2.

Thirty-third Report from the House of Commons European Scrutiny Committee, *Democracy and Accountability in the EU and the Role of National Parliaments*, HC 152, 2001–2.

Audit Commission for Local Authorities and the NHS of England and Wales, *Kingston Upon Hull Corporate Governance Inspection Report*, July 2002, Audit Commission, London.

Fifth Report from the Select Committee on the Procedure of the House, HL 148, 2001–2.

Chancellor of the Exchequer, *Comprehensive Spending Review and Public Service Agreements*, July 2002.

Office of the Deputy Prime Minister, *Tackling Poor Performance in Local Government*, Consultation Paper, August 2002.

Second Report from the Modernization Committee, *A Reform Programme*, HC 1168, 2001–2.

Comptroller and Auditor-General's Report, *Inpatient and outpatient waiting in the NHS*, HC 221, 2001–2.

Comptroller and Auditor-General's Report, *Inappropriate Adjustments to NHS Waiting Lists*, HC 452, 2001–2.

Forty-sixth Report from the Committee of Public Accounts, *Inappropriate Adjustments to NHS Waiting Lists*, HC 517, 2001–2.

Scottish Civic Forum, *Audit of Public Participation*, November 2002. Edinburgh, Scottish Civic Forum.

Eighth Report of the Committee on Standards in Public Life, *Standards of Conduct in the House of Commons*, Cm. 5663, November 2002.

Electoral Commission (2002), *Election 2001 Campaign Spending*. London, Electoral Commission.

Select Committee on Public Administration, *Ministerial Accountability and Parliamentary Questions: The Government's Response to the Committee's Ninth Report of Session 2001–2*, HC 136, 2002–3.

First Report from the Joint Committee on House of Lords Reform, HL 17, HC 171, 2002–3.

Select Committee on Public Administration, First Special Report, *The Public Service Ethos: Government's Response to the Committee's Seventh Report of Session 2001–2*, HC 61, 2002–3.

Audit Commission, *Comprehensive Performance Assessment*, 12 December 2002. London, Audit Commission.

Office of the Deputy Prime Minister, '*Tackling Poor Performance in Local Government*', Response to Consultation Exercise, 13 December 2002. London, Office of the Deputy Prime Minister.

References

ALEXANDER, LORD (2001). 'The Role of the Lord Chancellor', Denning Society lecture, *The Times*, 30 October 2001.

ALI, R., and O'CINNEIDE, C. (2002). *Our House? Race and Representation in British Politics*. London: Institute of Public Policy Research.

ALLAN, T. R. S. (1993). *Law, Liberty and Justice: The Legal Foundations of British Constitutionalism*. Oxford: Clarendon Press.

—— (2001). *Constitutional Justice. A Liberal Theory of the Rule of Law*. Oxford: Oxford University Press.

ALLISON, J. (1999). *A Continental Distinction in the Common Law*, 2nd edn. Oxford: Oxford University Press.

ALSTON, P. (1999). *The EU and Human Rights*. Oxford: Oxford University Press.

AUSTIN, J. (1832). *The Province of Jurisprudence Determined*, H. L. A. Hart, 1954. London: Weidenfeld & Nicolson.

AUSTIN, R. (2000). 'Freedom of information: the constitutional impact' in J. Jowell and D. Oliver (eds.) (2000). *The Changing Constitution*, 4th edn. Oxford: Oxford University Press, 319–71.

BALLS, E. (2002). 'The Treasury' (lecture reported in *The Times*, 13 June 2002).

BAMFORTH, N. (1998). 'Parliamentary sovereignty and the Human Rights Act 1998', [1998] *Public Law* 572.

BARAK, A. (1999). 'The role of the Supreme Court in a democracy', 33 *Israel Law Review*, 1.

BARENDT, E. (1998). *An Introduction to Constitutional Law*. Oxford: Clarendon Press.

BARKER, A. (1982). *Quangos in Britain*. London: Macmillan.

—— 1997) 'Other people's quangos: quasi-government in seven countries' in M. Flinders, I. Harden, and D. Marquand (eds.) (1997). *How to Make Quangos Democratic*. London: Charter 88 and Political Economy Research Centre.

—— (1998). 'Political responsibility for UK prison security—ministers escape again', 76 *Public Administration* 1–23.

BARNETT, H. (2002). *Constitutional and Administrative Law*, 4th edn. London: Cavendish.

BARRON, A. and SCOTT, C. (1992). 'The Citizen's Charter programme', 55 *Modern Law Review* 526–46.

BEER, S. (1982). *Britain Against Itself*. London: Faber & Faber.

BEETHAM, D. (ed.) (1994). *Defining and Measuring Democracy*. London: Sage.

BELL, D. (2002). *The Barnett Formula* (unpublished memo, Dept. of Economics, University of Sterling).

—— and CHRISTIE, A. (2001). 'Finance—The Barnett Formula: Nobody's Child?' in A. Trench (ed.) (2001). *The State of the Nation 2001*. Thorverton: Imprint Academic.

BELL, J. (1992). *French Constitutional Law*. Oxford: Clarendon Press.

—— (2002) 'Review of Schwarze: *A Birth of a European Constitutional Order*', [2002] *Public Law* 191.

BELLAMY, R. (1999). *Liberalism and Pluralism: Towards a Politics of Compromise*. London: Routledge.

—— (2001). 'Constitutive citizenship versus constitutional rights: Republican reflections on the EU Charter and the Human Rights Act' in Campbell, T., Ewing, K.D., and Tomkins, A., (eds.) (2001). *Sceptical Essays on Human Rights*. Oxford: Oxford University Press.

BINGHAM, LORD (2000). 'The highest court in the land', Millennium lecture, unpublished.

BINGHAM, LORD (2002). *A New Supreme Court for the United Kingdom*. London: Constitution Unit.

BIRCH, A. H. (1964). *Representative and Responsible Government*. London: George Allen and Unwin.

BIRKINSHAW, P. (1991). *Reforming the Secret State*. Milton Keynes: Open University Press.

—— (1998). 'An all-singin' and all dancin' affair: the new Labour government's proposals for freedom of information', [1998] *Public Law* 176.

—— (2001a). *Freedom of Information: The Law, the Practice and the Ideal*, 3rd edn. London: Butterworths.

—— (2001b). 'British Report' in J. Schwarze, *The Birth of a European Constitutional Order*. Baden-Baden: Nomos Verlag.

—— and PARKIN, A. (1999). 'Freedom of Information' in R. Blackburn and Lord Plant (eds.) (1999). *Constitutional Reform*. London: Longman Press.

BLACKBURN, R. (1995). *The Electoral System in Britain*. London: Macmillan.

—— and PLANT, LORD (eds.) (1999). *Constitutional Reform. The Labour Government's Constitutional Reform Agenda*. Longman: London.

BLACKSTONE, SIR WILLIAM (1765–69). *Commentaries on the Laws of England*. Chicago: Chicago University Press.

BOGDANOR, V. (1981). *The People and the Party System: The Referendum and Electoral Reform in British Politics*. Cambridge: Cambridge University Press.

—— (1999). *Devolution in the United Kingdom*. Oxford: Oxford University Press.

BOSTON, J., MARTIN, J., PALLOT, J., and WALSH, P. (1996). *Public Management: The New Zealand Model*. Auckland: Oxford University Press.

BOYLE, K., and HADDEN, T. (1999). 'Northern Ireland' in R. Blackburn and Lord Plant (eds.) (1999). *Constitutional Reform. The Labour Government's Constitutional Reform Agenda*. Longman: London.

BRADLEY, A. W. (2000). 'The sovereignty of Parliament—in Perpetuity?' in J. Jowell and D. Oliver, (eds.) (2000). *The Changing Constitution*, 4th edn. Oxford: Clarendon Press.

—— and EWING, K. D. (2002). *Constitutional and Administrative Law*, 13th edn. London: Longman.

BRAZIER, R. (1998) *Constitutional Reform*, 2nd edn. Oxford: Oxford University Press.

—— (2001) 'How near is a written constitution?', 52 *NILQ* 1–19.

BROMLEY, C., CURTICE, J., and SEYD, B. (2001). 'Political engagement, trust and constitutional reform' in A. Park et al. (eds.) (2001). *British Social Attitudes: The 18th Report*. London: Sage.

BROWN, L. N., and BELL. J. (1998). *French Administrative Law*, 5th edn. Oxford: Clarendon Press.

BULPITT, J. (1983). *Territory and Power in the United Kingdom: An Interpretation*. Manchester: Manchester University Press.

BURKE, E. (1774). 'Speech to the Electors of Bristol' in F. G. Selby (ed.) (1963). *Burke's Speeches*. London: Macmillan.

BURROWS, N. (2000). *Devolution*. London: Sweet & Maxwell.

BUXTON, SIR RICHARD (2000). 'The Human Rights Act and private law', 116 *LQR* 48.

BYNOE, I. (1996). *Beyond the Citizen's Charter. New Directions for Social Rights*. London: IPPR.

CAMDESSUS, M. (1998) *The IMF and Good Governance*. Paris: IMF.

CAMPAIGN FOR A SCOTTISH ASSEMBLY (1988). *A Claim of Right for Scotland*. Edinburgh: Campaign for a Scottish Assembly.

CAMPBELL, D., and LEWIS, N. D. (eds.) (1999). *Promoting Participation: Law or Politics?* London: Cavendish Publishing.

—— and YOUNG, J. (2002) 'The metric martyrs and the entrenchment jurisprudence of Lord Justice Laws', [2002] *Public Law* 399–406.

CAMPBELL, T., EWING, K. D., and TOMKINS, A. (eds.) (2001). *Sceptical Essays on Human Rights*. Oxford: Oxford University Press.

CHAPMAN, R. (1988). *Ethics in the British Civil Service*. London: Routledge.

Chartered Institute of Public Finance and Accountability (1994). *Corporate Governance in the Public Services*. London: CIPFA.

CLAYTON, R. (2001). 'Regaining a sense of proportion: The Human Rights Act and the proportionality principle', 6 *EHRLR* 504.

—— and TOMLINSON, H. (2000). *The Law of Human Rights*. Oxford: Oxford University Press.

COLE, M. (2001). 'Local government modernisation: The executive and scrutiny model', 72 *Political Quarterly*, 239.

COLEMAN, S. (ed.) (2001). *Elections in the Age of the Internet*. London: Hansard Society.

COMMISSION ON ELECTORAL REFORM (1976). *Report*. London: Hansard Society.

COMMISSION ON THE CONDUCT OF REFERENDUMS (1996). *Report*. London: Constitution Unit.

COMMISSION TO STRENGTHEN PARLIAMENT (2000). *Strengthening Parliament*. London: Conservative Party.

CONSTITUTION UNIT (1996a). *Scotland's Parliament. Fundamentals for a New Scotland Act*. London: Constitution Unit.

—— (1996b). *An Assembly for Wales*. London: Constitution Unit.

COOK, R. (2002). *Parliament and the People: Modernisation of the House of Commons*. London: Hansard Society.

COOTE, A. (1992). *The Welfare of Citizens. Developing New Social Rights*. London: Institute of Public Policy Research.

CORNES, R. (2000). 'Intergovernmental Relations in a Devolved United Kingdom: Making Devolution Work' in R. Hazell (ed.) (2000). *The State and the Nations*. London: Imprint Academic.

COULSON, A. (1989). *Devolving Power. The Case for Regional Government* (Fabian Society Tract no. 537). London: Fabian Society.

COWLEY, P. (1996). 'Crossing the floor: representative theory and practice in Britain', [1996] *Public Law* 214.

CRAIG, P. P. (1990). *Public Law and Democracy in the United Kingdom and the United States of America*. Oxford: Clarendon Press.

—— (1991). 'Sovereignty of the United Kingdom Parliament after *Factortame*'. 11 *Yearbook of European Law* 221.

—— (1998). 'Ultra vires and the foundations of judicial review', 57 *Camb. L.J.* 63, repr. in Forsyth (2000).

—— (1999a). 'Competing models of judicial review', [1999] *Public Law* 428–447.

—— (1999b). *Administrative Law*, 4th edn., 1999. London: Sweet & Maxwell.

—— (2000). 'Britain in the European Union' in J. Jowell and D. Oliver (eds.) (2000). *The Changing Constitution*, 4th edn. Oxford: Oxford University Press.

—— (2001). 'The courts, the Human Rights Act and judicial review', 117 LQR 589.

—— and De Burca, G. (2002). *EC Law: Text, Cases, and Materials*, 3rd edn. Oxford: Oxford University Press.

—— and WALTERS, M. (1999). 'The courts, devolution and judicial review', [1999] *Public Law* 274.

CRICK, B. (2000). *In Defence of Politics*, 5th edn. London: Continuum.

CROFT, J. (2000). *Whitehall and the Human Rights Act 1998*. London: Constitution Unit.

—— (2001). 'Whitehall and the Human Rights Act 1998', 6 *EHRLR* 392.

CURTICE, J. (2001). 'Hopes dashed and fears assuaged? What the public makes of it so far' in Trench (ed.) (2001). The *State of the Nation 2001*. Thorverton: Imprint Academic.

—— and SEYD, B. (2000). *Wise after the Event? Attitudes to Voting Reform Following the 1999 Scottish and Welsh Elections*. London: Constitution Unit.

CYGAN, A. (2002). 'The white paper on European Governance—have glasnost and perestroika finally arrived to the European Union?', 65 *MLR* 229.

DAHRENDORF, R. (1988). 'Citizenship and the modern social conflict' in R. Holme and M. Elliott (eds.) (1988). *1688–1988: Time for a New Constitution.* Basingstoke: Macmillan.

DAINTITH, T. C. (1979). 'Regulation by contract: the new prerogative', [1979] *Current Legal Problems* 41.

—— (2002). 'A very good day to bring out anything we want to bury', [2002] *Public Law* 13.

—— and PAGE, A. (1999). *The Executive in the Constitution.* Oxford: Oxford University Press.

DAVIES, R. (1999). *Devolution: A Process, not an Event.* Cardiff: Institute of Welsh Affairs.

DE SMITH, S., WOOLF, LORD, and JOWELL, J. (1996). *Judicial Review of Administrative Action,* 5th edn. London: Sweet & Maxwell.

DEAKIN, N. (1994). 'Accentuating the apostrophe: The Citizen's Charter', 15 *Policy Studies,* 55.

—— and WRIGHT, A. (eds.) (1989). *Consuming Public Services.* London: Routledge.

DE BURCA, G. (1998). 'The principle of subsidiarity and the Court of Justice as an institutional actor', 36(2) *JCMS* 217.

DICEY, A. V., (1959). *Introduction to the Study of the Law of the Constitution,* 10th edn. London: Macmillan.

DICKSON, B., and CARMICHAEL, P. (eds.) (1999). *The House of Lords. Its Parliamentary and Judicial Roles.* Oxford: Hart Publishing.

DOIG, A. (2002). 'Sleaze Fatigue: The House of Ill-Repute', 55 *Parliamentary Affairs,* 389–99.

—— and WILSON, J. (1998). 'What price New Public Management?', 69 *Political Quarterly,* 267.

DONAGHY, P. J., and NEWTON, M. T. (1987). *Spain: A Guide to Political and Economic Institutions.* Cambridge: Cambridge University Press.

DOUGLAS-SCOTT, S. (2002). *Constitutional Law of the European Union.* London: Longman.

DREWRY, G. (1983). 'Lord Haldane's Ministry of Justice—Stillborn or strangled at birth?', 61 *Public Administration* 396–414.

—— (1989). *The New Select Committees,* 2nd edn. Oxford: Clarendon Press.

—— (2002). 'Whatever happened to the Citizen's Charter?', [2002] *Public Law* 9.

—— and BUTCHER, T. (1991). *The Civil Service Today,* 2nd edn. Oxford: Basil Blackwell.

DUMMETT, A., and NICOL, A. (1990). *Subjects, Citizens, Aliens and Others.* London: Weidenfeld & Nicolson.

DYSON, K. (1980). *The State Tradition in Western Europe.* Martin Robertson: Oxford.

EDWARDS, R. (2002). 'Judicial deference under the Human Rights Act', 65 *MLR* 859.

ELDER, N. (1970). *Government in Sweden.* Oxford: Pergamon Press.

ELLIOTT, M. (1996). 'The ultra vires rule and the foundations of judicial review', 57 *Camb. L.J.* 129.

—— (1999) 'The ultra vires rule in a constitutional setting: still the central principle of administrative law', 58 *Camb. L.J.* 129, and repr. in Forsyth (ed.) (2000). *Judicial Review and the Constitution.* Oxford: Hart Publishing.

—— (2001). *The Constitutional Foundations of Judicial Review.* Oxford: Hart Publishing.

—— (2002). 'Parliamentary sovereignty and the new constitutional order: Legislative freedom, political reality and convention', 22 *Legal Studies* 340.

ELSENAAR, M. (1999). 'Law, accountability and the Private Finance Initiative in the National Health Service', [1999] *Public Law* 35–42.

EMILIOU, N. (1992) 'Subsidiarity: An effective barrier against "the Enterprise of Ambition"?', 17 *ELRev* 383.

ERSKINE MAY, T. (1997). *The Law, Privileges, Proceedings and Usages of Parliament,* 22nd edn. London: Butterworths.

ESKRIDGE, W. N., and FEREJOHN, J. (2001). 'Super-statutes', 50 *Duke Law Journal* 1215–76.

EWING, K. D. (1987). *The Funding of Political Parties in Britain.* Cambridge: Cambridge University Press.

—— (1996). 'Human rights, social democracy and constitutional reform' in C. Gearty and A. Tomkins (eds.) (1996). *Understanding Human Rights*. London: Mansell.

—— (1999*a*). 'The Human Rights Act and parliamentary democracy', 62 *MLR* 79.

—— (1999*b*). 'Social rights and constitutional law', [1999] *Public Law* 104.

—— (2000). 'A theory of democratic adjudication. Towards a representative, accountable and independent judiciary', 38 *Alberta Law Review* 708.

—— (2001*a*). 'The unbalanced Constitution' in T. Campbell, K. D. Ewing, and A. Tomkins (eds.) (2001). *Sceptical Essays on Human Rights*. Oxford: Oxford University Press.

—— (2001*b*). 'Transparency, accountability and equality: The Political Parties, Elections and Referendums Act 2000', [2001] *Public Law* 542.

—— (2001*c*). Constitutional reform and human rights: Unfinished business?', 5 *Edinburgh Law Review* 297.

—— and GEARTY, C. A. (1990). *Freedom under Thatcher*. Oxford: Clarendon Press.

FAULKNER, D. (1998). 'Public services, citizenship and the state—the British experience 1967–97' in M. Freedland and S. Sciarra (eds.) (1998). *Public Services and Citizenship in Public and Labour Law*. Oxford: Clarendon Press.

FELDMAN, D. (2002*a*). *Civil Liberties and Human Rights*, 2nd edn. Oxford: Oxford University Press.

—— (2002*b*). 'Parliamentary scrutiny of legislation and human rights', [2002] *Public Law* 323.

FENWICK, H. (2002). *Civil Liberties and Human Rights*, 3rd edn. London: Cavendish.

FINER, S. E. (1975). *Adversary Politics and Electoral Reform*. London: Anthony Wigram.

FLINDERS, M., HARDEN, I., and MARQUAND, D. (eds.) (1997). *How to Make Quangos Democratic*. London: Charter 88 and Political Economy Research Centre.

FLYNN, N. (1999). 'Modernising British government', 52 *Parliamentary Affairs* 582.

FORMAN, F. N. (2002). *Constitutional Change in the United Kingdom*. London: Routledge.

FORSYTH, C. (1996). 'Of fig leaves and fairy tales: The ultra vires doctrine, the sovereignty of Parliament and judicial review', 55 *Camb. L.J.* 122, repr. in Forsyth, 2000.

—— (2000). *Judicial Review and the Constitution*. Oxford: Hart Publishing.

FOSTER, C. D., and PLOWDEN, F. J. (1996). *The State Under Stress*. Buckingham: Open University Press.

FOUCAULT, M. (1979). 'Governmentality', 6 *Ideology and Consciousness* 5.

—— (2000). 'The ethic of the concern for self as a practice of freedom' in Rabinow, P. (2000). *Ethics: Subjectivity and Truth*. London: Penguin.

FOX, A. (1974). *Beyond Contract: Work, Power and Trust Relations*. London: Faber & Faber.

FREDMAN, S., McCRUDDEN, C., and FREEDLAND, M. (2000). 'An E.U. charter of fundamental rights', [2000] *Public Law* 178–86.

FREEDLAND, M. (1998). 'Public law and private finance—Placing the private finance initiative in a public law frame', [1998] *Public Law* 288–307.

—— and SCIARRA, S. (eds.) (1998). *Public Services and Citizenship in European Law*. Oxford: Clarendon Press.

FRY, G. (1997). 'The Conservatives and the civil service: "One step forwards, two steps back"?', 75 *Public Administration* 695–710.

FUKUYAMA, F. (1995). *Trust: The Social Virtues and the Creation of Prosperity*. London: Hamish Hamilton.

GALBRAITH, J. K. (1983). *The Anatomy of Power*. Boston: Houghton Mifflin Company.

GAMBLE, A., and WRIGHT, T. (eds.) (1999). *The New Social Democracy*. Oxford: Blackwell.

GANZ, G. (1987). *Quasi Legislation*. London: Sweet & Maxwell.

GARDNER, J. P. (1990). 'What lawyers mean by citizenship' in Speaker's Commission *Encouraging Citizenship. Report of the Commission on Citizenship.* London: HMSO.

GAY, O. (2002*a*). *The Regulation of Parliamentary Standards—A Comparative Perspective.* London: Constitution Unit.

—— (2002*b*). 'The regulation of parliamentary standards after devolution', [2002] *Public Law* 422–37.

GEARTY, C., and TOMKINS, A. (eds.) (1996). *Understanding Human Rights.* London: Mansell.

GENN, H. (1999). *Paths to Justice: What people do and think about going to law.* Oxford: Hart Publishing.

GIDDENS, A. (1998). *The Third Way.* Cambridge: Polity Press.

GOLDSWORTHY, J. (1999). *The Sovereignty of Parliament.* Oxford: Oxford University Press.

GREEN, SIR GUY (1985). 'The rationale and some aspects of judicial independence', 59 *Australian Law Journal* 135–50.

GRIFFITH, J. A. G. (1979). 'The political constitution', 42 *MLR* 1–21.

—— (1991). *The Politics of the Judiciary,* 4th edn. Glasgow: Fontana.

—— (1993). *Judicial Politics since 1920.* Oxford: Blackwell.

—— (2000). 'The brave new world of Sir John Laws', 63 *MLR* 159–76.

—— (2001). 'The common law and the political constitution', 117 *LQR* 42–67.

GYFORD, J., LEACH, S., and GAME, C. (1990). *The Changing Politics of Local Government.* London: Unwin Hyman.

HADFIELD, B. (2000). 'The foundations of judicial review: Devolved power and delegated power' in C. Forsyth (2000). *Judicial Review and the Constitution.* Oxford: Hart Publishing.

—— (2001). 'Seeing it through? The multifaceted implementation of the Belfast Agreement' in R. Wilford (ed.) (2001). *Aspects of the Belfast Agreement.* Oxford: Oxford University Press.

—— (2002). 'Towards an English constitution', [2002] *Current Legal Problems,* (forthcoming).

HAILSHAM, LORD (1976). *Elective Dictatorship.* London: British Broadcasting Corporation.

—— (1978). *The Dilemma of Democracy.* London: Collins.

HALE, DAME BRENDA (2001). 'Equality and the judiciary: Why should we want more women judges?', [2001] *Public Law* 494–509.

HANSARD SOCIETY (2002) *Technology: Enhancing Representative Democracy? A Report on the use of new communication technologies in Westminster and the devolved legislatures.* London: Hansard Society.

HANSARD SOCIETY COMMISSION ON ELECTION CAMPAIGNS (1991). *Agenda for Change.* London: Hansard Society.

HANSARD SOCIETY COMMISSION ON THE LEGISLATIVE PROCESS (1992). *Making the Law.* London: Hansard Society.

HANSARD SOCIETY COMMISSION ON PARLIAMENTARY SCRUTINY (2001). *The Challenge for Parliament. Making Government Accountable.* London: Vacher Dod Publishing Ltd.

HANSARD SOCIETY COMMISSION UPON THE FINANCING OF POLITICAL PARTIES (1981). *Paying for Politics.* London: Hansard Society.

HARDEN, I. (1992). *The Contracting State.* Buckingham: Open University Press.

HARLOW, C. (1999). 'Accountability, New Public Management, and the problems of the Child Support Agency', 26 *Journal of Law and Society* 150–74.

—— and RAWLINGS, R. (1997). *Law and Administration,* 2nd edn. London: Butterworths.

HARMON, M., and MAYER, R. (1986). *Organisation Theory for Public Administration.* Boston: Little, Brown.

HART, H. L. A. (1994). *The Concept of Law,* 2nd edn. Oxford: Clarendon Press.

HART ELY, J. (1981). *Democracy and Distrust.* London: Harvard University Press.

HARTLEY, T. (1998). *The Foundations of European Community Law*, 4th edn. Oxford: Oxford University Press.

HAYEK, F. A. VON (1960). *The Constitution of Liberty*. London: Routledge & Kegan Paul.

HAZELL, R. (2001). 'The English question: can Westminster be a proxy for an English parliament?', [2001] *Public Law* 268–80.

—— (ed.) (2000*a*). *The State and the Nations. The First Year of Devolution in the United Kingdom*. Thorverton (Essex): Academic Imprint.

—— (2000*b*). 'Intergovernmental relations: Whitehall rules OK?' in R. Hazell (ed.) (2000). *The State and the Nations. The First Year of Devolution in the United Kingdom*. Thorverton (Essex): Academic Imprint.

HEATER, D. (1990). *Citizenship. The Civic Ideal in World History, Politics and Education*. London: Longman.

HENNESSY, P. (1990) *Whitehall*. London: Fontana.

—— (1996). *The Hidden Wiring. Unearthing the British Constitution*. London: Indigo.

HEYWOOD, P. (ed.) (1997). *Political Corruption*, Oxford: Blackwell.

—— (2000). *Spanish Regionalism: A Case Study*. London: Constitution Unit.

HIMSWORTH, C. M. G. (1999). 'Securing the tenure of Scottish judges: a somewhat academic exercise', [1999] *Public Law* 14–22.

HOOD, C. (1991). 'A public management for all seasons?', 69 *Public Administration* 3–19.

—— SCOTT, C., JAMES, O., JONES, G., and TRAVERS, T. (1999). *Regulation inside Government. Waste-Watchers, Quality Police, and Sleaze-Busters*. Oxford: Oxford University Press.

HOROWITZ, D. (2001). 'The Northern Ireland Agreement: consociationalist, maximalist, and risky' in J. McGarry, (ed.) (2001). *Northern Ireland and the Divided World*. Oxford: Oxford University Press.

HUGHES, O. (1998). *Public Management and Administration: an introduction*, 2nd edn. Basingstoke: Macmillan.

HUNT, M. (1998). 'The "horizontal effect" of the Human Rights Act', [1998] *Public Law* 423.

INSTITUTE OF PUBLIC POLICY RESEARCH (1991). *The Constitution of the United Kingdom*. London: IPPR.

IRVINE, LORD, of LAIRG (1996). 'Judges and decision makers: The theory and practice of Wednesbury review', [1996] *Public Law* 59–78.

JACKSON, P. M. (2001). 'Public sector added value: Can bureaucracy survive?', 79 *Public Administration* 5–28.

JOHNSTON, R., and PATTIE, C. (1995). 'The impact of spending on party constituency campaigns in recent British general elections', 1 (2) *Party Politics* 261–73.

JOINT CONSULTATIVE COMMITTEE ON CONSTITUTIONAL REFORM (1997). *Report* (the Cook/Maclennan Report). London: Labour Party, Liberal Democrats.

JONES, T. (1999). 'Judicial bias and disqualification in the *Pinochet* case', [1999] Public Law 391–9.

JOSEPH, P. A. (1998). 'Constitutional review now', [1998] *N.Z.Law Rev.* 85.

—— (2000). 'The demise of *ultra vires*— judicial review in the New Zealand courts', [2000] *Public Law* 354.

JOWELL, J. (1999). 'Of vires and vacuums: The Constitutional context of judicial review', [1999] *Public Law* 448.

—— (2000). 'Beyond the rule of law: Towards constitutional judicial review', [2000] *Public Law* 671.

—— and LESTER, A. (1987). 'Beyond *Wednesbury*: substantive principles of administrative law', [1987] *Public Law* 368–82.

—— —— (1988). 'Proportionality: neither novel nor dangerous' in J. Jowell and D. Oliver (eds.) (1988). *New Directions in Judicial Review*. London: Sweet & Maxwell.

—— and OLIVER, D. (eds.) (1988). *New Directions in Judicial Review*. London: Sweet & Maxwell.

KELSEN, H. (1949). *General Theory of Law and State.* Cambridge: Mass.

KENNON, A. (2000). *The Commons: Reform or Modernisation.* London: Constitution Unit.

KICKERT, W. (1993). 'Autopoiesis and the science of (public) administration: essence, sense and nonsense', 14 *Organisational Studies* 261–78.

KING, A. (2001). *Does the United Kingdom still have a Constitution?* London: Sweet & Maxwell.

KINGSFORD-SMITH, D., and OLIVER, D. (eds.) (1990). *Economical with the Truth: The Law and the Media in a Democratic Society.* Oxford: ESC Publishing.

KLUG, F., STARMER, K., and WEIR, S. (1996). *The Three Pillars of Liberty. Political Rights and Freedoms in the United Kingdom.* London: Routledge.

LABOUR PARTY (1995). *A Choice for England.* London: Labour Party.

—— (1996). *New Voice for English Regions.* London: Labour Party.

—— (1997). *Manifesto.* London: Labour Party.

LAWS, SIR JOHN (1993). 'Is the High Court the guardian of fundamental constitutional rights?', [1993] *Public Law* 59.

—— (1994).'Judicial remedies and the constitution', 57 *MLR* 213.

—— (1995). 'Law and democracy', [1995] *Public Law* 72–93.

LEDUC, L. et al. (eds.) (2002). *Comparing Democracies,* 2nd edn. London: Sage.

LEFTWICH, A. (1993). 'Governance, democracy and development in the Third World', 14 *Third World Quarterly* 605–24.

LEGG, SIR THOMAS (2001). 'Judges for the new century', [2001] *Public Law* 62–76.

LEIGH, I. (2000). *Law, Politics and Local Democracy.* Oxford: Oxford University Press.

—— and LUSTGARTEN, L. (1989). 'The Security Service Act 1989', 52 *MLR* 801–40.

LEOPOLD, P. (1998). 'The application of civil and criminal law to members of Parliament and parliamentary proceedings' in D. Oliver and G. Drewry (eds.) (1998). *The Law and Parliament.* Butterworths: London.

LESTER, A., and PANNICK, D. (eds.) (1999). *Human Rights Law and Practice.* Butterworths: London.

LE SUEUR, A. (1996). 'The judicial review debate: From partnership to friction', 31 *Government and Opposition* 8–26.

—— (2001). *What is the Future of the Judicial Committee of the Privy Council?* London: Constitution Unit.

—— and CORNES, R. (2001). *The Future of the United Kingdom's Highest Courts.* London: Constitution Unit.

LEWIS, D. (1997). *Hidden Agendas: Politics, Law and Disorder.* London: Hamish Hamilton.

LEWIS, N., and SENEVIRATNE, M. (1992). 'A social charter for Britain' in A. Coote (1992). *The Welfare of Citizens. Developing New Social Rights.* London: Institute of Public Policy Research.

LEWIS, N. D. (1998). 'A Civil Service Act for the United Kingdom', [1998] *Public Law* 463.

—— (1999). 'The constitutional implications of participation' in D. Campbell and N. D. Lewis (eds.) (1999). *Promoting Participation: Law or Politics?* London: Cavendish Publishing.

—— (2001). *Law and Governance.* London: Cavendish.

LIBERAL DEMOCRATS (1990). "*We the People . . .*"*—Towards a Written Constitution* (Federal Green Paper No. 13). Dorchester: Liberal Democrat Publications.

—— (1993). *Here We Stand.* London: Liberal Democrats.

LOUGHLIN, M. (1992). *Public Law and Political Theory.* Oxford: Oxford University Press.

—— (1996). *Legality and Locality. The Role of Law in Central-Local Government Relations.* Oxford: Clarendon Press.

—— (2000*a*). *Swords and Scales. An Examination of the Relationship between Law and Politics*. Oxford: Hart Publishing.

—— (2000*b*). 'Restructuring of central-local government relations' in J. Jowell and D. Oliver (eds.) (2000). *The Changing Constitution*, 4th edn. Oxford: Oxford University Press.

Lundvik, U. (1983). 'Sweden' in G. Caiden (ed.) (1983). *International Handbook of the Ombudsman*. Greenwood Press, 179–85.

MacCormick, N. (1999). *Questioning Sovereignty: Law, State and Practical Reason*. Oxford: Oxford University Press.

McCrudden, C. (2001). 'Not the way forward', 52 *Northern Ireland Legal Quarterly* 372.

Macdonald, J. (1990). 'Draft Constitution in "We, The People . . ."—Towards a Written Constitution' (Liberal Democrat Federal Green Paper No. 13). Dorchester: Liberal Democrat Publications.

McDonald, O. (1992*a*). *Swedish Models. The Swedish Model of Central Government*. London: IPPR.

—— (1992*b*). *The Future of Whitehall*. London: Weidenfeld & Nicolson.

McEldowney, J. (2000). 'The control of public expenditure' in J. Jowell and D. Oliver (eds.) (2000). *The Changing Constitution*, 4th edn. Oxford: Oxford University Press.

McFarland, A. S. (1992). 'Interest groups and the policy making process' in M. M. Petracca, *The Politics of Interest*. Boulder: Westview Press.

McGlynn, C. (1998). *The Woman Lawyer: making the difference*. Butterworths: London.

MacTaggart, F. (2000). *Women in Parliament: Their Contribution to Labour's First 1000 Days*. London: Fabian Society.

Malleson, K. (1997). *The Use of Judicial Appointments Commissions: A Review of the US and Canadian Models*, Lord Chancellor's Department, Research Paper no. 6. London: Lord Chancellor's Department.

—— (1999). 'Assessing the Performance of the Judicial Service Commission', 116 *South African Law Journal* 41–5.

—— and Banda, F. (2000). *Factors Affecting the Decision to apply for silk and judicial office*, Lord Chancellor's Department Research Series No 2/00, June 2000. London: Lord Chancellor's Department.

Mancuso, M. (1993). 'Ethical attitudes of British MPs', 46 *Parliamentary Affairs* 180.

Marsh, D., and Rhodes, R. A. W. (1992). *Policy Networks in British Government*. Oxford: Oxford University Press.

Marsh, I. (1990). 'Liberal priorities, the Lib-Lab pact and the requirements for policy influence', 43 *Parliamentary Affairs* 292–321.

Marshall, G. (1984). *Constitutional Conventions*. Oxford: Clarendon Press.

—— (1989). *Ministerial Responsibility*. Oxford: Oxford University Press.

—— (1998). 'Interpreting interpretation in the Human Rights Bill', [1998] *Public Law* 167.

Marshall, T. H. (1950). *Citizenship and Social Class*. Cambridge: Cambridge University Press.

Martin, S. (2000). 'Implementing "Best Value": Local public services in transition', 78 *Public Administration* 209–27.

Massot, J. (2001). 'Legislative drafting in France: The role of the Conseil d'Etat', 22 *Statute Law Review*, 96–107.

Mead, L. (1986). *Beyond Entitlement*. New York: Free Press.

—— and Field, F. (1997). *From Welfare to Work*. London: Institute of Economic Affairs.

Megarry, R. (1944). 'Administrative quasi-legislation', 60 *LQR* 125.

Middlemas, K. (1979). *Politics in Industrial Society*. London: Deutsch.

Miers, D., and Page, A. (1990). *Legislation*, 2nd edn. London: Sweet and Maxwell.

MILL, J. S. (1975). 'Representative Government' (first published in 1861), ch. 15 in J. S. Mill, *Three Essays*. Oxford: Oxford University Press.

MORGAN, J. P. (1975). *The House of Lords and the Labour Government 1964–70.* Oxford: Clarendon Press.

MORISON, J. (1998). 'The case against constitutional reform', 25 *Journal of Law and Society* 510–35.

—— (2001). 'Democracy, Governance and Governmentality: Civil public space and constitutional renewal in Northern Ireland', 21 *Oxford Journal of Legal Studies* 287–310.

MORRISON, J. (2001). *Reforming Britain. New Labour, New Constitution?* London: Reuters.

MOWBRAY, A. (1999). 'The role of the European Court of Human Rights in the promotion of democracy', [1999] *Public Law* 703–25.

MUNRO, C. (1983). 'What is a constitution?', [1983] *Public Law* 563.

NEWMAN, J. (2001). *Modernising Governance. New Labour, Policy and Society.* London: Sage Publications.

NICOL, D. (2001). *EC Membership and the Judicialisation of British Politics.* Oxford: Oxford University Press.

NOLAN, LORD, and SEDLEY, SIR STEPHEN (1997). *The Making and Remaking of the British Constitution.* London: Blackstone Press.

NORTON, P. (1980). *Dissension in the House of Commons 1974–79.* Oxford: Clarendon Press.

NORTON-TAYLOR, R. (1990). *In Defence of the Realm? The Case for Accountable Security Services.* London: Civil Liberties Trust.

NOZICK, R. (1984). *Anarchy, State and Utopia.* Oxford: Blackwell.

OLDFIELD, A. (1990). 'Citizenship: an unnatural practice?', 61 *Political Quarterly*, 177–98.

OLIVER, D. (1981). 'The constitutional implications of the Labour party reforms', [1981] *Public Law* 151.

—— (1992). 'Written constitutions: principles and problems.', 45 *Parliamentary Affairs* 135–52.

—— (1994). 'The Lord Chancellor's Department and the judges', [1994] *Public Law* 157–63.

—— (1996). 'The Scott Report', [1996] *Public Law* 357.

—— (1997). 'Regulating the conduct of MPs. The British experience of combating corruption' in P. Heywood (ed.) (1997). *Political Corruption.* Oxford: Blackwell.

—— (1999). 'The Lord Chancellor, the Judicial Committee of the Privy Council and devolution', [1999] *Public Law* 1–5.

—— (2000). 'The frontiers of the state. Public authorities and public functions under the Human Rights Act', [2000] *Public Law* 476.

—— and AUSTIN, R. (1987). 'Political and constitutional aspects of the Westland affair', 40 *Parliamentary Affairs* 20–40.

—— and DREWRY, G. (1996). *Public Service Reforms. Issues of Accountability and Public Law.* London: Pinter.

—— —— (eds.) (1998). *The Law and Parliament.* Butterworths: London.

OLOWOFOYEKU, A. (1999). 'Decentralising the UK: The federal argument', 3 *Edinburgh Law Review* 57–84.

—— (2000). 'The *Nemo Iudex* rule: The case against automatic disqualification for bias', [2000] *Public Law* 456–93.

O'NEILL, O. (2002). *A Question of Trust* (Reith Lectures, 2002). Cambridge: Cambridge University Press.

OSBORNE, D., and GAEBLER, T. (1992). *Reinventing Government.* New York: Addison Wesley.

OSMOND, J. (2000). 'A Constitutional Convention by other means: The first year of the National Assembly for Wales' in R. Hazell (ed.) (2000a). *The State and the Nations. The First Year of Devolution in the United Kingdom.* Thorverton (Essex): Academic Imprint.

—— (2001). 'In search of stability. Coalition politics in the second year of the National Assembly for Wales', in A. Trench (ed.) (2001). *The State of the Nation 2001*. Thorverton: Imprint Academic.

PAGE, A., and BATEY, A. (2002). 'Scotland's other Parliament: Westminster legislation about devolved matters in Scotland since devolution', [2002] *Public Law* 501–23.

PALMER, G. (1987). *Unbridled Power*. Oxford: Oxford University Press.

PATTERSON, S. C., and MUGHAN, A. (1999). *Senates. Bicameralism in the Contemporary World*. Columbus: Ohio State University Press.

PENNER, R. (1996). 'The Canadian experience with the Charter of Rights: Are there lessons for the United Kingdom?', [1996] *Public Law* 104.

PERRI 6 (1999). 'A constitutional culture for more participation: what would it look like?' in D. Campbell and N. D. Lewis (eds.) (1999). *Promoting Participation: Law or Politics?* London: Cavendish Publishing.

PETTIT, P. (1999). *Republicanism: A Theory of Freedom and Government*, 2nd edn. Oxford: Clarendon Press.

PHILLIPSON, G. (1999). 'The Human Rights Act, "horizontal effect" and the common law: A bang or a whimper?', 62 *MLR* 824.

PHILP, M. (1997), 'Defining political corruption' in P. Heywood (ed.) (1997). *Political Corruption*. Oxford: Blackwell.

POIRIER, J. (2001). 'The functions of intergovernmental agreements: Post-devolution concordats in a comparative perspective', [2001] *Public Law* 134–57.

POWER, M. (1994). *The Audit Explosion*. London: Demos.

—— (1999). *The Audit Society. Rituals of Verification*. Oxford: Oxford University Press.

PRATCHETT, L. (2002). 'Local government: From modernisation to consolidation', 55 *Parliamentary Affairs*, 330–46.

PROSSER, T. (1997). *Law and the Regulators*. Oxford: Clarendon Press.

PURCHAS, SIR FRANCIS, (1994). 'Lord Mackay and the judiciary', 144 *New L.J.* 527.

RAWLINGS, R. (1998). 'The New Model Wales', 25 *Journal of Law and Society* 461–509.

—— (2000). 'Concordats of the Constitution', 116 *LQR* 257–86.

—— (2001) 'Quasi-legislative devolution: powers and principles', 52 *NILQ* 54–80.

RHODES, R. A. W. (1991). 'Introduction' to 69 *Public Administration*, (special issue on New Public Management).

—— (1994). 'The hollowing out of the state', 65 *Political Quarterly* 138–51.

—— (1997). *Understanding Governance. Policy Networks, Governance, Reflexivity and Accountability*. Buckingham: Open University Press.

RICHARD, I., and WELFARE, D. (1999). *Unfinished Business. Reforming the House of Lords*. London: Vintage.

RICHARDSON, J. J. (1982). 'Programme evaluation in Britain and Sweden', 35 *Parliamentary Affairs* 160–80.

—— and JORDAN, C. (1979). *Governing under Pressure: The Policy Process in a Post-Parliamentary Democracy*. Oxford: Martin Robertson.

ROGALY, J. (1976). *Parliament for the People*. London: Temple Smith.

ROKKAN, S., and URWIN, D. (eds.) (1982). *The Politics of Territorial Identities: Studies in European Regionalism*. London: Sage.

—— and D. URWIN (1982). 'Introduction: Centres and peripheries in Western Europe' in S. Rokkan and D. Urwin (eds.) (1982). *The Politics of Territorial Identities: Studies in European Regionalism*. London: Sage.

ROSE, R. (1976). *The Problem of Party Government*. Harmondsworth: Penguin Books.

RUSH, M. (1998). 'The law relating to Members' conduct' in D. Oliver and G. Drewry (eds.) (1998). *The Law and Parliament*. London: Butterworths.

RUSSELL, M. (2000). *Reforming the House of Lords. Lessons from Overseas.* Oxford: Oxford University Press.

RYDIN, Y. (1999). 'Environmental governance for sustainable urban development: A European model', 4(1) *Local Environment* 61–4.

SAGGAR, S. (2000). *Race and Representation.* Manchester: Manchester University Press.

SANDFORD, M. (2002). *A Commentary on the Regional Government White Paper Cm. 5511.* London: Constitution Unit.

—— and McQUAIL, P. (2001). *Unexplored Territory: Elected Regional Assemblies in England.* London: Constitution Unit.

SCARMAN, SIR LESLIE (1974). *English Law – The New Dimension.* London: Stevens & Sons.

SCHOFIELD, P. (1990). 'Bentham on public opinion and the press' in D. Kingsford-Smith and D. Oliver (eds.) (1990). *Economical with the Truth: The Law and the Media in a Democratic Society.* Oxford: ESC Publishing.

SCHWARZE, J. (ed.) (2001*a*). *The Birth of a European Constitutional Order.* Baden-Baden: Nomos Verlag.

—— (2001*b*). 'German Report' in J. Schwarze (ed.) (2002). *The Birth of a European Constitutional Order.* Baden-Baden: Nomos Verlag.

SCOTT, A. (2001). 'The role of concordats in the new governance of Britain: Taking subsidiarity seriously', 5 *Edinburgh Law Review* 21.

SCOTT, C. (1999). 'Regulation inside government: re-badging the Citizens' Charter', [1999] *Public Law* 595–603.

SCOTTISH CONSTITUTIONAL CONVENTION (1989). *Towards a Scottish Parliament.* Edinburgh: Scottish Constitutional Convention.

SCOTTISH CONSTITUTIONAL CONVENTION (1990). *Key Elements of Proposals for Scottish Parliament.* Edinburgh: Scottish Constitutional Convention.

SCOTTISH CONSTITUTIONAL CONVENTION (1995). *Scotland's Parliament. Scotland's Right,* Scottish Constitutional Convention, Edinburgh.

SEAR, C. (2002). *Short Money,* House of Commons SN/PC/1663, 22 August 2002. London: House of Commons.

SEDLEY, SIR STEPHEN (1995). 'Human Rights—a twenty-first century agenda', [1995] *Public Law* 386–400.

—— (1997). 'The common law and the constitution' in Lord Nolan and Sir Stephen Sedley, *The Making and Remaking of the British Constitution.* London: Blackstone Press.

—— (1994). 'The sound of silence: Constitutional law without a constitution', 110 *Law Quarterly Review* 270.

SELBOURNE, D. (1994). *The Principle of Duty.* London: Sinclair Stevenson.

SENEVIRATNE, M. (2000). ' "Joining up" the ombudsmen – the Review of Public Sector Ombudsmen in England' [2000] *Public Law* 582.

SEYD, B. (1998). *Elections under Regional Lists.* London: Constitution Unit.

SHAPIRO, M., and STONE (1994). A 'The new constitutional politics of Europe', 26 *Comparative Political Studies* 397.

SHETREET, S. (1976). *Judges on Trial.* Oxford: North-Holland.

SIEDENTOP, L. (2000). *Democracy in Europe.* London: Allen Lane/Penguin Press.

SKORDALI, E. (1991). *Judicial Appointments. An International Review of Existing Models* (Research and Policy Planning Unit of the Law Society). London: Law Society.

SORABJEE, S. (1994). 'Obliging government to control itself: Recent developments in Indian administrative law', [1994] *Public Law* 39.

STEEL, D. (1980). *A House Divided.* London: Weidenfeld & Nicolson.

STEVENS, R. (1993). *The Independence of the Judiciary: The View from the Lord Chancellor's Office.* Oxford: Oxford University Press.

STEWART, J., and WALSH, K. (1992). 'Change in the management of public services', 70 *Public Administration*, 499.

STEYN, LORD (1997). 'The weakest and least dangerous department of government', [1997] *Public Law* 84–95.

—— (1999). *The Constitutionalisation of Public Law*, London: Constitution Unit.

—— (2002a). 'The case for a Supreme Court', 118 *LQR* 382–96.

—— (2002b). 'Human Rights: The Legacy of Mrs Roosevelt', [2002] *Public Law* 473.

STRAW, J., and BOATENG, P. (1996). *Bringing Rights Home: Labour's Plans to incorporate the European Convention on Human Rights into United Kingdom Law*. London: Labour Party.

SUNKIN, M., and PAYNE, S. (eds.) (1999). *The Nature of the Crown – A Legal and Political Analysis*. Oxford: Clarendon Press.

THAIN, C., and WRIGHT, M. (1995). *The Treasury and Whitehall: The Planning and Control of Public Expenditure, 1976–1993*. Oxford: Clarendon Press.

THOMAS, C., and MALLESON, K. (1997). *Judicial Appointments Commissions: the European and North American Experience and the Possible Implications for the United Kingdom*. London: Lord Chancellor's Department.

TOMANEY, J. (2000). 'The Regional Governance of England' in R. Hazell (ed.) (2000a). *The State and the Nations. The First Year of Devolution in the United Kingdom*. Thorverton (Essex): Academic Imprint.

—— (2001). 'Reshaping the English Regions' in A. Trench (ed.) (2001). *The State of the Nation 2001*. Thorverton (Essex): Imprint Academic.

—— and HETHERINGTON, P. (2001). *Monitoring the English Regions: Report No. 2*. London: Constitution Unit.

TOMKINS, A. (1998). *The Constitution after Scott*. Oxford: Clarendon Press.

—— (1999). 'Of constitutional spectres'.

Review of Eric Barendt: *An Introduction to Constitutional Law*, [1999] *Public Law* 525–40.

—— (2002). 'In defence of the political constitution', 22 *OJLS* 157.

TRANSPARENCY INTERNATIONAL (2001). *Corrupt Perceptions Index 2001*. Paris: Transparency International.

TRENCH, A. (ed.) (2001). *The State of the Nation 2001*. Thorverton (Essex): Imprint Academic.

VALLINDER, T. (1994). 'The judicialization of politics—A world-wide phenomenon', 15 *International Political Science Review* 91.

VAN BUEREN, G. (2002). 'Including the excluded: The case for an economic, social and cultural Human Rights Act', [2002] *Public Law* 456–72.

WADE, SIR WILLIAM (1998). 'The United Kingdom's Bill of Rights' in *Constitutional Reform in the United Kingdom*. Oxford: Hart Publishing.

—— (2000). 'Horizons of horizontality', 116 *LQR* 217.

—— and FORSYTH, C. (2002). *Administrative Law*, 9th edn. Oxford: Clarendon Press.

WADHAM, J., GRIFFITHS, J., and RIGBY, B. (2001). *Blackstone's Guide to the Freedom of Information Act 2000*. London: Blackstone Press.

WALDRON, J. (1999). *Law and Disagreement*. Oxford: Oxford University Press.

WALKER, C., and AKDENIZ, Y. (1998). 'Virtual democracy', [1998] *Public Law* 489–506.

WARD, A. J. (2000). 'Devolution: Labour's strange constitutional "design"' in J. Jowell and D. Oliver (eds.) (2000). *The Changing Constitution*, 4th edn. Oxford: Oxford University Press.

WEILER, J. (1995). 'Does Europe need a constitution? Demos, Telos and the German Maastricht decision', 1 *ELJ* 217.

WEINRIB, L.-E. (1999). 'Canada's constitutional revolution: from legislative to constitutional state', 33 *Israel Law Review* 13–50.

WEIR, S., and BEETHAM, D. (1999). *Political Power and Democratic Control in Britain. The Democratic Audit of the United Kingdom.* London: Routledge.

—— and HALL, W. (eds.) (1994). *EGOTRIP: Extra-governmental organisations in the United Kingdom and their Accountability.* London: Charter 88 Trust.

WHEARE, K. C. (1963). *Federal Government,* 4th edn. Oxford: Oxford University Press.

—— (1966). *Modern Constitutions.* 2nd edn. Oxford: Oxford University Press.

WICKS, E. (2000). 'The United Kingdom government's perception of the European Convention on Human Rights at the time of entry', [2000] *Public Law* 438.

WILFORD, R. (2001). *Aspects of the Belfast Agreement.* Oxford: Oxford University Press.

—— and WILSON, R. (2000). 'A "Bare Knuckle Ride": Northern Ireland' in R. Hazell (ed.) (2000). *The State and the Nations. The First Year of Devolution in the United Kingdom,* 2000. Thorverton (Essex): Imprint Academic.

—— —— (2001a). 'Northern Ireland: End-game' in A. Trench (ed.) (2001). *The State of the Nation 2001.* Thorverton: Imprint Academic.

—— —— (2001b). *A Democratic Design? The political style of the Northern Ireland Assembly.* London: Constitution Unit.

WILKE, M., and WALLACE, H. (1990). *Subsidiarity: Approaches to Power-Sharing in the European Community* (Royal Institute of International Affairs. Discussion Paper 27). London: Royal Institute of International Affairs.

WINETROBE, B. (1998). 'The autonomy of Parliament', in D. Oliver and G. Drewry (eds.) (1998). *The Law and Parliament,* Butterworths: London.

—— (2001a). 'Counter-devolution? The Sewel Convention on devolved legislation at Westminster', 6 *Scottish Law and Practice Quarterly* 286–92.

—— (2001b). *Realising the Vision: a Parliament with a Purpose.* London: Constitution Unit.

WISTRICH, E. (1992). 'Restructuring Government New Zealand style', 70 *Public Administration,* 119–35.

WONG, G. (2000). 'Towards the nutcracker principle: Reconsidering the objections to proportionality', [2000] *Public Law* 92.

WOODHOUSE, D. (1997a). *In Pursuit of Good Administration.* Oxford: Clarendon Press.

—— (1997b). 'Ministerial Responsibility: Something Old, Something New', [1997] *Public Law* 262.

—— (1998). 'The Office of Lord Chancellor', [1998] *Public Law* 617–32.

—— (2001). *The Office of Lord Chancellor.* Oxford: Hart Publishing.

WOOLF, LORD (1995). 'Droit public—English style', [1995] *Public Law* 57–71.

WOOLF, SIR HARRY (1990). *Protection of the Public—A New Challenge.* London: Stevens & Sons.

WOOLF, LORD, JOWELL, J. L., and LE SUEUR, A. (eds.) (1999). *De Smith, Woolf and Jowell's Principles of Judicial Review,* London: Sweet & Maxwell.

WRIGHT, T., and GAMBLE, A. (2002). 'Is the party over?', 73 *Political Quarterly* 123–124.

ZIAMOU, T. (1999). 'New Process Rights for Citizens', [1999] *Public Law* 726.

Index